Orwell

By the same author

Fiction

Great Eastern Land
Real Life
English Settlement
After Bathing at Baxter's: Stories
Trespass
The Comedy Man

Non-fiction

A Vain Conceit: British Fiction in the 1980s
Other People: Portraits from the '90s (with Marcus Berkmann)
After the War: The Novel and England Since 1945
Thackeray

ORWELL

D. J. Taylor

Chatto & Windus
LONDON

Published by Chatto & Windus 2003

2 4 6 8 10 9 7 5 3 1

First published in Great Britain in 2003 by
Chatto & Windus
Random House, 20 Vauxhall Bridge Road,
London SW1V 2SA

Random House Australia (Pty) Limited
20 Alfred Street, Milsons Point, Sydney,
New South Wales 2061, Australia

Random House New Zealand Limited
18 Poland Road, Glenfield,
Auckland 10, New Zealand

Random House (Pty) Limited
Endulini, 5A Jubilee Road, Parktown 2193, South Africa

The Random House Group Limited Reg. No. 954009
www.randomhouse.co.uk

A CIP catalogue record for this book
is available from the British Library

ISBN 0 7011 69192

Papers used by Random House are natural, recyclable products made from wood
grown in sustainable forests; the manufacturing processes conform to the
environmental regulations of the country of origin

Typeset by SX Composing DTP, Rayleigh, Essex
Printed and bound in Great Britain

Richard Paul Hore (1928–2002)

Requiescat

How much do we need to know about a writer, personally? The answer is that it doesn't matter. Nothing or everything is equally satisfactory. Who cares in the end? As Northrop Frye has said, the only evidence we have of Shakespeare's existence, apart from the poems and plays, is the portrait of a man who was clearly an idiot. Biography is there for the curious; and curiosity gives out where boredom begins. – Martin Amis, *The War Against Cliché*

Obviously, no full explanation of a man is ever possible. – Richard Rees, *George Orwell: Fugitive from the Camp of Victory*

Contents

Contents

List of Illustrations

The author and publishers would like to thank the following for kind permission to reproduce illustrations: The Orwell Archive, University College, London (1, 2, 6, 9, 12, 13, 22, 26, 35); BBC Photo Library (33); Susannah Collings and Elizabeth Doria (19, 20, 21); Pauline McGregor Currien (10, 11); Estate of Vernon Richards (40, 41); Mrs Esme Goldsmith (16); the late Mrs Celia Goodman (34); Mrs Dora Hammond (18); Mrs Deirdre Levi (6, 7); the late Mr George Summers (20); Mrs Kathleen Symons (30).

Acknowledgements

The most substantial of the many debts accumulated during the four years in which this book was written is to Peter Davison. It is fair to say that Orwell studies would scarcely exist in their present form without the decade and a half that Professor Davison spent in compiling his magisterial edition of the complete works. For his help, advice, willingness to answer enquiries and persistent enthusiasm, often in the face of serious ill health, I am profoundly grateful. Ian Angus, who assisted Professor Davison in his labours, having previously co-edited the four-volume *Collected Essays, Journalism and Letters* with Orwell's widow Sonia, was also a mine of information and a welcome source of encouragement.

Several people allowed me to use unpublished or partially published material in their possession. In particular I am grateful to Richard Ingrams, who provided an unexpurgated typescript of Malcolm Muggeridge's journals from the period 1948–50 and Leonard Muggeridge for kindly allowing me to quote them, Kenneth Sinclair-Loutit, who sent me the relevant sections of his autobiography, David Holbrook, who supplied a copy of the relevant pages of an unpublished novel, and Malcolm Edwards, Managing Director of the Orion Publishing Group Trade Division, who enabled me to consult papers in the archive of Victor Gollancz Ltd.

For permission to reproduce extracts from Orwell's published writings, I am immensely grateful to the Orwell estate, in the person of Bill Hamilton of A.M. Heath. I should also like to thank the Buswell Memorial Library, Wheaton College, Illinois for allowing me to make use of the previously unpublished letters from Orwell to Malcolm Muggeridge in their possession, and in particular David Malone and Judy Truesdale of its special collections department.

Among friends of Orwell and those with personal knowledge of him who allowed themselves to be interviewed, I should particularly like to thank the late David Astor, Mr George Bumstead, the Rt. Hon. Michael Foot, Lucian Freud (via his biographer, William Feaver), Mrs Esmé Goldsmith, the late Celia Goodman, Mrs Dora Hammond, David Holbrook, Denzil Jacobs, the late Michael Meyer, Janetta Parladé, the late Lady Violet Powell, Michael Sayers, the late Mr George Summers, Kathleen Symons, Peter Vansittart and Francis Wyndham.

Of the many others who responded to requests for information or suggested promising lines of enquiry, I am grateful to Anne Olivier Bell, Derek and Judy Brooke-Wavell, Susannah Collings, Ian Collins, Mrs Winifred Cook, Fr. O. Cramero, Professor Sir Bernard Crick, Mr Dudley Crick, Pauline McGregor Currien, Sarah Curtis, Miss Norah Denny, Margo Ewart, William Feaver, Mrs Rita Field, Mrs Dorothy Frankford, Gill Furlong of the Orwell Archive at University College London, Nicky Gathorne-Hardy, Miriam Gross, Valerie Grove, Anthony Hobson, the late Rt. Hon. Lord Jenkins of Hillhead, the late Austin Kark, Robert Kee, Francis King, Jeremy Lewis, the late Earl of Longford, Bronia Awdas McDonald, Michael Meredith, Leonard Miall, Simon Morgan, editor of the *Blyth Bugle*, Annie Murray, Frances Partridge, the late Anthony Powell, John Powell, Tristram Powell, Piers Paul Read, the late Vernon Richards, Sidney Sheldon, Hilary Spurling, Elaine Steabler, Professor John Sutherland, the late David Sylvester, Mr E.J. Tooke of 'Trash 'n' Carry' Southwold, Ion Trewin, Natasha Walter, Mr Ronnie Waters, Dr George Watson, Professor Roger Webster, Francis Wheen, Tiffany White and Paul Willetts.

At Chatto & Windus I should like to thank my publisher, Alison Samuel, for her constant encouragement and support. As ever I am immensely grateful to my editor, Jenny Uglow, for her enthusiasm and tact, and to my literary agent Gill Coleridge and her assistant Lucy Luck.

Numbers of literary editors and other professional colleagues kept me supplied with relevant books and commissions. They include Adrian Hamilton, Boyd Tonkin, Nick Coleman, Catherine Pepinster, Simon O'Hagan, Laurence Earle, Claire Armitstead, Giles Foden, Annalena McAffee, Ian Katz, Stephen Moss, Caroline Gascoigne, Andrew Holgate, Peter Wilby, Jason Cowley, Lisa Allardyce, Boris Johnson, Stuart Reid, Mark Amory, Clare Asquith, Nancy Sladek, Alan Jenkins and Holly Eley. The staff of the London Library were as courteous and efficient as ever.

I owe a special debt of gratitude to Rachel, Felix, Benjy and Leo for tolerating the customary absences from hearth and supper-table.

Norwich, 2003

I

An Oxfordshire Tomb

In a shortish working career of a little over two decades, Orwell produced nearly two million published words. The twenty volumes that Peter Davison's monumental *Complete Works* needed to accommodate them take up nearly four feet of shelf space. If he lived to be seventy, Orwell once proposed, comparing his professional output with that of the average coal-miner, the chances were that he would leave a shelf-full of books. He died young, the novels and essays that would have occupied his fifties and sixties were never written, and yet post-humously at any rate, with the help of devoted editors and compilers, he achieved his ambition. Again – and these comparisons say some-thing about the way in which his mind worked – Orwell once calculated that the lifetime output for a prolific writer of boys' school stories would, were the pages to be lined end to end, have carpeted the best part of an acre. His own *oeuvre* spread out sheet by sheet would occupy an area roughly the size of Norwich city centre. The fifty years since his death have brought perhaps two million words more: biographies, critical studies, memoirs by literary colleagues and childhood friends, even a novel (David Caute's *Dr Orwell and Mr Blair*) in which he plays a starring role. Why add to them?

Thackeray once declared that when he read a book all that remained in his head was a picture of the author. This defies all known precepts of modern literary theory, but the point remains. Orwell has obsessed me for the best part of a quarter of a century. The first 'adult' novel I ever picked off the bookshelf in my parents' house was a Penguin paperback of *A Clergyman's Daughter* that some ineluctable instinct had led my mother to buy in the early 1960s. The GCSE O-level English paper essay that I prophetically set out on a year or so later was: 'Whose biography would you most like to write?' Always in my adolescence, Orwell was there, the ghostly figure on the back of the book jacket urging me on. The sense of sheer personality that rises from his work – that urgent need to communicate vital things – is immensely strong, all the more so if you are a teenager who barely knows that books exist.

'He knows all about me,' you feel, 'he wrote this for me' – which, curiously enough, is what Orwell himself wrote about Henry Miller. Were I ever to meet his shade in the celestial equivalent of the Groucho Club – not, you suspect, somewhere Orwell would ever allow himself to be found – I should say what Philip Larkin maintained that he said to Cyril Connolly when the two of them were introduced at Auden's memorial service: 'Sir, you formed me.' Cheap Penguins in those days, procurable at fifty pence a throw from the University of East Anglia bookshop, the four volumes of Sonia Orwell and Ian Angus' *Collected Essays, Journalism and Letters* were my private cornucopia in the sixth-form years, a vast, sprawling bran tub into which repeated scoops yielded up anything but bran. Dickens, Thackeray, Gissing, Smollett, hosts of minor writers washed up on the early-twentieth-century shore: hardly any of the people who came to occupy my mental lumber room would have taken up residence there had it not been for Orwell.

There was more to it than this, of course. Marking down Orwell's collected works as a hugely idiosyncratic version of the *Good Book Guide* is perhaps the equivalent of regarding Sir Winston Churchill as a moderately effective leader of the Conservative Party. For Orwell is, above all, a moral force, a light glinting in the darkness, a way through the murk. His status as a kind of ethical litmus paper stems not so much from the repeated injunctions to 'behave decently', and some of the implications of behaving decently for the average western lifestyle, as from the armature that supported them. Broadly speaking he realised – and he did so a great deal earlier than most commentators of either Right or Left – that the single most important crisis of the twentieth century was the decline in mass religious belief and, its corollary, in personal immortality. God was dead and yet the secular substitutes put in His place, whether totalitarianism or western consumer capitalism, merely travestied human ideals and aspirations. The task facing modern man, as Orwell saw it, was to take control of that immense reservoir of essentially spiritual feeling – all that moral sensibility looking for a home – and use it to irrigate millions of ordinary and finite lives. The atrocities of Nazi Germany and Stalinist Russia – and this point is repeated endlessly in his later writings – could only have been designed by the godless because they presuppose a world in which there is no moral reckoning, and where the only power that matters is the ability to control not only your fellow men but the history of which they are a part and the knowledge on which that history rests. The idea that there was a life after death was unsustainable, but the moral baggage that accompanied that belief was indispensable. As it happens, and for reasons it is superfluous to explore here, I don't believe that God is altogether dead, but I do believe in the materials which Orwell used to construct his opposition to – that eternally memorable phrase from an essay published in 1940 – 'the smelly little orthodoxies which are now contending for our souls'. It is worth pointing out that these orthodoxies still exist sixty years later, if in rather different forms and wearing yet more elaborate disguises, and that it is our duty to resist them with exactly the same vigour with which Orwell resisted Hitler and Stalin.

And so in a curious way I always knew that I would end up writing about Orwell, that the contents of the Oxford history syllabus were as nothing compared to – say – the essay 'Oysters and Brown Stout', which first alerted me to the fact that there was a writer called Thackeray, or the essay on Dickens, which leaves you with the feeling that Dickens and for that matter Orwell himself are sitting in the room talking to you as you read. The intensity of this fixation was such that it took me most of my twenties to establish the areas in which Orwell, mysteriously, was fallible, principally those breathtaking generalisations which close, adult inspection reveals to be a little less watertight than they seem. Take the famous statement that 'Good prose is like a window-pane'. One doesn't have to be a literary theorist to know that this is nonsense. Ronald Firbank, Marcel Proust and James Joyce (the last of whom at least Orwell profoundly admired) wrote varieties of 'good prose' and none of their sentences is remotely like a window-pane. Transparency, surely, is not the only virtue? It is the same with some of Orwell's no-nonsense prescriptions for linguistic frankness, his hatred, for example, of those double-negative formulations of the 'His was a not insignificant talent' type. Arguably the complexities hinted at when one writer remarks of another that his talent was not insignificant are worth going into, something that redounds to language's credit rather than its capacity for obfuscation. I believe, for example, that Orwell's own attitude to the Jews was not unprejudiced. Equally, one suspects that Orwell, in one of his less hard-line moments, would have seen this.

Meanwhile the process of finding out about Orwell, of accumulating, both openly and surreptitiously, that stock of Orwell lore went on. Any sixtysomething littérateur with some kind of track record met in early days around literary London was immediately pinioned with the question 'Did you know George Orwell?' The first book I ever reviewed – sniffily: how dare anyone crash in on my private party? – was Bernard Crick's *George Orwell: A Biography*. All this – the harassing of literary notables, the snootiness over Professor Crick – was undertaken not in a spirit of fluttering antiquarianism but in the absolute conviction that Orwell, to borrow the original title of Christopher Hitchens' recent polemic, *matters* in a way that ninety-nine out of a hundred writers do not. As a reader I have always been wary of 'relevance' in literature: so often it means the cast-off manuscripts of Group Theatre, Soviet social realism and novels with titles like *Brixton Superfly*. All art, Orwell famously suggested, is propaganda; equally, not all propaganda is art. At the same time it is accurate to say that in the fifty years since his death Orwell has managed to colonise vast areas of political thinking and ordinary language in a way that would have seemed remarkable to the friends who gathered round his deathbed. As with Dickens – perhaps the writer whose absorption into the national subconscious Orwell's case most closely resembles – several of his most resonant utterances are used on an almost daily basis by people who have never read a line of his books. Again, as with Dickens, people mysteriously *know* about Orwell at second hand: that all animals are equal but some are more equal than others; that Big Brother is watching you; that Room 101 is where you go to be confronted by your worst horrors.

This centrality to a whole area of our national life was confirmed, on one very narrow level, by the tumult of approbation that greeted Peter Davison's edition of the *Complete Works* on its appearance in 1998, and on another, much more expansive plateau, in media reaction to the events of 11 September 2001. Without warning Orwell was every-where: mentor, guide, motivating spirit, conscience. As readily as one commentator inveighed against the 'pansy left' and proposed that every British soldier sent to Afghanistan should have an edition of Orwell's essays packed in his rucksack, so another would dole out some of his less comforting observations about war's inescapable moral consequences. All this may seem a considerable distance from the emaciated figure dying in a hospital bed half a century and more ago, and not the least fascinating speculation about Orwell is what he might have made of it all. Distinguishing the reality from the myth was difficult enough in the week after his death, Malcolm Muggeridge thought. Fifty-three years later it is harder still. And yet it is this contemporary fixation with Orwell, with that grey and curiously *sorrowful* face staring remorselessly

4

back across time, that justifies the attempt to get inside his head: to establish not only what can be said about him and the world he inhabited, but what he can tell us about ourselves.

The tortuous history of Orwell biography is largely down to its subject. Orwell requested in his will that no biography of him should be written. Orwell's widow Sonia spent many years trying to enforce this edict against increasingly sophisticated opposition. The first critical studies of Orwell's work by Laurence Brander (who had known him at the BBC) and John Atkins appeared within a few years of his death. By the late 1950s there was a ready market for Orwell reminiscences. Paul Potts' memoir 'Don Quixote on a Bicycle' appeared in the *London Magazine* in 1957. Richard Rees' full-length study, *Fugitive from the Camp of Victory*, which contains many biographical fragments, followed four years later, along with his sister Avril's radio broadcast 'My Brother, George Orwell'. Sonia's response to this rising tide of interest was twofold. On the one hand she set to work with Ian Angus, then Deputy Librarian at University College, London, on what eventually became the four-volume *Collected Journalism, Letters and Essays*, published by Secker & Warburg in 1968. On the other she appointed Malcolm Muggeridge, a close friend of Orwell's in the 1940s, as official biographer. The Muggeridge benediction, it now seems clear, was a deliberate spoiler. A full-time editor, television presenter and contro-versialist, Muggeridge – as Sonia, one imagines, had foreseen – found the demands of a full-scale biography beyond him. His preliminary research survives, but there is no evidence that he made any serious effort to complete the book. In any case Sonia intended the four-volume, 1,500-page selection of Orwell's work to be his memorial. As for the real biographical monument, there were other interested parties at work. Peter Stansky and William Abrahams' *The Unknown Orwell*, uncountenanced by Sonia but displaying the fruits of a great deal of painstaking research, was well received on its publication in 1972. Cyril Connolly was moved to declare that the years he and Orwell had had in common were 'described with so much tenderness and insight that I am often deluded that the writers were there'. It was this that apparently decided Sonia to appoint a new 'official' biographer and ensure that he actually produced a biography. Having read and been impressed by something he had written, she selected the then Birkbeck politics don Bernard Crick. *George Orwell: A Biography* duly appeared in late 1980. Sonia, who survived long enough to read the proofs, supposedly went to her grave believing that she had betrayed her late husband's memory.

Quite why Sonia took this view of a punctilious and in many ways ground-breaking account of Orwell's life is uncertain. You suspect that by this stage in the proceedings any biography would have fallen short of the exacting yardsticks she had in mind. Sonia, as this book will perhaps show, was an odd woman and an odder literary widow: loyal, protective, keen to do the right thing, but simultaneously erratic in her judgement and capricious in her personal likes and dislikes. In her absence the floodgates of Orwell studies were opened. The year 1984, inevitably, brought a deluge of material: Audrey Coppard and Bernard Crick's assemblage of first-hand testimony, *Orwell Remembered*; a similar collection, *Remembering Orwell*, edited by Stephen Wadhams; W.J. West's *Orwell: The War Broadcasts*, based on scripts discovered in the BBC archives at Caversham. (A companion volume, *Orwell: The War Commentaries*, appeared the following year.) Subsequently the tide became a torrent: a second biography by the American scholar Michael Shelden in 1991; a third by Jeffrey Meyers in 2000. In between these high-water marks there have been studies of Orwell's fiction, of the intellectual climate in which his books were published and received, further reminiscences and dissections of the 'Orwell myth'. This is a well-trodden path, and the scenery can be distressingly familiar. Writing once to a woman to whom Orwell had diffidently proposed marriage in 1946, I got back a letter which amongst other information listed the seven previous researchers who had come to interview her. What more was there to be said? this lady wondered.

It was, and is, a good question. Practically anyone of any consequence who came across him during the decade and a half of his life on the public stage has left a record of the encounter. The Orwell who turns up in the recollections of ordinary people is a rather different figure: less touched by fifty years of posthumous sanctification, more human. Three years ago, for example, I went to a village near Didcot in Oxfordshire to interview an old gentleman named George Summers, then in his early nineties. As it happened, I had met Mr Summers nearly two decades before when I was at college with his daughter Annie and had heard rumours of his connection with Orwell even then. Mr Summers, re-encountered in his front room, was affable but cagey. The story itself, pieced together through numberless digressions, involved Orwell's attempt, back in Suffolk in the early 1930s, to worm his way into the affections of Mr Summers's then fiancée, a woman named Dorothy Rogers. It ended with a chase – Orwell on foot, Mr Summers pursuing on a motorcycle – across Southwold common, remembered by the pursuer sixty-five years later as follows (this is a direct transcription from the tape): 'I tried . . . I missed him . . . I went I suppose fifty yards, and there he was, and there was she . . . I was the guardian angel . . . I ran up the bank . . . I sort of pushed him off . . . I didn't kill him,' Mr Summers innocuously concluded.

However laboriously reassembled in a ninety-year-old's memory, this is an extraordinary image: the vengeful figure crouched over the handlebars; the lanky interloper fleeing before him over the springy turf. (It is worth asking, too, what Dorothy was doing. Following behind? Watching the chase from the vantage point of the bank? Carrying on home, leaving the boys to fight it out?) However incongruous, nothing in twenty years of reading and writing about Orwell has quite so narrowly conveyed to me what, in a certain sense, Orwell was like. It took perhaps three-quarters of an hour for Mr Summers to finish, and embellish, his tale. Later Annie and I drove to Sutton Courtenay, a few miles away over the back roads, to examine Orwell's grave in the village churchyard plot secured for him by his friend David Astor. Not the least of the many ironies that have attached themselves to Orwell is that this professional man of the people should have been buried amidst the Oxfordshire verdure, through the agency of an Anglo-American aristocrat.

Just over fifty years earlier another couple could have been found lingering in the graveyard at Sutton Courtenay: a striking blonde woman in her early thirties, pale with strain and anxiety, supported by a slightly older man. The two of them – David Astor, editor of the *Observer*, and Sonia, Orwell's widow – were not alone. They came accompanied by a solicitor, an undertaker's van and its attendants and a very long coffin. Orwell's funeral and interment took place on 26 January 1950. Among several interested spectators who left records of the event, Malcolm Muggeridge was perhaps the most intrigued. It is Muggeridge, more than anyone else, who conveys something of the sheer difficulty involved in getting the deceased underground. Somewhat to the general surprise, Orwell had requested in his will that his funeral service should follow the rites of the Church of England and that he should be buried in a cemetery. For one who had never professed Christian beliefs, still less been affiliated to any place of worship – at any rate in his later years – this demand would be difficult to realise. In the end the idea of a London burial place was abandoned and Astor influence was brought to bear on the vicar of Sutton Courtenay. Meanwhile, Muggeridge and Orwell's close friend Anthony Powell ('churchy' people, according to Astor, and aware of the protocols involved) engaged the vicar of Christ Church, Albany Street, where the Powells worshipped, to conduct the service in London. Muggeridge, who had an eye for this kind of detail, was interested to find that the undertaker knew the Reverend Rose, in fact was lunching with him the same day to talk over future business. Sonia, deeply distressed by the events of the past few days, was consulted but took no active part in the arrangements. She was 'quite helpless in the matter', Muggeridge noted.

Thursday 26 January was bitterly cold. London lay in the grip of winter. Travelling to the church in a taxi with Orwell's sister Avril, and seeking to break the ice with a woman who had little small-talk, David Astor asked her who she thought that Orwell had most admired. Avril misunderstood the question – Astor meant an individual rather than a type – and shot back 'the working-class mother of eight children'. Sonia had not felt up to greeting the mourners as they entered the church. Instead the vestibule was manned by Orwell's publisher, Fred Warburg, and his business partner Roger Senhouse, both of them behaving 'as if it were a publisher's party', according to Lady Violet Powell. Stationed inside, Muggeridge allowed his wintry eye to rove over the congregation. Largely Jewish, he decided, and almost entirely unbelievers. The Reverend Rose was 'excessively parsonical' and his church unheated. As for the mourners themselves, Fred Warburg and his wife Pamela occupied the front row, followed by a file of relations of Eileen O'Shaughnessy, Orwell's first wife, whose obvious grief seemed to Muggeridge 'practically the only real element in the whole affair'. However artificial Muggeridge may have thought the proceedings, he was impressed by the lesson (chosen by Powell) from the twelfth chapter of Ecclesiastes: 'man goeth to his long home, and the mourners go about the streets . . . Then shall the dust return to the earth as it was: and the spirit shall return unto God who gave it'. This was, everyone agreed, a desperately sad affair: not some ancient literary eminence called to his eternal rest in a blaze of pomp and glory but a man of forty-six who had not survived long enough to taste the fruits of his success. Sonia seemed 'dazed'. Muggeridge felt a pang as the coffin was removed, particularly because of its length: 'Somehow this circumstance, reflecting George's tallness, was poignant.' A quarter of a century later Anthony Powell remembered the service as one of the most harrowing he had ever attended.

Afterwards the majority of the congregation repaired to the Powells' house in Chester Gate. Astor, Sonia and the hearse departed for Oxfordshire. Following the burial service, read by the Reverend Gordon Dunstan from the Book of Common Prayer, the 'small company' (the vicar's words) proceeded outside. By chance the graveyard at Sutton Courtenay abutted a government building used for testing water samples from the Thames. Apart from Sonia, himself and their professional attendants, Astor recalled, Orwell's interment had only a single spectator: a scientist in a lab coat smoking a cigarette and looking, Astor thought, horribly like an extra from *Nineteen Eighty-Four*. Back in London, reading through the obituaries by Arthur Koestler, V.S. Pritchett, Julian Symons and others, Muggeridge felt that he saw in them 'how the legend of a human being is created'.

Part One
1903–1927

2

A Question of Upbringing

I can't stop thinking about the young days with you & Guin &
Prosper. – Letter to Jacintha Buddicom, 15 February 1949

No one can look back on his schooldays and say with truth that
they were altogether unhappy. – 'Such, Such Were the Joys'
(1968)

Like most rebels, his friend Anthony Powell maintained, Orwell was
half in love with the thing he was rebelling against. In Orwell's case, the
thing he was half in love with but lost no opportunity to criticise
throughout a twenty-year career in print was his upbringing, down in
the soft, prosperous, but by no means invulnerable core of early
twentieth-century England. As a grown man, another of his friends
thought, he was 'steeped in the illusions of 1910'. Richard Rees, who
observed him quietly for the best part of two decades, noted that his
conservatism extended to every aspect of his make-up except politics.
How the writer George Orwell, born Eric Blair, came by those illusions,
and the steps he took to rid himself of them – some successful, others
transparently half-hearted – is perhaps the chief emotional panorama of
his life.

The mature Orwell was, investigation insists, a complex man:
ambitious, but curiously detached from the theatres of his ambition,
sceptical yet given to bouts of self-dramatisation, distrustful of power
but not averse to power's exercise. Inevitably, the roots of this
complexity lie somewhere in childhood and the huge portmanteau of
family baggage that he carried with him into adult life. The Blairs, by
the time Eric arrived among them, were casualties of a distinctive shift
in early nineteenth-century English social history: the flight from the
land. Eric's great-great-great-grandfather was an earl; his father was a
medium-grade Imperial civil servant. For the earl's great-great-great

grandson, the words Evelyn Waugh puts into the mouth of his hero John Plant's Royal Academician father in *Work Suspended* (1942) would have had an uncomfortable resonance. 'Seventy years ago the politicians and the tradesmen were in alliance,' Plant senior laments:

'they destroyed the gentry by destroying the value of land; some of the gentry became politicians themselves, others tradesmen; out of what was left they created the new class into which I was born, the moneyless, landless, educated gentry who managed the country for them. My grandfather was a canon of Christchurch, my father was in the Bengal Civil Service. All the capital they left their sons was education and moral principle.'

This is an exaggeration, but its central point remains. The history of the Blair family in the nineteenth century is the history of a decline. Each of the descendants of Charles Blair (1743–1801), who married the daughter of the Fane Earl of Westmorland, was somehow less distinguished than his immediate predecessor. The family fortunes, built on the now decaying Jamaican sugar and slave trades, were sharply diminished. Thereafter the path ran down and ever down. Orwell's grandfather Richard Arthur Blair, born in 1802, was ordained a Church of England deacon at Calcutta in 1839 and spent a decade or so attached to the Indian army before returning to England in 1854. There was still a certain amount of aristocratic lustre to hand – the Reverend Blair used his Fane connections to acquire the prosperous ecclesiastical living of Milborne St Andrew in Dorset – but the pattern was unshiftable. With his shrewd eye for categorisation, Orwell was keenly aware of the social class in which he had fetched up. His family, he later wrote, 'was one of those ordinary middle-class families of soldiers, clergymen, government officials, teachers, lawyers, doctors'. Such family myths and legends as the Blairs allowed themselves were faintly prosaic. One, recalled by Orwell's sister Avril, had the Reverend Blair, *en route* to furlough in England, stopping at the Cape. Here he became acquainted with a family called Hare (the name recurs in *A Clergyman's Daughter*) and, prior to resuming his journey, engaged himself to one of the daughters. Returning a few months later he discovered that his fiancée had married someone else. 'Oh well,' the disappointed suitor is supposed to have remarked, having inspected the remaining members of the family, 'if Emily's married it doesn't matter. I'll have Fanny instead.' Orwell's paternal grandmother was at this stage a young lady of fifteen who continued to play with her dolls for some time after her marriage.

The Blairs were pattern examples of the Victorian upper-middle class: professionally – and sentimentally – attached to the Empire, their money mostly gone, but sustained by the thought of a fine and more prosperous past. The memory of this heritage strayed into Orwell's own inner landscapes. The fastidious rector in *A Clergyman's Daughter* – where Orwell is sufficiently knowledgeable about genteel clergymen to be able to call his parish by the technically correct term of a 'cure' – dreams reminiscently of his Oxford days as an antidote to present-day penury and looks down his nose at the local petty gentry. Orwell's poem 'A Happy Vicar I Might Have Been' ('A happy vicar I might have been/two hundred years ago/to preach upon eternal doom/and watch my walnuts grow . . .') glances back at a lost, Elysian world, full of certainty, conviction and money. Here at the end of the nineteenth century the happy vicars were gone. Their descendants looked out on to a world of civil service examinations, prudent marriages and the disagreeable necessity of earning a living.

The mid-Victorian generation of Blairs added to their problems by being philoprogenitive. Even by the standards of the nineteenth century the ten children of Richard Blair, however cunningly dispersed around the Dorsetshire rectory, would have been a source of financial strain. The tenth, Richard Walmesley Blair, Orwell's father (born in 1857), probably had little say in his choice of career. In 1875, aged eighteen, he followed the family spoor east by joining the Government of India's Opium Department with the rank of Assistant Sub-Deputy Opium Agent, 5th grade. Opium, legalised as recently as 1870 and mostly exported to China, was already a key component of the revenues annually remitted to the Imperial exchequer, but the status of its administrative department was not high. Not much is known of Richard Blair's early life. Conservative in his tastes, without the literary interests that had distinguished earlier generations of his family – there had been Fane playwrights and Fane poets – he spent his early manhood in permanent transit across India, monitoring the production and distribution of a drug of whose consequences he must have been painfully aware. Promotion came slowly. By the time of his son's birth, when he was already in his mid-forties, he had climbed only as far up the hierarchical ladder as Sub-Deputy Opium Agent, 4th grade. Such a lifestyle, and such an income – at its height his salary did not exceed £650 a year – may not have encouraged a romantic outlook on life. At any rate, Richard Blair married late. He was thirty-nine when he attached himself to Ida Mabel Limouzin, a young woman eighteen years his junior, born in Surrey but brought up in India by her French father and English mother. The Limouzins, whose family base lay at the port of Moulmein, south of Rangoon, were long established in Burma as shipbuilders and teak merchants. As well as long-term residence in the East they shared another characteristic with the Blairs: fading fortunes. Ida, who had been working as a governess in India, apparently accepted her husband on the rebound, having been jilted by another man to whom she had been engaged. One should be chary of pronouncing on the emotional lives of people who left no record of themselves, but it does not seem to have been a marriage made in heaven.

Searching for an adjective to describe this low-key, late-Victorian landscape, I thought of Thackeray's 'shabby-genteel'. Orwell admired Thackeray: his 1943 *Tribune* essay reveals a deep fascination with the concept, painstakingly outlined in *Vanity Fair*, of living well on nothing a year. The Blairs were not prosperous, but they were near enough to prosperity to know what it looked like and appreciate its sheen. At the same time, even in the lower reaches of its professional class, this was a world of enormous security and self-belief. The gentility of the average lower-upper-middle-class Indian civil servant's son (Orwell's careful diagnosis of where he stood socially) might be 'almost purely theoretical'; as an animating spirit it mattered far more than, say, a belief in God. The Blairs had an heraldic crest and a case of family silver – Orwell ended up pawning the knives and forks in the 1930s to raise the money to go to Spain – even if there was little opportunity to put them on display. They knew how to behave in 'society' even if society's doors were not always flung wide to greet them. In *The Road to Wigan Pier*, a book in which the awareness of class distinctions becomes a kind of mania, Orwell tried to map out the chasm that ran between the lower and upper ends of the pre-Great War bourgeoisie. 'A great gulf existed between those on £400 a year and those on £2,000, but it was a gulf which those on £400 did their best to ignore.' The people in this stratum owned no land, but felt that they were landowners in the sight of God. They kept up this 'semi-aristocratic' outlook by going into the professions rather than trade. To mark all this down as a kind of mental confidence trick is to ignore the strict, and genuine, social demarcations on which it depended. In retirement on the Suffolk coast, Richard Blair was remembered as a benign old man, happy to send a wedding present to his greengrocer but also capable of cutting that tradesman dead if he met him in the street on a Sunday.

However much he may have resented it, the fact that he was by birth and appearance a 'gentleman' hung irremovably over Orwell's life, and persistently undermined his attempts to 'connect' with the lower orders. The minor officials who came across him in his tramping days knew him instantly for what he was: a toff trading under a false prospectus. Like Ravelston, the wealthy magazine proprietor of *Keep the Aspidistra Flying*, the shabbiness of his corduroy trousers only drew attention to the fact that they had been made by a very good tailor. Gentility often made Orwell a shrewd observer of the social scenes he infiltrated, with an eye for detail that less detached explorers would have missed, but it could sometimes leave him in a state of uneasy suspension, halfway between an environment where he felt materially at home and the world to which he was drawn by instinct and curiosity. A world, more to the point, from which upbringing and ancestry left him, in the end, eternally debarred.

All this, though, lay in the future. The early married life of the Blairs followed a time-honoured Anglo-Indian routine: constant removals brought about by Mr Blair's job; the eventual retreat home. Marjorie, their elder daughter, was born in 1898 during a stay at Tehta. Just over four years later Richard Blair was transferred to a new post at Motihari in Bengal, not far from the border with Nepal. It was here, on 25 June 1903, that his only son was born. Christened Eric Arthur – a photograph survives of a chubby baby clasped in the arms of his ayah – the child was sent back to England with his mother and sister some time in the following year. Undoubtedly this early severance set the pattern for the young Eric's relationship with his parents. Barring a solitary leave of absence in 1907 Mr Blair did not reappear in his son's life until Eric was almost nine: the formative influences were all administered in the nursery. These were not quite as conventional as the other parts of Orwell's upbringing might have suggested. With her French ancestry and her habit of dressing in 'a vaguely artistic way', Mrs Blair cut a faintly exotic figure in Home Counties Edwardian society. She was interested in art, and later in life took lessons in a Suffolk studio run by a resident French artist. The Limouzin side expressed itself strongly in Eric. Anthony Powell noted how in adulthood his physical presence conjured up thoughts of France. Ida's sisters, too, were unconventional by the exacting standards of the day, offering invitations to Fabian tea parties, or, in the case of Eric's Aunt Nellie, decamping to Paris to live with an Esperantist. All this gave Ida an individuality which was not lost on her son, or indeed on her husband, whom she called 'Dick' and was occasionally inclined to order about.

A telegraphic diary survives from the time of Ida's first months back in England. It contains no reference to Mr Blair. Amid a round of social engagements and genteel diversions, Eric features as 'baby'. The account of his doings is oddly prophetic. In early 1905 he is ill with 'bronchitis'; 11 February finds him much better and 'calling things "beastly"'. On 6 March 'baby went out for the first time today for more than a month'. Baby could be adventurous – on 14 June he climbed out into the garden by way of the drawing-room window – but he remained prone to bad health. He was ill again in late July – Mrs Blair, away in London, was summoned home by the nurse – and again in September. On 4 November, Ida recorded 'Baby worse so sent for doctor.' Four days later, presumably recovered, 'Baby came downstairs'. No comparable record exists for later stages of Eric's childhood, but his infancy was punctuated by a series of short illnesses, invariably related to his chest. All the early photographs of him show a plump, chubby boy, but the roots of his perpetual ill health – defective bronchial tubes – lie here in infancy. From these very early days in England, too, came his abiding love for the countryside of the Oxfordshire/Berkshire border. By late 1905 Mrs Blair and her two children – Marjorie was now seven, Eric just turned two – were established at 'Ermadale' (an amalgam of the two infant Christian names), Vicarage Road, Henley-on-Thames. The market town and the Thames Valley in which it lay left an indelible mark on Orwell's consciousness. *Coming up for Air*, written in his mid-thirties and in the shadow of approaching war, is a desperate love letter to the sights and scenes of childhood, full of odd fragments of hoarded detail recalled across the decades. Behind it, however carefully disguised – the Bowlings are small shopkeepers of the kind that Mr Blair would presumably have cut dead in the street – lies a conception of family life and the mature writer's view of the process of growing up.

'I hope you love your family?' Orwell once demanded of his friend Richard Rees. The idea of the family, both as a social unit and as a metaphorical conceit, meant a great deal to him. His writings come crammed with idealised pictures of cosy working-class interiors: father reading the paper in front of a roaring fire, mother drowsing over her knitting, children skirmishing on the hearthrug. England, he once suggested, was a family with the wrong members in control. The image of a nation as a restless, rackety household ruled over by feeble uncles and mad aunts is a captivating one, and it shows the depth, or rather the fervour, of Orwell's collectivism. As an adult he was an intensely solitary man who believed steadfastly in the benefits of a communal life. For all this theoretical enthusiasm, the families in his novels are consistently unhappy, breaking down, about to fall apart. The Reverend Hare in *A Clergyman's Daughter* is a vain, autocratic widower who seems to have violently abused his late wife (the scenes between them witnessed by Dorothy, their daughter, have been enough to put her off sex for life) and regards Dorothy, who combines the roles of housekeeper, parish administrator and secretary, as a kind of upper servant. The Comstocks in *Keep the Aspidistra Flying* are 'a peculiarly dull, shabby, dead-alive, ineffectual family. They lacked vitality to an extent that was surprising.' Flory in *Burmese Days* is entirely detached from family life: parents dead, sisters horsy women living in England with whom he has altogether lost touch. George Bowling in *Coming up for Air*, of all the imaginary people created by Orwell perhaps the most family oriented, ends up married to a paragon of penny-pinching dreariness. In a novel hugely absorbed by the idea of childhood, his own children are barely described. Throughout a fictional world that extends to half a dozen novels, only once, in the figure of Bowling, does Orwell attempt to recreate a child's-eye view of the world. Ominously, perhaps, the world of young George, the son of a stolid minor tradesman who dies before the bankruptcy court can claim him, is the most distant from his own experience.

However ground down by parental anxieties or the prospect of a changing world that neither he nor they can comprehend, George Bowling's childhood and his family life are undeniably happy. What did Orwell think of his own upbringing? His father seemed an aged, remote figure. Reflecting on the biblical injunction to 'Honour Thy Father and Mother' repeatedly dished out at his prep school, Orwell noted that 'I knew very well that I merely disliked my own father, who I had barely seen before I was eight and who appeared to me simply as a gruff-voiced elderly man for ever saying "don't".' His affection for his mother, on the other hand, and she for him (Mrs Blair referred to her children as 'my chicks' in letters to third parties) is abundantly clear. Late in life – the evidence comes from a notebook entry made shortly before his death – Orwell divined that he had been his mother's favourite child. But did he realise this at the time? Working out what the individual members of the Blair family thought of each other, singly and collectively, is complicated by the fact that, in perfect accordance with the standards of their day, they were not emotional people. Such social equals as noted down their impressions of them were aware of this hostility to the open display of 'feelings', made allowances for it and detected nothing out of the ordinary in what remained. Avril Blair believed that they were all devoted to each other. 'They lived on the undemonstrative terms that seem to have been normal for members of their family,' Richard Rees noted of Eric and his younger sister Avril's behaviour to each other on Jura in the late 1940s. (Another visitor, alternatively, remembered unspeakably dreary conversations inching forward in monosyllables over the kitchen table as Avril listlessly plucked a goose.) To an observer from lower down the social scale, the Blairs could seem neither happy nor close. The daughter of their 'daily' in Suffolk in the late 1920s recalled distinctly the feeling that Richard and Ida Blair 'didn't hit it off', and that, additionally, Mrs Blair was 'a hard woman'. This may seem a fair distance away from a neighbour's recollection of a handsome woman, adorning herself with agate drop earrings, producing enticing dishes of cabbage *en casserole*, rather than the usual overcooked English slops, but it is perhaps only a measure of how the Blairs seemed to people who were not on their social wavelength. It took something extraordinary to knock them off balance, to prod what may now seem quite ordinary emotions to the surface.

Such was the degree of detachment Orwell extended to members of his family, Avril remembered, that even the modest revelations of *Down and Out in Paris and London* came as a bewildering surprise. The Blairs were interested in the book and eager to read it, 'but it almost seemed as if it had been written by a different person'. Orwell's surviving letters to his father from the late 1930s are respectful and affectionate, but they are not complicit. Perhaps we should not expect them to be. Whatever their collective imperfections, their diffidence, their endless anti-emotionalism (and you suspect that Orwell had his own relations in mind when he described the Comstocks as a family in which 'nothing ever happened') the Blairs offered a unit, an attitude and an outlook from which their son could never quite extricate himself. 'He seemed to think himself rather a rebel,' a girl who knew him in the 1930s shrewdly remarked, 'but I don't think he could ever quite make it.'

The world of the upper-middle-class Edwardian childhood has been endlessly revisited by late-twentieth-century autobiographers. Among

Orwell's contemporaries, Anthony Powell, Evelyn Waugh and Cyril Connolly – to name only three – left accounts of an upbringing that was not substantially different from his. To a greater extent than he would perhaps have wanted to admit, Orwell conformed to the prevailing patterns of his class. Powell and Connolly's fathers were army officers. Arthur Waugh was a publisher. Richard Blair, who would end his days in the Indian Civil Service as Sub-Deputy Opium Agent, 1st grade, lagged just a little way behind them in terms of professional prestige. Now turned fifty, and with only a five-year stretch in front of him before retirement, he returned to England for three months' leave in 1907, begat a third child, Avril, born the following year, and then went away again. By this time the family had moved again to a house called the Nutshell, and the older children had begun to attend a convent school, Sunnydale, staffed by Anglican nuns. It was here, Orwell revealed, that he first fell violently, if remotely, in love with a much older girl named Elsie (the name is given to George Bowling's shopgirl sweetheart, later glimpsed in slatternly decline, in *Coming up for Air*). There was a more tangible friendship with the children of a neighbouring plumber with whom he went bird-nesting and played mildly erotic games until Mrs Blair stepped in and snuffed out the connection on class grounds. Slightly later, as a boy of seven or eight, Eric featured as the cadet member of a teenaged gang led by a fifteen-year-old local doctor's son named Humphrey Dakin (again, the 'Black Hand Gang', whose initiation ritual involves eating a live earthworm, turns up in *Coming up for Air*). Dakin was not impressed by his younger confederate: 'A rather nasty fat little boy with a constant grievance. It took him a long time to grow out of it.'

The passage of time in *Coming up for Air*, with war looming on the horizon and the scent of disturbance in the air, has a peculiarly rapt hallucinatory quality. 'And time was slipping away,' George Bowling reflects. '1910, 1911, 1912 . . . I tell you it was a good time to be alive.' To Bowling 'before the war' was always summer – a delusion, as he very well knows, 'but that's how I remember it. The white dusty road stretching out between the chestnut trees, the smell of nightstock, the green pools under the willows, the splash of Burford Weir – that's what I see when I shut my eyes and think of "before the war . . ."' Towards the end of his life Orwell allowed himself a certain amount of nostalgia over this prelapsarian round of endless summers and village sweet shops. (Bowling provides a page-long description of Edwardian confectionery, with prices included.) A review of *Great Morning*, the first volume of Osbert Sitwell's long-winded autobiography, maintains that its author is probably right to insist that English life in the immediately pre-1914 era had 'a kind of gaiety' that has never been recovered. The cultural baggage that Orwell drags in as evidence – Chaliapin and the *Ballet Russe*, ragtime, the tango, young men-about-town in grey top-hats, houseboats, 'a splashing to and fro of wealth unseen since the early Roman Empire', is probably not the kind that would have occurred to a child. Equally, no one can doubt the fervour with which it is marshalled against the world of forty years hence. Orwell's 'As I Please' columns, written for the left-wing weekly *Tribune* in the mid-1940s, and much of his other journalism, are awash with this type of rhapsodising: paragraphs on the popular songs of the Edwardian age ('Rhoda had a pagoda', the earliest he could remember, dated from 1907–8); meticulous descriptions of children's toys such as peg-tops – there were two kinds, Orwell remembered, one thrown over your shoulder, the other curled out underhand – or, 'one of the greatest joys of childhood', the brass cannons mounted on wooden gun carriages which cost the substantial sum of 10 shillings and went off 'like the day of judgment'. For all its parental restrictions, there was a degree of licence about the early twentieth-century childhood, an absence of rules and regulations, that appealed to Orwell's anarchic side. The gunpowder needed to detonate the miniature cannon could be bought across the counter, while Orwell recalled buying his first firearm, a lethal-looking weapon known as a Saloon Rifle, 'with no questions asked' at the age of ten.

Only by resurrecting our own memories of childhood, Orwell once suggested, can we begin to appreciate quite how distorted is the average child's view of the world it inhabits. The marked absence of children from his novels does not mean that Orwell took no interest in childhood in general or his own in particular. A twitch on the invisible thread that connected him to the world of pre-war Henley could produce dramatic results. 'I can't stop thinking about the young days,' he wrote to a childhood friend, not seen for nearly thirty years, who had contacted him after chancing upon the real identity of the author of *Animal Farm*. But the idea of childhood was important to Orwell for other reasons, in that it confirmed and justified the view he took of himself. The impression of Orwell the child conveyed by his published writings is of a solitary, diffident, aloof boy, permanently on the edge of things, fundamentally detached from the ebb and flow of juvenile life. Avril Blair, who observed this existence at close hand for thirteen years, was concerned to scotch the 'myth' of Orwell's miserable upbringing. 'It has been said that Eric had an unhappy childhood,' she wrote in a memoir published ten years after her brother's death. 'I don't think that was in the least true, although he did give out that impression when he was grown-up.' Avril took up this line again some years later when Jacintha Buddicom announced her intention of writing the reminiscences that became *Eric and Us*. The question of his solitude having once more arisen, Avril suggested that 'Eric had all the friends he wanted. In any case, he was an aloof, undemonstrative person, which doesn't necessarily mean to say that he had a blighted childhood.'

Steering a course through these opposing currents is made all the more difficult in that, with one significant exception, Orwell left no detailed account of his formative years. What he remembered, or what he remembered out loud, came in fragments. The key public event of his childhood, he maintained, was the loss of the *Titanic* on 15 April 1912. The accounts of this disaster, read out over the family breakfast table, filled him with horror. In particular, the fate of the passengers in the stern, flung 300 feet in the air as the ship up-ended itself before being plunged downward, produced a sinking sensation in his stomach thirty years later. Then there was a whole string of memories conveying the sense of class difference and class privilege: his admiration for working-class people – the kindly farmhands met on family holidays in Cornwall, the labourers working at the house next door who taught him to swear – balanced by an awareness of the elemental fissures that ran through the society of which he was a part; his shock at the local squire who countermanded the umpire at a village cricket match and ordered a dismissed batsman back to the wicket. Hindsight, and subsequent adult skirmishes in the class war, may have distorted some of these memories, but the care with which they are burnished up and dealt out conveys something of their importance to Orwell's sense of himself and the world he grew up in. Leaving aside Humphrey Dakin ('stinking little Eric') those around him recalled a detached but not unfriendly child, unfailingly polite, with a marked fondness for reading. Introduced to books by his elder sister, Eric subsisted on a diet that ranged from children's classics such as *Gulliver's Travels* and R. M. Ballantyne's *The Coral Island* to newer authors such as Beatrix Potter and the contemporary jingoism offered by Bartimeus's *Naval Occasions* or Ole-Luk-Oie's *The Green Curve*, the prophecies of a professional soldier who forecast, among other things, air raids and a German invasion. Mrs Blair detected literary talent. Orwell preserved a memory of himself, aged four, dictating a poem containing the phrase 'chair-like teeth', which he fancied was derived from Blake. Significantly, perhaps, the mature Orwell was anxious to connect this with the wider view that he took of his childhood. 'I had the lonely child's habit of making up stories and holding conversations with imaginary persons,' he explained, 'and I think from the very start my literary ambitions were mixed up with the feeling of being isolated and undervalued.'

This is hindsight again but it points towards an important truth. Orwell went through life in ceaseless cultivation of what might be called his personal myth. On one level his work is a constant stream of propaganda for the view that he took of himself, his childhood, his personality, and the great stretches of past time of which he had been a part. Nowhere, perhaps, is this tendency more pronounced than in the vision he conceived of his early education.

By early 1911 Eric was nearly eight: the age at which most boys of his background would be entered at a preparatory school. Mrs Blair, in whose hands the matter rested, took up the task of planning her son's education with some enthusiasm. Transparently ambitious on his behalf – this much is clear from her eventual choice – she was keen, in the light of the family's modest finances, to find somewhere capable of training him up to the level required for a public school scholarship. At last, with the help of her brother Charles, who lived on the south coast, she came up with a school named St Cyprian's, outside Eastbourne. Eric was accepted as a pupil in the summer of 1911 and began what was to turn into a five-year stint there in the autumn term. So much has been written about St Cyprian's in the past half-century – most of it by famous old boys with grudges to nurture – that it is sometimes difficult to remember that it was simply a school rather than a mythological seed-bed. By the formal standards of its time – not always high – it was an exceptional place: laid out on a five-acre site, with spacious living quarters, a substantial dining hall, a gymnasium and even a small chapel. This spruce little colony, with perhaps a hundred pupils, was the private fiefdom of its proprietors, Mr and Mrs Vaughan Wilkes, known to the boys as 'Sambo' and 'Flip' (Mrs Wilkes' nickname derived from her uncorseted breasts). Academic standards, annually monitored by external examiners, were impressive. 'I can fairly say that St Cyprian's need not fear being compared with standards of work done at its competitors,' Sir Charles Grant-Roberts, a Fellow of All Souls, pronounced at about this time. The curriculum stuck rigidly to the subjects required for public school entry: Latin, Greek, English, History and a smattering of Mathematics. Efforts were made to teach the boys such newfangled accomplishments as French, Science and Drawing, but the Wilkeses' speciality, in common with their scholarship-hungry competitors, was the Classics. As to where all this proficiency might lead, although there was a strong connection with Harrow School, St Cyprians preferred to emphasise a rather more tenuous link with Eton College.

Again, vats of ink have been expended on analyses of the school's social catchment area. While St Cyprian's in Orwell's time certainly touted its aristocratic élite – the second son of the Duke of Devonshire, even a Siamese prince – there is a suspicion that most of the pupils came from a slightly less exalted category. A boy who arrived the year after Eric left remembered a preponderance of *nouveaux riches*, children whose parents had done well out of the war. The young Orwell himself marked most of his schoolmates down as scions of 'the non-aristocratic rich, the sort of people who live in huge shrubberied houses in Bournemouth or Richmond, and who have cars and butlers but not country estates'. Landless gentry, then, but of a higher status than the Blairs. Eric's own particular upper-middle-class redoubt was firmly represented. Keen on talent of whatever income bracket, the Wilkeses were prepared to accept boys at half-fees (£90 per annum instead of £180) if they thought them potential scholarship winners. Eric, unexceptionably, and, as far as we can make out, silently, was one of these.

The formal record of this five-year stay in the shadow of the South Downs – its winter chill is memorably evoked in Bowling's account of his time at an Eastbourne convalescent hospital after being invalided home from the Western Front – reveals only an utterly conventional middle-class English childhood. St Cyprian's kept to a spartan, but not notably severe, regime: early morning swimming in the school's plunge pool, followed by PE, chapel and breakfast (huge slices of bread and margarine and porridge served up in pewter pots) in the dining hall. Mrs Wilkes, on the other hand, was furnished with a grapefruit. A religious atmosphere was encouraged. Scripture, one old boy recalled, 'began almost before the end of the meal' with the learning of Bible verses by heart. On Sundays Sambo volleyed questions that required the boys to have memorised at least a chapter of the Old or New Testament. Time not spent in the classroom was taken up with sport, brisk walks across the Downs and the writing of letters home.

Eric's early dispatches back from St Cyprian's, written in the period

1911–12, are painfully innocuous. Though presumably touched up by the Wilkeses, with one eye on the parental audience of the breakfast table, they give no hint of the trouble that lay ahead. On 14 September 1911, a few days into his first term, he wrote to his mother: 'I suppose you want to know what school is like, its alright we have fun in the mornings.' There are references to Togo, the family's wire-haired terrier, another boy's birthday, sports results. Towards the end of 1911 the compositional style picks up rapidly. The high points of prep-school life tick metronomically by: 3rd in a swimming race, 2nd in Arithmetic, 1st in Latin. He was clearly prone to illness: a letter from the following February finds him in the sickroom 'again', but the steady progress in class makes it plain that the Wilkeses had picked a winner. 'Second in everything,' he reported back shortly afterwards. Later there are accounts of a football match ('I was goalkeeper in the second half and they only got past the half-line twice') in which – a good phrase for an eight-year-old – 'they were running at me like angry dogs', summer cricket and an end-of-year fancy dress dance. Eric informed his parents that he went 'as a footman in a red velvet coat and a white silk flowered waistcoast, and red silk trousers, and black stockings, and a lace frill, and a wig'. The careful itemising betrays his fascination.

In the minds of his schoolmates, Eric was a distinct but not obtrusive figure. Sir John Grotian, whose older brother Brent was Eric's exact contemporary, remembered the two classmates being bullied, chased around the school by a mob of boys until they were finally cornered up against the wall of the gym. Cyril Connolly, three months Orwell's junior and later, as the editor of *Horizon*, one of his most reliable literary sponsors, recalled physical details: a big boy, outwardly strong, but always 'chesty' and 'bronchial'. Their shared love was books: years later Orwell would remember excursions through the silent dormitories at dawn to retrieve a half-read copy of H.G. Wells' *The Country of the Blind* from his friend's bedside table. There are occasional, fleeting glimpses of him in the school magazine. The cricket report for the summer term of 1914 – in later life Orwell admitted to a 'hopeless' boyhood passion for cricket – represents 'Blair' as having improved very much of late, able with care to bat very well and a good, though insufficiently agile, catcher of the ball. Meanwhile, his home life was subject to change. Richard Blair had retired from the Opium Department in 1912, aged fifty-five, and come home for good, while the family had moved to the village of Shiplake, two miles out of Henley. Roselawn, their new house, was a substantial property, set in an acre of ground. Mr Blair's annual pension of £400, nearly a quarter of which was laid out on his son's school fees, went a long way in south Oxfordshire in the years before the Great War.

Some starker realities lay to hand. The prospect of war hung ominously over Orwell's early adolescence. The uneasy pre-war atmosphere of *Coming up for Air,* the realisation that 'this here German Emperor' was getting too big for his boots and that 'it' was coming some time, is sharply observed. It was at this time, too, that he met one of the most punctilious of his early observers, whose recollections form the only extended portrait of what Eric Blair as a boy was actually like. Jacintha Buddicom's memories should be treated with a certain amount of caution. Just as the adult Orwell nurtured a defining vision of himself which no amount of contrary evidence would ever shift, so the elderly Miss Buddicom took a similarly weighted view of her youthful playmate. *Eric and Us* is not exactly a propagandist work, but the idea of Orwell's 'normality' drifts in the air above it like woodsmoke. And yet for all the deliberateness of intent, the paraphernalia of Orwell's early teendom is vividly laid out. He was like that, you feel, and in however stage-managed a way the memorialist is being true to his memory. There were three Buddicom children: Jacintha, two years older than Eric; Prosper, a year younger; and Guinever, who was the same age as Avril. In addition to Quarry House, Shiplake, where they lived with their mother (there was an increasingly absentee father, a former curator of Plymouth Museum turned market-gardener), the Buddicoms owned a thatched cottage in a field to the north-west. Here, one summer day, they noticed a boy in the adjoining field standing on his head. Asked to explain himself, the boy replied, 'You are noticed more if you stand on your head than if you are the right way up.' It was the start of a considerable intimacy, so far as we can make out the chief intimacy of Orwell's early years. Certainly Jacintha remembered the Blairs *as a family.* Marjorie, then in her mid-teens, seemed practically grown-up. Mrs Blair impressed her as 'vivacious, spirited'; her husband as the reverse, 'very ancient and not sympathetic'. Their son seemed 'a notably reserved and rather self-contained boy', but humorous and quizzical (he referred to his Limouzin relatives as 'the Lemonskins' or 'the Automobiles'). Above all, Jacintha stresses, the Blairs were a happy family. Judging from her sharp eye for detail, any indications to the contrary would have travelled back across the years along with the headstands and the summer afternoons in Oxfordshire meadows.

While it was Prosper with whom Eric spent most of his time in the holidays – conducting 'chemical experiments' and at one point manufacturing a whisky still whose detonation caused a slumbering cook to give notice – the thirteen-year-old schoolgirl and her new friend shared literary interests. A particular enthusiasm was for the children's writer E. Nesbit, with whom Eric, making use of his aunt's Fabian connections, had even contrived to have tea. His desire to become a FAMOUS AUTHOR expressed itself in long, sub-Shakespearian dramas. One of them, 'The Man and the Maid', clearly derived from *The Tempest* (it features a sorcerer named 'Miraldo') and probably dating from a year or so later, survives in an old notebook labelled 'Masterpieces II'. All of this – the chemical experiments, the baked hedgehogs, the Wardour Street English of the dramas (LUCIUS: 'Mother Gaffins is a long while a coming'. MIRALDO: 'I doubt not she is a trifle rheumatic. Perchance I might sell her a cure for it') read aloud to the silent schoolgirl – is a relief, for looking at Orwell's *oeuvre* as a whole one sometimes wonders whether, like Mr Smallweed in *Bleak House*, he ever had a childhood. As one Orwell scholar once put it, it takes a real imaginative effort to think of his ever being young. The letter he wrote to Jacintha in 1949 when she renewed contact, with its passionate elegisings sits oddly alongside the reactions to *Nineteen Eighty-Four* and the gloom about his failing health, but it is actually quite commonplace: a middle-aged man brought unexpectedly face to face with his past.

He had other things to occupy himself with during this last golden summer of 1914. Practically every English writer of that late-Victorian/early Edwardian generation has left some account of the weeks immediately preceding and following the outbreak of the Great War. To Anthony Powell, living in an army house near Aldershot where his father's regiment was quartered, the war was something sharp, hard and actual: embarkation, news of casualties, young officers who a month ago had been chatting in the hallway as they changed into tennis shoes now dead in Flanders. Evelyn Waugh's elder brother Alec remembered watching Kent play cricket at Blackheath, with a stream of telegraph boys arriving on bicycles to present the players with their summonses to call-up. In *Coming up for Air* George Bowling is conscious of an immense climacteric looming into view: 'For several days . . . there was a strange, stifled feeling, a kind of waiting hush, like the moment before a thunderstorm breaks, as though the whole of England was silent and listening.' A quarter of a century later, in the essay 'My Country Right or Left', written in the early days of another war, Orwell recorded his three chief memories of the time: a cartoon of the Kaiser that appeared in the newspapers in the last days of July; the Henley cabman bursting into tears in the marketplace when his horse was requisitioned; crowds of young men, clad in the fashions of the day – high collars, tightish trousers and bowler hats – scrabbling for the green-coloured evening papers as they arrived in bundles at the station off the London train. 'And then one afternoon a boy came rushing down the High Street with an armful of papers, and people were coming into their doorways to shout across the street: "We've come in! We've come in!"'

Orwell may not have witnessed this particular incident, but it seems clear that he saw something very like it, that the onset of war left a deep impression on him. Avril's first coherent memory of her brother, which she fancied might even have come from the day war broke out, was of him sitting on the floor of his mother's bedroom talking to her 'in a very grown-up manner' while his six-year-old sister knitted him a scarf in the St Cyprian's colours. Not long after this, inspired by the army recruiting campaigns, he wrote a patriotic poem – 'Awake! Young Men of England' – which somebody, presumably Mrs Blair, sent to the local paper, the *Henley and South Oxfordshire Standard*, who printed it early in October.

> Oh! give me the strength of the lion,
> The wisdom of Reynard the fox,
> And then I'll hurl troops at the Germans,
> And give them the hardest of knocks.

There were two more verses, climaxing in a call for instant enlistment ('For if, when your Country's in need/You do not enlist by the thousand/You truly are cowards indeed'). The poem was well received at St Cyprian's, where Mrs Wilkes read it aloud to the assembled school.

It is a tableau out of a boy's school story: the approving headmaster and his wife; the modestly gratified pupil; the respectful silence. Had Mr and Mrs Wilkes been able to foresee the time bomb ticking away quietly in the prize pupil's imagination they would have been less impressed. What Eric thought about St Cyprian's during the five years he spent there is not recorded. What he thought about it as a grown man is one of the most damning indictments of an educational system ever committed to paper. No one knows exactly when the long essay 'Such, Such Were the Joys' (not published in Britain until 1968, the year after Mrs Wilkes' death, for fear of libel proceedings) was written, but the first hint of its genesis comes in two letters sent by Orwell to his fellow-Cyprian Cyril Connolly in 1938. Connolly, then at work on *Enemies of Promise*, which contained his own version of life with the Wilkeses, had turned up some schoolboy correspondence. 'What you say about finding old letters of mine makes me apprehensive,' Orwell wrote. 'I wonder how you can write about St Cyprian's. It's all like an awful nightmare to me, & sometimes I think I can still taste the porridge ...' Another letter, from later in the year, analyses their respective standings in the school – Connolly, Orwell thought, 'was in every way more of a success'; his own position, on the other hand, was 'complicated and in fact dominated by the fact that I had much less money than most of the people around me' – and recalls their shared literary enthusiasms: the dawn raids in pursuit of H.G. Wells and the row that broke out when Eric was discovered with a copy of Compton Mackenzie's incendiary *Sinister Street*. Though it predates the essay, perhaps by several years, the second letter conveys its essential elements in a couple of sentences: his belief that he was not a success; his consciousness of relative poverty; and, above all, his hatred of 'that filthy old sow Mrs Wilkes'.

Nearly 15,000 words long, and showing evidence of careful composition, 'Such, Such Were the Joys' is an exposé of the teaching profession on a par with the Dotheboys Hall scenes in *Nicholas Nickleby* or Samuel Butler's *The Way of All Flesh*. To read it, in fact, is to be constantly reminded of Butler's advice to schoolmasters: never look at one of your pupils, half asleep over his books in the back row, without remembering that this, possibly, may be someone who, long years distant, will tell the world what manner of man you were. The charges it levels against the Wilkeses are many and various, but they can be divided into perhaps half a dozen key areas: cruelty (the essay opens with an account of Eric being thrashed by Mr Wilkes with a riding crop); snobbishness; the continual emphasis on Eric's status as a charity boy; the general squalor of the school, its poor food and wretched living conditions; poor teaching; and, in some ways dominating the charge-sheet to the exclusion of all else, the terrible, domineering, capricious figure of 'Flip'.

No thumbnail sketch of 'Such, Such Were the Joys' can ever quite do justice to the feeling of sheer horror that rises up from its pages, the thought of a childhood lived out at a bedrock level of misery and desperation, in a nightmare world where one's every action is liable to rebuke by stern, unyielding and above all arbitrary authority. Its tone is instantly conveyed by the opening scene. Flogged by Mr Wilkes with such viciousness that the riding crop actually breaks in mid-stroke, Orwell represents himself as bursting into tears. Pain, the thought that tears were 'expected' of him and genuine repentance all played a part, but also present was 'a deeper grief which is peculiar to childhood and not easy to convey: a sense of desolate loneliness and helplessness, of being locked up not only in a hostile world but in a world of good and evil where the rules were such that it was actually impossible for me to keep them'. It is a world, too, of intensely ritualised snobbery, where all the rich boys are blatantly favoured ('I doubt if Sambo ever caned a boy whose father's income was much over £2,000 a year') while Eric's own position as a potential scholar on half-fees is constantly rubbed into him by lectures on avoiding unnecessary expense ('Your parents wouldn't be able to afford it') and warnings as to his probable destiny should the scholarship not materialise ('a little office boy on £40 a year'). Then there is the ghastliness of the environment: the flakes of ancient porridge stuck under the rims of the pewter bowls, the stinking water of the plunge bath and the filthy lavatories. Orwell maintained that he couldn't think of St Cyprian's 'without seeming to breathe in a whiff of something cold and evil-smelling – a sort of compound of sweaty stockings, dirty towels, faecal smells blowing along corridors, forks with old food between the prongs, neck-of-mutton stew, and the banging doors of the lavatories and the echoing chamber pots in the dormitories'. As for the teaching style espoused by the Wilkeses and their underlings, this consists of tedious rote-learning designed solely with the aim of allowing a boy to appear to advantage in a scholarship exam. Atop the heap sits Mrs Wilkes, with her favouritism, her endless reproaches, her sinister and malign intrusions, to whom Orwell imagined that in the last resort he felt 'a sort of guilt-stricken loyalty'.

There are one or two passages in 'Such, Such Were the Joys' that indicate a striving for balance. 'No one can look back on his schooldays and say with truth that they were altogether unhappy,' Orwell remarks. There were excursions over the Downs to Beachy Head, cricket, natural history – most of his 'good' memories from before the age of twenty, he claims, were to do with animals – and above all books, the discoveries he made with Connolly, the copy of *Vanity Fair* found in Mrs Wilkes's private library. There were even, he acknowledged, two members of the school's staff that he liked and responded to – 'Mr Batchelor' (a man named Knowles) and 'Mr Sillars' (Brown): the latter taught Geography and Drawing, as well as organising nature trips, and showed Eric the plated, pearl-handled revolver he kept in his room. The overall verdict, though, is profoundly, and disquietingly, negative. Orwell's memories, he concluded, were 'largely memories of disgust', undercut by a sense of deep, unalterable worthlessness. 'I had no money. I was weak. I was unpopular. I had a chronic cough. I was cowardly. I smelt.' Five years at St Cyprian's reinforced a conviction that coloured his entire boyhood: 'that I was no good, that I was wasting my time, wrecking my talents, behaving with monstrous folly and wickedness and ingratitude . . .'

Even allowing for Orwell's legendary fastidiousness and susceptibility to hurt, this is quite a catalogue. Plenty of distinguished ex-St Cyprian schoolboys – Connolly, Gavin Maxwell, the golfer Henry Longhurst – published their memories of Mr and Mrs Wilkes: none marshalled quite so much venom. How much of what Orwell says should we believe? There are several contextual points to be borne in mind. Clever, sensitive little boys have a habit of feeling the slights of upbringing more keenly than their classmates, the majority of whom simply get on with the task in hand. Mrs Wilkes, tracked down in old age by some early biographers, had her own distinctive view of the young Orwell: there was no warmth in him, she recalled. Her son, Eric's near-contemporary, remembered his mother having a 'great respect' for this backsliding ingrate. This is voting for one's party, perhaps, but a trawl through the reminiscences of several old boys supplies evidence to rebut, or at any rate call seriously into question, nearly all of Orwell's allegations. Far from being a sadistic flogger, Mr Wilkes was remembered as a shy and notably unaggressive character. Snobbishness there certainly was, but this was endemic to the prep school culture of the time. In seeking to bulk out their form lists with earls' grandchildren, the Wilkeses were simply representative of their class. No one, additionally, remembered any pupil let in on the half-fee system being publicly, or even privately, reminded of the fact. As for the supposed squalor of the school, this, for nearly half the duration of Eric's stay, was the Great War, when food was scarce and comfort at a premium. Prep school food, countless reminiscences insist, was uniformly dreadful. With regard to the teaching, the school's academic record, attested to by its external examiners, speaks for itself. As for Mrs Wilkes, several of her pupils may have (retrospectively) lamented her favouritism and split-second mood swings; others recall her as an inspired teacher, whose knowledge of, and enthusiasm for, the English classics would not have disgraced a university don. In later life they wrote to her and kept up with her. In 1951, 250 of them attended a celebration dinner in her honour, and Henry Longhurst was happy to acknowledge her as 'the outstanding woman of my life'.

The early twentieth-century English prep school was, history suggests, a fairly dismal place. While allowing that nothing particularly horrible happened to him at his own establishment, the New Beacon, Anthony Powell confessed himself unwilling to live five minutes of it again. Even Alec Waugh, who adored school and reverenced his teachers, remembered being forced to eat the contents of a breakfast bowl into which he had recently vomited. Jacintha Buddicom's opinion is worth having here. She recalled several conversations between Orwell and her brother Prosper about school beatings, but was left with the impression that they were the exception rather than the rule. Talking once of Mrs Wilkes, Orwell remarked that 'to be a favourite with old Mum you have to be a Duke in a kilt', but this was said humorously; there was no element of rancour. As for the self-accusing litany of weakness, cowardice, ill health, unpopularity and body odour, this Miss Buddicom briskly dismissed. He was a perfectly normal, happy boy, well-built – certainly in surviving photographs he towers over Prosper – independent-minded to the degree that popularity, or its absence, never troubled him. St Cyprian's was his 'scapegoat'.

What one wants, amid this barrage of claim and counter-claim, is the testimony of someone whose background, or at any rate family income, was similar to Orwell's. It can be found, perhaps, in the memories of Alaric Jacob – like Orwell, admitted on half-fees – who entered St Cyprian's a term or so after Orwell had left. Jacob's *Scenes from a Bourgeois Life*, which contains his prep school memories (the school features as 'St Saviour's,' and its proprietors as 'Mr and Mrs Arbuthnot'), has interesting Orwell associations – it was issued by Secker & Warburg, his publisher, a year before his death, carries an epigraph from Connolly's *The Unquiet Grave* and was conceivably seen by Orwell before he died. Jacob, who arrived at the age of eight, describes the school as being administered 'with great shrewdness and efficiency by the headmaster's wife'. Mrs Wilkes, he stresses, had a good heart, using her husband's profits to subsidise what he calls 'the careers of the new poor', and was an excellent teacher. At the same time she displayed 'a violent and indiscriminate temper'. A small boy who had the misfortune to offend her at the start of the term might spend the next ten weeks vainly trying to make amends. Jacob claims literally to have found a friend kneeling beside his bed repeating the words 'Oh God, deliver me from evil and grant that I may keep in Mrs Arbuthnot's favour all this term, through Jesus Christ Our Lord Amen.' As for the prevailing atmosphere of locker room and dormitory, this was 'an education in *snobisme*'. Few spectacles were so repulsive as that of a group of small boys lying on a cricket field discussing why so-and-so's parents looked so queer and why it was that the lower classes were so funny. This has the authentic Orwellian note – Jacob survived by means of his 'presentable' parents, the key to entry to the St Cyprian's inner circle – but he is careful to note that the constant cries of 'How much have *your* people got?' were not the work of Mrs Wilkes. Rather, they were endemic to the system over which she presided.

But perhaps one ought to go back to Orwell's text. What kind of a piece of writing is 'Such, Such Were the Joys?' Malcolm Muggeridge left an intriguing record of a day in February 1950 when, during a visit to Secker & Warburg with Orwell's widow Sonia and his great friend Tosco Fyvel, the question of printing the unpublished essay in a posthumous collection arose. Roger Senhouse, a partner in the firm, found the piece repugnant, 'full of self-pity'. Muggeridge agreed, 'but then so was George, and so was David Copperfield'. In a way, Muggeridge thought, the essay rather resembled Dickens's autobiographical novel, 'only dehydrated'. Unquestionably, Orwell intended it to be taken as literally true, which, equally unquestionably, it is not. One may not go so far as Robert Pierce, who suggests, after a minute survey of the evidence, that Orwell neither wet his bed nor was beaten, yet, like a great deal of Orwell's writing, the air of menace it stokes up and the literary devices used to bring off its effects are strikingly artificial. Take, for example, the final sentence in which Orwell proclaims that the school's magic 'works no longer, and I have not even enough animosity left to make me hope that Flip and Sambo are dead or that the story of the school burning down was true'. This is clearly false: St Cyprian's did continue to work its spell, or Orwell would not have taken the trouble to recreate it so lavishly. As for the animosity, 'Such, Such Were the Joys' is dripping with it. Throughout the essay we can see a mythologising spirit at work, fastening on symbolic incidents (the 10-shilling cricket bat whose purchase is denied on the grounds that 'Your parents couldn't afford it') building up to the hauntingly powerful picture of the lost, excluded outsider, the whole gathered up in a grandly sinister metaphor: the police state, with Sambo as its all-seeing, ever-vigilant eye. One of the stories Orwell recounts is of being sent on an errand to Eastbourne and straying off the prescribed path to buy chocolate in a sweet shop. He emerges to find a man staring intently at his school cap. Obviously, Orwell represents his younger self as realising, the man was a spy placed there by Sambo. This seemed a perfectly logical explanation. 'Sambo was all-powerful: it was natural that his agents should be everywhere.'

All this – the references to Sambo's 'spies', and his being 'all powerful' – points us in a rather different direction, the question of when 'Such, Such Were the Joys' was written. The woman who acted as Orwell's secretary in the mid-1940s remembered making a fair copy from a bleary and apparently much-travelled typescript. This was submitted to Secker & Warburg in 1947. But who typed the original, and when? A possible completion date is 1939–40 (Orwell announced his intention of 'writing a book about St Cyprian's' back in 1938). Or it could have been written and typed – or rewritten and re-typed – in 1945–6 when Orwell engaged an additional typist to do work for him. At any rate it is highly probable that a considerable part of the work on 'Such, Such Were the Joys' was done when Orwell was incubating, or indeed writing, what became *Nineteen Eighty-Four*. Over the years many a critic has speculated that this exposé of the totalitarian mind is on one level a projection of his infant misery, an autocratic world that has its roots in a boys' boarding-school. But it could be argued, equally plausibly, that the trick is being played the other way round – that Orwell's mature views on authoritarianism and its psychological consequences encouraged him to recast his memories of St Cyprian's in a more sinister shape. The idea of the school as a police state, Mrs Wilkes with her arbitrary favouritism – all this, it could be said, is the mental baggage of *Nineteen Eighty-Four* shifted back in time. Whatever the answer to this riddle, there is some kind of relationship between the essay on boyhood and the dystopian novel, certainly sufficient to suggest that both existed in Orwell's mental landscape at the same time.

And whether or not Orwell's account of St Cyprian's is literally true, other old boys who wrote about Mr and Mrs Wilkes later acknowledged the influence of prejudicial hindsight. Connolly, having settled his own scores in *Enemies of Promise* (1938), got a letter of 'bitter reproach' from his old headmistress. Looking over his parents' papers after their deaths he came to appreciate the pains that the Wilkeses had taken on his behalf. The adult Connolly decided that what he had caricatured was simply exaggerated enthusiasm. In 1967, hoping to make some kind of posthumous reparation, he turned up at Mrs Wilkes's sparsely attended funeral. Nobody spoke to him. His final verdict was that 'History, if it can be bothered, will probably show Mr Wilkes to have been an extremely conscientious, though unimaginative man; and Mrs Wilkes to have used too much physical violence and emotional blackmail, and to have vented some personal bitterness on the boys. Yet she was warm-hearted and an inspired teacher.' All the same, Connolly could not resist mentioning the 'voodoo-like' quality of the place, and the reports he had heard of old boys who taught their children to shake their fists at the now deserted playing fields (the rumour Orwell had heard was correct – the school did burn down in a fire in 1939) as they drove past.

Whatever Orwell may have thought about St Cyprian's, he and Connolly were two of the Wilkeses' prize pupils and, as such, prime candidates for a public school scholarship. By his twelfth year the thought of this step up to the next rung of the educational ladder hung dramatically in the air. Jacintha Buddicom remembered late-afternoon sessions in the garden at Quarry House being interrupted by Mr Blair arriving to remind his son to post the answers required to the questions set by a St Cyprian's master with whom he did correspondence coaching in the holidays. The Blairs had moved back to Henley (where Mr Blair now officiated as secretary to the local golf club) once again in 1915, to a smaller, semi-detached house at 36 St Mark's Road. No schoolfriends came to stay; neither did Eric go on visits of his own, though there were mentions of his great friend 'CC'. Extra-curricular activities extended to the role of Prince Charming in a Christmas 1915 panto got up under the auspices of a local peer whom Mr Blair had met at the golf club. He was a terrible actor, another member of the cast recalled, and above all shy.

In 1915 Eric won the school English prize. The pressure on him to succeed grew ever more intense. He states in 'Such, Such Were the Joys' what probably was a literal truth: that never in his life did he work harder than when urged on by Mr and Mrs Wilkes. The formal record of his final year is simply a catalogue of triumph. In February 1916 he was dispatched to Wellington College, together with Connolly (the latter 'hated every moment: the blue-suited prefects bustling about the dismal brick and slate, the Wellingtonias and rhododendrons, infertile flora of the Bagshot sand'), emerging with the first open scholarship in Classics. There followed a two-and-a-half-day examination and interview at Eton. He came 13th overall, and, with only twelve scholarships immediately available, would, if he wished to take up his place, have to wait until a vacancy arose. Back at St Cyprian's he won the Classics prize and in June came second to Connolly in a fine old anachronism of memory testing called the Harrow History Prize. In the year's external examiner's report he and Connolly feature as the school's undoubted star pupils, Connolly the champion at English, Orwell better at Latin and Greek. There was a second appearance in print, too, when the school was set the task of writing a poem to commemorate the recent death of Lord Kitchener. Again, Orwell's attempt was sent – by himself, according to Connolly – to the *Henley and South Oxfordshire Standard*, where it appeared on 21 July. It is a conventional piece, and probably of less interest to Orwell scholars than the column devoted to 'The Problem of the Tramp', a consideration of local vagrancy statistics, that appears on the same page.

He eventually left St Cyprian's at the end of 1916, having finished third in the school's senior diving competition and played Mr Wardle in the Dickensian sketch 'Mr Jingle's Wedding' (exceedingly good in a difficult part, thought the school magazine) staged at a local army camp and two nearby military hospitals. The solitary letter home that survives from this period is a much more sophisticated performance than his earlier notes, full of references to 'unspeakably horrid' teas and 'ripping picnics'. There is no hint of the misery under which he supposedly laboured. At some point in mid-December he took his leave of Mrs Wilkes. The adult Orwell claimed to detect 'a sort of patronage, almost a sneer' in her farewell. Despite his achievements, he was 'not a good type of boy'. What emotions did he believe he felt on that cold Sussex morning in the middle of the Great War? 'Failure, failure, failure – failure behind me, failure ahead of me – that was by far the deepest conviction that I carried away.' And so the thirteen-year-old boy, with his brace of scholarships and his teetering stack of prizes, packed his bags and disappeared into the rest of his teenage life.

3

Eton Medley

A boy with a permanent chip on his shoulder. – John Wilkes, Eton contemporary

He never was very successful at school – he did no work and won no prizes – but he managed to develop his brain along the lines that suited it. He read the books which the headmaster denounced from the pulpit, and developed unorthodox opinions about the C. of E., patriotism and the Old Boys' Tie . . . – *Keep the Aspidistra Flying* (1936)

After Christmas, no Eton vacancy having yet emerged, Eric made the short journey down into Berkshire to spend the spring term of 1917 at Wellington College. Wellington, though undoubtedly what Mr Levy in *Decline and Fall* (1928) would have classified as a 'leading school', had a somewhat austere atmosphere. Founded by the Prince Consort in the mid-nineteenth century, it had little of the grandeur associated with ancient foundations such as Harrow and Rugby, and the reputation of having been designed for 'the sons of soldiers unlikely to be rich'. Not much is known of the short time – no more than nine weeks – Eric spent in its chilly purlieus. A younger friend who knew him much later in life, and discussed the school with him, got the impression that he found it 'terrifically spartan', even after the discomfort of St Cyprian's. Jacintha Buddicom characterised it as a 'cold-douche disappointment' – the only activity in which Eric took any pleasure, she gathered, was skating on the lake during a long, late-winter freeze-up. Nevertheless, he remained sufficiently *au fait* with the school's traditions and its paraphernalia to recognise the Old Wellingtonian tie a quarter of a century later, and took an interest in the reforms initiated by his Eton friend Robert ('Bobbie') Longden, a young headmaster who met an untimely death in a Second World War bombing raid. Under Longden,

Orwell maintained, Wellington had become 'quite enlightened'. In many ways this is typical of Orwell's have-your-cake-and-eat-it attitude to the traditions in which he was raised: affecting to despise the lure of the old boys' tie but capable of recognising it when he saw it. Meanwhile, the Wellington Enlightenment lay in the future, and, an Eton place finally turning up – one of the last of the scholarship intake ('election') of 1916 – he happily left the school shortly after Easter, proceeding to Shropshire to spend part of the holidays with the Buddicom children in their grandfather's house at Tinklerton. In the context of the time, and in the light of what followed, Mr and Mrs Blair's decision to take him away from Wellington is a significant one. With its more middle-class tone and a parental catchment area much more in keeping with his father's profession, the school might have been made for a boy like Eric Blair. Nonetheless, given the opportunity, both he and his parents unhesitatingly preferred Eton.

The Great War, by now over halfway through its third year, was bogged down in stalemate. Later Orwell would remember this as a time when enthusiasm for the war among the non-combatant young dwindled into indifference. Taught by elderly schoolmasters dragged out of retirement to replace those sent to the Front, living in conditions of increasing discomfort, many schoolboys had become almost immune to world events; even the Russian Revolution of autumn that year 'made no impression', Orwell maintained. The outsize map of the Western Front pinned up on a blackboard in the school library, where advances and retreats were represented by silk threads stretched over drawing pins, went unregarded. Fire-breathing young officers on leave from Flanders were listened to without enthusiasm. Yet war was having a considerable effect on the Blairs. In 1917 Richard Blair, in a notably gallant and patriotic gesture, gave up his duties at the golf club and enlisted as a second lieutenant (at sixty he was thought to be one of the oldest junior officers in the British army). Sent to France, he ended up in charge of a pack-mule depot at Marseilles. In his absence Mrs Blair decamped to London to take up war work at the Ministry of Pensions. With Marjorie employed as a dispatch rider with the Women's Legion – mother and daughter lived at first in a tiny flat in Earls Court before removing to slightly larger premises in Notting Hill – and the two younger children at boarding-school, 36 St Mark's Road was let out on a series of short tenancies. Family reunions became difficult to convene. One practical consequence of this fracture was a greater intimacy with the

Buddicoms. At Christmas 1917, for example, Eric and Avril stayed at Shiplake as paying guests ('I feel it is most dreadfully cool of me asking you this,' Mrs Blair apologised to Mrs Buddicom, 'but these are such extraordinary times that one is forced to do out-of-the-way things') at £1 a week each. The arrangement was repeated a year later.

No amount of relocation or living out of suitcases could quite take the gloss from Eton, where he arrived in May 1917. The Eton experience has been raptly analysed in a shelf-full of memoirs. Looking back on his time at the school over ten years after it had ended, Anthony Powell – a man whose sensibilities could to some extent be said to have been paralysed by Eton – tried to convey something of the initial impression that the place made on him. Staring out of his study window a day or so after his arrival, Powell observed a boy of about fifteen coming along the far side of the street. One hand was in his pocket. The other supported a pile of books against his thigh. The boy's top-hat – these were *de rigueur* until the 1940s – pushed to the back of his head, was no less startling than his exceptionally short trouser-legs and light-coloured socks. One of his shoulders was higher than the other. This, together with a slight sag at the knees, produced a perfect specimen of what was known as the 'Eton slouch'. As a final garnish, he was singing a popular song of the day. Powell was instantly transfixed. 'This was the most sophisticated thing I had ever seen.' His verdict on the wider Eton atmosphere was that it offered 'a florid interlude, coloured by a sort of hobgoblin realism, like a picture by Breughel'. Above all, Powell was impressed by the absolute conviction of the standards on display, next to which the poise of his 'Brideshead generation' Oxford contemporaries seemed merely self-conscious. It was not just that one saw the names of former prime ministers carved into desk-tops, rather that the whole government of the country was seen as a personal responsibility. It was as if, rather than saying 'If you don't learn to speak French properly you'll never be able to enjoy yourself in Paris', the Eton authorities were insisting, however silently, that 'If you don't learn some sort of civilised behaviour, England will become uninhabitable for everybody.' Powell was not alone in experiencing this sensation. Connolly had a similar moment on Windsor bridge during the scholarship exam when he watched two languid Etonians appraising the rowing style of an oarsman who laboured beneath them. 'Really,' one of them drawled, 'that man Wilkinson's not at all a bad oar.'

Orwell's formal opinion of the four and a half years he spent at Eton was expressed in a few carefully chosen sentences supplied to professional reference books and written for the benefit of foreign audiences unfamiliar with his work. Once again, there is a sense of deliberateness – an unshiftable view of the past – in the sentiments conveyed. In a 1940 entry for *Twentieth Century Authors*, for example, he writes: 'I was educated at Eton, 1917–1921, as I had been lucky enough to win a scholarship, but I did no work there and learned very little, and I don't feel that Eton has been much of a formative influence in my life.' Five years later, in an autobiographical sketch for the American magazine *Commentary*, he insisted, 'I was only at Eton because I had a scholarship, and I don't belong to the social structures of most of the people who are educated there.' Shortly afterwards he offered a variation on this approach to readers of the Ukrainian translation of *Animal Farm*: 'I was educated at Eton, the most costly and snobbish of the English Public Schools. But I had got in there by means of a scholarship, otherwise my father could not have afforded to send me to a school of this type.' The implications of these three statements, composed over a period of five years, are clear: Eton was too good for him; he was there on sufferance; it left no impression on his mind or personality. The first two of these assumptions are questionable, but the third is highly misleading. Eton left a profound impression on Orwell which, if anything, became more marked the further he moved away from it.

Working out what Orwell made of his time at Eton is complicated by the extraordinary freemasonry that characterises the Etonian world, a series of unspoken assumptions about personal and collective behaviour that can render its atmosphere almost impenetrable to the outsider. It was at this time a largish establishment of nearly a thousand boys, divided up into as many as twenty houses – so large, in fact, that many of the pupils went through their five years there without ever coming across other boys with whom, at a smaller school, they would have been in almost daily contact. Thus Orwell was 'at Eton' at the same time, to take only the most obvious literary supporting acts, as Harold Acton, Anthony Powell, Cyril Connolly and Brian Howard. This does not mean that he knew any of them in the accepted schoolboy sense. Acton, a year younger, remembered him by sight; Powell, two and a half years his junior, not even that. Even Connolly, born in September 1903 and consequently entering the school three terms behind him, saw much less of Orwell at Eton than he had done at St Cyprian's. He recalled him as 'rather extreme and aloof', perpetually sneering at 'They', a compound of masters, Old Etonians, clergymen and reactionary fellow-pupils,

Lavishly distributed in numberless buildings grouped around the central site, a mile or so distant from Windsor, Eton's physical essence is similarly difficult to define: grandiose architecture, the sprawl of playing fields leading down to the watery glades of the river; resplendent in summer, in winter wreathed in Thames Valley mist. Powell's years of brooding on the locale produced this description, from the opening chapter of A *Question of Upbringing*:

> As winter advanced in that river valley, mist used to rise in late afternoon and spread over the flooded grass; until the house and all the outskirts of the town were enveloped in chilly vapour, tinted like cigar-smoke. The house looked on to other tenement-like structures, experiments in architectural insignificance, that intruded upon a central concentration of buildings, commanding and antiquated, laid out in a quadrilateral, though irregular, style. Silted-up residues of the years smouldered uninterruptedly – and not without melancholy – in the maroon brickwork of these medieval closes . . .

Other aspects of the school beyond the architectural surround seemed locked in the distant past. Orwell himself noted the atmosphere of almost pre-modern 'chaos' that prevailed. As an institution, Eton had virtually escaped the Arnoldian educational reforms out of which the nineteenth-century English public school system had been created. This, nearly everyone who went there agreed, made it a highly unusual place: a magisterial collective entity full of obscure secret fiefdoms; unfailingly orthodox in its make-up but quietly sympathetic to more maverick elements; aristocratic but not exclusively so; self-governing and *sui generis*. Orwell's position in this ant heap of poise, wealth and ambition was made more anomalous by his scholarship. As a King's Scholar (KS) absolved from all fees except basic living expenses (about £25 a year) he was part of what one contemporary called 'an intellectual elite within a social elite'. Quartered on their own premises in College, under the supervision of the Master in College, and distinct from the 900 'oppidans' (from the Latin 'town-dweller') the seventy or so King's Scholars were in one sense the wheel on which the school turned, providing the Captain of the School, ten members of the twenty-strong sixth form and numbers of the members of 'Pop', the Eton Society, a self-elected body of around twenty-eight boys, who acted as prefects and possessed certain privileges, usually in the field of recherché dress styles.

It is tempting to say that Eric Blair – the fourteenth member of his election – was a Colleger first and an Etonian second. Each Etonian house was a separate community – its doors locked at five in winter, its members providing teams for school sporting competitions – but Collegers were something more than this: a group of boys corralled together by dint of their intellect and the somewhat archaic arrangements of College itself. In their first year, for example, Eric and his companions inhabited the Lower Boys' chamber, which was separated into individual 'stalls' rising halfway to the ceiling. Eric was undoubtedly proud of this newfound status; there is a letter in which he refers to 'beastly oppidans', and he subsequently kept in touch with several members of a high-flying group that included Dennis Dannreuther, later a fellow of All Souls and barrister, Longden and the Byzantine historian Steven Runciman. There were familiar faces to hand, too, however indifferent his reaction to the presence of former St Cyprian's boys such as the Wilkeses' son John. At any rate his initial reports on the place were favourable. During a summer holiday with the Buddicoms, again spent at their grandfather's house in Shropshire, Jacintha was given to understand that while he had been neutral about St Cyprian's and thought Wellington 'beastly', he was 'interested and happy' at Eton. This assumption that Eric was like any other fourteen-year-old boy at the start of his public school career was reinforced by an inspection of surviving photographs from the summer of 1917: '*exactly like Eric at that age*', she rhapsodised, 'the happy, smiling schoolboy, with his happy, smiling face'. Whether happy or not, one thing Eric was determined upon, at any rate academically speaking, was to give himself a rest. There is little doubt that he frankly slacked at Eton. In the Michaelmas 'half' (the Eton word for 'term') of 1917, for example, he came bottom in Latin, a subject in which at St Cyprian's he had carried all before him. There was nothing unusual in this idleness – many boys were goaded so strenuously through their scholarship exams that they were happy to tread water for the next two or three years – but it was noted by his contemporaries. Unquestionably bright, ran the general verdict, but as Wilkes junior put it, 'I don't think he tried too hard'. This unwillingness to exert himself had immediate academic consequences. Initially marked down as a Classical specialist on account of his scholarship, Eric was soon transferred to the less exacting arena of Classical General. Later he tried Science for a while – the 'chemical experiments' with Prosper Buddicom had demonstrated his mild scientific bent – but without distinguishing himself. The Eton 'block' system meant that boys of similar intelligence were taught together subject by subject, to a certain extent irrespective of seniority. Within a year Eric had not only been overhauled by most of his election but seems quite cheerfully to have resigned himself to the fate of an academic makeweight.

None of Eric's Eton reports survives. This is a pity, as they – and the regular housemasters' letters home – tended to be shrewd and psychologically revealing documents: Anthony Powell's, for instance, offer a casebook of adolescent moodiness. But it seems clear that by an early stage in his Eton career, the prospect of any sort of academic distinction was remote. To go on to Oxford or Cambridge, Eric would have needed both a scholarship and a fair amount of parental belt-tightening. These he was plainly not going to get. All of which gives peculiar interest to a long conversation with Jacintha Buddicom, which she dates to September 1918 and an afternoon spent picking mush-rooms in the fields near Henley, 'about Oxford and the wonderful time we should have when we got there' (Jacintha, then aged seventeen, was at Oxford High School). It is difficult to know how much to read into this. None of Orwell's schoolfriends remembers him showing any interest in the idea of going on to university. The immediate conse-quence of these confidences over the mushrooms was a poem addressed to Jacintha and entitled 'The Pagan' (this refers to a disagreement between the Oxford High School authorities and the Buddicoms over the family's agnosticism). It is a rather solemn piece – most of Orwell's early poems are sombre affairs ('So here are you/and here am I/Where we may think our Gods to be;/Above the earth, beneath the sky/Naked souls alive and free') – ending with the thought of a 'mystic light' that ever in the recipient's head would shine. Jacintha, who was a critically minded girl, proposed several amendments, including the substitution of 'naked souls' with the less suggestive 'unarmoured'. These – mush-room hunts and solemn poems – naturally raise the question of Eric's romantic feelings towards Jacintha. Looking back, half a century later, Miss Buddicom was certain that there were none. Whatever the teenage boy may have felt for this slightly older girl in a world hedged round with parental proscription is permanently obscured by his well-documented adolescent reserve.

And yet Eric was undoubtedly close to Jacintha, made her the repository for many of his confidences and was not shy of talking to her about what remained his chief ambition. The FAMOUS AUTHOR conversations were still actively pursued, to the point of discussing suitable bindings for that far-off collected edition. As for the taste that might shape this literary career, Eric's enthusiasms, as declared to Jacintha, were very much of their time: Chesterton, E.W. Hornung, M.R. James, an outwardly benign figure who issued from the Provost's lodgings at Eton (where he arrived in 1918) some of the most macabre ghost stories in the English language, the Buddicoms' copy of Wells' *Modern Utopia*, which he read so often that Jacintha's parents made him a present of it (she remembered his disappointment at missing Wells at one of the Limouzins' Fabian tea parties). The modern movement in literature – Joyce, Pound and Firbank – lay beyond the horizon, but there were other writers with whom chance brought him together. Walking into the study of one of his Eton masters, and finding him out, he picked up off the table a magazine with a blue cover. This turned out to be a copy of Ford Madox Ford's *The English Review*, a decisive influence in shaping highbrow taste in the early twentieth century (D.H. Lawrence's inamorata Jessie Chambers remarked, 'What a joy it was to get the solid, handsome journal from our local newsagent, and feel it was a link with the world of literature'). By his own admission, Eric's idea of a 'good' poem was Rupert Brooke. He was consequently overwhelmed by Lawrence's 'Love on the Farm', in which a woman watches from a cottage window as her husband advances across the fields, plucks a rabbit from a snare, kills it, throws it on the kitchen table and passionately embraces her. Lawrence cast a substantial shadow over Orwell's literary development: the hunting scenes in *Burmese Days*, notably the moment where Flory and Elizabeth are exalted by slaughtering a leopard, show a discernible Lawrentian trace.

For the moment, such juvenilia as he produced was determinedly conventional: humorous pieces in the style of the comic writer Barry Pain; a detective story called 'The Vernon Murder' (this looks like a private joke, as one of the characters is called 'Leonard Vernon' and another 'Cyril Tipley'; Connolly's Christian names were 'Cyril Vernon'); a fragmentary sketch about a man trying to light a cigarette in a freezing waiting room, 'Mr Puffin and the Missing Matches'. Eton friends noted a liking for esoterica, in Eton terms probably not much more than a fondness for Wells and Samuel Butler. Steven Runciman recalled his habit of 'airing his knowledge, particularly to the masters, who were very slightly shocked to find someone so well read in books which they thought a bit too grown up for the young'. Like Gordon Comstock, perhaps, in *Keep the Aspidistra Flying*, Eric was content to let his mind develop along the lines that suited it, picking up along the way the enthusiasms and behavioural tics that would stay with him for the rest of his life. Reading Jacintha's accounts of her teenage days in Oxfordshire one is constantly struck by how much of the mature Orwell – a man whom Jacintha never knew – seems to be present: faintly aloof, spare and ironical in his speech, following his own intellectual paths, cultivating private interests that were sometimes markedly out of the way. Jacintha remembered, for example, his collection of comic post-cards. There was a comparatively mild selection which she was allowed to read. A second, more *risqué*, set was kept out of sight in a manila envelope.

The slightly dispersed quality of the young Orwell's teenage life – the lack of a fixed base, family scattered by wartime – persisted beyond the war's end in November 1918. The Christmas following Eric's fifth term at Eton found Mrs Blair's younger children billeted once more on the Buddicoms. As earlier biographers have noted, there is a mystery about this arrangement. Mr Blair remained in France, but surely Mrs Blair would have wanted to see her children at Christmas. Space at Notting Hill Chambers was at a premium, but could she not visit? What kept them apart? The severance is all the more puzzling in the light of the motherly tone of her letter of 21 December to Mrs Buddicom, with its fond references to her 'chicks' and Eric's Christmas presents (25 shillings from his father, five shillings from Aunt Nellie Limouzin). This Christmas produced another poem for Jacintha, a portentous sonnet beginning with the lines 'Our minds are married,/but we are too young/for wedlock by the custom of this age' and ending with the assurance that the two of them would remember 'when our hair is white,/these clouded days revealed in radiant light'. Jacintha recalled him writing it in a corner of the Buddicoms' dining room while the younger children sat playing card games at the table. However juvenile, it sets the tone for most of Orwell's later poetic excursions: formal, conventionally rhymed, altogether stuck in the Housman, or even pre-Housman, groove. Come January he, Prosper and Guinever decamped to Brighton to stay with one of Prosper's schoolfriends. The letters to Jacintha flowed back and forth on a weekly basis: plays seen, books read. Judging by later letters sent to women friends about literature, these were determinedly didactic.

Most of Eric's interests at this point existed *outside* the classroom. He quite enjoyed Eton and relished the relative freedom it offered, but its curriculum held little to interest him. Neither, too, did the people administering it. Orwell's tutor for much of his time at Eton was the legendary A.S.F. Gow, subsequently a Fellow of Trinity College, Cambridge, known to generations of Eton schoolboys as 'Grannie Gow'. According to Denys King-Farlow, Orwell's exact contemporary – the two arrived in College on the same day in May 1917 – Gow tried to encourage Eric in his studies, but the interest was never reciprocated. Certainly Gow, who like several other Eton masters moved in worlds beyond his professional calling, left some mark on Orwell: this much is proved by their later contact. For the moment Eric's response was limited to squibs disparaging his love of Homer and interest in Italian painting. His relationship with Crace, the Master in College, who had overall charge of the Eton scholars, was, if anything, even worse. An April 1920 number of *College Days*, a handwritten ephemeral in the ancient Eton tradition, to which Eric is known to have contributed, carried the spoof personal ad, 'A.R.D. After rooms – JANNEY'. 'A.R.D.' was a boy named A.R.D. Watkins; 'Janney' Crace's nickname. Crace, though furious, was unable to exact much retribution, as to have done so would have been to acknowledge the favouritism to which the squib refers. None of the staff, not even G.H. Lyttelton, whose extra English classes were the nursery for a riot of celebrated literary figures, seems to have inspired Orwell, or to have been themselves inspired, although Orwell and Runciman were impressed by the gangling, myopic figure of Aldous Huxley, who briefly taught them French. Runciman recalled that Orwell was the only person with whom he discussed Huxley's work. There was no chance of any extra-curricular fraternisation, though. Huxley, to whom Eton figured as a purgatorial interlude in his writing career, made a rapid exit from the classroom after the lesson ended.

However much his later career may have surprised them, Eric's Eton contemporaries recognised his distinctive personality. 'Standing aside from things,' a boy named Christopher Eastwood remembered, 'observing, always observing'. Christopher Hollis, two years above him in the school library, later a Tory MP and Catholic publisher, started to take notice of Eric as a result of an incident involving a boy named Johnson Major. The junior Johnson reported that Blair K.S. had taken a violent dislike to his brother, apparently on grounds of noisiness, constructed an effigy of him out of a bar of soap, stuck pins in it and kept it on the bracket below the mirror in his cubicle (the reference to the cubicle dates this to Eric's first year in College) in the hope of paranormal vengeance. Curiously Johnson Major was then beaten twice in three days. Intrigued, Hollis – though not supposed to associate with 'Lower Boys' – sought him out. Hollis recalled Eric above all as a humorist, 'a boy saying and doing funny things'. Noel Blakiston, who achieved posthumous fame as the (unyielding) object of Cyril Connolly's schoolboy affections, recalled him 'collecting the religions of the new boys'. Was he Cyrenian, Sceptic, Epicurean, Cynic, Neoplatonist, Confucian or Zoroastrian? Eric asked one of these newcomers. The boy replied that he was a Christian. 'Oh, we haven't had one of those,' Eric deadpanned back. There was another episode involving an obscure dispute over a tennis ball in which it was proposed to beat every one of the fourteen boys in Eric's election. Eric offered himself as scapegoat – a futile gesture, as it turned out, as the authorities went ahead with the original plan. The incident stuck in Hollis' head as, watching the mass punishment with the other Collegers, he noticed the extreme shininess of Eric's trousers – the only hint that came to him during their schooldays 'that he was perhaps poorer than the rest of us'.

The tenor of these reminiscences is unusually consistent. As a boy in his mid to late teens, Eric was neither unpopular nor insignificant – in the midst of a school whose hierarchies were especially complicated; he merely followed his own path. He was certainly rated a bit of a 'Bolshie', to use the shorthand of the day, but as Hollis points out this was standard for the era. The winds of change 'blew like a gale at Eton and particularly in College'. Dealings with him were always stimulating, Runciman thought, because one never felt confidence in his friendship. However self-absorbed, he managed to take part in most of the traditional Eton amusements, played in the house football matches and the legendarily complex Wall Game, went swimming at the bathing place known as Athens – a photograph taken by King-Farlow shows him posing insouciantly with Runciman and three other boys – and fished in Jordan, a tiny tributary of the Thames. He also took an active part in preserving the Eton tradition of ephemeral magazines, contributing to the handwritten *Election Times* in 1918 and conducting three issues of the much more professional *College Days* (the fifth number, got up for the Eton–Harrow cricket match of 1920 and full of smart adverts, was supposed to have netted King-Farlow and himself £128). The Athens photo shows a tall, well-built boy retaining the plump face of childhood. Eric's height shot up during his time at Eton.

Five feet seven in his mid-teens, he was six feet three by the time he left. Yet his health was never good. He had pneumonia twice in his teens, in 1918 and 1921. A letter sent back from one of the Shropshire holidays by a Buddicom aunt notes that 'Eric has a bit of a cough. He says it is chronic . . .' It would be easy to claim, in the light of this kind of evidence, that Eric was in some sense 'neglected'. Modern school medical arrangements would have diagnosed his weak lungs at an early stage: eighty years ago schools and parents were less vigilant.

Less characteristically, in the light of what came later, he was also capable of joining in another traditional, though less conspicuous, Eton pastime – cultivating crushes on younger boys. Long years afterwards Cyril Connolly turned up a lost note, originally reproduced in a letter to a third party, in which Orwell confessed himself 'gone' on Eastwood and imploring Connolly, judged to have ambitions in the field himself, not to interfere. 'If I had not written to you, about 3 weeks into next half you would notice how things stood,' Orwell explained, 'your proprietary instincts would have been aroused & having a lot of influence over Eastwood you would probably have put him against me somehow.' Given the sheaf of testimonies to his habitual schoolboy reserve, this is a revealing document (two other boys are named), instantly conjuring up a teeming and furtive world of adolescent passions expended in glances across the schoolyard and waves from distant windows. But it would be wrong to draw any serious conclusions from it about Orwell's sexuality. Sentimental attachments of this sort were commonplace at Eton and rarely took physical form. As Connolly notes, the point of the letter rests on the age difference. As Eastwood, like Connolly, was in the election below they would naturally have seen much more of each other in the course of their daily routine.

Richard Blair was finally demobilised in 1919. Nothing, everyone was uneasily aware, would ever be the same again. This was true even of the family life of the Blairs, where routines learned in wartime proved difficult to set aside. Mr Blair resumed his duties at the golf club and the family returned to St Mark's Road, but the Notting Hill flat was kept up as a *pied-à-terre*, possibly occupied in Mrs Blair's absence by Marjorie or one of the Limouzins. Marjorie's removal from the family hearth – she was now in her early twenties – became permanent not long afterwards when she married the Humphrey Dakin who had so disliked her younger brother trailing after him in the fields around Henley. Christmas 1919 was the first the family had spent together for three years. Keeping up his interest in the macabre, Eric gave Jacintha a copy of *Dracula* and a crucifix. By this stage Eric had become a fixture in Buddicom family life. Prosper's diary from the spring holiday of 1920 shows that he spent twenty-one out of the twenty-six available days with Eric, shooting, taking tea at the golf club or going on trips to the cinema in Reading. The school calendar offered further opportunities to see his friends during the following term. Late in June, for example, he wrote to Mrs Buddicom asking if he could watch the Henley Regatta from their punt, while early in July he managed to spend two days of the Eton–Harrow match at Lord's in the Buddicom family box (Prosper was by now at Harrow) supposedly annoying a Buddicom uncle who complained of his 'flirtation' with Jacintha.

In the exams that ended the summer half of 1920, Blair KS came 117th out of the 140 boys in his year and bottom of his election. It was not a distinguished performance. Shortly afterwards, though, came an incident which foreshadowed one important side of his adult life. He spent the first week of the vacation at the school OTC camp on Salisbury Plain, intending to take the train down to Cornwall to join the rest of the Blairs on holiday in Cornwall when the camp broke up. A misreading of the timetable left him stranded in Plymouth, late in the evening, with only sevenpence halfpenny in his pocket. There followed what Orwell described in a letter to Steven Runciman as 'my first adventure as an amateur tramp'. The choice lay between a bed at the YMCA and nothing to eat or food and vagrancy. The young Orwell chose the latter, spending sixpence on a bag of buns and wandering around the outskirts of Plymouth – in his greatcoat he was taken for a recently demobbed soldier – until he found a corner of a field next to some allotments where he could doss down for the night. After missing the early train he finally left Plymouth at 7.45 a.m. 'I am very proud of this adventure', he told Runciman, 'but I would not repeat it.' After the Cornish holiday there was a further jaunt, nearer home, to Maidensgrove four miles north-west of Henley, where the Blairs rented a tumbledown cottage. Eric amused himself by constructing a hut in the wood with the name 'Aston Villa' done in pebbles outside the entrance. Jacintha was away staying with her grandmother, so much of the rest of the vacation was spent with Prosper. They rounded off the holiday with a trip to London to see Galsworthy's *The Skin Game*, before Prosper travelled on to Harrow.

The question of Eric's future was now looming large in the Blairs' deliberations, one of several conundrums that had to be solved as he reached his late teens. With Richard Blair well into his sixties, he and his wife were looking for somewhere to retire to. A letter from Eric to Prosper at Christmas 1920 tells the younger boy to send his reply to an address near Ipswich. This suggests that they may already have been looking eastward rather than in their usual Thames Valley haunts. At seventeen, Eric was still treading water at Eton. A further year of education lay ahead of him (*Keep the Aspidistra Flying* notes the 'strange idealistic snobbishness' of the Comstocks, who are 'willing to go to the workhouse' rather than let Gordon leave school before the age of eighteen) and then . . . what exactly? The only real guide to this debate is Jacintha Buddicom. Early in 1921 Prosper went down with a bad attack of influenza (Eric's proposed stay at Quarry House had to be cancelled and he wrote a commiserating letter from Suffolk). In the end the illness was so severe that his heart was affected. The Buddicoms decided to move to Harrow so that he could attend the school as a day boy. The Blairs, having given up 36 St Mark's Road without finding a replacement, were by this stage effectively homeless. Summer 1921 consequently found Mrs Blair, Eric and Avril (Mr Blair's whereabouts are unknown) combining with the Buddicoms to rent a house called Glencroft in Rickmansworth. Fifty years later the recollection of this month in semi-rural Middlesex still burned brightly in Jacintha's memory. The teenage contingent amused themselves playing tennis, listening to records on the gramophone that came with the house or making excursions to a billiard hall in the village. There was another of Eric's poems to digest, a typically grave affair that ran:

> Friendship and love are closely intertwined,
> My heart belongs to your befriending mind:
> But chilling sunlit fields, cloud-shadows fall –
> My love can't reach your heedless heart at all.

Jacintha, a prudent girl, responded with:

> By light
> too bright
> Are dazzled eyes betrayed:
> It's best
> to rest
> content in tranquil shade.

But at the heart of the stay, apparently, lay 'interminable conversations'

51

between Ida Blair and a sympathetic Mrs Buddicom about Eric's career. Jacintha represents this as a straightforward clash of diametric opposites: Mr Blair regarding the Indian Civil Service as 'the only career he would tolerate for his son', to Eric's horror; Mrs Blair pleading for the boy to be given his chance to try for university. According to Jacintha, the conflict developed into a desperate rearguard action fought by mother and son, backed up by a 'vigorous' correspondence from Mrs Buddicom, that was in the end unable to break down Mr Blair's resolve. While nobody can doubt that words were spoken and letters exchanged, it seems likely that the issues at stake were rather more complex than this. Whether or not Eric wanted to go to Oxford, the chances of him obtaining any kind of scholarship were negligible. Unlike Connolly who later that year became a Brackenbury Scholar of Balliol, he was bottom of his election and outwardly indifferent to prolonging his education. 'Eric rather took the line of slightly despising us for going to the university,' one of his contemporaries recalled. Set against the lure of the dreaming spires was the pull of family connection.

The five years Orwell eventually spent in Burma are sometimes portrayed as a dreadful, meaningless exile. In fact both sides of his family had deep roots in the East. Several of his relatives, notably his maternal grandmother, still lived there. It was an age, too, where the idea of a family profession had far more importance than it does now. Steven Runciman remembers his friend being 'determined' to go to Burma, and having sentimental longings for the East. Whatever the heat and duration of the argument, a decision was reached, made or, perhaps, imposed. Eric would go back to Eton for a final term before beginning the process of seeking entry to the Indian Imperial Police. Returning for the autumn half of 1921, now aged eighteen, he was belatedly admitted to the sixth form, and among other privileges acquired the services of a fag. Anthony Wagner, later as Sir Anthony Wagner the Garter Knight of Arms, who briefly occupied this post, recalled him as 'a kind and considerate fagmaster' while admitting that 'he did not talk much'.

Eric spent fourteen terms at Eton, just over four and a half years. What effect did it have on him? As an adult he was determined to convey the impression that he was there on sufferance, socially unsuited to the place and despised for his poverty. Each of these claims should be treated with a degree of scepticism. Certainly Eton was awash with wealth and grandeur. Equally there were plenty of boys – Anthony Powell was one – whose families were willing to make sacrifices in order that their sons could enjoy a good education. Almost without exception, Orwell's contemporaries are suspicious of the idea that he was excluded from the Eton mainstream on account of his background. Runciman, for example, thought it 'dishonest' of him to maintain that he was miserable because he was poor. Eton was full of boys from modest homes dragging themselves up by their bootstraps. To the outward eye Eric's position was no different from anyone else's: he had the same teenage indulgences, money for treats, his mother followed the school custom of arriving on half-holidays to take her son and his friends out for tea. Moreover, Etonian snobbishness, everyone is keen to stress, consisted only of a generalised contempt for non-Etonians. Monetary or class differences were of little account. The first real glimpse into the snob-world of upper English society, Powell thought, came at Oxford, not Eton. 'I wouldn't have known whose parents had money and whose didn't,' Eastwood claimed. No one knows what Orwell truly felt about his time at the school, but we do know that he was capable of misrepresenting incidents that occurred at Eton if they could serve some later literary purpose. *The Road to Wigan Pier,* for instance, contains an account of the Eton peace celebrations of 1919. Here, according to Orwell, the boys, ordered to march into the schoolyard in darkness carrying torches and singing patriotic songs, guyed the whole proceedings and substituted their own 'blasphemous and seditious' verses. In fact, Christopher Hollis suggests, this was merely a protest against an unpopular OTC, 'a straightforward rag' without the element of principle that Orwell attached to it. The Provost noted only that 'The boys all stood with torches raised and were perfectly silent.'

Undoubtedly the personal myth that Orwell erected above his time at Eton was almost as strong as his reinvention of St Cyprian's. Yet there was another Eton from which he was permanently, if not deliberately, barred. Consider, for example, the career of his exact contemporary Alec Dunglass, later the 14th Earl of Home and as Sir Alec Douglas-Home Prime Minister in 1963–4, who arrived at the school as an oppidan on the same day that Eric Blair took up residence in College. Lord Dunglass, as he was then styled, had been destined for Eton since birth. There was no question of him going anywhere else, or of having to sit scholarship exams. 'It was a natural progression,' his biographer commented. Life at the school had its unpleasant side, Sir

Alec conceded, especially in the last year of the war when rations ran low. To balance this was a 'vintage lot' of schoolmasters. Snobbery and money-consciousness there may have been, but Dunglass missed them. It was rather that – again the quotation comes from his authorised biography – 'his perspective was different'. The future Earl played for the First Eleven at cricket, represented the school at Eton fives, became President of Pop and departed to Christ Church trailing clouds of glory behind him alongside a stack of Etonian friends and future cabinet colleagues.

But this is what upper-class English life was like eighty years ago: an infinitely adaptable mansion capable of housing embryo 14th earls and candidates for the Indian Imperial Police alike. However much Orwell may have tried to escape it, the legacy of Eton overhung his work, friendships and opinions. Most obviously, any Old Etonians who came across him later in life tended immediately to greet him as one of their own. Several claimed that they would have identified him as an OE merely from his published writings. Orwell's affinity with people who had attended his old school – friends from this source included Richard Rees, David Astor, L.H. Myers and Anthony Powell – is rather marked. Meeting one he could instantly slip into Etonian habits. A visitor to Jura in the late 1940s remembered being relegated to the kitchen when the island's Old Etonian laird came to call. Orwell's attitude to this Eton connection, although at first largely indifferent, seems to have undergone a decisive change in the mid-1930s. By 1937 he was back in contact with Connolly (who introduced him to Powell), Dannreuther (shortly before the latter's premature death) and King-Farlow. Eton left its mark, too, on his outward persona, his way of talking, his attitudes, even his turns of phrase. Jack Common, watching him saunter into the *Adelphi* office ten years later, knew immediately that here was a public school man. A much younger friend from the 1940s marked him down as an 'obvious ex-public school boy' from the start.

And curiously the Eton atmosphere had a habit of insinuating itself into his work. Reviewing a novel by Pearl S. Buck ten years later he could turn aside to remark that the author was handicapped by 'the style of [Andrew] Lang's crib to the *Odyssey*'. No doubt the readers of Richard Rees's free-thinking, left-leaning organ appreciated the analogy. One of the waiters in *Down and Out in Paris and London*, in his tail coat and white collar, is described as looking like an Eton boy. This reservoir of public school imagery even extended to rival establishments. Thus the piece of fashionable headgear worn by Gordon

Comstock's girlfriend Rosemary in *Keep the Aspidistra Flying* is 'cocked down over her eyes like a Harrow boy's straw hat'; a simile that perhaps one in a thousand of Orwell's readers would understand. Eton, in fact, remained an inescapable presence in his life. The suspicion lingers that, in the last resort, he did not want to escape it. Later letters to Connolly come crammed with references to the Eton–Harrow match. Stafford Cottman, who served with him in Spain, was startled to be asked one morning in the trenches if he could remember the Eton boating song (he obliged, much to Orwell's delight). By his early forties Orwell, if not exactly a professional Old Etonian, was certainly someone caught up in the various networks with which the school perpetuated itself. In April 1946, for instance, he was in touch with no fewer than three former Eton masters: Gow; M.D. Hill, who wrote to him apropos the essay on 'Boys' Weeklies'; and George Lyttelton, who wanted him to write a book for a series he was editing.

This is not to underplay the bitterness of some of Orwell's criticisms of Eton. The futility of a classical education seemed manifest to him in the fact that at thirty-three he had forgotten the Greek alphabet. You suspect, too, that at least some of Orwell's later hostility to the pansy aesthetes, the left-leaning literary homosexuals of the 1930s and 1940s, took root here in his schooldays. As far as we know he had no connection with the Eton Society of the Arts, its presiding spirits Harold Acton and Brian Howard, and the activities that produced the *Eton Candle*, a celebrated avant-garde one-off, published shortly after his departure, but it seems unlikely that the school's flamboyant aesthetic fringe escaped his notice; Acton and Howard were conspicuous boys who left a lasting impression on most of their schoolmates. Some of the assaults in *Keep the Aspidistra Flying* on the 'moneyed young beasts' of the 1930s literary circuit look as if they can be tracked back to this source. All this combined to produce an attitude to Eton that sometimes broke out as outright hatred. A younger friend from the 1940s, himself an ex-public school boy, recalled a conversation with him about the probable demise of the public school system and the 'joy' in Orwell's face when he expressed a hope that the school would disappear. A piece of esoteric Eton slang incautiously dropped by Richard Rees on Jura produced a paroxysm of facial misery. But by the end of his life he was capable of turning unexpectedly emollient. One of the last book reviews he ever wrote, for the *Observer* in 1948, was of B.W. Hill's *Eton Medley*. Ivor Brown, no lover of the Eton system, had commissioned the piece on the assumption that Orwell would share his own hostility. To his surprise, Orwell produced a balanced piece in which familiar criticisms were mitigated by praise for 'a tolerant and civilised atmosphere which gives each boy a fair chance of developing his own ability'. Asked by David Astor, late in life, if he would ever consider sending his son there, he complained only of the dress code, which 'made a fool of a boy'. Astor retained a lasting impression that Orwell was grateful to Eton for giving him the chance to pursue his own interests, a breathing space in a more or less congenial environment. Another, lesser, public school would have been harder going.

A few fragments remain from Eric's final term. At the October recitations – an important event in the Eton calendar when selected pupils declaimed literary works to an audience of boys and parents – he read from Stevenson's 'The Suicide Club'. The *Eton College Chronicle* approved: 'Blair's speech was skilfully chosen ... the even and unmoved coolness with which Blair let the story make its own effect was certainly very successful.' There was a curious incident when he and a boy named John Heygate – later to achieve notoriety as the man who eloped with Evelyn Waugh's first wife – acted as the two sixth-form attendants or 'praepostors' at a birching administered by the headmaster, Cyril Alington. Heygate included such an episode in his Eton novel *Decent Fellows*, reducing the number of praepostors to one. According to Anthony Powell, who knew both men, Orwell took offence at a description of the sixth-form boy, who has previously held out the cane with 'shy reverence', pretending to look out of the window 'in pain and dignity', detecting a sneer at his squeamishness. Finally he made a dramatic appearance in the Wall Game played between College and an Oppidan team on 29 November 1921. In the Wall Game the common score is a 'shy'. As in rugby union, when a 'shy' is scored the scoring side then attempts to convert it into a goal. This is achieved at one end of the playing area by throwing a ball against a garden door and at the other by hitting a mark on a tree. Scoring a goal is notoriously difficult, for years no one had achieved the feat, and yet this was exactly what Eric did, hurling the ball back to Longden who passed on to the door. No doubt the episode's symbolism occurred to him: a rare moment of formal success in a school career lived more or less below surface level. Three weeks later Eric packed his trunks, said goodbye to his College friends, presented Wagner with a copy of Robert Service's *Rhymes of a Rolling Stone* as a parting gift, and left Eton for good.

Orwell's face

Orwell was interested in faces. Above all, he was fascinated by their ability to convey the characteristics – the personality, in extreme cases the ideology – of what lay beneath the skin. The poem inspired by the Italian militiaman who shook his hand at the Lenin Barracks in Barcelona ends with the words: 'But the thing that I saw in your face/No power can disinherit/No bomb that ever burst/Shatters the crystal spirit.' One of the last things he wrote in his hospital notebook was the valedictory epigram: 'At fifty, every man has the face he deserves.' Primed to tell him about the mentalities they concealed, faces stared up at him from print. Whenever you read a strongly individual piece of writing, he believed, the features of the author could be glimpsed somewhere behind the page: not always accurate portraits, but a figurative projection. Reading Dickens, famously, he saw 'the face of a man who is always fighting against something, but who fights in the open and is not frightened, the face of a man who is *generously angry*.'

It would be surprising, given the importance that Orwell ascribed to human features, if they didn't merit lavish descriptions in his work. Each of his early novels opens with a shrewd little survey of the physiognomy of the principal character. These are not generally prepossessing. Even without his hideous birthmark, Flory in *Burmese Days* has a face grown 'very haggard in spite of the sunburn, with lank cheeks and a sunken, withered look round the eyes'. Dorothy Hare in *A Clergyman's Daughter*, on the other hand, sees in the mirror 'a thin, blonde, unremarkable kind of face, with pale eyes and a nose just a shade too long: and if you looked closely you could see crows' feet round the eyes, and the mouth, when it was in repose, looked tired.' Gordon Comstock in *Keep the Aspidistra Flying*, catching sight of his reflection in the window of Mr McKechnie's bookshop, divines that it is 'not a good face. Not thirty yet, but moth-eaten already. Very pale, with

57

bitter, ineradicable lines.' The single exception to this rule, perhaps, is George Bowling – the least cast-down of Orwell's 1930s creations – who decides that he 'hasn't such a bad face, really. It's one of those brick-red faces that go with butter-coloured hair and pale-blue eyes.' Even Bowling, though, has just lost the last of his natural teeth.

And these, it should be pointed out, are Orwell's heroes and heroine, the people with whom he sympathises and regards, in however complex a way, as emblems of himself. Turn to his minor characters and one might as well be inspecting a line of Victorian waxworks. Dorothy's solitary companion at early morning Communion is the venerable Miss Mayfill, in whose ancient, bloodless face the mouth is 'surprisingly large, loose and wet. The under lip, pendulous with age, slobbered forward, exposing a strip of gum and a row of false teeth as yellow as the keys of an old piano.' If Miss Mayfill resembles an elderly bloodhound, Julia, Gordon's sister, might be taken for a large, lumbering bird: 'a tall, ungainly girl . . . with a thin face just a little too long – one of those girls who even at their most youthful remind one irresistibly of a goose'. As for Lieutenant Verrall, the cavalry officer who supplants Flory in Elizabeth Lackersteen's affections, however hard, brutal and fearless its contours, his face in the last resort is that of a rabbit. To move a bit deeper into the text, into its world of momentary glimpses and fleeting impressions, is to fetch up instantly in a chamber of horrors. 'A bad face he had,' Gordon thinks, looking out of the bookshop window at a browsing passer-by. 'Pale, heavy . . . Welsh, by the look of him.' 'Corner Table', whose bland features stare down from the Bovex ad that Gordon so despises, has 'an idiotic, grinning face, like the face of a self-satisfied rat'. Bloodhounds, geese, rabbits, rats: the seeds of Orwell's anthropomorphic farmyard were sown many years before *Animal Farm*.

None of these faces – Flory's, Comstock's, Bowling's – is recognisably Orwell's own, although his friend Richard Rees believed that in describing Dorothy Hare's features he was describing a feminised version of himself. At the same time, certain adjectives recur: 'thin', for example, and 'pale'. Like their creator, Orwell's characters look old before their time: even Rosemary's freshness in *Keep the Aspidistra Flying* is somehow compromised by the two white hairs on her crown which she declines to pull out. Youthfulness, where it exists, is practically a guarantee of irresponsibility. Bowling's retired public school Classics master chum Porteous, for instance, has a 'thin, dreamy kind of face that's a bit discoloured but might almost belong to a boy, though he must be nearly sixty'. Porteous, with his refusal to take Hitler seriously and his belief in the 'eternal verities', has never grown up.

With the possible exception of Verrall's ('a rabbit, perhaps, but a tough and martial rabbit') none of these faces embodies or represents any kind of power. In some ways their weakness is a result of the detail lavished on them. Significantly, when Orwell came to describe faces – actual or fictional – with the ability to put millions of men on the march his language is much more abstract and imprecise. Big Brother's head, which pursues Winston Smith from every hoarding and every tele-screen, is simply 'black-haired, black-moustachioed, full of power and mysterious calm'. The qualities that give the face its resonance, its capacity to command and subdue, hang in the ether. Confronted with a real-life tyrant, too, Orwell's response is oddly unsatisfactory. There is a curious review of *Mein Kampf*, written in the spring of 1940, which discusses the standard publicity photographs of Hitler. It was, Orwell decided, 'a pathetic, dog-like face, the face of a man suffering under intolerable wrongs. In a rather more manly way it reproduces the expression of innumerable pictures of Christ crucified.' Most con-temporary commentators were inclined to be a little less charitable than this, but Orwell had detected something in Hitler's face to which he invariably reacted: self-pity.

All this raises the question of what Orwell thought of his own face, and what other people thought of it. Anthony Powell was not alone in detecting a resemblance to Doré's version of Don Quixote – in fact Paul Potts' affectionate 1950s memoir is entitled 'Don Quixote on a Bicycle'. An East End woman who met him during his tramping days was reminded of Stan Laurel. In certain respects – a throwback to his Limouzin forebears – it was not an English face. Powell, again, noted the similarity to French workmen seen contemplating life in Parisian estaminets. Orwell himself was uninterested in, in fact downright indifferent to, his own personal appearance. Requests later on in his career for publicity photographs invariably ran into trouble. The problem was only solved in 1946 when his friend Vernon Richards was commissioned to take a portfolio of pictures in the flat (the camera eventually moves out into the surrounding streets) at Canonbury Square, Islington. And yet for all this indifference Orwell's face is, to my mind, one of the most extraordinary things about him: extraordinary for the way it changes, and, ultimately, its almost complete separation from the template of youth. Place a picture of Thackeray in his white-haired old buffer phase next to Maclise's portrait of the twenty-two-year-old club lounger and you can at least recognise the similarity of the facial lines. It would be possible to set the famous 'Orwell at the microphone' BBC photograph alongside Jacintha Buddicom's childhood snaps without realising that they are the same person. 'What have you in common with the child of five whose photograph your mother keeps on the mantelpiece?' he asked in *The Lion and the Unicorn*. In Orwell's case, not even a physical similarity.

The degeneration of Orwell's features between childhood and young manhood is quite startling. The Eton pictures, even the solitary Burma Police shot, show a chubby, almost moon-faced boy. By the time of Dennis Collings's Southwold beach photograph of 1934 – he was then thirty-one – he looks forty. In the line of Spanish comrades snapped at an ILP summer school three years later he looks nearer fifty. Friends who picked up with him again in the 1930s after a decade and a half's gap were shocked by this contrast: Connolly noted the gulf between the ravaged grooves of Orwell's face and his own plump, cigar-smoking persona. And finally there are Vernon Richards's photographs, the last-known photographs of Orwell in existence, taken in the Islington flat six months after the publication of *Animal Farm*. Encouraged by the presence of a friend – two friends, as Richards brought his wife, Marie-Louise – Orwell looks more relaxed than in any previous incarnation. Absorbed, kindly, still a little detached from the proceedings, he changes his son Richard's trousers, types, rolls cigarettes, takes the child for a walk in his pram, examines a Burmese sword half-drawn from its scabbard and performs various manoeuvres in his workshop. In by far the most striking portrait he sits bolt upright and expressionless in his chair. It is an impassive, elongated face, the eyes fixed on everything and nothing. At forty-two, he could be any age between fifty and seventy-five, 'full of power and mysterious calm'.

4

White Man's Burden

The life of the Anglo-Indian official is not all jam. In comfortless camps, in sweltering offices, in gloomy dak bungalows smelling of earth-oil, they earn, perhaps, the right to be a little disagreeable. – *Burmese Days*

Eric returned from Eton not to Henley but to the seaside town of Southwold, eighty miles out of Liverpool Street on the north Suffolk coast. It was here that Richard and Ida Blair – he now in his mid-sixties, she nearing fifty – had decided to retire. Southwold was, and is, a rather remote locale, although in those days possessing its own rail link to the Suffolk county town of Ipswich, but there were good reasons why the Blairs should think it a congenial spot in which to pass their declining years. The town was a well-known haunt of Anglo-Indians that offered, at any rate in its upper reaches, a genteel seclusion not easily come by in the Home Counties. They may even have chosen it – the initial recommendation came from the parents of one of Mrs Blair's Notting Hill neighbours – with their son's immediate interests in mind. Amongst other attractions – pier, sailors' reading room, gentleman's club – Southwold contained a 'crammer'. To gain entry into the Indian Imperial Police Orwell would have to pass an entrance exam whose subjects included not merely the public school staples of Latin and Greek but Mathematics and Freehand Drawing. 'Craighurst', run by a former Dulwich College master named Philip Hope, lay on a chilly corner of the front overlooking the beach huts and the grey North Sea, a short step from the Blairs' house in Stradbroke Road, which runs south from St James's Green, near the town's epicentre of High Street, church and brewery. Here, in January 1922, with the north wind rattling the windows, Eric began his new routine.

Not much is known about his life in the ten months he spent in Southwold prior to his departure for Burma. One of his enduring early friendships, with Dennis Collings, the son of the local dentist, dates from this period, although Collings, at sixteen, was a couple of years younger: their real intimacy came some years later. Eric's Eton contemporaries were dispersing, to Oxford, Cambridge and jobs in the City. Faced with this parade of lustre and éclat – Connolly, for instance, with his Balliol scholarship – it is tempting to write Orwell off as a deracinated figure, permanently exiled to an Imperial backwater. But the Indian Imperial Police was a highly respectable, if not particularly glamorous, profession for a young man – especially one with Eric's colonial connections. The Buddicoms, too, whatever their initial agitation about Eric 'having his chance', accepted it as a thoroughly reasonable choice of career. A hundred and forty miles distant, and separated by London, Eric saw less of the Buddicoms during the remainder of his time in England. A sentence from a letter he wrote to Prosper around this time passed into family history: 'Millions of people at this crammer shoot – at least three of them.' But he stayed at Quarry House again in April, where Jacintha – now a grown-up young lady of twenty – remembered him flailing at Prosper's punchbag and learning to ride his friend's motorbike. 'I don't mind so much about *starting* it,' she recalled him complaining, 'I want to know how to stop the damn thing.'

The minimum age for entry into the India Police was nineteen. Eric would reach this on 25 June. A testimonial was solicited from the long-suffering Crace, who – showing perhaps how few Etonians proceeded to this part of the Empire – declared himself ignorant of the procedure. 'I do not know at all what is required for candidates for the India Police,' he replied to the India Office authorities. 'I send a formal certificate which is perhaps all that is necessary . . .' The exam, lasting a week, began two days after Eric's birthday. Even to an Eton slacker, the intellectual level needed was not high. The English paper, for instance, required the candidate to write a letter to a relation describing a visit to the theatre. The History paper invited him to speculate on the identity of the greatest prime minister since Pitt. Eric's strength lay in the classical training he had so disliked at Eton. His best mark was in Latin (1,782 out of a possible 2,000) declining to 174 out of 400 in Freehand Drawing. With a pass mark set at 6,000 out of a possible 12,400 he came seventh out of the twenty-six candidates who exceeded it. In a riding test, taken early in the autumn, for which he had prepared himself with lessons at a local stables, he did less well – twenty-first out of the successful twenty-three. But he was through. Asked to state his preferred choice of posting he placed Burma first, ahead of the United Provinces, on the grounds that he had relatives in the former (notably his grandmother, still living in Moulmein) and that his father had served in the latter. Burma was not a fashionable posting, if the India Police could be said to possess such things, but the choice makes plain Eric's immersion in his own background, and the sheer ordinariness of the destiny he had planned out – or had had planned out – for himself. He was going to be an Imperial servant in a place familiar to him from family legend, where his mother had spent much of her childhood, near to the Indian postings of his father's entire professional career, and where he would possess a swathe of family connections. Exile it was not.

Now, there were three months to while away before he left. An odd episode brought his stay at Craighurst to an abrupt end, when he and a fellow pupil, remembered as 'a wild young man' who had previously been expelled from Malvern, fell foul of the Southwold borough surveyor Mr Hurst. Discovering the date of Hurst's birthday, they sent him a dead rat together with a signed greeting. A fuss having been made, Eric and his accomplice were expelled: a futile punishment in Eric's case as he had already sat the police exam. The only real witness to the summer of 1922, once again, is Jacintha. She was 'sure' that he joined the family at the Eton–Harrow match in the second week of July, and that he went on holiday with them again to Shropshire. She recalled eavesdropping on a three-way conversation between Orwell, Prosper and one of Prosper's Harrow friends in which they discussed the ghost stories of Orwell's 'great hero' M.R. James. On what terms did Eric and Jacintha part? Nearly thirty years later Orwell wrote her a letter in which he cheerily accused her of 'abandoning' him to Burma. The fact that Jacintha – ominously precise in most of her recollections – could not remember their last meeting suggests that neither she nor Eric was deeply moved. Jacintha was twenty-one and marriageable. Eric was nineteen and about to begin a career on the other side of the world. Each would have known that their relationship, such as it was, was destined to founder.

Two of the other recruits had opted and been accepted for the Burma Police. One, C.W.R. Beadon, had left in early October. The other, H.J. Jones, followed with Orwell from Liverpool on 27 October. The month-long, 8,000-mile journey via the Mediterranean, the Suez Canal, the Red Sea and the Indian Ocean left an indelible impression on Orwell's mind. In an 'As I Please' column from 1947, when England languished in conditions of post-war austerity, he wrote of the luxurious environment which the SS *Herefordshire* offered to its first-class passengers. When not asleep or playing deck games the two recruits seemed always to be eating. The meals were 'of that stupendous kind that steamship companies used to vie with one another in providing'. Ceylon, where the ship docked along the way, furnished a breathtaking gateway to the East. (Flory in *Burmese Days* remembers sailing into Colombo 'through green glassy water, where turtles and black snakes floated basking'.) The trip brought two symbolic incidents of the kind that litter Orwell's writings. The first took place during the voyage when Orwell noticed the SS *Herefordshire*'s European quartermaster, a bronzed figure for whom he had conceived an intense admiration, scurrying out of the cookhouse carrying a pie dish containing half a baked custard pudding. The spectacle of a man he admired furtively absconding with pilfered food while the first-class passengers gorged themselves a few yards away, Orwell believed, 'taught me more than I could have learned from half-a-dozen Socialist pamphlets'. The second happened at Colombo harbour when a mob of coolies swarmed on board to deal with the luggage of those passengers who were disembarking. One, having mishandled a tin trunk, was viciously kicked on the backside by a white police sergeant, to the evident approval of the onlookers. As parables of, on the one hand, social division and, on the other, racial superiority, these are almost too neatly realised. There is no doubt that Orwell witnessed them – if nothing else, there is the sheer detail of the baked custard pudding – but at the same time you wonder if he saw them in quite the same way that they are put down on the page: the necessity to him of symbolism of this kind, and the lengths to which he would go to make symbolism work for him, are a feature of his writing.

From Colombo the ship ploughed on towards the mouth of the Irrawaddy, past the myriad factory chimneys and the tops of the river-side pagodas, to Rangoon. Here after a round of calls to, among others, His Excellency the Governor, Sir Harcourt Brace, and the Inspector-General of Police, Colonel Macdonald, he and Jones boarded the mail train on the afternoon of 28 November and made the sixteen-hour journey to Mandalay, site of the police training school. Beadon, who had arrived earlier in the month, was among the officers gathered to greet this 'sallow-faced, tall, thin and gangling' boy whose clothes 'no matter how well cut, seemed to hang on him . . .'

Where had he come? And what lay in store? The Burma of the early 1920s was a recent annexation to the British Empire. Modern Burmese history had begun barely four decades before when on the intervention of the Secretary of State, Lord Randolph Churchill, a British Expeditionary Force led by General Sir Harry Prendergast had entered Mandalay and ordered the Burmese King Thibaw's immediate and unconditional surrender. There was some faint precedent for this invasion. Britain had fought two previous wars against the Burmese, in 1824–6 and 1852–3, but until the late nineteenth century Upper Burma at least had retained its territorial integrity. Though the country's internal troubles had been used as a justification, the real reasons for the Churchill fiat were commercial. Keen on the idea of cheap rice, oil and timber, businessmen in London and Calcutta had been pressing for government action since the 1860s. When it came, it did so with a vengeance. Rather than imposing direct rule, or governing by way of a protectorate – the usual means by which the Empire administered newly acquired territory – the British simply wiped out Burma's existing institutions on the spot. The monarchy (Thibaw spent the remaining thirty years of his life in exile on the Indian coast); nobility; army; royal agencies – all these went down practically overnight before the advancing colonial tide. British and Indian troops poured over the frontier – the Burmese garrison was 40,000 strong in the early years of the twentieth century – closely followed by railway contractors and Calcutta timber merchants. By 1913 the Burmah Oil Company was extracting 200 million gallons annually, three-quarters of the country's total output, while a handful of British firms accounted for the same percentage of teak production.

All this – the razed forests, the oil prospecting and the rice cartels – bred deep resentments. These were exacerbated by Burma's exclusion from the general pattern of Imperial political development. The 1918 Montagu-Chelmsford report had recommended constitutional reforms in India, of which Burma had technically been a part since 1886: mysteriously, the proposals turned out to apply to India alone. Widespread unrest, fomented by the Young Men's Buddhist Association, originally founded as a mildly pro-British social club but since metamorphosed into a hotbed of sedition, eventually produced a compromise: Burma was allowed a legislative council, three-quarters of whose members would be elected on a limited property franchise extending to about a quarter of the province's adult male population. This made it very different from India, a centuries-old part of the Empire with carefully nurtured administrative structures and a native autocracy. Burma, which only thirty years before had possessed its own king and its own army, was effectively under martial law. Orwell arrived there at a time when serious political disturbance had only recently come to an end and the rising crime wave that had replaced it was thought to have a political basis. An official report from the 1920s, for example, noted that while village assemblies were beginning to lose their bitter anti-government tone, a contempt for authority 'inspired by political agitation' lay beneath the upsurge in theft and robbery. Burmese crime statistics, minutely documented by the colonial administration, give some idea of the task facing its 13,000-strong police force: 47,000 reported incidents in 1923–4, over 800 murders in the year following, a 25 per cent increase in reported crime in the year after that, 'including several instances of horrible savagery'. The prison population hovered at 16,000. There were around seventy hangings a year.

None of this, though, quite conveys the sheer strangeness of Burma to the average European incomer. Substantial parts of it existed beyond the civilising Imperial net: the Wa hills, near the Chinese border in the north, were still unpacified in the 1930s. Wildernesses of scrub and jungle surrounded the major population centres. Here, quite literally, danger lurked. Throughout Orwell's time in Burma the annual mortality statistics from attacks by wild animals ran into three figures. Then, at any rate to the Western eye, there was the deeply unpromising climate – scorching heat from February to May, a long monsoon reaching into September, followed by a short winter when, as *Burmese Days* puts it, 'Upper Burma seemed haunted by the ghost of England'. All this made a vivid impression on visiting Englishmen and women, whose reactions varied from fascination with a hitherto unknown landscape and culture to queasiness over the primitive nature of the customs on display. An Englishwoman on a jungle tour in the 1930s was horrified by the spectacle of a girl in childbirth attended by two old women whose notion of midwifery was to put a plank on her stomach and jump on it in the hope of forcing the baby out. This gave the experience of living in Burma a queer, lop-sided feel. On the one hand it was a land of strict hierarchies and protocols – Mrs Lackersteen in *Burmese Days* pores over the Civil List like a duchess reading Debrett – governed by the most elemental urgings of Imperial theatre: the big event of 1922, for instance, had been the visit of the Prince of Wales. Yet behind the surface pomp lay dirt, deprivation, squalor and an infant mortality rate approaching 20 per cent. There was a tendency for European visitors to overstate the backwardness of early twentieth-century Burma, and modern Burmese historians are keen to stress the various ways in which even the pre-British state was trying to adapt itself to the modern age. All the same, from the point of view of the British administrator, the rare amenities of Burmese life tended to be imports from the West.

The countless testimonies of old Burma hands show something of the odd effect that the country had on the specimen English sensibility. On the most basic, visual level Orwell was both appalled and fascinated by the world he saw around him. He later claimed to have written *Burmese Days* simply to get the landscape out of his system: 'In all novels about the East the scenery is the real subject matter.' Whatever he may subsequently have thought about the colonial administrators he was, with a few dramatic exceptions, charmed by the native population. Reviewing C.V. Warren's *Burmese Interlude,* many years later, he noted that like every European whose experience was not confined to the big towns the author had conceived a deep affection for the Burmese. This sympathy, he thought, was partly the result of the prevailing social conditions. Census records of the time show the presence of 200,000 'foreigners', but most of these were Indians and Chinese. The percentage of Europeans was relatively small; that of European women even smaller. In between these two sectors lay an indeterminate class of 'Eurasians' of the kind whose appearance at the church service in *Burmese Days* so horrifies Elizabeth Lackersteen ('Couldn't something be done about them?' etc.), mostly the product of relationships between European men and their Burmese mistresses, tolerated by native Burmans but roundly despised by the ruling class. The comparative isolation of the colonial élite again produced a situation very different to India, forcing Englishmen to associate much more closely with 'native' subordinates.

Orwell would have been made welcome in Burma, and not only by his fellow-recruits. The Burma Police had an excellent reputation among the European community: 'a very good lot', according to one colonial civil servant of the time. Their camaraderie may have helped to compensate for the disadvantages of Mandalay, remembered by Flory as 'rather a disagreeable town', dusty and hot and remarkable for five main products beginning with the letter 'p' – pagodas, pariahs, pigs, priests and prostitutes. Like many Burmese towns of the post-Occupation period it was effectively split in two: the British fort, a mile square, with a sprawling native quarter behind. The police school was largely given over to the training of native sub-inspectors; the much smaller contingent of British assistant superintendents (ASPs) formed a discrete unit, set to take courses in Burmese, Hindustani, Law and police procedure. Orwell's new home possessed, by all acounts, a rather rackety atmosphere. Young men recently arrived from England often found the place too much for them – one room was kept permanently empty on the grounds that its final occupant had committed suicide – and recruits were encouraged to keep their spirits up. However excellent the force's reputation, it did not extend to sobriety. Ominously, the ramshackle collection of inebriates that populated the service's upper levels in the 1920s were all protégés of a hard-drinking ex-training-school colonel who expected his trainees to follow his example. The preliminary training course took six months. Orwell's proficiency in languages was remarked – by its close he was apparently capable of 'high-flown' conversations with the Burmese priests – but he was not thought to be clubbable. 'Rather shy, retiring,' remembered Roger Beadon, who was slightly surprised to find an Old Etonian here in the dust of Mandalay. Yet the 'rather lugubrious' figure was still capable of amusing himself. There were excursions by motorbike, for which Orwell produced an extraordinary low-slung American machine. On another occasion Orwell asked Beadon if he wanted to come on a tiger shoot. Armed with Beadon's Luger and a shotgun borrowed from the school's principal they drove hopefully along the jungle tracks in a bullock cart – the customary means of transport in Burma – but without finding anything. At some point, too, Orwell made the acquaintance of the famous Captain H.F. Robinson, an Indian army officer seconded to the Burma police and cashiered after a scandal involving his native mistress, whose exploits after he was dismissed from the service included converting to Buddhism, trying to start a gold-mine and surviving an attempt at suicide.

Orwell left no formal account of his four and three-quarter years in Burma. All that remain are the official records of his postings and the reminiscences of a handful of people who came across him at the time: generally unrevealing (while stressing his apparent detachment) and giving no clue as to what was going on in his mind. Early on in his stay he wrote three letters to Jacintha Buddicom. None of them survives, but Jacintha remembered the first as a lament along the lines of 'You could never understand how awful it is if you hadn't been here'. She replied asking why, if it were so bad, he didn't come home. Two more letters in a similar vein followed, after which Jacintha stopped answering. Orwell was due to complete his police exams early in 1924.

Before this, at the end of the preceding November, he was posted to Maymyo for a month's service with a British regiment, the South Suffolks. According to the passage in *The Road to Wigan Pier* where this experience is used as a litmus test of Orwell's class consciousness, he admired these 'hefty, cheery youths' five years older than himself with the medals of the Great War on their chests while remaining faintly repelled by the vision of sweaty working-class manhood that they conjured up. But he was entranced by the locale.

Maymyo was Burma's principal hill station, on the edge of the Shan peninsula, to which the Rangoon government repaired in hot weather. The journey involved a train ride through mountains so precipitous that two engines were needed, one to pull and another to push. Many years later the startling contrast with Mandalay ('the scorching sunlight, the dusty palms, the smells of fish and spice and garlic, the squashy tropical fruit, the swarming dark-faced human beings') was still fresh in Orwell's memory. Tumbling out of the train, mentally prepared for the atmosphere of the Eastern city they had left behind, visitors to Maymyo suddenly found themselves breathing air 'that might be that of England' in a landscape of green grass, bracken and fir trees, complete with hill women selling baskets of strawberries. The vividness of these impressions – not written down until a decade after he left Burma – are a mark of the way in which the place preyed on his mind. *Burmese Days* is full of striking juxtapositions of this kind, in which the familiar and the bizarre come scrambled together: blistering white heat and the thudding of the bullock carts giving way to dusty clubrooms lined with mildewed English novels and month-old copies of *Punch*. Maymyo even had a golf club, to which Orwell was invited by Beadon and his father. Orwell would have been familiar with the ambience – much of his boyhood holidays, after all, had been spent at the Henley club where his father officiated – but, as Beadon noted, 'he didn't mix very well'.

From Mandalay, where he returned shortly before Christmas 1923, he was sent to his first posting proper: Myaungma, a frontier outpost of the Raj in the Irrawaddy delta. It was not a good first job, according to the standards of the Burma Police, with onerous duties: as headquarters assistant to the District Superintendent, the twenty-year-old Orwell was responsible for a police station with a strength of thirty to fifty men, made more exacting by the remote location. Twante, his next destination, was little better: a far-flung town in the Hathaway district, a thirty-six-hour steamer trip from Rangoon. Again the degree of responsibility ran far ahead of Orwell's experience. As Sub-Divisional

Officer, with a remit to oversee the workings of the police station while touring the local villages to gather intelligence, he was effectively in charge of the security of nearly 200,000 people. Worse, perhaps, was the scarcity of Europeans. Much of his time was spent on his own – in a memoir written by a contemporary in nearby Bassein he figures merely as 'the police officer at Twante' – making solitary excursions from one village headman to another. A district superintendent who met him once or twice at official conferences remembered a tall, good-looking young man, pleasant to talk to and easy of manner, in no way distinct from any of his colleagues.

Things improved at the end of 1924, when, with his two-year probationary period at a close, and newly promoted to Assistant District Superintendent (the salary was £65 a month, most of which could be saved), he was posted to Syriam. The Syriam force's chief task was to ensure the safety of the local Burmah Oil Company refinery. The advantage of belonging to it lay in the town's proximity to Rangoon, the Burmese capital and the only population centre for hundreds of miles capable of offering Western-style amenities. Cut in two by the railway line, up-market residential districts in one direction and the native city in the other, Rangoon offered a clutch of diversions, ranging from the exclusive Gymkhana Club to the Burra Bazaar, drenched in the smell of fruit and spices sold from the cave-like rooms huddled within its vast interior, the official Government House receptions and Smart and Mookerdum's bookshop, which sold the latest titles sent out from England. *Burmese Days*, where Flory remembers 'the joy of those Rangoon trips . . . the dinner at Anderson's, with beefsteak and butter that had travelled eight thousand miles on ice, the glorious drinking bout . . .', hints at Orwell's relish of the hours he spent there. For the first time in his stay he could enjoy a proper social life, amongst a circle that included Leo Robertson, an Old Etonian businessman in his early thirties who had 'gone native' and married a Burmese woman, and Alfred White, an under-secretary in the government administration who had come across him at Twante. It was at Robertson's house that he was briefly reunited with Christopher Hollis, on his way back to England after a round-the-world tour with the Oxford Union debating team. One might expect Orwell to have been reasonably forthcoming with someone he had known at school and with whom he had friends and experiences in common. On the contrary, three years out of Eton he struck Hollis merely as a diligent and conventionally minded servant of the Raj. Rangoon, too, provided the setting for an odd episode that foreshadows both a key scene in his first novel and a submerged side to his personality.

Maung Htn Aung, then a student, subsequently one of the first native Burmans to take an interest in Orwell's work, was waiting on the platform at the Pagoda Road railway station when he noticed a tall young Englishman descending the stairs with the aim of taking a train to the Mission Road station, near the site of the Gymkhana Club. Surrounded and jostled by a throng of schoolboys – a time-honoured act of minor civil disobedience – Orwell lost his temper and hit out at the boys' backs with the cane he carried before being pursued on to the train by a mob of undergraduates from the city's university, where the argument continued in a compartment. Suitably recast, the station incident turned up ten years later in *Burmese Days*, where the timber merchant Ellis strikes a boy he imagines is mocking him. Mistreated by a quack doctor, the boy loses his sight, thereby sparking a full-scale assault on the Kyauktada club. It is a revealing episode that illustrates both the tension that underlay daily life even in so civilised a milieu as up-town Rangoon and also the violent streak that periodically bobs up in defiance of Orwell's customarily easygoing manner. Above all, perhaps, it shows how few qualms Orwell had in resorting to the traditional stances of pukka-sahibdom when he thought the situation demanded it. His outward appropriateness to the role he had chosen for himself at this point in his life was noted by less transient observers than Hollis. During his time at Syriam he spent several days with another officer named De Vine billeted on one of the BOC refinery chemists. Installed on the veranda one night, pyjama-clad, after an evening of boozy singsongs, Orwell complained about the lack of good modern comic songs. The chemist decided, quite reasonably on the evidence, that his guest was a 'typical public school boy' who betrayed no literary interests. Even the mention of Aldous Huxley's name brought no real response. All Orwell would say was that Huxley had taught at Eton during his time there and was nearly blind.

It would be easy – a bit too easy, perhaps – to characterise the Orwell who wandered through 1920s Burma as the darkest of dark horses, an intellectual fifth columnist endlessly concealing his real intentions from the people around him. And yet it is perfectly possible that there was nothing very much to conceal, that the man who lounged on bungalow verandas singing bawdy songs into the small hours of the morning was merely being true to his nature. Orwell later claimed that he spent his early twenties consciously trying not to be a writer. His manifest keenness on the off-duty routines of the Burma Police may have been a part of this attempt. Yet the testimony of his Burma colleagues suggests that, along with the conventional outlook, they detected something out of the ordinary, were left, in the last resort, with the impression that there were sides to Orwell's character that were carefully kept under wraps. In September 1925 he was transferred to Insein, again within striking distance of Rangoon, where Roger Beadon visited him at his house. Beadon, who tried to keep his own quarters in some kind of order, was shocked by the prevailing chaos. Goats, geese, ducks and other livestock roamed through the downstairs rooms. Further evidence of eccentricity came in Orwell's habit of attending the local churches of the Burmese Karen tribe, many of whom had been converted to Christianity by American missionaries: not, he explained, because he was religious, but because talking to the priest was more interesting than the conversation on offer at the English club.

Insein was the home of the second-largest jail in Burma. From here, in April 1926, Orwell moved on to Moulmein, again as Assistant Superintendent. Moulmein would have been a more congenial spot than some of his earlier postings. Unlike the frontier backwaters it was a decent-sized town with a substantial European population. It also contained two of his Limouzin relatives: his grandmother, known for her 'eccentric' (that is, native) dress sense, and his Aunt Nora, married to Henry Branson Ward, Deputy Conservator of the Forestry Department. Orwell may or may not have attended his grandmother's celebrated bi-weekly 'at homes', but he certainly accompanied her to social events. An older colleague remembered meeting him at a sporting competition with two older ladies, one of whom asked his advice about 'Eric's' prospects. It would be very unlikely for this lady not to have been Mrs Limouzin. There are other fragmentary glimpses of Orwell's time in Moulmein. Maung Htn Aung, who toured the area some years later in search of eyewitness acounts, uncovered memories of a 'skilful centre-forward' who scored many goals for the Moulmein police team (Orwell refers in 'Shooting an Elephant' to playing football against nimble and not always over-scrupulous Burmans). A half-Burman woman, May Hearsey, married unusually for the time to an English police inspector, came across him at this period when her husband, who was looking for a job, turned up at nearby Martabar. They were met by 'a tall, gaunt, young man dressed in khaki shorts and shirt and holding a police helmet in his hand'. In his capacity as the station's second-in-command, Orwell gave Hearsey a job as a detective, and proved unexpectedly sympathetic when the new recruit worried about his unsuitability for the post, eventually helping him to get a transfer to the river police.

Finally, shortly before Christmas 1926 Orwell was transferred to Katha, to the west of Mandalay, set amidst the luxuriant landscape and vegetation which provided the backdrop to *Burmese Days*. 'Kyauktada' is characterised as a 'fairly typical' Upper Burman town, unchanged between the time of Marco Polo and 1910, when it offered a convenient spot for a railway terminus and a district headquarters, with an administrative network of lawcourts, hospital, school and jail burgeoning in its wake. Beyond the town the Irrawaddy 'flowed huge and ochreous, glittering like diamonds in the patches that caught the sun; and beyond the river stretched great wastes of paddy fields, ending up in a range of blackish hills'. The European population was small: Flory in *Burmese Days* has exactly six white compatriots. To identify them with the collection of boozers, club-loungers and Imperial time-servers depicted in the novel is a logical step, but it ignores the fact that we know nothing of Orwell's time in Katha other than that he caught dengue fever, a debilitating illness caused by a virus transmitted by mosquito, applied for leave on a medical certificate (he would have been entitled to leave in any case come November, having completed five years in the service) and was granted six months' absence by the India Office Service and General Department beginning on 1 July 1927. He had just turned twenty-four.

At an age when most of the members of the Edwardian-born literary generation were setting out on their professional careers, having enjoyed three not very productive years at university (Connolly idled, Waugh and Powell both took thirds) he was emerging from half a decade's punishing hard work on the margins – sometimes beyond the margins – of the civilised world. Asking what Orwell was 'like' in his early twenties, in the sense that it can be asked of writers such as Waugh and Powell, is a fruitless endeavour. Nobody knows. To take an obvious comparison – and the two men appreciated each other's work and met later in life – Evelyn Waugh's career as an undergraduate, failed schoolmaster and young man-about-town was monitored by half a dozen sharp-eyed young contemporaries, each with sufficient social and intellectual nous to make something of what they saw. Orwell's observers were a handful of colleagues, none of whom showed any special interest in him because no special interest seemed warranted by either his personality or his behaviour. George Stuart, for example, who seems to have known him towards the end of his time in Burma, possibly in the Moulmein days, recalled an easygoing young man, keen on his job – to which he brought distinctive linguistic skills – who enjoyed parties and was fond of animals. Much of this rings true, especially the aptitude for languages and the love of animals, as does the memory of Orwell's untidiness: Mrs Stuart was apparently commissioned to keep his clothes in repair. Here and there, though, come hints of the way in which he spent his free time and the things that occupied his mind. Unusually for a Burma police officer – and unlike his grandmother, whom he once disparaged for spending forty years in Burma without troubling to learn the language – he took a serious interest in Burmese culture. The rapturous accounts of the native entertainment to which Flory escorts Elizabeth Lackersteen in *Burmese Days* are clearly based on first-hand observation. This interest extended to native folklore and custom: discussing the possibility of legally changing his name to 'George Orwell' with a friend in the early 1940s, he once remarked, half seriously, that if he did this he would have to take another name to write with as the Burmese practice was that a man had one name which he used and another known only to his priest. He was keen, too, on Burmese cinema, able to reminisce, accurately, about the craze for local versions of American cowboy films that hit the country in the mid-1920s when the Rangoon screens were suddenly full of native actors wearing five-gallon hats and buckskins.

Yet, inevitably, the strongest twitch on the thread came from home. The *Rangoon Gazette*, standard reading for expatriates, printed a steady stream of material calculated to appeal to homesick Imperial servants. As in his teens, the popular songs of the period stuck in Orwell's head: 1923's big smash 'Yes, we have no bananas'; 'It ain't gonna rain no more', the hit of the following year; and 'Show me the way to go home'. The first two of these, he later wrote, 'went round the world like an influenza epidemic, and were sung even by primitive tribes in the remotest parts of Asia and South America'. They were sung in upper Burma: Flory hears the gramophone in the club at Kyauktada playing 'Show me the way to go home' as Elizabeth and his arch-rival Lieutenant Verrall dance together under the fans. And always, too, there were books: a reliable way of assuaging loneliness, a glimpse into a world beyond the jungle and the dirt-track roads. Flory, who reads rapaciously, has 'learned to live in books when life was tiresome'. Orwell's reading material took in both the doughtier late-Victorian iconoclasm he had enjoyed in his teens – he mentions a volume of

Samuel Butler's *Notebooks*, mildewed by years of Burma damp – and stock middlebrow bestsellers (he was affected 'almost to tears' by Margaret Kennedy's *The Constant Nymph*, the publishing sensation of 1924) but at the same time he was expanding his idea of what fiction could do. In Burma he came across Lawrence's 'The Prussian Officer' and 'The Thorn in the Flesh'. Reading the former, as the servant of an Imperial power in a country more or less under military rule, Orwell was struck not only by Lawrence's horror of military discipline but also by his understanding of its nature. Something told Orwell that Lawrence had never been a soldier, but somehow he was able to project himself into the atmosphere of army life, the German army at that.

It would be easy enough, on the strength of his forays into native culture and the hours spent reading books in dak bungalows, to mark Orwell down as a closet highbrow, quietly despising – as does Flory – the culture represented by the imported copies of *Blackwood's Magazine* (to which Mr Macgregor in *Burmese Days* makes bland contributions) and pining for solitude and the life of the mind. This would be a mistake. Flory is an older man in his thirties who has had the time to grow bitter and aloof, whereas Orwell, still in his early twenties, seems to have enjoyed some of the conventional social diversions of Burma. One characteristic of Flory's that he may have shared is an interest in Burmese women. Traditionally, bachelor police officers and civil servants in far-flung towns where the number of European women could be counted on the fingers of one hand kept native mistresses. Orwell remarked on this habit to friends, without ever revealing whether he kept one himself. Roger Beadon noted that 'I never saw him with a woman', which proves nothing. A mistress would have been kept out of the way, although one suspects that her existence would have been common knowledge. Beadon's visit to Orwell's house at Insein turned up only livestock. Flory contributes some atmospheric memories of the Eurasian girl Rosa McFee that he seduced in Mandalay in 1913, while Harold Acton, who did not meet Orwell until twenty years later, claims to have listened to some lubricious recollections of Burmese women. None of this, though, is conclusive. Neither is Leo Robertson's suggestion, made to Hollis, that his friend enjoyed prowling the waterfront brothels of Rangoon's red light district. Here and there, on the other hand, come hints that in depicting the relationship between Flory and his native mistress Ma Hla May Orwell knew what he was talking about. Among his unpublished papers, and written either while he was living in Burma or shortly afterwards, are two poems about sleeping with Burmese women. 'A mingled scent of sandalwood, garlic, coco-nut oil and the jasmine in her hair floated from her,' runs *Burmese Days'* account of Ma Hla May's distinctive smell as she sets about her preliminary manoeuvres. 'It was a scent that always made his teeth tingle.' The forensic detail suggests that Orwell had known at least one Burmese woman fairly intimately.

And now he was going home. His motives are unclear. He had not, at this stage, resigned from the service, and the leave he was about to take had been procured through a medical certificate. Yet the illness seems not to have been mentioned to his family back in England. The statements Orwell later made about his decision to leave his job with the Burma Police are quite as emphatic as his estimates of St Cyprian's or Eton. He gave up his job, he told the compilers of *Twentieth Century Authors* in 1940, 'partly because the climate had ruined my health, partly because I already had a vague idea of writing books, but mostly because I could not go on any longer serving an imperialism which I had come to regard as very largely a racket'. As with his statements about St Cyprian's and Eton, one wonders how much of this resolute conviction was retrospective, initial inklings confirmed and solidified by time. Was he right about his health? In a 1923 training school group photograph he still looks reasonably fresh-faced, but most of the contemporary accounts of his time in Burma describe him as 'thin' and 'gaunt'. Stuart noted his weak chest, which the moist Burma climate could hardly have helped. Then there is Orwell's professional anti-Imperialism, the idea that even during the later stages of his police career he was a kind of agitator *manqué* silently incubating seditious thoughts as he questioned suspects or wheedled intelligence out of village elders. The sections in *The Road to Wigan Pier* that deal with his time in Burma are full of symbolic moments – the overnight train journey to Mandalay spent damning the Empire with a member of the education service, ending in the 'haggard morning light' when the two men parted 'as guiltily as any adulterous couple', the American missionary who, watching one of Orwell's Burmese subordinates bullying a suspect, remarked, 'I wouldn't want your job'. These are vivid passages that give an impression of having grown out of years of brooding. But however firmly Orwell's anti-Imperialist convictions may have taken root at this time, they were well hidden from his colleagues. Naturally, no serving officer in an Imperial force would go out of his way to draw attention to unorthodox views, but the people who knew Orwell in Burma regarded his opinions as absolutely standard for the milieu. Stuart never thought him anti-establishment. Marrison, the BOC chemist, considered him a perfectly representative type. Hollis, an observer who had, additionally, known Orwell in another world, found no trace of liberal opinions. 'He was at pains to be the imperial policeman, emphasising that these theories of no punishment and no beatings were all very well at public schools but they did not work with the Burmese . . .' Granted, Orwell had a well-developed talent for irony, along with a near-unfathomable reserve, but with Hollis, surely, he would have unbent a little and revealed something of his true feelings?

Going back to the specific circumstances of his departure, he seems to have left when he did primarily because of illness – it wanted only a few months, after all, to the statutory leave that would have followed his five years' service. This is not to discount various rumours put about by colleagues. Beadon, for instance, thought that his departure was brought about by a bullying district superintendent. The officer asked for advice by Mrs Limouzin remembered suggesting that if Orwell was unhappy in his job he should get out while he still had time to start a fresh career.

The probability is that in mid-1927, ill, longing for England and doubting the value of what he was doing, Orwell had no clear idea of his future direction. It took the months that followed to develop these feelings to the point where they could be publicly expressed. Two years later, in an article for a French newspaper, he would write that 'if we are correct, it is true that the British are robbing and pilfering Burma quite shamefully'. Flory claims that 'the British Empire is simply a device for giving trade monopolies to the English – or rather to gangs of Jews and Scotchmen'. There follows an informed analysis of Imperial depredations on the teak, rice and oil industries, and the suppression of other native trades such as muslin manufacture and shipbuilding in order to squeeze out competition. At the centre of Flory's thoughts, and 'poisoning everything', is 'the ever bitterer hatred of the atmosphere of Imperialism in which he lived'. The mature Orwell was prepared to draw distinctions, between principled men and time-servers, between the civil administration and the commercial interest, under whose 'sloth and greed' the Far Eastern promise of the Empire had rotted. Moreover his attitude to Burma and its people was always realistic. He had no illusions about the prospect of Burmese 'democracy'. Burma was a small, agricultural country, he wrote in 1942, and talk of independence was nonsense, 'in the sense that it will never be independent'. In a world of international power politics, satellite status was about the best an ex-colony could hope for.

But this is advancing Orwell's view of world affairs deep into the 1940s. From the angle of 1927, there is a suspicion that, as in earlier parts of his life, attitudes that were inchoate at the time of departure took a certain amount of time to harden into something tangible. Inevitably, they find their fullest expression in his creative work. This falls into three distinct categories: some early poems and a fragmentary try-out for *Burmese Days*; the novel itself, first published in 1934 but worked on for some years before this; and two of his finest sketches, 'A Hanging', published in the *Adelphi* in August 1931, and 'Shooting an Elephant', which appeared in John Lehmann's *New Writing* five years later. Most of the poems have a recognisable tone: gloomy, self-pitying, intensely romantic in their anti-romanticism ('. . . I do not care what comes/When I am gone, though kings or peoples rot,/Though life itself grow cold; I do not care/Though all the streams & all the sea ran blood.') 'The Lesser Evil', one of the poems about sleeping with Burmese women, has perhaps some faint interest in that it sets up an opposition between the spiritual – a church where old maids caterwaul 'A dismal tale of thorns and blood' – and the secular (visits to 'the house of sin') that was to preoccupy him in the future. The rest is doom, gloom and futility, culminating in a terrible poem entitled 'When the Franks Have Lost Their Sway' which talks about empires being torn asunder and finally demands of the reader:

> Is it not dreadful thus to contemplate
> These mighty ills that will beset the world
> When we are dead & won't be bothered with them?
> Do not these future woes transcend our own?

Dreadful is perhaps putting it mildly. The dry-runs for *Burmese Days*, on the other hand, include an extract from Flory's 'autobiography', which relates it more closely to Orwell's own early life. Although thirteen years older than his creator, here Flory has a father who served in the Indian Civil Service and a brace of sisters, though both are older than him. Of his relationship with his father he suggests that 'they might have been called friends. The reticence that lies between all blood relatives held us apart, & then I had scarcely seen him till I was thirteen years old.'

'A Hanging' and 'Shooting an Elephant' would make a good introduction for anyone who had never read Orwell and wanted to know what the fuss was about. The first sketch describes the execution of a native prisoner in a Burmese jail; the second takes in the shooting of a rogue elephant which has killed a man, carried out in front of a huge crowd of expectant Burmans, and eventually undertaken, the reader is given to understand, because the writer fears losing face. Each, ultimately, is about the futility, and the moral consequences, of taking a life. In a sense, though, the precise circumstances don't matter. In the end the emotional kick of the writing is more important than the autobiographical roots. If Orwell did witness an execution during his time in Burma – and such attendances were not part of the police routine – then a likely spot was Insein, owing to the size of its jail. Certainly the detail of 'A Hanging' is highly convincing: the look on the face of the condemned man, the way in which he skips to one side to avoid a puddle on his way to the block. We know, too, that Orwell was familiar with the procedures of Burmese executions: he notes elsewhere the difficulty of procuring executioners, a job that was usually done by convicts themselves. And yet one of the signature marks of Orwell's early writing is its use of models, well-known literary templates which the tyro writer could adapt to his own design. Without in any way plagiarising it, 'A Hanging' belongs to the same tradition of anti-capital-punishment literature as Thackeray's 'Going to See a Man Hanged': there is the same bitter attention to detail, the same sharp focus on the figure of the victim, the same valedictory widening of the gaze, so that the personal turns universal.

Ambiguity also hangs over 'Shooting an Elephant' – full of intent, densely realised description, but incapable of being fixed to a particular date or locale, and referred to only once, and that indirectly, elsewhere in Orwell's writings. (Elizabeth in *Burmese Days* is 'quite thrilled' when Flory describes 'the murder of an elephant he had perpetrated some years earlier'.) George Stuart claimed to have been at the club in Moulmein when the message about the rogue elephant came through, prompting Orwell to borrow a rifle and set out in pursuit, but this memory of the episode may not have been wholly accurate. He also maintains that the transfer to Katha was a punishment for destroying something of value (the sketch records only an argument between the Europeans as to whether Orwell had done the right thing) handed out by the Chief of the Police Service, Colonel Wellbourne. Certainly Wellbourne, an unwitting bigamist (he married his third wife before the second had been legally disposed of), thought to possess 'no great charm' by an associate, would have been capable of this. Another of Orwell's contemporaries thought that he remembered a report of the incident in the *Rangoon Gazette*, and indeed there is such a report, dated 22 March 1926. However, the protagonist was not Orwell but Major E.C. Kenny, subdivisional officer at Yamethin, who shot an elephant that had killed a man five miles east of the Tatkon township 'to the delight of the villagers'. Far from being upbraided, Kenny was subsequently promoted Deputy Commissioner.

'A Hanging' and 'Shooting an Elephant' are figurative snapshots, no more than a few pages long. The most complete statement of Orwell's view of Burma is found in *Burmese Days*. Re-read nearly seventy years after its first publication, *Burmese Days* is an odd book: an 'Eastern' novel built on a conventional foundation – the obvious influence is Somerset Maugham – but decked with the most fantastic figurative garnishes. Flory, its chief character, is a disillusioned teak merchant in his thirties, unmarried (though he has a Burmese mistress, Ma Hla May), bored with the handful of local Europeans with whom he is forced to associate, and finding civilised conversation – and an audience for his harangues about the Raj – only in the company of an Indian hospital doctor, Veraswami. To make matters worse, Flory is disfigured by a hideous birthmark. The arrival in Kyauktada of Elizabeth, the twenty-year-old niece of hard-drinking Mr Lackersteen, gives Flory unexpected hope, only for him to be mercilessly cut out by an aristocratic army officer, Lieutenant Verrall. Meanwhile, Kyauktada generally is subject to the machinations of an unscrupulous native magnate, U Po Kyin, who is cheerfully blackmailing and bullying himself to prominence. Having seen off Verrall and covered himself in glory by performing heroically in a failed uprising, Flory is thrown over by Elizabeth when U Po Kyin bribes the now discarded Ma Hla May to make a public scene in, of all places, the Kyauktada church. Flory shoots himself.

All this is accompanied by some pattern dissections of the iniquities of British rule and devastating portraits of the whisky-sodden wrecks and amateur humorists who infest the club, and yet the most striking thing about the novel is the extravagance of its language: a riot of rococo imagery that gets dangerously out of hand. This is apparent even in the preliminary description of U Po Kyin breakfasting on the veranda of his bungalow, where his servant's face recalls 'a coffee blancmange', while U Po Kyin himself dresses in a pink *paso* which glitters in the sun 'like a satin praline'. Later, in the gardens of the European club, a native servant moves through the jungle of flowers 'like some large nectar-sucking bird'. Subsequently, in the space of two pages, a lizard clings to the wall of Flory's house 'like a heraldic dragon', light rains down 'like glistening white oil' and the noise of doves produces 'a sleepy sound, but with the sleepiness of chloroform rather than a lullaby'. Towards the end of the book the figurative touches would not disgrace a Beardsley-era aesthete. Camp-fire flames dance 'like red holly', U Po Kyin's betel-stained teeth gleam in the lamplight 'like red tin-foil', Flory and Elizabeth's canoes move through the water 'like long curved needles threading through embroidery'. Finally, the language loses all relation to the things it is trying to describe. The moon rises out of a cloud-bank 'like a sick woman creeping out of bed', and storms chase each other across the sky likes squads of cavalry. This is a testimony to the impact of Burma on Orwell's imagination, but it is also the mark of a 'modernist' if faintly old-fashioned aesthetic sensibility – like something out of an 1890s poem by Richard Le Gallienne – which would take nearly a decade to subdue.

Given the identification of Kyauktada with Katha, the temptation is to mark *Burmese Days* instantly down as a *roman-à-clef*, and to assume that the principal Europeans – Mr Macgregor, the Assistant District Commissioner, Ellis the spiteful timber merchant, Westfield, Maxwell and the Lackersteens – are thinly disguised representations of real people. The manuscript of the novel so alarmed Victor Gollancz that he initially declined to publish it for fear of libel. When Gollancz did finally feel able to proceed, Orwell was ordered to consult the official directories of the time to ensure that the names of 'Macgregor', 'Westfield', 'Maxwell' and 'Lackersteen' were not those of serving Anglo-Indian officials. Orwell reported that he had looked through the 1929 Burma Civil List – earlier volumes were apparently unobtainable – and found nothing. This is correct. And yet Orwell's covering up of his tracks in the cast list for *Burmese Days* is not quite conclusive. Several of the characters' names, for example, are simply lifted from back numbers of the *Rangoon Gazette*. On 14 September 1923 a Mr J.C.J. Macgregor, a well-known timber merchant, was reported as returning to Liverpool from Rangoon, while on 19 October in the same year a Mr Lackersteen arrived in Rangoon; 'B.J. Ellis' left Liverpool on the same day. There was a real U Po Kyin, a native Burman at the Mandalay training school (he appears in the 1923 photograph) and an Indian doctor who served at Katha whose name has the same suffix as Dr Veraswami. But there is another plausible candidate for Mr Macgregor, the bumbling but essentially good-natured ADC. Had Orwell looked through the 1929 Burma *military* directory he would have emerged with the name of Colonel F.H. McGregor, commander of the Rangoon Third Field Brigade. A shipping merchant who doubled up as an army officer – joint roles of this kind were common in inter-war Burma – McGregor was at one point stationed in Syriam during Orwell's time in Burma and additionally lived in a Rangoon suburb. He was a well-known personality, and it is inconceivable that Orwell could have spent five years in the country without coming across him in some capacity. Photographs of the Colonel (born in 1880) show a bulky, bespectacled character, oddly reminiscent of Orwell's portrait of the chief bore of the Kyauktada club: 'a large, heavy man, rather past forty, with a kindly, puggy face, wearing gold-rimmed spectacles. His bulky shoulders, and a trick he had of thrusting his head forward, reminded one curiously of a tortoise.'

Orwell left Burma in late July. He never went back. Flory, plotting his retirement in England, imagines that he 'would forget Burma, the horrible country that had come near ruining him'. But Burma haunted Orwell's imagination, both as a practical demonstration of Imperial wrongdoing and as a more elemental sensory tug. Dorothy in *A Clergyman's Daughter*, for instance, on her knees by the Suffolk roadside smelling a bunch of fennel, imagines suddenly 'Scent of spice-drenched islands in the warm foam of eastern seas.' For the rest of his life Burma offered an instant point of comparison for the landscapes Orwell encountered. At home, the north of England caravan colonies of *The Road to Wigan Pier* reminded him of the 'filthy kennels' of the Burmese coolies. Abroad, Morocco found him adducing endless parallels between the ethnic peoples, agricultural arrangements and colonial society. There is even a hint of the anthropomorphism of *Animal Farm* in his early review of a Pearl S. Buck novel, *The Good Earth*, in which he laments the fate of the Burmese rickshaw pullers, 'men running between shafts, like horses'. For the next twenty years the spectre of Burma rose continually in Orwell's mental life, in fragments of memory – the strange boy met in Rangoon who, questioned as to his origins, replied that he was a *Joo* – and personal connection. As late as 1949 he was trying to use David Astor's influence to find his old friend Leo Robertson a job. At the very end of his life his thoughts returned to the experiences of a quarter-century before. 'A Smoking Room Story', the rough plan for a novel sketched out not long before his death, features a character named 'Curly Johnson' ('a tallish, shapely youth, moving with a grace of which he is not conscious'). Johnson, sent home from

Burma by his firm, combines a dislike of the American and English businessmen on the ship with social insecurity: he is wary of the bright young people who swarm aboard at Colombo. There is also mention of a Burmese woman, Ma Yi (his mistress), and the 'dust and squalor of his house, the worn gramophone records, the piled up whiskey bottles . . .'

What had been the impact of Burma on the personality of this reserved and apparently unremarkable young man? He had arrived there immature and impressionable. He left it older in both body and spirit, and, temperamentally, split in half. Reflecting ten years later on an environment that had simultaneously jogged both the conservative and the anarchic sides of his mind, he gave this unresolved tension a violently dramatic focus. Half of him, *The Road to Wigan Pier* maintains, thought that Imperialism was a racket; the other half wanted nothing better than to plunge a bayonet into a Buddhist priest's guts. Burma, it might be said, established one of the central oppositions in Orwell's life and writings: the conflict between his commitment to fair play and liberal principles and a latent authoritarianism constantly breaking out in complaints about grinning yellow faces. Occasionally this took on a symbolic focus. On the one hand Orwell subscribed to the free-thinking, left-leaning *Adelphi*, a magazine in which some of his earliest journalism appeared, while he was in Burma. On the other, he was quite capable of nailing copies to a tree and taking pot-shots at them when their brand of idealistic left-wing politics became too irksome to be borne. As a Burma police officer whose working life was spent dealing with the practical consequences of Imperialism, Orwell was constantly annoyed by the sheer gaucherie of most anti-Imperial polemic. What sickened him about left-wing people, he once told his friend Jack Common, was their ignorance of how life had to be lived 8,000 miles away from Britain. 'I was always struck by that when I was in Burma and used to read anti-imperialist stuff'. Now he was on his way back: a month's sea voyage would see him home. The inter-war years were the great era of the literary man's voyage by sea: Evelyn Waugh sightseeing around the Mediterranean on the trip that produced his travel book *Labels*, his older brother Alec on the Messageries Maritimes boat to Tahiti, Mr and Mrs Huxley following Orwell's own earlier route up the Irrawaddy. For the tall, gaunt twenty-four-year-old scribbling his way through the pile of government paper filched from some police headquarters in Upper Burma, as the liner moved on slowly through the Indian Ocean, much sterner realities lay ahead.

Part Two
1927–1936

5

Cross-Channel

How I wish I were with you in Paris, now that spring is there. –
Letter to Celia Paget, 27 May 1948

The voyage home brought another of those pieces of symbolism that, in retrospect, seem to have wound themselves through Orwell's life like loosestrife. Towards the end of the third week in August the boat stopped at Marseilles. France, at any rate working-class France, was currently in uproar over the forthcoming execution in America of two Italian anarchists, Sacco and Vanzetti, recently convicted for crimes against the state. Presumably unaware of this agitation – although news of the case had gone round the world in the summer of 1927 – Orwell found himself standing on the steps of one of the English banks talking to a clerk as before them a vast procession of the French proletariat marched by, their banners proclaiming *Sauvons Sacco et Vanzetti!* It was a futile protest: the Italians were executed a few days later.

Writing the episode up nearly five years later, in a state of markedly greater political awareness, Orwell believed that he had detected a genuine cultural difference. Such a thing might have happened in England in the 1840s, the age of Chartism and mass dissent: it could not happen now; but the French were indignant at what seemed a piece of rank injustice. Orwell's suspicion that he had chanced on a fundamental national divide was confirmed by the matter-of-fact response of the English clerk: 'Oh well, you've got to hang those blasted anarchists.' Even if they were not guilty? the returning Burma policeman wondered. The bank clerk seemed surprised. Anarchists, as far as he was concerned, were there to be hanged. But for Orwell the demonstration revealed something profoundly important about French culture when compared to the arrangements beyond the Channel: it was a country where a certain amount of civil disturbance was seen as an inevitable process, where 'the highly socialized mind, which makes a kind of composite god out of the rich, the government, the police and the larger newspapers has not been developed . . .' As with many of the other figurative episodes from Orwell's early life, the gap between observation and deduction – in this case five years – is significant. The Orwell who wrote the incident up for the *Adelphi* in 1932 was able to put his finger on one of the key processes of modern, civilised life. The young man who witnessed it in 1927, fresh from a world in which 'anarchism' and 'protest march' were simply words, was less sure of the importance of what he saw.

But his old life – the life of month-long sea voyages, efflorescent landscapes, the endless toll of the Imperial tocsin – was nearly over. From Marseilles he made his way home to Southwold. In the five years since his departure the Blairs had moved house from Stradbroke Road to 3 Queen Street, a narrow thoroughfare set at a 45 degree angle to the market square and a short step from the seafront. Avril, now a young woman of twenty, was struck by the change in her older brother. Hair grown darker since his straw-coloured teens, and sporting a toothbrush moustache, he looked much more like his father. Five years in the East had also made him chronically untidy, Avril deduced: when he smoked a cigarette, he threw the butt and the match on the floor and expected them to be swept up. At this point, apparently, Orwell's bombshell was undropped. It fell during the course of a family holiday to Cornwall in September. Here, in front of hitherto unsuspecting parents, he declared his intention of leaving the Burma Police and setting up as a writer. The only witness to this bolt from the blue was Avril. She remembered her mother being 'rather horrified', which, given the Blair tendency to understatement, may be translated as 'very upset indeed'. Richard Blair's reaction was much worse. His only recorded comment, recalled by a friend who met Orwell a couple of years later, was that his son was behaving like 'a dilettante', but all the signs, both in Avril's reminiscences and in Orwell's sporadic references to his father, point to an actual estrangement, not repaired for several years. But however crushing the weight of parental disapproval, Orwell would not be gainsaid. A letter was sent to the India Office, and his resignation set to take effect from 1 July 1927. If nothing else all this – the row with his parents, the resignation letter – is a mark of Orwell's determination. His desire to quit Burma for good may only have been inchoate when he left it, but his comment about the 'first sniff of English air' deciding him looks all too accurate. It is worth pointing out, for example, that he decided not to play the health card – after all, he went home on a medical certificate, and a niece who attended the Cornish holiday has a vague memory of him being ill in bed – and by formally resigning he lost his entitlement to full pay (£140, the equivalent of £5,500 today) during his leave of absence.

From Cornwall the Blairs returned to Suffolk. No doubt as a respite from the tensions of Queen Street, Orwell renewed his acquaintance with various Southwold friends he had made during his stay there five years before. Dennis Collings, having spent time growing sisal in Mozambique, was back in England prior to studying Anthropology at Cambridge. So, too, was Sharp, his fellow-student from Mr Hope's crammer, whose mother had settled in Southwold. Sharp remembered the revenant as 'very tall, very shy . . . and rather untidily dressed', while suggesting – sentiments that were probably shared by family friends in town – that 'Blair senior must have been horrified when his son left the Indian police'. The difference between the nineteen-year-old who had left England for a safe, if unglamorous, job on the outer margin of the Empire and the twenty-four-year-old who returned to it with only a vague ambition 'to write' (presumably whatever Orwell thought about Imperialism was kept from Richard Blair) struck observers beyond the family circle. At some time in the early autumn of 1927 Orwell spent a fortnight with the Buddicoms at their Aunt Lilian's house in Shropshire. Prosper and Guinever were present during this stay; Jacintha was not. Describing the holiday to her niece, Aunt Lilian reported that Eric seemed 'very different'.

Again – and this is characteristic of Orwell's whole pre-1930 life – one can recreate the environments through which the migrant passed, but Orwell himself is impossible to pin down. Only a handful of glimpses survive of his early Southwold period, none from anyone with whom he enjoyed anything resembling intimacy. The Southwold tailor, Mr Denny, from whose aunt Richard and Ida Blair later bought a house, fitted him out for the rigours of an English winter: a three-piece suit in September, a pair of flannel trousers a month later, an overcoat the following January. It was cloth thrown away, Mr Denny thought. His client was 'one of those people who put on a suit and don't look well-dressed even when they put it on new'. At the same time the ménage in Queen Street had another, silent observer. The Blairs had a daily help, Mrs May, a talkative Southwold matriarch – the Mays were a famous local family – who became a great crony of Ida's. Esmé, her daughter, who was twelve at the time, vividly recalled 'Eric's presence on the premises in the winter of 1927/8'. Her recollections of the Blairs *en famille* reflect the attitude of ordinary Suffolk people to what, for all Orwell's disparagement of his social background, were essentially, and by the exacting standards of Southwold, gentlefolk. The Blairs, in the mind of a girl from the local council school, were 'high class'. Richard Blair was 'a gentleman'. As for his son, he was 'a loner', who was 'not quite all there', clad in a ramshackle get-up typified by woollen scarves wound three times round his neck but still descending to his knees.

There was a further visit that autumn, to see Gow at Cambridge. Entertained by his old tutor – he was placed next to his great hero A.E. Housman at dinner at Trinity high table – Orwell, while stressing his determination to write, asked for advice. Gow, a veteran of these confidences, was noncommittal while pointing out some of the difficulties of the literary life. One of these, naturally enough, was finding an entrée to the environments in which it could be lived. Clearly, if he was serious about writing Orwell had to move in circles where writers could be found, and in the orbit of editors who might commission, or at any rate encourage, his work. In fact he needed to be in London. Orwell's solution was to write from Southwold to Ruth Pitter, a neighbour from the old Mall Chambers days, asking if she could help him to find a room. Pitter, already embarked on what was to be a distinguished career as a poet, remembered him as an Eton schoolboy ('a tall young man with hair the colour of honey and a brown tweed suit sitting at a table by the window cleaning a sporting gun'), and was happy to help. His lodgings, a single room in a house in the Portobello Road, were overseen by the immensely snobbish Mrs Craig, formerly lady's maid to an ornament of the aristocracy, who features in one of Orwell's symbolic vignettes of English life. At one point, Orwell recalled, all the occupants were locked out of the house. This mischance obliged Orwell and Mr Craig to travel some distance to borrow a ladder from one of the Craigs' relatives. The couple had spent fourteen years not speaking to their neighbours and did not intend to begin now.

All this – the London lodgings, the seriousness about wanting to write – is a testimony to Orwell's resolve, his sense of himself at what must have been a difficult stage in his career, and yet there is a feeling that certain aspects of this new life were still provisional. December brought a letter from the India Office confirming his departure, but the resignation was not widely known outside the Blairs' immediate circle or much referred to by Orwell himself. Ruth Pitter, for example, only found out once he was installed at Portobello Road. Like everyone else, she thought it a bad mistake, 'like turning down a cheque for 5,000 or 10,000 pounds', as well as being rough on his parents. A note of uncertainty, too, hangs over his attendance around this time at a dinner staged by members of the 1916 Eton election, fixed up by an Old Etonian acquaintance named Maurice Whittome. Such was Orwell's diffidence, and so little did he say, that Whittome came away with the impression that a decision about the Burma Police was still pending and any thoughts about what might replace it were altogether unformed.

This may have been Orwell lapsing into a typical display of company manners: the dark horse, giving nothing away. On the other hand, it may have proceeded from a genuine uncertainty. Other aspects of Orwell's life at this time suggest that he had yet to drift very far from the routes mapped out by upbringing and education: socially, he was happy enough to spend time with Dennis Collings or keep up with his Eton contemporary Alan Clutton-Brock. The only real witness, to whom in any case he confided very little, is Ruth Pitter. Slightly older than Orwell, and preoccupied with her own affairs – she was later to run a pottery studio with her friend Kathleen O'Hara – Pitter liked her younger acquaintance while always feeling able to laugh at what she thought were his absurdities. She noted that he seemed ill and was additionally troubled by a 'nasty foot' that needed treatment. Despite Mr Denny's efforts the cold of an English winter upset him. He never seemed to have enough clothes, she remembered, and would warm his hands over a candle flame before starting work. At the heart of these memories, perhaps, is the thought of something faintly exotic, out of kilter with the west London life of the late 1920s. There were trunks of clothes brought back from Burma including some great, spreading hats: when Orwell wore these in the street, he was trailed by bands of interested children. More significant, perhaps, is that Pitter sees this exotic vagrant not simply as himself but as part of a family unit she had been observing for the best part of a decade. In contrast to the respectful Suffolk working class, she tended to see the Blairs as 'rather tatty', while enjoying the company of Aunt Nellie, then living nearby and keen to issue invitations to supper ('she gave us fearsome dishes such as one would have in Paris if one was a native Parisian and dreadfully hard-up'). Moreover, with the exception of Jacintha Buddicom and perhaps Connolly, she was the first person to be shown Orwell's apprentice literary work. Predictably, as a published poet Pitter found these early efforts irretrievably gauche, 'like a cow with a musket'. One short story began 'Inside the park the crocuses were out'. She and

Kathleen amused themselves by correcting the misspelt rude words with which these early manuscripts were garnished.

It was Ruth Pitter, too, who monitored Orwell's first decisive attempt to collect literary material and set out on the path that ended with the publication of his first book – a tramping excursion to the East End. In *The Road to Wigan Pier*, published ten years later, Orwell's account of why he put on ragged clothes and set out into the poorest working-class district of east London is starkly and convincingly set out. Five years as the servant of an oppressive system had left him with a 'bad conscience'. As a result he felt he had to escape not just from Imperialism 'but from every form of man's dominion over man'. Failure seemed the only virtue. This line of thought had pointed him in the direction of the English working class, symbolic victims of injustice who, he imagined, occupied the same role in England as the Burmans in Burma, their position exaggerated by the prevailing economic situation. This was late 1927, a year and a half after a General Strike in which, as one historian put it, the British working classes had picked up a loaded revolver and then silently put it down. 'Unemployment', which had barely existed when Orwell left home in 1922, marched through every newspaper column. At this stage, however, the shabby-genteel sub-world of which most unemployment consisted had not yet come Orwell's way. To him not having a job meant destitution, 'brute starvation'. He wanted to seek out people on the absolute margins of English life: tramps, down-and-outs, beggars, pavement artists. The account of this descent, again given in *The Road to Wigan Pier*, is carefully constructed. Heading east from the City Orwell stopped before a lodging house in Limehouse Causeway advertising 'good beds for single men'. The charge was ninepence. It was a Saturday night. Stevedores, navvies and a few sailors sat about playing draughts. Seeing the newcomer, a burly drunk launched himself forward. Orwell braced himself for trouble, only for the man to collapse matily on to his shoulders. 'Ave a cup of tea, chum,' he declared. Orwell had a cup of tea. 'It was a kind of baptism.'

Or was it? No one doubts that the encounter with the drunken stevedore in the Limehouse kip took place more or less as Orwell describes it. But the account of how he arrived there is both a rationalisation and a telescoping of a complex mental process. The ideological armature, you feel, came later. Like so much of his early work Orwell's forays among the tramps, his stays in casual wards (where tramps could sleep for a night, known as spikes) and his eventual holiday among the Kentish hop-pickers had a specific literary context. Among a certain stratum of early twentieth-century literary men, an absorption in low life, in out-of-the-way existences lived on the social frontier, was a perfectly conventional professional interest. Several of the authors Orwell most admired in his early twenties featured tramps in their writings, and the vagrant – fat, drink-sodden and bearing no relation to his real-life equivalent – had been a staple of English humour for nearly a century. The hero of H.G. Wells's *The History of Mr Polly* (1910) ends up as a tramp. Orwell was familiar with W.H. Davies's *The Autobiography of a Super-tramp* (1908), even more so with Jack London's exposé of East End social conditions, *The People of the Abyss* (1903). Among other similarities, Davies' account follows the same geography and the same sequence of events: the Saturday night journey to Limehouse, the drunken reception at the lodging house cut short, for Davies, not by a cup of tea but by the landlady shepherding him upstairs to the dormitory. (Davies was a genuine tramp, on both sides of the Atlantic, who later wrote a whimsically favourable review of *Down and Out in Paris and London*.) Unquestionably Orwell was sincere in what he was about – no one who reads a line of his social reportage could doubt his sympathy for the people he came across in the course of his travels – but he was also a literary apprentice in search of material. Throughout the early excursions into a world that would emerge five years later in *Down and Out* the stirrings of a political purpose, the need for 'copy' and sheer curiosity march side by side.

The same sense of a well-trodden literary path hangs over his decision, taken in the spring of 1928, to go to Paris. This is occasionally depicted as a conscious attempt to seek out and explore the lower reaches of an alien culture. In fact it was a good deal less than this. In the late 1920s, lured by the plummeting exchange rate – the pound was then worth 120 francs – and a bohemian tradition that went back to the novels of Murger and Paul de Kock, writers and apprentice writers flocked to Paris in an ever-replenished horde. Orwell's relocation to 6 rue du Pot de Fer in the 5th *arrondissement* followed a route taken by any number of his contemporaries. Cyril Connolly later discovered that he had spent the early months of the following year living a few streets away. Orwell was not living among the proletariat but in the middle of the Latin Quarter: out-at-elbow, polyglot but essentially bohemian rather than impoverished. The opening lines of *Down and Out*, with their vista of 'leprous houses lurching towards one another in queer attitudes as though they had all been frozen in the act of collapse', are an exaggeration. Orwell saw poverty in Paris, and later experienced it, but his first year in the city was spent as much in the company of fellow-foreigners as native Parisians. Always a magnet for expatriate artists, Paris was crammed to bursting point with the literary class to which Orwell aspired. Hemingway had lived a few hundred yards beyond the rue du Pot de Fer earlier in the 1920s. F. Scott Fitzgerald was a twenty-minute walk away. Orwell wondered whether he had seen James Joyce at the celebrated Deux Magots café, but could not be sure as, before the age of publicity photographs, 'J was not of distinctive appearance.' Legend – some of which Orwell himself helped to create – has tended to portray inter-war Paris as an open-all-hours nightclub staffed by aristocratic Russian commissionaires ruined by the Revolution and patronised by dollar-rich Americans itching to write the novel that would knock Proust into a cocked hat. Certain aspects of the reality lagged only a short way behind. The American novelist John Dos Passos, for example, remembered 'loafing around in little old bars full of the teasing fragrances of history ... talking bad French with taxi-drivers, riverbank loafers, workmen, petites femmes, keepers of bistros, *poilus* on leave, we young hopefuls eagerly collected intimations of the urge towards the common good'.

Though he would probably have balked at characterising himself in these terms, Orwell certainly fell into the Dos Passos category of young hopeful. And if it was a good time to be in Paris, it was definitely a good time to be a writer, whether in Paris or anywhere else. To examine the nuts and bolts of literary life in the late 1920s is to be constantly struck by the sheer profusion of outlets that existed for creative work. London, for instance, ran to half a dozen morning and evening newspapers, and there were any number of middlebrow 'literary' magazines – *John o' London's Weekly*, the *London Mercury*, the *Royal* and the *Sphere* – of a kind that has altogether ceased to exist. A short story, Alec Waugh once remarked, had to be very bad or very good – that is, defiantly highbrow – not to find a home. Orwell's must have been very bad, as no fiction at all survives from this period in his life. Yet his father's charge of aimless trifling was misplaced. He worked hard during his time in Paris. We know that he wrote two novels – an early version of *Burmese Days* and a second manuscript which he destroyed after a single publisher's rejection letter – but there were also several short stories of which some record survives, and a wad of newspaper articles. This probably represents only a fraction of his work. But what kind of writer did Orwell imagine himself to be? To judge from the titles of the material that he submitted to a newspaper syndication agency in 1929, he inclined to the staider kind of 'Georgianism' peddled by Somerset Maugham and Walter de la Mare. A letter from the McClure agency, over the signature of its London representative L.I. Bailey, refers to three pieces of short fiction: 'The Sea God' (Bailey thought this immature and containing too much sex), 'The Partition Crown' (over-descriptive) and 'The Man in Kid Gloves' (excellent, but again too much sex). Though there is no way of divining the subject matter or treatment, each sounds like a thoroughly representative magazine story of the period.

He had better luck with his journalism. In fact he had been barely six months in Paris before publishing his first signed article, 'La Censore en Angleterre', 'Censorship in England', in *Monde,* a highly regarded French literary journal, not to be confused with the mass circulation daily newspaper of the same name. The piece is conventional in scope, playing up the absurdities of the age-old English proscription of incendiary literature for the benefit of an audience that considered English 'morals' faintly macabre, but making a good historical point about the rise of the Victorian bourgeoisie. Even in the eighteenth century, Orwell suggested, the age of Fielding, Smollett and Sterne, England had possessed a puritan middle class, yet it had not been able to prevent *Tom Jones.* It was only a century later, when this emerging class could make itself felt politically, that censorship really took root. He followed this foreign début with his first appearance in a British periodical, an article in *G.K.'s Weekly* on 'A Farthing Newspaper'. The French newspaper in question was *Les Amis du Peuple,* owned by the millionaire perfumier Coty, whose vast sales presented Orwell with a dilemma that he was regularly to address over the next twenty years. *Les Amis du Peuple,* though undeniably popular, was virulently right-wing. What could one do about genuine expressions of popular taste if they happened not to coincide with one's own opinions? Why shouldn't England have its own cheap newspaper? he concluded. At least the 'poor devils' who bought it would be getting value for money.

The articles for *G.K.'s Weekly* and *Monde* were what a modern commissioning editor would call 'think pieces': miniature essays which move forward from the original subject to make wider historical observations. In a series for *Le Progrès Civique,* published in late December 1928 and January 1929, he made direct use of some of his London material. The three pieces – 'Unemployment', 'A Day in the Life of a Tramp' and 'Beggars in London' – appeared under the general heading 'Civic Progress in England: The Plight of the British Working Class'. They survive only as translations of Orwell's originals, and are written up according to the French newspaper style (single-line sentences peppered with exclamation marks) while remaining full of eye-catching detail. *Le Progrès Civique* paid its new contributor E.A. Blair 235 francs per article – just under £2, not a great deal by the standards of the day but worth having in a city where a packet of soup cost a farthing. Orwell wrote one further piece for the paper four months later which rehearses some of the arguments of *Burmese Days*. There was also a second essay for *Monde* on John Galsworthy, full of officious pieces of throat-clearing ('we should note') but locating Galsworthy's appeal in the conflict that existed in his work between the haves and have-nots, the weak and the strong, the sensitive and the obtuse. The choice of an ageing Nobel laureate to be – now regarded as somewhat out of date two decades on from his Edwardian heyday – as a suitable subject for a newspaper essay points to the particular literary culture from which Orwell emerged and of which he considered himself a part. Evelyn Waugh's first serious piece of literary criticism was an essay on Firbank; Cyril Connolly busied himself appraising the latest avant-garde novels. Orwell's natural *métier*, at this stage in his development, was the rather dusty figure of the author of *On Forsyte Change*.

What kind of life was Orwell living in Paris, here at the age of twenty-five? The narrator of *Down and Out in Paris and London* seems horribly alone, apart from his friend Boris, the Russian ex-cavalry officer, and nodding acquaintances from the bistro. In contrast, Orwell's life in the boarding-house at rue du Pot de Fer was far from solitary. Aunt Nellie was living in Paris with her Esperantist husband (an echo of Mr Adam survives in a *Tribune* essay of 1944 where Orwell notes that 'for sheer dirtiness of fighting the feuds between the inventors of various of the international languages would take some beating'), and we know that she was sufficiently a part of his social circle to be introduced to his friends. The letter from Mr Bailey at the McClure agency mentions 'your aunt', as does a note from a woman named Ruth Graves which Orwell received a bare six months before he died. Ms Graves, now living in America and stirred to write by an appreciative radio reference to *Animal Farm*, recalled evenings in Paris when the two of them took turns preparing Saturday dinner 'and the hours of good talk later in my little cluttered place in Rue de la Grande Chaumière'. Twenty years later she treasured the memories of her time in Paris, including the conversation 'of a tall young man in a wide-brimmed pair of Breton hats, who was as kind as he was keen of mind'.

Who was Ruth Graves? There is no reference to her anywhere in Orwell's writings, nor to their mutual friend 'Edith Morgan', also mentioned in this fond remembrance of time past. Clearly, though, Orwell was hardly friendless during his time in Paris. All the evidence suggests that he had an agreeable time living the life of the struggling literary expatriate and exploring a city that he was always to remember with pleasure. Like Hemingway he admired the plane trees in spring, relishing the fact that the bark was not blackened with smoke like the trees in the London squares, and he conceived a fondness for the Jardin des Plantes, even if the affection was undercut by a typical Orwellian grotesquerie. There was nothing there of interest, he explained to a friend twenty years later, except the rats which had overrun the place and grown so tame that they would eat out of your hand.

Come spring 1929 this routine of Saturday night suppers, occasional newspaper articles and hard work on his novels was badly upset. Towards the end of February he fell ill, and early in March was admitted to the Hôpital Cochin in the 15th *arrondissement* 'pour une grippe'. In 'How the Poor Die', the grisly essay that commemorates this stay – among other indignities he was cupped and buckled into a hot poultice – Orwell maintained that he was suffering from pneumonia, but 'une grippe' is usually translated as 'influenza'. Similarly, the fact that he was discharged after a bare fifteen days makes a bad attack of flu seem the more likely explanation. Whatever the precise nature of his illness he was well enough, four days after this, to attend the funeral of Marshal Foch at Les Invalides. According to the account of this piece of Gallic ceremonial that Orwell offered to his readers in the *Tribune* in 1947, this was chiefly memorable for its glimpse of Foch's charismatic contemporary Marshal Pétain: 'a tall, lean, very erect figure, though he must have been seventy years old or thereabouts, with great spreading moustaches like the wings of a gull'. At the sight of this ancient warrior in the procession a vast, susurrating whisper of 'Voilà Pétain!' ran through the crowd. Orwell had a weakness for public spectacles of this kind: eight years later he managed to be present at the funeral of George V.

Shortly afterwards another crisis declared itself when an Italian staying at the lodging house broke into the guests' rooms and made off with their money. This is the account given in *Down and Out in Paris and London*. According to Mabel Fierz, whom Orwell had not yet met but to whom he later confided various semi-intimate details, the culprit was a 'little trollop' named Suzanne, picked up in a café, with whom he was currently infatuated. Suzanne, in the Fierz version, had an Arab boyfriend with whom Orwell was involved in some kind of fracas. Whatever the truth of this explanation, as with the Burmese girls and other later episodes, there is a sense that one never quite knows with Orwell, that vast areas of his personal life stretch out into impenetrable blackness. The theft began the chain of events described in *Down and Out*. Using money received from *Le Progrès Civique* for his Burma article for rent, Orwell spent three weeks in a state of semi-starvation with his friend Boris before landing a *plongeur* or dishwasher's job at a big hotel (variously identified as the Lotti or the Crillon) and subsequently transferring – with Boris in the role of head waiter – to a similar post in a newly established restaurant called the Auberge de Jehan Cotard.

The first half of *Down and Out in Paris and London*, which purports to describe this four- or five-month period in Orwell's life, is a vivid piece of writing, a primer to the range of special effects that characterise his work: the wintry eye for detail (only Orwell, you feel, would notice the way in which the consistency of human saliva changes in conditions of near-starvation); the eternal fastidiousness over dirt, squalor and bugs tumbling into the milk; the unfeigned sympathy for people who, unlike the narrator, will be chained to this environment for the rest of their lives. Practically any page of *Down and Out*, opened at random, will turn up some odd vignette from a world of hoarded centimes and half-starved men wolfing down stale bread: the psychology of pawning clothes in one of the French state pawnshops; the subterranean passageways of the Hotel X which remind him of the lower decks of cruise liners ('there was the same heat and cramped space and warm reek of food, and a humming, whirring noise (it came from the kitchen furnace) just like the whirr of engines'); the ghastly atmosphere of the restaurant, where there is never enough money to pay for anything and the fat cook with her 'crise de nerfs' is abused by a kitchen staff made callous by sheer fatigue. All this carries a painful air of authenticity. It would be difficult, you feel, for anyone to make up an incident as bizarre as Orwell's visit to the bogus Communist cell where he is instructed in future to bring decoy bags of laundry and commissioned to write articles on 'le sport' for a Russian newspaper. The man who described the scene below stairs at the Hotel X – 'a dozen waiters with their coats off, showing their sweaty arm-pits, sat at the table mixing salads and sticking their thumbs into the creampot. The room had a dirty, mixed smell of food and sweat' – had clearly witnessed it at first hand. And yet this does not mean that the book is 'true' in the literal sense, and certainly not that the events depicted in it took place in exactly the way that they are set down. This is not to accuse Orwell of fabricating the evidence, merely to point out the gap between a scene observed and a scene recreated on the page, and the inevitable degree of artifice, selection and discrimination that intervene.

A first edition of *Down and Out* presented to Orwell's Southwold friend Brenda Salkeld contains many annotations in his own hand. Boris is 'as described'. The account of the trip to the Communist secret society is marked 'This happened very much as described'. Of the experience of going without food for three days, Orwell wrote 'This all happened', whereas the description of the Hotel X is glossed 'All as exact as I could make it.' At the beginning of the third chapter, which offers a kind of user's guide to life on the poverty line, are the words 'Succeeding chapters not actually autobiography, but drawn from what I have seen.' Not long after he produced these notes for Miss Salkeld, in 1934, Orwell wrote an introduction for the French edition of the book. He has not exaggerated, he assures prospective readers, except by selection. Moreover, 'everything I have described did take place at one time or another'. The characters are individuals but 'intended more as representative types'. All this begs several questions. What, for example, is a character who is simultaneously an individual and a representative type? At the very least the first half of *Down and Out* is a conspicuously Gallic affair, full of somewhat stagy 'French' conversation, whose local colour has been laid on with a trowel. In amongst the authentic low-life detail – rubbing garlic on to your bread so that the taste lingers and gives you the illusion of having eaten recently – are what look suspiciously like a selection of Parisian tall stories. Charlie's account of his seduction of a quivering virgin in a Sadean brothel, which takes up an entire chapter, has clearly wandered in from some late-nineteenth-century decadent's confessional. I never did believe the story of Roucolle the miser who is swindled into buying a consignment of face powder which he imagines to be cocaine. The letter that Boris supposedly receives from an ex-mistress to whom he has applied for succour strikes an oddly unconvincing note, while offering a point of comparison with an earlier collection of Anglophile writings on Paris. Thackeray's *Paris Sketch Book* (1840), to which *Down and Out in Paris and London* bears occasional slight resemblances, contains an account of the suicide of a resident Englishman. Found among his papers is a brief, poignant note from his mistress, 'Fifine'. Reading it, one is conscious that if he did not transcribe the original word for word Thackeray at any rate accurately remembered its gist. In contrast, Yvonne's salutations to her 'little cherished wolf' and her memory of the 'so dear kisses I have received from thy lips' seems somehow tuppence coloured. One doesn't so much disbelieve them – it is a mark of *Down and Out*'s attack that the reader swallows practically everything that is offered to him – as become aware that the level of the writing has shifted down a gear.

These changes in perspective give the book an odd, topsy-turvy feel, the sense of fragments of autobiography, fantasy and straightforward social comment mixed uncomfortably together. For all that, even in its wildest flights the figure who wanders through the maze of hotel passageways and restaurant ante-rooms is recognisably Orwell. Some of the most revealing moments in *Down and Out* come when Orwell can be seen unconsciously measuring the people around him against his own social yardsticks, demonstrating his affiliations and prejudices in a way that can often seem sharply incongruous. Told to shave off his moustache by an indignant superior, for instance, he realises that he has infringed a rule of etiquette, 'like not wearing a white tie with a dinner-jacket'. Best of all, perhaps, is the undisguised snobbishness directed at the rich Americans who frequent the Hotel X. Apparently knowing 'nothing whatever about good food', these guests stuff themselves with disgusting American 'cereals', eat marmalade at tea, drink vermouth after dinner and order *poulet à la reine* at 100 francs only to souse it in Worcester sauce. 'Perhaps it hardly matters if such people are swindled or not,' Orwell grandly concludes. Perhaps it doesn't, but explosions of this sort immediately change the angle from which the world of *Down and Out* is perceived. All at once Orwell is no longer a downtrodden *plongeur* living in a flyblown boarding-house and drinking *bouillon zip* at 50 centimes a packet but the ghost of an upper-class Englishman silently despising the frightful foreigners with whom chance has brought him into contact.

Passages of this kind offer up another riddle. Why did Orwell choose to starve with Boris in a cheap lodging house and drudge below stairs in a hotel? The impression conveyed by the book is that Orwell was, literally, destitute and yet, as we know, Aunt Nellie was living a few streets away, not to mention the friends of the Saturday night suppers. The existence of this phantom safety net serves to differentiate the book from the genuine life-on-the-breadline confessionals with which it is occasionally compared. Then there is Orwell's device for concluding the French half of his narrative and getting him back to England, the mysterious 'B' who promises him a job looking after a congenital idiot. 'B' has no real-life equivalent, although Orwell did some months later spend part of a summer tutoring a 'backward boy' in very different circumstances. In reality Orwell seems to have planned his return home with a certain amount of care, sending out feelers to literary magazines and advising people of his future whereabouts. In August 1929 – presumably about the time when the narrator and Boris are pawning their overcoats and fishing for dace in the Seine – Orwell sent a copy of a new piece of tramping reportage, 'The Spike', to the *Adelphi*, following this up with an enquiring letter a month later. During the autumn Orwell's drudgery would have been lightened by the news that the magazine had accepted it for publication. He replied on 12 December, accepting the terms proposed and giving his parents' house in Southwold as an address for future correspondence. It was time to be going home.

He had been away for nearly a year and three-quarters. Although Orwell never referred much to his time in Paris, confining himself to the most mundane remarks about the workings of the Métro, he clearly relished the experience. Mindful of its subject matter, his preface to the French edition of *Down and Out* notes that he would be distressed if French readers imagined he bore the least animosity towards a city of which 'I have very happy memories'. Towards the end of his life the memories hardened into a desperate nostalgia. 'I wish I were with you in Paris,' he wrote to a young woman friend working there in 1948, wondering if Marshal Ney's statue had been restored to its place outside the Closerie des Lilas. (This raises the spectre of Boris, whose admiration for Ney had led him to loiter in the café opposite.) A visit to the war-torn wreckage in 1945 plunged him in gloom. In fact Paris for Orwell never really existed beyond this early encounter. 'It's lucky for you you're too young to have seen it in the 'twenties,' he wrote to the same friend; 'it always seemed a bit ghostlike after that, even before the war.' Aside from the first half of *Down and Out*, his Paris experiences re-emerge in only one other substantial piece, 'How the Poor Die', first published in 1946 in the anarchist magazine *Now* but probably written during the early part of the war. Though separated by nearly a decade there are distinct similarities of approach. While full of authentic horrors – the patient who suffers agonies when he urinates, the primitive treatments that would have seemed out of date in the

Victorian age – 'How the Poor Die' has a vein of feeling running beneath its surface that goes back to the nineteenth century. With its nod to the fictional doctors in Thackeray and Trollope and its evocation of Tennyson's famous tear-jerker 'In the Children's Hospital', it turns in the end into a meditation on the pre-chloroform era of medicine, in which Orwell's own experiences, however sharply rendered, act as the trigger releasing a variety of literary and historical material that had previously lain dormant in his mind.

Some time in the fortnight before Christmas 1929 he said goodbye to his Paris friends and left for England. *Down and Out in Paris and London* has him travelling third class via Dunkirk and Tilbury, and then taking the train to B's office where his friend informs him that the congenital idiot's family have taken him away for a month but he supposes Orwell can hang on until then? Orwell has only nineteen shillings and sixpence in his pocket, thereby setting up the second half of the book ('I was outside in the street before it occurred to me to borrow some more money . . . For a long time I could not make up my mind what to do'). Not having the 'faintest notion' of how to get a cheap lodging house, the narrator spends the night in a 'family hotel' before beginning his descent into the abyss. The reality was more – or rather less – prosaic. He went back to Southwold.

Orwell's voice

Despite his years at the BBC, despite countless one-man broadcasts and dozens of panel discussions, no record of Orwell's voice survives. For an idea of what he sounded like and the words that he used – diction, delivery, phrasing – one can only turn to the testimonies of his friends.

The Spanish surgeon who treated the bullet wound in his throat in 1937 assured him that the power of speech would never return. As it turned out, this was unduly pessimistic. His voice came back, but it had lost its vigour. In a crowded room, or against background noise, Orwell had trouble making himself heard. A friend from the 1940s remembered him at a packed luncheon table trying once or twice to raise the necessary decibels and then abandoning the attempt, to pass the rest of the meal in silence.

One thing all Orwell's friends were agreed upon was that his accent was upper-class. In an age when locution was quite as important as the clothes one wore, Orwell's vocal register immediately enveloped its owner in a pair of spiritual plus-fours. 'Markedly Old Etonian,' thought his young friend Michael Meyer, by which he meant simultaneously high-pitched and drawling. No doubt Orwell was aware of his elevated tone. The young George Bowling, joining a west London tennis club in *Coming up for Air*, listens to its middle-class suburban members calling out the score in voices that are 'a passable imitation of the upper crust'. His creator's was the real thing, ripe for modification if he thought the social circumstances demanded it. There were occasional forays, for example, into the style known as 'Duke of Windsor cockney'. A BBC colleague once heard him assuring an Asian contributor that skin tone played no part in their relationship: 'The fack that you're black and I'm white has *nudding woddever to do wiv it*.' On down and out excursions he tried to stick with cockney impersonations. In fact the tramps and the Kentish hop-pickers noticed simply that he talked 'different'.

Amidst a Babel tower of contemporary regional accents, not everyone located his vocal distinctiveness in class. Yet however drawled and languid Orwell's voice, there was something peculiar about it – a peculiarity that seems to have preceded the Fascist bullet. Gow remembered that he 'croaked discordantly' at Eton. A teenage girl met in Suffolk years before the Spanish trip was struck by his 'jerky sentences'. David Astor noted a distinctive, staccato way of talking, 'husky rather than indistinct', but, given that his first wife apparently adopted several of its mannerisms, clearly imitable by those in close proximity to it. Lucian Freud had the curious impression of a voice struggling to overcome some kind of obstruction, 'literally monotone'. Powell, perhaps predictably, saw it as a question of upbringing – a way of speaking brought back to him when talking to former forestry officials from India and Africa, an intonation possibly even subconsciously copied from Richard Blair.

Such voices are suited to the dead-pan. Orwell's humour seems to have been intimately connected to the way in which he delivered his words. Astor asked him once what the Marxists thought of him. Orwell itemised some choice pieces of invective. 'A Fascist hyena . . . A Fascist octopus.' There was a pause. 'They're very fond of animals.'

6

Down There on a Visit

It is a great mistake to be too afraid of dirt. – Letter to Brenda
Salkeld, July 1931

You take my tip & *never* sleep in Trafalgar Square. – Letter to
Dennis Collings, 27 August 1931

The *Adelphi* wanted revisions. Given that the magazine was a quarterly,
'The Spike' would not appear until April 1931, twenty months after it
was first submitted. Orwell must have chafed at the delay, conscious
that this was the best piece of writing he had yet produced. The articles
published in the Parisian newspapers were competent, but there is no
hint of anything remarkable running beneath their surface. In contrast,
Orwell's account of two days spent in a casual ward is full of closely
observed details: still showing the odd looseness of style and excess
verbiage that characterises much of his early work, but creating its best
effects out of terseness. 'It was late afternoon. Forty-nine of us, forty-
eight men and one woman, lay on the grass waiting for the spike to
open . . .' Like many a 'Georgian' writer of the period, Orwell was still
unable to resist the purple patch: 'Overhead the chestnut branches
were covered with blossom, and beyond that great woolly clouds floated
almost motionless in a clear sky', the opening paragraph continues.
Significantly, though, luxuriance of this kind is nearly always there to
be deflated by the squalor of what moves beneath. 'Littered on the
grass,' Orwell goes on, 'we seemed dingy, urban riff-raff.' Favourite
stylistic tics, too, are beginning to declare themselves. A bit later
uneaten food in the workhouse kitchen is 'defiled' by the tea-leaves
thrown on it. In the closing scene, when a tramp named Scotty chases
after Orwell to replace some borrowed tobacco, the cigarette ends
dropped into his palm are described as 'debauched'. The figurative
undertow of this kind of imagery is striking, as if the thought of ordinary

things being tampered with or twisted out of their normal use revolted Orwell in an almost sexual way. Suitably reworked, 'The Spike' would eventually re-emerge in two of the later chapters of *Down and Out*. In the meantime, Orwell was quick to use the promise of future publication to establish a connection with the *Adelphi* and the people who ran it.

Founded by Katherine Mansfield's consort Middleton Murry in the 1920s, the *Adelphi* was a characteristic small-circulation journal of its time: 'progressive', fascinated by what was still known as the 'Soviet experiment', determinedly literary while occasionally looking rather old-fashioned in some of its tastes. Orwell pokes mild fun at it in *Keep the Aspidistra Flying*, remarking of its alter ego, *Antichrist*, that it appeared to be edited by an ardent nonconformist who had transferred his allegiance from God to Marx while getting mixed up with a gang of *vers libre* poets along the way. The joke still manages to convey something of the odd mixture of seriousness (denial of God's existence balanced by an uneasy awareness of the continuing significance of God to human affairs) and occasional bouts of aestheticism in which the paper specialised. At this point in its history, Murry having recently retired, the *Adelphi* was being jointly edited by Sir Richard Rees and Max Plowman. Rees, three years older than his new contributor, an Old Etonian, ex-diplomat and Workers' Educational Association lecturer, was a wealthy young baronet happy to pay the magazine's bills and subsidise some of his harder-up protégés. He features in *Keep the Aspidistra Flying* as 'Ravelston', a well-meaning patrician silently appalled by some of the grimmer manifestations of working-class culture. 'Practically anything got printed in *Antichrist* if Ravelston suspected that its author was starving.' Plowman, then in his late forties, represented a slightly older kind of progressivism. He was a dedicated pacifist scarred by his experience on the Western Front – his memoir, *A Subaltern on the Somme* had appeared in 1927 – who went on to become general secretary of one of the country's chief anti-war ginger groups, the Peace Pledge Union.

Rees, who observed Orwell on and off for the best part of two decades, is a key early witness both to his personality and to what at this stage were barely decipherable political leanings, possibly the first person with whom he came into contact who both shared his background and at the same time understood the kind of literary-cum-political world in which he wanted to operate. At first Rees was not particularly impressed. His recollection of their first meeting, early in

1930 in New Oxford Street, hard by the *Adelphi* offices in Bloomsbury Street, was that Orwell made a 'pleasant impression' while seeming to be 'rather lacking in vitality'. There was nothing outwardly remarkable about him. Looking back on his friend's political views, Rees diagnosed a 'Bohemian Tory' whose time among the working classes was pointing him towards Socialism. Orwell's own memories seem to confirm this. He became a Socialist, he later wrote, 'more out of disgust with the oppressed and neglected life of the poorer sector of the industrial worker than out of any theoretical understanding of a planned society'. But at this stage Orwell's attitude to Socialism, the *Adelphi* and presumably Rees himself was still embryonic. This, after all, was a magazine that he had used for target practice only a few years ago in Burma. Yet he clearly found Rees and Plowman congenial companions, keeping up with them (Plowman died in 1941) for the rest of his life. Through them he made a third friend, a young Tynesider named Jack Common who sold subscriptions for the magazine. Common, who later wrote *Kiddar's Luck*, one of the great working-class novels of the era, quickly established Orwell's relation to the social orbit in which his patrons moved. Initially nonplussed by the apparent 'outsider' status of the scruffily dressed newcomer, he rapidly detected a 'public school presence'.

However shrewd the first impressions of Rees, Common and others, it was above all an elusive presence. The really striking feature of Orwell's life in the early 1930s, surrounded as he was by friends and family, the literary citadels before him waiting to be stormed, is how little we know about him and how few verifiable facts remain. His day-to-day existence, routines – even his whereabouts – are a mystery for months on end. Yet his base throughout this period, in fact until the mid-1930s, was his parents' house in Southwold. By 1930 the Blairs had been living on the north Suffolk coast for the best part of a decade and were fixtures in the town. Richard Blair, now in his mid-seventies and known to his intimates as 'Toby', was a pillar of the Southwold gentlemen's club, the Blyth (tradespeople vigorously excluded), at which he and his wife played bridge. If this makes the elder Blairs sound like the stuffiest kind of small-town conservatives, then it should also be said that their acquaintance extended into more bohemian areas. They were on friendly terms with Madame Tabois, the town's resident French artist, whose studio lay along Ferry Road near the harbour, and from whom Ida Blair took lessons. Avril, meanwhile, had branched out on her own and become proprietress of a high-class tea-shop, the

Refreshment Rooms, later rechristened the Copper Kettle, next door to the family's rented Queen Street house. It is a mark of the paralysing snobbery of Southwold in the 1930s that even this modest commercial venture was frowned on in the town's more exclusive circles. All the same, there are distinctions to be made. No doubt Southwold's genteel villas of the inter-war period were simply awash with old ladies who stuck pins into effigies of Mr Cook, the firebrand miners' leader, and believed that if you gave the working classes baths they would keep coal in them. But the impression occasionally given in books about Orwell that the town was simply a retirement home for the upper bourgeoisie is a mistake. Although best known in the public imagination at this time as one of the sites of the Duke of York's camp – a well-intentioned scheme conceived by the future King George VI that brought public school boys and their working-class counterparts together under canvas on the common – Southwold had its earthier side. There were substantial pockets of poverty, especially among the fishing community, and Church Street, in particular, was remembered by one former inhabitant as 'awful'. Despite the influx of retired gentlefolk it was still a small port – coal was regularly unloaded at the harbour – as well as offering a range of commercial concerns such as the Homeknit factory on Pier Avenue and the Adnams brewery, the reek of whose malt hung over the High Street six days out of seven. Yet it was not, we can safely assume, Orwell's kind of place. Knype Hill in *A Clergyman's Daughter* is not, strictly speaking, a recreation of Southwold. Inland and dominated by a sugar-beet factory, it bears a closer resemblance to Bury St Edmunds. However, the description of the High Street, forking after a couple of hundred yards to form a small marketplace, is unmistakably drawn from the life. It is, additionally, 'one of those sleepy, old-fashioned streets that look so intensely peaceful on a casual visit and so very different when you live in them and have an enemy or a creditor in every window'. Avril was more matter-of-fact: 'Eric loathed Southwold'.

And yet Southwold, and some of its inhabitants, were to play a decisive part in Orwell's life over the next few years. However much he may have disliked the place, however tense his relationship with his father, however reluctant he may have been to involve himself in its anodyne social life, there was congenial company to hand. Through his parents he came to know the Morgan family – Mrs Morgan was a widow who added to her income by supplying board and lodgings to boys studying at Mr Hope's crammer – whose attractions included an exceptionally pretty daughter named Roma. No evidence of their relationship survives, but there is a persistent family legend that a brief engagement was contracted. Dennis Collings came back at regular intervals from his Cambridge Anthropology course. It was probably through Collings that Orwell re-encountered an attractive young woman named Eleanor Jaques (the Jaqueses had previously lived next door to the Blairs in Stradbroke Road) whose family lived at a house called Long Acre in nearby Reydon. He also spent a great deal of time with Brenda Salkeld, the daughter of a Bedfordshire clergyman who taught gym at St Felix's, a girls' boarding-school whose premises lay a couple of miles inland. Through these new friends, and through his family, he was introduced to older people: a Yorkshire barrister named Colin Pulleyne who lived in the town with his mother; a Mrs Carr who lived along the High Street near the house that the Blairs themselves would eventually buy; Miss Fanny Forster, later the town's mayoress, who had literary interests and lent him books. He also seems to have mixed with the Southwold 'gentry' on their own terms. The town museum, for example, has a copy of *Burmese Days* inscribed to Tony Fox, a wealthy stockbroker who owned property near the seafront and later founded a charitable trust with the aim of refurbishing houses for the benefit of local people rather than allowing them to be turned into holiday homes.

Southwold was a small place – not more than 2,000 inhabitants – and, demarcations of status notwithstanding, its social patterns were nearly always interconnected. The Blairs' daily help, Mrs May, also worked for the Jaqueses in Reydon. Her daughters Esmé, Marjorie and Olive worked for Avril at the Copper Kettle ('a high class' establishment, one of their cousins recalled, 'very special'). However much Orwell may have wanted to distance himself from the routines of small-town social life, he could scarcely avoid being caught up in them. As a newcomer to Southwold with no visible means of support, he became an approved subject for comment, speculation and mild disapproval. He was a particular favourite with Mrs May, who noted and sympathised with his poor health ('Poor boy, I feel so sorry for him'). The general impression conveyed by the people who remember him from this time is of a detached, rather vague figure, assumed to be sponging off his parents, legendarily untidy ('He always seemed to be three days away from a shave'). Well wrapped up in thrice-wound scarves against the winter cold, he was known to spend long hours shut up in his bedroom or walking around the town 'in a dream'.

No doubt this picture of a minor black sheep silently outraging his conventional family has become calcified by time. Still, there was something odd about Orwell in the context of 1930s Southwold: introverted, detached, literally vagrant. Rumours of his tramping exploits were a regular source of local gossip. However scandalised the Blairs may have been (Mrs Blair commented enigmatically on one of these disappearances that her son had 'gone with nothing'), Mrs May was even more upset. There is a relentlessness about Orwell's low-life fixation at this time. His letters to Brenda Salkeld are full of bantering attempts to shock. If they are to meet in London perhaps she won't object to three days' growth of beard? At any rate he can promise no lice, etc. etc. Orwell's interest in social conditions and the plight of the dispossessed was quite genuine – it shines out of everything he wrote and said on the subject. At the same time there is a sense of something more fundamental moving beneath, a compulsion to immerse himself in an activity from which his more sensitive side revolted. David Astor, with whom Orwell later discussed his tramping adventures, believed that on one level he undertook them simply to try to overcome his ingrained fastidiousness, his fear of dirt and sweat, to see how far he could push himself. A piece like 'The Spike' offers a portrait of a man in whom limitless moral sympathy and outright physical disgust are uneasily contending. It is this tension that gives Orwell's writing about down-and-outs and the squalor of the sevenpenny doss houses its sheen. There are private terrors here, you feel, only narrowly concealed by print. Other friends could not see the point in these excursions. Brenda Salkeld, at whose parents' house he turned up during one of these trips, was simply exasperated. 'All that business about being a tramp was just ludicrous. He had a home, he had a nice family . . .'

Other elements of the 'nice family' were capable of providing a refuge. Come the early spring Orwell left for an extended stay with Marjorie and family at Bramley on the outskirts of Leeds, where Humphrey Dakin had just started on a new job in the Civil Service. Dakin, unimpressed as ever, advised his brother-in-law to get a proper job rather than persevere with the chancy business of writing. He was also struck by Orwell's reluctance to immerse himself in the atmosphere of the cheery working-class 'local'. 'He used to sit in a corner . . . looking like death.' Here and back at Queen Street Orwell worked hard on the manuscript of what became *Down and Out in Paris and London*, at this point concentrated on his French adventures and entitled 'A Scullion's Diary'. An early version, presented in straightforward diary form, was submitted to, and rejected by, Jonathan Cape around this time. The Mays, in particular, were impressed by his dedication and also slightly alarmed by his unwillingness to leave the bedroom in which he wrote. Esmé remembered him sequestering himself in there for days on end. 'Go and take that poor boy something up,' Mrs May would eventually command. To the teenage girl ferrying cups of tea and snacks the son of her mother's employer seemed an eccentric figure: 'he never dressed up or anything'.

As well as labouring over 'A Scullion's Diary', Orwell was cutting his teeth as a reviewer on the *Adelphi*'s books pages. A notice in the May 1930 number of Lewis Mumford's biography of Melville shows him laying several of the foundations for his mature critical style: arresting epigrams; positions about human behaviour shrewdly taken up. 'Melville had a wretched life, and was generally poor and harassed, but at least he had an improvident youth behind him . . . He had not been bred, like so many Europeans, into respectability and despair.' In the August number he compared Edith Sitwell's study of Pope with Sherard Vines's *The Course of English Classicism,* while in October he conducted an all-out assault on J.B. Priestley's middlebrow bestseller, *Angel Pavement.* 'One wonders incredulously whether anyone has really mistaken Mr Priestley for a master. His work has no damning faults, but neither has it a single gleam of beauty, nor any profundity of thought, nor even memorable humour.' The novel was simply a 'middle article' spun out to 600 pages, spirited, conscientiously witty and exhibiting an 'utter lack of anything intensely conveyed'. This is an interesting complaint, for it lists the qualities that the twenty-seven-year-old apprentice looked for in fiction: 'beauty', 'profundity of thought' and 'memorable humour', with the final stricture about the lack of anything intensely conveyed sounding uncannily like F.R. Leavis. At first sight Orwell's hostility to Priestley looks faintly gratuitous, as the subject matter of *Angel Pavement,* with its pinched clerks and thwarted spinsters, would in ordinary circumstances have been very much to his taste. At the time, though, Priestley-baiting was a popular literary parlour game. Early works by Waugh, Powell and Graham Greene are full of feline disparagement of a writer whom serious people thought seriously overrated: Greene's *Stamboul Train* (1932) had to be temporarily withdrawn after Priestley had detected libellous intentions in the portrait of a complacent popular novelist named 'Mr Savory'.

By the summer of 1930 Orwell's life in Southwold assumes a sharper focus. At some point in their walks across the common he proposed marriage to Brenda Salkeld. But Miss Salkeld turned him down, preferring friendship, and also, one suspects – judging from the contents of some of Orwell's later letters – not wanting to be lectured about books. Some of his time was taken up across the river in Walberswick where he acted as tutor to a boy named Bryan Morgan – unconnected to the Southwold Morgans – then in his early teens, crippled by polio and rather 'backward'. The Morgans were well-to-do (there may have been a connection through the 'Edith Morgan' Orwell had known in Paris), living in a house on one side of the main Walberswick Road and also owning land on the other. Migrating to this second plot to supervise Bryan, Orwell was frequently observed by a teenage girl named Dora Georges, a friend of the older Morgan children. Sixteen-year-old Dora considered the private tutor to be 'rather an awkward customer' who spoke in 'jerky sentences' and was something of a figure of fun to his employer's family: 'We used to make jokes about him.' Sometimes when Orwell and Bryan were roaming in the field, Dora went across the road to chat. On one of these occasions Orwell pushed a piece of paper into her hand. This turned out to be a poem, headed 'Ode to a Dark Lady'. Dora, who thought nothing of the writer's 'very gauche manner', was unimpressed. The poem was thrown away. There is something intensely Orwellian about the scene, though: the formal expression of regard; the poem pushed silently into the hand of someone who secretly thinks the donor rather comical. Ten years later Orwell supplied an odd footnote to his time with the Morgans in a letter to Sacheverell Sitwell, apropos a review he had written of Sitwell's *Poltergeists*. Out walking with Bryan on Walberswick Common they had come across a cardboard box lined with cloth and containing tiny pieces of furniture arranged to look like the contents of a doll's house. 'Puzzled' by the discovery, Orwell was convinced that there was something sinister about it, that the box was meant to be found, like something out of one of M.R. James' ghost stories.

There was a second teaching job that summer, supervising the three Peters boys, sons of a female friend of Mrs Blair's. The eldest, Richard, later a distinguished academic, left a vivid portrait of the 'rather strange but very nice' young man who took them on nature rambles, talked to them about books, showed them how to catch roach in the Walberswick mill pond and conducted bomb-making experiments; one of these blew up a stretch of the family garden. For relaxation he went bathing or set up an easel on the beach. It was while out painting, one day in August, that he got into conversation with a holidaying couple walking along the beach. Francis Fierz was an executive in a steel manufacturing firm. Mabel, his wife, then in her late thirties, had literary interests and, in addition, a forceful personality which she was prepared to put at Orwell's service. The Fierzes – Mabel in particular – took a shine to Orwell. Over the next few years he stayed repeatedly at their house in Oakwood Road, Hampstead Garden Suburb (Max Plowman lived nearby, which was a further attraction), and Mabel was to play a decisive part in getting his first book published.

Summer passed. The Fierzes went back to London. The tutoring jobs came to an end. For nearly a year there is scarcely a clue as to Orwell's whereabouts. In late autumn he was at Queen Street, from which a couple of letters were addressed to Max Plowman asking about, and then dealing with, revisions to 'The Spike'. Some of his time was spent in London – other letters were sent from the Fierzes – and there were certainly more tramping expeditions. There is an odd, infinitely beguiling, glimpse of him at around this time from a woman whose family lived in Limehouse in the early 1930s. With ten people residing in the 'old, cold, inconvenient' house, domestic help was at a premium. One day a friend who lived in the Rowton House (a superior lodgement for single men) in Whitechapel brought back one of the other occupants with a view to offering him work. It was eventually agreed that the newcomer would act as a kind of male charwoman, cleaning the house for half a crown a day plus a midday meal. Tall, thin, nicknamed Laurel on account of his faint resemblance to Oliver Hardy's sidekick Stan, the stranger was an object of deep curiosity to the family, not least because of his educated accent, remembered as 'plum-in-the-mouth, BBC English'. Coming back from school to find him in the house, one of the younger children was taken aback when Laurel bowed slightly, kissed her mother's hand and remarked 'Goodbye, Queen of the Kitchen', adding to the girl, 'Your mother is a fine lady and a splendid cook.' His employer was 'consumed with pity', revealing that Laurel had scrubbed floors, cleaned two outside lavatories and polished up a blacklead kitchen range before having to be ordered to stop. Half a century later, coming across Orwell's picture in a book (probably Bernard Crick's biography), the girl was able to establish Laurel's real identity.

However welcome the half-crowns picked up charring in Limehouse, Orwell was still trying hard to establish himself as a literary man, putting his name forward to editors and touting for work. The letter he wrote to Max Plowman in January 1931 setting out the kind of books he liked to review was probably one among many. Orwell's interests as outlined here include India, low-life in London, Villon, Swift, Smollett and among contemporaries 'anything by M.P. Shiel or Somerset Maugham'. Keeping up his involvement with working-class life, he reviewed Lionel Britton's *Hunger and Love*, in which a slum child's attempts to educate himself are scuppered by the war, for the April *Adelphi*. Britton's novel seemed chiefly memorable for a flaw that was to run throughout most working-class fiction of the period. Most novels, Orwell suggested – rehearsing a famous later remark – are written 'by the well-fed, about the well-fed, for the well-fed'. Anything that broke the genteel stranglehold of middle-class writers writing about middle-class subject matter was to be welcomed, and yet it was possible to produce a valuable social document that was worthless as a novel. Orwell's fastening on this stand-off between form and content is something more than the routine complaint of a ground-down fiction reviewer: the dilemma was one that characterised his own early work. Meanwhile, as his journalism had not yet appeared anywhere else, he was becoming known as one of the *Adelphi*'s regular contributors ('A Hanging' appeared there in August 1931). The magazine had a modest circulation, no more than a few thousand copies, but it was a start. And in the intervals of this apprentice work he completed a new version of 'A Scullion's Diary', now in more or less the book's final shape, and dispatched it once again to Cape, from whom some time in the autumn it was once again returned.

Orwell was planning his most ambitious tramping excursion to date. This was first advertised in a letter written in July to Brenda Salkeld suggesting a meeting before she departed for the school holidays. It would be fun if they could go hopping together, he innocuously proposed. 'But I suppose your exaggerated fear of dirt would deter you.' It was a great mistake to be too afraid of dirt, he added sententiously. Working in the Kentish hop fields over late August and September was a traditional East End way of taking a late summer holiday: Orwell, knowing that the material he picked up would make good journalistic copy, intended to observe conditions in the fields at first hand. He spent the first part of the summer in Southwold, catching a glimpse – or so he thought – of a ghost in Walberswick churchyard (a man's figure in what might have been brown vestments seen out of the tail of one eye) before proceeding to London and the Fierzes. Then on 25 August, with fourteen shillings in hand, he spent the night in Lew Levy's kip in the Westminster Bridge Road, followed by a two-day stint on the bum amongst the floating population of Trafalgar Square. 'You take my tip,' he sagely advised Dennis Collings, to whom a record of this adventure was dispatched two days later, '& *never* sleep in Trafalgar Square.' Things were 'tolerably comfortable' until midnight, he reported, after which paralysing cold set in. At 4 a.m. he got hold of a pile of newspaper posters to wrap himself up in. An hour later he migrated with some of the other square-sleepers to a coffee shop in St Martin's Lane where one could sit undisturbed over a twopenny cup of tea. Above all, Orwell was fascinated by the unwritten rules of the square. Until noon you could do anything you liked – even shave in the fountains – except sleep, in which case you would be woken by the police. From noon till nine you could sit on the benches or the pedestals of the statues but were moved on if you sat on the ground. From nine until midnight the police would wake you every five minutes, after midnight every half an hour, all 'for no ostensible reason'.

Orwell's anxiety to return from Kent with some form of 'copy' is made clear by the detailed diary he kept for the next six weeks, much of it later reproduced wholesale in *A Clergyman's Daughter*. After a night in another lodging house in the Southwark Bridge Road, one of the few sevenpenny kips in London 'and looks it' (the beds were only five feet apart and the kitchen a cellar where the deputy sat with a tray of jam tarts a yard or so from the lavatory door), he set off for Kent with three mates picked up along the way. 'Ginger', the leading personality in this trio, inspired Orwell to a brief character sketch. An ex-soldier and a fairly typical petty criminal, Orwell thought, he had probably, when not in prison, broken the law every day for the previous five years. Orwell clearly rather admired Ginger – there is a more substantial portrait of him as 'Nobby' in *A Clergyman's Daughter* – noted his proficiency at begging and his technical expertise. He was less keen on the friend brought along by the second man, 'Young Ginger'. This was 'a little Liverpool Jew of eighteen, a thorough guttersnipe'. All of a sudden the guillotine of class descends. Orwell approves of Ginger for his insouciance and resourcefulness; the Jewish teenager merely disgusts him. By this point around six of Orwell's original fourteen shillings remained. Carrying their utensils – cadged tins, cutlery that had been stolen from Woolworth's – and supplies of bread, margarine and tea, they took the twopenny tram to Bromley, brewed up on a rubbish heap and spent the night sleeping in long wet grass on the edge of a recreation ground. The morning of the next day was spent robbing an orchard. Orwell's conscience pricked him at this but he consented to stand guard. Then, stealing and begging as they went, the three vagrants and one Old Etonian continued in the direction of Sevenoaks. A detour to the spike at Ide Hill served to split the company in half. It was then late on Saturday. The supervisor, known as the 'tramp major', had orders to keep men admitted in until Tuesday; the workhouse master was keen on extracting a full day's labour from 'casuals' but would not allow them to work on Sunday. With their companions opting for three nights inside, Orwell and Ginger slept on the edge of a park abutting the church.

On Sunday morning they passed through Sevenoaks into the heart of Kent. Government inspectors were at large in the county enforcing the recent legislation introduced by the Labour government to the effect that all hop-pickers should have accommodation. However, there were ways of circumventing the new laws. An old Irishwoman they fell in with near Maidstone advised them that she had got a job on one of the farms merely by claiming that she had lodgings nearby: in fact she was sleeping clandestinely in a tool-shed. Once again Orwell's conscience had a bad moment when Ginger and the Irishwoman used him as a front while they palmed cigarettes and apples from under the nose of a local shopkeeper. The three of them spent the night in a half-built house. On the next day, 1 September, with money running low, they failed to get taken on at Chalmers' Farm. When they were 'tapping' a gentleman picnicker, the man became so friendly that Orwell forgot to put on his *faux*-cockney accent and was courteously presented with a shilling. A lift from a lorry driver took them to the spike at West Malling where, next morning, they secured jobs at Blest's farm and were immediately sent out into the fields. The financial situation was now becoming desperate. With only threepence left in his pocket Orwell wrote back to Southwold asking for ten shillings to be sent care of the nearest post office. It came two days later. Not for the first time, Orwell noted the innate generosity of the working-class families clustered round the hop-bines. He and Ginger would have had practically nothing to eat had the other pickers not fed them.

The next seventeen days, or rather fifteen, as no work was done on a Sunday, were spent picking hops. Orwell's account of the culture of the hop-field shows his customary eye for detail. The pay was twopence a bushel, and it was theoretically possible to earn thirty shillings a week, although in practice he doubted that anyone made half this, as the rules were expressly designed to exploit the fact that most of the workers regarded their employment as a paying holiday. Orwell identified three more or less distinct groups of pickers: East Enders down from Whitechapel and Bow; gypsies and itinerant agricultural labourers; and a sprinkling of tramps. He was struck by the kindness of a coster and his wife who befriended him and repeatedly gave him food. 'They were the kind of people who are generally drunk on Saturday nights and who tack a "fucking" on to every noun, yet I have never seen anything that exceeded their kindness and delicacy.' It seems clear, though, from various hints in the diary, that many of the hop-pickers regarded Orwell as a special case, an exotic migrant from beyond the narrow world of the hop-field and the East End. When it became too much of a chore to keep up the cockney accent, people noticed, as so often, that he talked 'different', and yet far from despising him as an outsider or, worse, a fifth columnist, were still more friendly. They seemed to think it particularly dreadful to have 'come down in the world', which could be the only plausible explanation for Orwell's presence on the farm.

The routines of the hoppers' camp were carefully set down three years later in *A Clergyman's Daughter*: a breakfast of bacon, bread and tea in the chilly dawn, the mile-and-a-half walk to the fields, ten or eleven hours' work tearing off hops from bines dragged down ('huge, tapering strands of foliage, like the plaits of Rapunzel's hair') across the picking bins. Rain was an occupational hazard. 'We are slopping about here in the most appalling seas of slush, unable to work & with no occupation but trying to start fires from wet wood,' he reported to Dennis Collings two days after his arrival at Blest's. 'Still it is rather fun for a short while, & I shall at any rate be able to make a saleable newspaper article.' Several of the minor characters from *A Clergyman's Daughter* were already wandering through his field of vision: Deafie, the self-absorbed exhibitionist tramp; Barret, a travelling agricultural labourer who reminisced gluttonously about food. Towards the middle of the month the nights began to turn colder. The hop-picking season was nearly over. For Dorothy in the novel this is a serious problem: she has nowhere to go. For Orwell it represented the end of an interesting experiment. He was paid off on 19 September. Several pickers who were illiterate brought Orwell and other 'scholards' their tally books to be reckoned up. Arriving at the local rail station to catch the hop-pickers' train back to London, Ginger having cheated a tobacconist's assistant out of fourpence in farewell to Kent, they came upon Deafie sitting on the grass with a newspaper over his unfastened trousers periodically exposing himself to passing women and children. Orwell confessed himself 'surprised' at the spectacle, while noting that there was scarcely a tramp alive without some sexual aberration. Weaving across the county to pick up other bands of pickers from stations along the line dense with late summer foliage, the train took five hours to reach London. At London Bridge Deafie stood them a pint, before Orwell and Ginger went off to a kip in nearby Tooley Street. The two of them had operated a joint tally book. Orwell calculated that they had made twenty-six shillings each, reduced to sixteen after deducting the train fares.

The Tooley Street kip was cheap, only sevenpence a night, 'probably the best sevenpenny one in London', Orwell, now a connoisseur of such premises, decided. His fellow-lodgers, unfortunately, were a 'pretty low lot', mostly unskilled Irish labourers and out of work at that. He was keen to write up his hop-picking diary, a task largely accomplished in Bermondsey Public Library, but on several mornings he and Ginger went in search of work at Billingsgate fish market. Helping a porter push his barrow 'up the hill' paid twopence a time and the competition was fierce: Orwell reckoned that he never made more than eighteen pence out of the dawn-to-midday shift. There is a nice symbolism, not of Orwell's making, about his presence here in Billingsgate in late September 1931, for it coincided with the financial crisis going on a quarter of a mile away in the heart of the City which ultimately led to the government taking the decision to go off the Gold Standard to protect the pound. This retreat came to be seen as definitive proof of the nation's post-war economic insecurity: as one contemporary observer put it, the end of parity between gold and sterling was 'for most Britons born before 1910 . . . the biggest shock that we had known or were to know'. On Friday, 18 September, despite the herculean efforts of the Governor of the Bank of England, Montagu Norman, to shore up sterling, the bank had lost nearly £19 million. On Monday the 21st, a few hours after Orwell and Ginger left for work, the Stock Exchange closed for the day in response to the mounting panic.

By now the diary was written up. Tooley Street was beginning to get on his nerves. It was noisy, hot, without privacy, and as ever he was revolted by the dirt. Orwell's almost forensic accounts of the cheap lodging houses in which he stayed show the horror they must have aroused in him. The Tooley Street kitchen smelt permanently of fish, and the sinks were blocked with rotting fish guts which stank horribly. The dormitory, too, was a perpetual din of coughing and spitting. Again Orwell wrote to Southwold for money and upgraded his accommodation to the area of the Blairs' old London haunts – a room at

Windsor Street near the Harrow Road. From here, a day or so later, he sent the hop-picking diary (presumably only in manuscript at this point, though it was later typed) to Collings, with a request that it should also be shown to Colin Pulleyne and to Eleanor Jaques 'if she would like to see it'. This is the first reference to Eleanor in Orwell's letters. There were to be many more.

He seems to have spent the time in Windsor Street working. The letter to Collings mentions short stories intended for a forthcoming magazine named *Modern Youth* ('a poisonous name for a poisonous paper'). Later in the month, having procured an introduction from Richard Rees, he boldly addressed T.S. Eliot at the offices of Faber & Faber, proposing to translate a French low-life novel Jacques Roberti's *A la Belle de Nuit*. Orwell's early letters to editors and publishers were always diffident. Listing his qualifications for undertaking the work he would say only that he was used to mixing in the kind of French society depicted in the novel and that he knew French slang better than the majority of Englishmen. Eliot asked to see the novel but as might have been expected, given the obscurity of the author and the even greater obscurity of the potential translator, nothing came of the project. For amusement Orwell read copiously – a letter to Brenda Salkeld from around this time offers an extensive reading list – and walked round Kensal Green cemetery, the resting place of many a Victorian literary man, inspecting the gravestones. *Modern Youth*, meanwhile, had postponed publication: it had failed to meet its printers' bills. Orwell left Windsor Street shortly before Christmas, having tried one final but ultimately fruitless low-life adventure – an attempt to get himself arrested for drunkenness. Picked up by the police in the Mile End Road on a Saturday he was kept in the cells over the weekend, fined six shillings on the Monday morning and confined for the rest of the day owing to his inability to pay. Never one to squander promising material, Orwell swiftly wrote the episode up for the *Adelphi* and later cannibalised it for Gordon's spectacular Soho drinking bout in *Keep the Aspidistra Flying*.

Some time in the latter part of the year, from an address in Sussex, he wrote his first letter to a man who was to play an important part in his career. Leonard Moore, a partner in the literary agency of Christy & Moore, was an acquaintance of Francis Fierz: Orwell seems to have been pushed into writing to him by Mabel. What Moore made of the letter, which was diffident to the point of self-effacement, is anyone's guess. Orwell doubts that he has anything in hand that would be of the smallest interest, but is sending two short stories which Moore *might* be able to use. The manuscript of 'A Scullion's Diary', meanwhile, had been sent to Faber, Orwell naturally being keen to exploit his faint connection with Eliot. There were also two more stories which he was trying to retrieve from *Modern Youth*'s printers, who in default of payment had impounded the magazine's copy. All this was hardly calculated to whet Moore's appetite, but he read the stories. The verdict was unfavourable. Writing from the Fierzes' early in January Orwell replied gloomily that he knew they were no good, but should Faber show an interest in 'A Scullion's Diary' he would put the business in Moore's hands. Prompted by an enquiring letter in mid-February, Faber rejected it. Orwell bestowed the manuscript upon Mabel Fierz, telling her to throw it away but to keep the paperclips.

Happily, Mrs Fierz was made of sterner stuff. Having read the book she took it to Moore's office in the Strand and prevailed upon him to read it too, following this up with an exhortatory letter. A further letter to Moore from Orwell, sent in late April after the agent had expressed an interest in representing him, restated the book's history: an early attempt sent to Cape in mid-1930; a revised version submitted in summer 1931; Eliot's verdict of interesting but too short. If by any chance it was to be accepted, Orwell instructed, could he please make sure that it was published anonymously 'as I am not proud of it'. So why try to get it published in the first place? Orwell's early letters to Moore are riven by an almost spectacular blockheadedness over the nature of publishing and the requirements of the people who worked in it. Over the next few years his agent was to become habituated to a stream of amateurish suggestions, requests for translation work, apparent bewilderment over the most straightforward publishing processes. Here in this first instalment Orwell mentions a long poem he is working on describing a day out in London 'which *may* be finished by the end of this term'. Then a sudden shaft of realism strikes him. 'I should not think there is any money for anybody in this kind of thing'. There was not. Neither was he likely to get much joy out of Chatto & Windus with a proposal to translate one of Zola's novels. It says something for Moore's patience, and his genuine interest in Orwell's work, that he was prepared to put up with this naivety. At the same time it reveals Orwell's great uncertainty at this point in his fledgling career over the kind of writer he wanted to be. Social reportage; novels; translation work; 'long' poems (a genre even then fading into antiquity) – all these at one time or another in the early 1930s seem to have suited his conception of the literary path he wanted to follow. The London poem occupied him on and off for years, surfacing finally as 'London Pleasures', the great futile pursuit of Gordon Comstock's leisure hours in *Keep the Aspidistra Flying*.

The reference to 'term' indicates another shift in the pattern of Orwell's erratic early 1930s life. By this time, like many another struggling writer of the inter-war era, he had passed into the murky landscapes of low-grade private education. How he came by the job at the Hawthorns High School for Boys in Hayes on the west London fringe is unknown: quite probably he applied to one of the city's numerous scholastic agencies. For an Old Etonian, taught – however much he may have disliked the experience – by one of the great classical scholars of the age, the Hawthorns must have seemed something of a comedown. There were fewer than twenty boys, drawn from the sons of the local *petit bourgeoisie*, their parents too proud to make use of council schools, and only one other master. Orwell found himself quartered in two rooms on the ground floor of a nearby house inhabited by the school's proprietor, an employee of the local HMV factory named Eunson, and his family. Fetched up in a nondescript part of west London, in a job he had been forced to take for financial reasons, he was acutely miserable. A midsummer letter to Eleanor refers to 'the above foul place' – in other words, the address written at the top of the paper – and describes Hayes as 'one of the most godforsaken places I have ever struck' (its atmosphere is faithfully reproduced in the penultimate section of *A Clergyman's Daughter*). Orwell's friendship with Eleanor had not yet progressed very far; though the letter was written nearly two months into the school term she is clearly not expected to know of his whereabouts. The Hawthorns' pupils remembered their teacher as strict in the classroom, but less buttoned up outside it, prepared to offer lessons in oil painting and taking one protégé on an excursion to the local marsh to trap marsh gas in jars. The same boy remembered being unable to sit down for a week after being caned by the 'rather harsh' Mr Blair, although such was the rapport between master and pupil, he bore no grudge. There was also a school play, 'King Charles II' – this, too, made its way into *A Clergyman's Daughter* – an elaborate affair involving complex sets and costume design.

Sequestered in west London with only limited opportunities for escape, Orwell took an unexpected turn in his writing. Looking at the letters and reviews from this time, it is impossible not to be struck by their interest – occasionally bantering, but nonetheless sincere – in religion; an interest, more to the point, that proceeded from a detailed knowledge of religious paraphernalia and a profound awareness of the issues that lay at stake. It would be wrong, perhaps, to talk about Orwell's religious 'side': he once assured David Astor that the test of a person's honesty was whether he or she believed in life after death, the implication being that anyone who did hold this belief was being dishonest. And yet, from a very early stage in his career, Orwell was obsessed by the problem of what might be called displaced religious sensibility. The greatest challenge facing both the state and the individual, he believed, was to recognise and put to positive use the intense human emotions that until fairly recently had been channelled into religious observance. Human beings had lost their souls, runs the argument of half a dozen of his essays, without finding anything to put in their place. When they did find something – this was a danger that became sharply apparent as the 1930s progressed – it was likely to be a form of totalitarian autocracy interested only in manipulating the past and ignoring the future. Significantly, in the same conversation with Astor, Orwell suggested that the proof of a person's moral feeling rested on whether they cared what happened after their death.

At this stage Orwell's views on personal morality in the absence of God lay in the future, but his interest in the question of spiritual belief was quite unfeigned. It is sharply apparent, for example, in a review for the *New English Weekly* of a book lent to him by the Roman Catholic Mrs Carr, his parents' friend from Southwold: Karl Adam's *The Spirit of Catholicism*. As well as airing his familiarity with contemporary religious politics, Orwell, though not uncritical, winds up on a respectful note: 'Very few people, apart from Catholics themselves, seem to have grasped that the church is to be taken seriously.' For a brief moment controversy raised its head. The great Catholic apologist Father Martindale, who knew Mrs Carr – it is possible that she also lent Orwell his *The Roman Faith*, referred to in the review – wrote to her saying that he would like to meet this young controversialist with a view to correcting various of his religious errors. This was the great age of the Catholic revival. Its luminaries – Monsignor Knox and Father D'Arcy – were well known to newspaper readers and high-life conversions were much in vogue. The kind of questions that Orwell discusses in the piece on Karl Adam were receiving an airing in every pulpit and serious newspaper in the country. It is easy enough to smile at the idea of Orwell as a potential Catholic convert – presumably the reason for Mrs Carr's zeal – yet to the literary man of the 1930s Catholicism could seem a highly seductive refuge. Gordon in *Keep the Aspidistra Flying*, who tells Ravelston that the only choice for a civilised man in the twentieth century is between Catholicism and Bolshevism, is over-stating his case, but it was a choice that plenty of civilised twentieth-century men, literary men especially, were prepared to make.

Half out of loneliness, half out of genuine interest, possibly in the hope of impressing Eleanor Jacques (remembered by her daughter as 'a very spiritual woman'), Orwell made a friend of the curate, a young man slightly older than himself named Ernest Parker, and attended the local Anglican church in Hayes. The church was ritualistic and 'high' and he had some difficulty in following its exacting protocols, but he was enthusiastic enough to volunteer to paint one of the church idols, an image of the Virgin Mary. He was trying to make it look as much like an illustration in *La Vie Parisienne* as possible, he told Eleanor. He would take Communion, too, he suggested, only he felt the bread would stick in his throat. Orwell's precise motives for sitting through Anglo-Catholic church services are unfathomable. Why, having taken the trouble to attend, could he not bring himself to take part in the Church's most important rite? He liked Ernest Parker, the curate ('a very good fellow'). Surely enjoying his company while secretly mocking the world of which he was a part would have constituted an act of betrayal? Was the satirical tone of his remarks to Eleanor merely a way of distancing himself from a series of inner confusions and affiliations that he could not yet rationalise? Whatever the explanation, he was keen to cultivate Eleanor as an audience, diffidently suggesting a rendezvous, wondering if she might like to procure some puss moth eggs for the boys' nature study, noting that he wasn't yet sure whether he would be in Southwold over the summer but wanted to get on with his novel. A Saturday meeting fell through when he received her letter too late to change his arrangements. Further incentive to press on with the manuscript of *Burmese Days*, parts of which were now at least four years old, came towards the end of June when Moore reported that the firm of Victor Gollancz was prepared to publish 'A Scullion's Diary', subject to worries over libel and certain inflammatory passages. At £40, the advance was on the low side (exactly the office boy's annual salary that Sambo had threatened him with all those years ago) but Orwell had every reason to be pleased. Though only in his infancy as a publisher – the firm had been founded as recently as 1928 – Gollancz was young, go-ahead, progressive in spirit and publicity-conscious. A young author signing his first contract in the early 1930s could have done a great deal worse. At the end of the month Orwell visited Gollancz at his office in Henrietta Street and received the list of proposed alterations, mostly to do with bad language and conspicuous names, but involving a rewrite of Charlie's account of his brothel visit. As for the title, which Gollancz disliked, Orwell at this stage favoured 'The Lady Poverty' or 'Lady Poverty' after the poem by Alice Meynell.

Term ended. Despite his previous indecision, Orwell went back to Southwold. There were good reasons for this, both domestic and emotional. After years of living in rented accommodation, and benefiting from a legacy from one of Ida's relatives, Mr and Mrs Blair had found the money (probably no more than a few hundred pounds, as it was sold for £1,100 two years after Ida's death) to buy their own home. Montague House, at the lower end of the High Street, purchased from the great-aunt of Orwell's tailor Mr Denny, was a decent-sized dwelling, opening on to the street but with relatively spacious rooms. As their parents were away visiting Marjorie and her husband in the north of England, Orwell and Avril had the place to themselves while they attempted to make it habitable. Avril remembered the supply of light bulbs being limited to two, taken with them as they moved from room to room. There was also a reawakening of the spirit of the 'chemical experiments' Orwell had undertaken with Prosper Buddicom. Unfortunately the attempt to distil rum from a kettle full of black treacle and boiling water through a length of rubber tube produced only a quantity of pure alcohol that tasted of rubber.

When not spring cleaning, Orwell worked late into the night on *Burmese Days*: the children of the grocer who lived on the other side of the street remembered hearing the noise of his typewriter clacking on into the darkness. But he had another quarry in view. A letter to Eleanor from mid-August shows a sharp rise in the emotional temperature. 'Dearest Eleanor' is enjoined not to forget Tuesday's meeting (2.15 p.m. by Smith's bookstall) and 'as you love me, do not *change your mind*'. Though there are earlier letters to Brenda Salkeld, this is the first of his relationships to unfold on the page, so to speak, and raises the whole question of the young Orwell's attitude to, and pursuit of, women. There is a distinct, though unspecific, memory among elderly residents of Southwold that he had the reputation of a convinced, though gauche and often unsuccessful, ladies' man. Certainly his relationship with Mabel Fierz looks as if it went beyond the roles of patroness and protégé at one point, and there is a letter in the Orwell archive in which she refers to him as her 'lover'. With Eleanor the situation was complicated by the presence of Dennis Collings, yet their closeness in the summer of 1932 – presumably Dennis was elsewhere – is beyond doubt. Immensely fond of Eleanor, Orwell could also be proprietorial (he complained bitterly when she had her hair permed without consulting him) and downright whimsical, suggesting that she might like to help with his research for a *New Statesman* article on common lodging houses by visiting a women's doss house. Two letters from the autumn shed some light on what took place in those summer walks along the River Blyth. In one Orwell recalls 'that day in the wood along past Blythburgh Lodge – you remember, where the deep beds of moss were – I shall always remember that, & your nice white body in the dark green moss'. Orwell's novels reveal a fondness for *plein air* frolics: they probably had their origin here. The other, written in mid-October, strikes a more plaintive note. 'It was so nice of you to say that you looked back to your days with me with pleasure. I hope you will let me make love to you again sometime, but if you don't it doesn't matter. I shall always be grateful to you for your kindness to me.' By this time, as far as can be deduced, Eleanor seems to have decided that the future lay with Dennis. This would have been a rather public choice: much of Southwold was in on the dilemma. Esmé May recalled that the rivalry was common knowledge, and that Orwell was 'not pleased, although he wouldn't say anything about it'. Years later Eleanor's daughter remembered her mother saying that she hadn't married Orwell 'because he was either too cynical or too sardonic' and that, however fond of him she was, 'she always knew she would marry Dennis'.

Whatever his romantic disappointments, he was keeping up a bustling work-rate. 'Clink' appeared in the August number of the *Adelphi* (the manuscript of this was lent to the Pulleyns but Orwell advised Eleanor, commissioned to retrieve it, not to show it to her parents; presumably the same went for Richard and Ida Blair), shortly to be followed by a back-scratching review of Ruth Pitter's *Persephone in Hades* – the *Adelphi* was now publishing monthly – and the *New Statesman* lodging-house piece. Back in Hayes, however, the days resumed their habitual dreary cast. The rough draft of *Burmese Days* depressed him horribly, he told Brenda Salkeld. He was still keeping up his interest in religious matters, going to church where he beheld the original of Miss Mayfill in *A Clergyman's Daughter* ('a moribund hag who stinks of mothballs & gin, & has to be more or less carried to & from the altar at communion'). He would have to communicate himself soon, he thought, or the curate would think his absence from the altar rail strange. It seemed rather mean to go to Holy Communion when one didn't believe, he explained, but 'I have passed myself off for pious & there is nothing for it but to keep up the deception.' This is an odd declaration. If Orwell was, as he puts it, shamming piety then why was he also reading *Belief in God* by Bishop Gore ('seemingly quite sound in doctrine'), who had confirmed him at Eton, and taking in the *Church Times*?

He was keen to see Eleanor again, confiding that Dennis had invited him to Cambridge for half-term but that there were two or three people there that he was anxious not to meet. Meanwhile the publication date of what had now been formally titled *Down and Out in Paris and London* was set for early January. On receipt of the proofs, in mid-November, Orwell wrote a wonderfully obtuse letter to Moore. There were two sets. Which one should he correct? One for the reader's objections and the other misprints? For safety's sake he had begun to do both. He was serious, too, about the pseudonym. Would 'X' be suitable? he wondered. Moore could have told him instantly that it would not. 'The reason I ask is if this book doesn't flop as I anticipate, it might be better to have a pseudonym I could also use for my next one.'

The question of why and how it was that late in 1932 'Eric Blair' became 'George Orwell' (by no means a clear-cut division, as Orwell continued to sign journalism under his real name for the next two years) has exercised literary historians for half a century. The temptation is to suppose that it represented some cataclysmic change of personality, motive and resolve, and yet the explanation is almost certainly more prosaic. Orwell wanted to publish *Down and Out* under an assumed name largely because he wished to spare his parents' blushes over its relatively seedy subject matter. Additionally, he had always disliked the prim Victorian connotations of his Christian name, with its nod to Dean Farrar's pious children's book *Eric, or Little by Little*. Some time between 15 and 19 November – the dates of the two relevant letters to Moore – he devised a list of aliases: Kenneth Miles, George Orwell and H. Lewis Allways. There was also mention of 'P.S. Burton', a name he had occasionally used while tramping. Of these, Orwell was his favourite. Eleanor Jaques remembered him coming back from Ipswich, through which the River Orwell ran, and announcing 'I'm going to call myself George Orwell, because it's a good round English name.' Richard Rees, alternatively, remembered the question of names awakening Orwell's pronounced superstitious side. If your name appeared in print, he claimed – Rees assumed he was being serious – it might allow an enemy to get hold of it and 'work some kind of magic on it'. Whatever the precise nature of the stimulus, some time in late November Gollancz's compositors were instructed to place the name 'George Orwell' on the title page. 'Kenneth Miles' and 'H. Lewis Allways' became footnotes to literary history.

He did manage a date with Eleanor in London on the last Saturday of November, when they met up outside the Old Vic. Another plaintive note survives from four days later proposing a Sunday trip to the country and noting that no mention had been made of further sexual opportunities. Nothing could be accomplished if Dennis were in Southwold, of course, but otherwise? 'You mustn't if you don't want to, but I hope you will.' However much Eleanor may now have been keeping him at arm's length, their relationship was still intimate. There is a possibility that she was working temporarily in London at this point – a letter of 17 December wonders whether she is selling any stockings and asks when she is 'going down' (i.e. returning to Southwold). A proposed walk in the country fell through but they met on 21 December outside the National Gallery and travelled back to Suffolk together two days later. Arriving at Montague House for Christmas Orwell was greeted by a stack of advance copies of *Down and Out*. What, he wondered naïvely to Moore, did 'a recommendation of the Book Society' on the cover mean? Five days later he journeyed to the Salkelds' family home in Bedfordshire to present Brenda with her copy. The process had taken five years since his return from Burma, but it was done. He was a writer.

7

Clergymen's Daughters

I am so miserable all alone. – Letter to Brenda Salkeld, August
1934

This age makes me so sick that sometimes I am compelled to stop
at a corner and start calling down curses from Heaven. – Letter to
Brenda Salkeld, September 1934

Down and Out in Paris and London was published on 9 January 1933.
The reviews, broadly favourable, were not without controversy. An
outraged restaurateur wrote to *The Times* complaining that the book
unfairly disparaged his profession. The passage objected to did not refer
to Parisian hotels in general but to one in particular, Orwell countered
omnisciently a few days later: as M. Possenti was ignorant of its identity
he had no way of challenging Orwell's estimate. At Montague House,
to which copies of these criticisms were sent, Richard and Ida Blair were
interested and at the same time slightly taken aback. Like most people
of their class and generation they disapproved of emotional and
physical frankness. Avril recalled that 'there was never any discussion
of sex or his love affairs or anything of that nature at all'. Their son's
apparent immersion in scenes that could have been painted by
Brueghel consequently came as a shock. And yet authorship, however
delicate the subject matter, was a profession which the Blairs would
have comprehended, and to a certain extent approved of. Presumably
they were pleased by the first signs of his success. Orwell went back to
Hayes in the third week of January, leaving a 100-page chunk of
Burmese Days with Moore *en route*, in the wake of another of his highly
ingenuous letters. The book, he reported, had been listed among the
Sunday Express 'best sellers of the week'. Did this mean anything
definite?

He was nearly thirty, and in the context of 1930s literary life rather a late starter. Evelyn Waugh had published his first book at twenty-three, Anthony Powell at twenty-five, Graham Greene at twenty-four. He was also – media circles being no less tightly knit then they are now – almost entirely beyond the palisades of contemporary bookworld fashion. He did not write for 'smart' magazines or work in publishing, and his file of literary contacts was painfully small. No doubt many of the rants put into the mouth of Gordon Comstock in *Keep the Aspidistra Flying* stemmed from Orwell's consciousness of his outsider status in the cut-throat world of early 1930s literary power-broking. 'The sods! The bloody sods!' Gordon apostrophises the editors of the fictitious *Primrose Quarterly*. 'Why not say outright: "We don't want your bloody poems. We only take poems from chaps we were at Cambridge with."' It is worth pointing out, of course, that several of Orwell's poems were accepted by people he had been to Eton with, but this is not to belittle an occasionally quite justifiable sense of exclusion. The early 1930s was an era notorious for its literary rackets. Sir John Squire, the wire-pulling editor of the *London Mercury*, and his stooges controlled half a dozen literary magazines and newspaper books pages between them, and Virginia Woolf allowed herself several scathing remarks about the kind of smart literary careerist – her particular bugbear was Cyril Connolly – who seemed to advance himself by way of alliances originally formed at school and university.

None of this, though, answers the more fundamental questions that need to be asked about Orwell at this time. What was he like? What preoccupied him? What were his ambitions? A trawl through the handful of early sightings suggests that people liked him, while finding him distant and detached. No one thought him particularly remark-able. Nor did he fit into any recognisable literary mould. Richard Rees detected several qualities that set him apart from the archetypal young literary thruster of the day – a Connolly, say, or a Stephen Spender. A friendly and considerate companion, Rees thought, entirely lacking in the pushy self-confidence that one might have expected. But while obviously intelligent and able, 'he did not seem especially original or gifted'. And if the man seemed rather old-fashioned, so did his writing: scrupulous realism alternating with self-conscious aesthetic flourishes; poems in dull, deliberate, sub-Housman quatrains. There is a way in which Orwell, even at the age of thirty, already looks like a figure from a vanished age; a way, too, in which he is already set apart from most of his contemporaries. One or two prominent exceptions notwith-standing, the image of the 'thirties writer' conjured up by most literary biography is of a metropolitan sophisticate. Orwell, loafing on Southwold common, exclaiming (in a letter to Brenda Salkeld) over the baby hedgehogs who scuttled in through the french windows of Montague House, was not like this. The letter about the hedgehogs seems, in retrospect, a perfect demonstration of the kind of person Orwell, or one part of Orwell, was. 'The hedgehogs keep coming into the house, and last night we found one in the bathroom: a little tiny hedgehog no bigger than an orange. The only thing I could think was that it was a baby of one of the others, though it was fully formed – I mean, it had its prickles.' There is a lot on display here – not only the deep absorption in 'nature' and the love and concern for animals, but the naturalist's eye for detail; above all, a lack of self-consciousness – Orwell is not, like most writers, playing to an unseen audience but simply writing things down. Significantly, the encounter with the hedgehog follows an immensely gloomy lamentation about the state of the world ('This age makes me so sick that sometimes I am compelled to stop at a corner and start calling down curses from Heaven'). The first passage is a slightly disillusioned young man generalising from the particular. The second passage is Orwell being Orwell.

One notes, even at this stage, the essential unreality of much of Orwell's approach to life. Later accounts of him are full of bizarre juxtapositions – Orwell arriving at smart parties in shabby tweeds innocently to enquire if it was all right to come in like this; stranded on a remote Scottish island after a boating accident and apparently more interested in the habits of the local bird population than the prospect of rescue. Orwell's early letters to Leonard Moore have the same brand of ingenuousness. Anyone who reads his letters to friends and professional acquaintances will be constantly pulled up by their lack of self-awareness. This is not to say that Orwell had no conception of the kind of person he was – he could be notably shrewd about himself if the circumstances demanded it – merely that he was sometimes altogether unconscious of the figure he cut in company. At the heart of the man who 'walked about in a dream', as the Southwold people put it, lay a deep vein of seriousness, often extending to outright melancholy. He was not a happy man in his early thirties, and it shows. Part of the explanation was the straightforward – if such an emotion is ever straightforward – loneliness of a man with an uncertain future stuck in a country town watching his friends disappear, but behind it is a much more integral problem. At thirty Orwell was still in the process of shaking off one kind of life and many of the affiliations that gave it substance. The new kind of life he was reaching towards had not yet taken shape. Much of this confusion, a fundamental uncertainty over how to proceed with the business of life, is symbolised by Orwell's grapplings with religion. *A Clergyman's Daughter*, the novel he completed shortly before leaving Southwold for good, has a theme that was becoming old-fashioned fifty years before in the days of Mrs Humphry Ward: the loss of religious faith. The book's central thread twists itself through much of Orwell's journalism from the period. Reviewing a study of Baudelaire for the *Adelphi* in July 1934, for example, he decided that the poet 'clung to the ethical and the imaginative background of Christianity, because he had been brought up in the Christian tradition and because he perceived that such notions as sin, damnation etc., were in a sense truer and more real than anything he could get from sloppy humanitarian atheism'. It could be Orwell talking about himself.

Meanwhile, there were several more immediate dilemmas. He had written a book, but could not yet live off his writing and was reduced to lowly teaching jobs. The girl he most admired (Eleanor) was in love with another man whom she would all too rapidly marry. The other girl he admired (Brenda) wanted nothing more than friendship. Professionally, despite the agreeable stir caused by *Down and Out*, he remained on the margins. The two-year gap between publishing his first book and finally escaping to the first faint semblance of the London literary charivari was an uneasy period, and the evidence of his dissatisfaction lies everywhere to hand. Orwell's letters from late 1934 are notable for their self-pity, a personal uncertainty rarely glimpsed in the remaining decade and a half of his life.

The initial news in the early part of 1933 was good. Moore swiftly disposed of the American rights to *Down and Out*: a French translation would soon follow. Back in Hayes for the spring term, Orwell was avid for a meeting with Eleanor. Was she coming up to town? he wondered in mid-February, while asking her to find out if the Pulleynes had received their copy of the book. A reference to a job with a fashion-plate artist suggests that Eleanor was looking for work in London. Orwell reported himself as suffering from a heavy cold. The April number of the *Adelphi* contained a notably grim poem:

> And I see the people thronging the street
> The death-marked people, they and I
> Godless, rootless, like leaves drifting,
> Blind to the earth and to the sky.

As poetry it is negligible, although one notes the influence of T.S. Eliot, but the sense of rootlessness is marked. Stuck in Hayes with only the friendly curate for company, Eleanor far away in Southwold and ambivalent in her affections, Orwell needed an outlet. He found one in Brenda, who for the next year and a half features as a sounding-board for literary and other enthusiasms. He wrote her a long letter in March, mocking her love of Shaw and trumpeting his newfound interest in James Joyce's *Ulysses*. Brenda, too, could be lured up to town. It was so nice at Burnham Beeches, he reminisced over a previous meeting, '& I should so like to go there again when the trees are budding'. Burnham Beeches, an innocuous piece of Thames Valley woodland, rapidly became an obsession with Orwell. Eleanor Jacques was enticed there. Dorothy in *A Clergyman's Daughter* picnics there on Christmas Day as a respite from her rebarbative employer Mrs Creevy over a copy of George Gissing's *The Odd Women*. Gordon Comstock tries and fails to have his way with Rosemary in the chilly autumn bracken. Teaching duties gave Orwell little free time – he also seems to have been inveigled into extra-curricular work at the weekends – but he was pressing on with *Burmese Days*, promising Moore another 100 pages by April. He was kept in Hayes until the middle of the month, but wrote again trying to fix up a meeting with a visiting representative of his American publisher, Harper Brothers. The lack of any definite break in his relationship with Eleanor can perhaps be caught from a letter from late May, written 'not knowing where you are' but sent to an address in Roehampton where she stayed when she was in London. Everything looks faintly uncertain. What about a long walk in the country? What are her summer plans? There was a chance that the Blairs would be letting Montague House for the holiday period: this might mean that Orwell would have to spend the time elsewhere. His working life was similarly unsatisfactory. He was already planning to leave the Hawthorns for another school in nearby Uxbridge, but it is clear that he regarded teaching as a stop-gap and that other options were under discussion. Aunt Nellie weighed in with a letter from Paris, enclosing both a subscription for the *Adelphi* and a cash gift for her favourite nephew, suggesting that he could try for a job as a travelling representative for Ruth Pitter's pottery company, and noting with an ingenuousness worthy of Orwell himself that Avril must have some patronage to dispense. In the meantime the letter sent in pursuit of Eleanor had obviously found its target as in early June he wrote planning a weekend jaunt. 'I think it would be nicest if we went somewhere where there are *woods*,' he proposed. Burnham Beeches it was, presumably reached by train from Paddington.

Whatever happened at a place which in *Keep the Aspidistra Flying* is the source of some of Orwell's most extravagant rhapsodies over 'nature' (Rosemary wades 'through a bank of drifted beech leaves that rustled about her, knee-deep, like a weightless, red-gold sea') and also of some of his bitterest misery, is lost in time, but Orwell's friendship with Eleanor was coming to an end. He wrote again in early July, chatting about the summer drought and the open-air baths at Southall, hoping that she would be in Southwold over the summer and ending with 'I am so pining to see you again'. By this stage his immediate destiny was fixed. He was transferring to a school called Fray's College in Uxbridge, an altogether larger establishment with nearly 200 pupils and a proper complement of staff, to teach French. This, too, was a source of anxiety, as he feared the school might want him to provide coaching in the holidays. A fortnight later he wrote again to Eleanor, reprising their exploits of the previous year: bathing and making tea along the Walberswick shore. He had no great hopes of the new job. 'I went over to see the prize-giving at the school and it looked pretty bloody'. But *Burmese Days* was finished, even if there were parts of it that he hated and wanted to change. This is the last of his letters to Eleanor that survives. By the summer of 1933 she seems to have made up her mind. At any rate she and Dennis Collings, whose reaction to the affair is unrecorded, were married the following year. The next six months are ominously blank. The only letters that remain are a handful to Moore. Such was the pressure of work at Fray's College that the revisions to *Burmese Days* took longer than Orwell expected, but by the end of November it was in a state to be delivered to Moore's house at Gerrards Cross. Characteristically, Orwell professed himself dissatisfied with the novel, 'but it is about up to the standard of what you saw . . .' Beyond the stresses of finishing a book that had occupied him on and off for over six years, ever since the first seeds had lodged in his mind on some Burmese veranda, he was still contributing reviews to the *Adelphi* and remained intrigued by Joyce, the subject of another long and faintly didactic letter to Brenda early in December. The fact was, he explained to Brenda, that Joyce interested him so much that he could not stop talking about him once he started. Within a few months there would be hard evidence of Joyce's influence on his own work.

Orwell made no friends among the staff at Fray's College. Hardly anything was remembered of him except his habit of taking his newly

acquired second-hand motorbike off on excursions through the surrounding countryside. On one of these trips he delivered the
manuscript of *Burmese Days* to Moore. A second jaunt proved his
undoing. Shortly before Christmas, out riding on a wet afternoon in
light clothes, he was soaked to the skin, caught a chill that developed
into pneumonia and was taken off to Uxbridge Cottage Hospital, where
for a time his life was thought to be in danger. Mrs Blair and Avril,
advised to come up from Southwold, arrived after the crisis had passed,
but the illness became part of family legend. Delirious, and presumably
imagining he was back in some ninepenny kip, Orwell kept muttering
to himself about money, in the sense, Avril remembered, of actually
wanting it beneath his pillow. By 28 December he was well enough to
write to Moore to thank him for dropping in to enquire after his
progress. His sharp eye for the routines of hospital life surfaced some
years later in 'How the Poor Die': a fellow-patient had died while they
were having tea, he remembered, but such was the nurses' dexterity
that the event passed almost unnoticed. Visiting him there Ruth Pitter
was told by the sister supervising the lung ward that those with red faces
would die and those with pale faces pull through. Discharged in the
second week of January, Orwell spent a couple of days in a hotel in
Ealing before returning to Southwold to recuperate. Again, the only
letters that survive are to Moore. Looked after by his family, he began
to recover to the extent of doing a little work and proposing to translate
a philosophical work written by a friend of Aunt Nellie's husband.
(Moore gallantly tried a couple of publishers without success.) Then,
some time in the early New Year, came the unexpected news that
Gollancz had turned down *Burmese Days*.

On the face of it Gollancz's decision was surprising. For a first book,
Down and Out had made a decided impact. Why reject a novel that, in
its mordant portrayal of Anglo-Burmese society, was likely to be quite
as controversial? But Victor Gollancz, unfortunately, was highly-
strung. A *News Chronicle* profile from the previous year gives a fair idea
of the stream of nervous energy that flowed daily through Henrietta
Street. Looking older than his thirty-nine years, body topped by a
dome-like, balding head, Gollancz was described as 'rather small,
humorous, shrewd', much given to pipe-smoking and pacing the room
as he talked. His aim, he told the sympathetic interviewer – the *News
Chronicle* was a progressive paper – was 'to help one day in the building,
nationally and internationally, of a more decent economic system'. As
well as owning to lofty ideals, Gollancz had a vigilant and occasionally

alarmist eye for the practical realities of publishing: his particular fear was the prospect of a damaging and financially ruinous court case. At the time at which the manuscript of *Burmese Days* arrived on his desk Gollancz was still smarting over the débâcle of *One Way of Love*, a novel by a young woman named Gamel Woolsey. This passingly frank account of a love affair had been accepted for publication, printed and bound, only for the publisher to lose his nerve over possible obscenity proceedings. The book languished and died, but Gollancz remained in a state of constant terror over potentially offensive passages in practically anything he published. Shortly after *l'affaire Woolsey*, he instructed his co-director Harold Rubinstein, 'I want everything done that can possibly be done to settle the matter rather than that we should have to fight it . . . I have a real horror of anything like a legal fight.' This explains both his reluctance to publish *Burmese Days* – a magnet, he imagined, for writs from real-life Indian civil servants – and his neurotic interference with Orwell's later books. *A Clergyman's Daughter* was heavily censored, including a scene in which Mr Warburton attempts to rape Dorothy. That these fears were not, in the last resort, unreasonable is demonstrated by the subsequent history of *Burmese Days*. Heinemann and Cape rejected it for the same reason. Harpers eventually accepted the manuscript, while demanding alterations, and – unusually for a fictional début by an English writer – the novel was first published in America. In the meantime, anxious to advance his career while the matter was resolved, Orwell proposed a short biography of Mark Twain. Harpers' chief editor advised him to try Chatto & Windus, but again the scheme found no sponsors.

Sequestered in his bedroom at Montague House as the spring winds rushed down across the Suffolk coast from Jutland, Orwell's frustration grew. He had begun work on another novel, which was to become *A Clergyman's Daughter*. The letters to Moore mention a mysterious project of the publisher Hamish Hamilton requiring 'specialist knowledge' which Orwell did not possess. 'On a Ruined Farm near His Majesty's Voice Gramophone Factory', a truly awful poem, inspired by the landscape near Hayes, that appeared in the April *Adelphi*, returns to the question of lost certainties:

> Yet when the trees were young, men still
> Could choose their path – the wingèd soul
> Not cursed with double doubts, could fly
> Arrow-like to a foreseen god . . .

The poet, stuck in the godless present, is 'both ways torn', motionless like Buridan's ass 'between the water and the corn'. Orwell's unhappiness at this time is plain from his letters to Brenda Salkeld. Yet it seems to have been Brenda on whom, once again, his emotional sights were now fixed. Her departure from Southwold at the end of the St Felix school term plunged him into gloom. 'How I wish you were here,' he lamented. A *Clergyman's Daughter* depressed him horribly. There were good passages in it, he knew, but somehow the whole would not cohere. Dennis and Eleanor, now married, were about to leave for the Far East. 'I can't stand this place when you're not here,' he told the real-life clergyman's daughter. If he were not fairly busy, he would go mad.

Orwell's distinctive brand of exaggerated self-pity is not to be taken with undue seriousness. Once he had finished his book, he intended to leave for London (a subsequent letter to Brenda foreshadows this). Yet the feeling of loneliness, determination to find company at any cost, probably explains a curious episode which it is possible to date to the summer of 1934. George Summers, six years younger than Orwell, was an antiques dealer with premises along Ferry Road near 'the point' at the further end of Southwold harbour. He seems to have moved in at least some of the local circles frequented by Richard and Ida Blair – he knew Mme Tabois, for example, who was a friend of his mother's – without having very much to do with them. But he knew 'Eric', first met in the Southwold ironmonger's shop, and had not taken to him. George Summers was friendly with, and may at this point have already been engaged to, a girl named Dorothy Rogers (by coincidence a friend of Dora Georges, to whom Orwell had presented his poem four years before), daughter of the proprietor of the Walberswick garage. Dorothy, remembered as 'the prettiest girl in the district', worked at a ladies' outfitting shop in Southwold named Griffin's where she was often to be seen by passers-by dressing the windows. Chatting one day to his future son-in-law, Mr Rogers enquired enigmatically: did his daughter ever go for walks on her own? Why yes, George replied: indeed, as her father must know, she had to walk home across Southwold common every afternoon from work to the chain bridge that ran over the Blyth to Walberswick. Mr Rogers offered a piece of advice. 'You look out . . . You guard it [the bridge] . . . You get on the end of that one evening with your motorbike . . . And if you see that feller there at the wrong time when she's supposed to be coming back from the shopping . . . run him down.' Intrigued, and somewhat suspicious, George turned up on his motorbike late one afternoon on the Southwold side of the bridge, just as Dorothy appeared in view at the point where the road wound down from the common. Waiting nearby was a tall and immediately recognisable figure. Some kind of altercation took place, ending with Orwell being chased back across the common by the avenging angel on the motorbike.

There were to be no more late-afternoon strolls by the Blyth. Brenda had gone to Ireland for the summer. Desperate for diversion, Orwell joined his father, with whom by now he seems to have been more or less reconciled, in one of the old man's favourite pastimes: watching films in the tiny local cinema in Duke of York's Road on the way to the common. A screening of *The Constant Nymph* took him back to his first reading of Margaret Kennedy's novel years before in Burma. Older and better read, Orwell cheerfully owned up to this lapse of judgement. But his underlying mood was grim. He was so miserable in Southwold, all alone, he told Brenda. The proofs of *Burmese Days*, recently received from America, made him 'spew'. *A Clergyman's Daughter*, now perhaps two-thirds done, was even worse. 'Do come back, dearest one,' he instructed her, before going on to recount another of those oddly Orwellian incidents with which his life is dotted. Walking along the nearby Easton Broad, deserted and gleaming in the summer sun, he had found the water so inviting that he had gone in naked, leaving his clothes in a heap at the water's edge. In an instant numbers of people came and sat down, including a coastguard 'who could have had me up for bathing naked'. Orwell's solution was to swim up and down for half an hour 'pretending to like it' until the spectators dispersed.

September came. Another gloomy letter to Brenda reported that the novel was going backwards. Moore was informed that it was 'rather fragmentary', but that there were (Orwell hoped) passages in it that people might find interesting. He filled in time not spent at his desk planting cabbages on the family allotment off the Blyth Road and making trips to Lowestoft and Norwich in search of bulbs. Finally, not satisfied with what he had done and feeling that he had made a mess of some promising ideas, he dispatched the manuscript to Moore in the first week of October.

A Clergyman's Daughter is a curious novel, one of the oddest things that Orwell ever wrote. Produced in a period of little over six months, awash with personal preoccupations and experiences, it is one of those books in which a writer's private demons contend with a mass of reportage masquerading as background. Dorothy Hare, who shares her

Christian name with the future Mrs George Summers, is the over-worked, downtrodden daughter of an ageing rector in Knype Hill, a moribund Suffolk parish. In her late twenties, but apparently already condemned to a life of spinsterdom owing to her terror of sex, Dorothy is in effect her father's unpaid housekeeper-cum-secretary, whose duties cover everything from typing his sermons to haggling with tradesmen and presiding over weekly meetings of the Mothers' Union. Dorothy is sustained in this life of semi-genteel bondage by a tiny handful of friends: Victor, the choirmaster, and a seedy middle-aged rake named Mr Warburton, an entertaining conversationalist whose conspicuous interest in her somewhat faded charms is a source of perennial disgust. Then, unexpectedly, after a hard day among her father's flock, culminating in an evening visit *chez* Warburton and a late-night session over the glue-pot manufacturing jackboots for a children's play, Dorothy suffers a breakdown. At any rate she is discovered sitting on the roadside in a London back street in a state of amnesia by a tramp named Nobby and his mates on their way to the Kentish hop-fields. Dazed and suggestible, Dorothy agrees to go with them. There follows a fortnight's hop-picking, during the course of which Dorothy finds out who she is. The prompt arrives courtesy of a tabloid report – chief witness the local gossip, Mrs Semprill – of a 'rector's daughter' vanished from the family hearth, having last been observed in a close embrace with Mr Warburton over the latter's garden gate. Migrating to London in the diaspora that follows the end of the picking session, her letters to her father unanswered, Dorothy ends up in a prostitutes' boarding-house in Lambeth Cut and finally on the streets, including an epic night in Trafalgar Square. Picked up by the police for begging, she is eventually rescued by her father's cousin, the baronet Sir Thomas Hare, and, as a means of getting her out of the way, he puts her to work in a dreadful private school in the west London suburbs. Sacked by her employer, the redoubtable Mrs Creevy, she is then rescued again, this time by the providential figure of Mr Warburton, who arrives unexpectedly in a taxi. Her chief accuser having recently been sued for libel, her reputation in Knype Hill is restored. Dorothy returns home, refusing Mr Warburton's offer of marriage along the way, to a slightly modified version of her previous circumstances.

Thus framed, *A Clergyman's Daughter* is essentially a matter of Orwell making use – sometimes clumsily, sometimes with considerable subtlety – of material drawn from his own life. Part One is a sharply drawn, naturalistic account of life in a Suffolk market town riven with snobbery and petty spite. Part Two, on the other hand, is simply an excuse for Orwell to reheat some of his tramping and hopping exploits. Then comes the night in Trafalgar Square, again making use of Orwell's experiences in the summer of 1931 but given an extra gloss by its pastiche of the 'Night town' scene in *Ulysses*. Part Four, framed by the memory of his own west London teaching days, intrudes an element of the grotesque not previously seen in his work. Mrs Creevy, for example – the terrifying ogress and child-queller of Ringwood House School, who announces that Christmas is a lot of nonsense got up by shop-keepers, cancels Christmas dinner but consents to pin up a couple of sprigs of the year before's holly – is a Dickensian pantomime dame when set against the more realistically drawn creations from the early part of the book. The juxtaposition of such disparate material – Suffolk, hop-picking, down-and-outs' London, private school-teaching – presented Orwell with huge technical problems. On one level the novel is merely an exercise in bridge-building in which the central character frequently tumbles into the water below. Reading it one is constantly struck by the way in which Dorothy falls in and out of the book, pushed aside by the torrents of reportage. The teaching job in 'Southbridge', for example, offers a splendid excuse for digressions on the shabbier end of the private school system ('There are, by the way, vast numbers of private schools in England . . .') and the sense of a novel endlessly pulling itself back from the brink of turning into a *New Statesman* article is rather too strong for comfort.

All this gives the book a faintly incongruous air, the feeling of personal experience, peculiar to the author, grafted on to an imagined psychology that is much less able to deal with it. As pontoon bridge after pontoon bridge is stealthily erected between the different clumps of material, the novel is consistently let down by sheer implausibility. The whole 'memory loss' episode is as unconvincing as Dorothy's rescue by the wildly improbable figure of Sir Thomas. Mr Warburton, too, seems oddly out of place as a *deus ex machina,* his shiftiness and unreliability now oddly replaced by a resolve to bear good tidings. Not for the last time in Orwell's work there is a sense of a writer resisting his own determinist impulses. Left to himself, you feel, Orwell might have sent Dorothy back to the streets rather than the thraldom of her father's gloomy rectory.

Orwell came to dislike *A Clergyman's Daughter*, famously described it as 'bollix', and would never allow it to be reprinted in his lifetime.

Such was the intensity of the proscription that after his death it took a further eleven years to realise a new edition. And yet for all its uncertainty of tone, and the constant spectacle of an author who has not yet established in his mind how fiction works, it is crammed with revealing details about the personality that constructed it. Lying beneath the down-and-out reportage and the depressing vistas of small-town Suffolk is a profound and genuine interest in questions of spiritual belief and religious observance, characterised above all by a fascination with the sheer paraphernalia of contemporary religious life. An early twenty-first-century academic meditating a thesis on 'Anglo-Catholicism versus Anglicanism. The Church of England in the Inter-war Era: Tensions and Dissent' would get a very fair idea of its underlying dynamic from the spiritual cauldron that is Knype Hill. At an early stage, for example, Orwell supplies a minute account of the contending brands of Christian observance on offer in this East Anglian backwater, from the 'modernist' St Edmund's (the name of the Southwold church, coincidentally enough) with its text from Blake's 'Jerusalem' blazoned over the altar and Communion wine sipped out of wine glasses to St Wedekind's, Anglo-Catholic and in a state of permanent warfare with the bishop. Again, there is Dorothy's long exchange with Victor while the schoolmaster rehearses the children's play, full of the most intricate period references to the *Church Times*, Bertrand Russell, Julian Huxley and the Bishop of Birmingham, and, when Victor turns to the rector's prosaic tastes in vestments ('On Easter Sunday he was actually wearing a Gothic cope with a modern Italian lace alb. Why, dash it, it's like wearing a top-hat with brown boots') straying into the realms of pastiche. The simile is Orwell's, you feel, rather than his character's.

The religious atmospherics are reinforced by the pull of the novel's figurative language and the range of its scriptural allusions. Dorothy exhorts herself by way of biblical quotations. Run to earth in the police cell she is compared by Sir Thomas' discreet butler to a rescued Magdalen. Even the bloomers that Mrs Creevy re-stitches of an evening in Southbridge 'seemed to carry upon them, as no nun's coif or anchorite's hair-shirt could ever have done, the impress of a frozen and awful chastity'. Running beneath are some much more temporal fixations. The most marked, perhaps, is an extreme desperate fastidious-ness which, when it surfaces, offers the spectacle of Orwell pushing his characters out of the way in his eagerness to play the parts himself. Dorothy's horror at the thought of having to sip from the chalice after old Miss Mayfill's venerable lips have slobbered over it is shot through with sinister physical detail: 'it was not an appetising mouth; not the kind of mouth that you would like to see drinking out of your cup'. Suddenly Miss Mayfill stops being a decrepit old woman smelling of gin and mothballs and turns into a ghastly subterranean creature capable of awakening Dorothy's innermost fears. There is even an echo of one of M.R. James' grislier ghost stories, in which a man stumbling about his bedroom in darkness reaches under his pillow to find 'a mouth, with teeth, and with hair about it, and, he declares, not the mouth of a human being'. In much the same way it is impossible to read more than a chapter or two without noting the obsession with money. Dorothy's battles with the household accounting are set down in the most minute detail, and in what other 1930s novel can one learn the price of a packet of spearmint bouncers or a pound of cheap Danish bacon?

And yet, in the end, all this is simply incidental. Where *A Clergyman's Daughter* finally declares itself is in a series of long, meditative passages in which Dorothy reflects on her recently dis-covered unbelief and the security of the environment in which she was nurtured:

> In another and deeper sense the atmosphere of the church was soothing and necessary to her, for she perceived that in all that happens in church, however absurd and cowardly its supposed purpose may be, there is something – it is hard to define, but something of decency, of spiritual comeliness – that is not easily found in the world outside. It seemed to her that even if you no longer believe, it is better to go to church than not; better to follow in the ancient ways than to drift in rootless freedom.

Dorothy knows very well that she will never be able to say a prayer again and mean it, but she also realises that for the rest of her life she will have to continue with this mental outlook: it is as much a part of her as her father's bilking of his tradesmen, looking the other way when you see the butcher, and bacon at fivepence a pound. The novel ends on an odd and slightly unsatisfactory note with Dorothy unable, or unwilling, to divert herself from the path on which she is set. Even Mr Warburton's sketch of her probable future, her father dead and the rest of his money frittered away, holds no real terror for her. But perhaps, she concedes, she will kneel at Miss Mayfill's left rather than her right at the Communion rail.

Orwell's time in Southwold was coming to an end. Barely a fortnight after Moore received the manuscript he was away. Aunt Nellie, using one of her husband's Esperanto connections, had found him a job. Francis and Myfanwy Westrope ran a bookshop in South End Drive, Hampstead. There was a vacancy for an assistant to work part-time; accommodation provided. The post offered an ideal solution to Orwell's difficulties – low wages but a base in London near the hub of the literary world and with several hours a day for him to get on with his writing. He left Southwold at the end of the third week in October. In a curious way, though, the place stuck in his mind; many of the fragments of experience picked up there never left him. There is, for example, a scene in *Nineteen Eighty-Four* in which Winston Smith, incarcerated in a cell at the Ministry of Love after the Thought Police have raided his and Julia's hideout, watches in fascinated horror as one of his cell mates tries to give a starving man a morsel of hoarded food. 'Bumstead', roars a voice from the telescreen, '2713 Bumstead J! Let fall that piece of bread.' Bumstead J – Jack Bumstead – was the son of the Southwold grocer whose shop lay across the High Street from Montague House, and whose brother George had lain awake listening to the sound of the typewriter tapping on into the small hours on the summer evenings of long ago.

Orwell and the rats

O'Brien picked up the cage and brought it across to the nearer table. He set it down carefully on the baize cloth. Winston could hear the blood singing in his ears. He had the feeling of sitting in utter loneliness. He was in the middle of a great empty plain, a flat desert drenched with sunlight, across which all sounds came to him out of immense distance. Yet the cage with the rats was not two metres away from him. They were at the age when a rat's muzzle grows blunt and fierce and his fur brown instead of grey. – *Nineteen Eighty-Four*

Orwell's obsession with – it would not be quite accurate to call it an aversion to – rats is widely attested. Rats are everywhere in his life, from the practical jokes of his adolescence to the macabre fantasies of his middle age. Undoubtedly some of the roots of this fixation lay in literature. We know that as a boy Orwell relished the works of Beatrix Potter, in which he must have come across Samuel Whiskers, and was addicted to M.R. James' ghost stories, a prime specimen of which is called simply 'Rats'. There is every chance, too, that at an early age he encountered W.H. Davies' poem 'The Rat': Orwell's 1943 *Observer* review of Davies' *Collected Poems* displays what looks like a long-standing familiarity with Davies' work, and specifically mentions 'The Rat':

> That woman there is almost dead,
> Her feet and hands like heavy lead;
> Her cat's gone out for his delight,
> He will not come again this night.
>
> Her husband in a pothouse drinks,

Her daughter at a soldier winks;
Her son is at his sweetest game,
Teasing the cobbler old and lame.

Now with these teeth that powder stones,
I'll pick out all of her cheek-bones;
When husband, son and daughter come,
They'll soon see who was left at home.

The poem betrays characteristic Orwellian elements: human vulnerability in the face of vicious animal intelligence ('They also attack sick or dying people,' O'Brien tells Winston in *Nineteen Eighty-Four*. 'They show astonishing intelligence in knowing when a human being is helpless'); above all, the idea of rats biting their victims in the face. Orwell had obviously studied rats at close hand. Writing about his time in Spain in 1937, hunting firewood in the shadow of the Fascist observation posts, he notes that 'If their machine-gunners spotted you, you had to flatten yourself out like a rat when it squirms under a door.' In his early life Orwell must have watched a rat squirming under a door, and the image had stayed with him to provide a neat little metaphor for his own affairs.

Subsequently the rodent tide flows endlessly through his work: an unappeasable furry brood piped in and out of the darkest reaches of his consciousness. Rats are all around him, dancing across the surface of his life like the two outsize specimens he saw first thing in the morning at the Auberge de Jehan Cotard sitting on the restaurant's kitchen table and eating from a ham that lay there. There is an enthusiastic letter to Prosper Buddicom from early 1921, sent from a holiday in Suffolk, about 'one of those big cage-rat traps' Orwell has bought and the sport to be had in letting a rat out and shooting it. 'It is also rather sport to go at night to a corn-stack with an acetylene bicycle lamp, & you can dazzle the rats that are running along the side & whack at them, – or shoot them with a rifle.' Rats crawled everywhere in Burma. Alarmed by its role as carrier of plague and disease, the colonial authorities regarded the rat as a public enemy. Local districts were obliged to furnish statistics of rat mortality, and there were carefully enumerated annual culls. Between 1922 and 1923, for example, nearly two million were exterminated in the province. In Rangoon, where the majority of this slaughter took place, it would have been impossible to walk down the average side street at certain times of the year without passing a mound of rat corpses. Neither, too, would it have been possible to avoid the presence of rats on more solemn occasions. There is a rather ghastly aside in *Burmese Days* where, in the middle of a description of the funeral of Maxwell, the murdered acting Divisional Forest Officer, the narrative pauses to consider the state of the cemetery: 'Among the jasmine, large rat-holes led down into the graves.' There is no doubt at all what will happen to Maxwell's body the moment that it is lowered into the earth. It was in the East, additionally, that Orwell would first have come across the most dreadful of *Nineteen Eighty-Four*'s many horrors. Starving rats, kept for days in a cage and then released on victims in a confined space, were an ancient Chinese torture.

Thereafter the rats wander in and out of his 1930s life. Staying in a sevenpenny kip in the Southwark Bridge Road in 1931 he notes that 'the rats are so bad that several cats have to be kept exclusively to deal with them'. On his hopping excursion later that year he recorded a fascinated encounter with the 'vermin man' from one of the big London restaurant chains. The rats were so numerous at one branch, Orwell's informant told him, that it was not safe to venture into the kitchen without a loaded revolver. This is like something out of a novel by James Herbert – the seething grey brood out for vengeance on trapped humanity. But it was Spain that cemented Orwell's alliance with the rat, to the extent that it sometimes seems that his chief interest is not so much his Fascist opponents as the hard eye glinting up from beneath the straw. At La Granja, for instance, he saw 'great bloated brutes that waddled over the beds of mud, too impudent even to run away unless you shot at them'. A barn which his unit occupied was 'alive with rats. The filthy brutes came swarming out of the ground on every side.' If there was one thing he hated, Orwell remarked, it was a rat running over him in the dark. 'However, I had the satisfaction of catching one of them a good punch that sent him flying.' Elsewhere he listens to rats splashing along a ditch 'making as much noise as if they were otters'. What one colleague called Orwell's 'phobia' could have unfortunate consequences. Thoroughly exasperated by a venturesome beast that had invaded his trench, Orwell pulled out his revolver and shot it. Spreading out from the enclosed space, the reverberations were enough to prompt both sides into action. The ensuing conflict left the cookhouse in ruins and destroyed two of the buses used to ferry reserve troops up to the front.

Davies' poem. The dead rat sent to the Southwold borough surveyor. The brandished revolver in the Spanish trench. All this is too big to be overlooked, too continuous, too nagging. On Jura, in the last part of his life, Orwell took his usual lively interest in the local rodent population. In June 1946 he noted that 'rats, hitherto non-existent, are bound to come after the corn has been put into the byre'. A buzzard, seen from afar, appeared to be carrying a rat in its claws. In April 1947 a trap borrowed from his neighbour 'killed an enormous rat in the byre'. Come June five specimens ('2 enormous') were dispatched in the byre in a fortnight. Orwell wondered at the ease with which the rats allowed themselves to be caught. 'The traps are simply set in the runs,' he noted, 'unbaited and almost unconcealed . . . I hear recently that two children at Ardlussa were bitten by rats (in the face, as usual)'. At almost exactly this time he would have been working away at *Nineteen Eighty-Four*, perhaps even writing the following exchange between Winston and Julia:

'Rats!' murmured Winston. 'In this room!'

'They're all over the place,' said Julia indifferently as she lay down again. 'We've even got them in the kitchen of the hostel. Some parts of London are swarming with them. Did you know they attack children? Yes, they do. In some of these streets a woman daren't leave a baby alone for two minutes. It's the great huge brown ones that do it. And the nasty thing is that the brutes always—'

'*Don't go on!*' said Winston, with his eyes tightly shut.

'Dearest! You've gone quite pale. What's the matter? Do they make you feel sick?'

'Of all the horrors in the world – a rat!'

Aged three

Lieutenant Blair on leave with
Ida, Eric and Avril

(*Left*) Jacintha

(*Above*) Prosper and Guinever Buddicom with Eric, Shropshire, 1917

(*Below*) Fishing with the Buddicoms

(*Above*) Illicit cigarette at Eton
(*Above right*) Cyril Connolly
at Eton

(Right) Connolly as an
undergraduate

Police Training School, Mandalay, 1923, (third from left, back row)

The real Mr Macgregor? Colonel F.H. McGregor, Third Rangoon Field Brigade (right)

EXTERIOR OF PREMISES

INTERIOR OF SHOWROOM

'Oh, the joy of those Rangoon trips! The visit to Smart & Mookerdum's bookshop for the new novels out from England…' – *Burmese Days*

Passport photo, mid-1920s   Richard Rees

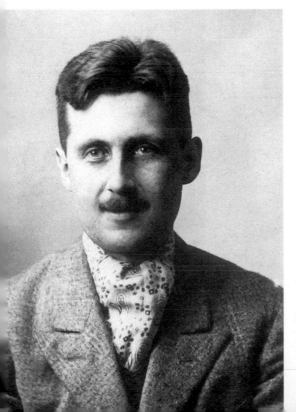

(*Above left*) The garden shed at Montague House

(*Main picture*) Southwold High Street, 1926

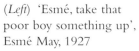

(*Left*) 'Esmé, take that poor boy something up', Esmé May, 1927

(*Right*) Mrs Jessie May

(*Above right*) 'The Dark Lady' –
Dora Georges, late 1920s

(*Right*)   Orwell on Walberswick beach, 1932

With Eleanor and friend on Southwold beach, 1932

(*Above*) George Summers, 1930s:
'I ran up the bank…I sort of
pushed him off…I didn't kill him.'

(*Right*) Mr and Mrs Dennis
Collings on their wedding day,
Cambridge, 1934

8

A Room with a View

And if we did get a writer worth reading should we know him
when we saw him, so choked as we are with trash? – *Keep the
Aspidistra Flying*

I want this one to be a work of art, & that can't be done without
much bloody sweat. – Letter to Brenda Salkeld, 16 February 1935

Booklovers' Corner lay on the southern slopes of Hampstead, on what
Keep the Aspidistra Flying would describe as 'a sort of shapeless square
where four streets converged'. Occupying a vague hinterland between
working-class Kentish Town and the leafier purlieus of NW3,
dominated by the nearby Playhouse cinema, it was also on a tram route,
the source of one of the novel's more grotesque 'modernist' images – a
tram 'like a raucous swan of steel' which glides groaning over the
cobbles.

No doubt the time spent staring out of the shop window encouraged
this kind of hallucinatory simile. In the evenings Orwell repaired to the
Westropes' flat at Warwick Mansions, Pond Street, the society of his
employers and his fellow-lodger Jon Kimche. Here, by all accounts, a
notably civilised atmosphere prevailed. Mr Westrope, tall and slightly
stooped, was described by one of his lodgers as being impressive in
appearance, 'rather like a quiet country solicitor'. His wife – they were
in late middle age – was more vivacious. Together they did their best to
make the young men who made up the shop's staff feel at home. There
was a pleasant sitting room which they were sometimes allowed to
borrow, and Orwell, used to the genteel observances of middle England,
was slightly startled when Mrs Westrope asked him if he intended to
bring women back to his room, not as a warning shot across the bows
but as an indication that his private life was his own. The social circle
of the Westropes' flat was only one of several to which Orwell, newly

arrived in London but with several useful contacts, had access. Gordon Comstock in *Keep the Aspidistra Flying* is an isolated figure. Essentially Rosemary, his girlfriend, and Ravelston, his guilt-ridden sponsor at *Antichrist* are his only friends, and the novel illustrates Orwell's trick – one carried all the way through to *Nineteen Eighty-Four* – of setting up a solitary anti-hero in opposition to a hostile world. In contrast, his own life at Warwick Mansions and the addresses to which he subsequently migrated was comparatively lively. Living permanently in London for the first time in his life, he was able to expand his range of acquaintances. He saw more of Rees and the group of writers associated with the *Adelphi*. He kept up his friendship with Mabel Fierz. Above all, he met the woman who was to become his first wife.

Orwell used *Keep the Aspidistra Flying* to express certain beliefs about the worlds – literary and emotional – in which he operated. But they were not all drawn from his own life. Most of his friends from the mid-1930s agreed that the bookshop in the novel is the gravest caricature. Here Mr Mckechnie, the shop's proprietor, slumbers over the gas fire with the snuff speckling his white beard while a dozen feet below his embittered assistant counts his diminishing store of cigarettes, expels tramps, defers to fruity-voiced women in search of dog books, presides with secret contempt over the shop's lending library and finds emotional release in kicking the spines of the Victorian classics at his side. But the atmosphere of Booklovers' Corner was markedly different. Past patrons remembered it as an excellent second-hand bookshop with a discriminating stock; its proprietors were a 'delightful couple' and only Orwell's account of the lending library offered any faint connection to the reality of the place. A twelve-year-old boy who browsed there in the mid-1930s recalled its cramped, dusty interior – the stock overflowing the shelves and stacked up to the ceiling – as 'rather exciting' for its promise of hidden treasures. Orwell's routine, set out in a letter to Brenda Salkeld, allowed for around five and a half hours' work a day (again, this distinguishes him from Gordon, who works a five-and-a-half-day week). Getting up at seven, he went down to open the shop at 8.45 and stayed there for an hour. From 10.30 until lunchtime he got on with his writing, returning to the shop at two and remaining there until 6.30.

There were worse constraints for a young novelist in the 1930s. Like Graham Greene, working on the sub-editor's desk at *The Times*, Orwell was fortunate in that his free time coincided with the hours when he was most mentally alert. He could yawn through the long afternoons with the real business of the day already behind him. A few glimpses of him in the role of bookseller's assistant survive. Kimche, who later fought with him in Spain and went on to become a colleague on *Tribune,* never saw him sit. Standing in the centre of the shop, he seemed 'a slightly forbidding figure'. As well as its stock of books and the lending library, the shop had various sidelines, among them second-hand typewriters and stamps. Kimche retained an abiding image of the tall, saturnine shop-walker 'almost like a gazelle' with a small boy, far below him, handing up a packet of stamps. There are other testimonies to the shop's faintly intimidating air when Orwell was on duty. The novelist Peter Vansittart, who visited Booklovers' Corner as a school-boy, remembered the 'slightly ungracious' assistant trying, unsuccessfully, to sell him a copy of *Trader Horn in Madagascar.* Vansittart stuck out for a copy of P.G. Wodehouse's *A Damsel in Distress.*

Although it ends on an up, *Keep the Aspidistra Flying,* the novel that occupied Orwell's time during his fifteen months at the Westropes' bookshop, is an end-of-tether book, deeply disillusioned both with the literary world which Gordon Comstock tries to infiltrate and with the wider environment glimpsed beyond the immediate irritations of rejection slips and professional snubs. While damning the rackets that compel him to prostitute his small but genuine talent, Gordon is uneasily conscious – something that perhaps marks him out as a 1930s anti-hero – that his struggles and resentment are increasingly irrelevant when set against the turmoil beyond the window. In some ways *Aspidistra* is less a novel about a struggling poet who feels himself to be excluded from the citadels of literary power than an attempt to foresee the future by a man who realises that the unsatisfactory arrangements of present-day life are set to be obliterated by something a great deal worse. For this reason it is important to see Orwell in the context of the environments in which he moved – professional, social and political – here in the mid-1930s, with the news from continental Europe growing steadily more alarming. Over six decades later it is easy enough to mark the 1930s down as a single, undifferentiated stretch of time: cloth-capped hordes at the dole queue; Stukas sweeping down over fleeing civilians at Guernica; torchlight glinting off spurred boots; the endless tide of lofted flags. These are characteristic images. To move back into Orwell's own professional terrain, it is impossible to read a serious English novel written after about 1935 without noting a deep sense of unease, often extending to outright dread. And yet contemporary evidence suggests that it is possible to separate the 1930s into several distinct phases: two years of deep depression, from 1929 to 1931, culminating in the formation of the National Government; a period of recovery when Hitler's rise was something that was going on elsewhere; the moment in 1936 when Franco seized the Spanish colonial possessions and began the three-year civil war; followed by a definite 'pre-war' period (again, one sees this in the novels of the time) when everyone knew that armed aggression was inevitable. 'The years 1933–6 were on the whole pleasant ones,' Alec Waugh wrote nearly half a century later in his autobiography. Waugh was a playboy novelist with a rich wife who came no closer to the privations of Jarrow than the cinema newsreels, but plenty of other people without four-figure incomes thought so too. It was the age of *Kristallnacht* and the reclamation of the Rhineland, but it was also the age of Stanley Baldwin's 'Safety First' and Lord Halifax's suave diplomatising.

The literary context in which Orwell can be located needs a similar readjustment. We tend to see the 1930s as the era of Auden, Spender, Isherwood and, occasionally dominating them to the exclusion of all else, Orwell himself. They were this, of course, but they were also a great deal more. As ever, English literary life offered a bewildering spectacle of contending interest groups, hierarchies old and new, mavericks, wire-pullers and the frankly unclassifiable. The old 1920s power bases operated by Bloomsbury and the Sitwells were still going strong. Newer, fashionable writers could be found grouped around such standards as the short-lived magazine *Night and Day* (Graham Greene, Evelyn Waugh, Elizabeth Bowen, Peter Fleming, Cyril Connolly). Beyond London a corpus of narrowly realist and defiantly working-class literature, exemplified by Walter Greenwood's *Love on the Dole* (1933), was taking root in the English regions. However, little of this inno-vation, experiment and political purpose disturbed the placid surfaces of middle-class taste. The great middlebrow bestsellers – Priestley, Walpole, Deeping – all the famous names that Gordon anathematises in *Aspidistra*, sailed on unbuffeted by the modernist tide. It was the great age of the Boot's Library, of the literary tea party, of the sedative fireside chats offered up by Ralph Straus, the chief critic of the *Sunday Times*. The programme of the 1936 *Sunday Times* Book Club exhibition, staged over a two-week period at the Dorland Hall, Lower Regent Street, gives a fair idea of the kind of material favoured by the contemporary mass taste. Here audiences could listen to A.E.W. Mason on 'The Historical Novel', watch Alec Waugh whip the cover from 'A Story-teller's Workbench', hear Peter Fleming describe the experience of 'Travelling

Light', thrill with Dorothy L. Sayers over 'The Tendency to Murder', or respectfully assimilate the Rt. Hon. Duff Cooper's thoughts on 'Biography'. Orwell was not a part of this world, either socially or economically – the average advance for a bestselling 'commercial' novel in the 1930s was £500, about three times his annual income – but this does not mean that he was altogether excluded from the literary networks. *Aspidistra* contains a terrific scene in which Gordon, invited to a party by an influential critic, turns up on the wrong day, is convinced that the mistake is deliberate and meant to humiliate him, writes an abusive reply to his host's note of apology and thereby burns his remaining bridge to the official literary world. Orwell, on the other hand, used the publication of *Burmese Days* to renew his friendship with Cyril Connolly, a useful man to know in his *New Statesman* phase. Connolly would become one of his most reliable and supportive patrons. The idea of Orwell as central to the literary movements of his time is a nonsense. But so, too, is the notion of the eternal, embittered outsider.

Above all, it was an age in which literary life became steadily more politicised. This was true even of the literary society perpetuated by the likes of the *Sunday Times* Book Club. Fact-finding missions to Moscow, under the auspices of the Soviet authorities, became the 1930s equivalent of the modern international literary festival. Even Beverley Nichols, the era's best-known literary socialite, spent a week in a Glasgow tenement in a fruitless search for copy. While Orwell had not yet arrived at anything resembling a coherent set of political beliefs, the Hampstead job placed him, for the first time in his life, in the day-to-day company of people for whom politics – left-wing politics – was a consuming interest. Part of this immersion was down to Rees (Ravelston in *Keep the Aspidistra Flying* has been trying 'for years' to convert Gordon to Socialism without ever succeeding in interesting him in it) but a greater impetus may have come from the Westropes, who were longstanding and proselytising members of the Independent Labour Party (ILP). Bernard Crick has pointed out the consistent allure of the ILP to the averagely discontented left-leaning 1930s intellectual. Founded as long ago as 1893 under the aegis of Keir Hardie himself, it had been instrumental in forging the great Socialist alliances of the early 1900s in which trade unions, middle-class Fabians and dis-illusioned liberals were brought together in the Labour Representation Committee. Scarcely a single ornament of the early Parliamentary Labour Party had failed to cut his or her teeth in the ILP – the notable exception was Attlee – and Ramsay MacDonald and Philip Snowden, later to become the first Labour Chancellor, had both been leading lights. Thirty years later, though, the ILP was no more than a tiny and exclusive sect (Aneurin Bevan used to twit his fiancée Jennie Lee over her 'virginity' in preferring it to the broad church of the 1930s Labour Party proper) personified in the figure of Ellen Wilkinson, the left-wing MP for Jarrow and author of an incendiary book describing her constituency's Depression-era poverty, *The Town That Was Murdered*. Nonetheless, the ILP's maverick status, anti-reactionary but democratic, not quite pacifist, avowedly revolutionary, gave it a definite appeal to disillusioned Socialists beyond the Labour mainstream. Simultaneously, the Westropes' contacts went well beyond it, in fact almost to the margins of respectable political discourse. It was through them, for example, that Orwell met Reg Groves, the celebrated Trotskyist firebrand who had preceded him in the shop. At the very least these new connections extended Orwell's political range. They may not have encouraged him to join a political party, but they prompted him to think about social and economic problems in terms that wouldn't previously have occurred, or appealed, to him.

Outside working hours Orwell was far from being the bedsit-bound recluse of *Aspidistra*, clandestinely flushing used tea-leaves down the WC when his landlady's back is turned. Evening chats with Kimche focused on Roman Catholicism and its baleful influence on public life: Orwell was reluctant to talk about his work, Kimche remembered. He was off, too, on his habitual quest for female company. 'Sally', a commercial artist who provided the professional background for Gordon's girlfriend Rosemary, kept him at arm's length, but he was on much more intimate terms with a girl named Kay Ekevall, whom he met in the shop some time in the autumn of 1934. Eight years younger than Orwell, independent-minded to a degree with which he would not have been familiar (Brenda Salkeld and Eleanor Jaques, by comparison, were nice middle-class girls living in provincial sequestration), she seems to have been fond of him while finding many of his attitudes faintly ridiculous. Kay was struck by her boyfriend's bad health. He was 'a nice-looking fellow' but somehow desiccated, with a pale, dry skin 'as if he'd been dried up in the Burma heat'. Liking Orwell, and prepared to go to bed with him, which many of her contemporaries would not have been, she was conscious of a relationship impeded on the surface by what to her seemed archaic social observances and beneath by a much more fundamental divide. Going Dutch on a date, for instance, was always problematic in the light of Orwell's 'ultra-masculine' tendencies. Beyond this she believed that while Orwell liked women well enough, 'I don't think he regarded them as a force in life'.

The real action, Kay implies, was to be found in all-male literary chat or at the solitary writer's desk. Strolling with him across Hampstead Heath or lounging in the nearby cafés, Kay noted several other distinctive traits. One of them was an obsession with money, frequently colliding with, or perhaps only offering a symptom of, a profound self-pity. Orwell, according to Kay, imagined himself 'the victim of injustice because he was poor and couldn't afford the things he felt he ought to have and had to struggle for things . . .' Rather like Gordon, who gets riotously drunk after cashing a cheque for an American magazine, he was fond of making a splash when in funds. There was a suspicion, too, of a man who though broadly progressive in outlook (Kay had to listen to many an anti-Imperial harangue) failed to confront many of the shibboleths of his upbringing: 'I don't think he faced up to a lot of his prejudices. I think he preserved them carefully.' Prone to portraying himself as rather a rebel, Orwell remained inextricably welded to the upper-middle-class value system he had grown up with, affecting to despise the advantages of a public school education but, Kay observed, finding it difficult to talk to anyone who was not on his intellectual wavelength. Undoubtedly much of the gap between them was generational – one notes a similar tone of amused affection in the reminiscences of other younger friends from this period in his life – but there is also a sense of someone failing to meet the exacting standards of the 1930s progressive package, still happily mired in the conditioning of his early life.

Much as he enjoyed his evenings with Kay, and the after-hours chats with whichever guests the Westropes might happen to have on the premises, Orwell's chief concern in the latter months of 1934 was his professional life. He was continuing to write for the *Adelphi* and still absorbed in rather esoteric theological works. The November issue found him reviewing Christopher Dawson's *Medieval Religion* ('What a relief to find that even in England there are Roman Catholic writers who can give us something better than the braying of Belloc or the twittering of Knox'). But his principal interest lay in the progress of *A Clergyman's Daughter*, then making its way through the legal and editorial minefield laid around it by Victor Gollancz. The ever-wary Gollancz had commissioned no fewer than three readers' reports, all of which praised the novel while expressing certain reservations. Gerald

Gould, the firm's chief reader and an influential figure on the reviewing circuit (he was chief critic of the *Observer*) thought the book an extraordinary piece of work while considering the school scenes overdrawn and the 'Night town' pastiche, though powerfully done, an artistic mistake. Harold Rubinstein, appraising the manuscript from both a forensic and an aesthetic angle, thought that the legal difficulties might be overcome, while complaining that the novel's five different sections were too loosely connected. Norman Collins, Gollancz's junior director, advised changes which he suspected that Orwell would be unwilling to make. Though Orwell was agreeable to revisions, Gollancz continued to worry about libel for several months, almost until the eve of publication the following spring. In a letter of mid-November Orwell admits to Moore that the school scenes are 'overdone'. Having seen Gollancz in Henrietta Street five days later, he agreed to tone them down. The typescript went back in mid-December ('Reference to Roman Catholic priest cut out ... Reference to Sunday Express cut out'), the Ringwood House extravagances blue-pencilled. As late as February Gollancz was still torturing himself over the Blifil-Gordon sugar-beet refinery, Ye Olde Tea Shoppe, Miss Mayfill, Mrs Semprill and countless other minor points of detail.

Meanwhile, inspired by his new surroundings and the dusty atmosphere of the shop, Orwell had begun a new novel. Initial progress was slow, although he did manage to complete a poem, 'St Andrew's Day', ultimately attributed to Gordon Comstock in *Aspidistra*, first published in the *Adelphi* in late 1935 but undoubtedly going back to the November of the previous year. Though conservative in form, it is one of Orwell's best performances in verse, vividly evoking the sweep of the north London roof-tops:

> Sharply the menacing wind sweeps over
> The bending poplars, newly bare,
> And the dark ribbons of the chimneys
> Veer downward, flicked by wisps of air,
> Torn posters flutter; coldly sounds
> The boom of trams and the rattle of hooves,
> And the clerks who hurry to the station
> Look, shuddering over the endless rooves ...

The poem then turns into a mordant appraisal of 'the money-god' who, among other iniquities, is responsible for contraception, laying 'the sleek, estranging shield' (i.e. a condom) 'between the lover and his bride'.

Work, both at Booklovers' Corner and at his desk at Warwick Mansions, together with an exhausting social life, left him tired. He was keeping odd hours, he told Brenda early in the New Year, coming home from a friend's house on a Sunday night, forced to walk several miles in drizzle owing to the absence of buses or trams, and then arriving in Hampstead to find himself locked out. But there was encouraging news about *Burmese Days*. Having nervously considered the matter and balanced his fear of the law with the conviction that Orwell was one of his most promising younger writers, Gollancz was prepared to go ahead if, in Orwell's words, 'time was taken'. Effectively this meant Orwell producing, with the help of contemporary directories, concrete proof that no *roman-à-clef* element survived. These negotiations coincided with a move from Warwick Mansions – Mrs Westrope was ill and the presence of a lodger was inconvenient – to a flat at nearby 77 Parliament Hill, found for him by Mabel Fierz, who knew the landlady, Mrs Rosalind Obermeyer. The removal aside, Orwell was concentrating on work. Not much was happening, he reported to Brenda at the end of February. As for the work in progress, 'I want this one to be a work of art, & that can't be done without much bloody sweat.' That Orwell was prepared to devote 'bloody sweat' to what was to be his fourth published work suggests that he had a slightly rosier view of his professional prospects. *A Clergyman's Daughter* was in the press. *Burmese Days* – provided he could convince Gollancz that it was fiction – would follow shortly afterwards. Publishers' lead-times were shorter seventy years ago. An author who delivered his manuscript in late summer could usually expect to see it in print in October. In the event Orwell would end up publishing three novels in a year. Another meeting at Henrietta Street, to which Orwell took a sketch map of 'Kyauktada', presumably to demonstrate its detachment from Katha, cleared the way for *Burmese Days*. 'A few trifling changes which will not take a week,' Orwell reported to Moore, a shade airily in the circumstances as the revisions ultimately enforced by Gollancz and his advisers were relatively extensive.

An advance copy of *A Clergyman's Daughter* went off to Brenda early in March 1935. Orwell pronounced it 'tripe' with the exception of the Trafalgar Square section. An account of his routines at Mrs Obermeyer's was appended: the purchase of a gas stove known as a 'Bachelor Griller' which could grill, boil and fry and allowed him modestly to entertain; a trip to the Coliseum to see the modish Negro dance troop the Blackbirds ('bored stiff'); book-buying excursions for the Westropes. He was also, both through the Fierzes and his landlady, making new friends. Chief among them was Rayner Heppenstall, a young Yorkshireman, recently graduated from Leeds University and a passionate balletomane, first encountered at a dinner at Bertorelli's in a party where the young Dylan Thomas was among the guests. Both Heppenstall and Kay Ekevall were part of a circle that included the young Communist poet Michael Sayers, who cemented the alliance by reviewing *A Clergyman's Daughter* (favourably) in the *Adelphi*. Orwell, though later prone to complain about literary rackets, was not above using his own connections in the marketplace.

A Clergyman's Daughter was officially published on 11 March, to mixed reviews. L.P. Hartley in the *Observer* found the thesis 'neither new nor convincing' but was impressed by the treatment ('sure and bold') and the dialogue. V.S. Pritchett in the *Spectator*, while approving the Trafalgar Square scene's 'immense knowledge of low life', regretted the 'stunt Joyce' style. Orwell was essentially a satirist, Pritchett thought, who by the end of the novel had been lured away into 'the glib amenities of caricature'. Peter Quennell in the *New Statesman* noted Dorothy's curiously cipher-like quality, complaining that 'she is a literary abstraction to whom things happen . . . We have no feeling that her flight from home and her return to the rectory have any valid connection with the young woman herself.' As critical judgement most of this is unarguable, but Orwell could perhaps have consoled himself with the distinction of the reviewers. This, after all, was his fictional début in England, at a time when most first novelists were lucky to be reviewed at all: however far short he may have fallen of Olympus, at least he was being taken seriously. Victor Gollancz remained upbeat, telling Moore that he thought Orwell had the talent to become one of the half-dozen leading authors on a list that in the 1930s included Dorothy L. Sayers and A.J. Cronin.

Looking at Orwell's life at this time – mornings at his desk in Parliament Hill, afternoons in the shop, evenings spent over the Bachelor Griller or sauntering around Hampstead Heath – one is struck by its compartmentalisation. Throughout his adult life, Orwell maintained numberless different 'sides' of which even close friends were barely aware: in more than one case the realisation was knocked to the surface only at his funeral. Even here in his early thirties the alliances he formed and the worlds in which he moved followed no set pattern.

He was an Old Etonian who worked in a second-hand bookshop, an ex-Imperial policeman who wrote interesting but old-fashioned novels and whose younger acquaintances reckoned him rather quaint, a conservative but self-consciously rebellious young man moving towards the outer fringes of the Labour Party. Doubtless the 1930s literary scene offered stranger juxtapositions than this – Anthony Powell, the regular army officer's son carousing in the Wheatsheaf with the bohemian artist Nina Hamnett, or Major Connolly's heir loafing among the expatriate bohemians of the South of France (the background to Connolly's solitary novel, *The Rock Pool*). With Orwell, though, the oppositions seem starker, more incongruous. An account of his activities over the May Bank Holiday weekend granted to mark George V's Silver Jubilee, supplied to Brenda, gives some idea of the various levels on which Orwell was capable simultaneously of living. On the Saturday he went down to Brighton for the day, picked bluebells, inspected birds' nests and returned to London to spend the evening in Chelsea. Short of funds for the rest of the weekend, and with the banks closed, he called at Richard Rees' flat in the hope of borrowing money. Here a kind of Socialist discussion group was in progress. Orwell found himself being harangued by seven or eight left-wingers, including a South Wales miner who told him, 'quite good-naturedly, however', that if he were a dictator Orwell would be instantly shot. There is something faintly mysterious about the distancing procedure that the letter sets in motion. Brenda is invited to regard Orwell as a naïve passer-by walking in off the street to be subjected to a bizarre left-wing shouting match. But the real Orwell knew Rees intimately, knew the kind of people likely to be meeting at his flat, would not have stayed for the three-hour period mentioned had he not been interested in and reasonably *au fait* with the issues at stake. It would be overstating the case to say that Orwell is trying to conceal something in this account of practical politics *chez* Rees, but there is a distinct sense of someone trying hard to preserve an air of detachment.

Late June, barely three months after his last date with the critics, brought the UK publication of *Burmese Days*. The novel was positively received, barring the odd sniff from conservative quarters such as the *Times Literary Supplement*, whose anonymous reviewer – possibly an old Burma hand – thought that 'the inaccuracies are no worse than in pleasant books which idealise the East' and that, additionally, Orwell's strictures on the work-rates of colonial bureaucrats show that 'he can hardly have mixed with the men who really run the country'. Sean

O'Faolain in the *Spectator*, alternatively, thought that 'Mr Orwell has his own merits and his own methods and they are absolutely competent in their class'. The book had important personal consequences. Among the correspondence it provoked was a letter from the anthropologist Geoffrey Gorer, who remained a close friend for the rest of Orwell's life. Cyril Connolly had admired the novel too – he reviewed it in the *New Statesman* – and the upshot was a reunion at Mrs Obermeyer's flat where the Bachelor Griller was pressed into service to provide *bifteck aux pommes*. Thirteen years on from his last sighting, Connolly was taken aback by his old friend's prematurely aged look. 'Well, Connolly, I can see you've worn a good deal better than I have,' was Orwell's opening remark. Connolly supposed that Orwell would be quite as discountenanced by his own fat, cigar-smoking persona, but the alliance, once reforged, persisted until death.

Presumably Connolly's appearance on Mrs Obermeyer's carpet – the epitome of the well-connected young literary man – brought some of *Keep the Aspidistra Flying*'s subject matter into sharper focus. The novel wasn't getting on too badly, he told Moore in May. He was also exploiting a recently acquired outlet for his literary journalism. Though by no means as prestigious as the *Spectator* or the *New Statesman*, the *New English Weekly* offered a venue for some of Orwell's best pieces of late 1930s criticism. His review of Henry Miller's *Tropic of Cancer* – a book which made a lasting impression on him – appeared there later in the year. Another early piece for the paper's editor Philip Mairet, was a round-up of three recent novels, including one that he might have been expected to like. This was the single-volume edition of Patrick Hamilton's enormous London trilogy, *Twenty Thousand Streets under the Sky*. Orwell's initial distrust ('a huge, well-meaning book, as shapeless and inert as a clot of frogspawn') is odd, as the milieu, a compound of mean streets, desperate love affairs and shabby-genteel parlours, was one in which he specialised himself. The likelihood is that he was simply put off, if not by envy (Hamilton's stage play *Rope*, later filmed by Hitchcock, had made him a wealthy young man) then by the comparisons to J.B. Priestley, who contributed a foreword: in later life Hamilton was one of the contemporary novelists that younger *Tribune* writers remembered him admiring.

It was at about this time – though the original stimulus came a month or two before – that Orwell's vagrant emotional life underwent a decisive shift. The affair with Kay had now been going on for some time. The fervent sign-offs to the regular letters to Brenda Salkeld ('With much love and many kisses') suggest that Orwell still hoped for some consolation in that quarter. But in the spring of 1935 Orwell and his landlady gave a joint party at Parliament Hill. Mrs Obermeyer was studying Psychology at University College London. She invited several of her fellow-students, one of whom was a dark-haired, pale-skinned girl named Eileen O'Shaughnessy. Eileen, two years younger, talkative and lively, made a distinct impression on the co-host. That was the kind of girl he would like to marry, he informed his landlady before the evening was out. Orwell being Orwell, with serious intentions on display, the early stages of their courtship included horse-riding on Blackheath, near the O'Shaughnessys' home at Greenwich. Within three weeks Orwell had as good as proposed. He got an equivocal response. Eileen was intrigued, without being at all ready to commit herself.

Rather like her angular suitor, Eileen had a varied career behind her. Of Irish descent, but born in South Shields where her father worked for the Customs and Excise, she was unusual among women of her generation in possessing an Oxford English degree. Subsequently she taught in a girls' boarding-school, took odd clerical and administrative jobs and then ran her own typing agency, giving it up in her late twenties to study for the UCL Master's degree. Of medium height, with a 'heart-shaped face' and 'Irish colouring', pretty rather than beautiful, Eileen never quite comes wholly into view in the recollections of Orwell's closer friends. Anthony Powell and his wife were fond of her while remembering her 'defensive' side. A friend puzzled over her 'curiously elusive personality'. Publicly, cheerfulness and efficiency were well to the fore. An ILP volunteer who came across her two years later in Spain, likened her to 'a pleasant young schoolmistress', briskly setting the affairs of the ILP contingent in order. Cyril Connolly's compliments are sincere but unrevealing: charming, intelligent, independent. However enigmatic she may ultimately have been, however ineluctable her qualities, there is widespread agreement among Orwell's friends at the time that Eileen cheered him up, took him out of himself, gave him confidence in his abilities. Kay, who met her once or twice, was happy to recede into the background: 'she was gay and lively and interesting, and much more on his level'. At the same time Eileen was under no illusions. Devoted to her brother Laurence, a thoracic surgeon to whom she occasionally acted as secretary, she was aware that blood ran deeper. 'If we were at opposite sides of the world and I sent him a telegram saying "come at once" he would come,' she once told a friend. 'George would not do that. For him work comes before anything.' Eileen's letters, of which several survive, are wonderful things: full of wit, affection and exuberance. Yet in the retrospective glare of Orwell's reputation, she never quite exists in her own right. One could read Orwell's account of the time they spent together in Morocco – sedulous nature notes and climatic observation – without ever realising that another person was there.

Orwell concentrated his gaze on Eileen in a way that, with the possible exception of Eleanor Jacques three years previously, he had never done before. Their relationship developed steadily through the summer, presumably furthered by another change of address. Early in August, Orwell established a male *ménage à trois* consisting of himself, Heppenstall and Sayers at 56 Lawford Road NW5. This was in Kentish Town, a resolutely working-class district to the south of Booklovers' Corner, and consisted of a three-bedroom first-floor flat; the ground floor and basement were occupied, respectively, by a tram-driver and his wife and a plumber and his family. Though the rent was split three ways the flat mostly contained only Orwell and Heppenstall, Sayers, 'the generally absent third tenant' in Heppenstall's words, preferring to use the premises only for assignations. In an atmosphere of mild semi-bohemianism – both Heppenstall and Sayers were aspiring literary men – Orwell figured as the somewhat more responsible senior partner. It was he, for example, who had his name on the rent book. Sayers recalled a somewhat 'severe' flatmate, strict about routine but happy to put himself out on his friends' behalf. Bringing Sayers a cup of tea as he lay in bed in the morning – cigarette always drooping from his mouth, the younger man remembered – he would deliver himself of such statements as 'Don't let me do any writing today, Michael. I'm full of malice and spite.' Looking back Heppenstall conceded that the younger men rather exploited 'old Eric': their attitude to a man eight years older and without the benefit of a university education contained a certain amount of condescension. Nevertheless Orwell was prepared to confide his romantic aspirations to Heppenstall, telling him in September that 'You are right about Eileen. She is the nicest person I have met for a long time.' Lawford Road was also the scene of a famous, and from the point of view of the injured party prophetic, incident. Late one night Heppenstall, whose interest in ballet extended to the pursuit of ballet girls, came back from the theatre so drunk that he was forced to crawl noisily up the stairs. There he found Orwell waiting for him. According to Heppenstall, writing the encounter up twenty years later, Orwell's monologue went as follows: '. . . Bit thick you know . . . This time of night . . . Wake up the whole street . . . I can put up with a lot . . . A bit of consideration . . . After all . . .'

Heppenstall, having remonstrated rather feebly, woke up ten minutes later with a bloodied nose. After crawling into the absent Sayers' room, he discovered that Orwell had locked him inside. Heppenstall battered at the door. He was then confronted by the sight of his flatmate brandishing a shooting-stick. Orwell first hit him across the legs, then raised the stick above his head with what Heppenstall describes as 'a curious mixture of fear and sadistic exaltation'. Rolling aside to dodge the blow, which descended on a chair, Heppenstall managed to evade further punishment, eventually being tidied up by the tram-driver and his wife.

It is a bizarre episode, but before erecting it as a monument to the 'darker side' that more than one critic has detected in Orwell several points should be borne in mind. The first is that the incident certainly happened. Mabel Fierz, with whom Heppenstall took refuge the next morning, confirmed this. The second is that it was recast many years later and in the light of new information about Orwell, and Orwell's writings, that was not then to hand (Heppenstall could not, for example, have produced a phrase like 'sadistic exaltation' before *Nineteen Eighty-Four*, to which the words clearly relate). The third is that in his writings about other writers Heppenstall nearly always has a secret agenda concealed below the surface. Famously touchy, liable to resent the superior literary talents that he came across in the course of his later professional life at the BBC – Evelyn Waugh was a notorious example – he was not above belittling their achievements indirectly. The question 'How can a man who hits a drunken friend with a stick still be a great writer?' is never stated in so many words in Heppenstall's account of the scuffle on the Lawford Road stairs, but it lurks there all the same, along with the retrospective glosses of fear and sadistic exaltation. Undoubtedly the middle-aged Heppenstall saw it as a great symbolic climacteric, and yet the evidence suggests it was simply a momentary quarrel between two friends, neither of them known for their flexibility. Michael Sayers's memory of the incident is that it had a political context, and was sparked off by Heppenstall's friendship with Middleton Murry, whom Orwell currently (and almost certainly wrongly) suspected of Mosleyite leanings. Significantly, the friendship endured and Orwell's letters from later in the year bear no trace of any lasting grievance. Confronted with a genuine sadist, you feel, Heppenstall would have kept him at arm's length.

Unquestionably, Orwell had an authoritarian side: he could scarcely have survived for five years in the Burma Police without one. What he said of Jack London – that he could foresee Fascism because he had a Fascist streak in himself – is probably quite as true of the mind that produced Big Brother, Room 101 and the cage of starving rats. Orwell's insights into the psychology of totalitarianism rarely look as if they were garnered second-hand – he knew all this, the reader feels; he worked it out for himself – but it would be a mistake to turn the lofted shooting-stick into the symbol of Orwell's totalitarian shadow.

Autumn came, and with it more work on *Keep the Aspidistra Flying*. It is a mark of Orwell's rising status that Moore had begun negotiating for him to write a serial for the *News Chronicle*. This kind of engage-ment for a popular newspaper was an accepted part of the pre-war literary man's routine. The formula was outlined by the celebrated literary agent A.D. Peters: 'A serial is 80,000 words. You write a five-thousand word first instalment, setting out the situation; the hero meets the heroine in the course of it; it must have a punch in the last line. Then you write a second instalment of three thousand words; that must have a punch-line too. The editor will commission it on the first two instalments.' These were lucrative commissions – the going rate was £350 – with an opportunity to turn the end result into a novel. Orwell, perhaps predictably, was singularly unsuited to the work. A letter of late September to Heppenstall talks of 'unspeakable torments' over its composition. No trace remains either of the story or of what it may have been about, though presumably the Peters template was followed. Finally after a week of 'agony', the 'beastly thing' was forwarded to Moore with 'small hope' that it would be any good. Orwell was right: it was his only attempt to write fiction for the popular press. But there was much else to think about. His novel was moving towards completion. He was planning a holiday in Southwold, from where he could travel up the coast to see Heppenstall who was staying with Middleton Murry in Norfolk. Eileen would not marry him as things stood – she had no real income and did not wish to be a drain on his resources – but held out hope for the following year, once she had finished her course. Testimony to his professional status came in an invitation to address the South Woodford Literary Society, from whose platform he spoke to over 400 people about *Down and Out* ('went over big', he told Heppenstall). The Lawford Road ménage was breaking up. By mid-autumn only Orwell remained, and the rent was putting a strain on his finances. Was there any prospect of an advance from Gollancz?

he wondered to Moore at the beginning of November: money worries were the last thing he wanted while he laboured over the closing sections of his book.

The *New English Weekly* review of *Tropic of Cancer* gives a hint of the direction in which his mind was moving. Fascinated by Miller's matter-of-fact recapitulation of bedrock bohemian life in 1930s Paris, he was quick to relate the novel's worm's-eye view of the world to the decay in religious belief. One result of this breakdown, Orwell suggested, had been 'a sloppy idealisation of the physical side of life'. A book like *Tropic of Cancer*, which dealt with sex by brutally insisting on the facts, probably swung the pendulum too far, but it was swinging it in the right direction. Man was not a Yahoo, Orwell concluded, but he was rather like a Yahoo and needed to be reminded of it from time to time. The same interest in lives examined from within stirs in an *Adelphi* review from earlier in the year of the working-class writer Jack Hilton's *Caliban Shrieks*. The book dealt with its subject *from the inside*, Orwell noted: instead of a catalogue of 'facts' relating to poverty the reader was left with a vivid notion of what it felt like to be poor. Orwell responded to books of this kind because they pushed him in a direction he wished to go himself, even if, as in *A Clergyman's Daughter*, the requirements of fiction occasionally got in the way.

And what, by extension, did it feel like to be Gordon Comstock, a moth-eaten young poet working in a dingy bookshop by day, frowsting in Mrs Wisbeach's ghastly boarding-house by night and pursuing the loving but virginal Rosemary – in other words, not at all like Orwell, who by the end of 1935 had published three books, lived in his own flat and was more or less engaged to be married? Of all the fiction that Orwell produced in the 1930s, *Keep the Aspidistra Flying* – the title tracks backwards to the mock-hymn warbled by the defrocked cleric Mr Tallboys in the Trafalgar Square scenes of *A Clergyman's Daughter* – is the one most closely associated with him as a writer. And yet it exists at a decidedly odd angle to the kind of person he was and was becoming – on the one hand providing yet another view of the world that can be identified with Orwell's own, on the other moving light years beyond it to magnify his obsessions and produce, in the end, a terminally ground-down feeling that many critics have linked to the immensely gloomy late-Victorian novelist George Gissing. *Aspidistra* is a transitional novel, the beginnings of a route out of the environments in which Orwell had previously dealt to a time when, as Anthony Powell put it, the Gissing had to stop. Gordon Comstock is the grandson of a self-made Victorian plutocrat whose vitality has dissipated itself among a tribe of ineffectual and by now impoverished descendants altogether crushed by the weight of his oppressive personality. A well-regarded poet – his solitary collection is thought to show 'exceptional promise' – Gordon is at war with both the appurtenances and the ethics of 'respectable' life (the aspidistra, which lurks in every room he has ever inhabited, is a potent symbol of this struggle) to the extent of giving up his job as an advertising agency copywriter (advertising is characterised as 'the last rattling of the swill-bucket') and taking refuge in Mr Mckechnie's bookshop. Gordon is supported in this endeavour by his chief professional patron, Ravelston, and his girlfriend Rosemary, the one because he respects Gordon's pursuit of principle, the other because she, albeit chastely, loves him. Each, though, is increasingly conscious – as also, deep down, is Gordon himself – that days spent in the dreadful pastiche version of Booklovers' Corner and nights husbanding his cigarettes *chez* Wisbeach don't offer the conditions in which poetry, or at any rate 'good poetry', gets written. Born of an atmosphere of penny-pinching, sexual frustration, envy and seediness, Gordon's serial fulminations on the state of the world, the literary rackets which he believes discriminate against him, women and money have a dreadful circularity. However much the reader is prepared to sympathise with him – and Gordon for some reason is a curiously attractive figure – one senses that he is quite unappeasable, that most of what he has to say is simply the projection of a vast inner dissatisfaction.

Before very long Gordon's affairs lurch towards crisis. Had up in court after a calamitous drinking bout – the result of an unexpected cheque from an American magazine – he loses his job and ends up staffing a threadbare twopenny lending library run by the rapacious Mr Cheeseman. Even by the standards of second-hand bookselling this is something of a comedown, but Gordon is defiant. The warm, careless 'underground' world of life on a few shillings a week is what he ardently desires. Ravelston, approving the principle, affects to support him while privately thinking Gordon's retreat from the pretence of a civilised life a mistake. Rosemary is merely uncomprehending. Then, visiting him one afternoon in his shabby lodgings ('Even in the bad light of the lamp she could see the state of filth the room was in – the litter of food and papers on the table, the grate full of cold ashes, the foul crocks in the fender, the dead aspidistra') she consents, finally, to sleep with him. Later, confronted with the inescapable fact of her pregnancy, Gordon is faced with a stark choice: either he abandons her or takes the path

back to respectability. Not without certain private misgivings he settles
for respectability and resumes his old job at the agency. The novel ends
with them, newly married, in their tiny flat off the Edgware Road, and
an ironic sign-off: 'once again, things were happening in the Comstock
family'.

The chief flaw in this luminous exercise in the shabby-genteel – as
Orwell, schooled in the fiction of the gloomy early twentieth-century
American naturalist tradition, would have known – is how little the
ending convinces. Gissing, to take the novelist with whom *Aspidistra*-
era Orwell is most frequently compared, is nearly always true to his
aesthetic principles. Having established an inexorable progress, or
descent, he sticks by it. Reardon, the unsuccessful novelist of *New Grub
Street*, and Peak, the frustrated anti-hero of *Born in Exile*, fail in their
ambitions: they die conscious of not having achieved the goals in life
they set out to capture. A proper determinist finale would have seen
Gordon simply frittering away his days in the slum bedsitter or engaged
in some squalid liaison with a woman of the streets, and Rosemary
ending up in a home for unmarried mothers. As it is, Gordon merely
turns over a new leaf, is miraculously given back the 'good' job he so
capriciously threw over and assumes, in the way that one puts on a new
overcoat, a system of values that he has spent the previous 200 pages of
the novel angrily repudiating.

Orwell's own personal circumstances are infinitely removed from the
essentially solitary world stalked by Gordon Comstock, the author of
Mice, but *Keep the Aspidistra Flying* is full of unobtrusive nuggets of autobiography – Gordon's schoolboy 'rebellion', the long poem on which he
desultorily works ('two thousand lines or so, in rhyme royal, describing
a day in London'); even the description of the police cell where Gordon
comes to ground is derived from the *Adelphi* essay of 1931. Simultaneously it offers a series of snapshots of how Orwell was developing as
a writer: the early aestheticism still much in evidence but being steadily
overlaid with an ominous, prefigurative gleam. Idling at an evening
street market, for example, Gordon watches three teenage girls, their
faces 'clustering side by side like a truss of blossom on a Sweet William
or Phlox'. When he stares at the most arresting of the trio, 'a delicate
flush like a wave of aquarelle flooded her face'. Elizabeth's face in
Burmese Days was described with exactly the same painterly precision.
Some of the rapturous nature notes that accompany Gordon and
Rosemary's excursion to Burnham Beeches would not look out of place
in the earlier novel:

Down the road the mist-dimmed hedges wore that strange purplish brown, the colour of brown medlar, that naked brushwood takes on in winter. Suddenly, as they came out on to the road again, the dew all down the hedge glittered with a diamond flash. The sun had pierced the clouds. The light came slanting and yellow across the fields, and delicate unexpected colours sprang out in everything, as though some giant's child had been let loose with a new paintbox.

The curious, though in Orwell's case by now predictable, thing about this is that it exists side by side with an habitual and ever more exaggerated fastidiousness about smells, squalor and decay. Here, for example, Gordon returns from the bar of the determinedly down-market working-class pub into which he has dragged the unwilling Ravelston, with two pint glasses of beer:

They were thick cheap glasses, thick as jam jars almost, and dim and greasy. A thin yellow froth was subsiding on the beer. The air was thick with gunpowdery tobacco smoke. Ravelston caught sight of a well-filled spittoon near the bar and averted his eye. It crossed his mind that this beer had been sucked up from some beetle-ridden cellar through yards of slimy tube, and that the glasses had never been washed in their lives, only rinsed in beery water.

Here in his early thirties half of Orwell is still hankering after an old-fashioned 1890s aestheticism, while the other half cheerfully extracts a Swiftian horror from the processes of ordinary life. Above them sounds a small but insistent prophetic note. 'Presently the aeroplanes are coming,' Gordon reflects early on in the proceedings. 'Zoom-whizz-crash! The whole world is going up in a roar of high explosive.' 'My poems are dead because I'm dead. You're dead. We're all dead. Dead people in a dead world,' Gordon lectures Rosemary in an uncannily accurate foreshadowing of *Nineteen Eighty-Four*. Even the poster advertising a preventative against sweaty feet that Gordon works on after his return to the agency – 'P.P. [pedic perspiration] WHAT ABOUT YOU?' (the slogan is reckoned to have a 'sinister simplicity') – seems only a short distance away from the world of Big Brother and the Thought Police.

Above all, *Keep the Aspidistra Flying* is a novel about the condition of being a writer and the environment in which the average literary life is lived, an inter-war instalment in a literary tradition that goes back to

Pendennis and *New Grub Street* and then on to a novel like Anthony Powell's *Books Do Furnish a Room*. As he reached the closing stages Orwell heard of something that would dramatically change his own writing environment, indeed have a decisive effect on the whole course of his future life. It came from Victor Gollancz and consisted of a proposal that Orwell should spend time researching social conditions in the north of England with the aim of producing a piece of extended reportage.

It would be wrong to present Orwell's acceptance of the offer that produced *The Road to Wigan Pier* as a Damascene conversion – the first step on the road to the full-blooded Socialism of the later 1930s. Neither, apparently, was there any strong financial inducement (although Orwell told Geoffrey Gorer that he could not have made the journey without Gollancz's support). Everything to do with the venture, in fact, was provisional. There was no guarantee that Orwell could produce a book about the depressed industrial heartland nor any undertaking that what he wrote would be published. Nevertheless early in 1936 he left Lawford Road, and camped for a few days at Warwick Mansions. The stay with the Westropes lasted just long enough for him to hand in his manuscript and write an essay on Kipling's death for the *New English Weekly* – a shrewd appreciation in which regret at Kipling's Imperialist tendencies is balanced by an awareness of the profound effect his work had had on Orwell's boyhood. Then, on 31 January, with the first salvoes over the new novel's potential for libel ringing in his ears, he left London for the north.

Part Three
1936–1939

9

English Journeys

The fact to which we have got to cling, as to a lifeboat, is that it *is*
possible to be a normal decent person and yet to be fully alive. –
Review of Cyril Connolly's *The Rock Pool*, 1936

I thought how dreadful a destiny it was to be kneeling in the gutter
of a back-alley in the bitter cold, prodding a stick up a blocked
drain. – Diary, 15 February 1936

On the last day of January 1936 Orwell travelled to Coventry by train.
The night was spent at a bed-and-breakfast – 'v. lousy', he recorded in
the journal he now began – at a charge of 3s. 6d. Over the next week
he made his way north by a combination of public transport and his own
two feet, walking enormous distances along the wintry Midlands roads.
The first day of February took him on foot to Birmingham, then by bus
to Stourbridge, then on foot again to a nearby youth hostel. The
account he left of this purposeful and observant progress is curiously
double-sided, awe and distaste for the dark, satanic landscapes mixed
with sedulous nature notes. Scarcely a rook pursued its reluctant mate
across the Staffordshire hedgerows, you sometimes feel, without Orwell
gamely following in the rear. By the end of his third day on the road he
had got as far as Stafford, putting up at a temperance hotel where the
bill for 'the usual dreadful room' was five shillings. By now something of
a connoisseur of down-market accommodation, Orwell was familiar
with its incidental discomforts. The Temperance Hotel's bathroom
turned up a commercial traveller developing his snapshots; eventually
he was prevailed upon to retire.

Orwell probably had no very clear idea where he was going. The
Adelphi had a string of regional representatives and agents, whose
addresses had been promised to him by Richard Rees, but these had not
yet arrived. Rees had been given a poste restante address in

Manchester. Before leaving London Orwell had written to Jack Hilton, author of *Caliban Shrieks*, asking if he could come and stay with him in Hilton's home town of Rochdale. Hilton, active in the burgeoning National Unemployed Workers' Movement (NUWM) and with the relevant statistics at his fingertips, had suggested Wigan as the best place for an incoming southerner to grasp the full magnitude of conditions in the depressed north. The likelihood is that Orwell intended to make for Manchester and then use Rees' list of contacts to plot a proper itinerary east and west of the Pennines. By 3 February he was moving on through the Pottery towns of Hanley and Burslem. Here it was bitterly cold. Signs of poverty were everywhere to hand, Orwell noted, in the streets full of draggled inhabitants and the poor shops. Rudyard Lake, a municipal amenity further along the trail, depressed him horribly. Shut up for the winter and frozen over, its surface covering of ice had broken into blocks which the wind had blown to the southern end and set clanking up and down. 'The most depressing noise I ever heard,' he thought, making a never-realised note to use the image in a novel with a cigarette packet bobbing up and down on the floes. He pressed on to another youth hostel, set in what seemed to be a sham nineteenth-century castle and consisting of endless stone passages, lit only by candles. By this stage money was running low. Orwell calculated that he had only 2s. 6d. left, scarcely enough for another night's decent lodging. The next morning dawned so cold that he had to thaw his hands over the fire before he could dress himself. Still heading north-west, he strode on to Macclesfield – another ten miles – ending up in Manchester in mid-afternoon. Here a crisis presented itself. The banks were already shut and it proved impossible to find anyone who would cash a cheque. Not fancying a night on the streets, Orwell pawned his scarf for 1s. 9d. and went to a common lodging house. Fortunately Rees' letter had arrived at the post office: he could now find people who could help him on his way.

The contrast between shabby-genteel London and the cobbled streets, factory chimneys and oily rivers of the north-west had an immediate impact on Orwell's imagination. There is a revealing moment in the first chapter of *The Road to Wigan Pier* when he finds himself alone in the lodging house bedroom with a cockney commercial traveller who somehow divines that Orwell is a fellow-southerner. 'The bastards!' he exclaims feelingly. 'The filthy bloody bastards!' This is a specific complaint about the standards in a particular Wigan boarding-house, but it goes deeper than this, symbolises, in fact, a great deal about divides, real and imagined, between North and South, Up Here and Down There, Decency and Squalor. Undoubtedly Orwell's sensitive, nature-loving side was appalled by what he found in the north: the fume-filled air, the factories leaking poison and the banks of shattered window-panes. Nothing in his previous experience of poverty, whether in Paris or the East End doss houses, had quite prepared him for the enormity of the caravan colonies of South Yorkshire. What follows is an intent voyage of discovery: the earnest solitary nosing his way forward through the wreckage of a civilisation. 'Monstrous', 'fearful', 'beastly' – all Orwell's favourite adjectival disparagements are in evidence in his accounts of England north of the Trent. At the same time the isolated figure at the heart of *The Road to Wigan Pier*, quite as much as the isolated figure at the heart of Orwell's novels, is not an accurate representation of the writer who produced it. One of the striking factors of what is offered up as reportage is the anonymity of the supporting cast. Orwell, it might be said, moves almost alone through a hostile world. In reality more or less his every step was abetted by well-wishers and hospitality-providers. This is not to question the value of the reportage, merely to emphasise the way in which the Orwell who appears in his books – *Down and Out* works a similar trick – manages to detach himself from the people around him.

Inevitably Orwell took with him on the train to Coventry all the other parts of his life – his relationship with Eileen (mentioned only in the diary from which *The Road to Wigan Pier* grew) and the erratic progress towards publication of his latest novel. In fact trouble about *Keep the Aspidistra Flying* dogged Orwell's path for several weeks. Shortly before he set out he had received a letter from Dorothy Horsman, one of Victor Gollancz' fellow-directors, enclosing Harold Rubinstein's comments on his solutions to the various suspect passages. Orwell replied to this and the manuscript was sent off to the printer. Then in mid-February Norman Collins wrote proposing further changes, mostly to do with spoof advertisements that were felt to be uncomfortably close to the real thing. The saga continued even beyond Orwell's return of the corrected proofs at the end of the month, when he was asked to make yet further corrections. Orwell's exasperation at what he believed to be not merely timorousness but outright incompetence – why, he wondered, hadn't he been asked to deal with this at an earlier stage of the proceedings? – spilled over in an indignant telegram to Gollancz and a protesting letter to Moore. The book had been 'ruined', he complained. His relationship with Norman Collins, with whom he had dealings during the war, never recovered from this falling-out. Above all, his irritation derived from what he regarded as a pointless distraction, pettifogging details that threatened the single-mindedness of his gaze. Looking at some of the changes that Gollancz required, in the light of the all too litigious contemporary publishing scene, one can see his point. Orwell, 150 miles away and utterly absorbed in a new task, could not.

The conventional view of the early months of 1936, which Orwell to a certain extent encouraged, goes something like this. Gollancz had commissioned him, at considerable expense, to go north to research a piece of reportage for his newly founded Left Book Club. The experience had, *inter alia*, the effect of converting Orwell to Socialism or at any rate strengthening an already serious interest in it; the book sprang seamlessly from what he saw. In fact, each part of this statement needs substantial qualification. The Left Book Club, in whose distinctive tangerine bindings *The Road to Wigan Pier* would eventually emerge, was at this stage barely a gleam in Gollancz's eye: the preliminary lunch between the publisher, the Labour politician Sir Stafford Cripps and the Marxist ideologue John Strachey at which the plan was hatched took place only a week or two before Orwell set out. Then there is the question of the advance Orwell was paid for writing it. According to Geoffrey Gorer, to whom Orwell apparently confided the details, Gollancz offered him £500 to underwrite the trip. By Orwell's standards this was an unprecedented sum – two years' normal income and, even more enticing, enough to get married on: he accepted on the spot. And yet, knowing what we do of Gollancz, this kind of munificence seems highly unlikely. Much as he admired Orwell's work, Gollancz was a prudent operator. In the three years that Orwell had published books under his imprint his total earnings had amounted to not much more than £400. The sum of £500 down, for a work whose final shape could only be guessed at, supposes a free-handedness altogether absent from the rest of Gollancz's long publishing career. (Kingsley Amis could be found twenty years later complaining at his sponsor's stinginess.) And if Orwell had been put in sudden receipt of two years' salary, why was he so manifestly hard up during the second part of 1936, eagerly taking on the role of Hertfordshire village shopkeeper to add to the proceeds of his literary journalism? It seems much more likely that Gorer is confusing the profit Orwell made out of the book after it was published with the much smaller sum – probably no more than £50 – that Gollancz may have handed over to subsidise his travels in February and March.

Another mark of the sketchy nature of the enterprise is that Orwell, when he set out and for some time afterwards, had only the vaguest notion of what he wanted to write. To Rees, a good four weeks into the trip, he reported that he had assembled reams of notes and statistics, 'though in what way I shall use them I haven't made up my mind yet'. As late as October, six months after his return, he was contemplating a book of essays. A letter from Gollancz to Moore from around this time wonders vaguely what Orwell is up to, rather than demanding delivery of a commissioned manuscript. If his ultimate purpose was at this stage uncertain, so, too, was the evidence of any commitment to or genuine understanding of Socialism. One of the people introduced to him by Rees, for example, is described as 'taking a prominent part in the Socialist Movement'. Orwell's distance from that movement is emphasised by the formality of the wording: it could equally well be the Temperance Movement or the Women's Movement. In much the same way a survey of municipal housing policy in Liverpool, which seemed to him essentially Socialist though instigated by Conservatives, inspired some notably amateurish reflections about Socialism and capitalism not being easily distinguishable beyond a certain point. In his thoughts about politics, as much as in the kind of book he intended to write, Orwell was still feeling his way.

So what sent him to the north of England in the first place? Like most modern historical phenomena, the great slump that followed in the wake of the 1929 Wall Street Crash swiftly amassed its own literature. Some of this was working class in origin. A great deal more was provided by middle-class onlookers. The tensions that this split perspective produced are evident in Orwell's own work and in its reception. Concentrated on the industrial heartlands of Lancashire and South Yorkshire – in the 1930s unemployment in Wigan, to which Jack Hilton had directed Orwell, was between 25 and 33 per cent of the population – the Depression was instrumental in effecting the rise of the proletarian writer. This process was not without its ironies. The Birmingham novelist Leslie Halward, for example, would probably never have picked up a pen had he not lost his job as a plasterer. Walter Greenwood, whose *Love on the Dole* (1933) remains one of the genre's enduring classics, began writing novels and plays after being sacked from his post in a Manchester department store. There were other Greenwoods. By the mid-1930s nearly every depressed area had a small and occasionally vociferous contingent of working-class writers: James Hanley in Liverpool, Harry Heslop and J.C. Grant in Durham, Walter

Brearley (author of the emblematically titled *Means-Test Man*) and F.C. Boden in Nottinghamshire. Heslop's *Last Cage Down* (1935), for instance, gives a vivid and dispiriting picture of a Tyneside laid waste by lost orders and mass lay-offs: 'Not a battleship being built. Not a crane moving. Not a man hitting a rivet with a hammer. A great, stultifying death.' As a contributor to a small-scale magazine receptive to this kind of talent – the *Adelphi* was a notable supporter of 'proletarian literature' – Orwell was aware of the phenomenon and had reviewed several of the books associated with it. As he noted in a review of Fred Bowen's *Rolling Stonemason*, 'One of the few encouraging results of universal education is that, at rather rare intervals, books written from a genuinely working-class standpoint are beginning to appear.'

They did so amid a swelling tide of middle-class reportage, typified if not inaugurated by J.B. Priestley's bestselling *English Journey* (1934). Post-Priestley, England north of the Trent became uncomfortably crowded by London literary gentlemen in search of copy. To name only one celebrated visitor, Aldous Huxley set out at exactly the same time as Orwell to inspect the Nottinghamshire coalfields, where he went down mines and visited areas of high unemployment. Further south Orwell had read and appreciated Hugh Massingham's *I Took Off My Tie* (1936) in which the author takes a job as an East End rent collector. Like Massingham's presence in Whitechapel, the books and the journalism that these excursions produced were greeted with considerable suspicion by those on the ground. Orwell's own relationship with Hilton, for example, was deeply uneasy. Having advised him to visit Wigan, Hilton was scathing about the result. 'So George went to Wigan,' he later commented, 'and he might have stayed at home. He wasted money, energy and wrote piffle ... The fatheads of readers, unassociated with what can be done in art with the rough stuff of prole life, got a colour that wasn't worth the paint-mixes.' Orwell's correspondence with Hilton – destroyed by Hilton after the war – would have been rather revealing. One draws attention to it not to call Orwell's motives into question, but to emphasise that none of this – excursions to the north, adventures among the working classes – took place in a vacuum, that there were sides to be taken, corners to be fought, and antagonisms that in the last resort could not be smoothed away.

Much of this lay in wait for Orwell, both in the eight weeks spent travelling on either side of the Pennines and in the months after *The Road to Wigan Pier*'s publication. Armed with Rees' list of contacts he spent a day in the Manchester lodging house before moving on to stay with a couple named Meade, a trade union official and his wife, in the Longsight district. Almost at once he noted some of the confusion provoked by the arrival of left-wing ideology into a conventional northern household. Husband and wife addressed him as 'comrade', although Mrs Meade was 'plainly uncomfortable about this'. The Meades gave him the address of a man named Jerry Kennan, an electrician and Labour activist who lived in Wigan and would be prepared to show him round the district. Orwell arrived on Kennan's doorstep on a Saturday afternoon, 'a tall feller with a pair of flannel bags, a fawn jacket, and a mac'. Under Kennan's escort the visitor was taken to a National Unemployed Workers' Movement centre – everyone was anxious to help, he noted, 'but I cannot get them to treat me precisely as an equal, however' – and was found lodgings with a family called Hornby at 72 Warrington Lane. This was Orwell's first contact with the kind of extended working-class household whose atmosphere *The Road to Wigan Pier* reproduces. As well as Mr Hornby – an out-of-work miner with the habitual pit-man's eye disease, nystagmus – and his wife, their teenage son and a cousin, the small house contained three male lodgers.

It was still terribly cold, with snow on the ground, but most of Orwell's time was taken up in tours around the locale. Turning up at the Co-operative Hall to hear Wal Hannington, the celebrated Socialist orator, he was disappointed: although capable of working up the crowd, Hannington was a poor speaker. The next day he went on a long walk along the town canal in search of the almost mythical pier that was to give his book its title, marvelling at the fearful landscape of slagheaps and blackened chimneys and noting the rats – weak with hunger, he assumed – faltering through the snow. His literary life continued to run briskly, if a shade incongruously, alongside. He was having a most interesting time and picking up all sorts of information, he told Moore on 13 February. Connolly, in whose forthcoming novel *The Rock Pool* he was taking a friendly interest, was informed that the miners were very nice people, warm-hearted and willing to take one for granted. Even more than the vistas of blackened brickwork and opaque skies, Orwell was shocked by the degree of human deprivation on display. Out with the NUWM collectors inspecting housing conditions and taken to a squalid caravan colony on the edge of the town he was struck by the degraded expressions on the faces of the people he met: one woman had a face like a death's head. Then, as he wandered up an alleyway, came an epiphanic moment which – slightly reworked to enhance its impact and supposedly seen from a train window – became one of *The Road to Wigan Pier*'s most unforgettable images: a young woman kneeling in the gutter poking a stick up the blocked waste-pipe. 'I thought how dreadful a destiny it was to be kneeling in the gutter of a back-alley in the bitter cold, prodding a stick up a blocked drain.' The woman looked up and caught his eye. Her expression was 'as desolate as I have ever seen'. It struck Orwell that she was thinking exactly the same thing.

Back at Warrington Lane Mrs Hornby was unwell, with consequent disruption to the household routine. Presumably directed by Jerry Kennan, Orwell changed his lodgings, moving to 22 Darlington Road, a house kept by a couple called the Forrests, who also ran a tripe shop from the lower floor. He noted instantly that though the social atmosphere was much the same as his previous digs the house was appreciably dirtier and smellier. Later this initial distaste would harden into a fabulous contempt for the Forrests (renamed the 'Brookers') and the supposed foulness of their existence. Number 22 Darlingon Road was to become the setting for *The Road to Wigan Pier*'s opening chapter, a Dantesque tour of backstreet squalor: Mr Brooker's black thumbprint on the bread; his semi-invalid wife lamenting the hardness of the world from her comfortable sofa; passing commercial travellers, unable to afford full board, making shamefaced meals out of food stored in their suitcases. Local opinion was divided about the Forrests' establishment, but it clearly had a reputation for being, as one observer put it, 'a bit on the low side, not quite as clean as you would expect it to be'. Lying in bed in the mornings, before descending to the Forrests' filthy breakfast table, Orwell listened to the mill girls clumping down the cobbled street in their clogs – an oddly formidable sound, he decided, like an army on the march. His travails with *Keep the Aspidistra Flying* were in full swing, culminating in a telegram to Gollancz on 19 February suggesting that the changes proposed were 'impossible'. Steadily more exasperated by the news from Henrietta Street, he continued to enquire into local social and political life, attending an NUWM 'social' in aid of the defence fund got up for Thaelmann, the German Communist leader arraigned by the Nazis – there was no *turbulence* left in England, he complained, having examined the docile audience – and going with an out-of-work miner named Paddy Grady to watch unemployed men robbing the 'broo', the train that brought coal dirt up from the mines to the slagheap.

A week into his stay at the Forrests', he was beginning to find the atmosphere intolerable. Particular low points included a full chamber-pot discovered under the breakfast table and his landlady's 'disgusting' habit of tearing off strips of newspaper to wipe her mouth and leaving the spit-sodden balls of paper strewn over the floor. The next few days brought two more eye-opening experiences. On 23 February, escorted by Kennan, he made his first trip down a mine. Kennan testifies to the physical discomfort Orwell notes in *The Road to Wigan Pier*. They had scarcely gone 300 yards along the first tunnel when Orwell was knocked flat by an unexpected change in the level of the roof. Later he was forced to walk doubled up, while the final stretch of the journey compelled him to fit his six-foot-three inch frame into a working space twenty-six inches high. Then, two days later, he travelled to Liverpool to visit John and May Deiner, the *Adelphi*'s agents in the city, and George Garrett, a docker and former seaman who wrote for the magazine under the pseudonym 'Matt Lowe'. Starting out early in the morning on the workers' train from Wigan, and still exhausted by his trip underground, Orwell arrived in a state of collapse and had to be put to bed. Mrs Deiner, who left a vivid account of the visit, remembered his reluctance to have medical help summoned: 'so we just did the best we could in those circumstances, gave him hot lemon'. Later he recovered sufficiently to tour the docks with the Deiners and Garrett in the former's baby Austin Seven, legs jack-knifed up in the rear seat like a grasshopper's. Here hundreds of men were waiting outside the dock gates, hoping to be taken on for unloading jobs. Orwell, 'very moved' according to his hosts, noted that they were selected by the foreman in the same way that cattle would be pulled out of the herd at an agricultural sale.

On 27 February he was back at Darlington Street, writing to tell Moore that he was going on to his sister Marjorie's home at Headingley in the Leeds suburbs, but then changing his mind. Instead, he informed Rees, he intended to stay in Sheffield under the auspices of another of the *Adelphi*'s working-class protégés, James Brown. Brown arranged for him to lodge at 154 Wallace Road with the Searles, an unemployed storekeeper and his wife. Orwell liked the Searles – he had seldom met people with more natural decency, he recorded – and enjoyed the three or four days he spent with them. He was less impressed with Sheffield. Stopping once in the course of a walk he decided to count all the factory chimneys he could see: the total was thirty-three. Never in his life, he thought, inspecting the shattered exteriors of some small engineering workshops, had he seen so many broken windows. Indeed, he would have assumed the buildings to be uninhabitable had he not seen the employees walking about inside. The city's leisure activities seemed quite as debased. Setting out one night to a men's association meeting at a Methodist church, he listened to an 'incredibly silly' talk by a clergyman, delivered to a listless audience who had clearly come for warmth rather than instruction. Shortly afterwards he said goodbye to the Searles, gravely impressed by the story of their life communicated to him a night or so before. Mrs Searle had been a charwoman who married her husband when he was unemployed. Forced to live in a single room, the family had endured desperate privations, including having to lay out a dead child in its pram: there was no other available space. Brown, a middle-aged ex-circus performer with a deformed hand, struck him less favourably. Though anxious to help, he was 'terribly embittered'. There was a tense moment towards the end of the trip when Orwell took him out to eat at a slightly expensive restaurant. Brown gnashed his teeth at the 'bourgeois atmosphere'.

From Sheffield Orwell moved on to Headingley to stay with the Dakins. Back in the world of the bourgeoisie he was immediately struck by the amount of elbow room allowed him. The household included five adults and three children (Marjorie's son Henry and her two daughters Jane and Lucy) but in contrast to the working-class interiors of Wigan, where the beds came jammed three to a room, it was still possible to be quiet. He spent the time paying a visit to the Brontë parsonage at nearby Haworth, where his eye was caught by a pair of Charlotte Brontë's tiny, cloth-topped boots, staying at the Dakins' cottage three miles out of Leeds on the edge of the moors, and reconnoitring the figure of his brother-in-law. Time had not softened Humphrey Dakin's asperities with regard to 'stinking little Eric'. In the various visits that Orwell made to Headingley at around this time – he seems also to have stayed there at Christmas a year or two before – Dakin features as a sceptical and occasionally disparaging spectator. While acknowledging Orwell's industry ('I've never known anyone that worked as hard as Eric did') and his habit of slipping upstairs to the typewriter as soon as the post-supper pleasantries were concluded, he continued to regard him as a slightly futile character who lacked the personal resonance required to accomplish some of the tasks he set himself. As a no-nonsense middle-class man who kept an eye on working-class life in the northern city he inhabited, Dakin's opinion of the Road to Wigan Pier journey is worth having. Among other observations, at this point he had no idea that Orwell had the slightest interest in politics. Later, having read the book, he commended its accuracy while noting the partiality of the view. Seedy boarding-houses might be a staple of backstreet life, but Orwell had never been to a football match or indeed any kind of popular entertainment where the working class could be seen enjoying itself. The thought of a failure to connect, an invisible barrier set down between observer and object, hangs over his reminiscences of Orwell's northern trip.

Dakin's memory of Orwell in down-market pubs where he 'never seemed to enjoy himself' raises the question of what the working-class people he met in Manchester, Liverpool and Sheffield thought of the tall, diffident ex-public school boy among them taking notes. Certainly one or two of the northerners he came across detected an unconscious air of superiority. 'He was kind of up in the air,' Kennan, the man who took him on his first visit to a mine, alleged, 'and a snob in some ways.' The Deiners, on the other hand, thought him deeply involved in what he did, moved by the signs of dereliction and despair he encountered, while conceding that he had little in the way of personal magnetism. All this was complicated by the confusion that the presence of a man with Orwell's accent and Orwell's demeanour could produce in a working-class environment seventy years ago, a brazen inappropriateness to milieu that could raise instinctive deference or bristling contempt. Amused by the unemployed miners' habit of calling him either 'comrade' or 'sir', he was not always meekly accepting of the reactions he provoked. Introduced to a militant Communist in Sheffield, who began a wholesale vilification of the bourgeoisie, he is supposed to have replied, 'Look here, I'm a bourgeois and my family are bourgeois. If you talk about them like that, I'll punch your head.' There were some skins that could not be shed.

By and large Orwell liked, appreciated and responded imaginatively to the people he met – *The Road to Wigan Pier* is an essay in human sympathy – but he was always aware of the gap that separated him from his subject matter. This is one of the book's great themes, reinforced, if unconsciously, by its figurative language. This, after all, was a man who could write: 'There is a widespread feeling that any civilisation in which Socialism was a reality would bear the same resemblance to our own as a brand-new bottle of colonial burgundy does to a few spoonfuls of first-class Beaujolais.' He wanted to connect, and yet the ties that restrained him were sometimes barely visible to him. At the same time he was keeping an observant eye on the society through which he travelled, and the class divisions that it incorporated. Working-class culture, he swiftly discovered, was far from homogeneous. Elevate a man like Meade to trade union officialdom and despite his habit of calling fellow-workers for the cause 'comrade' he rapidly passed into the ranks of the middle class. Significantly, the Meades were scandalised when they found out that their guest had spent his first night in Manchester staying in a common lodging house. The realisation that working-class English life had its own layers and its own antagonisms played an important part in the view that Orwell came to take of the class system. This was a complex arrangement, he believed, that could not be deciphered through simple economics. To watch the English class system being expounded by an orthodox Marxist, he wrote shortly after returning from the north, was like watching a roast duck being carved up with a chopper.

From Headingley at the end of the second week in March he moved on to Barnsley. The digs, fixed up by a man named Wilde, secretary of the South Yorkshire branch of the Working Men's Club & Institute Union, came courtesy of the Grey household: a miner and his wife, two little girls and the inevitable complement of lodgers. The house was clean and decent – Orwell noted the flannelette sheets on the bed approvingly – but he doubted that he would pick up much of interest. For one thing, Barnsley had no proper reference library. However, he did manage to see Sir Oswald Mosley address a public meeting in the town. Dismayed by the violence shown towards hecklers by the blackshirted retinue, he was still more depressed by Mosley's ability to carry the meeting with him. In his first experience of demagoguery at work, Orwell was struck by how easy it was to bamboozle an uneducated audience if, like Mosley, you had repartee to hand with which to evade awkward questions. Six weeks into his journey – even now he had only just sent back to Gollancz the last lot of corrections to *Keep the Aspidistra Flying* – some of the edge had gone off Orwell's enthusiasm. He was pining to be back in the languorous south, he told Jack Common in mid-March, and to be able to do some work. Two days later, back in South Yorkshire after a brief trip to the *Adelphi* office in Manchester, he went down a mine at Wentworth – a much easier proposition than the Wigan pit, as he could stand upright. Even so, he was grateful for the tin hat provided by his hosts. Without it, he calculated, he would have banged his head twenty times. As on his previous descent, Orwell admired the skill and physical endurance on display below ground. And yet, he discovered, professional expertise was relative. As he worked up his notes in the evening most of the

Greys would gather round to cast admiring glances at his typing. He went down a third pit at Grimethorpe two days later and found the effort required even less demanding. Here the nearest workings were a bare quarter of a mile away and he could walk almost without stooping. Barnsley, meanwhile, had proved more interesting than he had first anticipated. A Communist meeting in the marketplace was 'disappointing', the sentiments rendered opaque by Marxist jargon; but the monstrous slagheaps alongside the town's main colliery were an extraordinary sight, permanently aglow from the fires smouldering below their surfaces. In the Mapplewell district he found the worst housing conditions he had ever witnessed: a run-down terrace called Spring Gardens where the landlord had given half the row notice to quit on account of rent arrears. Entering one of these 'frightful interiors' with a man named Firth who was showing him round the area Orwell discovered a pitiable family group: the old father, 'horribly bewildered' by the apparent end of his twenty-two-year tenure, turning anxiously to the visitors with some idea that they might help; listless, undernourished sons. The house was 'terribly bare' – there were no bedclothes except overcoats; small children, naked but for cotton shifts, played in the mud at the back of the houses. Showing more confidence than he possessed, Orwell advised them that the landlord was bluffing, that they should stand their ground and if threatened with court action themselves threaten to counter-sue for lack of repairs. 'Hope I did the right thing,' he wrote in his diary.

He was nearing the end of his time in the north. Three days later he travelled to Headingley for another stay with the Dakins. By the end of March he was back in London. He had been away exactly two months. Although at this stage Orwell had no very clear idea of how he might recast the material acquired in the various northern towns and cities he had explored, he was conscious of the need for a cheap and congenial working environment in which the book could be written. As so often in his early life the helping hand was provided by Aunt Nellie, who until the spring of 1936 had been living in a tiny cottage in the Hertfordshire village of Wallington. The first mention of Wallington comes in a letter written halfway through the Wigan journey. During the second half of the trip he had made arrangements to take over Aunt Nellie's tenancy, and by 2 April he was installed. The move to Wallington, safely detached from the fleshpots of London, supports the idea that Orwell was acutely hard-up on his return from the north, and that any advance from Gollancz had come in the shape of travelling expenses. His rent was only 7s. 6d. a week, but he was already looking to expand his income. As for the accommodation itself, as he informed Jack Common (by chance Common was living under a dozen miles away), 'of course it isn't what you might call luxurious'. It wasn't. Wallington was a tiny enclave – the population never exceeded 100 inhabitants – with a single village pub providing its only point of communal focus. Even by the standards of the 1930s it was both uncomfortably remote – Baldock, the nearest place of any size, was three miles away – and uncomfortably primitive. 'The awfulness of his houses!' one of Orwell's friends generalised before offering grim particulars on the spartan conditions of Wallington. Antique in construction – it was thought to date from the early sixteenth century – the cottage was prey to damp. There were few modern amenities. 'They didn't even have an inside loo. You had to go to the bottom of the garden.' Within, the lower floor consisted of two small rooms and a tiny pantry with a sink, the latter more often than not blocked. In the absence of mains gas, cooking was done on a primus stove. Ancient, twisted stairs led upwards to a wide open landing and twin bedrooms. The staircase was always dark, guests remembered – no bulbs were ever put in the light sockets – and rendered even less navigable by a steadily encroaching tide of books. On and off, Orwell lived at the Stores for over a decade, and used it as a weekend retreat long after he had returned to London. As its name suggested, the cottage had recently doubled up as the village shop, business being transacted in one of the downstairs rooms, customers entering by way of the four-foot-six-inch front door. The counter stood in the middle of a space eleven feet square and was visible through slats in the upper door of the sitting room.

Despite its small size and remote location, Orwell seems to have been enchanted by the Stores. As well as offering the solitude necessary for literary work it also gave him the chance to indulge his market-gardening side. A goat and some hens were quickly introduced on to the premises. He was also thinking – provided the landlord was agreeable – of reopening the shop. Common, who had experience of running a small tobacconist-cum-newsagent's in Chelsea, was petitioned for advice. By mid-April Orwell had the landlord's consent, was making enquiries with the Baldock wholesalers, and had made a start on the garden, an 'Augean' task in which he turned up twelve discarded boots in two days. Amid this round of gardening and household chores, which Orwell always enjoyed, some of the themes of *The Road to Wigan Pier* were already taking shape in his imagination.

Jack Common was treated to an early rehearsal of his opinion of the average middle-class Socialist. So many of them, Orwell proposed, 'are the sort of eunuch type with a vegetarian smell who go about spreading sweetness and light and have at the back of their minds a vision of the working class as TT, well washed behind the ears . . . and talking with BBC accents'. As an expatriate northerner who worked for the *Adelphi* Common would have had his own views on parlour Socialism, but he was aware that Orwell's arrival as a Hertfordshire neighbour marked a new stage in their relationship, that the man found digging his overgrown garden was a slightly different proposition from the man he had entertained over the *Adelphi* gas fire. In Hertfordshire Common glimpsed Orwell's love of nature, his fondness for 'country-dwellers' talk'. Common remembered him showing 'far more interest than I'd expected' in his plan to make a garden out of a bare meadow.

Halfway through April Orwell announced his intention of paying a Sunday social call and Common went out to meet him. Eventually a solitary cyclist came slowly into view, labouring against the gradient. More than usually communicative – he was negotiating for a patch of land on the other side of the road, he told Common, where he could run his hens – Orwell allowed himself to be taken off to the local pub. Here Common witnessed, and was himself a part of, one of those curious incidents in which Orwell's distance from the people with whom he sought to assimilate himself became sharply apparent. The landlord, an ex-navy rating, addressed him as 'sir', with one eye on Common, the inference being that if the visitor belonged to the same social level as Common himself, Common would correct him. For some reason Common chose not to. It was the same in Wallington. Orwell was quite liked by his fellow-villagers, their testimonies insist, without ever being regarded as 'one of them'. Meanwhile, the routines of literary life were steadily reasserting themselves. He made a start on what was to become *The Road to Wigan Pier*, and wrote to Cyril Connolly asking him and his wife Jean to stay. *Keep the Aspidistra Flying* finally appeared on 20 April 1936. Receipt of the complimentary copies brought a good example of Orwell's curious delicacy. Having sent a copy to Mrs Meade, his hostess in Manchester, he followed it up with a nervous letter to Rees, who he knew to be staying in the north on *Adelphi* business. Could Rees kindly drop a hint, he wondered, to the effect that presentation copies didn't need to be read? Professionally he was carrying on where he left off: reviewing novels for the *New English Weekly*, fishing about for other introductions (he would start to write for the *Listener*, under its literary editor J.R. Ackerley, later in the year and also for *Time and Tide*, introduced there by Geoffrey Gorer), combining his literary work with the arrangements necessary to prepare the shop for its reopening in early May.

There is a conspicuous absentee from this round of literary and domestic tasks, the meetings with Jack Common and the writing of letters to the Baldock wholesalers: Eileen. Was she living at Wallington at this point? Did she come to stay? Practically the first hint of her existence, in the context of this new life in Hertfordshire, comes in a letter to Moore about the forthcoming American publication of *A Clergyman's Daughter*. Assembling 'picturesque details' for the composer of the blurb, Orwell suggested that it could be said of the author that 'he is thinking very seriously of getting married'.

Not very much is known of the circumstances of Orwell's marriage. The initial idea, aired the previous year, had been that Eileen would finish her Master's course at Birkbeck before taking any decisive step. In the end, rather to the disappointment of some of her friends, who thought it sat oddly with her reputation for independent-mindedness, she abandoned it before completion. There is scarcely any mention of the wedding preliminaries in Orwell's letters apart from an odd and faintly paranoiac murmur in a note to Geoffrey Gorer of late May. The shop by this time had been open a fortnight. Having listed the takings – he expected to make between 25 and 30 shillings in the second week – Orwell announced that he was getting married on 9 June, but that he and Eileen were telling as few people as possible lest their relations combined against them in some way to prevent it. What exactly Orwell meant by this is anyone's guess. He and his future wife were both in their thirties, unencumbered by previous attachments. No property was settled on them. Each had lived an independent life since early adulthood. The idea of their relatives somehow conspiring to obstruct their path to the altar seems faintly preposterous. One can only assume that this kind of staginess – possibly based on some mild hint of unease that had wafted up from Greenwich or down from Southwold – appealed to Orwell's sense of melodrama, that it suited him to magnify a local difficulty into a serious impediment. As for the economic basis of their union, he and Eileen seem to have assumed from the outset that money would always be tight and that they had better marry while they had the chance. He expected that they would rub along all right, 'as to money, I mean,' Orwell told Gorer. There is a sense in letters of this kind in which one never knows if Orwell is saying what he thinks or conducting an elaborate tease. The same note of almost paralysing diffidence is struck in a letter responding to John Lehmann's request for a contribution to the newly founded *New Writing*. With maximum self-deprecation, Orwell proposes the sketch that became 'Shooting an Elephant', going on to suggest that this might be too highbrow for the magazine, and in any case he doubted whether there was anything anti-Fascist in the shooting of an elephant. The obvious response to a letter of this kind, sent to an editor bent on commissioning new work from upcoming talent, is to wonder exactly what game Orwell is playing here. Is he simply being obtuse? Extracting some mysterious private fun at Lehmann's expense? Whatever the explanation, the tone is utterly characteristic of both his personal and professional life: polite, detached, determined, in the last resort, to follow his own inclinations.

Established in this new world of shopkeeping, impending marriage, running his smallholding and literary work, Orwell found several elements of his older life rising up to claim him. The early summer brought two letters from Old Etonians. Both had been instigated by Connolly. One – from Anthony Powell – would eventually produce one of his most substantial adult friendships. Powell, two and a half years younger and the author of four determinedly modernist novels, had been vaguely aware of Orwell's work for some time, having read *Down and Out in Paris and London* on the recommendation of his painter friend Adrian Daintrey. Like several of the reviewers of *Keep the Aspidistra Flying*, Powell was impressed by the novel's grimly realistic quality, while noting that the form, style and views expressed seemed markedly old-fashioned. Then, unexpectedly, Cyril remarked that he and Orwell were in touch. Connolly gave a sobering account of his friend, stressing his asceticism, the lines of 'suffering' and 'privation' etched on his hollow cheeks. The portrait, Powell conceded, was 'a disturbing one'. Intrigued, he sent a fan letter and a copy of *Caledonia*, his satirical poem on the contemporary cult of Scottishness printed up in celebration of his marriage to Lady Violet Pakenham eighteen months before. Orwell's reply, though perfectly polite, conveyed, Powell thought, a faint chill, making him feel, especially in the light of Connolly's report, that somehow Orwell was not for him. Another five years passed before they met in the flesh.

Orwell replied to Powell's letter the day before his marriage. The wedding morning itself found him writing to his fellow-Colleger Denys King-Farlow. What had happened to their old College friends? Orwell wondered. He supposed that they were all dons, civil servants and barristers. As for himself, 'I have had a bloody life a good deal of the time but in some ways an interesting one.' As in the letters to Geoffrey Gorer and John Lehmann it is impossible to guess how Orwell wanted this to be received. Certainly it conveys a sense of detachment, a warning to King-Farlow that Orwell imagined his life to be beyond the standard Old Etonian groove. And yet, it was a life that was to become increasingly populated by ex-Etonians. King-Farlow was swiftly invited to visit Wallington. Having written the letter, Orwell went off to get married. According to village legend he and Eileen walked together to the church, Eileen entering the grounds through the lych-gate, Orwell proceeding to the back gate, vaulting over it and joining her in the porch. The wedding party consisted of Richard, Ida and Avril Blair, who had come over from Southwold, Eileen's mother and her brother Laurence and his wife Gwen. It was a fortnight before Orwell's thirty-third birthday.

One wonders what Eileen, a bright, spirited woman who had given up her Master's degree for a life spent selling shillings' worth of groceries and watching her husband type, expected from her marriage. Eileen's friend Lydia Jackson remembered her expressing 'some dissatisfaction' during her first year at Wallington, the inference being that she had anticipated some involvement in Orwell's work but was effectively excluded from it. Wallington itself scarcely offered the materials for domestic comfort. Driven over by Richard Rees in October 1936, Mark Benney, a former burglar now launched on a literary career, was struck by this manifestation of what he was always to regard as Orwell's life of 'monastic poverty'. The door of the cottage was opened by 'a tall figure, face and clothes covered with coal smuts, who peered at us through a billowing cloud of smoke'. Orwell's first attempt at an autumn fire had been frustrated by a defective chimney. Almost immediately Benney was offered a demonstration of his host's curious sense of propriety. The granite blocks, suitable for stopping the hole, that he and Rees found in the garden were politely declined on the grounds that they were tombstone fragments from the nearby cemetery.

Whatever Eileen may have thought of the rushing East Anglian winds and smoking chimneys is beyond recreation. Surviving materials from the first six months of their marriage are painfully slight: a handful of letters, a few reviews, in particular a notably sharp piece about Connolly's *The Rock Pool*, which appeared in the *New English Weekly* towards the end of July. Orwell admired Connolly as a critic but his reaction to this account of the adventures of a gang of bohemian idlers lounging on the beaches of the south of France was essentially a moral one. Even to want to write about 'so-called artists who spend on sodomy what they get by sponging' betrayed a certain spiritual inadequacy. It was clear, too, that Connolly rather admired the 'disgusting beasts' he was writing about. Orwell's conclusion rose far above the dingy expatriate world of Connolly's novel. 'The fact to which we have got to cling, as to a lifebelt, is that it is possible to be a normal decent person and yet to be fully alive.' Art was not simply a matter of stylised behaviour.

The brisk review of *The Rock Pool* – Connolly, it should be pointed out, had noticed *Keep the Aspidistra Flying* in similarly no-nonsense terms – marks an important step in one of Orwell's chief intellectual preoccupations of the time: formulating what he felt about contemporary English writing and his own place within it. His current critical work – there was even a long, two-part essay in the *New English Weekly* later in the year boldly titled 'In Defence of the English Novel' – is full of attempts to take up positions, get to grips with the tide of literature he saw around him. In analysing Orwell's view of the 1930s literary scene it is important to try to reimagine that scene as it really was. In retrospect Orwell seems to dominate the pre-war literary world. In reality he existed on its margins. And his tastes, in an age of formal experiment and innovation, were old-fashioned. Essentially Orwell's view of the fiction that came his way in the late 1930s had three aspects. First he believed that most English writing was 'staid to the point of primness'. Comparisons with contemporary American writing would always be painful 'because in America the tradition of nineteenth century freedom is still alive, though no doubt the reality is as dead as it is here'. By and large – and this formulation recurs in Orwell's critical work – the English novel was written by literary gents, about literary gents and for literary gents; in other words locked in a tradition of limited subject matter and stock responses. Worse, at any rate in the hands of a modish avant-garder such as Connolly, it lacked the moral basis which Orwell thought inseparable from any form of art. Highbrow writers, in fact, were guilty of mocking the conventional lives and decent aspirations of the vast majority of their readership. At the same time the small proportion of contemporary literature demonstrably not written about or for literary gents was also suspect. Some of Orwell's greatest hostility at this time was reserved for writers such as Philip Henderson, author of *Marxism and the Novel*, and Alec Brown: middle-class Marxists, Orwell believed, trying to tailor life to ideology.

Understandably, left-wing critics who have approached Orwell's view of the literature of the 1930s have been sharply opposed to this line. Andy Croft, for example, has accused him of an 'exaggerated panic' in assuming the central stream of English literature as 'more or less under Communist control'. In fact, Croft suggests, Henderson and Brown were intellectually isolated even in the left-wing circles in which they moved, severely criticised as ultra-leftists who disregarded the primacy of aesthetic judgement. Here, the Marxist argument runs, Orwell was shooting paper tigers. Elsewhere he was ignoring what lay in front of his face. One of *The Road to Wigan Pier*'s many strictures on professional socialists is that writers on the Left 'have always been dull, empty windbags, while those of genuine talent are usually indifferent to Socialism'. Left-wing literary historians, conversely, would argue that much of the resistance to totalitarianism had its roots in popular fiction, that the 1930s brought a politicisation of the popular novel that helped to stimulate resistance to Fascism. Looking at some of the politically inclined bestsellers of the period – A.J. Cronin's *The Stars Look Down*, for example, which follows the fortunes of an ex-miner MP who loses his seat in the 1931 Labour meltdown to a corrupt Conservative fellow-worker – one can see what Orwell's left-wing critics are getting at.

There were other positions to be formulated, far beyond – though still connected to – the narrow confines of English literary politics. In mid-July 1936 the Popular Front government newly elected to power in Spain was plunged into crisis by a military revolt begun in Spanish Morocco and the Canary Islands under the leadership of the resourceful General Franco. The right-wing conspiracy was intended to produce a *coup d'état*, not a long-drawn-out military conflict, but the rebels' hesitancy, together with the government's decision to arm the trade union militias, produced a very different result. A week later Spain was split into two contending camps, Nationalist and Republican, each in search of military and financial resources, and civil war had begun. Orwell took a close interest in Spain. King-Farlow, who visited him at Wallington in the early autumn, remembered him following the progress of the conflict in the newspapers – Franco's establishment of his power base, the first waves of (mostly Republican) sympathisers flocking across the French border. His political contacts buzzed with its importance – a democratic government overthrown by aristocratic feudalism – and it would have been much discussed at the *Adelphi* summer school he attended at Langham in Essex in early August where he spoke (with Heppenstall in the chair) on 'An

Outsider Sees the Distressed Areas'. *The Road to Wigan Pier*, too, on which he was now busily engaged, is transparently a book written in the shadow of great events. The personal dilemmas that afflicted him at this time, set in sharp relief by the Spanish war, underlay a poem, one of the best that Orwell ever wrote, sent to the *Adelphi* early that October:

> A happy vicar I might have been
> Two hundred years ago;
> To preach upon eternal doom
> And watch my walnuts grow;
>
> But born, alas, in an evil time,
> I missed that pleasant haven,
> For the hair has grown on my upper lip
> And the clergy are all clean-shaven . . .

Here in the modern world, the poem goes on, it is 'forbidden to dream again; we maim our joys or kill them'. Man's soul is fought over by the priest and the commissar:

> I dreamt I dwelt in marble halls,
> And woke to find it true;
> I wasn't born for an age like this;
> Was Smith? Was Jones? Were you?

It is the age-old writer's dilemma, translated to the mid-twentieth century. Half the average literary gaze, it might be said, is directed firmly backwards, into a time that the writer suspects may have been a great deal more congenial than the one he or she currently inhabits. The other half is uneasily conscious that it is going to have to make some accommodation with the modern age, that the writer who does not, who takes refuge in the past, is simply not a functioning part of his environment. The polemical second half of *The Road to Wigan Pier*, to which Victor Gollancz and others took such violent exception, in which Orwell discusses the nature of Socialism without having any clear idea of what Socialism consists, is in some ways an extension of this, conveying the thought of a sensibility that would much rather not have to be dealing with these questions – that would much rather be sitting in a country rectory writing works of no ideological significance whatsoever – but knows, in its heart of hearts, that such options are no longer available.

The Road to Wigan Pier, now moving to its conclusion here in the Wallington cottage as the news from Spain grew daily more ominous, is a pattern demonstration of the way in which Orwell's writing was now capable of bringing off its effects. At once vivid, charged and persuasive, its first two chapters – describing life in the Brookers' grimy lodging house and the trip down the Wigan mine – are a dramatic exercise in literary artifice, whose principal technique is straightforward exaggeration. Almost from the outset, Orwell stokes up the atmosphere by means of highly emotive linguistic tricks. The lodgers' bedroom, for example, is represented as 'beastly', 'defiled', with 'hideous furniture' and 'squalid' beds jammed amid 'wreckage' – a nightmarish hell-hole rather than a shabby place where a collection of down-at-heel itinerants are woken out of their slumber by the mill-girls' march. Then there is the way in which Orwell makes most of his points by way of generalisation. 'Like all people with permanently dirty hands,' Mr Brooker has 'a peculiarly intimate, lingering manner of handling things'. Joe, the lodger on the PAC (Public Assistance Committee), is 'the kind of person who has no surname . . . the typical unmarried unemployed man'. As for the Brookers as an economic unit, they are 'the kind of people who run a business chiefly in order to have something to complain about'. Invariably, supporting evidence of the Brookers' unmitigated awfulness comes by hearsay. Of the tripe hole: 'Black beetles were said to swarm there.' Of the Old Age Pensioners whose presence in the house landlord and landlady are said to resent: 'It was said that they [the Brookers] were overheard anxiously asking the insurance-tout "how long people lived when they'd got cancer".' Who saw the black beetles? Who overheard the insurance agent's catechism? Orwell never says. Much of this is manifestly unfair: monstrous, comic, infinitely believable, but unfair all the same. Reinvented by this pitiless literary gaze the Brookers cease to be a pair of draggled lodging-house keepers with some disagreeable personal habits and are transformed into lurid pantomime grotesques. But the way in which Orwell loads the evidence against them is quite unignorable. There is a grisly portrait of Mr Brooker sitting by the fire with a tub of filthy water peeling potatoes at the speed of a slow-motion picture – to which it might be said that it would be odd if the water in which potatoes had been peeled stayed clean! Even the food served up on the Brookers' sticky, multi-layered table-top is morally wanting. For supper, for example, there was 'the pale flabby Lancashire cheese and biscuits'. The Brookers refer to the biscuits 'reverently' as 'cream crackers'. Even this, it turns out, is compounding the original offence by glozing over the fact that there is only cheese for supper.

It is instructive to compare the techniques used to demolish the Brookers with those of the following chapter 'Down the Mine'. The language is of the same exaggerated type – 'monstrous' boulders, dust heaps like 'hideous grey mountains' – and yet that much easier to accept. To the reader, who has probably never been down a coal-mine in his life, these are fantastic, undreamed-of landscapes that need the Brobdingnagian gloss Orwell imparts to them if they are to cohere. 'Down the Mine' carries, too, the sense of something unforced, a reaction that has not been silently inflated by the pejorative use of language. 'Watching coal-miners at work,' Orwell remarks, 'you realize momentarily what different universes different people inhabit.' Even here, though, far underground, simultaneously marvelling at human fortitude and analysing the economic system that put it to work, he was capable of overplaying an exceptionally good hand. There is an odd moment, for example, in which he puts out his fingers and discovers 'some dreadful slimy thing' oozing among the coal dust. A dead rat? Something yet more horrible? The object turns out to be a chewed quid of tobacco – an unpleasant thing to fall into your hand, granted, but there are worse items lying around beneath the earth.

In the intervals of working up the *Wigan Pier* material he was continuing to extend the range of his literary journalism, writing an evocative memoir of his time at Booklovers' Corner for the *Fortnightly*, reviewing travel books for *Time and Tide* and producing the long essay on contemporary fiction for the *New English Weekly*. This essay aired another of his perennial complaints about the literary climate, the poor quality of most contemporary book-reviewing. Somehow the average critic who reviewed books for a newspaper had to remember the wider literary context in which they existed, and yet trying to apply a respectable standard to the ordinary run of novels was, Orwell suggested, like weighing a flea on a spring-balance designed for elephants.

All the while, too, he was monitoring the news from Spain. Here, as the autumn wore on, Franco's Army of Africa was pushing towards Madrid in a series of military advances characterised by the slaughter of leftist militiamen and Republican activists. In the event Madrid survived – it probably would have fallen had Franco not made a detour east in order to relieve Toledo – but the Republic was in an increasingly desperate position. Already, in a movement led by the Communist-dominated International Brigade, thousands of foreign sympathisers were making their way to Spain. At some point in the autumn Orwell decided to join them. Again, little is known of the stages by which this decision was reached. The only evidence exists in a series of letters making the various arrangements. On 8 December he was issued with a passport. Two days later he got Moore to guarantee a £50 overdraft at the bank. Preparations for departure and the final adjustments to the manuscript of *The Road to Wigan Pier* proceeded side by side. Finally the book was sent to Gollancz on 15 December. A formal letter was lodged with Christy & Moore empowering Eileen to deal with Orwell's literary affairs in his absence and arrangements made to pay all moneys into her bank account. Orwell was habitually restless to complete a task – Eileen would have remembered the haste with which he had left London earlier in the year – and doubtless wanted to leave for Spain as soon as he could. However, 19 December brought a telegram from Victor Gollancz requesting a meeting on the grounds that there was a chance of *The Road to Wigan Pier* being selected for publication by the Left Book Club.

Since Gollancz's original lunch with Cripps and Strachey back in January, the Left Book Club had grown far beyond the expectations of its founders. (Orwell had already reviewed one of its early publications, Wilfred Macartney's Parkhurst memoir *Walls Have Mouths*.) The initial plan had been to launch a left-leaning newspaper, but Gollancz lobbied for a literary venture. Solvency required a minimum of 2,500 subscribers, but in the event 40,000 supporters came on board in the first year, buttressed by a network of discussion groups and think-tanks. Five and a half decades since its dissolution it would be hard to think of a better symbol for the lofty idealism – and the sheer wrong-headedness – of left-wing politics in the 1930s than the stream of books that was issued under its imprint over the next dozen years. Boasting, at any rate in its salad days, a readership of over a quarter of a million, it was both a highly influential experiment in consciousness-raising and a demonstration of one of the great truths of left-wing political life in Britain: that high-mindedness and exceptional silliness are drawn together by a kind of natural law. Both of these qualities were much in evidence in the reception and publication by Gollancz of *The Road to Wigan Pier*. Impressed by the searing reportage of the first section, Gollancz was less sure of the merits of the second, polemical half. This, as well as offending his own conception of the Socialist ideal, would, he calculated, annoy many of his subscribers. The exact sequence of events is difficult to reconstruct, but Orwell is known to have come up to London on 21 December to make more Spanish arrangements. A meeting took place with Gollancz, and an advance of £100 was proposed, but as late as Christmas Eve Gollancz had still not decided whether the book should be a Club choice.

Meanwhile – and the two strands of Orwell's life are probably connected – the author was trying to find an organisation under whose auspices he could procure entry to Spain. He began by visiting Communist Party HQ in King Street and applying to the General Secretary of the British Communist Party, Harry Pollitt. Given the close links between King Street and Gollancz' office, where Communist sympathisers were much in evidence, it is quite possible that Pollitt had already received intimations of Orwell's political unorthodoxy. At any rate, getting an unsatisfactory answer to the question of whether Orwell wanted to join the International Brigade – he would prefer to make up his mind when he got there, Orwell replied – he advised him to get a safe passage from the Spanish embassy in Paris. Undeterred, Orwell used his ILP connections and obtained a letter to John McNair, the party's representative in Barcelona. The ILP's General Secretary, Fenner Brockway, remembered his militant mood when he turned up at the ILP headquarters. The trip would probably produce a book, he admitted, but his immediate aim was to take part in the struggle against Franco. Shortly before Christmas he left England for France. Several characteristic stories survive from these preliminaries: of Orwell remarking to Jack Common, wistfully but as if determined to prove a point, that if everyone who went to Spain killed a Fascist then there wouldn't be so many left; of his arrival in the office of the *New English Weekly* to tell the editor, Philip Mairet, gravely that 'something had to be done'. A persistent legend is that he and Eileen pawned the family silver to pay his travel costs, telling the Blairs that it had been sent away for engraving. One thing seems certain, however. Despite his later claim that he had gone to Spain with a vague thought of writing newspaper articles, Orwell had a much more definite purpose in mind. He wanted to fight.

Orwell and the Jews

In February 1933 Victor Gollancz received a letter from a Mr S.M. Lipsey, a recent reader of *Down and Out in Paris and London*. It was not complimentary. 'On its merits or otherwise I have no desire to comment,' he commented, 'but I am appalled that a book containing insulting and odious remarks about Jews should be published by a firm bearing the name Gollancz.' A spirited correspondence followed – Gollancz was not the man to take slights of this kind lying down – there were threats of legal action and finally the row fizzled out. Its shadow, though, hangs over much of Orwell's early writings and indeed his whole attitude towards Jews, Jewishness and, later on, the foundation of a Zionist state. It is also apparent in an odd remark made by Malcolm Muggeridge in his private account of Orwell's funeral. Muggeridge was intrigued by the large number of Jews present, believing the dead man to have been 'at heart strongly anti-semitic'.

Orwell's later writings show a serious interest in the idea of Jewishness, or at any rate in the somewhat abstract notion of 'the Jew'. Among other items he wrote a long essay for the *Contempory Jewish Record* on 'Anti-Semitism in Britain', reviews of books on Jewish subjects (including a notice of Sartre's *Portrait of the Anti-Semite*) and several 'As I Please' columns which turn, directly or indirectly, on the question of anti-Jewish prejudice. His friend Tosco Fyvel, who later made a careful survey of these articles, divided Orwell's thoughts on Jewishness into three categories. On the one hand Orwell was shocked by the sheer vehemence and extent of the anti-Jewish feeling he detected. On the other he was anxious to demonstrate that the arguments in favour of anti-Semitism were irrational, usually nothing more than an attempt to find a scapegoat for an economic grievance. And yet there was a third side, Fyvel believed, which was uneasily conscious that expressions of popular feeling had to have a cause. In the

196

last resort the man in the tobacconist's queue who referred mockingly to the 'chosen race' did not do so quite arbitrarily. Anti-Semitism, it seemed to Orwell, must have an explanation, however misguided the stimulus or doubtful the evidence.

Some context is in order. English novels of the 1930s are full of what in retrospect we might want to mark down as disparaging references to the Jews. Equally, the English novelists who made them – and their number included Waugh, Greene and Priestley – would have laughed at the imputation of anti-Semitism. Anthony Powell, when someone pointed out a Jewish reference in *Afternoon Men* (1931) sixty years after the book first appeared, replied somewhat stiffly that it was simply what one wrote at the time. To step back into the English literature of the century before is to enter a spiritual locker room full of the deadliest insults to 'low, disgusting Jews' (Trollope) or grotesque caricatures of 'sheenies' (Thackeray). 'Jew-baiting' – which incidentally Orwell was concerned to distinguish from anti-Semitism – turns up as regularly in the Victorian novel as sadism or the misplaced will. Orwell recognised the existence of this tradition, to which he several times refers and by implication deplores. Nevertheless, there is an odd intensity to some of his early references to the Jews, which would have struck many a less vigilant reader than S.M. Lipsey.

Down and Out in Paris and London, for example, has barely entered its third chapter before Orwell is describing a 'red-haired Jew, an extraordinarily disagreeable man' to whom he used to sell clothes at a shop in the rue de la Montagne Ste-Geneviève. 'It would have been a pleasure to flatten the Jew's nose, if only one could have afforded it.' Then there are the anti-Jew rants put into the mouth of Boris, his partner in grime, bearing on the latter's experiences in the Imperial Russian army. '"Have I ever told you, *mon ami*, that . . . it was considered bad form to spit on a Jew? Yes, we thought a Russian officer's spittle was too precious to be wasted on a Jew . . ."' This is reportage, obviously, the recollection of another person's harangue, but there is something fascinated in it, and the phrasing (Boris is allowed to go on for half a page) is clearly Orwell's own. As is its characteristic: the abstract conception of 'the Jew', a figure seen in terms of his Jewishness *and nothing more.* Coming back to England, practically the first thing that Orwell does is to wander into a coffee shop at Tower Hill where 'in a corner by himself a Jew, muzzle down in the plate, was guiltily wolfing bacon'. Not even 'a Jewish-looking man', you see, simply 'a Jew'. If it comes to that, how does Orwell know that the emotion he detects is guilt? There is something gratuitous, too, about the reference to 'muzzle' – as if the man in the café is not quite human and the explanation for this sub-humanity has something to do with his being Jewish.

'The Jew' makes regular appearances in Orwell's diaries over the next ten years. Out tramping in the summer of 1931 he fell in with 'a little Liverpool Jew of eighteen, a thorough guttersnipe. I do not know when I have seen anyone who disgusted me quite as much as this boy,' Orwell noted solemnly, going on to record his revulsion at 'a face that recalled some low-down carrion-eating bird'. Queerest of all, perhaps, is an entry from October 1940 describing the wartime confusion of the London Underground. Detecting 'a higher proportion of Jews than one would normally see in a crowd of this size', Orwell decided that what was 'bad' about the Jews was that they were not only conspicuous but went out of their way to make themselves so. He was particularly annoyed by the sight of 'a fearful Jewish woman, a regular comic-paper cartoon of a Jewess', who 'fought her way off the train at Oxford Circus, landing blows on anyone who stood in the way'. Now, it is perfectly possible that the woman in question resembled an extra from *Fiddler on the Roof* and that the incident took place exactly as Orwell recorded it. Even so, it is a safe bet that few early twenty-first-century onlookers will be able to read it without clenching their teeth.

If the rumours of the 1930s had awakened liberal consciences to the Jewish question, then the Second World War made the plight of the Jews in Nazi Europe unignorable. There was also the debate about what would happen after the war's end and the possible creation of a Jewish state. 'The Jew' was no longer a slightly sinister English comic-book staple but a symbol of the evil that men could do to one another. Orwell, who had countless Jewish friends (Koestler, Fyvel), Jewish publishers (Gollancz, Warburg) and Jewish work colleagues (Jon Kimche and Evelyn Anderson at *Tribune*) would have had this pointed out to him unceasingly. Undoubtedly it made him reflect on his attitude to Jewishness, what could and could not be said about it, and what in the past he had said about it himself. 'I have no doubt that Fyvel thinks *I* am anti-semitic,' he ventured in a letter to Julian Symons, who – neatly enough – was half-Jewish himself. Roy Fuller, who had complained that a *Tribune* reviewer had alleged he was anti-Semitic, was reassured that it was impossible to mention the Jews in print 'either favourably or unfavourably' without getting into trouble. In one way Orwell's public musings on Jewishness, which begin around 1944, may have been an attempt to make amends for past insensitivity. There is an odd vignette in the *Contemporary Jewish Record* essay when he recalls being accosted by a ragged boy in Rangoon in the 1920s, 'whose manners and appearance were difficult to place'. '"I am a *Joo*, sir,"' the boy explained, when questioned. 'He admits it openly,' Orwell represents himself as remarking to the friend he was with. Yet he was still intrigued by anti-Semitism's popular roots, the idea that in the end it is not quite without foundation. An *Observer* review from January 1944 of two books on Jewish themes distinguishes between 'true anti-semitism, an essentially magical doctrine' and straightforward xenophobia. The problem, as Orwell saw it, was to determine why persecution of the Jews, pre-Christian in origin, had begun and why it had endured when so many similar superstitions had perished. Two weeks later he returned to this theme in *Tribune*. The weakness of the left-wing attitude to anti-Semitism, he alleged, was that it approached the subject from a rational angle. This could never explain the deep-seated resentment of Jews that runs through English literature and the countless passages (perhaps including his own) 'which would be called anti-semitic if they had been written since Hitler came to power'.

It would be idle to classify Orwell as 'anti-Semitic'. The complexities of what he thought and wrote about the Jews defy easy summary. And yet there is something odd in the implication that insulting Jews is acceptable as long as one knows they won't end up in a gas oven. Tosco Fyvel, a long-term and essentially sympathetic registrar of Orwell's attitudes to Jewishness, remembered this argument surfacing in a discussion of 'Jew' references in T.S. Eliot's early verse. These, Orwell thought, were 'legitimate barbs for the time'. Despite Orwell's opposition to the idea of a Zionist state – he had a 'curiously distant' attitude, Fyvel noted, to the post-war fate of the Jews of Eastern Europe – they had only one serious quarrel. This arose out of the 1945 article 'Revenge is Sour', a report of Orwell's tour of a former concentration camp in south Germany where, among other things, he witnessed a Viennese Jew in the uniform of a US officer (referred to throughout as 'the Jew') kicking a captured SS man. Here, Fyvel protested, was a by-blow of the greatest crime in history and Orwell had given it a single, dismissive paragraph. And why call the man a Jew when he came from Vienna and wore an American uniform? Somewhat astonished by this reproach, Orwell taxed his friend with over-sensitivity. But the rebuke had its effect. In the remaining five years of his life there were no more references to 'the Jew'.

10

Spanish Bombs

I ask your pardon, half of them cannot read,
Your forbearance if, for a while, they cannot pay,
Forgive them, it is disgusting to watch them bleed,
I beg you to excuse, they have not time to pray.
Here is a people, you know it as well as he does,
Franco, you can see it as plain as they do,
Who are forced to fight, for the simplest rights, foes
Richer, stupider, stronger than you, or I, or they, too.
And so while the German bombs burst in their wombs,
And poor Moors are loosed on the unhappy,
And Italian bayonets go through their towns like combs,
Spare a thought, a thought for all these Spanish tombs,
And for a people in danger, shooting from breaking rooms,
For a people in danger, grieving in falling homes.

– Brian Howard, 'For Those with Investments in Spain: 1937', first
published in number 6 of a series of poetry leaflets, *Les Poètes du
monde deféndent le peuple espagnol*

And so in the last days of 1936 – he probably set out on 23 December
– Orwell travelled to Spain via Paris. It was his first visit to the city for
seven years, and he marked it by paying a call on Henry Miller in his
Montparnasse studio. Miller was a writer who preyed on Orwell's mind
in the late 1930s. Only a few months before he had written to thank
him for a copy of his second novel, *Black Spring*: Orwell 'liked part of it
very much' while fearing that it lacked the resonance of *Tropic of
Cancer*. Three years later Miller was to provide the impetus to one of
his greatest essays, *Inside the Whale*. The arrival of the 'tallish,
emaciated Englishman' a day or so after Christmas was recorded by
Miller's friend Alfred Perlès, who left a thoughtful account of their
meeting. Not much of the conversation survives, but during the course

of it Orwell confided to Miller that the experience of serving in the Burma Police had left an indelible mark on him. Miller, who knew something of Orwell's history from his long autobiographical letter, wondered why, given all that he had been through, he should want to push himself towards a further ordeal. Wasn't he more use to the world alive than dead? Orwell replied 'earnestly and humbly' that in extraordinary times there could be no thought of avoiding self-sacrifice. Miller, the arch-quietist, was impressed in spite of himself, and smiling at Orwell's 'Savile Row suit' (in fact, as Orwell protested, the suit came from the Charing Cross Road) presented him with his corduroy jacket, a contribution to the Republican war effort. Perlès notes that Miller tactfully refrained from adding that Orwell would have been welcome to the jacket even if he had been fighting for Franco. Watching the two of them together Perlès was struck by the sharp contrast in personality and temperament, Miller with his 'semi-oriental detachment', Orwell 'tough, resilient and politically-minded, ever striving in his bid to improve the world'. The Paris stay was memorable for one other episode – another of those guilt-ridden encounters which Orwell later set down for the benefit of his *Tribune* readers – when a mix-up over addresses found him hiring a taxi to carry him a distance of a few hundred yards. The taxi-driver was incensed, and the ensuing row ended with both men screaming abuse at each other. Furious at the time, Orwell later came to appreciate the view that the man had taken of him: simply another moneyed foreigner traversing the Paris boulevards while 500 miles away the class struggle was in full swing. He went south by train across the Spanish border, transfixed by the sight of labourers in the fields rising from their work to give the anti-Fascist salute.

Spain, it can safely be said, was the defining experience of Orwell's life. Much more emphatically than the disillusionment of Burma, his trips among the embankment sleepers or his journeys among the unemployed, it gave him a sense of what he wanted from life and the goals that he wished to achieve. Or rather it gave him a context – intense, dazzling and unforgettable – for many of the previous experiences in which his view of life had taken root and grown. This much is clear from the stream of reviews and articles he wrote about the Spanish war and its consequences after his return, but it is also apparent in the memories of the friends who watched him go. Richard Rees noted that it was only when Orwell went to Spain that he began to realise how extraordinary he was. For all these clouds of retrospective glory, Orwell's arrival in Barcelona two or three days before the end of the year had its farcical side. Jennie Lee remembered meeting him in the lobby of a hotel where she was sitting with friends, a pair of boots dangling over his shoulder, wondering where he could join up. Suspicious of his lack of credentials, she was won over by the boots, so large (Orwell took a size 12) as to be more or less unprocurable in Spain. Eventually Orwell found his way to John McNair in the ILP's Barcelona office. McNair, too, was initially wary of the tall ex-public school boy with the drawling upper-class accent, but turned out to have read two of his books. While not denying a literary motive – he wanted to write about the situation in Spain to stir working-class opinion in England – Orwell declared himself anxious to join the Republican militia. While this was being fixed up, McNair produced a Catalan journalist, Victor Alba, who was commissioned to show him round the city. Alba, an enthusiastic young man who provided a '1936 style tour' concentrating on the sites of the street fighting of six months before, was unimpressed by his mostly silent companion. Low-voiced and wrapped up in himself, he seemed merely a 'bored journalist' with scant knowledge of the country he had come to survey. *Homage to Catalonia*, which Alba read in exile in Mexico, came as a revelation.

Barcelona, Orwell discovered, was full of foreigners. By this stage in its progress the Spanish war had rapidly developed into the *cause célèbre* of contemporary international politics. Something of the passions it stirred can be glimpsed in Nancy Cunard's assemblage *Authors Take Sides on the Spanish War*, published as a *Left Review* pamphlet in the autumn of the following year. Of the 148 contributors, the vast majority took the government side, while only five – among them Edmund Blunden and Evelyn Waugh – offered responses that could in any way be construed as pro-Franco. (A last-minute intervention from George Bernard Shaw beginning 'In Spain both the Right and the Left so thoroughly disgraced themselves in the turns they took in trying to govern their country before the Right revolted that it is impossible to say which of them is the more incompetent . . .' had to be filed under 'unclassified'.) The general tone was set in a statement from Brian Howard, an exemplary 1920s aesthete now ablaze with recently acquired political consciousness: 'A people, nearly half of whom has been denied the opportunity to learn to read, is struggling for bread, liberty and life against the most unscrupulous and reactionary plutocracy in existence . . . With all my anger and love, I am for the people of Republican Spain.' Orwell later acquired sufficient knowledge of the realities of Spain to hold the convenors of *Authors Take Sides* in the deepest contempt, but the fervour that such publications reflected lay at the heart of pro-Republican feeling, sending thousands of in some cases absurdly youthful volunteers off to Spain to fight for the Communist-run International Brigade. Kenneth Sinclair-Loutit, then a twenty-two-year-old Cambridge graduate, who arrived there in the autumn of 1936 with a medical relief agency, remembered the feeling of compulsion that the situation inspired. 'Spain had become my life . . . all my other loyalties, pleasing my parents, finishing my studies, my life in London . . . all had vanished below the horizon.' For the Left, Spain – both then and in the decades that followed – became a touchstone of 'commitment'. Treece, the well-meaning liberal English professor of Malcolm Bradbury's *Eating People is Wrong* (1959) knows that in some way his life has been blighted by the comic misunderstanding that, as a young man sympathetic to the cause to end all liberal causes, kept him in England.

Like Vietnam thirty years later, Spain had the capacity to inflame British public opinion at every level of society. Simultaneously, these divisions were by no means precise. Staying in London in late 1936 while he arranged a transfer to the International Brigade, Sinclair-Loutit was struck by the lack of hostility that his presence evoked among the members of the ultra-conservative Junior Constitutional Club. This was characteristic of the time. However one may have conceived the Spanish war – a defence of democracy, a test of national self-determination in an age of power politics, an opportunity for social revolution – the issues at stake were rarely clear-cut. Orwell himself admitted to Anthony Powell that the sides native Spaniards fought on depended largely on the part of Spain in which they lived.

These confusions are sharply apparent in the background to the first phase of the war. Nearly six months after the generals' revolt, Spain was divided up into Nationalist and Republican areas. Franco's assault on Madrid – which was the capital and, until the Republican administration hastily decamped to Valencia, the seat of government – was bogged down in stalemate but there had been significant Nationalist advances to the south and north. It had already become clear, within weeks of the onset of hostilities, that whatever happened in Spain was not likely to be left to the Spanish themselves. As a democratically elected government of a leftist slant, the Giral administration had applied to its near-neighbour France for aid. France's Socialist premier Blum was sympathetic, but the modest supplies of aircraft shipped south in the first weeks of the war were cut short by divisions in the French cabinet. Blum's solution was to propose that all European governments should agree a policy of non-intervention. The inevitable effect of this agreement was to polarise the conflict into contending ideological extremes. On the one side, Hitler had provided the Junkers JU-52 transports that carried Franco's Army of Africa to the Spanish mainland. On the other, in the absence of all but the most rudimentary overseas aid, it was obvious that Soviet policy would play a pivotal role. At this point Russian foreign policy was a year or so into its 'Popular Front' phase – a strategy for resisting Fascism that involved support for 'bourgeois democracy' governments threatened by the authoritarian Right. In a purely local context, this had the effect of helping the Spanish Communist Party, in parliamentary terms a small-scale organisation with only seventeen seats in the Cortes, but it was not the chief objective. Historians continue to argue over the precise nature of Soviet war aims in Spain and the real scope of Soviet involvement, but as Russian aid – and Russian agents – began to flood into the country in October 1936 one aspect of its strategy at least was certain: it was not intended to promote any kind of social revolution.

And yet, as much of the country's infrastructure continued to disintegrate and regional towns and cities made their own *ad hoc* arrangements, in many areas of Spain under Republican control the first six months of the war had precisely this effect. Armed by the government, their communal energy harnessed by the initial resistance of July and August 1936, organisations such as the anarchist-leaning CNT (National Confederation of Labour) and in Catalonia the POUM (the United Workers' Marxist Party), left-wing but anti-Stalinist, seized the opportunity to undermine existing social arrangements. Across Republican Spain as a whole this was an uneven process, but in Catalonia, as Orwell soon discovered, it was enthusiastically supported by both the rural peasantry and the urban working class. The middle classes, less certain, lay low. In the meantime, early in September 1936, a genuine Popular Front government, including both Socialists and Communists, had come into being under the premiership of Francisco Largo Caballero, a former plasterer who had left school at seven and who was leader of Spain's largest trade union, the UGT (Unión General de Trabajadores). Beneath this broad umbrella of armed resistance to Franco's alliance of industrialists, landowners and the Catholic Church, lurked a significant divergence of views. Certain parts of the Left coalition (notably the POUM and the smaller Socialist groups) believed that all-out social revolution was the point of the struggle. The antirevolutionary tendencies of more centrist parties – the Spanish Socialist party was historically cautious and reformist – therefore coincided with Communist policy. Communist influence, consequently, expanded out of all proportion to the party's parliamentary representation or popular support. Caballero, while keen to moderate the coalition's revolutionary tendencies, was irritated by the Communists, who in turn maintained that he was not prosecuting the war effectively.

It was amid this atmosphere of growing tension and internal faction fighting that Orwell turned up in Barcelona, knowing little about the extremely complex political situation that the war had brought into being and wanting only to kill Fascists: the views he later took about Spanish politics had at this point scarcely begun to take shape. Arriving in the heart of Catalonia he was immediately plunged into the company of POUM supporters, but his initial sympathies, as he admitted, were for the Communists who at least seemed to want to get things done. But he would also have been made instantly aware of the profound differences that separated parts of the Popular Front alliance. To Sinclair-Loutit, then attached to the Thaelmann Centuria, a German-Communist-dominated part of the International Brigade, these had been evident in Barcelona since the early autumn. On leave with his girlfriend, Sinclair-Loutit stopped at a café table in front of one of the old houses at the lower end of the Ramblas, Barcelona's principal thoroughfare. Barely had they sat themselves down when a microphone descended from the balcony of the floor above and a young woman pulled up a chair to introduce herself as a journalist from Radio Verdad, 'the only broadcasting service that uses reality in preference to make-believe'. After a few moments' desultory talk about the progress of the war on the Aragon Front, Sinclair-Loutit declared that he was not prepared to give an interview. It was too late. 'This is the POUM station,' the girl interjected. 'We not only believe in liberty, but we practise it.' The interview had already taken place. Conscious of having committed a major blunder, Sinclair-Loutit beat a retreat.

In retrospect Spain was full of dazzling symbols and experiences that brought home to Orwell the magnitude of what he had stumbled upon. One encounter took place in the Lenin Barracks in Barcelona, a cavalry HQ taken over and rechristened the previous summer, on the day before he joined the militia when an Italian militiaman, divining that he was an English volunteer, greeted him with a wordless handshake. The meeting realised perhaps the most quoted of all Orwell's poems 'The Italian Soldiers Shook my Hand':

But the thing that I saw in your face
No power can disinherit
No bomb that ever burst
Shatters the crystal spirit.

Though the romantic side of his nature should never be discounted, Orwell was not a romantic Socialist – his concentration on the material necessities of life can occasionally come as a shock – but the spectacle of a city in which most of the traditional social usages had been overthrown awakened a crusading zeal in him. The opening chapter of *Homage to Catalonia* introduces a note of vagueness to his original motive – 'I had come to Spain with some notion of writing newspaper articles' – while stressing the inevitability of practical involvement once he had seen what was going on. At this time, and in that atmosphere, joining the militia seemed the only conceivable thing to do. The revolutionary atmosphere of Catalonia coloured the simplest social transaction. Practically his first experience was receiving a lecture from a hotel manager for trying to tip the lift boy. Outwardly, at any rate – the reality turned out to be a good deal more complex – the ruling classes had ceased to exist.

There was certainly little sign of them at the Lenin Barracks. The native Spaniards that Orwell came across – there was only one other Englishman, a man named Williams – were solidly working class: blacksmiths, porters, factory operatives. It was a bad time to be joining up, he swiftly discovered: six months into the war many of the original militia volunteers were either exhausted or dead. Having been told, after his introduction to the divisional commander José Rovira, that he would be sent to the Aragon Front the next day, he had to wait until the next *centuria* was assembled. In the meantime the experience of staying in a military barracks – a Spanish military barracks at that – awakened all his customary fastidiousness. The cavalry horses had been seized and sent to the Front 'but the whole place still smelt of horse-piss and rotten oats'. The communal drinking bottle handed round by the militiamen – made of glass with a pointed spout and uncomfortably reminiscent of a hospital bed bottle – revolted him: Orwell asked for a cup. Squalor and barbaric drinking implements aside, conditions at the barracks revealed a more integral sense of chaos. Uniforms were issued piecemeal. The recruits were mostly teenage boys from the Barcelona back streets whom it was impossible to persuade to stand in line. Worse, the absence of discipline was compounded by a democratising spirit that prompted officers to rebuke men who addressed them as 'sir' and to appeal to their better nature rather than military law. Worst of all, perhaps, they were taught nothing about weaponry (there were in fact no weapons: Orwell believed that in the whole of the barracks only the sentries had rifles), only the antiquated drill that he had learned with the Eton OTC. And yet 'How easy it is to make friends in Spain!' Orwell was short on personal resonance, habitually reserved in his dealings with other people. Here in Spain, cheek by jowl with working-class Spaniards whose Catalan dialect he still had great difficulty in comprehending, he was overwhelmed by hospitality and widespread appreciation of the simple fact that he was there.

It was by now early January 1937. After much rumour and procrastination the unit was suddenly ordered to the front at two hours' notice. At once the barracks was alive with women helping their sons and husbands to pack. Orwell had to be shown how to put on his new leather cartridge boxes by Williams' Spanish wife, herself a veteran of the July street battles. Amongst other things, *Homage to Catalonia* is a study of the Spanish temperament. Several aspects of this were on display at the Lenin Barracks in the hours before departure. In particular Orwell noted the combination of ceremoniousness and ceremonials, often apparently conducted for their own sake, with administrative confusion. Lit by torchlight, decorated by a sea of red flags, the scene in the square where the men were finally marshalled was one of terrific uproar and excitement. A political commissar made a speech in Catalan beneath huge rolling red banners – Orwell makes it sound rather like a left-wing version of the Nuremberg rallies – after which the file, under the command of one of Rovira's General Staff, Georges Kopp, was marched off to the station (taking the longest route, to achieve maximum public impact) and placed on a train packed so tight with bodies that there was barely room to sit on the floor. Then, at a snail's pace – something under 20 kilometres an hour, Orwell estimated – they set off uphill towards the Aragon plateau. From the station at Barbastro they went by lorry to Siétamo, and then westward to Alcubierre just behind the line fronting Zaragoza. Here, 1,500 feet above sea level in the depth of winter, the cold was impregnated by what Orwell deduced was the characteristic smell of war, a compound of excrement and decaying food. Alcubierre in particular, though untouched by bombs, was a sea of filth. Striding up to the front line, Orwell found himself looking at the troops on either side of him with horror. They were teenage boys whose slogans, shouted along the way with the aim of keeping their spirits up, 'sounded as pathetic as the cries of kittens'. The Front itself was similarly disillusioning, merely a chain of hilltop 'positions'. In the clefts behind these promontories, Orwell's roving eye soon established, lay the refuse of months. In the middle distance, along the next chain of hilltops, microscopic figures could occasionally be seen. It was the Fascist line, 700 yards away.

Orwell stayed on the Aragon Front for nearly five months. Militarily speaking it was a backwater. Heavy fighting took place around Huesca, but Orwell's unit played only a minor part in this. The rest was night patrols, the occasional sniper bullet winging its way across the valley and what Orwell called 'the mingled boredom and discomfort of stationary warfare'. There were, as he soon discovered, good reasons for this stagnation. The first was the sheer impregnability of the opposing lines, built as they were on hilltops overlooking a deep valley. The second was the complete absence of most of the materials with which war could be prosecuted. The trench mortars, for example, were regarded as too precious to be fired and were kept at Alcubierre. Most of the rifles were useless. There were, additionally, no maps, charts, range-finders, telescopes or field-glasses, flares, Very lights, wire cutters or armourers' tools. Reading Orwell's account of what was by his own admission little more than a shambles, it is difficult not to be struck by the thought that the presence of the Republican army on the Aragon Front was largely symbolic. This is the narrow, practical complaint – as opposed to the wider, theoretical issues – levelled at Orwell by some of his left-wing critics: that he was tucked away, as one of them put it 'on a front that did not count ... where he was serving no useful military purpose'. There are degrees of usefulness, of course, not all of them military. Orwell was well aware of the drawbacks of his posting and by the end of his time there chafed to leave it, but his early weeks on the mountain-tops were simply enveloped in practicalities, the far from straightforward business of establishing a routine here amid the piercing cold, the piles of rusty tins, the rats and the mounds of excrement. Five things were important in trench warfare, he ruefully acknowledged: firewood, food, tobacco, candles and – a very bad fifth – the enemy. The search for warmth quickly established itself as the main priority of front-line life. One night on duty Orwell carefully itemised the garments he was wearing: a thick vest and pants, a flannel shirt, two pullovers, a woollen jacket, a pigskin jacket, corduroy breeches, puttees, thick socks, boots, a trench-coat, a muffler, lined leather gloves and a woollen cap.

Sanitation was non-existent. The troops were allowed a quart of water a day for both washing and drinking. The personal habits of the militiamen left much to be desired. Some had a habit of defecating in the trench, 'a disgusting thing when one had to walk round it in the darkness'. Despite these privations there is a boyishness about Orwell's accounts of trench warfare, the sense almost of an Etonian lark: 'it was rather fun wandering about the dark valley with the stray bullets flying overhead like redshanks whistling'. A later, daylight patrol was 'not bad fun in a Boy Scoutish way', he reported. Again, as so often with Orwell, one wonders how this is meant to be interpreted. Insouciance? Self-deprecation? In the end you suspect that these, quite simply, were the only terms on which Orwell could respond to the experience of scuttling across a Spanish valley in the dark. Simultaneously, although warfare brought out the teenage boy in Orwell it also invested him with authority. Older than most of his fellow-recruits, he was also, as a result of his time in the Burma Police, vastly more experienced. He was swiftly promoted to *cabot,* or corporal, in charge of ten men by the unit commander, a twenty-year-old Pole named Benjamin Lewinski, and set to impose some kind of order on what was effectively an untrained mob. The revolutionary style of discipline he had first encountered in the Lenin Barracks turned out to be more reliable than he had expected, but the work – training youngsters how to shoot and take cover – hardly placed him at the cutting edge of the Republican war effort.

Meanwhile, there was disturbing news from home. Orwell's letters to Eileen from the first three months of 1937 do not survive; neither do those she sent in reply. Some of their contents, though, can be guessed at, notably the continuing struggle over publication of *The Road to Wigan Pier,* now set for the spring. Still alarmed by the book's provocative second half, Victor Gollancz had first tried to dispense with it altogether. In this he had been stoutly repulsed by Moore and Eileen. Not able to bring himself to turn the book down, he compromised by writing his own preface to the Left Book Club edition, taking issue with what he regarded as ill-informed comments on the nature of Socialism. Orwell's view on Socialist 'crankiness', the idea that the Soviet Union 'glorified' industrialism, the 'curious indiscretion' of his description of Soviet commissars as 'gangsters' – all this is piously rebutted in a short essay dated 11 January, provoked, according to the opening paragraph, by the worry that readers might think that Orwell's book reflected the views of the three men (Gollancz, Strachey and Harold Laski) who had chosen it for publication or that it represented Left Book Club 'policy'.

Keen on Orwell's autobiographical lead-in to Part Two ('I know, in fact, of no other book in which a member of the middle class exposes with such complete frankness the shameful way in which he was brought up to think of large numbers of his fellow men'), Gollancz was less impressed by some of his thoughts on typical Socialists ('I have a fairly wide acquaintance among Socialists of every colour, and I feel that the whole of this section is based on a misunderstanding'). The Gollancz introduction is a fascinating period piece: high-minded, sincere, painfully conscious of its duty both to author and to subject, yet reduced to almost neurotic distress by the thought that any of the achievements of the Soviet Revolution could be so amateurishly called into question. Clearly, though, Eileen – in so far as this was possible in the rushed circumstances of the book's publication – was keeping an eye on Gollancz. Her letter from mid-January to Moore's office states that she appreciates the book is being brought out in great haste, and that proofs could not be let out of the publisher's office (in the event she got to see them for twenty-four hours) but hopes that the proof-correctors have not made too many 'emendations'. Here, as in other letters from early 1937, Eileen passes on data sent back from the Front. Orwell had had time to send a postcard from Siétamo admiring the stoicism of the local peasantry, who carried on as if nothing had happened even though buildings were almost smashed to pieces by bombs and shell-fire. Promotion to corporal had annoyed him, she reported, as he had to get up early to turn out the guard. However there was compensation in the shape of a dug-out 'in which he can make tea'.

Only six months married, and presumably at a loose end now that she no longer attended lectures at Birkbeck, Eileen itched to be in Spain herself. She wrote a final letter to Moore dealing with the presentation copies of *The Road to Wigan Pier* (they included one to 'Mrs Dennis Collings') in early February, shortly before her own departure to Barcelona to take up a volunteer's post in John McNair's office. Aunt Nellie was reinstalled at the Stores and commissioned to maintain the shop. By this time Orwell's own position had altered. Three weeks into his stay an ILP contingent had turned up at Alcubierre. It was thought expedient to keep the English together so Williams and Orwell were sent to join the newcomers at a new position at Monte Oscuro, several miles to the west and in sight of Zaragoza. Orwell liked his new companions – there was a solitary Spaniard, Williams' brother-in-law Ramón, together with a dozen native anarchist machine-gunners – commending them, rather in the tones of an Eton housemaster, as 'an exceptionally good crowd, both physically and mentally', and they, with a few prominent exceptions, liked him. Eyewitness accounts of Orwell in Spain stress his distinctiveness, while occasionally differing over its source. Even in an army with no dress code his appearance was sufficiently outlandish to cause comment. Bob Edwards, who became a Labour MP in the first post-war parliament, remembered seeing him for the first time hung round in a 'grotesque' mixture of clothing and accessories: 'corduroy riding breeches, khaki puttees and huge boots caked with mud, a yellow pigskin jerkin, a chocolate-coloured balaclava helmet with a knitted khaki scarf of immeasurable length wrapped round and round his neck and face up to his ears, an old-fashioned German rifle over his shoulders and two hand-grenades hanging from his belt'. Younger members of the platoon noted an air of authority and expertise: he was, for example, adept at retrieving potatoes and kindling from the slope. One man remembered a night patrol, by moonlight. There was no need to crouch down, Orwell reassured him: he would not be seen.

Above these reminiscences hangs the eternal question of whether he 'fitted in'. To the eighteen-year-old Stafford Cottman, he was the most popular man in the contingent, disliked only by a handful of malcontents who murmured over his accent 'or the fact that he'd been disdainful over some subject or other'. One of them – later to become a thorn in Orwell's flesh – was Frank Frankford, who detected only condescension: 'You always got the impression that he felt Socialism was alright as long as the workers didn't run it.' Another volunteer, Jack Branthwaite, whose father had been a miner, was impressed by the human warmth that flowed out of *The Road to Wigan Pier*: it was written from the heart, he decided. And yet Orwell was not a 'mixer' in the accepted sense. Edwards noted his bravery. During one Fascist attack the machine-guns malfunctioned. The Spanish gunners refused to lie down in the face of enemy bombardment, thinking it beneath their dignity. Orwell joined them – a fearless thing to do, Edwards thought, but stemming from an urge to 'prove himself'. Off duty, he had a habit of sitting by himself writing ('the bloody scribbler', Edwards nicknamed him) or reading: Shakespeare and Charles Reade's *Hard Cash* featured on his Aragon list. He was not strong, caught cold easily and liked his comforts, chiefly proper English tea ordered by Eileen from Fortnum and Mason or the Army and Navy Stores and sent up from Barcelona.

There is something characteristic in the thought of Orwell bringing these aspects of his Englishness with him to Zaragoza: reading Victorian novels and brewing his tea in a dug-out overlooking the Aragon Front. The photographs that survive from Eileen's visit in March, when she was driven up in a staff car by Georges Kopp, have something of this air. The members of the ILP contingent are posed behind one of the Spanish machine-gunners. Orwell dominates the group by virtue of his height. Eileen crouches at his side. The trip was not without its risks – the Fascist guns opened up at one point – but the faces could be staring out from a seaside charabanc. Orwell's reaction to the life going on around him, both human and natural, is also very typical. *Homage to Catalonia* is full of nature notes along the way – the trees not yet budding, blades of winter barley poking up through the lumpy soil – breaking out every so often into purple patches reminiscent of his previous attempts to get to grips with the landscapes of Burma. In general he found the mountain scenery oppressive to the eye.

> But sometimes the dawn breaking behind the hill-tops in our rear, the first narrow streaks of gold, like swords slitting the darkness, and then the growing light and the seas of carmine cloud stretching away into inconceivable distances were worth watching even when you had been up all night, when your legs were numb from the knees down and you were sullenly reflecting that there was no hope of food for another three hours.

Shortly before Eileen's arrival in Barcelona the unit left Monte Oscuro and together with the POUM troops in the sector were sent fifty miles across the Catalan plain to join the Republican army surrounding Huesca in a siege that had been going on for months. Six weeks into active service, relocated to a part of the line where the prospect of actual combat was much more immediate, Orwell would have been able to bring greater clarity to the question of what he was doing in Spain and what he hoped to achieve. What, when it came down to it, was he fighting for? *Homage to Catalonia* includes a chapter of self-examination along these lines, revealing in that it acknowledges the naïvety with which Orwell set out in Kopp's procession to the Barcelona railway station. What was at stake – a key Orwell phrase by this time – was 'common decency'. Orwell had joined the POUM militia simply because he arrived in Barcelona with ILP papers. At this point he knew little of the fault-lines that separated the Spanish political parties and less of the special character of Spanish Fascism.

Backed by the aristocracy and the Church – institutions that tended to have serious doubts about other right-wing European autocrats such as Hitler and Mussolini – Franco's aim, close inspection revealed, could be more properly described as an attempt to restore feudalism. Unlike the Nazi visions of a thousand-year Reich, it looked backwards, not to the future. Moreover, what went on inside the country's borders was being seriously misrepresented beyond them. 'Outside Spain few people grasped that there was a revolution; inside Spain nobody doubted it.'

Many of these distinctions had yet to impress themselves on Orwell's mind. The 'line' peddled by the PSUC (Partido Socialista Unificada de Cataluña), and their Communist allies – that nothing mattered except winning the war – deeply appealed to him, to the extent that he wanted to transfer to the International Column. This single-mindedness was noted by his comrades in the ILP contingent. According to a young American volunteer, 'He had no political consciousness at the time. He didn't comprehend the role that the Communists were playing in Spain.' There was also a suspicion, emanating from Edwards, that Orwell preferred the International Brigade because it would provide better copy. Frankford was emphatic about this. Orwell wanted to join the International Brigade, he claimed, 'because he was a journalist'. This is unfair to Orwell, but evidently the solitary note-taking – Eileen refers to the diary he was keeping at this time and acknowledges that a book will eventually emerge out of his experiences – had not gone unnoticed.

Spring was coming to Huesca. Searching the ditches Orwell found violets and a variety of wild hyacinth. Food remained a problem, the chief resort being a nearby potato patch with practically no cover from the Fascist machine-gunners. By now life in the trenches was having an adverse effect on his health. A letter from Eileen to her mother, sent in late March from the office of the POUM journal *Spanish Revolution*, reporting on her visit to the Front, describes him as 'fairly well'. He had recently been examined by a Spanish doctor at Monflorite, a few miles behind the Front, who pronounced him to be suffering from nothing worse than cold and fatigue. Eileen, unimpressed by both the doctor ('quite ignorant and incredibly dirty') and his hospital – not much more than a dressing station for casualties brought up from the Front – abandoned a scheme to stay there as a nurse and went back to Barcelona, thinking that her husband's interests were best served by the supplies of tea, chocolate and, when procurable, cigars. However, Orwell was soon back at Monflorite, on this occasion with a poisoned hand that required ten days' rest. The light-fingered Spanish hospital orderlies stole practically everything he possessed, including the photographs from Eileen's visit, but there was compensation in some 'blissful days' spent walking around the countryside. Here in a drinking pond used by the village mules he turned up some 'exquisite green frogs, the size of a penny, so brilliant that the young grass looked dull beside them'. He wrote to Eileen thanking her for a fresh consignment of supplies and the reviews of *The Road To Wigan Pier* she had sent on. These, Orwell considered, were better than could be expected, with the predictable exception of Harry Pollitt in the *Daily Worker*.

Back on the Huesca Front he was involved in what turned out to be one of the most dangerous episodes of his military career. The Republican line was advancing. In a seven-hour night manoeuvre 600 militiamen constructed a vast expanse of trench and parapet only a few hundred yards from the Fascist positions. Subsequently volunteers were requested for a night attack on an enemy redoubt under the direction of the battalion commander, Jorge Roca. The account of the sortie given in *Homage to Catalonia* – it can be supplemented by a dramatic reconstruction in the *New Leader* ('Our boys of the good old ILP did their job and damn well') – is a curious mixture of immediacy and reflective detachment. The thirty or so volunteers moved forward over the wet ground with the aim of getting within bombing distance before being overheard. At the same time another force would attack further up the line. Orwell was taken back to his Burmese hunting days: 'I have felt exactly the same thing when stalking a wild animal, the same agonised desire to get within range, the same dream-like certainty that it is impossible.' They got to within a few yards of the line before the Fascists saw them. There was panic when Orwell found himself caught between enemy fire and the shots of his own troops, but in the end the parapet was breached and the attackers poured over. According to the *Leader* Orwell's figure could be seen 'coolly strolling forward through the storm of fire' (a fellow-militiaman remembered him standing up to shout 'Come on, you bastards!' to which he replied 'For Christ's sake, Eric, get down').

Inside the enemy position Orwell found himself chasing a retreating Fascist along a communication trench with a bayonet. This, too, took him back twenty years to the school boxing instructor explaining in vivid pantomime how he had bayoneted a Turk at the Dardanelles. The man escaped; his colleagues were dead or disappearing. Boxes of ammunition and an enormous telescope were found – both of immense value to the badly supplied Republican army – but an attempt to remove them faltered when the Fascists began to attack from a position further up the line which the Republican shock troops had obviously failed to take. The militiamen tried to erect a barricade on the unprotected side but the enemy was closing in. Orwell borrowed a bomb from a man named Moyle and threw it precisely where he judged the rifle fire to have come from. There was a dreadful outcry of screams and groans. Orwell admitted to a 'vague sorrow' as he heard the man yelling. The unit retreated with a captured box of ammunition to find that Roca and an Englishman named Hiddleton were missing. Volunteering to search, Orwell, Moyle and three Spaniards discovered that the Fascists had regrouped in strength and were chased back. The two missing men turned out to have been wounded and removed to a dressing station. Later Kopp assured them that the attack, diverting troops from another part of the line where an assault was in progress, was a 'success'.

It was Orwell's last substantial engagement. As the spring days grew longer and the abundant flowers produced incongruous effects – wild roses with blooms the size of saucers straggled over the shell-holes behind the Front – he grew darkly conscious of the fact that he was doing no good. He had spent 115 days in the line, he calculated, 'and at the time this period seemed to me to have been one of the most futile of my entire life'. Retrospect insisted that this was not so, that the three and a half months formed an interregnum quite different from anything he had experienced before in which he learned things he could not have acquired in any other way, but for the moment his greatest wish was to join the International Brigade and get to Madrid. He was due leave and his discharge papers had been sent in – much to the dismay of some members of the ILP contingent. Bob Edwards had left Spain some weeks before – the 'bloody scribbler', it may be pointed out, was still there – but he had told Orwell what he knew about the activities of the International Brigade's political commissars. Harry Milton, who travelled back on leave with him, made the point in even starker terms: 'They won't take you, but if they do, they'll knock you off.' But Orwell was not to be dissuaded. On 25 April he and Milton went back to Monflorite and slept for a few hours in a barn. Then they caught the early train at Babastro and transferred to an express at Lerica. They were in Barcelona by three o'clock in the afternoon. Richard Rees had been in the city only a few days before. During his stay he had called on Eileen at the POUM office, where she was working. He found her in what struck him as a very strange mental state – absent-minded, preoccupied, apparently dazed. At first Rees assumed this was the result of worrying about her husband, but when she began to talk of the risk, to Rees, of being seen with her in the street the explanation no longer seemed to fit. Later Rees settled on a different reason for Eileen's distress. She was, he realised, the first person in whom he had witnessed 'the effects of living under a political terror'.

Barcelona

Curiously enough the whole experience has left me with not less but more belief in the decency of human beings. – Homage to Catalonia

Despite the various minor ailments he had suffered at the Front, Eileen thought Orwell in good health on his return to Barcelona. His clothes were in shreds, his boots practically disintegrating – Jennie Lee had been right about the difficulty of finding size 12s in Spain – and his body slightly lousy and burned dark brown by the sun, but he was, she considered, 'looking really well'. Unfortunately, within a few days of joining her at the Hotel Continental he went down with some kind of stomach complaint: probably the result of too much food and drink after the frugality of the trenches, he thought. Nevertheless he was determined to enjoy his leave in a city previously only glimpsed in the depths of winter.

In his absence Eileen, now ten weeks in Spain, had got to know Barcelona well. She had been there during the March aerial bombardment – the habitual noisiness of the Spanish was stifled in times of emergency, she reported – and had taken advantage of what, even in wartime, was an enticing night-life. A letter to her mother written towards the end of March notes that she had had '3 superb dinners in succession' and that instead of going home early to write letters had arrived back at the hotel in the small hours of the following morning. Undoubtedly some of these dinners came courtesy of her husband's commandant Georges Kopp, whose relationship with Eileen is one of the enigmas of the Orwells' Spanish trip. Two years older than Eileen and evasive about his personal life – much of the information he supplied to Orwell turned out to be false – Kopp was an odd character, whose partiality for the company of Mrs Blair was noted by one or two members of the ILP contingent. A friend of Eileen's, Rosalind

Obermeyer, who co-hosted the party at which she and Orwell first met, recalled how in later years Eileen's face would light up at the mention of Kopp's name. None of this proves anything about their association, but Kopp is consistently, if unobtrusively, present in both husband's and wife's accounts of the events of May and June 1937: ferrying Eileen to the Front in his car; writing letters on her behalf. He could not have known then that much of the Orwells' final days in Spain would be taken up in trying to rescue him from what seemed the prospect of certain death.

As ever, the Orwells' thoughts were not solely concentrated on Spain. There was English post to deal with, including the copies of the Left Book Club edition of *The Road to Wigan Pier* with Gollancz's introduction, which Orwell had not yet seen, and news of Wallington. The shop was declining under Aunt Nellie's negligent supervision and there was money owing locally. Eileen commissioned her brother Laurence to sort things out and dispose of the remaining goods. Presumably Aunt Nellie had moved out by this time as there was a plan, never realised, to allow Orwell's badly wounded ILP comrade Arthur Clinton to recuperate there. For all these distractions, Orwell's chief interest, wandering in and out of the Hotel Continental after tending his upset stomach with a couple of days in bed, lay in the enormous changes that had come over Barcelona in the four months since he had last been there. In the light of the previous year's social revolution, many of these seemed distinctly ominous. Most obviously, the civilian population had lost much of their interest in the war: it was simply something that rumbled on in the remote distance, and as such an impediment to 'normal' life. The old divisions between rich and poor and master and servant were reasserting themselves. Servility, conspicuously absent from the Barcelona shops and hotels at the turn of the year, was now conspicuously renascent. Taking Eileen into a hosiery shop on the Ramblas, Orwell was surprised to find the shopman bowing and scraping in a way that would have seemed excessive in Oxford Street. Meanwhile, there was more formal evidence of changing times. In particular Orwell noted a systematic propaganda campaign directed against the party militias and in favour of the 'Popular Army', into which all the armed forces had since February been theoretically incorporated.

Although he was dimly aware that the political landscape of Republican Spain was beginning to shift beneath his feet, Orwell, by his own admission, still regarded party political differences as secondary to his aim of getting to the Madrid Front. If he wanted to get to Madrid he would have to join the International Column, which meant obtaining a recommendation from a Communist party member. Then there was the problem of what to do about Eileen. Madrid would probably be closed to her, but staying in Barcelona would be pointless. Eileen assumed her ultimate destiny would be Valencia, the seat of the Republican government. A letter sent on May Day to her brother discloses some of the practical realities of the war effort. The Orwells realised that they were 'politically suspect' to the International Brigade, but when they had explained matters to the Brigade representative, the man 'was practically offering me an executive job by the end of half an hour, & I gather they will take George'. Eileen acknowledged the incongruity of the choice, 'but it is what he thought he was doing in the first place, & it's the only way of getting to Madrid'. Orwell had already applied for his discharge papers, but he was prevented by his illness from calling at the barracks to collect them. The International Brigade was apparently keen to recruit from the ILP contingent: had he been in better health he might have been accepted on the spot. However, he was ill, he had another week's leave remaining, and having resorted to the expedient of ordering a new pair of boots, which were still being made, he had nothing to march in. Orwell – significantly, given the events of the next week – decided to stay put.

Beneath the outwardly placid surface of Barcelona – the crowds flocking along the Ramblas and the noisy commerce of the streets – huge antagonisms were stirring. Much of this unrest was fuelled by political assassinations carried out by feuding Republican groups, followed by lavish funerals. Much of this was attributable to the longstanding hostility between the anarchists and the more orthodox Left, the latter now much more susceptible to Communist influence. At the same time the divisions that now split the anti-Franco coalition were growing ever more complex. At the end of April, for example, after the murder of a prominent member of the UGT, the government ordered all the shops to close and staged an enormous funeral procession, largely made up of Popular Army troops, which took two hours to pass. Orwell watched it from his window at the Hotel Continental. That night he and Eileen were woken by a fusillade of shots from the direction of the Plaza de Cataluña a hundred yards away, later revealed as the murder of a CNT man. There was talk of a May Day demonstration in which both the CNT, whose moderate leader-ship was working for reconciliation, and the UGT would take part, but in the end it was called off for fear of rioting. It was an odd state of affairs, Orwell reflected, that Barcelona, of all places, should turn out to be probably the only major city in non-Fascist Europe not to celebrate the twentieth anniversary of the Soviet Revolution. However remote the civil war might now seem to the Barcelona bourgeoisie, its ramifications were alarmingly close at hand. Each day brought a further rise in the political temperature. Orwell's ILP compatriot Jack Branthwaite remembered being with him at the Hotel Continental when a street fight broke out nearby. 'We were sitting there, and a shot came through the window. We all ducked. We didn't know what it was all about.'

Matters came to a head on 3 May, when several lorryloads of Civil Guards drove up to the Barcelona telephone exchange, mainly operated by CNT workers, and tried to place it under official control. Alerted to the disturbance halfway down the Ramblas, where he saw shots being exchanged between some anarchists and someone in a nearby church tower, Orwell was on his way back to the hotel when he bumped into an American army doctor he had met at the Front, who explained the situation to him. Together the two men set off for the Hotel Falcon, then operating as a kind of POUM boarding-house, at the further end of the Ramblas. Here everything was in confusion. At the POUM's local office practically opposite rifles were being handed out on the understanding that the Civil Guard were in hot pursuit of the CNT and seizing strategic spots that overlooked other buildings belonging to the workers. In the absence of hard information, the potential defenders settled down to wait. Orwell had managed to procure a rifle but had it stolen from him by a young militia boy. Eventually he was able to reach McNair, the ILP representative, by telephone. McNair reported that everything was OK. It would be OK at the POUM Comité Locale, Orwell riposted, if they had any cigarettes. Half an hour later, having been stopped twice on the way by Anarchist patrols, McNair appeared bearing two packets of Lucky Strike. By this time, with the evening wearing on, the militiamen had had time to take stock of their situation. There were hardly any weapons on the premises: the armoury was practically empty. In addition the place was crowded with passers-by who had taken shelter when the trouble started. They spent an uncomfortable night sleeping on the floor. The building had formerly operated as a cabaret theatre. Orwell tore down a curtain from one of the stages, wrapped himself up in it and managed to sleep until 3 a.m. when he was given a rifle and placed on guard at a window.

By morning there were barricades in the street. Disarmed once more, his rifle having been requisitioned, Orwell and another Englishman decided to go back to the Hotel Continental. They got as far as the food market halfway along the Ramblas when firing broke out. A barricade was up on the street corner where Orwell had seen shooting the day before, and a man hiding behind it warned him that there were Civil Guards in the church tower sniping at anyone who passed. As Orwell crossed the street at a run, a bullet cracked past 'uncomfortably close'. When he drew level with the POUM Executive building, still on the other side of the street, he heard shouts coming from some shock troopers standing in the doorway. Separated by trees and a newspaper kiosk, Orwell could not see what they were pointing at. Having got back to the hotel, made sure that Eileen was safe and washed his face, he went back to the Executive building to ask for orders. By this time the noise of rifle and machine-gun fire had risen in a crescendo. Orwell's conversation with Kopp, whom he discovered there, was interrupted by a series of appalling crashes from below. Hurrying downstairs to investigate, they found a group of shock troopers inside the doorway bowling bombs down the street as if they were playing skittles. The head of Orwell's American militia comrade Harry Milton, with whom he had travelled down on leave, could be seen sticking up above the kiosk like a coconut. It turned out that the Civil Guard had barricaded themselves into the nearby Café Moka, attempted to fight their way out, been repulsed, fled back into the café and then opened fire on Milton, who happened to be walking down the street, causing him to dive for shelter.

Kopp, whose coolness under fire Orwell greatly admired, immediately took charge of the situation and attempted to broker a truce. Standing on the pavement, and in full view of the café, he took off his pistol and laid it on the ground. Then, together with two Spanish militia officers, he walked up to the doorway that concealed the Civil Guard riflemen. The shirt-sleeved man who emerged to parley pointed nervously to two unexploded bombs that lay on the pavement. Kopp returned and told his own men to touch them off with rifle fire. Orwell, using a rifle borrowed from one of the shock troops, took aim at the second bomb and the solitary shot he fired during the whole disturbance missed its target. There followed a tense and long-drawn-out stand-off. Their orders, Kopp explained to Orwell once they were safely back inside the POUM building, were to defend themselves if attacked but not to open fire if it could possibly be avoided. As for the best method of defence, immediately opposite was a cinema named the Poliorama, on whose upper storey was a museum and then an observatory with twin domes that commanded the street. Guards had already been posted. Orwell joined them and, taking breaks for meals, spent the next three days on the roof-top looking down over the tree-lined street. Reflecting on this protracted stake-out in *Homage to Catalonia*, he was keen to emphasise that he suffered from nothing worse than hunger and boredom, 'yet it was one of the most unbearable periods of my life'. The city, large parts of which fanned out beneath and around him, lay 'locked in a sort of violent inertia'. However, there were compensations. One was an unofficial non-aggression pact which Kopp had negotiated with the Civil Guards, whose material result was a present of fifteen bottles of beer looted from the Café Moka's storeroom. Another was the unexpected presence of Jon Kimche, Orwell's friend from Booklovers' Corner. Struck by the ease with which they renewed their acquaintance ('it was like we were resuming the conversations we had in Hampstead') Kimche remembered Orwell criticising the inefficiency of the militia and the shortcomings of their equipment.

Orwell spent most of his time on the roof reading a supply of Penguin paperbacks, darkly conscious of the Civil Guard, who had established their own post fifty yards away above the café. Only once did it look as if trouble was about to break out, when someone in the street took a shot at the adjoining building, but it was soon smoothed over. The only bullet fired in anger at Orwell came from a building further down the street, but it went so wide that it failed even to hit the observatory roof. Meanwhile food was running short. Although supplies could be brought in from the Hotel Falcon under cover of darkness, there was never enough to go round and the men – Orwell put their number at between fifteen and twenty – were encouraged to slip out to the Hotel Continental for meals. Here the militiamen discovered an extra-ordinary collection of people: flotsam from the streets, foreign journalists, political suspects, and an immensely sinister character nicknamed 'Charlie Chan'; everyone supposed him to be a Russian secret service agent, and his get-up included a revolver and a miniature bomb attached to his waistband. Two or three days into confrontation a change seemed to come over the atmosphere. The barricades were still in place and the CNT rank and file were insisting on the return of the telephone exchange and the disbanding of the Civil Guard. Had the municipal authorities made these two concessions and ended food profiteering then, Orwell believed, the barriers would have been dismantled in a couple of hours. But it was clear that the city administration was inflexible. All kinds of rumours were afloat: that the Valencia government was sending a 6,000-strong force to occupy the city; that 5,000 Anarchist and POUM troops had abandoned the Aragon Front to head them off. The first of these turned out to be true. Kopp told Orwell that he had just heard that the government was about to outlaw the POUM and declare a state of war. In this event Kopp would have to seize the Café Moka, so the militiamen spent the evening of 5 May barricading and fortifying their building. One interested spectator was Eileen, who had hurried up from the Hotel Continental to volunteer as a nurse. Another rumour suggesting that the water was about to be cut off had them filling every basin, bucket and bottle on the premises. By this time Orwell had gone nearly sixty hours without proper rest. He lay down on a sofa thinking he would snatch a few minutes' rest before the attack on the café. When he woke up it was broad daylight and Eileen was standing beside him. Apart from sporadic firing in the streets, everything seemed more or less normal.

Still, though, all was subterfuge and rumour. On the afternoon of 6 May the ghost of an armistice rose up and people rushed out to buy food, only for the gunfire to resume. Orwell returned to the roof. Amongst the mob of safety-seekers inside the Hotel Continental a 'horrible atmosphere of suspicion' had arisen. The supposed Russian agent was cornering foreign refugees and explaining that the whole thing was an anarchist plot. Orwell watched him with disdainful fascination, 'for it was the first time I had seen a person whose profession was telling lies' – unless, that is, one counted journalists. That evening the principal dinner dish offered to the Hotel Continental's thronged and polyglot clientele was a single sardine per head. The only item in abundant supply was oranges, provided by some stranded French lorry drivers. Orwell passed a further night on the roof, but by the next day – Friday – it looked finally as if the disturbance was coming to an end. The government radio broadcasts were emollient and threatening by turns, urging everyone to go home and warning that after a certain hour anyone found carrying arms would be arrested. The barricades were steadily depopulated, the trams began to return to service and the black anarchist flag was taken down from above the telephone exchange. Later that evening government troops from Valencia – crack Assault Guards, the pride of the Republican army – appeared on the streets. There remained the delicate problem – given the prohibition on the carrying of arms – of returning the six rifles used for guarding the observatory back across the street to the POUM building under the gaze of the Civil Guards in the Café Moka. Eventually Orwell and a Spanish boy smuggled them over concealed in their clothing. Even Orwell's 34-inch inside legs had difficulty coping with the barrels of the Long Mausers, but in the end the task was accomplished. On the next day the Assault Guards were everywhere, 'walking the streets like conquerors'.

It was an altogether queer time, Orwell later acknowledged, a time of things happening very fast and not happening at all, a time when the city's outward return to normality failed to disguise the tensions that ran beneath. Above all, it was clear that old scores remained to be settled. Whatever the ultimate cause of the Barcelona fighting it would allow the Valencia government to dominate Catalonia to a degree that had not been possible during the revolutionary atmosphere of the autumn of 1936. The worker militias would be broken up, their members parcelled out among the Popular Army. The POUM were declared to be covert Fascists: a cartoon in circulation depicted a mask emblazoned with a hammer and sickle being slipped off a face, to reveal the swastika beneath. Despite the tide of official pronouncements the air was full of uncertainty as individuals tried to establish what these commands might mean for their own communal or personal fiefdoms. Life on the ground, where these policy changes were at best provisional, proceeded in a much less absolutist way. Orwell was surprised to receive a further approach from his Communist friend, asking if he still wanted to transfer into the International Brigade. Surely, Orwell wondered, the government papers had him marked down as a Fascist? Ah, the Communist replied, but he was only obeying orders. In the following weeks, in Barcelona and elsewhere, this defence cut little ice.

All around him entirely innocent people were being arrested or forced to go to ground. An ILP friend, wounded at the Front and sent back to Barcelona when the fighting started, spent eight days in a cell so crowded with prisoners that there was no room to lie down. A German girl who had no papers contrived to dodge the police by pretending to be someone's mistress. Orwell remembered the look of 'shame and misery' on her face when he accidentally bumped into her emerging from the man's room. To read the accounts of the Republican government's descent on Barcelona is instantly to become aware of its importance for Orwell's later work and the view he developed of the authoritarian state. 'You had all the while a hateful feeling that someone hitherto your friend might be denouncing you to the secret police.' Yet more bizarre was the way in which ordinary life went on alongside the police raids and the overflowing cells: a fashionably dressed woman sauntering down the Ramblas with a poodle at her heels and a shopping basket over her arm as the rifles cracked a street or two away; a group of people clad in black (a funeral party, Orwell deduced) trying for perhaps an hour to cross the Plaza de Cataluña but always driven back by a machine-gunner in an overlooking hotel. The people in the shoe-shop making Orwell's boots – he made several calls before, during and after the fighting – seemed completely indifferent despite, their customer suspected, being his political opponents. Perhaps a majority of the city's inhabitants had not the slightest interest in what was going on around them, he believed.

Chastened by his experience Orwell had decided to return to the Aragon Front. Given his past affiliations and present unease, there seemed no real alternative. Sinclair-Loutit, back on leave from the Madrid Front, came across him one afternoon in the same POUM café on the Ramblas where he had been unwittingly cross-questioned by Radio Verdad. Their discussion of the progress of the war left Sinclair-Loutit puzzled. Both men had provided virtually identical analyses of the military situation, 'but, paradoxically, his solution ignored the crucial role of Madrid. So he was to return to his unit on the dead Aragon front'. In fact Orwell was well aware of the crucial role of the Spanish capital. It seems much more likely that, suspicious of Sinclair-Loutit's political sympathies (as he continued to be when the two met again in England) he decided to keep his cards close to his chest. From the Hotel Continental, on 9 May, Orwell wrote what was in the circumstances a marvellously nonchalant letter to Victor Gollancz, claiming to like his introduction to *The Road to Wigan Pier* and ascribing the delay in his response to his being 'rather occupied'. He was returning to the Front in a few days, he told Gollancz, and expected to be there until August. 'After that I think I shall come home, as it will be about time I started another book.' As it turned out, through no fault of his own, and by the skin of his teeth, he would be back in England in a bare six weeks.

There was, as Kenneth Sinclair-Loutit had pointed out, not a great deal happening on the Aragon Front. The chief trouble was snipers: although the Fascist trenches were more than 150 yards distant they were on higher ground and on two sides. First thing in the morning, as the dawn began to rise over the valley, Orwell had the habit of lighting a cigarette and standing smoking it immediately behind the parapet of the Republican trench. This had been built for Spaniards, men six or eight inches smaller, which meant that his head and shoulders were outlined in silhouette against the sky. 'Eric, you know, one of these days you're going to get shot,' Branthwaite had cautioned him. Dawn on 20 May broke with an unusual clarity: 'a beautiful, beautiful sunrise,' Harry Milton, who had stood guard during the small hours, remembered. At 5 a.m. Orwell came to relieve him, climbed on to the sandbagged step and stuck his head over the parapet. A shot rang out – from the Fascist-occupied church near the POUM line, Branthwaite believed – and he toppled over. In *Homage to Catalonia* Orwell sat down to analyse the sensations of being shot with all his customary detachment. He had the feeling, he recalled, of being at the centre of an explosion: a loud bang, a blinding flash of light, an almost electrical shock, bringing with it a wave of paralysing lassitude, of being stricken and shrivelled away to nothing. His first thought was that a rifle had gone off nearby and shot him accidentally. Then he realised that the bullet had struck him somewhere in the front of the body. The speed of the bullet's flight had sealed up the entrance to the wound but when Milton cradled Orwell's head in his arms a puddle of blood appeared beneath. When he tried to speak he found he had no voice, but at the second attempt he managed to ask in a squeak where he had been hit. In the throat, he was told. Lifted up, with blood pouring from his mouth, Orwell heard a Spanish militiaman behind him say that the bullet had gone clean through his neck.

Reasoning that he could not have been shot through the throat without damage to his carotid artery, Orwell assumed he was dying. He was reassured, once laid on a stretcher, when his right arm – numb since the moment of impact – came back to life and started hurting. Carried by four bearers he was borne off a mile and a half behind the lines to an ambulance, where a doctor bandaged his wound, administered morphine and dispatched him to Siétamo. Later, when sufficient sick and wounded had accumulated to make the trip worthwhile, the ambulance went on to Barbastro – a terrible journey over pot-holed roads which reminded Orwell of a fairground ride on something called the Wiggle Woggle taken as a child at the White City Exhibition. Worse, the Siétamo orderlies had forgotten to tie the patients to their stretchers. Orwell had the strength to cling on but one man spilled out on to the vehicle's floor. Finally from Barbastro he was sent on to the big hospital at Lerida, which treated militiamen and civilians alike.

It was here, early on the morning of 22 May, driven up from Barcelona by Kopp, that Eileen got to see him. He was in a reasonable state, complaining of an aching right arm and a pain in his left side which seemed connected to his collapse in the trench rather than the throat wound. His voice was hoarse, but he could be understood. Returning to Barcelona, Eileen sent a carefully worded telegram to Southwold stressing Orwell's 'excellent' progress and emphasising that there was no cause for alarm. This may have been the case, but in fact Orwell had not yet received any diagnosis or treatment. Even Lerida, he found, was essentially a grander version of the medical transit camps near the Front, a stopping-off point at which men were left 'hanging about' for days until such time as they could be shipped on to specialist hospitals at Barcelona and Tarragona. Initially confined to bed, Orwell kept his usual beady eye on the toings and froings of the ward, noting for example that the man in the adjoining bed had been given medicine that turned his urine bright green. Two teenage militiamen whom Orwell had met in his first week at the Front arrived in the hospital to visit a friend. Unable to think of anything to say they unloaded their tobacco on him before fleeing in embarrassment. Though still in pain from his arm and the injury to his side – but not, mysteriously, from his wound – Orwell was soon well enough to get up. There was a garden in the hospital grounds with a pool filled with goldfish and a breed of small grey fish that his fisherman's eye marked down as bleak which he sat and watched for hours while he awaited his transfer. Many others, some of them in much worse states, were in the same position. Men with dreadful wounds or smashed bones lay on beds in the wards with their injuries swathed in casings made of bandages and plaster of Paris, with a description of the damage pencilled on the outside. Usually the casing was not removed until the patient reached Barcelona or Tarragona as much as ten days later.

Orwell had been told that he would be sent to Barcelona. In fact on 27 May he was transferred to Tarragona – another nightmarish journey in a third-class railway carriage crammed with badly wounded men who were in a state of collapse. Their arrival brought a symbolic vignette of the nature of war: a trainful of men from the International Column moving out while the medical train crept in. It was like an allegorical picture, Orwell reflected: the fresh men gliding proudly up the line; the maimed men sliding slowly down; the guns on the open truck making one's heart leap and reviving 'the pernicious feeling, so difficult to get rid of, that war *is* glorious after all'. Most of the men – they were Italian volunteers – would be killed at Huesca a few weeks later.

Orwell spent nearly three days at Tarragona. His strength was slowly returning and he managed one day to walk as far as the beach. Here life seemed to be going on much as normal, although characteristically Orwell contrived to see a bather drowned, 'which one would have thought impossible in that shallow and tepid sea'. Finally his wound was examined by a doctor. He was told that he would never get his voice back, as the larynx was 'broken'. The bullet had missed the main artery by a hair's breadth. The pain in his arm, it was established, came from a bunch of nerves in the back of his neck pierced by the bullet's exit. A further transfer was thought desirable and late on 29 May Eileen and Kopp arrived to take him the sixty miles to the Sanatorium Maurin, a POUM-run hospital in the Barcelona suburbs. By the following day his voice, previously inaudible beyond the range of a few feet, had improved, as had his appetite. He found several other Englishmen on the premises, including Arthur Clinton and Stafford Cottman who had been sent back from the Front with suspected TB.

Orwell would take no further part in the war. On 1 June he received a thorough examination by Professor Grau of the University of Barcelona. Grau diagnosed 'incomplete semi-paralysis of the larynx due to abrasion on the right side larynx dilating nerve'. The bullet had passed between the trachea and the carotid artery. All that could be recommended by way of treatment was electrotherapy, and he was referred to a Dr Barraquer at the city's General Hospital, who specialised in the electric treatment of nervous disturbance. Kopp – ever vigilant in pursuit of Orwell's interests – wrote a report on his condition which was sent to Eileen's brother. Thereafter, in the early days of June, a routine established itself. Eileen remained at the Hotel Continental, with Orwell coming up from the suburbs for his electrotherapy. By now he had decided to return to England. He was certified medically unfit, but to obtain an official discharge he would have to appear before a medical board at one of the hospitals near the Front and then go back to Siétamo to get his papers stamped at the POUM headquarters. A letter to Cyril Connolly proposes an early meeting in London. 'If I can get my discharge papers I ought to be home in about a fortnight.' Battered, hoarse and still in pain, he was anxious to share his experiences of Spain: 'I have seen wonderful things, and at last really believe in Socialism, which I never did before.' Writing to

Laurence O'Shaughnessy a couple of days later, Eileen reported that he was better – voice improving, and more feeling in his arm – though *utterly* depressed, which Eileen, knowing her husband's psychology, thought was a good thing.

It was now nearly the middle of June. The political situation in Barcelona, which had escaped Orwell's eye for nearly a month, was still dangerously disturbed. Many prominent POUM people, including Bob Smillie, the charismatic grandson of the famous miners' leader, were still in jail, and foreigners continued to be arrested as 'deserters'. Assault Guards patrolled the streets and there was a widespread fear that street fighting would return. The wider political situation was disquieting. Back in mid-May the Communists had orchestrated a cabinet crisis. Caballero resigned as premier, to be replaced by Negrin at the head of an administration purged of left-wingers which the anarchists chose not to join. The revolution was in retreat: the influence of the Soviet Union could only increase. Ominously, this sinister turn of events seems to have been long-planned. Orlov, head of the NKVD in Spain, had assured his headquarters in Moscow as long ago as December 1936, that 'The Trotskyist organisation POUM can easily be liquidated.' Though aware of the rumours flying around Barcelona, Orwell had his own private objectives to accomplish. After seeing Kopp, who was off to Valencia in search of a special appointment in the engineering section, he left for Siétamo. He arrived to find an attack in progress and the call for reservists likely to go out at any moment, and spent the night sleeping on the ground with a cartridge box for a pillow. Subsequently he spent several days traipsing from hospital to hospital in pursuit of his discharge, fetching up at Monzon hospital. A cheerful doctor signed the certificate, assuring him that he would never speak again. Waiting to be examined, Orwell heard the screams of a patient being operated on without anaesthetic inside the surgery. He entered the room to find chairs flung about and the floor covered with blood and urine.

Nevertheless he had his discharge, stamped with the seal of the 29th Division, and a medical certificate in which he was 'declared useless'. He was at liberty to go back to England. Luxuriating in this newfound freedom, Orwell felt able at last to 'look at Spain'. Accordingly he spent a day at Barbastro observing the local arts and crafts. Unsurprisingly, this realised some typical Orwellian detail. Watching a man make a skin bottle, for example, he discovered 'with great interest' that the design was accomplished with the fur on the inside, so that in drinking water from a goatskin bottle one was actually drinking distilled goat hair. Suddenly, away from the rat-infested trenches and the piles of excrement, he caught a glimpse of the Spain that existed in his imagination: white sierra, Moorish palaces, lemon groves, girls in black mantillas. The mood persisted in Barcelona in the restaurant where he stopped for dinner on the way back to the Hotel Continental. Had he liked Spain? a fatherly waiter wondered. Would he come back? Oh yes, Orwell assured him in his still-squeaky voice, he would come back.

Back at the Hotel Continental this illusion of amity, genteel tourism and romantic Spain was abruptly shattered. He arrived to find Eileen sitting in the lounge. She came up to him in a casual way, put her arm round his neck, smiled encouragingly and then hissed the words 'Get out'. Orwell was so taken aback that the instruction had to be repeated. In the end he allowed himself to be led away downstairs. Halfway down they met a Frenchman known to them both who advised Orwell to take himself off before the police were called. A POUM member on the hotel staff skipped out of a lift to say the same thing. In the street Eileen explained what had happened in his absence. The POUM had been suppressed, its buildings seized and practically everyone connected with it who could be found imprisoned. All this had begun on 15 June – the day Orwell had left for Siétamo – with the arrest of the POUM leader Andres Nin and a raid on the Hotel Falcon. On the next day the party was declared illegal and within a few hours nearly all the members of its forty-strong executive committee were in prison. Now, nearly a week after the initial proscription – Orwell seems to have got back to Barcelona on the evening of 21 June, four days before his thirty-fourth birthday – a rumour had reached the city that Nin had been shot. Inevitably the move against the POUM had involved a high degree of subterfuge. It had, for instance, been kept secret from the military draft that left for the Front in mid-June to prevent the possibility of the men simply throwing down their weapons. In the intervening days, Orwell calculated, several men must have been assassinated in complete ignorance of the fact that the Republican newspapers were denouncing them as Fascists.

What was to be done? What, in particular, had happened to his friends? The Sanatorium Maurin had been raided: Williams and Cottman were in hiding. So was McNair. Kopp, however, was in jail, seized on his return to the Hotel Continental to fetch his kitbags *en route* to the front. Eileen had escaped, Orwell realised, only through her value as a decoy. Two nights earlier, in the small hours, six plainclothes policemen had invaded her hotel room and searched it. They took

Orwell's diaries, his books and press cuttings and even a bundle of his dirty linen, but missed passport and chequebook. Even now Orwell had difficulty in grasping the reality of the situation he and Eileen had fallen into. It was almost impossible to believe he was in any danger. 'The whole thing seemed too meaningless.' Gradually Eileen convinced him of the seriousness of their predicament. The only thing to do while they tried to rally their remaining friends in the city and plan an escape route from Spain was to lie low and conceal their connection with the POUM. As a first step, Eileen made him tear up his militiaman's card and an incriminating photograph of a group of soldiers with a POUM flag flying in the background. They agreed to meet next day at the British consulate, where Cottman and McNair were also expected, knowing that the British consul alone could not guarantee them safe passage. Anyone trying to leave Spain had to have their passport stamped in triplicate by the Chief of Police, the French Consulate and the Catalan immigration authorities. There was no safe house or hiding place. In the end, after walking a long way, Orwell fetched up somewhere near the General Hospital where until a few days previously he had gone for his electrotherapy. He tried an air-raid shelter, but it was newly dug and dripping with damp. Finally he came upon the ruins of a burnt-out church where, in a hollow hedged about with lumps of broken masonry, he managed to achieve a few hours' rest.

The exact conditions of life on the streets of Barcelona for anyone connected with the POUM in the last days of June 1937 are impossible to recreate. Several survivors – not only those politically opposed to Orwell – maintained that the dangers were exaggerated. As one of them put it, 'I walked round those streets on my own, and I never made any secret of the fact I was with the POUM ... No one ever said anything. I never felt any antagonism.' Branthwaite on the other hand, back in Barcelona on leave, had already got wind of the situation in Lerida where people had urged him to get rid of his uniform and destroy his papers. What is undeniable, though, is that Orwell's life was in danger. A warrant was issued for his and Eileen's arrest, while a report to the Tribunal for Espionage and High Treason at Valencia from the following month denounced them, on the strength of seized correspondence, as 'confirmed Trotskyists' and ILP agents of the POUM. Had Orwell and Eileen remained in Spain they would almost certainly have been shot. Meanwhile they were stuck in Barcelona with time running out and a complex series of protocols to negotiate before they could escape. Waking up in the hollow of the burnt-out church, Orwell walked back to the city centre. There were Republican flags flying over the POUM building and the public noticeboard at the end of the Ramblas was plastered with copies of anti-POUM cartoons. Near the quay he discovered a row of POUM militiamen sprawling exhaustedly in the bootblacks' chairs, having spent the night in the streets. At ten he arrived at the British consulate to meet Eileen. McNair and Cottman turned up shortly afterwards with the news that Bob Smillie was dead in the Valencia jail, supposedly of appendicitis. At some point they came upon Moyle and Branthwaite, the latter in an even worse position with regard to 'papers' in that he had arrived in Spain on a short-term Cook's ticket which was now well out of date.

That afternoon – an act of considerable bravery in the circumstances – they went to visit Kopp in jail. The two rooms requisitioned to hold political prisoners – originally the ground floor of a shop, Orwell noted – contained nearly a hundred people, including several of the wounded from the Sanatorium Maurin. Kopp, characteristically, turned out to be in excellent spirits. 'I suppose we shall all be shot,' he remarked as he came towards them through the crowd. But there was a solitary ray of hope. Among Kopp's papers, said to be lying in the office of the Chief of Police, was a letter from the Ministry of War addressed to the colonel commanding engineering operations. If it could be retrieved it would establish Kopp's bona fides. However, this could only be accomplished by the person to whom it was addressed. Undeterred by the bureaucratic labyrinth or the personal risk, Orwell found a taxi and had himself conveyed to the War Department near the quay. To his surprise he was allowed to see the colonel's ADC. Having had the circumstances of the case explained to him, the officer agreed that a mistake had been made. And what force had Major Kopp served in? Although shocked by Orwell's revelation that he and Kopp were POUM, the officer disappeared into the colonel's room. Here the sound of an agitated conversation could clearly be heard. Presently, however, he re-emerged and signalled to Orwell to follow. The letter was retrieved from the Chief of Police's office and the officer promised that it would be delivered. Orwell was touched that the man shook hands with him publicly outside the Chief of Police's office in front of a gang of *agents provocateurs*. 'It was like publicly shaking hands with a German during the Great War.'

Orwell and Cottman spent the night sleeping in long grass at the edge of a derelict building lot. As Orwell later acknowledged, they were leading a curious kind of double life – skulking around the city's back streets by night; by day masquerading as moneyed English tourists. On the next afternoon he and Eileen went to see Kopp for the last time. There was nothing they could do. Kopp's military superior had been unable to spring him from jail. By now, thanks to the British consulate, their passports were in order. The initial plan was to catch the 7.30 p.m. train to Port Bou, but Orwell arrived at the station to find that it had already left. Eileen went back to the hotel. Orwell, McNair and Cottman had dinner in a restaurant near the station, established that the proprietor was a CNT member and were allowed to sleep in a three-bedded room upstairs. It was the first time in five nights, Orwell calculated, that he had been able to sleep with his clothes off. Joined by Eileen early the next morning they boarded the train and crossed the frontier without incident. Cottman remembered McNair encouraging him to read a proffered copy of John Masefield's poems as a way of emphasising their innocuousness to the authorities. In the event they need not have worried. Their names were not on the list of suspects at the frontier passport office and after the guards had searched them from head to foot they were allowed through the barrier on to French soil. After six months in Spain Orwell discovered that all he had to show for his stay was a goatskin water bottle and one of the tiny lamps in which the Aragon peasants burned olive oil. Their first act on reaching France was to rush to a kiosk and buy all the cigars and cigarettes they could stuff in their pockets. As a memento of what they had left behind, the first French newspaper they saw carried – bizarrely – a full report on McNair's arrest for espionage.

McNair and Cottman were travelling on to Paris, but Orwell and Eileen decided to get off at Banyuls-sur-mer, the first stop down the line, thinking they would like a few days in the tranquillity of a French seaside town. Unhappily the place turned out to be solidly pro-Franco: Orwell remembered the glance which the Fascist-sympathising Spanish waiter at the café they frequented shot him when he brought an aperitif. It was different in Perpignan, an hour's drive away, where various government factions were caballing against each other and there were POUM supporters. Fenner Brockway, then trying to enter Spain in his capacity as chairman of the ILP, came across them here and spent a few hours with them. Thin and hoarse, Orwell was violently angry at what he had seen. He celebrated his thirty-fourth birthday at Banyuls, bored and disappointed. The weather was bad, the water dull and choppy. Within a few days, obscurely let down, feeling that they ought to be doing something about the sink of ill-will and shattered ideals that they had left behind, but knowing there was nothing they could do, the Orwells had had enough of their seaside holiday. They set off northward to Paris through a countryside that seemed to become greener and softer by the mile after the poverty of Spain, crossed the Channel and took the train up through the placid landscape of southern England. Looking out of the window at the sleek summer grass, Orwell marvelled at the curious sense of detachment that filled his mind. It was difficult, he thought, passing through the green fields and their level hedgerows, 'especially when you are peacefully recovering from sea-sickness with the plush cushions of a boat-train carriage under your bum', to believe that anything was really happening anywhere.

Orwell in view

Just as there is no extant recording of Orwell's voice, so there is no filmed representation of him. This is not altogether surprising. Television, after all, was in its infancy: Orwell never appeared on it. And yet by the end of his life early versions of the cine-camera had made their way into many a middle-class home. Surely someone, somewhere, at some point in the period 1930–50 must have pointed the lens in the direction of, say, the family party, the ILP summer school contingent on the Hertfordshire lawn, the Home Guard platoon digging out trenches in Regent's Park, and fetched up with the image of a tall, haggard man with a toothbrush moustache? Perhaps, in the end, someone did.

The most assiduous of Southwold's twentieth-century historians was a man named Barrett Jenkins. Mr Jenkins, now deceased, was the son of the town's first professional photographer. In this capacity he was a silent presence at most of Southwold's formal social occasions in the years between the two wars: at first with a Box Brownie, then with what one assumes from the fixed perspective of the surviving films was a tripod-mounted cine. Mr Jenkins' *oeuvre*, shot in faltering two-tone, gives a good idea of the place Southwold was in the 1920s and 1930s, the kind of diversions on offer to its townsfolk and the high degree of communality that these inspired. Judging from this visual account, the town's inhabitants liked nothing better than to assemble *en masse* with the aim of beating the bounds, marking the final journey of the Halesworth to Southwold railway (which closed in 1929) or celebrating George V's Silver Jubilee six years later. Most students of Orwell's time in Southwold, noting the uncomplimentary remarks about small-town Suffolk life smuggled into the portrait of 'Knype Hill' in A *Clergyman's Daughter*, have assumed that it was a dreary place, where any sign of individuality was instantly snuffed out beneath a blanket of bourgeois disapproval. The Jenkins archive shows something different: a warm, if faintly ceremonious, provincial life in which people were anxious to participate – whether it was in the *Daily Mail*-sponsored pushball matches on the common (a pushball was a gigantic spheroid about thirty feet round which most teams ended up balancing on their outstretched palms) or planting trees outside St Edmund's church.

Presented with the throng of Southwold citizenry, the forests of flat caps, cloche hats and bare-kneed schoolchildren, one looks for figures in the crowd. There is one at the very beginning of Mr Jenkins' three-minute encapsulation of the beating of the parish bounds, conducted on 6 August 1928 – Orwell would have been in Paris at the time – when a dapper, elderly man wearing a Panama hat and a summer suit is caught for a second or two among the High Street motley. Having studied it alongside the photographs in the Orwell archive, I have a hunch that this is Richard Walmesley Blair taking a gentle constitutional to see what all the fuss was about, but I cannot be sure. But there is an incontrovertible sighting in a brief film of some shirt-sleeved labourers on the beach piling up sand for the sea defences. Sauntering among them, cigarette protruding from beneath flat cap, a summer-frocked woman at his side, is a stout little man with a moustache who bears a distinct resemblance to mid-career photos of H.G. Wells. This, it turns out, is Mr Hurst the borough surveyor to whom, some years before, the disaffected young gentlemen of Mr Hope's crammer sent the rat.

And what about Orwell? Where is he? I went looking among the rows of onlookers convened to watch the pushball contest between the ladies' hockey club and the employees of the Homeknit factory, the final ride of the rackety Southwold train, the autumn's first sprats glinting in their nets on Southwold beach, and found nothing: only the endless flat caps and the canny Suffolk faces, Mayor Critten in his gown, the mace-bearer looking like Mr Bumble out of *Oliver Twist* and the vicar in his clerical bands. And yet . . . In the summer of 1930 Mr Jenkins shot some footage of one of the great Southwold occasions: the arrival of the fair. Much of this is simply crowd shots – the Mayor and Corporation solemnly taking the first ride on the roundabout – but for a moment or two the camera lingers over the procession of traction engines labouring up the High Street. On the left-hand pavement, separable from the flock of attendant schoolboys by virtue of being nearly two feet taller, a thin, short-haired character in a high collar wanders – half promenading, half loafing – alongside. No amount of pause-buttoning will ever produce a result. Freeze-framing film of this antiquity creates only a blur. On the negative side is the undoubted fact that the figure is smoking a cigarette out of a holder, which Orwell was never known to do. Nevertheless, there is something rather wonderful in the thought that it could be him, stepping out of his parents' house on a summer's evening in 1930 to watch the traction engines lumber in from Reydon, here amid the cloche-hatted women and the skirmishing children – all that lost Suffolk life that he hated but that remained, inexorably, a part of the world in which he moved.

12

Wintering Out

I am not a Marxist and I don't hold with all this stuff that boils
down to 'Anything is right which advances the cause of the party.'
– Letter to Frank Jellinek, 20 December 1938

I cannot tell you how deeply I wish to keep alive, out of jail, and
out of money worries for the next few years. – Letter to Jack
Common, 26 December 1938

Spain left an indelible mark on Orwell, quite apart from the bullet-hole
in his throat. The next two years of his life were lived in its shadow,
attempting to promulgate his own version of what had taken place
there, and dealing with legacies that were as much personal as political.
For the rest of his days, in fact, the six months spent on the Aragon
Front and on the streets of Barcelona ran on unappeasably through his
mind. Visiting him in hospital a few weeks before he died, Malcolm
Muggeridge noted that he talked incessantly about 'the Home Guard,
and the Spanish Civil War'. Above all, Orwell was conscious that he
had seen 'great things', as a letter to Cyril Connolly puts it. At the same
time he was keenly aware that the horrors of the Aragon trenches and
the Barcelona alleyways – blood, treachery and murder – had not
disillusioned him, but had, he maintained, 'left me with not less but
more belief in the decency of human beings'. As ever, his memories
soon took on a symbolic focus. In the essay 'Looking Back on the
Spanish War', written five years later in the midst of another conflict,
he recalled a Fascist infantryman scurrying along the top of a trench
whom he declined to shoot as the man was pulling up his trousers. A
second memory was more complex and, Orwell thought, shameful. A
boy from the Barcelona slums, suspected of stealing from his fellow-
militiamen (some of Orwell's cigars were among the plundered items),
was strip-searched but found to be innocent. Orwell, who had believed

him to be guilty, tried to make amends by taking him to the cinema and plying him with brandy and chocolate, an attempt at reparation that seemed to him 'horrible'. Somehow this insensitive treatment was made to seem worse in the course of a row that broke out when Orwell, in his capacity as corporal, had to drag a recalcitrant soldier to his post. The 'wild boy' from Barcelona turned out to be his most ardent defender.

The roll-call of Spanish names and dead Spanish faces was still vividly alive to Orwell in 1943. Many of the seeds of *Nineteen Eighty-Four* were sown here in Catalonia. It was in Spain that, for the first time in his life, Orwell saw newspaper articles that bore no relation to the known facts, read accounts of battles where no fighting had taken place, saw troops who had fought valiantly denounced as cowards and traitors. Spain provided the first intimation that the concept of objective truth was 'falling out of the world'. Its future history books would be written according to the prescriptions of whoever was in power. Significantly – for it marks his first attempt to connect his earlier thoughts about religion with the shadow of totalitarianism – Orwell linked this abandonment to the decay of belief in an afterlife. 'The major problem of our time is the decay of belief in personal immortality,' he wrote. In the absence of any hope of divine judgment, or even the assumption that what happened on earth after one was dead mattered, autocrats could do what they liked. The challenge was to harness the displaced religious sensibility of a world without God to some common purpose.

Throughout the tens of thousands of words written about his own and others' experience of the Spanish war, he remained surprisingly objective. The root causes of individual actions were often not instantly explicable in textbook political terms, he realised. 'I would not say that there is a case for Fascism,' he told a correspondent around this time, 'but I do think there is a case for many individual Fascists.' Wars, the argument runs, are fought by people: ideology is merely a backdrop. In this spirit he was moved by reports of the siege of Alcazar, where a beleaguered Nationalist force had held out for seventy-two days: there was no need, merely because one's sympathies lay on the other side, to pretend this wasn't a heroic exploit. For all this even-handedness, Spain politicised Orwell in a way that no previous stretch of his life had managed to do – confirming his belief in the indomitability of the human spirit; above all, perhaps, giving him a context in which he could approach and come to terms with the much greater European conflagration that lay two years beyond the horizon. In contrast to the faintly naïve operator of the Hampstead/Wigan period, the Orwell of 1937–9 is a much more political animal, prepared for the first time to join a political party, to sign manifestos, even – as the Second World War became inevitable – to take direct political action. All this, one infers, has its roots in the Spanish conflict. So, too, did his developing view of what Socialism might be thought to represent for the ordinary people who looked to it as a means of bettering their lives. Orwell was never a romantic Socialist of the type – very common in the 1930s – who yearned wistfully for primitive, William-Morris-style communitarianism and for whom machines were simply evil-smelling agents of destruction. 'How right the working classes are in their materialism,' he wrote in 'Looking Back on the Spanish War'; 'How right they are to realise that the belly comes before the soul, not in the scale of values but in point of time.'

Spain had left another, more disquieting legacy: it had shattered his health. Despite the gloomy prognoses of the Spanish doctors, Orwell's voice eventually returned to something near its full strength. His real problem, though, had nothing to do with the sniper's bullet. As an adult – certainly from the time he came back from Burma – Orwell was never really well. By the age of thirty-four, for example, he had already suffered from four bouts of pneumonia – a much more serious affliction in the pre-antibiotic days – not to mention the attack of dengue fever that had brought him back from the East. Practically every eyewitness account of Orwell from this period emphasises his thinness, the gauntness of his face. The freezing dawns and the damp trenches of the Aragon Front worsened this underlying frailty. Significantly, the post-Spain period brought months of protracted ill health and, it is fair to say, the onset of the long downward path that led to his premature death. Quite apart from the state of his chest, these were difficult times for husband and wife. Hard-up – Orwell's income during late 1937 and early 1938 was probably no more than £2 a week – their finances further straitened by Orwell's illness, they were reduced to borrowing money from friends, while the subsequent trip to Morocco, taken to protect Orwell's lungs from a harsh English winter, was only made possible by the subsidy of an anonymous benefactor. Professionally, too, Orwell was in low water, his career afflicted by poor sales and a temporary falling-out with his publisher. A vein of dissatisfaction runs through Orwell's private utterances, in which ill health, professional setbacks and consciousness of the storm clouds gathering beyond the Channel all played their part. It seemed to him that they might as well all pack their bags for the concentration camp, he gloomily suggested to Cyril Connolly in March 1938.

Spain was everywhere – in the books he reviewed (the torrent of Spanish literature did not dry up until the end of the 1930s), in the letters he sent in defence of politically suspect friends, in the articles he wrote with the aim of correcting the misrepresentations of the English press. Predictably, Orwell's position with regard to press reporting of the Spanish Civil War was unorthodox. The majority of mainstream English newspapers were, to a greater or lesser degree, pro-Franco. Of the minority that supported the Spanish government some (notably the *Manchester Guardian*, to whose editor Orwell wrote in commendation) maintained a reasonably objective reporting style. Others, notably the *Daily Worker*, slavishly followed the line from King Street. What might be called the Hard Left opposition to Orwell's view took a number of different forms. Non-POUM left-wingers who had fought in Spain were not necessarily hostile to him as an individual. Neither did they believe that the atrocity stories from Barcelona were necessarily untrue. Rather, they thought him guilty of a serious misjudgement. This, essentially, is Kenneth Sinclair-Loutit's charge. Orwell's suspicion of and enmity towards the Communists, whom he rightly regarded as dominating the Popular Front, clouded his understanding. He failed to accept that the POUM represented only a small intellectual splinter group, and that the real foreign enemies of the Spanish Republic were German Nazis and Italian Fascists. In the context of the mid-1930s European balance of power, only Soviet support could ensure the survival of Republican Spain. The Spanish revolution was not 'betrayed' by the Communists, as Frank Frankford later put it, because only Communism could keep that revolution alive. To a certain kind of International Brigade veteran, consequently, Orwell's eagerness to disclose what he had seen on the streets of Barcelona was insufficient excuse for his attack on Soviet involvement in Spain. 'I don't think his dislike of the Communists was justification for doing dirt on the Spanish Republic the way he did,' one of them complained. These, it should be pointed out, are the views of people who had served in Spain, were aware of the complex circumstances in which wars get fought and are understandably keen to emphasise the very real confusion about Republican Socialism that existed in Orwell's mind throughout the early part of 1937.

There is also another kind of Marxist critic of Orwell who did not serve in Spain and whose conclusions are intended to serve somewhat narrower ideological ends, or rather to deflect any blame that might attach itself to the Soviet Union. Here, for example, is a passage from Raymond Williams' 1971 'Modern Masters' study of Orwell:

> Most historians have taken the view that the revolution – mainly anarcho-syndicalist but with the POUM taking part – was an irrelevant distraction from a desperate war. Some, at the time and after, have gone so far as to describe it as deliberate sabotage of the war effort. Only a few have argued on the other side that the suppression of the revolution by the main body of Republican forces was an act of power politics, related to Soviet policy . . .

As Christopher Hitchens points out in his notably unforgiving study *Orwell's Victory*, even thirty years after it was written, with Williams dead and the whole Marxist historiographical tradition in which he laboured reduced to ashes, one reads this with a fair amount of incredulity. Who, it may be wondered, are 'most historians'? 'Suppression' is certainly one way of describing the presence of Soviet-sponsored hit-squads on the streets of Barcelona, mass imprisonment, rigged trials and summary executions. Then there is that marvellously innocuous 'related to Soviet policy', as if what happened in Spain in the early summer of 1937 had a faint, incidental connection to Russian foreign policy rather than being its direct result. In Williams' defence, it can be said that some of the contemporary misrepresentations of the POUM were no less insidious. There had been a preliminary skirmish or two in the reviews of *The Road to Wigan Pier*, but the real fight between Orwell and the unreconstituted, Stalinist Left, an argument that was to splutter on for the best part of half a century, begins here in the summer of 1937, in – and occasionally beyond – the pages of some time-honoured English literary magazines.

Arriving back in England at the end of June, the Orwells put up at what was now their chief London base: the O'Shaughnessy house at Greenwich. Picking up some of the literary contacts he had put down six months before, Orwell found – not hugely to his surprise – that he was already embroiled in controversy. His immediate priority, before settling down to work on his Spanish book, was to sell an account of his experiences in Barcelona to some sympathetic English editor. Impressed by reports on the war that he had read in the *New Statesman and Nation*, he had already telegraphed from France to the paper's legendarily high-minded editor, Kingsley Martin, to ask if he would commission a piece. Martin accepted the offer but not the article ('Eye-witness in Barcelona') that followed a few days later, on the grounds that it would 'cause trouble'. The precise wording of the rejection, which seems to have been made by telephone, is past recovery, but the underlying principle was confirmed by letter. Whether as a sop, or merely in acknowledgement of his newfound status as a Spanish expert, Orwell was then offered the chance to review the Spanish book of the moment, Franz Borkenau's *The Spanish Cockpit*. This piece, too, was rejected – again by Martin, rather than the paper's literary editor, Raymond Mortimer – on the grounds that it contravened editorial policy. Both articles subsequently appeared in print, 'Eye-witness in Barcelona' in an obscure publication called *Controversy: The Socialist Forum*, the Borkenau review in *Time and Tide*, but the damage was done and the incident remains one of the great stand-offs of contemporary literary politics, endlessly fought over by partisans on both sides.

To Orwell the issue was clear-cut: the suppression of truth and free speech in pursuit of ideological ends. And yet to write off Kingsley Martin, a luminous and almost sacerdotal figure whom younger acolytes regarded as the model of probity, as a Marxist stooge clearly will not do. ('If, all one's life, one is looking for who one truly is, one has to remain open to other people, hoping to learn from them, hoping to find something new which one can incorporate into oneself, and thus strengthen and build one's identity' was one tribute to his ceaseless voyage of self-exploration.) Martin's defence, stuck to for the rest of his life, was that the press was dominated by anti-Republican propaganda, each side in the conflict had behaved with appalling cruelty, but 'I had to make my decision on general public grounds, *to the end that one side might win rather than the other side*'. Orwell's first article was, in Martin's view, pro-enemy propaganda, although true. The book review, on the other hand, was not strictly speaking a notice of the book (this was eventually undertaken some months later by V.S. Pritchett) but a restatement of Orwell's political opinions. Both articles attacked the Republican government on atrocity grounds, and although Martin had no reason to doubt their accuracy he believed that they would be out of place in the only weekly paper of its kind that wasn't shoulder to shoulder with Franco. Orwell, who had plenty of space at his disposal in other magazines, should go elsewhere.

Orwell never forgave Martin for this episode. There is a famous story of how, years later, he spotted Martin on the far side of a crowded restaurant and asked his lunch guest, Malcolm Muggeridge, to change places with him in order to spare Orwell the sight of 'that corrupt face'. The kill-fee for the unpublished review, proferred and declined, was inevitably marked down as 'hush money' (to which Martin's biographer tartly responded 'If that was hush money, a good many of us have been hushed by the *New Statesman*, usually making the simpler assumption that we hadn't this time delivered the goods and yet the paper didn't want to lose us'). Martin himself clearly had deep misgivings about his role in what has since become one of the *causes célèbres* of English literary censorship, continuing to justify himself for the rest of his life – he died in 1967 – with appeals to the greater good. They were brilliant articles, he told Muggeridge, who had presumably questioned his own use as a kind of cordon sanitaire, and they were true, but they would have damaged the Republic. Moreover they were 'unlike' *Homage to Catalonia*, whose 'balance' Martin admired. Ominously, in the same week that Martin turned down 'Eye-witness in Barcelona', Orwell was already running into trouble with the as yet unwritten account of his Spanish adventures. The crash course in practical left-wing politics he had undergone in the past six months had convinced him that Gollancz, with his hot-line to King Street, would turn a jaundiced eye on anything that could be construed as an assault on Republican solidarity. In the first week of July, consequently, he travelled up from Greenwich to Henrietta Street to see how the land lay. Gollancz was away, but a meeting with Norman Collins, whose dealings with him over the corrections to *Keep the Aspidistra Flying* still rankled, left him in no doubt as to what Gollancz' opinion would be. That Gollancz was both monitoring the situation and determined to nip unorthodoxy in the bud seems clear from a letter of 5 July responding to the vigilant Collins' report, in which he thought it 'probable' that he would not want to publish whatever Orwell produced.

Happily Gollancz's letter coincided with an approach from the firm of Secker & Warburg, in the person of its managing director, Fred Warburg. Alerted to Orwell's difficulties by a couple of his ILP contacts, Reg Reynolds and John Aplin, Warburg invited him to call on the following day. Although interest was also expressed by Duckworth, Orwell was impressed by this new suitor. Established the previous year by an alliance between Warburg and the firm originally founded by Martin Secker in 1910, Secker & Warburg were left-wing but independent-minded, and in Orwell's view 'more suitable' than more mainstream sponsors. Having undertaken to provide an outline, submitted to Leonard Moore in the middle of July, he and Eileen went back to Wallington. Here everything was in disarray. Aunt Nellie, who had left some months ago, had let things slide. The shop had been abandoned. Rather than reopen it the Orwells decided to concentrate on animal husbandry, initially by way of a pair of goats and a rooster named Henry Ford. They also acquired a clipped poodle whom Orwell christened Marx.

Even here in the depths of a Hertfordshire summer the fall-out from their Spanish experiences continued to descend. Kopp, still imprisoned in Barcelona, was about to go on hunger strike. Recapitulating his recent dealings with the *New Statesman* for the benefit of Rayner Heppenstall, Orwell complained that it was impossible to get a word about the anti-Trotskyist assault into the English press. This was not quite true, as the first section of a two-part essay on 'Spilling the Spanish Beans' had already appeared in the *New English Weekly* on 29 July (in it Orwell maintained that left-wing papers 'with their far subtler methods of distortion' had prevented the British public from grasping the true nature of the Spanish struggle); the two pieces rejected by Martin would soon follow elsewhere. And yet in mid-1937 the streak of paranoia that ran beneath the surface of Orwell's mind seems more than justified by the circumstances in which he found himself. In the space of a month, after all, he had seen a piece of reportage, a review and a proposal for a book turned down on ideological grounds by people he had known and dealt with for years. Gollancz, he told Heppenstall, was part of the Communist racket. It was while he was in this agitated mental state that a copy of Nancy Cunard's *Authors Take Sides on the Spanish War* questionnaire, possibly the second or third dispatch, caught up with him. Orwell's 'reply' was one of the most intemperate paragraphs he ever committed to paper:

> Will you please stop sending me this bloody rubbish. This is the second or third time I have had it. I am not one of your fashionable pansies like Auden and Spender, I was six months in Spain, most of the time fighting, I have a bullet-hole in me at present and I am not going to write blah about defending democracy or gallant little anybody.

If he did manage to compress what he knew about the situation in Spain, and what had been happening on the government side into six lines, Orwell went on, the compilers wouldn't dare to print it. 'You wouldn't have the guts.' There was a final, incendiary sign-off.

By the way, tell your pansy friend Spender that I am preserving specimens of his war-heroics and that when the time comes when he squirms for shame at having written it, as the people who wrote the war-propaganda in the Great War are squirming now, I shall rub it in good and hard.

Quite why Orwell should have selected Stephen Spender as the luckless victim of his asperity is not immediately obvious: amid the tide of poems, statements and propagandisings about Spain that spilled into English literary life in the late 1930s there were worse offenders than the twenty-eight-year-old author of *Vienna* (1934) and *The Destructive Element* (1935). Essentially he seems to have settled on Spender, at this point known to him only by newspaper articles, as the epitome of the well-intentioned, left-leaning non-combatant whose enthusiasm bordered on the simplistic and whose understanding of the issues at stake was painfully limited. Auden was to come in for similarly rough treatment a couple of years later.

With occasional visits to London and elsewhere, Orwell spent the second half of 1937 in Wallington tending his animals, working at his garden and writing what was to become *Homage to Catalonia*. Looking at his life at this period one is struck by how much had happened in such a comparatively short stretch of time. Barely eighteen months before he had been a bachelor working in a Hampstead bookshop. Now he was a married man with an abiding sense of political conviction and a bullet-hole in his throat working a Hertfordshire smallholding. As his own life had changed, so had the world beyond the window. War was looming: Orwell's letters and journals from this time are full of sinister prophecies of the turmoil to come. At the same time past horrors could not be put to one side. Several of his trips beyond Wallington in the summer of 1937 were on Spanish business. At the end of July, for example, he went down to Bristol to attend a meeting in support of Stafford Cottman, whose involvement with the POUM had had him drummed out of the local Young Communist League and seen his house picketed by outraged former comrades. In early August he was present at the ILP summer school at nearby Letchworth, where John McNair reported on the nine months of fighting. There was a two minutes' silence for the fallen – Arthur Chambers and Bob Smillie – and several men, including Moyle, Branthwaite and a reluctant Orwell, supplied eyewitness accounts of their experiences.

From this time, too, presumably, dates a curious encounter recalled many years later by Rayner Heppenstall. The newly married Heppenstall was living with his wife in a Hampstead bedsitter. Having entertained Orwell with a cheap meal at a local Italian restaurant, they invited him to stay the night. Short on furniture, the Heppenstalls did, however, possess a 'multi-purpose chair'. This was opened up for their guest. All three of them then prepared to go to bed in the single room. Some time later Margaret Heppenstall awoke to find Orwell, stark naked, wandering around. Polite but unembarrassed, he apologised for disturbing her and explained that he was trying to find his way to the lavatory. The journey was eventually accomplished, although Margaret Heppenstall made sure that she was facing the wall when he came back. There is something faintly characteristic about this: Orwell's non-chalance; Orwell's apparent ease in situations where another man might have been nonplussed. The same note is struck in an episode, dating from several years later, recounted by Anthony Powell. Arriving in shabby corduroys at a relatively smart party at which most of those present wore evening dress, Orwell stopped to enquire vaguely of his host: was it all right his coming in dressed like this? What, Powell wondered, would his response have been had the answer been no? It would be an exaggeration, perhaps, to talk of the unreality of Orwell's approach to life, and yet his self-absorption, imperviousness to the air around him, can occasionally seem acute.

Yet Orwell cared very much what people thought about him, particularly if – as in the months after his return from Barcelona – their motives were hostile. Late in August he wrote a long letter to Victor Gollancz urging him to intervene on his behalf with the staff of the *Daily Worker*, with whom Gollancz was closely connected. The *Daily Worker*'s interest in Orwell dated from March, when Harry Pollitt had amused himself at the expense of *The Road to Wigan Pier* ('One thing I am certain of, and it is this – if Mr Orwell could only hear what Left Book circles will say about this book, then he would make a resolution never to write again on any subject that he does not understand'). Thereafter it had continued to attribute to him the belief that 'The working classes smell' (in fact Orwell had claimed that the middle classes were taught to believe this – a rather different thing). Orwell asked Gollancz to tell the newspaper's editorial staff that if they repeated this 'lie' he would publish a reply. At the same time he drew attention to the much more serious campaign of 'organised libel' currently being waged against POUM veterans recently returned from Spain. Cottman, for example, as well as having his house spied on and being expelled from the Young Communist League – arguably a less severe hardship – had been described in a letter as 'in the pay of Franco'. If a similar statement were to be made about Orwell, he would sue. There were no more references to the working classes 'smelling', and yet within a month Orwell was to feature again, albeit anonymously, in the *Daily Worker*'s campaign against the POUM. The originator of this dispute was an unwelcome revenant from the ILP's Aragon contingent, Frank Frankford. Although he had been at large in Barcelona at the time of the Orwells' escape, having effectively deserted his post, Frankford had remained in the city and eventually been briefly imprisoned – not, as it turned out, for political unorthodoxy but for stealing pictures from a church. Back in London he made two visits to the ILP's offices in early September, on the second occasion to collect the money offered to all returning Spanish veterans. A week later the *Daily Worker* published a statement over the name of 'F.A. Frankfort', dated from Barcelona three weeks before and accusing the POUM of operating as a Fascist fifth column. Specific charges included 'open fraternisation' between POUM troops and Nationalists and the nightly transit of a cart across the Fascist lines at Alcubierre while the sentries in Kopp's contingent looked the other way. Frankford's motive in promulgating these obvious lies is obscure. Spite certainly had something to do with it. His later utterances on Orwell are shot through with a very personal distaste. Political conviction may have played a part. But the sub-text of Orwell's rejoinder, published in the *New Leader* of 24 September and signed by all the contactable members of the unit, dwells on the personal factor. Frankford had noted that 'the POUM seemed very glad to get rid of me'. In fact, having walked out of the line without leave, he was lucky not to have been shot. Orwell concluded that the statement had been drafted by a Barcelona journalist and that Frankford had agreed to sign it to 'save his skin'. Whatever the truth of this, it is clear that Frankford was one of those mischievous scamps attracted to enterprises of this kind like bluebottles to dead meat, whose opinion on this and other matters to do with Orwell are not to be taken seriously. Corresponding with Anthony Powell many years later, for instance, he claimed to have been talking to Orwell at the moment when he was shot, but this, too, seems unlikely. Orwell's companion at the time was the American militiaman Harry Milton.

The autumn wore on in Wallington and *Homage to Catalonia* began to take shape. As he followed the slow but remorseless advance of Franco's forces into Republican territory, Orwell's enthusiasm for the things he had seen was balanced by an awareness of the Republic's eventual destiny. He had had a 'most interesting time', he reported to Connolly from Southwold in October (Connolly had tried to see Orwell in Spain but had got no further than Fraga) but it was 'heartbreaking' to witness the subsequent course of the war. Money was tight, but the experiences of the last eighteen months had at least provided him with specialist literary fields he could till, and he continued to review both Spanish books and, an increasingly common sub-genre, reports from Depression-era Britain. A *Time and Tide* round-up from the autumn, for example, covered James Hanley's *Grey Children*, Wal Hannington of the NUWM's *The Problem of the Distressed Areas* and a history of Chartism. Early December found him reporting to Moore that a rough draft of *Homage to Catalonia* was complete. There was also mention of a novel about 'a man who is having a holiday and trying to make a temporary escape from his responsibilities, public and private'. This is the first reference to what was to become *Coming up for Air*.

Orwell probably envisaged nothing more than a life consisting of a book a year, the Wallington smallholding and Eileen. But the trials of the past few months had taken their toll. He was unwell and, it seems reasonable to assume, worsened his condition by not allowing his body time to recover from the privations of the trenches. Wallington, too, offered a bleak prospect for the semi-invalid in winter. Rayner Heppenstall, who visited the Stores early in 1938, was struck by the place's sequestered, run-down air. It was 'not a pretty cottage', he decided, and the adjoining village was 'desolate'. Two goats in a stinking shed seemed the extent of the Orwells' animal husbandry. Across the road lay a strip of land where vegetables were grown: here he and Orwell dug. For all the marked air of austerity and the lack of heating, Heppenstall noted the conspicuous affection which husband and wife displayed towards each other. With his book finished and set for spring publication, Orwell's mind was still dominated by the events of the previous year. He reviewed Arthur Koestler's *Spanish Testament* – Koestler, the *News Chronicle*'s correspondent in Spain, had been imprisoned without trial after the fall of Málaga – and responded in *Time and Tide* to a reader's enquiry wondering why there had so far been no Anarchist books about the conflict by spilling the beans about his treatment at the hands of the *New Statesman*. No confidences were betrayed – the *New Statesman* was described as a 'well-known weekly' – but nobody involved in the original dispute would have been in any doubt as to whom or what Orwell was referring. The letter brought a polite but indignant response from Raymond Mortimer ('what you say is not quite true') who had not had the full circumstances of the case explained to him by his editor. Persuaded that Orwell had been censored on grounds of policy, Mortimer had the grace to apologise. Although Orwell did not sever all relations with it, and subsequently reviewed for the paper on several occasions, immediate olive branches were declined. 'I do not think you can blame me if I feel that the *New Statesman* has its share of blame for the one-sided view that has been presented,' he told Mortimer, with whom he remained on good terms. A later meeting probably took place with Kingsley Martin to discuss what Martin continued to refer to as a 'misunderstanding'. Here, though, there could be no forgiveness.

The faint sense of drift that hangs over Orwell's life in the pre-war age – old avenues closing down, new ones not yet opened up – seems marked in the early part of 1938. He had thrown over his main commercial sponsor, Gollancz, for a firm which, although enthusiastic, was not in the same commercial league. His book was in the press, but the market in which it would take its place was already saturated. The lack of immediate prospects perhaps explains his interest – reluctant but genuine – in the offer of a job on the *Lucknow Pioneer*, a proposal he took with sufficient seriousness to travel up to London in mid-February for vetting by A. Houghton Joyce of the India Office. Joyce felt that Orwell was a security risk, that should his contract on the paper be terminated he would stay in India and take to 'extremist work'. Covert representations were made to the *Pioneer*'s editor, Desmond Young, but Orwell seems to have regarded the matter as more or less settled. He had seldom wanted to do anything less, he told Jack Common two days before the meeting with Joyce, but it would be an opportunity to see 'interesting' (that trademark Orwell adjective) things. What he really wanted to do, was to 'vegetate' for a few months and think about his novel.

In the event India, the novel and everything else were pushed to one side by his deteriorating health. In early March this worsened dramatically. The exact circumstances are not wholly decipherable, but according to Eileen he was first 'laid up' on 8 March and became progressively worse during the following week. A letter of 14 March to Connolly reports that he is spitting blood and going to a sanatorium in Kent to be X-rayed. The sanatorium was Preston Hall near Aylesford, to which Laurence O'Shaughnessy was attached as a consultant surgeon. At some time after this letter was written, however, Orwell's condition worsened to the extent that his life was in danger. A letter of 15 March from Eileen to Jack Common talks about 'the drama of yesterday' – Common had apparently been summoned to help from his neighbouring village – and bleeding that seemed to go on for ever. Orwell was admitted to Preston Hall on 15 March which, given the distance involved, suggests an emergency trip by ambulance late on the previous day. Throughout, Orwell seems to have remained characteristically diffident about his illness. No doubt the doctors would find that he was OK, he assured Cyril Connolly a few hours before he began haemorrhaging; in any case it was a good excuse for not going to India, which he had never wanted to do. In fact he was very seriously ill, prescribed absolute bed-rest for weeks and not discharged until 1 September – five and a half months from the date of his admission.

What was wrong with him? The most plausible candidate, naturally enough, was tuberculosis. A letter from Eileen to Denys King-Farlow written towards the end of June, three days before Orwell's thirty-fifth birthday, suggested that for the first two months he appeared to have TB in both lungs, which would have been 'pretty hopeless'. In the end, however, Orwell's doctors decided that the primary condition from which he suffered appeared to be bronchiectasis, a legacy of the defective bronchial tubes with which he had been born. Even to a layman this seems an odd diagnosis, especially given the fact that, as Orwell's medical records show, he had coughed up blood on three previous occasions. But these were early days in the development of pulmonary medicine. X-ray techniques were still in their infancy: it would take another decade and new drugs even to establish the existence of TB-resembling conditions such as sarcoid. Whatever the verdict on Orwell's chest – and the doctors certainly discovered an old, non-infectious lesion in one lung dating back to the 1920s – the treatment would have been the same: rest, building up, avoidance of strain. Orwell, in contrast to those close to him, refused to alarm himself. A letter to Jack Common written a week or two after his admission is mostly about Common's forthcoming book, *Seven Shifts*. 'I don't think there's really much wrong with me,' he gamely deposed.

There is an echo of another famous literary casualty from lung disease here: D.H. Lawrence, who went practically to his death maintaining that his symptoms were 'bronchial'. For Orwell, recovery would be a slow process. He was forbidden to work, and for the most part confined to bed, occupying his enforced leisure with crossword puzzles and low-key fraternisation with the other inmates. The patient in the next cubicle recalled 'a very quiet man' whose idiosyncrasy lay in his clothes: outsize shoes, a jacket that hung flapping from his spindly frame, a roll-necked red pullover. His solitary diversion was the stream of people who came to see him. In addition to closer friends such as Common and Heppenstall, the former *Adelphi* editor Max Plowman and his wife Dorothy came, bringing the novelist L.H. Myers who would go on to play a considerable role in Orwell's life. John Sceats, an insurance agent met through their joint involvement with *Controversy*, in which 'Eye-witness in Barcelona' had been published, was there when the Plowmans appeared, and talk turned to the international situation. War ought to be opposed, Orwell implied. Ironically, given the scribbled comments on the back of Nancy Cunard's circular, Connolly arrived in the company of Stephen Spender. Both men at this point figured as the sponsors of a new political ginger group, the *Solidaridad Internacional Antifascista* (International Anti-Fascist Solidarity) and, as ever, Orwell's sense of scrupulousness was touched by a personal connection with someone he had roundly abused only six months before. Writing to Spender early in April he apologised for his 'angry reply'. The disparaging reference stemmed from the fact of 'not knowing you personally at that time'. Spender was puzzled by this apparent about-face. Why, he wondered, should Orwell want to with-draw his attack merely because the two of them had met? Personal resonance was more important than the false impression of print, Orwell assured him. 'Even if when I met you I had not happened to like you, I should still have been bound to change my attitude, because when you meet anyone in the flesh you realise immediately that he is a human being and not a sort of caricature embodying certain ideas.'

Homage to Catalonia, meanwhile, was published at the end of April. Orwell had high hopes for the book – even three months later he was confidently predicting it would sell 3,000 copies – but despite some encouraging reviews (and a predictable savaging in the *Daily Worker*) it was a resounding commercial flop. Only 700 copies had been disposed of by the end of the year, there was no further edition until after Orwell's death, and the translation produced by Orwell's French admirer Madame Davet remained unpublished until 1955. It was small consolation that the book's failure had little to do with its merits. The Spanish conflict had been in progress for nearly two years now; there was a glut of war books. Moreover the entrenchment of political attitudes was reflected in absurdly partisan reviewing. In the week after publication Orwell wrote to both the *Times Literary Supplement* and the

Listener complaining of misrepresentation. The *TLS* reviewer, he suggested, had merely used the book as a means of discrediting the Spanish militia on the Aragon Front. Eighty per cent of the *Listener*'s space had been taken up in resurrecting the claim that the POUM was a Fascist fifth column. Orwell won this particular dispute – the reviewer, Philip Jordan, was publicly rebuked by his editor – but such slights rankled.

Frustrated by his sequestration, he believed, or affected to believe, that his health was improving, telling Geoffrey Gorer at the end of April – again – that he doubted whether there was anything wrong with him. Certainly he put on a little weight at Preston Hall, but the 11 stone 9 pounds reached a few days before the Gorer letter was still painfully thin for a man of his size. Reading these protests about his state of health – and they recur throughout the rest of his life – one wonders very much about the mental attitudes that underlay them. Did Orwell believe, despite the evidence of bloody handkerchiefs and ambulance rides, that his doctors were being unnecessarily cautious? Or was he merely deluding himself on Lawrentian lines? At any rate there is a stoicism at the heart of Orwell's attitude to his health, a detachment from physical sensation – his later accounts of streptomycin treatment have an eerie, scientific quality – that can sometimes seem faintly inhuman. However sanguine he may have been to friends, the fact remains that he was not allowed out of bed until the beginning of June, and then only for an hour a day, subsequently increased to three. He supposed he would be there for another month or two, he told Jack Common at the end of May: in fact he spent the summer at Preston Hall.

On 1 June, however, he was transferred from the main body of the sanatorium to the New Hostel, an ancillary boarding-house in which patients who had passed the initial stage of their treatment could recuperate. Soon he was roaming about the nearby Kentish countryside, alternating trips to St Peter's, the Aylesford parish church and bus rides to Rochester Cathedral with his customarily self-engrossed nature rambles. One of his fellow-patients remembered coming across him in a hayfield watching a pair of caterpillars negotiate a twig. It is easy to imagine that a certain amount of the desperate nostalgia for the rapidly receding world of the English countryside that suffuses *Coming up for Air* took root in these summer strolls around the Medway towns. But Orwell was also in pursuit of something, or someone, else: one of his wife's best friends. Lydia Jackson, later under the name of 'Elisaveta

Fen', a writer and translator of Chekhov, visited Preston Hall some time that summer. Orwell, found fully dressed and lounging in a deckchair, proposed a walk. Beyond sight of the buildings an 'awkward situation' arose.

Looking back on the encounter, Lydia Jackson was emphatic about her response. She was not in the least attracted by Orwell, even less so in his current cadaverous state. Her chief loyalty, additionally, was to Eileen. She decided that she must not take the incident seriously and must treat it as a sick man's vagary. Clearly, however, it was something more than this. Beneath the formal record of Orwell's marriage to Eileen, it is fair to say, exists a dimly glimpsed sub-world of more or less furtive liaisons and casual affairs. We know that Orwell was unfaithful to Eileen during their marriage – he admitted this to friends – but the exact depths of his undercover emotional life are impossible to fathom. He seems, for example, still to have been fruitlessly in pursuit of Brenda Salkeld at this time; there were other entanglements – some known to Eileen, others not – in the early 1940s. To say that they cast a shadow over what we may feel about Orwell isn't perhaps the point, for their chief characteristics are ambiguity and elusiveness. The relationship with Lydia Jackson, which on paper alone extends to two dozen letters, is a case in point. If she was not attracted by Orwell and thought him a bad influence on Eileen (she is on record as regretting her friend's marriage) then why did she continue to have dealings with him? The letters that Orwell addressed to her in the following year have an archness that may simply have been Orwell's idea of correct romantic protocol, but here and there emerges a definite sense of complicity.

As the summer of 1938 wore on, Orwell's doctors were able to note a sustained improvement in his condition. By early July he had regained his highest recorded weight, of twelve stone. Already the question of where he might go when he left Preston Hall was under discussion. The original plan seems to have been that he and Eileen would look for a 'perfect cottage', albeit costing not more than 7s. 6d. a week, in the south of England where he could continue to recuperate. Ideally Orwell's chest needed a winter abroad in a hot climate (Cyril Connolly was sounded out on the subject of cottages in France) but there was little money and, until Orwell regained his strength, little prospect of adding to it. Clearly the Orwells' plight must have been discussed in their immediate circle, as during the summer the Plowmans revealed that an anonymous benefactor (in fact L.H. Myers) was prepared to lend them £300 to underwrite a foreign trip. With Myers' identity kept secret, the Orwells accepted.

Sixty years after his death, Myers remains an enigmatic figure. Highly regarded as a novelist in his day – the original *Pelican Guide to English Literature* allows him a chapter all to himself – his reputation has since fallen into apparently terminal decline. An immensely wealthy Old Etonian who inherited a fortune in his early twenties, he lived what his friend the novelist L.P. Hartley called a 'leisured and uneventful' life. All this might seem to place Myers rather beyond his younger protégé's coign of vantage, and yet one suspects that Orwell would have found the inner turmoil under which Myers laboured highly attractive. A depressive hypochondriac, at this point in his life obsessed with Communism, his novels tended to turn on the conflict between the material and spiritual worlds. His tetralogy *The Near and the Far* (1929), for example, though set in an imaginary sixteenth-century India, is full of contemporary shadings. According to Myers's biographer, he 'sees the inadequacy of liberal humanism for the sort of being man is . . . He had, that is, a sense of evil.' Plainly, this kind of thing found an echo in a man who was to spend the last decade of his life exploring some of the limits of liberal humanism himself, as did Myers' desperate, though essentially unfulfilled, need to 'connect'. This, after all, was an author who once observed that the idea of one of his characters walking down Piccadilly 'oppressed and frustrated' him. Not much is known about Orwell's friendship with Myers – the ultimate source of the £300 was never revealed to him, even after Myers's death (he committed suicide) in 1944 – but the two men kept up during the early years of the war, and several of Myers's oracular pronouncements on the wartime political situation get an approving mention in Orwell's diary.

The Myers connection is a further sign of the direction in which Orwell's mind was moving in the late 1930s with the news from continental Europe growing steadily harder to ignore. Whereas before his departure to Spain, he had been merely interested in left-wing politics, now he was politically engaged. One mark of this newfound involvement in the practical processes of politics was his decision to join a political party. Given that the party in question was the ILP – a small burr sticking to the shaggy hide of English Socialism proper – this may seem a fairly negligible gesture, but the statement he provided to the *New Leader* at the end of June ('Why I join the ILP') is a good place to start in any analysis of his emerging political beliefs. Above all, it is an emphatic repudiation of quietism. In an age of power politics, the writer's instinctive impulse is to keep to one side, and yet at a time when 'the era of free speech is closing down' detachment of this sort is simply unfeasible. The time is coming, in fact, when a writer will be forced to choose between being sidelined altogether or tolerated as a marginal entertainer, 'producing the dope that a privileged minority demands'. In an age when the triumph of Fascism means creative sterility, one has to be an active Socialist rather than merely sympathetic to Socialism. Spain had brought home to Orwell the danger of 'mere negative anti-Fascism'. With the Communists simply an instrument of Soviet foreign policy and mainstream Labour fatally in thrall to a reactionary establishment (even in the post-1945 era, Orwell was notably lukewarm about the Labour leader Clement Attlee) the ILP was the only British political party he felt able to support. This is stirring stuff – Orwell's statements of political intent generally are – but what did it actually mean? And what, in particular, did he think about the great dilemma then obsessing the British Left: how to react to the prospect of war? One obvious point to make about his position at this time is that he was involved with some very free-floating left-wing company. The *Solidaridad Internacional Antifascista* (SIA), for example, brought him into contact with home-grown anarchists. Reg Reynolds, who had put him in touch with Warburg, was on the ILP's pacifist wing. These were not orthodox Socialist circles, and as many of his statements over the next year and a half show, Orwell was feeling his way towards a personal political programme. The chief problem facing men of goodwill who wished to oppose an intolerant enemy had already become clear to him. It is, for example, starkly set down in the review of Koestler's *Spanish Testament*: 'The only apparent alternatives are to smash dwelling houses to powder, blow out human entrails and burn holes in children with lumps of thermite, or to be enslaved by people who are more willing to do these things than you are yourself.'

By the end of June Eileen could tell Denys King-Farlow that 'Eric isn't so ill as they thought'. Great care, though, would have to be taken and he was still only up to the occasional piece of journalism: a review of Common's *The Freedom of the Streets* for the *New English Weekly* in mid-June, for instance. A contract with the firm of Nelson for a book with the working title 'Poverty in Practice' had to be shelved and *Coming up for Air* was still no more than a tentative outline. He had sketched the novel out, he told Moore, but didn't want to start until he felt fit. The same letter contains further proof of Orwell's conception of himself as a 'political' writer in an intriguing reference to a pamphlet he had written 'more or less on the subject of pacifism'. Never published – the ILP publications committee turned it down on the grounds that it was 'too long and too absolutist' – and never traced, this doubtless gathered the random fragments of the pre-war period into a more coherent whole. His narrower interest in literary politics endured, and there are several letters to Common foreshadowing later anatomies of the publishing racket. Orwell's point, here and afterwards, was that the length and tone of a book's review depended largely on the amount its publisher spent on advertising. Rather like the lost pacifist pamphlet, this, too, is a good example of Orwell's 'absolutism' on a subject he felt passionately about. Certainly there was at this time, had been and always would be, a relationship between books reviewed and publishers' advertising – the 1930s were a notoriously corrupt decade in this respect – and yet the Orwell who inveighed against what he called the 'reviewing ramp' must have been uneasily conscious of his own role in it, a few rungs further down the ladder than the hacks of the *Observer* and the *Sunday Times*. Orwell had noticed his friend Jack Common's book just a couple of months before Geoffrey Gorer noticed his friend Orwell's. Low-level conspiring of this type is endemic to any literary age, of course, but one stresses its existence in the world stretching out from the sanatorium at Aylesford to make the point that Orwell was, in his way, a sharp literary operator capable of benefiting, as his career progressed, from a network of alliances and well-disposed friends. Isolated he may have been at this stage in his career, but he did not lack supporters. Already this sphere of influence ranged from, at the top, well-connected *flâneurs* such as Connolly, whose forthcoming *Enemies of Promise* would make him the most highly rated young critic in England, to, at the bottom, journeymen labourers from the minor weeklies such as Jack Common. Common seems to have been close to his Hertfordshire neighbour at this time. It was arranged that he should take over the cottage, whose lack of amenities was immediately sketched in by its owners ('You know what our cottage is like. It's bloody awful,' Orwell reminded him, while Eileen provided further details of the absence of hot water and the propensity to flooding.)

By August 1938 Orwell was able to report to his mother that they had more or less settled on Morocco for the winter trip and were in the process of making arrangements. Old Mr Blair, now past eighty, had been ill and a Southwold visit was in prospect. Orwell spent a further fortnight at Aylesford, taking a lively interest in the progress of the crops and visiting Maidstone zoo, then stayed briefly in Suffolk ('cold tea is good fertiliser for geraniums,' runs a specimen diary entry) before returning to Kent to prepare for the journey. In amongst the ordering of guidebooks from his old employer, Francis Westrope, and the detailed hints on goat husbandry compiled for Jack Common, one notes Orwell's characteristic vagueness when confronted with projects of this kind. He and Eileen's geography was so poor, it turned out, that they assumed French Morocco abutted the Mediterranean rather than the Atlantic. The original scheme had been to travel via Paris (where Orwell had hoped to see Mme Davet) and Marseilles, but this would have meant approaching their destination via Spanish Morocco – inadvisable for anyone who held a passport showing they had spent time in loyalist Spain. In the end they went by boat from Tilbury via Gibraltar and Tangier. Gibraltar, which they reached at the close of the first week in September, produced several indications of the continuing nearby turmoil, in particular a Spanish destroyer flying the Republican flag drawn up in the harbour with a huge shell-hole in its side. By 10 September they were in Tangier: pro- and anti-Franco slogans on the walls about equally distributed, Orwell thought. Both unwell from the journey, they entered the country by early morning train, survived the labyrinthine Customs and police interrogations, spent nearly a day in Casablanca waiting for their luggage to catch up with them and then proceeded to their initial stopping-off point, Marrakech.

French Morocco was a popular destination for the 1930s literary traveller. Evelyn Waugh had stayed there in 1934 – the experience was later put to use in *Work Suspended* – alternating blasé letters recounting his exploits in the Fez brothels ('It was very gay and there were little Arab girls of fifteen & sixteen for ten francs each and a cup of mint tea') with more exalted compositions to his gentlewomanly friend Lady Katherine Asquith. Sacheverell Sitwell, too, passed through the country in 1938: an extraordinary excursion staffed by Sitwell, dressed in a Savile Row suit, accompanied by a train of beautiful women and a guide travelling in two chauffeur-driven cars. However otherworldly his eye, Sitwell gives a good idea of some of the splendours and miseries that awaited the Orwells in the main square at Marrakech, the Djemaa el Fna, at sunset.

A huge square with, in the middle, as it were a circus ring. A crowd of thousands moves round it, while its inner side, towards the centre, has circle after circle watching; moving on. Over all, hangs a haze of dust. The noise is such you cannot hear a person speak. In a moment you are lost in it. This is the Djemaa el Fna, and there is nothing like it in the world.

The tourist trail pursued by these exotics was not Orwell's. Sitwell, in the sixteen breathless pages devoted to Morocco in *Mauretania: Warrior, Man and Woman* (1940), sees a combination of spectacle and heritage: the veiled prostitutes whose appearance brought back the Arab world of the caliphate, the horrors of the witch doctors' pharmacopoeia ('a tray of disgusting objects, concoctions of bat or frog . . . the carcass of a raven looking like a body which has been dragged through a town at the horse's tail'). Orwell, in the only substantial piece he wrote about his stay ('Marrakech', published in John Lehmann's *New Writing*) sees poverty, marching men – Marrakesh was an important French garrison town – swarms of flies chasing after the coffin-borne corpses. In general he did not enjoy the six months he spent there. 'Morocco seems to me a beastly dull country,' he told Connolly: 'no forests and literally no wild animals', with the people of the big towns 'debauched' by the combination of poverty and the tourist trade. His health suffered at least one set-back and he chafed at his absence from England at a time of national emergency: this was the period of Chamberlain's flight to Berlin and the postponement of war. Nevertheless, it forms a significant interlude in his life. It was in Morocco, for example, that he wrote *Coming up for Air*, renewed an acquaintance with Dickens (the books sent out by the Westropes) that was to bear immediate fruit in a substantial essay written in the summer of 1939, and, most important of all, continued to brood about war and his attitude towards it.

The Orwells began by staying in the Hotel Continental, remaining for a day in what was fairly obviously a brothel largely because, as Eileen put it, 'Eric didn't notice anything odd about it until he tried to live in it.' Having relocated to the Majestic, and thence to an address in rue Edmond Doutte, they made arrangements to rent a villa five or six miles out on the Casablanca road owned by a Frenchman named Simont. Eileen believed that this would be 'fun from our point of view' – the villa was surrounded by orange groves, they intended to buy cheap French furniture, there was even a plan for Avril to come and stay – and yet neither felt any particular interest in their environment. Though he made his usual careful notes about the local agricultural methods, Orwell admitted as much in a letter to Jack Common a fortnight later.

'I don't care much for this country and am already pining to be back in England.' Depressed by the prospect of war – in which, Eileen noted, none of the French settlers seemed in the least interested – neither of them liked Marrakech. Assembling some of the details that would surface in the *New Writing* piece, Orwell noted the terrible poverty of the Jewish quarter, the universal child labour, the pervasive stench of disease and decay. In a fifty-yard saunter down the street it was quite usual to see three or four blind people. The Villa Simont would not be available until mid-October. Already, though, Orwell had begun to establish a routine: beginning on his novel, Eileen reported, and knocking up boxes for the goats and chickens he intended to rear over the next few months. There was a local doctor at hand to monitor his chest, but the habitual stoicism had already supervened. There was, of course, 'nothing wrong with me really', he briskly informed Common at the end of September.

Orwell's letters home in the winter of 1938–9, often to Common, are an odd mixture of small and large things unselfconsciously mixed: the seriousness of the European situation; the deficiencies of the Wallington cottage WC; comparisons of the colonial regimes of France and Britain; Hertfordshire animal husbandry ('I'm sorry about the hens, but I suppose they *must* lay soon'). By mid-October, now installed at the villa – furnished at a cost of around £10, Eileen calculated – he was devoting most of his energy to his novel. In particular, there were a couple of letters to John Sceats, the insurance agent who had visited him at Preston Hall, asking for information about his hero's proposed professional background ('I have only a very vague idea as to what an insurance agent does'). Undoubtedly Morocco, about whose dullness he continued to complain, provided an indirect spur to the creative impulse that lies at the heart of *Coming up for Air*, for it is nothing less than an elegy for a bygone England.

Orwell's trick in his previous novels had been to project various aspects of himself on to characters with whom he cannot quite wholeheartedly be identified. *Coming up for Air* is the most ingenious, and arguably the most effective, of these projections. John Flory, Dorothy Hare and Gordon Comstock had each been drawn from a social class to which Orwell had some kind of affiliation, but George Bowling, his new protagonist, existed several steps further down the hierarchical ladder. Bowling, a fat, middle-aged *homme moyen sensuel* living with his joyless and socially superior wife Hilda and their curiously anonymous children on the western fringes of London, is struck by a sudden desire to revisit the scenes of his Oxfordshire childhood in a town where his father was a struggling small tradesman. The journey, deviously accomplished in the face of Hilda's suspicion, takes place in the shadow of war: Bowling's mind is crowded with visions of exploding bombs and roads crammed with fleeing refugees. It is, inevitably, a failure – Lower Binfield has changed beyond recognition, the symbolic pond where the teenaged fisherman first came upon a brood of monstrous carp is a refuse heap. Worse, his carefully pre-planned alibi is no match for Hilda's wiles. The novel ends on a queer, anticipatory note, the business unfinished, the real conclusion drifting beyond the horizon, the only solidity glimpsed in a past that, however lavishly recreated, is no longer there.

Unsurprisingly, perhaps, for a novel whose hero's father is a put-upon small shopkeeper in a flyblown market town, *Coming up for Air's* most obvious debt is to the H.G. Wells of *The History of Mr Polly*. One of the absconding Mr Polly's key encounters – when he returns to his old home, now a tea-shop, and is served by his wife – is mirrored by Bowling's half-minute in the tobacconist's shop behind whose counter stands Elsie, his first love, now a slack-jawed hag. But there is an ominous foreshadowing, too. One of Bowling's friends is a retired public school master named Porteous, at whose feet George sits, we are given to understand, as a way of imbibing a hint of the 'culture' that was absent from his own upbringing. Porteous is not especially convincing as a character – his detachment from the modern world is so absolute that you always wonder how it was that he and the fat insurance agent ever came across each other – but he is indirectly responsible for what is perhaps the novel's most prophetic moment. Bowling has enquired what Porteous thinks of Hitler. After establishing Hitler's utter ephemerality, Porteous reads his friend a poem. For the first time the soothing, rhapsodical public school voice fails to work its magic. Bowling is struck by a curious sensation. '*He's dead.* He's a ghost. All people like that are dead.' The note had already been struck in Gordon Comstock's harangues; it would be struck again in the famous exchange between Winston and Julia in *Nineteen Eighty-Four*.

Coming up for Air would occupy Orwell for most of his time in Morocco, but there were other literary tasks in prospect. He continued to review books about Spain, not uncontroversially (a joint review of E. Allison Peers' *The Church in Spain 1737–1937* and Eoin O'Duffy's *Crusade in Spain* brought protests from both authors) and supplied a piece to the *Adelphi* headed 'Political Reflections on the Crisis'. His conclusion was that the British people would go to war if they were told to, while remaining essentially pacific and prepared to vote against any party that went war-mongering. In this atmosphere the Left Book Club agitation about a war in defence of democracy had gone some way towards losing the Labour Party the anticipated general election. Although he assured Moore that the climate was doing him good, Orwell's health was still giving cause for concern. Writing to Jack Common's wife May early in December, Eileen reported that he had been ill for a week (Eileen had also been ill herself), noting enigmatically that 'His illness was a sort of necessary stage in getting better; he had been worse here than I've ever seen him.' What does Eileen mean by this? Does 'worse here' mean a depression of spirits (it is followed by a complaint about the tedium of life in Morocco) or actual physical prostration? Eileen's letter gives a good idea of the routines of the villa – their servant, who arrived early in the morning, bringing fresh bread and milk for breakfast, simple meals of eggs, butter and fruit – without dwelling on what must have been a fairly isolated existence. Orwell's diary, though punctiliously kept up, offers nothing of great interest: agricultural methods, systems of land tenure, Arab funerals 'the wretchedest I have seen', consisting of a rough wooden bier, a hole not more than two feet deep, the body dumped in with nothing covering it except a mound of earth and either a brick or a broken pot placed at one end.

Christmas out on the Casablanca road was a perfunctory affair. A cold snap had frozen the fruit trees, Eileen was ill, the Christmas pudding had yet to arrive from England and Orwell confessed that it was not until the evening that he remembered what day it was. End of year letters sent his mind coursing back to the last days in Barcelona. The day that news arrived of Kopp's release from jail, after eighteen months' detention, found him writing to Frank Jellinek, the left-wing Spanish correspondent of the *Manchester Guardian*. With characteristic bluntness Orwell noted that he believed he had seen Jellinek in a pavement café shortly before his escape and would have crossed the road to speak to him had he not been ready to believe that every Communist was a spy. ('I am not a Marxist,' Orwell wrote, 'and I don't hold with all this stuff that boils down to "Anything is all right which advances the cause of the party."') For all this, Orwell's comments on Kopp's release were sharply realistic. After what they'd done to him the Republican authorities were 'bloody fools' to let him go. On Boxing Day he wrote a revealing letter to Jack Common containing more about the unproductive Wallington hens ('It seems to me that if it were any definite illness they would die of it and not merely stop laying'), a little about the local Arab population, whom he liked but could find no way of communicating with, and something about his literary plans. *Coming up for Air* would be done by April. Orwell reckoned the manuscript was a mess, while conceding that he liked parts of it and thought it had opened up a big subject which he had not had the time adequately to work out. There is an intriguing reference, too, to an enormous book 'in several volumes' which would take years to plan and execute. There is something faintly plaintive in all this, the thought of an intelligence oppressed by financial and health problems, monitoring the darkening clouds over Europe and wanting only the time to write. 'I can't tell you how deeply I wish to keep alive, out of jail, and out of money worries for the next few years.'

But he was conscious that for those on the independent-minded Left, time was running out. Back in September he had signed an ILP manifesto printed in the *New Leader* under the heading 'If War Comes We Shall Resist It'. A letter from January 1939 to Herbert Read, who had sent a copy of his personal call-to-arms *Towards a Free Revolutionary Art*, gives an idea of what shape this resistance might take. It was time to start organising for illegal activities, Orwell maintained – getting hold of stocks of paper and printing presses with a view to producing anti-war pamphlets. Was Read interested? A second letter, written a couple of months later, emphasises how comparatively revolutionary Orwell's stance was in the context of the time and his proximity to contemporary anarchist positions. There is, for example, mention of the journal *Revolt*, which published half a dozen issues in the early months of 1939, and an assertion – counter to Read's suggestion that it was absurd to prepare for an underground campaign if one didn't know who was going to campaign and what for – that those who failed to make some preparations would be helpless when anything happened. Meanwhile, he predicted, the greater part of the Left would simply associate themselves with 'the fascizing process'.

A first draft of *Coming up for Air* was nearly complete: the Orwells intended to return to England in April. He was feeling better, Orwell told Geoffrey Gorer, didn't cough much and had gained half a stone in weight. The *longueurs* of the stony, treeless landscape beyond the Villa Simont had been temporarily dispersed by a visit to Taddert, high in the Atlas mountains sixty miles from Marrakech, where Orwell admired the local Berber tribesmen and their 'exquisitely beautiful' womenfolk.

Notwithstanding the threat of war ('A nightmare to me,' he told Lady Rees, Richard Rees's mother) enthusiasm for 'home' becomes almost palpable in his letters as the spring progresses. In the end they fixed their departure date for 23 March. The news was conveyed to Lydia Jackson in a somewhat arch letter noting that the writer is 'so looking forward to seeing you', has been thinking of her constantly and warning her to 'be clever & burn this, won't you'. A plan to find the Dorsetshire cottage canvassed the previous summer fell through, probably on grounds of expense. The Orwells would be going back to Wallington. Another scheme to install Kopp, then quartered on the O'Shaughnessys in Greenwich, in the cottage for the time between Jack Common's departure and their return also fell through. Orwell confessed that he was longing to see England. At the end of the third week in March they set off for Marrakech and thence to Casablanca. Here, as their original boat had been delayed, they secured a passage on a Japanese ship dropping off a consignment of tea. In the meantime the signs from afar grew steadily more ominous. Five thousand French troops had passed the villa a few days before their departure. Then, in a Casablanca cinema, they watched a film on the life of the soldier, accompanied by a cine-reel demonising Germany. Such propagandising in this out-of-the-way corner of the French empire could mean only one thing, Orwell decided: war was certain.

Never one to waste time where the processes of publishing were concerned – and probably anxious about the money involved – Orwell left the completed manuscript of *Coming up for Air* at Moore's office within a few hours of arriving back in England on 30 March 1939. His immediate destination was Southwold, where old Mr Blair was now terminally ill, but he had time to leave a postcard at Lydia Jackson's London flat suggesting that he could look in for an hour the next morning before leaving for Suffolk. Miss Jackson prudently absented herself from the premises, prompting him to write to her later in the day ('I rang up 3 times. Are you angry with me?') and canvassing a rendezvous on his return from Southwold two or three days later. In the event he was forced to spend nearly a week in Southwold confined to bed with a cold. The original idea was that Eileen should stay in Greenwich, but discovering that Mrs Blair, too, was ill, with phlebitis, she travelled up to Suffolk to help out. Orwell's chest had 'behaved very nicely', she reported to Mary Common, and he was now convalescent. Husband and wife finally returned to Wallington on 11 April.

Leaving aside the mounting international crisis, both Orwell's personal and professional lives were subject to tension. He continued to write surreptitious letters to Lydia Jackson, and yet the strain evident in the Orwells' marriage seems to have had its roots in quite another quarter. Fastening on Lydia as a confidante, Eileen revealed that their relationship was going badly wrong, the cause being 'a schoolmistress or something' whom Orwell had known before marrying her and continued to see, apparently in full view of the villagers, in Wallington. This can only have been Brenda Salkeld, presumably visiting in the school holidays from her parents' house in Bedfordshire. Simul-taneously, Eileen was worried that Gollancz might make trouble about *Coming up for Air*, which Orwell rightly judged to have pacifist tendencies as well as containing a satirical account of a Left Book Club meeting, and within days of Moore's receipt of the book was worrying whether it might not be better to change his fiction to a different publisher. As it turned out, Gollancz had declined to listen to what Orwell imagined were siren voices from King Street and proposed only minor alterations. *Coming up for Air* was published almost at once at the beginning of June. It was well reviewed – there was even a friendly notice in the *Daily Worker* – and sold out its edition of 2,000 copies (Orwell's earnings from it amounted to a welcome £125) but this was not, Orwell knew, a good time to be publishing a novel. Anthony Powell remembered the depressing effect on publishing in general, and on his own novel *What's Become of Waring* (1939) in particular, caused by Hitler's decision a couple of months earlier to send troops into the international free port of Memel. Orwell's three-part saga – referred to again in a letter to Moore – would have to wait. As a follow-up to *Coming up for Air* he proposed a collection of essays, whose centrepiece would be a long meditation on Dickens, recently re-read in the long evenings at the Villa Simont. This kind of thing was a drug on the market, as Orwell with his experience of the publishing game well knew, but Gollancz was persuaded to declare an interest. A rough draft of 'Charles Dickens' was finished by early July. The Dickens essay marks a decisive twist in Orwell's trajectory as a writer. Not only is it one of the finest pieces of literary criticism he ever wrote, instantly seeing the point of Dickens' humour and his moral stance while salvaging him from the myriad constituencies who claimed him as their own, but it also draws Dickens squarely into the moral vision that Orwell was trying to construct around his own feelings towards 'England' and 'Englishness'. A review of Clarence L. Streit's *Union Now*, written for the *Adelphi* at around this time, confirms this centralising gaze. The slide to war was happening, Orwell argued, 'because nearly all the Socialist leaders, when it comes to the pinch, are merely His Majesty's Opposition, and nobody else knows how to mobilise the decency of the English people, which one meets with everywhere when one talks to human beings instead of reading newspapers'.

Work on the essay had to be put aside for a week at the end of June when word came from Southwold that Mr Blair was about to die. Now aged eighty-two, and suffering from intestinal cancer, the old man had for some time been reconciled to his wayward son. Orwell was glad, he told Moore, that 'latterly he had not been so disappointed in me as before'. In fact Richard Blair's last moments of consciousness were spent listening to a favourable review of *Coming up for Air* read out to him from the *Sunday Times*. After he died there occurred another of those odd little Orwellian moments that gain their oddity from Orwell's retelling of them. Having removed the copper pennies placed on the deceased's eyelids in the customary way, Orwell wondered what to do with them. In the end he walked down the High Street to the promenade and threw them into the North Sea.

Back in Wallington, as the summer rose to its height, he began to keep a diary of events. Composed of countless press cuttings, taken from sources as diverse as the *Daily Telegraph* and the *Smallholder*, it is a quintessential Orwell document, endlessly revealing of the things his mind was inclined to fasten on. There is fighting on the Manchukwo–Mongolian border. Egg production in England and Wales stands at 3,250 million units. A large-scale ARP practice is taking place across south-eastern England (8 July) and the native rat population is put between four and five million. Some newspapers are appealing for the inclusion of Churchill in the cabinet, while the crowd attending the Eton–Harrow match is put at 10,000 and said to be the smartest gathering for some years. A week later he wrote to Moore enclosing a summary of the contents of what was to become *Inside the Whale* ('Charles Dickens', 'Boys' Weeklies' and the title-piece discussion of Henry Miller). Worried about his future – notwithstanding his current anti-war stance, it would have been clear to him that he was unfit for any serious war work – Orwell was anxious about money, even going so far as to wonder whether the 'Poverty in Practice' project might not be revived. Meanwhile 60,000 German troops had marched into Danzig and the prospect of war invaded every thought and professional engagement. Reviewing a collection of books for *Time and Tide* early in

August, he noted that they all revolved 'at varying distances around the same subject . . . I suppose it is unnecessary to say what that subject is.' There was a disquieting incident on 12 August when two detectives arrived at the cottage with orders to seize all books 'received through the post'. The books in question were supposedly 'obscene' items published by Jack Kahane's Paris-based Obelisk Press, Henry Miller's publisher. The authorities had been alerted, Orwell discovered, by a letter to the press intercepted at the Hitchin sorting office. This episode has occasionally been given a highly symbolic role in Orwell studies – the first grasp of the totalitarian hand on the collar – and yet Orwell, at any rate with hindsight, was concerned to downplay its significance. The police were only carrying out orders, and even the public prosecutor wrote to say that he understood that as a writer Orwell might have a need for books which it was illegal to possess. On the other hand, two days after the raid Orwell noted in the diary a remark made by an unidentified friend: 'it appears that the opening of letters to persons connected with left-wing parties is now so normal as to excite no remark'.

Hitler was poised to invade Poland. Across Britain preparations for war ground into gear. Eileen, ironically enough, had secured a job at the Censorship Department at Whitehall – a post that would mean spending the working week in London. More policemen arrived in Wallington, this time to arrange for the billeting of soldiers. On 24 August, Orwell left for Ringwood in Hampshire to stay with L.H. Myers. Nothing is immediately known of this visit other than that he was impressed by his host's understanding of the international situation and the information he had gleaned from his well-connected acquaintance (Myers knew Churchill, whom he reported to be deeply pessimistic). The British ambassador to Berlin flew back and forth with ultimata and responses. Nazi troops marched across the Polish border. On 3 September, the day on which Chamberlain made his broadcast declaring war, Orwell made his way back via Waterloo to the O'Shaughnessys' house in Greenwich. Mobilisation had been proclaimed. All over the country literary men turned to their diaries in a spirit of disbelieving apprehension. 'I feel as if I could not write again . . .' Stephen Spender wrote that morning. 'I must put out my hands and grasp the handfuls of facts. How extraordinary things are.' The aluminium barrage balloons, Spender thought, seemed nailed into the sky like bolts.

Part Four
1939–1945

13

Life during Wartime

I should like to put it on record that I have never been able to dislike Hitler. – Review of *Mein Kampf*, *New English Weekly*, 21 March 1940

My chief hope for the future is that the common people have never parted company with their moral code. – Letter to Humphry House, 11 April 1940

Orwell left Myers's house some time on 3 September and made his way to Waterloo. Here the platforms were crammed with troops setting off for unknown destinations. Despite the circumstances – Chamberlain's mid-morning announcement of a declaration of war had been followed by a false air-raid alarm – there was no panic. Neither, Orwell deduced from his observation of the milling crowds, was there much enthusiasm. In fact, the onset of hostilities seemed to inspire little interest. Yet the visible signs of war lay everywhere to hand. The sky above London was packed with barrage balloons. The newspapers announced that three million people were in the process of being evacuated. Churchill and Eden joined the cabinet; senior Labour politicians declined office for the time being. After forty-eight hours at the O'Shaughnessys' house in Greenwich Orwell headed back to Wallington, where more mundane matters demanded his attention. In his absence the late summer heat wave had wreaked havoc on the garden. He spent the next few days restoring order in the knowledge that there were plans to be made and decisions to be followed up. Eileen was already working at the Whitehall Censorship Department. At this stage Orwell presumed that he would follow her to London. The Stores would be shut up once more, the hens sold and the goats given away to a neighbour. In the event he was to stay at the Wallington cottage for another nine months.

Orwell's literary generation spent the six years of the Second World War in a variety of occupations. Anthony Powell proceeded from a commission in the Welch Regiment to military intelligence and thence to a post as an Allied liaison officer. Cyril Connolly sat in an editorial chair. Henry Green joined the Auxiliary Fire Service. Auden, notoriously, left for America. Orwell, whose health would always render him unfit for military service, was frankly envious of those of his contemporaries who contrived to put on uniform. Why couldn't someone on the Left do that? he grumbled when the news came through that Evelyn Waugh was serving in a Commando unit. That he was able to take up this attitude to literary combatants says something for the profound transformation in his thinking about the war since August 1939. According to 'My Country Right or Left', written a year later, this was practically an instantaneous conversion. It took place on 25 August, the night before the announcement of the Russo-German pact. Lying in bed at Myers' house in Hampshire, Orwell dreamed that war had begun. This had a curious effect on him. In his semi-conscious state two things, in particular, were immediately apparent: first, that he was relieved that the years of uncertainty had finally come to an end; second, that he was a patriot, that he would support the war, even if it meant lining up alongside the hated Chamberlain government, and if possible fight in it. The dream was prophetic. He came downstairs the next morning to find the newspapers announcing that Ribbentrop, the Nazi foreign minister, had flown to Moscow, and that war was now inevitable. Having reached this decision, and effectively turned his back on much of what he had written and said over the past two years, he was subsequently forced to explain it to his friends on the ILP's pacifist and anarchist fringe. An exchange of letters with Reg Reynolds' wife Ethel Mannin, treasurer of the SIA, contains her rather plaintive reproach, 'I thought you thought it all crazy, this smashing of Nazi faces.' There were probably other remonstrances of this kind in the autumn of 1939, but Orwell's mind was made up. A few days after the outbreak of war, with the garden trained back, the early potatoes harvested and the windfall apples made into apple jelly, he wrote to the authorities expressing his willingness to join the war effort.

But joining the war effort, especially for a thirty-six-year-old man with damaged lungs, was not as easy as it sounded. Here in the pre-conscription days, even Orwell's healthy contemporaries found themselves having to rely on the intervention of highly placed friends. The bitter sense of frustration that hangs over Orwell's life in the early

1940s stems from this inability to contribute, or to be allowed to contribute, to the war. Set against the news from beyond the Channel, his professional tasks seemed worse than trivial. 'Everything is disintegrating,' he wrote in June 1940. 'It makes me sick to be writing book reviews at such a time, & even angers me that such time-wasting should be permitted.' Writing was impossible – Orwell's letters from this time are shot through with the realisation that at a time of international crisis creative artists were simply unable to function – but what else was he to do? The consciousness of missed opportunities, of settling down in a stagnant ooze of inanition, oppressed him. His characterisation of the Anglo-French novelist Julian Green, whose *Personal Record 1928–1939* he reviewed in April 1940, is effectively a description of himself: 'young enough to expect something from life and old enough to remember "before the war"'.

Here in the autumn of 1939 there was very little to expect. The period 1939–41 is one of Orwell's blackest periods. He spent much of the first part of it in Wallington waiting for Eileen to join him on alternate weekends. He was hard-up, earning little from journalism, with no novel in prospect, and fighting humiliating battles with the taxman. A friend remembered him saying at this time that he simply tore up letters from the Inland Revenue unread. But he was steadily sowing the seeds of his literary and professional future. In the early years of the war he cemented his connection with Connolly's *Horizon*, wrote the first of his regular 'London Letters' to the American political magazine *Partisan Review* and began to take up speaking and scripting engagements with the BBC. All this was to bear substantial long-term fruit. So, too, was the view of 'Englishness' that he was continuing to formulate, and its relation to the political future he saw taking shape around him. Much of his writing reeks of dissatisfaction – the horrors of the Blitz, the thump of bombs in the distance, the search for someone who might employ him – and yet looking back from the vantage point of 1941 at the 'strange boring nightmare' he had an inexplicable feeling that he had learned something from it, just as he had learned things from Spain. War, quite as much as peace, could be a formative experience. Perhaps in the end, he mused, it would turn out to be a blessing in disguise, 'though certainly it is a very deep disguise at present'.

It is also a period when Orwell is at his most elusive, when the trail grows intermittently cold. The domestic diary from his time at Wallington, a painstaking document recording the egg harvest and the state of the garden, has a ten-day gap at the start of September, during which Orwell says he has been 'travelling', but there is no indication where to and on what business. Possibly it was in pursuit of war work. If so, the optimism of the first weeks of the month was soon dashed. A letter to Moore from early October, enquiring about the circulation of the magazines that would feature in 'Boys' Weeklies', announces a change of plan. In the absence of an official job, he intended to stay in Wallington, finish *Inside the Whale* and get the garden in trim for the winter. It was a lonely existence, marked out by trips to Baldock, the punctilious nature notes – a bird that was surely a golden plover, solitary excitement over a 'phosphorescent worm or millipede' found on the evening lawn which, ferried indoors in a test-tube, rapidly began to fade – and 'experimental' apple jam which did not, he acknowledged, seem a great success. His friends, even those not in khaki, seemed much more usefully employed. Rayner Heppenstall would soon join the army and leave for Northern Ireland. Connolly was hatching literary plans. He kept in touch with the political acquaintances made in the pre-war era, knowing that he no longer shared their aims. Nevertheless, at weekends it was possible to recreate a miniaturised version of pre-war social life. He spent a couple of days with Eileen and Lydia Jackson picking blackberries in the Hertfordshire lanes. Connolly came up from London. Professionally he was scratching a surface living from the *Listener*, *Time and Tide* and the *Adelphi*. As publishing schedules habitually lagged behind the rush of world events, several of the books he reviewed dragged him back to an older time. He wrote a mournful piece about Nancy Johnstone's *Hotel in Flight*, which covered the last eighteen months of the Spanish Civil War, praising its authenticity and going on to wonder what, in the end, the conflict had meant to the Spanish people whom it had been intended to benefit. Reviewing the casual contacts he had made with peasants, shopkeepers, street-hawkers and even militiamen, he was conscious that the great majority simply had no feelings about the war, except for wanting it to cease. If a really good book were ever to be written about the war, it would probably be produced by a Spaniard, and not a 'politically conscious' Spaniard at that. Good war books, Orwell went on, widening the focus of his enquiry, were nearly always written from the angle of the visitor. What robbed the outlook of most foreigners in Spain – especially the English and the Americans – of the necessary realism was the thought, lurking in the back of their minds, that they at least would live to tell the tale.

Meanwhile the 'phoney' war, a period of intense preparation on either side of the Channel but little actual military activity, ground on. Each night the black-out arrived a few minutes earlier. The London pavements were piled with sandbags. Windows were taped up with strips of paper. Fine autumn weather, the balloons in the sky, the threat somehow submerged behind civilian routines, made the south of England seem 'interesting and almost gay', Stephen Spender thought. All over the country writers were coming to terms with the changed situation, wondering how they could make themselves useful; what – if anything – they were expected to do. Lunching with Spender, T.S. Eliot proposed that the important thing was that writers should keep writing, that as many literary people as possible should remain detached and not take an official post. Orwell's detachment, on the other hand, was simply wished upon him. Throughout the autumn he continued to work on the three essays that would go to make up *Inside the Whale*. The long consideration of Dickens had been finished before the war began. To it he added the essay on 'Boys' Weeklies' and the title-piece analysis of Henry Miller, which opened out into an analysis of the environment in which contemporary literature was written. Orwell admired Miller – 'the only imaginative prose-writer of the slightest value who has appeared among the English-speaking races for some years past' – while regretting his quietism. The literary history of the 1930s seemed to justify this position, and yet in a world of power politics detachment, whether of the pure 'aesthetic' kind or Miller's hard-boiled amoralism, had lost its sheen. *Tropic of Cancer*, consequently, demonstrated only the impossibility of any major literature until the world had 'shaken itself into new shape'. By early December the book was ready, although Orwell wondered to Moore whether Gollancz would want to publish it, 'as there is at any rate one passage that probably won't appeal to him'. There is something faintly paranoid about this – it would have taken a much more hard-line ideologue than Gollancz to reject a manuscript on the strength of a single passage – and Orwell already seems to have had Warburg waiting in the wings, should the Henrietta Street connection turn sour. Happily, Gollancz liked the book, despite his offer of a paltry £20 advance, and scheduled it for spring publication.

Orwell had been busy arranging his own advance publicity, informing Moore that Connolly and Spender wanted to see the manuscript for *Horizon*. This is the first reference to a connection that was to serve Orwell for the next half-dozen years. First appearing in the New Year of 1940 but a hot topic of book world gossip throughout the preceding autumn, *Horizon* was the literary sensation of the phoney war. Anxious to unload the unfinished novel on which he had been working when the war broke out, Evelyn Waugh wondered to his agent at about this time whether it would be possible to sell it to 'a highbrow paper', noting that 'Connolly has started one backed by a pansy of means named Watson'. This is hugely unfair to the enigmatic figure of Peter Watson, who has some claims to be regarded as the great literary patron of the 1940s. But cheered by an offer for the serial rights of what became *Work Suspended*, Waugh – though prone to mock some of the modernist propaganda that featured in *Horizon*'s pages – swiftly revised his opinion. Writing to Connolly twenty years later, and ten years after the magazine's demise, he was able to assure him that 'it is very proper that you should have proud memories ... It was the outstanding publication of its decade.' Though Waugh's letter is in part a disguised attempt to distance himself from the charge of having satirised Connolly in his 1961 novel *Unconditional Surrender* (which features a wartime magazine named *Survival* and its risible editor Everard Spruce) he spoke nothing but the truth. No single publication, perhaps, contributed as much to the literature of the 1940s as *Horizon*. Nothing, equally, has a greater claim to be regarded as Connolly's lasting monument. Run from offices beneath Peter Watson's flat in Lansdowne Terrace (the atmosphere is memorably evoked in J. Maclaren-Ross's *Memoirs of the Forties*) selling only a few thousand copies a month and kept alive on Watson's money, *Horizon* managed to combine high, if not Olympian, literary aspirations with an indisputable chic. It was prepared to take risks – devoting an entire number later on in the 1940s to Waugh's *The Loved One* – while acting as a showcase for upcoming talent. Maclaren-Ross and Angus Wilson were only two of the writers whose names Connolly effectively made during the course of the decade. Above all, and to a degree rarely seen in English letters, it was Europeanised in a way conspicuous for the time. Connolly's heart lay in France: the 'West' conceptualised in his famous valedictory editorial ('. . . it is closing time in the gardens of the West, and from now on a writer will be judged only by the resonance of his solitude or the quality of his despair') went a very long way beyond Calais.

Thus constituted, *Horizon* provided Orwell with a ready-made medium for his work, administered by an editor who was prepared to sympathise almost indefinitely with what he wanted to say. 'Boys' Weeklies' appeared in March 1940, the month of *Inside the Whale*'s publication. Subsequently, along with smaller reviews, Connolly was to print a substantial chunk of Orwell's *The Lion and the Unicorn: Socialism and the English Genius* (December 1940), 'Wells, Hitler and the World State' (August 1941), 'The Art of Donald McGill' (September 1941), 'Raffles and Miss Blandish' (October 1944) and 'Politics and the English Language' (April 1946). The symbiosis at work had profound advantages for both sides. Orwell, developing as an essayist in the field of popular culture, needed a medium in which he could perform without space constraints or editorial bias. In Connolly he found an editor who, within reason, was prepared to back his contributor's judgement. Connolly may not have taken everything offered to him – 'How the Poor Die' was probably intended for *Horizon* rather than George Woodcock's small circulation *Now* in which it eventually appeared, and 'Such, Such Were the Joys' was debarred on libel grounds – but in general he offered Orwell a platform which most youngish writers moving on into mid-career are desperate to achieve. There were other advantages, too. In becoming part and parcel of the *Horizon* set-up, Orwell began to move, however imperceptibly, in a more glamorous literary world. Editors, Connolly felt, had social obligations. Even Evelyn Waugh, who was occasionally disposed to poke fun at the atmosphere of the *Horizon* office, with its succession of well-bred young secretaries, remembered 'the delightful parties you gave'. In one sense the magazine was Orwell's first introduction to London literary life proper. And there was something else. On one of his visits to the office he would certainly have come across Connolly's editorial assistants. Among them was a striking dark-haired girl named Janetta Woolley, one of whose first jobs was to ink out by hand the swear-words in Maclaren-Ross' story 'A Bit of a Smash in Madras', who would later be present at his second marriage. So, in a rather different capacity, would another, a fresh-faced blonde woman in her early twenties, devoted to Connolly but hero-worshipping his homosexual patron. Her name was Sonia Brownell.

The Orwells spent much of December, including Christmas, together in Greenwich. Returning to Wallington, Orwell found that the hens had laid 101 eggs in his absence but that the mice were very bad ('must try poisoning them'). It had been snowing, and despite a temporary thaw on the afternoon of Old Year's Night, he spent a chilly New Year's Day among the Hertfordshire frosts. His immediate prospects looked equally barren. There was still no war work, and still no prospect of finding anything permanent to do in London. Anxious to maintain his literary output, and to involve himself directly in the intellectual ferment created by the war, Orwell was keen to accept an invitation that reached him in the early days of 1940. Although he was still prepared to be published by Victor Gollancz (who had retained an option on his next two novels) Orwell had been careful to maintain his links with Fred Warburg. It was in this capacity that he was asked to the initial meeting of a group of writers convened by Warburg in January to discuss 'war issues'. The gathering had both professional and personal consequences for Orwell. It led eventually to one of his most sustained pieces of wartime commentary, while bringing him into the orbit of a man who was to become one of his close friends.

T.R. ('Tosco') Fyvel was in his early thirties, the son of one of the early Zionist leaders, who had left the Switzerland of his upbringing for a minor English public school and a place at Cambridge. He admired Orwell's work and left a vivid account of the first meeting of Warburg's discussion group, held at the St John's Wood home of the German-Jewish expatriate Hans Lothar, formerly deputy editor of the liberal newspaper *Frankfurter Zeitung*. Here he found 'a very tall, thin man with a long, thin, haggard face, with deep-set blue eyes, a poor, small moustache and deep lines etched in grooves down his face'. He was shabbily dressed, but in his manner and bearing reminded Fyvel of some of the British colonial officials he had met in the Middle East. But above these vestiges of sahibdom hung a whiff of something exotically French, detectable in the dark blue working man's shirt and his habit of rolling cigarettes 'incessantly' out of blackish, acrid tobacco. Somehow this was not what Fyvel had expected. It was clear, too, that the opinions Fyvel had been monitoring in print over the past eighteen months had undergone practically a 180-degree turn. Orwell recounted the story of his dream – this seems to have been something of a party piece – and aired his belief that there was no sign of any British Fascism or, less encouragingly, any kind of social revolution. Fyvel was struck, apropos of a discussion of 'Not Counting Niggers', the title of Orwell's review of Streit's *Union Now* in the *Adelphi* piece printed a few weeks before the war began, by his insistence on the link between opposition to Hitler and freedom for India, and also by his doubts about common Anglo-Soviet war aims. Even if Hitler were eventually to attack Russia, Orwell prophesied, how could the move towards a Socialist Britain be squared with Stalin's absolutism?

The two men got on well. Fyvel remembered going over Orwell's sombre view of any future Anglo-Soviet alliance as he took the late-night train back to Hastings where he and his wife were then living. Come the spring, a social get-together was arranged in London, also involving Eileen and Mary Fyvel. The Fyvels liked Eileen, despite her obvious tiredness: although 'rather echoing' Orwell, she remained a distinctive personality in her own right. Orwell was gloomy about war's general effect on culture and its particular effect on himself. The English novel had become a purely upper-middle-class artform, he argued (wrongly, as it turned out); there was still no war work in the offing and he was earning very little. He talked about the Wallington livestock and his plans to raise potatoes as a hedge against the Nazi submarine blockade. Fyvel's memories of Orwell and Eileen from the early part of 1940 are one of the few accounts of husband and wife in tandem, and give a vivid picture of what they must have been like as a marital double act: Eileen talking about her work in the occasionally bizarre atmosphere of the Censorship Department or humorously recasting incidents from their time together in Spain; Orwell recalling their first struggles to make ends meet in the Wallington shop. But there was a fantastic and unfathomable side to all this camaraderie. Mary Fyvel remembered Orwell telling her of his obsession with the teenaged Arab prostitutes in Marrakesh: in the end Eileen had allowed him to have one. The Fyvels did not quite know what to make of this ('True or imagined? It did not matter,' Fyvel concluded) but it lent an odd gloss to an otherwise conventional relationship, the thought of shadowy, secret recesses stretching away beneath the surface of their public lives.

The same could be said of the way in which Orwell's creative life was moving on, here at a time of comparative inertia. It was Gollancz who teased out the link between Orwell's current preoccupations and what was to come. Writing in early January to assure him how much he liked *Inside the Whale*, Gollancz wondered whether he was being over-pessimistic about the chances of freedom of thought surviving into an economically totalitarian society. Orwell was inclined to agree. Nothing was certain until a true collective economy had been tried out in the West. What worried him was whether ordinary people in countries like England grasped the difference between democracy and despotism well enough to want to defend their liberties. 'However, perhaps when the pinch comes the common people will turn out to be more intelligent than the clever ones. I certainly hope so.' This is uncannily prophetic of the great declaration of *Nineteen Eighty-Four* ('If there is hope it lies in the proles') and yet ghostly prefigurations of this kind run silently through a great deal of Orwell's work in 1940–41. A few months later, for example, he discussed the case of Sir Richard Acland, a Liberal MP and later founder of the idealistic Common Wealth party, in a letter to the Dickens scholar Humphry House. Acland was a well-meaning ass, Orwell thought, incapable of seeing anything wrong with the Soviet regime. British intellectuals, he argued, had become infatuated with the 'inherently materialist Marxist notion' that technical advances will necessarily have a moral effect. 'My chief hope for the future is that the common people have never parted company with their moral code.' Shortly after this he wrote a group review of four reprinted 'dystopian' texts for *Tribune*. The novels in question were Jack London's *The Iron Heel*, Wells' *The Sleeper Wakes*, Huxley's *Brave New World* and – a lesser known but no less interesting work – Ernest Bramah's *The Secret of the League*, in which a Labour government achieves such a huge majority that it cannot be dislodged and is eventually overthrown by a middle-class conspiracy.

Orwell's comments on this quartet, at least two of which may be thought to have a direct effect on his own work, are highly revealing. *The Iron Heel* was inferior to Wells, he thought, but because of his own streak of personal savagery London could grasp something that Wells apparently could not – that hedonistic societies do not survive. This was his complaint about *Brave New World*, with its pleasuredomes and ceaseless pursuit of sensual satisfaction. A ruling class needed a strict moral basis, a quasi-religious belief in itself, a mystique. No society of the kind Huxley envisaged could last more than a generation or two owing to the decadence of its élite. Taking these themes yet further, in January the following year he wrote a piece on Koestler's novel *Darkness at Noon*. Here, in a withering projection of the Moscow show trials, Rubaskov, one of the last survivors of the original Central Committee of the Communist Party, is arrested, charged with incredible crimes, denies them, is tortured, confesses everything and is shot in the back of the neck. 'For the good of the party,' Orwell notes, is probably the final argument.

But the journey to Orwell's own dystopian world had scarcely begun. In the meantime he was gloomy and out of sorts, conscious that professionally he ought to 'lie fallow' after the excitements of the past few years and desperate for the chance to do something in the fight against Fascism. A letter sent to Geoffrey Gorer early in January 1940 recapitulates his life over the past year: Morocco, his father's death, his inability to procure war work. The idea that he ought to husband his resources was, as usual, rendered a nonsense by the hand-to-mouth conditions of his professional life. In 1940, for instance, he reviewed over 100 books. Not much survives from this period of his life, when he was still stuck in Wallington and seeing Eileen every ten days or so. He was reading *Mein Kampf*, recently republished in an English translation, with, he told Moore, 'some interest'. Recovering from one of his habitual bouts of winter chest trouble, he would have been pleased by the reception accorded to the simultaneous appearance of 'Boys' Weeklies' in *Horizon* and Gollancz's publication of *Inside the Whale*. 'Boys' Weeklies' marks the start of something new in Orwell's work: the examination not just of life at bedrock, but also of the influences that go to make up and direct that life. Orwell's analysis of the world of the *Magnet* and the *Gem* stops marginally short of labelling the whole phenomenon a capitalist plot, but underlying it is a penetrating awareness of the way in which literature gets written. It is also, or rather was, transparently his own world, as this summary of the landscape inhabited by Harry Wharton and Bob Cherry makes clear:

> The year is 1910 – or 1940, but it is all the same. You are at Greyfriars, a rosy-cheeked boy of fourteen in posh, tailor-made clothes, sitting down to tea in your study on the Remove passage after an exciting game of football which was won by an odd goal in the last half-minute. There is a cosy fire in the study and outside the wind is whistling. The ivy clusters thickly around the old grey stones. The king is on his throne and the pound is worth a pound. Over in Europe the comic foreigners are jabbering and gesticulating, but the grim grey battleships of the British fleet are steaming up the channel and at the outposts of Empire the monocled Englishmen are holding the niggers at bay.

Orwell, as Cyril Connolly once observed, was a rebel in love with 1910. 'Boys' Weeklies', too, emphasises the immense complexity of the attitude Orwell adopted towards the past, which his excursions into popular culture attempt to define: an unquestioning love of its atmosphere and paraphernalia set against a sharp awareness of the ideological current running beneath. There was an amusing coda to the essay's publication in *Horizon*, when a letter arrived from 'Frank Richards', author of the *Gem* and *Magnet* series, whom Orwell, on the strength of his voluminous output, had supposed to be a collective pseudonym. 'Frank Richards Replies to George Orwell', which more than holds its own with some of Orwell's more emphatic claims, and is especially acute on the prospects for a left-wing boys' paper ('I hope that it is, and will remain, impossible') appeared in the May number. By this time *Inside the Whale* had garnered a stack of appreciative reviews – the Dickens essay was recognised as an imaginative piece of salvage, and even Mrs Leavis descended from the mountain of *Scrutiny* to suggest, in a rather back-handed compliment, that 'if he would give up trying to be a novelist Mr Orwell might find his *métier* in literary criticism, in a special line of it peculiar to himself which is particularly needed now.' Predictably, *Inside the Whale* did not sell well. Gollancz printed only 1,000 copies, and some of these were later destroyed in a bombing raid. But it had given Orwell a clearer sight of the writer he wanted to be.

For the *New English Weekly* at the end of March Orwell wrote a characteristic piece about *Mein Kampf*, noting that the Nazi dictator would never have succeeded had it not been for the attraction of his personality. 'I should like to put it on record that I have never been able to dislike Hitler.' The photographs of him in his early Brownshirt days showed 'the face of a man suffering under intolerable wrongs', his expression not unlike that of the crucified Christ. Anticipating the remarks on Huxley made later that summer, Orwell noted that Hitler's success lay in his ability to grasp the falsity of the hedonistic attitude to life. Human beings did not only want comfort, safety and shorter working hours; they also, at least intermittently, craved struggle, self-sacrifice, drums, flags and loyalty parades.

The particular human being was still drifting on the tide. Everything was very quiet on the Wallington front, he reported to Gorer early in April. At the moment he was trying to join a government training centre and learn machine draughtsmanship. There were several reasons for this: he wanted a job; the work, which would suit his ever-present 'practical' side, appealed to him; moreover, in the event of universal conscription, he would prefer to do something skilled – if nothing else it would be useful to emerge from the war having learned a trade. Once his affairs were settled he wanted to get Eileen out of the Censorship Department simply because she was being worked to death, as well as spending most of her time in London. As for their finances, they could get by if he stuck to his writing, but he was anxious to slow down. The idea for the long novel that had taken root in his mind before the war was still there, but there was no prospect of starting it in the immediate future. There were reviews to write, the never-ending reviews – Malcolm Muggeridge's book about the 1930s, Havelock Ellis' autobiography – and the spring sowing to be done. An ambitious plan to raise half a ton of potatoes on the Wallington plot was revised down to six hundredweight. Unable to be present at the *Adelphi* Easter conference, he sent a lecture to be read by someone else, 'attacking pacifism for all I was worth'. This has not survived, but clearly Orwell was anxious to gauge the audience reaction, enquiring of Rayner Heppenstall if he had been in the room: 'I don't know how they liked it and would like to hear from someone who was there.' And then, finally, something – not much, but something – came up. *Time and Tide*, the weekly for which he had reviewed books for some years, offered him the post of theatre critic with the possibility of contributing additional film reviews. It was not an obvious job for someone of Orwell's interests, and not particularly well paid (the magazine was run on a shoestring by its feminist proprietor, Lady Rhondda) but it would give him the chance to finance cheap lodgings in London and be with Eileen, and he jumped at it.

The incongruity of having to pursue the mundane tasks of reviewing at a time when there seemed every chance that the country would shortly be invaded was not lost on the literary journalists of 1940. Both Richard Church and Hugh Walpole began their round-ups of the week's books one morning in June with the reflection that it was strange to be sitting down at a familiar desk doing a routine review that might never appear because England had been overrun. Orwell himself first heard about the retreat to Dunkirk between the acts at a play at the Duke of York's theatre. The drama of all-out war was being enacted with frightening speed. Professional duties faded into insignificance. Composed in an atmosphere of extreme unease, Orwell's theatre reviews are not the most penetrating things he ever wrote. The productions he was sent to see covered the entire range of the contemporary stage, from the Old Vic *Tempest*, starring John Gielgud as Prospero and Jessica Tandy as Miranda, at the top, to ephemeral burlesques at the bottom. At both ends of the spectrum his eye tended to alight not on the incidental detail of the performance but on the wider cultural framework. The lesson of *The Tempest*, for example, was that apart from half a dozen well-known plays Shakespeare would remain unstageable until the general public had taken to reading him. Watching *Applesauce* at the Holborn Empire, alternatively, he detected in Max Miller 'one of a long line of English comedians who have specialised in the Sancho Panza side of life, in real *lowness*'. It was important that such people existed,

Orwell thought, as they expressed something which was valuable to our civilisation, without which humanity would lose sight of an element that was integral to itself.

Happily London theatreland lay only a short distance from the Orwells' new home: a flat at Dorset Chambers, a mansion block in Chagford Street, NW1. It was a curious kind of double life: professional duties running side by side with the disastrous news from France. On 25 May 1940, for instance, as the British Expeditionary Force fell back towards the French coast, Orwell was at the Comedy Theatre in Panton Street talking to the annual gathering of the Dickens Fellowship. Though he remained a punctilious observer of the frenzied wartime scene – the diary he resumed at this time is full of vivid period detail – there was something faintly detached about his attitude. June found him 'thinking always of my island in the Hebrides, which I suppose I shall never see'. This is the first reference to Jura, the bolt-hole that sustained him in his last years, but the matter-of-factness of the comment suggests that the idea had lodged in his consciousness a long time before. There was literary work to hand: the diary was originally conceived as a joint project with his friend Inez Holden, a long-time attendant on the London literary scene (Duckworth had published her novel *Sweet Charlatan* as far back as 1932, and she is the model for Roberta Payne in Powell's *What's Become of Waring*). Even with the lurking threat of invasion, routines began to establish themselves – reviews, twice- or thrice-weekly trips to the theatre – but there was a sense in which he had ceased to care. The reviews, he noted in mid-June, on which he had lavished such tender care at the start of his career, were now written straight on to the typewriter. Like the rest of London, perhaps, he seemed to be sleepwalking, wandering through a sedative private world where sterner realities barely penetrated. At the end of May, with the BEF falling back on Dunkirk, he could still see 'no evidence of any interest in the war'. Attending a revue entitled *Swinging the Gate* at the Ambassadors Theatre, he was struck by the paucity of references to the conflict.

By this stage his and Eileen's fears about the news from beyond the Channel had taken on an immediate, personal dimension. Eileen's much-loved brother Laurence had been serving in the medical corps attached to the BEF. There was no news of his whereabouts. As successive days passed, Eileen became paralysed with anxiety. The London railway termini were clogged with returning troops and refugees and on Saturday, 1 June Orwell went to Waterloo and Victoria

to see if he could pick up any news. Out again in London on the following day he noted the usual Sunday crowds drifting around the capital
with no obvious sign that they grasped the seriousness of the situation.
Laurence would never come back from France. Eileen, whose
admiration for him had known no bounds, was distraught. To Orwell,
everything was 'disintegrating'. An interview at the War Office brought
no offers of work. On 12 June, as Nazi troops swept across France, he
and Eileen walked through central London to see if the newspaper
reports of attacks on Italian shops were accurate: the Soho trattorias
and small provisions shops had hastily reinvented themselves as
'British'. Two days later the Germans were in Paris. On 17 June came
news of the French surrender. 'Horribly depressed by the way things are
turning out,' runs a diary entry from the end of June. An appearance in
front of the Medical Board produced a 'C' grading: unfit for any kind of
military service. Orwell professed himself 'appalled' by the lack of
imagination shown by a system that could find no room for a man below
the average level of fitness who was not actually an invalid. There was
no solace in literary work. Beyond bread-and-butter reviewing, he was
incapable of picking up a pen. John Lehmann, who had asked for
something else for *New Writing*, received only an apology. 'I just can't
write with this kind of thing going on.'

It was at this point, fortunately, that some kind of outlet for his
energies did emerge. The great sensation of the Home Front, as the
news from the continent grew ever more threatening, had been the
foundation of the Local Defence Volunteers (LDV). Born out of a radio
broadcast by Anthony Eden, and shortly afterwards rechristened the
Home Guard, it had gripped the public's imagination. Eden got a
quarter of a million men in twenty-four hours: more were to follow.
With his service in Burma and Spain, and in particular his experience
of street-fighting in Barcelona, Orwell was a natural recruit. In mid-
June he attended a local LDV group conference, held in the committee
room at Lord's Cricket Ground (the last occasion he had visited Lord's,
Orwell calculated, had been nineteen years before for the 1921
Eton–Harrow match). The St John's Wood volunteers eventually
became C Company of the 5th London Battalion – their first drill took
place a week later – and Orwell entered into his duties with enthusiasm.
Undoubtedly, this zeal on behalf of the Home Guard had an underlying
political agenda. With the memory of Spain fresh in his mind, he
envisaged it as a kind of people's army that might play a pivotal role in
domestic consciousness-raising. In this spirit he wrote a no-nonsense

letter to *Time and Tide* advocating the slogan ARM THE PEOPLE. The example of Barcelona showed that a few hundred men with machine-guns could paralyse the life of a large city. And yet, as Orwell knew, the Home Guard would have to struggle to avoid a middle-class bias. He himself was quickly promoted to sergeant, but there was considerable official suspicion of left-wing Spanish veterans. Many of his public utterances about the organisation over the next two years, conse-quently, consisted of warnings about the 'blimpish' forces of reaction. A *Tribune* piece from the end of 1940, for example, takes issue with ILP complaints about the Home Guard's supposedly 'Fascist' nature, emphasising the 'decisive' difference that could be made if left-wingers would join it. If there were any British equivalent to Pétainism – the French Vichy administration which governed at the Nazis' behest – then 'the existence of a popular militia, armed and politically conscious, and capable of influencing the regular forces, will be of profound importance'.

Much of this, inevitably, would be wishful thinking, as can be seen from the arrangements in St John's Wood. The unit to which Orwell was attached consisted of nine or ten people: Denzil Jacobs, a boy in his late teens waiting to be called up by the RAF, his Great War veteran uncle, Dennis Wells, who owned a nearby garage, two wealthy bourgeois from Loudon Road named Chandler and Hadrill, a Selfridge's van driver named Jones, and two other men named Davidson and Launchbury. Thus constituted, the group met twice weekly at the local headquarters, an old house in Grove End Road, before setting out to undertake such tasks as guarding the local telephone exchange and other strategic points. Periods off duty were spent at a small-hours poker school, superintended by some of the older men. Jacobs remembered 'Blair' losing ten shillings at the first of these conventions, declaring 'That's my lot' and taking the boy off to chat. Nearly twenty years younger than the tall, diffident NCO, Jacobs was fascinated by the older man. Represented by the others as 'a bit of a lefty', he was, nonetheless, strongly anti-Soviet. 'Are you a Communist?' Jacobs once enquired. 'It depends what you mean,' Orwell told him. Behind their conversation, as ever, lurked the shadow of the dark horse. After several months of shared guard duty Jacobs knew only that his colleague was some kind of journalist: no other details of his livelihood were ever vouchsafed. At some point, it came out that he had been a King's Scholar at Eton. Jacobs was frankly astonished. 'Anybody less likely to have been at Eton, as I had envisaged Eton, was Blair.' He was clearly unwell, Jacobs remembered, gaunt and with a chest that rattled ominously when he slept, but a dedicated and conscientious soldier, willing to give up his Sunday mornings to sit in a room above a garage in Abbey Road with other members of the unit making bombs. Yet in the context of the middle-class camaraderie of the guard post, Jacobs was struck by his singularity and his interest in what Jacobs thought of the topics of the day, an interest increased by Jacobs' Jewishness. The difference between husband and wife, too, seemed marked. This was the period when Eileen was prostrate from the death of her brother, and yet her 'outgoing' nature contrasted with Orwell's 'rather peculiar' character.

To the routines of twice-weekly guard duties in St John's Wood and theatregoing could be added a third point of focus. In the summer of 1940 the Fyvels moved from Hastings to set up house with Fred Warburg and his wife Pamela at Scarlett's Farm near Twyford in Berkshire. The Orwells were regular weekend visitors, so much so that, looking back from a distance of forty years, Fyvel found that the entire period had reduced itself to a tableau of cloudless, sunny days during which he and Orwell sat talking in the lush Berkshire grass. Warburg's plan to bring writers together in pursuit of war 'issues' had gradually crystallised into a publishing venture, appearing under the Secker imprint, that would go under the name of Searchlight Books. The *émigré* German journalist Sebastian Haffner would write about the correct way to treat a post-Nazi Germany. William Connor ('Cassandra' of the *Daily Mirror*) was approached for a book about shortcomings in the popular war effort. Orwell would begin the series with what Fyvel called 'an optimistic book about the future of a democratic socialist Britain'. It was an odd time to be launching any collective literary effort. All manner of professional commitments and personal vanities stood in the way – Fyvel remembered a long conversation between Orwell and the egocentric Connor in which the two simply failed to communicate – and yet by the second half of the year the project began to take shape. Fyvel recalled other fragments from Scarlett's Farm: Orwell in frayed shirt and ragged trousers sitting patiently in a chair as Pamela Warburg painted his portrait; again, lying on his back in the grass chuckling as he held the Fyvels' small daughter above his head. But above all, perhaps, Fyvel remembered the presence of Eileen, tired, drawn and untidily dressed, sitting in 'unmoving' silence on the gathering's edge. Several other witnesses attest to Eileen's severe traumatisation in the months after her brother's death, a condition which, one friend suggested, verged on muteness. Put side by side the two pictures – the tall, frail man laughing with the baby girl, the silent, ground-down wife – raise once again the question of Orwell's marriage and in particular its childlessness. Undoubtedly Orwell yearned for children. There is a rather wistful letter from earlier in the year in which he congratulates Rayner Heppenstall on the birth of a daughter: 'What a wonderful thing to have a kid of one's own. I've always wanted one so.' Pamela Warburg, who had a knack of securing confidences of this kind, told Fyvel that Orwell had told her that he was, or believed himself to be, sterile. Eileen had her own health problems, which may have stood in the way of conceiving a child. As with so much of their relationship, there is no way of knowing for sure.

Increasingly the al fresco conversations of Scarlett's Farm took place against an aerial accompaniment. Fyvel connects the opening sentence of *The Lion and the Unicorn* ('As I write, highly civilised human beings are flying overhead, trying to kill me') with an afternoon on the lawn as the Battle of Britain raged on above. Life had become a mixture of the familiar and the outlandish, past and present colliding in unexpected ways: two 'glorious days' in mid-August at Wallington, where they were harvesting the oats and Orwell took Marx out in search of rabbits, the news of Trotsky's assassination in Mexico, coalescing with the view, in Portman Square, of 'a four-wheeler cab, in quite good trim with a good horse and a cabman quite of the pre-1914 type'. The Blitz had begun. A few days later Orwell was walking out of the front door in Greenwich when the East India Docks were hit. An acquaintance who had returned from Cardiff reported bodies brought up in pails after a direct hit on a ship lying in harbour. The next few days consisted only of 'insanities'. On 7 September, as another massive assault began on Docklands, he was on his way by bus to have tea with Connolly at the latter's flat in Piccadilly. Two women sitting in front insisted that the shell bursts were descending parachutists. Subsequently he took shelter in a Piccadilly doorway, just as he might have done if sheltering from a summer rain shower, and then sat in Connolly's flat with their mutual friend Hugh Slater, currently a leading light in the development of the Home Guard. Slater, a Spanish veteran, was reminded of his days in Madrid. Only Connolly, Orwell thought, was suitably impressed, exclaiming that it was the end of capitalism and 'a judgment on us'. Most of the night of 9 September was spent in 'frightful discomfort' in a public shelter. A week later he saw a plane shot down for the first time. London was rapidly succumbing to the confusions of war: bomb craters everywhere, displaced persons on the street. So much pavement was roped off owing to unexploded bombs that coming back from Baker Street, 300 yards away, was like penetrating a maze. Two girls, elegantly dressed but with dirty faces, stopped him to ask 'Please, sir, can you tell us where we are?' There were curious sights to be seen on every street corner. Walking past the John Lewis store in Oxford Street at the end of September, Orwell saw a pile of plaster mannequins: to his susceptible eye they looked exactly like corpses. Shortly afterwards he fell ill with a poisoned hand and had to spend a fortnight in Wallington, occupying the time with reviews and putting the finishing touches to *The Lion and the Unicorn*. There were now eleven evacuees in the village, he noted, and the potato crop had turned out well in spite of the dry weather.

Divided into three parts, 'England Your England', which Connolly published in the December *Horizon*, 'The English Revolution' and 'Shopkeepers at War', *The Lion and the Unicorn* (1941) is the first considerable statement of Orwell's view of 'Englishness' and national identity. He begins by attacking the myth that national loyalties and characteristics are simply arbitrary. In fact they are founded on real differences of outlook. To come back to England from a foreign country, consequently, is to register the sense of breathing a different air. The English, to note a few of the generalisations subsequently wheeled into view, are not intellectually gifted but at heart gentle and above all private: characteristics that manifest themselves both in formal 'official' culture and in a 'genuinely popular' culture that goes on unofficially beneath the surface. Above all, perhaps, in this opening sequence Orwell is keen to establish what English people feel about the fact of their being English. He notes the general weakening of national morale that had taken place in the 1930s – this was partly the fault of the left-wing intelligentsia, 'itself a kind of growth that had sprouted from the stagnation of the Empire' – and also the emergence of a different kind of civilisation, populated by a new phenomenon in English social life, people of indeterminate social class, dragged into being on the outskirts of great cities (significantly, two of the forcing houses of this new civilisation that Orwell lists are Letchworth and Hayes).

This, though, is merely a preamble to his analysis of the situation in which England currently found herself. Dunkirk, he argued, was a symbol of national inadequacy, proof that private capitalism did not work, a demonstration of that faltering hierarchy, 'a family with the wrong members in control' governed by the old and incompetent. Only a Socialist nation could fight effectively; only by revolution could the native genius of the English people be set free: 'What is wanted is a conscious open revolt by ordinary people against inefficiency, class privilege and the rule of the old.' Traditional English Socialism, in the shape of the Labour party, had failed to motivate the vast armies of ordinary people or to use the patriotism of the workers. It was impossible to win the war without establishing Socialism or to establish Socialism without winning the war. In the context of 1940 this was incendiary stuff. Its radicalism was emphasised by a six-point programme whose adoption would help the new-style English Socialist movement to prosper: large-scale nationalisation; limitation of incomes; democratic reform of the educational system; immediate Dominion status for India, with the power to secede from the Empire once the war was won; an Imperial General Council in which the coloured peoples would be represented; and a formal alliance with China, Abyssinia and 'all other victims of the Fascist powers'.

These aims demonstrate precisely how leftist Orwell's views were in the early years of the war: much more extreme than anything advocated by 90 per cent of Labour MPs. His final prediction – that within six months the country would see the creation of a new English Socialist movement, based on the old-style Labour party and the trade unions but transcending them through its appeal to the bourgeoisie – was far more sweeping than any of the material coming out of Transport House, for it presupposed the old-style Labour party's extinction. Afterwards Orwell would admit that he had misread the political situation in the post-Dunkirk era, that much of this was wishful thinking and that only gradualism would achieve any of the social and political changes he wished to institute. As a rallying cry it established him firmly in the tradition of radical pamphleteers that goes back as far as Winstanley's Diggers about whom he was later to write. 'The heirs of Nelson and Cromwell are not in the House of Lords. They are in the fields and the streets, in the factories and the armed forces, in the four-ale bar and the suburban back-garden; and at present they are still kept under by a nation of ghosts.'

Written at a time of grave national crisis, The Lion and the Unicorn glows with optimism, confident in the ability of men and women to improve their lot. The circumstances in which it was written were less roseate. Orwell noted in his diary in mid-October the 'unspeakable depression' of lighting the morning fire with hoarded newspapers from the previous year and getting glimpses of optimistic headlines literally going up in smoke. Back in London and returned to his customary round of novel-reviewing, he made another prediction about the narrower effect of the war on art: that the novel about people 'with pale sensitive faces in lovely old country houses would go the way of the dodo'. As with English Socialism, time was to prove him wrong. But he was launched on the task that would sustain him for the whole of the war period and beyond. Curiously, one of the last pieces of journalism he wrote in 1940 was a review of Charlie Chaplin's *The Great Dictator*. What was Chaplin's particular gift? he wondered. The answer was clear. It was his power 'to stand for a sort of concentrated essence of the common man, for the ineradicable belief in decency that still exists . . .' The same, in a slightly different way, could have been said of Orwell himself.

Orwell's paranoia

Orwell maintained a lively interest in 'them', the malign exterior forces whom he suspected of interfering in his and other people's lives. On one level *Nineteen Eighty-Four* is simply a gigantic metaphor: the all-seeing, authoritarian eye opening a window into men's souls. Critics have often speculated on the roots of this obsession, locating them – to note only a few examples – in the police raid on the Wallington cottage in search of obscene materials, the experience of working in the censorship-riven atmosphere of the wartime BBC, or even as far back as the days in Spain spent one jump ahead of the Communist witch-hunts. In fact Orwell's paranoia can be glimpsed in every stage of his career. While the outlines of Mr Vaughan Wilkes' prep school 'police state' in the shadow of the Sussex Downs are a retrospective gloss, Orwell certainly brought back from St Cyprian's a deep suspicion of vigilant, eavesdropping authority. It followed him to Burma – Jacintha Buddicom remembered the strong impression given by one of his letters that he thought he was being watched – and it wanders through the reminiscences of many of the people who knew him in the 1930s. Richard Rees recalled a curious exchange on the subject of his *nom de plume*: seeing his name in print gave him an unpleasant feeling, Orwell explained, because 'how can you be sure your enemy won't cut it out and work some sort of black magic on it?' This was whimsy, Rees thought, while noting that on occasions of this sort one could never be sure if Orwell was being serious or not. Jon Kimche, his companion in the Westropes' Hampstead flat, observed a much more elemental writerly fear: copyright theft. He was 'quite paranoiac' about this, Kimche maintained. 'He was convinced that someone would steal his ideas.'

It would be surprising if this fear of prying eyes didn't transfer itself to the printed work. Sure enough, one of the commonest sensations of the 1930s novels is the feeling of being spied on. Burma, inevitably, is awash with unspoken ukases over what can and cannot be said, but even the provincial backwater of Knype Hill in *A Clergyman's Daughter* is represented as a cauldron of spite and backbiting, scores being settled behind the lace curtains and the privet hedges, gross libels and calumnies crackling down the telephone wires. 'It was one of those sleepy, old-fashioned streets, that look so ideally peaceful on a casual visit and so very different when you live in them and have an enemy or a creditor behind every window.' *Every* window? Surely some of Knype Hill's 5,000 or so inhabitants practise Christian charity? But this is what Orwell does with his characters: cuts them off, places them – isolated, friendless – at the mercy of huge, unappeasable forces. There is a dreadful scene, also in *A Clergyman's Daughter*, in which Dorothy is harangued and humiliated by a gang of puritanically minded parents, having explained to her class a sexual reference in *Macbeth*. Her employer Mrs Creevy's role, both before and after, is that of head conspirator – ceaselessly keeping an eye on Dorothy, her whereabouts and her attitude to her job. Gordon in *Keep the Aspidistra Flying* is less intimidated by his gorgon of a landlady, but even so his life is a series of furtive concealments: brewing illicit cups of tea in his room while listening for the sound of feet on the stair. George Bowling in *Coming up for Air* has a terror of being found out. His journey in search of the Thames Valley haunts of his boyhood is coloured, and eventually undermined, by the thought that his wife's spies will be on his tail. When he half hears the emergency radio broadcast featuring a woman with the same name his first thought is that it is one of Hilda's dodges, an elaborate ruse dreamed up with the deliberate aim of making him suffer.

Towards the end of Orwell's life, with the horrors of the Second World War behind him, this fixation hardened into something that could seem faintly obtrusive to the casual onlooker. Isaac Deutscher who, as a fellow *Observer* correspondent, occasionally shared press corps accommodation with him in Occupied Europe in 1945, was taken aback by the stubbornness with which Orwell dwelt on 'conspiracies': 'his political reasoning struck me as a Freudian sublimation of persecution mania,' Deustcher maintained. 'He was, for instance, unshakeably convinced that Stalin, Churchill, and Roosevelt consciously plotted to divide the world, and to divide it for good, among themselves, and to subjugate it in common.' Clearly, these are the outlines of *Nineteen Eighty-Four*, and yet you sense that they go back beyond the immediate political situation; that they run deep into the foundations of Orwell's whole mental outlook. Stuck on Jura in the late 1940s, he imagined that he was being spied on by Communists, that people were opening his mail (Richard Rees received several warnings of this nature). All this adds up: the telescreen, *Nineteen Eighty-Four*'s great symbolic invention, is not an adventitious fictional device, but something central to the ideas he held about the world, in the last resort a metaphor for life.

14

London Calling

Now and again in this war, at intervals of months, you get your nose above water for a few moments and notice that the earth is still going round the sun. – Diary, 4 March 1941

Its atmosphere [the BBC] is something half-way between a girls' school and a lunatic asylum, and all we are doing at present is useless, or slightly worse than useless. – Diary, 14 March 1942

January 1941 began with a bitter cold snap that plunged the country into chilly inertia. The Bloomsbury diarist Frances Partridge's record of the wartime life she shared with her husband Ralph and son Burgo in their Wiltshire fastness of Ham Spray recounts a succession of frozen ponds and sunless days with dim light reflected off the surface of the snow, the silence broken only by the crackle of burning Christmas decorations in the hearth. Lord Woolton, Minister for Food and proponent of the famously frugal Woolton Pie, announced a further cut in the meat ration to 1s. 2d. per adult a week, including 2d. worth of corned beef. The Partridges made do with suppers of red herrings on toast. Bedded down in the snow, England was adrift with rumour. A cross-Channel invasion was expected within the next 30 to 60 days, probably involving the widespread use of gas.

Orwell spent the first days of the New Year working on a commission for the left-leaning American political journal *Partisan Review*. Clement Greenberg, its editor, had seen Orwell's work in *Horizon* (where he had published himself), and, having found out more about him from Connolly and the latter's American wife Jean, proposed that he should write a regular 'London Letter'. The brief was relatively open: topics of the day, naturally, but also his own personal observations, and even gossip if he felt like it. Over the next few years the letter became a reliable vehicle for Orwell's opinions about British political life and his prognoses of the future conduct of the war. Written on the hoof, his predictions are not always accurate, yet they offer revealing snapshots both of conditions on the Home Front as the war moved forward and of the way in which Orwell's mind was continuing to focus on the issues that obsessed him: the new kind of political movement which he hoped the war would bring into being; the prospect of social and economic upheaval once the war had ended. His first contribution, printed in the March/April number – there was generally a two-month gap between dispatch and publication – diagnosed a reactionary backlash. Back in 1940 what amounted to a 'revolutionary situation' had existed in England, he believed, but no one had taken advantage of it. Now there seemed to be no alternative between unthinking 'King and Country' patriotism and supporting Hitler. British pacifism, Orwell concluded, had suffered a 'moral collapse'. Orwell's continuing quarrel with pacifism – and with numbers of individual pacifists – is a constant theme of his writings from the early 1940s, winding in and out of his newspaper columns and his private correspondence and bringing together both home-grown pacifists and those occupying the wider international stage. A letter to a Welsh Congregationalist minister who had written to him about *The Lion and the Unicorn*, for example, disputes the idea that propaganda can ever be successful without a display of military force to back it up. Sir Richard Acland's recently published *Unser Kampf* seemed to assume that if we told the Germans we wanted peace they would simply lay down their weapons. In the end non-belligerence of this kind would merely strengthen the position of the forces it theoretically opposed. Gandhi, Orwell argued, had made it easier for the British to continue to manage India because of his distaste for the sort of direct action that would have put British rule in jeopardy.

If *Partisan Review* offered a formal venue for Orwell's hopes and expectations, the minutiae of life in wartime London tended to be confined to his diary. Visiting the western edge of the City early in February he was appalled by the devastation around St Paul's, the cathedral barely chipped by bombs and standing out like a rock from the piles of collapsed masonry. Shortly afterwards he went with Eileen's sister-in-law Gwen O'Shaughnessy to visit a shelter in a crypt beneath Greenwich church. It was less crowded than usual, his guides assured him – on particularly bad nights 250 people would pack inside and the stench was insupportable. The tour found Orwell's sense of propriety getting the better of his habitual fastidiousness. It seemed to him that it was far worse for children to be playing about in a vault full of corpses than that they should have to put up with a certain amount of 'living human smell'. A later raid set the church on fire while people were still sleeping beneath and obliterated much of the park outside, opposite the O'Shaughnessys' house. According to Orwell, a telephone conversation with Eileen that took place as the raid reached its height went as follows: 'What's that?' 'Only the windows falling in.' Despite the widespread disruption conventional patterns of life continued to assert themselves. Coming home late at night through tube stations colonised by armies of working-class Londoners, he was struck by the 'normal, domesticated' air: young married couples tucked up together under print counterpanes, larger families – mother, father and several children – 'all laid out in a row like rabbits on a slab'. The image may not be a particularly cheerful one – and the spectre of Winston Smith's childhood memories of taking shelter from the first nuclear explosions is never far away – but you sense that Orwell is impressed by the solidarity, the feeling that some kind of decent, communal life is still able to take place even here, down underground, with the bombs juddering the distant pavement. The same feeling suffuses wartime novels such as Monica Dickens's *The Fancy* (1943), set among a mixed band of factory operatives and clearly based on a perspective much the same as Orwell's.

Like the underground sleepers laid out on their slabs he was managing to preserve his own routines: work; film reviewing for *Time and Tide* – the general quality not high, although he liked Sydney Gilliat's version of *Kipps* ('It is a pleasure to be able to report, for once, that a novel has been filmed and remains recognisable'); occasional trips to Wallington. Weekending there early in March, with the spring crocuses out and hares glimpsed sitting in the winter wheat, he reflected that 'Now and again in this war, at intervals of months, you get your nose above water for a few moments and notice that the earth is still going round the sun.' The Home Guard continued to absorb his energies with its twice-weekly guard duties and Sunday morning bomb-making sessions (a wad of lecture notes on street-fighting techniques survives) although his reputation as a mortar expert was jeopardised by an incident at a local garage when by mistake he loaded the weapon with a drill bomb capable of leaving the muzzle at high velocity. The recoil, on a concrete floor, was tremendous – knocking out one man's teeth and putting another one in hospital. Orwell's attitude to the Home Guard continued to combine enthusiasm for its potential – political as much as military – with a marked distaste for its occasional blimpish excesses. He was appalled, for example, by what he regarded as the jingoistic and self-righteous air of its church parades. Despite morale-sapping delays in the delivery of weapons and munitions, it could at least be regarded as a serious force, he told his *Partisan Review* readers later in the year. Socially, too, its catchment area was improving. Many of the Great War veterans who had filled the ranks in the early days had been superannuated. With the advent of call-up, volunteers tended increasingly to be younger, working-class men looking for experience before they joined the armed forces. As a result the political discussions were more intelligent, Orwell thought, and the different social classes forced to mix with each other. He also approved of the radicalising influence of the Osterley Park Training Centre (he reviewed *Armies of Freedom* by its founder Tom Wintringham in the *New Statesman*) and supported Wintringham and his colleague Hugh Slater against a certain amount of official disapproval.

In the intervals between these contending commitments, there was still time for some sort of social life. Like much of Orwell's life, at any time in his existence, this occupied a variety of compartments: after-work drinks with comparatively humble literary acquaintances at times alternating with somewhat grander surroundings. On one of the latter occasions he and Eileen were having supper at the Café Royal with Inez Holden. Noticing that Anthony Powell and his wife Lady Violet were sitting at a table on the other side of the room, Inez Holden determined to introduce them. What followed is an illustration of what, to Powell, was Orwell's oddity, the sense he gave off of not, when it came down to it, being like anyone else. On leave from his unit of the Welch Regiment, Powell had decided to make more of the occasion by changing into patrol uniform, an outfit with brass buttons and a high collar. He felt certain that Orwell would disapprove of what might be interpreted as a display of militaristic preening. In fact Orwell's first words, 'spoken with considerable tenseness', reassured him:

'Do your trousers strap under the foot?'

Powell signified that they did. Orwell approved, explaining that he had worn similar trousers in Burma. 'Those straps under the foot give you a feeling like nothing else in life,' he volunteered. His voice, Powell noted, had 'a curious rasp'. Most of what Powell later defined as the 'essential unreality' of Orwell's approach to life is encapsulated here: the relish of incongruous detail; the immersion in patterns of thought that were entirely his own. The two Old Etonian novelists got on sufficiently well to keep in touch. When his stint with the Welch

Regiment came to an end and he returned to London, Powell was swiftly admitted to the circle of Orwell's closer friends.

Despite this ability to expand his social and professional range, both through people he met in the course of his work and acquaintances picked up more informally like the Powells, Orwell was conscious that he was turning in on himself. Looking back through his diary at the end of March 1941 he realised that it had grown sporadic, focusing much less on public events than on the details of his day-to-day existence. There was a feeling of helplessness 'growing in everyone', he thought. Newspapers and bus stops were full of rumours: activity in the Balkans; the sending of an expeditionary force to Greece, a prospect which Orwell – rightly, as it turned out – thought 'terribly dangerous'. Hedged about by this atmosphere of mystery and subterfuge, what the situation lacked was a moral point. It was difficult to persuade people to face hunger and deprivation when the war seemed to have no purpose, when an invasion had failed to materialise and the rich seemed to be carrying on just as before. The war's inability to iron out social inequalities was a subject for constant brooding and occasional sharp displays of principle. Peter Vansittart remembered being in Orwell's company when L.H. Myers invited him out to dinner at a fashionable restaurant in which Myers had an interest, politely extending the invitation to Vansittart. Orwell's reply, flung back without reference to his prospective fellow-guest, was along the lines of 'Oh no, Leo, we're not going to come and eat your black-market food.' (Vansittart, who would quite have liked an expensive meal, was taken aback.) The remedy for this introspection, he knew, lay in war work but his chances of official employment still seemed remote. At the end of March he wrote to the Air Ministry in search of a job in its Public Relations Department. This was a popular berth for literary men in wartime – the Bomber Command PR office was then being run by Orwell's Eton contemporary Alan Clutton-Brock. According to the reformed burglar Mark Benney, who knew Clutton-Brock, Orwell was suggested by Benney as a suitable recruit. Benney's memoirs contain an interesting account of Clutton-Brock, 'resplendent in his blue squadron leader's uniform', calling on Orwell effectively to interview him for the job. Though several of the details are inaccurate – Benney claims that Orwell and Clutton-Brock 'did not know each other', while Orwell, additionally, is represented as living in Paddington – the 'bizarre dialogue' he reproduces seems wholly authentic:

AC-B: 'I can't say anything about the work, of course, but I assure you it's tedious beyond belief. And the dreadful people you meet!'

GO: 'I wouldn't want a commission, you understand. I'd be quite happy in the ranks.'

AC-B: 'And you have to do six weeks of foot-training first – insufferable! In fact, until it occurred to me to think of the whole thing as a kind of ballet I didn't think I'd survive it!'

GO: 'But I like drills. I know the Manual by heart. I need the discipline!'

Despite the personal connection, the job fell through. The only outlet for his mental energies, consequently, was journalism: streams of reviews; three essays for the *Left News*, the organ of the Left Book Club; two contributions to Gollancz' public disavowal of his love affair with Communism, *The Betrayal of the Left*. Inevitably his political journalism at this point is a series of amplifications of the line taken in *The Lion and the Unicorn*. 'Our Opportunity', for instance, which appeared in the *Left News* early in the year, argues that the challenge is both to defend England and to turn it into a popular democracy. Middle-class patriotism was not a sham: the vital task for Socialists was to bring the bourgeoisie on board. 'These people will be with us,' Orwell claimed, with what even at the time seems unwarranted optimism, 'if they can be made to see that a victory over Hitler demands the destruction of Capitalism.'

To examine the literary memorials of the early part of the Second World War is to uncover a world of impermanence and fracture extending to outright vagrancy. Amid a widespread accommodation shortage made worse by extensive bomb damage, many Londoners existed in an atmosphere of hastily packed suitcases and skirmishes with hostile landladies. The colonies of the dispossessed coming together in the Belgravia townhouses of Evelyn Waugh's *Sword of Honour* trilogy are based on first-hand observation. Waugh's older brother Alec, back from France with the BEF and awaiting redeployment, ended up living in a flat the size of a box-room above his literary agent's office. There was nowhere else to go. The Orwells' progress around war-torn London is characteristic of the time. In early March they moved from Dorset Chambers to a one-bedroom flat on the seventh floor of Langford Court on Abbey Road in St John's Wood. Langford Court was a large, multinational block much inhabited by refugees. Eileen and another tenant once spontaneously embraced each other on the stairs after each divined that the other was English. High up in the foothills of the north London rise, it commanded a panoramic view of the city. Climbing up on to the roof one day, Orwell was startled by what he saw. A year on from the start of the Blitz, much of the East End was flattened beyond redemption and the financial district lay in ruins. Here in NW8, however, the prospect seemed quite unchanged apart from a few churches whose spires had been snapped off in the middle. Langford Court was handy for the Home Guard – Denzil Jacobs remembered calling there and meeting Eileen – but like so much of the accommodation fixed up by people in harassed transit across the capital, it was no more than a temporary refuge.

Meanwhile the war news was bad. In Greece and the Middle East the Allied forces were being thrown back. Rommel was at the Egyptian frontier. In mid-April there was a huge raid on north-west London. Bombs fell on Lord's and the St John's Wood churchyard. Still, though, Orwell detected no great interest in the progress of the war. The enemy seemed poised to fall upon the Suez Canal, and yet walking into a pub to listen to the nine o'clock news he was surprised to find the radio silent. At Wallington, far away from the bombs, he sowed several stone of seed potatoes while the Greek débâcle continued to unfold. With the native army said to have capitulated, no one knew how long the British could hold out. There would be hell to pay in Australia, Orwell noted, over the pointless loss of Anzac troops. The only minor consolation was that a full-scale row might lead to some discussion of Australia's position in the Empire and a 'democratization' of the conduct of the war. Back in London, in the midst of a small-hours bombing raid, he and Eileen were woken by a dramatic crash. Hearing shouts from the darkness that the building was hit, they went up to the roof to find fires burning on all sides. It appeared that a bomb had fallen on the neighbouring garage, setting light to the cars inside. The Orwells decamped to the Davidsons, who lived nearby, where they were given tea and a slab of chocolate which their hosts claimed to have been hoarding for months. Back in the flat they discovered that their faces were blackened with soot.

In an atmosphere of sleepless nights and sobering news from the Middle East, Orwell's low spirits sank still further. Already his thoughts were moving towards the post-war world. There seemed to be no chance of winning the war 'in any decent way'. Churchill – throughout his tenure as Prime Minister Orwell regarded Churchill with the deepest suspicion – was planning to give all Britain's overseas territories away and then win them back with American aeroplanes and rivers of blood. In a couple of years, he speculated gloomily, the UK would either be overrun or a Socialist republic 'fighting for its life, with a secret police and half the population starving' (interestingly enough, this was Oceania's condition in *Nineteen Eighty-Four*). Neither prospect was enticing. There is a faintly hysterical tone to some of these prognoses, undoubtedly brought about by the bad news and Orwell's misery over his perceived uselessness. A claim in his diary for mid-May that the British ruling classes had 'condemned themselves to death' by failing to occupy places such as the Canary Islands, Tangier and Syria takes no account of the logistical difficulties. This, after all, was a period when Britain was fighting the war more or less on her own: military caution was bred by lack of manpower rather than spinelessness or incompetence. Even the news – a day or so before his thirty-eighth birthday – that Germany had invaded Russia failed to rouse him. In novels of the period, this is always presented as the great climacteric to the war's opening phase, the moment at which dawn's first rays appear on an otherwise bleak horizon. Nick Jenkins in Powell's *The Soldier's Art*, for example, feels 'an immediate, overpowering, almost mystic sense of relief' take shape within him. 'I felt sure everything was going to be all right.' Orwell could only reflect glumly that 'the worst omen is that the Germans would probably not have attempted this unless certain that they can bring it off, and quite rapidly at that.' Listening to Stalin's speech on the radio a week or so later, he could think of no better example of the age's moral and emotional shallowness than the fact that the country's previous differences with Soviet Russia had apparently been forgotten overnight.

There is, it scarcely needs saying, something uncomfortably absolutist about this. If pacifists are not to be allowed their finer feelings about the war then why, it might be argued, should Orwell be allowed his? He could be notably hard-headed about the way wars had to be fought – upbraiding Kingsley Martin two years before over the 'conditions' on which the Left could support the government (as if war were 'a cricket match'), going on, a year or two later, to defend such tactics as the saturation bombing of enemy cities (it was only in propaganda films, he suggested, that the bombs fell on orphanages). Given that the inevitable result of war is that blood will be spilled and unspeakable horrors perpetrated in the name of victory, what is wrong about putting your ideological scruples aside for a while so that Fascism can be defeated? After all, according to the Orwell argument, if Germans are going to have to die it scarcely matters who kills them. If there was a consolation in the resultant Anglo-Soviet alliance, it was that working-class loyalty to the Soviet Union was no longer a positive force. Fifteen years ago no country except possibly Japan would have dared to attack Russia, he told the readers of *Partisan Review* later in the year, because the common soldiers could not have been trusted to use their weapons against the Socialist fatherland. A decade and a half's worth of pogroms and five-year plans had made patriotism a much more potent affair.

The second year of the war was nearing its end. Orwell's huge journalistic output continued to range over the surfaces of this out-landish, bomb-cratered world and at times to move deep within it. Stalin and Noël Coward. Goebbels and H.G. Wells. Within the space of a few days in July 1941 he reviewed *Blithe Spirit* for *Time and Tide*, surveyed 'English Writing in Total War' for the American *New Republic* (there was no chance of any literary revival of the kind that had happened in the Great War, he suggested, as the writers were either too busy or too depressed to write anything) and wrote a piece for the *Daily Express* on the need to crack down on the black market. And then, in early August, came the thing he had been looking for since he returned to London fifteen months before. He was offered a job.

Orwell's connection with the BBC went back to the end of the previous year, when he had taken part in a Home Service discussion of 'The Proletarian Writer' with Desmond Hawkins. Subsequently, in the spring of 1941, he was invited to contribute four short talks on the future of literary criticism to the Corporation's Eastern Service by the head of its Indian section Z(ulfaqar) A(li) Bokhari. It seems to have been on Bokhari's initiative that moves were set in train to recruit him for the Indian branch. The post – its professional title was 'Producer, Indian Section' – offered a salary of £640 per annum (slightly less, for purposes of comparison, than his earnings fifteen years before in the Burma Police) and required attendance at the BBC's central London locations – initially 55 Portland Place, subsequently 200 Oxford Street – five days a week, with extra hours on Saturday mornings. Officially he was E.A. Blair, 'Talks Assistant', although he reverted to 'George Orwell' when dealing with people who knew him by his professional name. For someone with no hands-on experience of radio broadcasting this was clearly going to be demanding work. Why did he take it up? The obvious answer is: precisely because of its exacting nature. It was classified as war work, it would involve working with other writers and it was focused on India, a country for which he felt an enduring affection and whose future became one of his chief obsessions as the war ground on. The satisfaction he felt in being involved, however marginally, in Indian affairs is clear from the text of a broadcast he gave in March 1942 outlining the schedule of a series called 'Through Eastern Eyes'. It was the first time that a non-Oriental speaker had been used: 'May I say how happy it makes me to be helping to organise these broadcasts,' Orwell summed up, 'broadcasts which I believe can be really helpful and constructive at a time like this – to the country in which I was born and with which I have many personal and family ties.' Orwell's disillusionment with the nature of what he was being asked to do and the sparseness of the audience who listened to him came later. For the moment he was simply happy to be a cog in the wheel of the war effort.

To a man accustomed to solitary days at his desk, this new environment would have been highly unfamiliar. The Indian Section of the BBC, under the general supervision of the Eastern Service Director (a new appointment, L.F. Rushbrook Williams, was made in October 1941), at this point consisted of Bokhari, three Hindu talks assistants and three secretaries. It broadcast twelve hours of programming a week, although this figure was soon increased. Orwell's remit, once he had grasped the fundamentals of the job, was to prepare three series of commentaries on the daily news, in English, for transmission to India, Malaya and Indonesia (both the latter territories were currently occupied by the Japanese). There were further, separate series translated into the vernacular languages of the subcontinent such as Gujarati, Tamil and Marathi, as well as programmes on educational, political and cultural issues. The general air was one of mild cultural uplift – exemplified, perhaps, by Orwell's earlier commission to talk on the future of literary criticism – and the guest speakers shepherded on to the air-waves were drawn from an eclectic pool of talent that ranged from well-known literary figures to minor celebrities of no particular distinction such as Lady Gertrude Grigg, wife of the Secretary of State for War. Orwell's first task was to attend a truncated BBC training course, held at the University of London's Bedford College site during the last two weeks in August (the poet and critic William Empson, a talks assistant in the Empire Department, was another of the inductees) where he received rudimentary instructions on programme techniques and Corporation protocol.

On the evening of the first day Empson accompanied his fellow-trainee back to Langford Court for a somewhat tense dinner with Inez Holden and the elderly H.G. Wells. Orwell's essay on his boyhood hero, 'Wells, Hitler and the World State', had appeared shortly beforehand in *Horizon*. This took a line that most modern critics would broadly accept: that Wells's greatest achievement resides in the succession of lower-middle-class novels that made his name in the decade before the Great War; what came afterwards represented a squandering of his talents. The two parties had met before, brought together by Inez. Typically Orwell did not imagine that the *Horizon* piece would be any bar to an enjoyable evening. Inez Holden's diary provides a memorable portrait of the considerable row that followed the dinner: Orwell wearing 'the look of an embarrassed prefect', both sides slapping down copies of the offending article on the dinner table, Wells accusing Orwell of 'defeatism'. Wells could be cantankerous in his old age, but Holden notes Orwell's mildness under attack. Going back to his house in Regent's Park with the diarist and a more or less incapacitated Empson, Wells conceded that he had enjoyed the evening. He was less pleased by a *Listener* article six months later. This produced a rejoinder urging Orwell to 'read my early works you shit'. Despite this remonstrance Orwell continued to proselytise on Wells's behalf. At least one friend recalled being 'made to read' a copy of *Love and Mr Lewisham*.

Two days before, Orwell had written in his diary, 'I am now definitely an employee of the BBC.' The German invasion of Russia was continuing. The stage seemed set for a long and exhausting war 'with everyone growing poorer all the time'. The quasi-revolutionary dawn in national life which he had detected in the aftermath of Dunkirk had disappeared. The diary was abandoned, not to be taken up again until March of the following year. In the early autumn of 1941 Orwell applied himself wholeheartedly to his new job, writing for example to a Dr P.H. Chatterjee to ask if he might contribute a talk on 'Rural District Councils' ('as we understand you have studied this subject') to the 'How it Works' series and commissioning the Sinhalese poet J. Meary Tambimuttu, a fixture of the wartime Fitzrovian literary scene that flourished almost on the BBC's doorstep, to appear on 'Through Eastern Eyes'. In mid-October he fell ill with bronchitis – his time at the BBC was punctuated by bouts of ill health – and it was not until November that he was back in harness. To look at the documentation that survives from the two years Orwell spent in the Indian Section – scripts, letters, booking forms, enough to fill three volumes of his collected works – is to be struck immediately by its predominantly routine nature and by the stifling blanket of BBC protocol. A certain amount of what he was asked to do – notably bringing well-known writers together on air in imaginative ways – was to his taste. Dr Chatterjee and the rural district council, one assumes, was not. These inconveniences Orwell would have been prepared to put up with in pursuit of the common good, but what if Dr Chatterjee had no listeners?

There are wider questions, too. Why was Orwell at the BBC, and what did the BBC expect from him? Undoubtedly Bokhari, his immediate superior, regarded him as a catch ('I am delighted and flattered to have your assistance,' he wrote, three weeks after the new producer had taken up his post). Among a certain kind of old BBC hand, alternatively, the arrival of Orwell and people like him – minor literary figures with no broadcasting experience – was regarded, as one of them put it, as a 'jobs-for-the-boys kind of billet' designed to get 'people like Guy Burgess and George Orwell on to the BBC payroll until they could be found more suitable appointments'. This may be true of Guy Burgess, whom Orwell certainly came across during his broadcasting days, but it is hugely unfair to Orwell, who whatever his lack of experience could hardly be accused of want of application. The one thing that can be said of his time at the BBC is how hard he worked. As well as supervising the production of hundreds of news broadcasts, he was constantly in search of ways to encourage new writers, especially those with an Indian background, or to put established talents to work in unusual forms. Peter Davison has noted that his fostering of performances of Indian drama was far in advance of its time. *Voice*, the innovative broadcast literary magazine that he conceived in 1942, may have been dominated by stars of the contemporary firmament such as Connolly, Lehmann and E.M. Forster, but there was space elsewhere for new and not necessarily orthodox contributors such as Mulk Raj Anand and Prem Chand. Even Reg Reynolds was allowed in to talk about 'Prison Literature' although the authorities jibbed at a suggestion canvassed towards the end of Orwell's time that he should broadcast on the Russian anarchist Kropotkin. None of this sounds like the dignified idling that undoubtedly did go on in certain corridors of Broadcasting House. Amongst his superiors – though there were occasional complaints about duplication and decisions taken unilaterally – he was generally admired for his dedication. A letter from Bokhari to the Empire

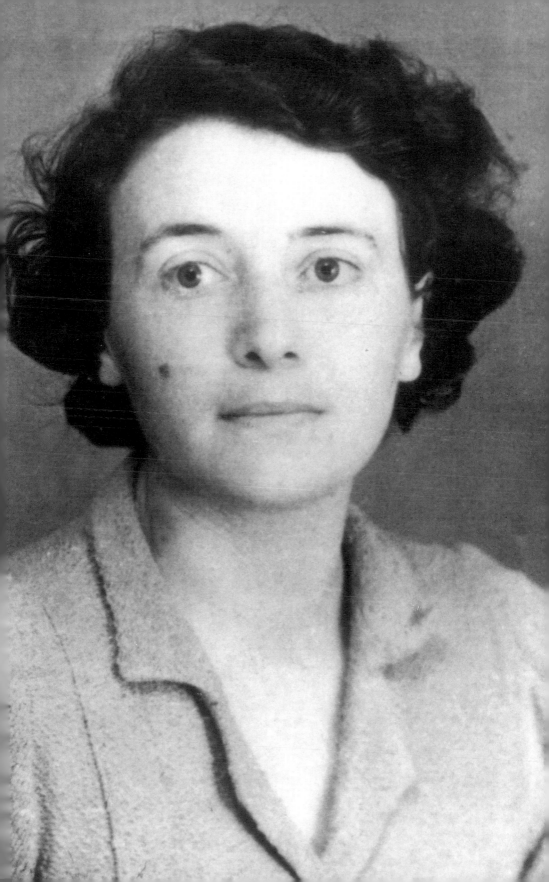

(*Previous page*) Eileen, 1930s

Jon Kimche

On the Huesca Front with
Eileen and ILP unit, March 1937

(*Above*) 'You see I've always been good with animals', Wallington, summer 1939

(*Left*) LDV exercise, Regent's Park, 1940: Orwell is on the extreme left.

Anthony & Violet Powell, 1942

David Astor

Julian Symons

Peter Vansittart, early 1940s

Arthur Koestler

Broadcasting days with
M.J. Tambimuttu,
T.S. Eliot, Una Marson,
Nancy Parratt, Mulk Raj
Anand, William Empson

Celia Paget

Sonia Brownell

Malcolm Muggeridge and Anthony Powell, 1946

Susan Watson

Fred Warburg

Michael Meyer

'Full of power and
mysterious calm' –
Nineteen Eighty-Four

With Richard, 1946

Executive in March 1942, for instance, notes his willingness to type his own letters in the absence of full-time secretarial support and worries about the weight of work entrusted to him.

In general Orwell's colleagues approved of his courtesy and unobtrusive efficiency. In an institution riven with hulking snobberies and departmental alliances, his attitude to the people who worked beneath and on either side of him was seen to be transparently good-humoured. The wife of a journalist whom he knew through the *New Statesman* remembered him as 'gentle, quiet and unassuming', with a slightly 'lost' look that called up a mothering instinct in women. He was ignorant of technical procedures – on learning of the existence of 'special effects', for instance, he zealously approached the relevant department with a request for a 'nice mixed lot'. Such gaucheness made him a ripe target for leg-pulling, apparently practised on him by all hierarchical ranks and nationalities. He caused some amusement by his enthusiasm for canteen food. By the standards of wartime London, where 'British Restaurants' offered previously unheard-of varieties of North Sea fish, BBC cuisine was unusually good. Orwell pronounced it *marvellous*. But then this was a man who once consumed a plate of jellied eels which Eileen had left out for the cat while his own supper simmered on unregarded in the oven.

As for the job itself, this required tact, diplomacy and the ability to deal with the sensitivities of large numbers of people only indirectly connected to the programme itself. Given the nationalist agitation that continued to inflame it, its proximity to the Eastern theatre of war and the question of its post-war political arrangements, India was dangerous territory. Plenty of people, inside and outside Broadcasting House, were disposed to interfere with what went out over its radio. The India Office's A.H. Joyce – the same A.H. Joyce who had worried about Orwell's suitability for a job on the *Lucknow Pioneer* four years before – complained about a script on the subject of trade unionism. Another old adversary, Norman Collins from Gollancz, surfaced in his wartime capacity as Empire Talks Manager and could at times cause trouble. Onlookers of this kind needed careful handling, as did certain of the regular contributors, notably Lady Grigg, whose exalted social position tended to deter criticism of her deficiencies as a broadcaster. Some of these difficulties had their amusing side, as when the man employed to undertake the Marathi translations was discovered to have forgotten his own language and subcontracted the work to a friend, but the sense of having to abide by a series of yardsticks that one could never fully comprehend came to grate on Orwell's nerves, and contributed to his thoroughgoing sense of exasperation.

The BBC atmosphere was 'something half-way between a girls' school and a lunatic asylum' he confided to his diary, on reopening it in March 1942, 'and all we are doing at present is useless, or slightly worse than useless.' But he was circumspect enough to know that this malaise was not exclusive to the BBC. It affected most of the institutions trying to cope with the contemporary turmoil. The 'impossibility of getting anything done' applied equally to the Home Guard, now two years on from its foundation but still incapable of providing any real training to its recruits. Another growing source of disillusionment was the thought that whatever enthusiasm and planning might have gone into the programming would be cancelled out by the sparseness of the audience.

Later in the 1940s Orwell discovered that there had been people listening – that in some cases his voice and the voices of his fellow-broadcasters had been lifelines to those huddled clandestinely around radios in occupied territory. But audience research was in its infancy and even his superiors fretted over the difficulties of gauging the extent of the listenership. Simultaneously, the atmosphere of the BBC, its endless corridors and rows of battery-farm offices, the heavy tread of footsteps on its polished floors, made a strong impression on him. Of all the things that he noticed, perhaps the most memorable was the sight of the charwomen sitting together in reception early in the morning waiting for their cleaning materials to be issued. Brooms in hand, they set off to scour the empty passages, singing in unison as they went. Undoubtedly a key scene in *Nineteen Eighty-Four* took root and grew here – the scene in which Winston hears the prole woman singing – but in some ways the picture offers more than this, provides in fact a metaphor for Orwell's dutiful but sometimes enraptured observation of a social class from which his upbringing would always exclude him. The great early twentieth-century diarist A.C. Benson once described the sight of two ladybirds signalling to each other from either side of the pane of glass which separated them as a 'parable'. The symbolism lay in the diarist's own inability truly to connect with the people around him. The spectacle of the BBC charwomen is Orwell's equivalent, a glimpse into a communal working-class world in which he was to invest most of his hopes for the preservation of the human spirit.

For someone who had never previously held down a full-time desk job, the Indian Section of the BBC imposed a strenuous regime. Despite these constraints Orwell's journalistic carerer proceeded side by side with it. It is not going too far to say that the BBC years, for all the demands they placed on his time, marked his appearance on a grander professional stage. Late 1941, for example, brought a letter from David Astor (the connection, like many of Orwell's literary links, came through Connolly) asking if he would be interested in writing for the *Observer*, the newspaper owned by Astor's father. The paper was not yet Astor's private fiefdom – J.L. Garvin remained editor until 1942, when he was replaced by Ivor Brown – and Orwell's early association with it did not always run smoothly, but Astor's interest signified another step up from the world of journeyman literary work. *Horizon*, too, continued to offer a showcase for his explorations of popular culture. The September 1941 number carried 'The Art of Donald McGill', his essay on the humour of the seaside comic postcard, an absorption that dated back to his teenage days in Henley with the Buddicoms. But if his life had a focus in the months of late 1941 and early 1942, it was the subcontinent to which he was broadcasting. Orwell had a habit of flagging the paths that his political opinions were taking in more straightforward literary pieces. A *Horizon* essay from early 1942 on Rudyard Kipling almost certainly grew out of his new role at the Indian Section, contemplating both the immediate problem of India's position in an empire at war and the question of her post-Imperial destiny. As ever Orwell is poised between a bitter understanding of Imperialism's consequences for a subject territory overrun by red-jacketed soldiers and a reluctant admiration for the personal dynamism that brought such entities into being. It was a mark of Kipling's closeness to the Imperial arrangements he wrote about that he failed to realise 'any more than the average soldier or colonial administrator' that an empire was primarily a commercial concern. Roads, railways, courthouses were all inextricably bound up with cartels and economic exploitation. And yet Orwell, an Anglo-Indian himself, could not shake off his allegiance to the caste that had created him. The nineteenth-century empire-builders were at least 'people who did things'. A reference perhaps, to Conrad's *Heart of Darkness*, where a character observes of a map of the world, 'There was a vast amount of red – good to see at any time, because one knows that some real work is done there.' If the prevailing Anglo-Indian attitude had been that of E.M. Forster, they could not have maintained themselves in power for a week. As in Orwell's agonisings over Burma ten years before, one sees the two sides of his nature – the authoritarian side and the part of him that believed in liberal principle – uneasily but honestly contending.

India gave him a cause, but it also, for perhaps the first time in his life, gave him a political hero. This was the gaunt figure of Sir Stafford Cripps, the so-called 'Red Squire', now a minister in the wartime coalition government. Tall, saturnine, ascetic, patrician, Cripps seemed to embody the moral fervour and determination to stick by one's personal beliefs that Orwell found so lacking in contemporary politics. One of the weekly 'News Reviews' from March 1942 notes that 'the outstanding thing about Sir Stafford Cripps . . . has always been his utter unwillingness to compromise his political principles'. The apparent failure of the Cripps mission to India that spring profoundly depressed Orwell. At the end of April he went to the House of Commons (in fact to the House of Lords, where the Commons, bombed out the previous year, now sat) to listen to the India debate. This was 'a poor show except for Cripps's speech'. The chamber had an out-at-elbow look and the MPs struck him as vague creatures, 'simply ghosts gibbering in some corner while the real events happen elsewhere'. In the early summer he managed to meet his hero when they spoke for a while in the House of Lords reception room. Subsequently, Cripps having expressed a wish to meet some 'literary people', Orwell, together with a motley collection of writers that included Empson, Jack Common and Guy Burgess, was one of the throng convened for the purpose. Perhaps inevitably, Cripps in the flesh was an appreciable distance from the Crippsian myth propagated by the newspapers. Orwell found him human and 'willing to listen', while prone to issuing what, at least to Orwell, were slightly 'horrifying' remarks. Orwell argued that it would be a disaster if the war ended without major social upheaval, but Cripps seemed not to understand. Orwell gathered that he did not feel it would make much difference whether the great powers of the post-war era were capitalists or Socialists. Later Orwell noted in his diary that he was up against 'the official mind'. It was not that Cripps had been corrupted – nothing so concrete – merely that ministerial responsibility stifled his zeal. Nevertheless Orwell maintained the connection, to the point where, later in the same summer, he could be shown (in strictest confidence by Cripps's secretary, David Owen) a draft of the Secretary of State for India L.S. Amery's statement on post-war policy towards Burma. This made gloomy reading: it envisaged direct rule and the re-establishment of the big British firms on much the same basis as before. 'Please God no document of this kind gets into enemy hands,' he noted.

By now he was nearing the end of his first year in the Corporation's service. His domestic life, too, had undergone several changes. In spring 1942 Eileen gave up her post at the Ministry of Information and transferred to the Ministry of Food in Portman Square. The work was much more to her taste – literally so, in that her chief job was to organise a Home Service programme called *The Kitchen Front,* aimed at encouraging ration-afflicted housewives to provide nutritious and low-cost meals. Like her husband, she was responsible for writing scripts and commissioning speakers, and Orwell asked her to organise a similar series, *In Your Kitchen,* for transmission on the Eastern Service. Though Eileen had to a certain degree recovered from the trauma of her brother's death, she was still immensely downcast. New friends of Orwell's who met her at this time noted her gravity, the difficulty of trying to lift her out of the slough of wartime routine. Anthony Powell noted that 'She was not usually given to making light of things, always appearing a little overwhelmed by the strain of keeping the household going . . .' The household, still located on the seventh floor of Langford Court, was, if not expanding, then receiving a larger than usual complement of visitors. In late 1941 or early 1942 Mrs Blair and Avril left Southwold for London with the aim of doing war work. Ida, now in her latish sixties, eventually took a job as a shop assistant at Selfridge's. Avril found employment at a sheet-metal factory near King's Cross station. Both were regularly entertained at Langford Court and became familiar faces in the curious, but in the context of the time by no means unusual, social life that the Orwells conducted in wartime London: a world of frugal late-night suppers punctuated by the thump of bombs, unexpected guests in search of a bed, spare rooms crowded out with passing migrants.

Some time in the summer of 1942 they moved again, to the ground floor and basement of 10 Mortimer Crescent NW6, a terraced house in Kilburn, further out into the north-west London sprawl. Built in the mid-nineteenth century, the property appealed to Orwell's Victorian side, conjuring up enticing visions of bygone middle-class life. The original owners would probably have kept a 'Buttons', he delightedly informed guests. More so perhaps than their previous flats, the Kilburn premises bore the imprint of Orwell's personality. The sitting room contained ancient family furniture. There were several eighteenth-century Blairs staring from the picture frames. The whole gave the impression that 'it might well have been the owner's study in a country house'. However incongruous it may have seemed to wartime visitors, making their way over the bomb-damaged pavements, the notion of the world of the country squire transferred to Kilburn seems in keeping with the view that Orwell took of himself, the deep sense of continuity and tradition that informed his idea of family life. Another side of his character – the practical, odd-jobbing side – was on display in the basement, where he installed a lathe. Anthony Powell spent a memorable night sleeping on a camp-bed beside it. The room was not entirely comfortless, he decided ('There was just about space'). Then, at around 4 a.m., an air raid began. Orwell came stumbling downstairs in the dark. He was 'rather glad' about the raid, he explained, as it meant there would be hot water in the morning: when not woken by gunfire from the local anti-aircraft battery he was usually too lazy to stoke the boiler.

Earlier in the year he had written a 'Mood of the Moment' column for the *Observer* complaining about the manifest inequalities of wartime life. People wanted equality of sacrifice at home, just as they wanted effective action abroad, and they believed that the two things were connected, he argued. Increasingly Orwell was beginning to wonder if his own sacrifices – the five-and-a-half-day week at the BBC – were worth it. Leaving aside complaints about the Corporation's pettifogging bureaucracy, his disquiet about his position in the Indian Section had two main points of focus. One was the question of whether anyone was actually listening (Laurence Brander, the Eastern Service intelligence officer, had been sent to India to investigate this in February). The other was what, in the sense of saying things that he did not believe, the job required him to do. It is often assumed that Orwell's eventual disaffection with the BBC stemmed from the fact that it was essentially a propagandist agency whose concern with 'truth' was secondary to military and political imperatives. This is a gross oversimplification of what was a relatively complex attitude to 'propaganda' and the uses to which it might be put. At bedrock level Orwell was simply disgusted by the lies which warfare seemed to excuse. 'We are all drowning in filth,' he wrote in his diary, having listened to an Italian radio report about supposed food shortages in London. Whenever he talked to or read the writings of anyone who had an axe to grind, he found that intellectual honesty and balanced judgement had vanished. He was similarly appalled by the script changes sometimes forced upon him by the BBC censors. One of his regular contributors, J.F. Horrabin, was always introduced to listeners as the cartographer for Wells' *Outline of History* and Nehru's *Glimpses of World History*. By August 1942 the political situation in India, where Nehru, Gandhi and the nationalist leaders were now behind bars, was such that Nehru's name was removed from Horrabin's CV. Yet however wary of propagandist pressures from on high – in January 1943 he told the European Service Talks Director that he was happy to do a proposed broadcast on social change in English towns, 'But I am not going to say anything I regard as untruthful' – he was also conscious of the value of propaganda to the war effort, if it was the right kind. His diagnosis of public reaction to the invasion of Madagascar in spring 1942 was that it had been mis-sold, interpreted across Asia as a piece of Imperialist land-grabbing. Effective propaganda could have produced a more positive result. In some ways he envied those propagandising to 'friendly' countries, he wrote on another occasion, for they were batting on such an easy wicket.

The military situation seemed to turn graver by the hour. A German invasion date had supposedly been set for 25 May. In the East the Japanese forces were ploughing through Burma. There was a danger that India itself might be overrun. Orwell's 'London Letter' of May 1942 to *Partisan Review* describes a country on the edge of a political crisis which he believed had been waiting to happen since Dunkirk; the difference being that in Cripps the disaffected elements now believed they had a genuine leader. Yet despite the mounting signs of international crisis, he continued to be struck by the 'normality' of London life – the lack of hurry, the mild demeanour of the crowds who drifted through the streets pushing prams or loitering in the squares to look at the hawthorn bushes. These were not propitious times for the creatively minded, and yet looking at the surviving correspondence from Orwell's BBC days one is constantly struck by the degree of imagination and keenness he brought to his talks producer's brief. There was a series on 'New Words' thrown up by the war, such as 'scorched earth', 'sabotage' and 'living space', a proposal to tackle 'great dramatists' (T.S. Eliot was invited to speak on Dryden), a scientific series involving such distinguished figures of the day as J.B.S. Haldane and Sir John Russell.

Most innovative of all, perhaps, was *Voice*, a literary magazine of the air-waves, whose first number went out in August 1942. It was, the producer acknowledged, 'the worst possible moment to be starting a magazine' – there were tank battles in Russia; the Pacific was aflame. He worried, too, that the medium was inappropriate for the kind of effects he wanted to achieve – 'Poetry on the air sounds like the muse in striped trousers,' he famously remarked – and yet in retrospect *Voice* looks like a remarkably successful literary experiment. Put out at the rate of a programme a month, both contributors (Empson, Eliot, Mulk

Raj Anand, Herbert Read, Edmund Blunden) and subject matter (war poetry, Eastern influences on English literature) ranged widely. There were also deliberate attempts to make enterprising use of the new medium – a short story by several hands, for example, rounded off by E.M. Forster. Surviving scripts reveal Orwell – constrained both by his script and the lurking presence of a switch censor who could cut off a speaker immediately – as a slightly stagy, mock-spontaneous impresario ('Is that true, Empson, in your opinion? Are there no war poets?' Someone mentions Auden's 'September 1939'. 'Oh yes, that's a very good one. I was forgetting that') but full of an interest that betrays nothing of the deep reservations he was beginning to feel. These anxieties were confirmed by a conversation he had with Laurence Brander after the intelligence officer's return from his six-month tour of India. Brander's conclusions were so depressing, Orwell confided to his diary, that he could hardly bear to write them down.

The regular *Partisan Review* letter, written at the end of August, reflects broader anxieties. Politically, the country seemed to be frozen into the 'crisis' he had reported three months before. Cripps, though still 'enigmatically' in his office, was thought to be biding his time, waiting for the right moment to break out and promote a revolutionary policy from beyond the government ranks. India was in turmoil, with the nationalist leaders in jail and Secretary of State Amery making inflammatory speeches. At home, one reminder of how things had changed was the arrival of American magazines 'with their enormous bulk, sleek paper and riot of brilliantly coloured adverts urging you to spend your money on trash'. (Orwell kept his eye on these weather-vanes of American capitalism and continued to make fascinated references to them deep into the 1940s.) Now into his second year at the Indian Section, he was irked by his inability to settle to any serious work. He had no time for anything except casual journalism, he told Moore in September. The plan to publish his 1940-41 diary alongside Inez Holden's had come to nothing – according to his co-author because she wanted to alter the substantial catalogue of entries which she disagreed with or found inaccurate. What journalism there was could be subject to upset. There was a row with the *Observer* (where Cyril Connolly had been installed as literary editor by David Astor) over Orwell's review of a book called *Retreat in the East*, rejected by the editor, Ivor Brown, on the grounds that Orwell's scathing attack on British businessmen in the Far East played into the hands of American commercial interests. Brown, for whom Orwell never had much time, was instantly marked down as a minor-league Kingsley Martin. Other review books were smartly returned. 'I don't write for papers which do not allow me at least a minimum of honesty,' he informed Connolly. All this was hugely irritating, but at the same time he was conscious that the war – and the BBC – was widening his range of contacts, putting him in touch with people into whose orbit he would not otherwise have strayed, even if they did not always live up to his expectations. Basil Liddell-Hart, the doyen of military strategy whom Orwell much admired, turned out to be mildly defeatist and 'pro-German subjectively'. There was, however, some amusement to be got out of a conversation with Osbert Sitwell, met at the same party as Liddell-Hart. Sitwell remarked that in Cornwall, should an invasion begin, the local Home Guard had orders to shoot all artists. Orwell deposed that in Cornwall this might be all for the best. Sitwell thought not. 'Some instinct would lead them to the good ones.'

Even here, though, amid a litter of journalism – mostly ground out late at night without time for revision – one can see many of the ideas Orwell had begun to formulate before the war being refined and in some cases refocused by the books that came his way. The stimulus could vary from a poem published the previous month to a novel published the previous century, but the effect was the same: a meditation on the nature of a totalitarian society, or the circumstances in which a totalitarian regime could take root and the psychological shifts that lay beneath it, all extracted from an individual human response. In the autumn of 1942, for example, a review of the first three of Eliot's *Four Quartets* for *Poetry London* offered the chance to conduct a detailed analysis of a poet who had meant a great deal to Orwell's early life. *Prufrock*'s theme might have been futility, Orwell suggested, but it was still a poem of wonderful vitality and power. The trouble was that conscious futility was a young man's game. The sedate Anglicanism of Eliot's middle years was psychologically compromised by the fact that in the mid-twentieth century 'hardly anyone . . . *feels* himself to be immortal'. Eliot was a man who did not feel his faith, but for complex reasons of his own merely assented to it. Two *Tribune* essays from this time on a pair of his favourite writers – Jack London and George Gissing – find him exploring the psychology of totalitarian movements. London's message was that while part of the average human being wanted comfort, safety and security, an equal part wanted blood, sweat and lofted banners. Gissing's novels, on the other hand, his tales of the downtrodden and harassed petit bourgeoisie, showed that the middle classes suffered far more from economic insecurity than people further down the social scale and, unlike them, were prepared to do something about it. Like Ernest Bramah, Gissing was a sensitive, idealistic man whose private fear of the mob turned him into a passionate anti-democrat.

In the wider world the battle for Stalingrad pressed on; there was an Australian offensive in New Guinea. Orwell noted the parallels with 1918 when Germany, having overrun countless territories, found that she could not transform them into paying concerns. Similarly, the Allied campaign in the Western desert was moving on towards victory. The final entry in Orwell's diary, made in mid-November, notes the ringing of church bells in celebration: 'the first time that I have heard them in over two years'. A week later a significant milestone was reached at the BBC when he was allowed to broadcast his first 'Weekly News Review' as George Orwell, the authorities having finally decided that his pro-India reputation might be welcomed by the native audience. But office life continued to wear him down. He could defend his work to a pacifist such as George Woodcock, who maintained that he was being 'used', but the attentions of the censors who refused to pass Anand's talk on the Spanish Civil War and the problems with 'difficult' speakers disheartened him. 'This morning everything went wrong that could have gone wrong,' he reported to Rushbrook Williams at the end of the year apropos of one of Lady Grigg's performances. In amongst the polite letters to potential speakers – Lord David Cecil, for example, or George Bernard Shaw, who could not be persuaded to contribute to 'Great Dramatists' – he was still trying to encourage less well known names. A year before he had thought he would stay at the BBC 'if the political changes I foresaw come off'. Manifestly, they had not. One hint as to his future direction came in the increasing volume of work he produced for the left-wing weekly *Tribune*: making one of his favourite points in a review of Anand's *Letters on India* that a major obstacle to colonial self-determination was the British worker's refusal to acknowledge that Indian poverty and his own relative affluence were connected; taking part in a long correspondence on the future of Burma (independence was no use to smaller nations if they could not fend for themselves, Orwell argued). One of his most interesting *Tribune* pieces from this period was a review of *Voice in the Darkness*, a study of the BBC's European Service. Could propaganda ever achieve anything on its own? he wondered. Now and again a well-aimed lie could produce a great effect, 'but in general propaganda cannot fight against the facts . . .' Orwell's own internal propaganda campaign to convince himself that his time in Oxford Street served either his own purposes or the wider national interest was coming to an end. There were other things urging him on. Above all, he had decided, he wanted to write a book.

Orwell's failure

He was a man who had long since resolved that his life should be a success. It would seem that all men would so resolve, if the matter was simply one of resolution. But the majority of men, as I take it, make no such resolution, and very many resolve that they will be unsuccessful. – Anthony Trollope, *The Small House at Allington*

Orwell was obsessed by the idea of failure. Life, he once wrote, was on balance a succession of defeats, and only the very young or the very foolish believed otherwise. To look back on past time was to be eternally cast down by a sense of your own insignificance. Leaving St Cyprian's at the age of thirteen with two public school scholarships under his belt he was uncomfortably aware that he had been judged and found wanting, and that the judgement would irreversibly continue. 'Failure, failure, failure – failure behind me, failure ahead of me – that was by far the deepest conviction that I carried away.' It was the same when he sat down to examine the down-at-heel, vagrant life of his mid- to late twenties. Disillusioned by the Imperial racket, thrown upon his own resources, he came, as he put it, to know both poverty and 'the sense of failure'. Glittering prizes lay strewn across the path of the Eton election of 1916 – All Souls fellowships, literary editorships and calls to the Bar – but Orwell knew, and according to his retrospective glosses seems always to have known, that they would never be his. Failure, he wrote in *The Road to Wigan Pier*, seemed the only positive virtue.

And if the man was a failure, so, too, was the work. Orwell's attitude to his books is generally that of bitter disparagement. Nowhere is this more apparent than in the essay 'Why I Write', written in 1946 for the little magazine *Gangrel* shortly after publication of the novel that had definitively made his name. Orwell hoped at some point in the near future to write another work of fiction, he told his readers. 'It is bound to be a failure, every book is a failure . . .' *Every* book? *Ulysses* and *Vanity Fair* and the *Origin of Species?* All of them? There is no getting away from this blanket disavowal of his own and everyone else's talent, for it had been there since the very start of his career. The idea of a pseudonym was first advanced to his agent back in 1932 on the slightly implausible grounds that he was 'not proud' of *Down and Out in Paris and London. A Clergyman's Daughter* was written off as 'bollix'. *Keep the Aspidistra Flying,* on which he claimed to have sweated blood at the time of writing, was later marked down as a pot-boiler, written simply to get his hands on Gollancz's £100. Neither would he allow to be reprinted in his lifetime. A new edition of *A Clergyman's Daughter* hung fire until as late as 1961. Generally speaking Orwell seems to have decided shortly after, or in some cases before, publication that what he had written was a mess in which a promising idea or good material had defied his ability to render it down. As for his workaday journalism, one need only read a sketch like 'Confessions of a Book Reviewer' to grasp the depths of professional futility by which he was regularly oppressed.

And if the books were failures, so – given that most of his leading characters are exercises in self-projection – were the people who wandered about in them. Each of Orwell's protagonists, in fact, is a study in failure, of life not sustaining its early promise, dreams cast down into dust. Flory in *Burmese Days* is a lonely fantasist, his best years squandered in drink and whoring; Dorothy in *A Clergyman's Daughter* an old maid at twenty-eight; Comstock in *Keep the Aspidistra Flying* a moth-eaten minor poet turned sour by his blighted hopes. Even George Bowling, the most resourceful of this shabby crew, is irrevocably caught up in the ooze and stagnation of a life lived out with the mirthless Hilda in the shadow of approaching war. Each of Orwell's novels, by extension, is the story of a rebellion that fails, of an individual – in the case of *Animal Farm* a mini-society – who, however feebly or obliquely, attempts to throw over the traces. Each ends in more or less the same way, with the protagonist humbled, defeated, sent back to square one. Flory shoots himself. Dorothy returns to the sedative thraldom of her father's rectory. Gordon succumbs to the insidious embrace of the money god. Winston, brainwashed and re-educated, knows that he loves Big Brother. There is no way out. The best one can hope for is a kind of coming to terms with this environmental quicksand, the 'he is dead but won't lie down' idea peddled by the epigraph to *Coming up for Air.*

When did Orwell begin to cultivate, or have cultivated for him, the notion of his personal inadequacy? Undoubtedly he felt that he had disappointed his parents, his father especially, by his choice of career, and yet the whole thing seems much more integral to him, much more bound up in his idea of who he was, than to have been a consequence of parental hurt. To go back to 'Why I Write', it is the off-handedness of the line about every book being destined to fail that really startles, the absence of gesture. It was Orwell, we can infer, who decided that he was a failure. The rest, the opinions of parents, schoolmasters and literary critics, was merely corroborative. At the same time it is important to distinguish what Orwell thought and said about himself from the habitual self-deprecation practised by other men of his age and background. To read accounts of the career of Ian Fleming's brother Peter, four years below Orwell at Eton, at least one of whose best-selling '30s travel books Orwell admired, is to descry a wall of quite impenetrable reserve, a stylisation of personal (and literary) manner founded on an almost painful diffidence. Orwell displayed many of the same characteristics – the laconic speech, the dry humour, the tolerant irony, the shirking from a limelight in which he might have performed to advantage – and yet, whatever his constant down-playing of his abilities, Fleming never seems to have thought he was a failure. He was only an upper-class Englishman, petrified by the thought that he might be 'showing off'.

Perhaps the strongest evidence of Orwell's sense of his own inadequacy comes in his dealings with women. By the standards of his time Orwell was a more than moderately successful ladies' man. And yet his surviving letters to women are shot through with trepidation, fear that they won't like him, that he has offended, certainty that something is bound to go wrong (significantly, one of his favourite poets was Housman, to whose sexual pessimism he clearly responded). The notes to Eleanor Jaques, for example, are full of plaintive self-pity. Those to Brenda Salkeld assume an uncharacteristic and therefore suspect bluffness. The ones to Lydia Jackson are just arch. The letters he addressed to Anne Popham in early 1946 are almost worse than this – an object lesson in how not to press a suit, an invitation to spurn what had been so kindly proposed. Seen with any kind of objectivity, Orwell's career is a riot of incident, hard work and achievement – an Eton scholarship, first book published before he was thirty, friendships with the great minds of his age, authorship of at least two novels that literally changed the way in which people thought. Reckoning up his life as he lay dying in University College Hospital, did Orwell imagine that it had been a success? Almost certainly the human skeleton in the hospital bed believed that in this, as in so many other compartments of his life, he had failed.

15

Gains and Losses

You will be glad to hear that I *am* writing a book again at last. –
Letter to Leonard Moore, 6 December 1943

George however is due home in the latter half of next month & he
is a curiously reliable man. – Eileen, 25 March 1945

Orwell maintained that the idea for *Animal Farm* came to him when
he was out walking in a country lane and he saw a small boy leading a
giant carthorse by the bridle. Always fond of animals, and aware since
his childhood reading of Beatrix Potter of the anthropomorphic uses to
which they could be put, he was struck by the inbred docility that
allowed man to tyrannise the animal world. What if the beasts could
be persuaded to throw off their shackles? Whatever the precise
creative stimulus, the mental processes that were to give depth and
context to this fleeting glimpse of horse and child had been a part of
his interior life for years. Since the start of the war – possibly even since
Spain – Orwell had been searching for a way to dramatise what he
believed was the human betrayal practised by the Soviet regime in
the twenty years since the Revolution. Now, in this tableau from the
country back-road, he had a foundation stone on which he could
build.

The first reference to this new project comes in a letter to Moore
from the end of 1943 – 'You will be glad to hear that I *am* writing a book
again,' Orwell discloses, guiltily aware that he had not produced a novel
for nearly five years – but *Animal Farm*'s gestation period probably
extends deep into the earlier part of the year. Many of his friends knew
he was working on it, even if at this stage the subject matter seemed
unpromising. Never a reliable summariser of book plots, Orwell
struggled to convey the outline of this new work to interested enquirers.
According to Michael Meyer, a younger friend met at around this time,

the scenario was represented as a 'kind of parable, about people who were blind to the dangers of totalitarianism, set on a farm where the animals take over and make such a bad job of it that they call in the humans again'. When the book eventually came into his hands two years later Meyer was 'staggered and delighted' that it bore no relation to this 'awful summary'.

Back at the BBC growing disillusionment had given way to a more or less open search for something else to do. There was no let-up in Orwell's work-rate – the scripts for news commentaries, educational talks and drama adaptations continued to pour forth – but he was conscious that he was wasting his time. Even among those people on the subcontinent who could be presumed to tune in, his name carried little weight. The intelligence unit had produced audience approval ratings for the principal speakers. This made grim reading: radio celebrities such as Priestley and the former *Times* editor, Henry Wickham-Stead, scored in the high sixties and seventies; Orwell languished at 16 per cent, even lower than his *bête noire*, Lady Grigg. There was, too, continuing interference from the upper reaches of the Corporation. A 'News Commentary' to Malaya in late May 1943 ran into trouble over its treatment of the dissolution of the Comintern. A fortnight later there was further trouble over Malaysia, culminating in a note from the Controller of Overseas Services to the Director-General of the BBC himself. The script does not survive and whatever Orwell may have said to provoke this high-level reaction is lost in time, but the resulting tension cannot have improved his morale. It was time to leave. By the summer he was actively in pursuit of another job, telling Rayner Heppenstall in August that 'I am definitely leaving it [the BBC] probably in about 3 months'. As to what might come next, Ivor Brown had asked him if he wanted to go to Algiers and Sicily for the *Observer*. Orwell was keen, but aware that his BBC contract obliged him to give two months' notice. Also, having gone fourteen months without a holiday, he was anxious for some time off. There was no hostility in his attitude to his employers: it was simply that a combination of circumstance and protocol made his job almost impossible. Left-wing attacks on the Corporation's usefulness generally had him rushing to its defence. In this spirit, in June 1943, he took part in a pseudonymous verse exchange with the young pacifist writer Alex Comfort in *Tribune*. (Comfort, under the alias of 'Obadiah Hornbrook', had written a 'Letter to an American Visitor'; Orwell replied as 'One Non-Combatant to Another'.) What really irked him was not so much the pacifism as the disparagement of the BBC:

> But your chief target is the radio hack
> The hired pep-talker – he's a safe objective
> Since he's unpopular and can't hit back.
> It doesn't need the eye of a detective
> To look down Portland Street and spot the whore,
> But there are men (I grant, not the most heeded)
> With twice your gifts and courage three times yours
> Who do the dirty work because it's needed;
> Not blindly, but for reasons they can balance
> They wear their seats out and lay waste their talents.

Writing to Comfort a month or so later – Orwell liked the younger man, despite this set-to, and contributed to his magazine *New Road* – he explained that it was the thought of William Empson's fruitless endeavours on behalf of the Chinese Service that made him so angry, 'though God knows I have the best means of judging what a mixture of whorehouse and lunatic asylum it is for the most part'. Nearly a year later he could still be found defending the BBC's impartiality. Even if the Corporation did pass on the official British line, he told readers of *Tribune*, it did at least make some effort to sift the others. Even in wartime, subject to a host of contending pressures and propaganda fiats, the ability to discriminate had not quite been lost.

Despite these defences of the organisation that paid his salary, he was conscious of his own uselessness. Most of his friends seemed busily engaged on the nation's behalf. A letter had come from Georges Kopp, now working officially for the French Ministry of Production but in fact spying for British intelligence (Kopp, who led a charmed life, was betrayed to the Gestapo but spirited out by plane before he could be arrested). Having taken a two-week holiday at the start of September, and still confident that something would come of the *Observer* scheme, Orwell decided to take the decisive step. A letter of resignation to Rushbrook Williams, written a few days after his return, is careful to stress that he has no grievance, merely a sense that he would be better elsewhere. 'I am tendering my resignation because for some time past I have been conscious that I was wasting my own time and the public money on work that produces no result.' He left his desk for the last time on 24 November 1943, having kept up his work rate to the end, trying (and failing) to sneak in Reg Reynolds' broadcast on Kropotkin, adapting *Macbeth* and a version of Hans Christian Andersen's 'The Emperor's New Clothes'.

The official line that Orwell took during his twenty-seven months in the Indian Section was that he had wasted his time. Clearly this is a substantial overstatement. Given the resources at his disposal he had been an innovator, albeit on a small and tightly regimented scale, and *Voice* bears at least some relation to the modern equivalent of the Third Programme, now Radio 3. In a minor yet significant way he had become a BBC figure, pointed out as such to trainee producers at parties and in canteens, and he carried several of his BBC connections with him into later life. For the moment, though, he was keen to shake the dust of Portland Place and 200 Oxford Street from his feet, and less than a week elapsed before he took up his new job. As he explained to Philip Rahv of *Partisan Review*, 'I have left the BBC after two wasted years in it and become literary editor of the *Tribune*, a left-wing weekly which you may have seen.' Orwell had been connected with *Tribune* since the early days of the war: joining its small editorial staff was a logical move. Its politics – leftist but anti-Stalin, supportive of the government if to a certain extent *faute de mieux* – were to his taste, as were the personalities that surrounded and conducted it. The capital for the paper's launch back in 1937 had been substantially put up by Cripps. The left-wing Labour MP Aneurin Bevan, whom Orwell admired, had become editor in the spring of 1942. Jon Kimche, his comrade of the Hampstead bookshop and the Barcelona roof-tops, was one of the editorial assistants. When a vacancy occurred with the departure of John Atkins – who later wrote one of the first critical studies of Orwell – to Mass Observation, Tosco Fyvel and others lobbied hard to secure Orwell as a replacement. He was hired to fill Atkins' role as literary editor, with the understanding that he would write a weekly personal column 'As I Please' and also contribute other, necessarily short, pieces and essays (like other newspapers *Tribune* suffered from paper rationing) when required at a salary of perhaps £500 a year.

Professionally the two years spent in *Tribune*'s cramped offices at 222 the Strand were among the happiest of Orwell's life. Bevan regarded him benignly, while acknowledging the existence of a deep temperamental fissure. Junior members of the staff recalled an editorial meeting at which Bevan, a notable friend of Israel, launched into a pro-Zionist speech. Orwell remarked that Zionists were merely 'a bunch of Wardour Street Jews who had a controlling interest over the British press'. Nothing anybody said could shake him from this view. In the context of the time the support that Bevan offered to his new recruit, often in the face of severe criticism from readers, was vitally important. The anti-Soviet strain that characterised Orwell's journalism in the latter stages of the war had few imitators: even right-wing commentators tended to pull their punches in respect of a supposedly benevolent 'Uncle Joe'. Michael Foot, who had not yet met Orwell but was intimately involved in *Tribune*'s affairs, remembered long conversations with Bevan about the controversies that Orwell's hostility to Stalin generated among the paper's readership. One makes this point to emphasise that *Tribune*'s line, or at any rate the line expected of it by many of its left-wing readers, was by no means clear-cut. The same tensions attended Orwell's post-war attacks on alleged Labour party fellow-travellers, many of whom, as Foot somewhat ruefully put it, 'were friends of mine'.

He was not, it scarcely needs saying, a good literary editor, largely owing to his reluctance to turn work down. The Canadian poet Paul Potts remembered seeing him stuff a ten shilling note into a stamped addressed envelope containing a manuscript that 'even he couldn't bring himself to print'. His successor, going through the desk drawers on his first day at work, came upon a cache of material of 'unspeakable badness' that he had not had the heart to reject outright. Nevertheless he tried conscientiously to improve the paper's books pages, whether by bringing in 'name' reviewers (both Eliot and F.R. Leavis regretfully declined) or fostering upcoming talent. One innovation with which younger contributors were happy to credit him was payment for contributions. This sometimes compensated for what, even in a left-field organ like *Tribune*, could be an esoteric choice of books. Peter Vansittart, for example, introduced to Orwell as a boy of nineteen by the equally youthful art critic David Sylvester, was paid £1 for his first contribution – a review of a history of the nineteenth-century Danish folk high school movement. Vansittart later became a *Tribune* regular, filling in on 'As I Please' at times when Orwell was away. The impression that rises from the surviving mass of Orwell's correspondence is of a man who is as anxious to please his contributors as they are to please him, always capable of doling out useful advice or hints on reviewing protocol. 'In a review of this kind it is all right to devote most of the space to exposition,' he advised R.S.R. Fitter, apropos his account of a life of Harriet Martineau, 'but I think we ought to just mention whether the author has done his work well or badly.' Apprentice reviewers appreciated this tolerance of habits that in other circumstances would have prompted a zealously wielded blue pen, just as they appreciated Orwell's approachability. Contributors who turned up at the office at around 5.30 could usually persuade him to join them in a nearby pub for an hour or so before he proceeded to Trafalgar Square and the number 53 bus that took him home to Kilburn.

Whatever Orwell's merits as a literary editor, it was the 'As I Please' column that cemented his relationship with the paper and provided the public face that here, in the later stages of the war, he offered to the world. Running to between 800 and 1,000 words and generally divided into three or four discrete sections, it offered a flexible medium for whatever he had in his head at the time of writing. Thoughts on the political situation, stray bits of reminiscence, odd scraps gleaned from books or plays, brain teasers – all these very disparate fragments were used to build what, in the end, became a surprisingly durable structure. The first 'As I Please', from early December 1943, turned on prevailing attitudes to American servicemen in England, pamphlet literature, Mark Rutherford and the London slums. Over the next few months he discussed his interest in artificial languages, reflected on the ugliness and vulgarity of political leaders and wrote an elegiac essay about the white rambler roses that had decorated the Wallington cottage. From the outset Orwell's tenure of 'As I Please' brought a series of lively correspondences (the essay about the roses provoked a steely exchange about 'bourgeois nostalgia'). One of the most engaging features of the column, read sequentially, is the sense of dialogue, points taken up, conceded or refuted, continuity rather than a trail of pronouncements which the reader could take or leave as he or she chose. Alongside the weekly column ran a series of short essays, often devoted to favourite writers such as Smollett or Thackeray. The sheer profusion of his *Tribune* work, and the ease with which it was thrown off, is a silent testimony to the frustrations of the previous two years. In fact the range of Orwell's output at this time in his career is startling. Along with his day job, his contributions to the *Observer* and *Partisan Review* and longer pieces for *Horizon*, he found time to write a weekly review for the *Manchester Evening News*. And always, for the first three months of 1944, as the upper deck of the 53 bus scanned its newspapers each morning for information about the long-awaited Second Front, there was *Animal Farm* burning into his mind. 'I am snowed under with work until I finish the book I am doing,' he explained to one of the *Political Review* staff in February 1944. The snow would continue to fall.

Orwell had turned forty in the summer, an age by which most writers have either achieved a reputation or gone some way towards establishing it. In the contemporary literary marketplace, he was, despite his *Horizon* and *Observer* pieces, still a faintly marginal figure. Peter Vansittart noted that his initial respect for Orwell derived entirely from the fact that he was a literary editor with patronage to bestow, not from any books he happened to have written. At the same time, his influence was far from negligible. Penguin, who had reissued *Down and Out in Paris and London* some years before, were now reprinting *Burmese Days*. They were also interested in *Keep the Aspidistra Flying* but Orwell, getting wind of this, stopped Moore's negotiations: he was not proud of the book, which he claimed had been written merely for money. There were more exalted mainstream commissions to hand as well, such as the 15,000-word letterpress to *The English People* in the Collins 'Britain in Pictures' series. A younger generation was discovering his work in university and sixth-form discussion groups. David Holbrook remembered coming across *Homage to Catalonia* and *Inside the Whale* at his Norwich grammar school during the early years of the war; in 1941 he spoke to an Oxford University Labour Club audience that included the teenaged Philip Larkin. Orwell's spoor was already being picked up by contemporary novelists. Julian Maclaren-Ross' *Of Love and Hunger* (1947), set in the penurious world of south coast vacuum cleaner salesmen in the months before the outbreak of war, is clearly indebted to *Coming up for Air* and contains, additionally, a minor character named Comstock.

The circles in which Orwell moved were not hermetically sealed: they sometimes shaded into one another with unexpected results. Most obviously there was his family. Richard Blair was four years dead. Ida, worn out by the strain of a demanding job undertaken in her late sixties, died of heart failure brought on by bronchitis and emphysema in March 1943. Avril remembered brother and sister visiting her in hospital – a copy of *Homage to Catalonia* lay on the bed – and Orwell's palpable distress. Avril herself continued to inhabit a flat not far from Mortimer Crescent and took some part in Orwell's social life. She was a dry-spoken woman by all accounts, retaining stray vestiges of youthful attractiveness (meeting her some years later, Anthony Powell reported to Malcolm Muggeridge that she was 'quite different from what one expected – very dotty, and of the twenties, but once quite good-looking'). Orwell kept up with Marjorie and her family, now living in Bristol, was fond of his Dakin nieces and nephew and at one point had the young Henry to stay for several months: Dakin recalled that they went to see Chaplin in *The Gold Rush*, where Orwell laughed louder than anyone else in the cinema. Aunt Nellie, too, continued to keep a fond eye on her nephew. To this group could be added Eileen's O'Shaughnessy relatives, in particular her sister-in-law Gwen, and Gwen's own half-sister Doreen who, on his return from France, was eventually to marry Georges Kopp. Orwell seems also to have fitted fairly easily into the group formed by Eileen's friends: Lydia Jackson (in whom he continued to take a friendly interest), the novelist Lettice Cooper, who was one of Eileen's work colleagues, and various survivors from university days such as the Jungian psychologist Margaret Branch.

Beyond this immediate family circle, understandably, Orwell's chief associates were other writers and literary people. Again, sharp distinctions can be made. On the one hand there were early sponsors and friends with whom he kept up, a category that included Richard Rees, Jack Common and Mabel Fierz: Mrs Fierz's son Adrian remembered Orwell attending his wedding in the early part of the war. Then came a group of men of about his own age – Powell, Koestler, Connolly, Muggeridge, Fyvel – with whom he was on fairly intimate terms. There were some more exalted connections – he continued to see something of T.S. Eliot and was on nodding terms with the Sitwells – but these links were not actively pursued. Orwell's natural milieu, certainly during the war years, seems to have been a Fitzrovian restaurant or a central London pub, with occasional forays into more glamorous haunts such as the Café Royal. It was here, for example, that he first came across the young artist Lucian Freud. Certainly, the pub was where he tended to meet a third category of literary acquaintance. These were younger writers, some barely out of their teens, several of whom – for example Alex Comfort and Kay Dick – edited little magazines to which he contributed. These relationships did not always get off on the right footing – Julian Symons, who inherited Orwell's *Manchester Evening News* slot, was initially suspected of Fascist tendencies – but Orwell's interest in promising newcomers, whom he introduced to publishers and promoted to commissioning editors, is one of his most attractive features. If only for geographical reasons, this group of tyro novelists and poets shaded into a fourth literary-cum-artistic grouping: the rackety bohemian world of the wartime Fitzrovia pubs and drinking dens. Orwell's connection to the out-at-elbows landscape of Tambimuttu's *Editions Poetry London* and Maclaren-Ross holding court at the bar of the Wheatsheaf is largely unrecorded in his work. Fitzrovia, though, was barely a stone's throw from the BBC and several of its denizens, notably Tambimuttu and Potts, were already known to him. Anthony Burgess remembered him arriving at the Wheatsheaf to drink a silent half-pint and stare fascinatedly at the local fauna, and he features in the list of personalities that Maclaren-Ross aimed to discuss in the unfinished section of his *Memoirs of the Forties.*

Equally, he had political interests to maintain. Through his BBC work and his *Tribune* job he already knew, in Cripps and Bevan, two of the architects of the future post-war Labour government. Then there came a handful of aspiring Labour politicians, many of whom dabbled in political journalism: Michael Foot, Richard Crossman (met at the *New Statesman*) and Patrick Gordon-Walker were all young MPs in the 1945 parliament whom Orwell knew to a greater or lesser degree. Michael Foot, for example, recalled meeting him for the first time at a lunch in Soho with Koestler shortly after the war's end. This was the formal world of 1940s parliamentary Socialism – and Orwell himself was subsequently approached by the Hendon Constituency Labour Party's Hampstead Garden Suburb branch to see if he would be interested in standing as a candidate. Beneath it ran a vein of much less respectable opinion, the world of unofficial ginger groups, 'causes' and protest meetings, in which he continued to wander, keeping up with many of his old ILP connections and some of the out-and-out anarchists met in the months after his return from Spain. Vernon Richards, for example, who first came across him in 1938 through his work for the SIA, was commissioned to take some of the last known photographs of Orwell eight years later and last saw him only a few weeks before his death.

Each of these groupings was characterised by Orwell's ability, not always evident among literary men, to 'keep up' with people met at previous stages of his life. These could be old Southwold acquaintances – the Collinges visited him at Wallington shortly before the outbreak of war – comrades from the Aragon Front such as Harry Milton and an Irishman named Paddy Donovan whom Orwell had employed to dig in the Wallington gardens (Jack Branthwaite, invited to the Stores, was surprised to find that evening dress was expected at dinner) or members of his Home Guard unit. The occasional blendings of these different parts of his life could lead to unexpected juxtapositions: Malcolm Muggeridge, for example, *Telegraph* journalist and right-wing polemicist dining *à trois* with Orwell and Kay Dick, lesbian novelist and editor of the *Windmill*; Paul Potts being suggested to Ivor Brown as a potential *Observer* writer; BBC colleagues inducted – at times with mixed results – on to *Tribune*'s reviewing staff. The young Francis Wyndham's solitary encounter with Orwell shortly after the war's end is a good example of how these various worlds could intersect. Wyndham and his mother rented the top half of a house in Trevor Square. Their downstairs neighbours were David Davidson, Orwell's Home Guard comrade, and his wife, the novelist Myra Meulen. Wyndham and Meulen were working on a one-off magazine, the *New Savoy*, for which she managed to procure permission to reprint 'A Hanging' (other contributors included Powell, Koestler and Olivia Manning). Proud of his friendship with Orwell, Davidson enjoyed having him to dinner. Summoned downstairs with his mother to one of these junkets, Wyndham sat shyly in the corner while Orwell ('polite' and talking 'rather low') and his host discoursed on politics.

What did the people who met him in the war years, that hectic and uncertain period of his life immediately before he achieved fame, think of him? To many observers he seemed a solitary, aloof figure, quietly eavesdropping on the conversations of the Fitzrovia drinkers but rarely joining in. Janetta Woolley retained the impression of a driven, hard-working man responsible for 'endless *Tribune* articles', a 'very serious, rather sad figure', neither outward-going nor convivial, 'sympathetic but rather difficult to get on with'. She remembered travelling back from a Connolly party with him on the top deck of a bus: the conversation failed to ignite. This habitual reserve occasionally snuffed out the attempts made by friends to introduce him to 'interesting people' with whom he might be supposed to have something in common. Anthony Powell once presided over a silent lunch party involving Orwell and the Catholic intellectual Alick Dru: 'There was no apparent antipathy; equally no communication.' The band of younger *Tribune* writers listened to him with respect, sometimes conscious that this deference was something he appreciated. 'He liked putting people in their place,' one young reviewer maintained. Any assumption of superiority would be mercilessly stamped on. Orwell's occasional officer-like tendencies ('I always saw him in uniform,' Peter Vansittart remembered) were noted by several of his friends. He had a mischievous side that was not always recognised or appreciated. John Morris, a colleague from BBC days, left an unflattering portrait of a man who, asked if any payment could be expected for a *Tribune* piece, replied that it was 'for the cause'. But this, according to other *Tribune* hands from the period, was simply a case of Morris failing to grasp the – admittedly idiosyncratic – way in which Orwell sometimes operated. Gaunt, thin, often in bad health – at work on the manuscript of *Animal Farm* he told Moore that he expected to finish by a certain date 'unless I get ill or something', a formulation that suggests he often did get ill – he often seemed to merit the art critic Michael Ayrton's nickname of 'Gloomy George'. Other friends, though, were impressed by his relaxed good nature and all-purpose enthusiasm. Regaling him with supper in Pimlico – where Orwell gnashed his way eagerly through some pork chops that his hosts thought uneatable – Julian Symons and his wife Kathleen found themselves involved in the lightest literary gossip. ('He was very easy to get on with,' Kathleen Symons remembered.) Michael Meyer, in his early twenties, is a good example of a younger friend encouraged for making an approach that another hard-worked middle-aged author might have rebuffed and swiftly admitted into a convivial friendship. Prompted by Tambimuttu to write a 'timid letter' proposing lunch at a Hungarian restaurant in Dean Street, Meyer was heartened by a courteous handwritten letter of acceptance. From this first meeting Meyer recalled Orwell's 'great height and thinness, his staring pale-blue eyes and his high-pitched drawl with its marked Old Etonian accent'. After a supper invitation to Mortimer Crescent the two settled into a congenial relationship of lunch and theatre visits, characterised by comparative high spirits. His silences, Meyer thought, were often a result of simply not being able to talk loudly enough. Taken to meet Meyer's voluble old college chum, the Labour MP Patrick Gordon-Walker, and unable to get a word in edgeways, he gave up.

Practically everyone was agreed on the faint air of 'unreality' that Orwell carried around with him, his bouts of abstraction, stark wonder at some of the most elementary social usages, disinclination to take sides. Unless the stakes were spectacularly high – and even Kingsley Martin, oddly enough, ended up broadcasting for the Indian Section – Orwell rarely bore a grudge. He could lend money, or solicit funds, for a writer like Cedric Dover of whose politics he profoundly disapproved. He was faintly surprised by the occasional coolness his actions provoked (the dispute with Wells, for example) on the grounds that one ought to be able to separate the human being from the words on the page. Above all, one notes the ability of Orwell's friendships to transcend the party line. In his old age the arch-Tory Powell reflected on the bafflement that his relationship with Orwell produced in young interviewers. And yet with their similar backgrounds, schooling and literary friends, Powell and Orwell had more in common than might at first be apparent. A colonel's son and a scion of the Indian Civil Service, both moving on from Eton to the world of books: it was on foundations such as these that upper-middle-class early twentieth-century life was built.

Whatever the occasional complaints about 'Gloomy George', there is a definite liveliness about Orwell's journalism in the early part of 1944, a feeling of shackles thrown off, a lightening of spirit that had previously been denied him. A photograph of Lord Beaverbrook, glimpsed in *Picture Post*, looked 'more like a monkey on a stick than you would think possible for anyone who was not doing it on purpose', he told his *Tribune* readers early in January. There was talk of a book of reprinted pieces (this became *Critical Essays*, not published until another two years had passed). Meanwhile, in the evenings and at weekends, he continued to work at *Animal Farm*, discussing it with Eileen, who provided regular bulletins on its progress to her work colleagues, and offering gnomic – and occasionally prophetic – updates to Moore. 'It is a fairy story but also a political allegory,' he explained, hazarding a March completion date, 'and I think we may have some difficulties about finding a publisher.' Here in the months before the Second Front, the problems involved in publicly criticising the leader of a major military ally were becoming apparent in other areas of Orwell's professional life. A month or so later the *Manchester Evening News* rejected a review of Harold Laski's *Faith, Reason and Civilization* because, Orwell believed, of its 'anti-Stalin implications'. If this was the case, one wonders why, as in the stand-off with the *New Statesman* six years before, Orwell did not turn the rejection into an issue of moral principle. In the end he continued to write for the paper for another two years.

If nothing else, the saga of *Animal Farm*'s labyrinthine route to publication displays the practicalities of wartime publishing, the influences that could be brought to bear and the covert pressure that could be exerted without most observers appreciating that it even existed. The initial problem, Orwell knew, would be with Gollancz, who though no longer an ardent believer in the Soviet cause – he had, after all, edited a volume entitled *The Betrayal of the Left* (1941) – would hardly want to sponsor a draught of undiluted anti-Stalinism. Such was

Orwell's conviction of Gollancz's hostility that, with a rather typical doggedness and defiance of all known publishing convention, he resolved to try to cut him out of the equation altogether. Why not tell Gollancz that the book wasn't likely to suit him, he suggested to Moore, and that it would only be sent if he definitely wanted to see it? As for other possible publishers, Warburg was not even to be considered at this stage as he 'probably wouldn't touch anything of this tendency' and in addition was short of paper (paper shortages, the bane of wartime publishers' lives, extended well into the late 1940s). Orwell had his eye on the new and lively firm of Nicolson & Watson, the optimistic sponsors of Tambimuttu's *Editions Poetry London*, Hutchinson or indeed anyone who had paper and, as he put it, wasn't in the arms of Stalin. Gollancz, diffidently addressed in mid-March ('I must tell you that it is – I think – completely unacceptable politically from your point of view?') and puzzled to be told that he wouldn't like something he hadn't yet seen, replied that he wasn't a Stalinist stooge and was keen to see the manuscript. However, his reaction was exactly what Orwell had predicted ('You were right and I was wrong'): Gollancz, for all his criticisms of Soviet Communism, could not bring himself to publish a satirical onslaught on its grandest panjandrum.

Shortly after this, despite the eagerness expressed by the firm's young editor André Deutsch, it was turned down by Nicolson & Watson on the same grounds as Gollancz. The next plan was to try Jonathan Cape, where Orwell knew one of the firm's readers, Veronica Wedgwood, or Faber, but already he was wondering whether he might not have to resort to unorthodox means to ensure publication. 'Failing all else I will try to get one of the small highbrow presses to do it,' he told Moore in mid-April. Inevitably some of these frustrations began to spill over into his journalism. Russophile feeling was stronger than ever, he told his *Partisan Review* readers in a 'London Letter' written a few days after the Nicolson & Watson rejection. Unless one relied on some diehard Catholic publishing house it was next to impossible to get anything anti-Russian printed. In the meantime the manuscript had made its way to Jonathan Cape's offices in Bloomsbury. Cape liked the book, Orwell reported after a visit to Bedford Square in the second week of May, although the details of his existing fiction contract with Gollancz would need careful handling. The letter to Moore made it clear that Orwell regarded Gollancz's attitude to *Animal Farm* as marking a significant breach between them. If Cape wished to make an option on Orwell's future works a condition of publication, then 'so be it'. Within the next fortnight Cape made a satisfactory offer. Moore began the task of unravelling the three-novel contract that Orwell had signed with Gollancz before the war. Cape might be asked if Gollancz could have the refusal of his next novel, Orwell deposed, but there would be no more works of non-fiction going to Henrietta Street: 'His politics change too fast for me'. Orwell's friends continued to follow developments with interest. Michael Meyer remembered that each successive meeting with his new friend during the summer of 1944 seemed to bring an account of some new publisher with whom negotiations had been opened, only for the book to be once more turned down. But for the moment, here in early June as the Allied armies moved across the Channel to France, the omens looked good.

The *Animal Farm* negotiations took place against the backdrop of an increasingly frenetic professional and social life. All but one of the pieces Orwell wanted to include in his new volume of essays was complete. The penultimate essay, 'Benefit of Clergy: Some Notes on Salvador Dali', in which he advanced the theory that it was perfectly possible to acclaim an artist as a man of genius and suggest that his work ought to be burned by the public hangman, was intended for the *Saturday Book* annual, but ultimately suppressed by the publisher, Hutchinson, on grounds of obscenity (it was physically sliced out of all but the advance copies). Meyer, finding that Orwell had never met his other great literary idol Graham Greene, arranged a lunch in Dean Street on 11 June to celebrate his twenty-third birthday. The two writers got on well, discovered shared literary interests – it was here that a plan was hatched for Orwell to write the introduction to a reprint of Leonard Merrick's Edwardian theatre novel *The Position of Peggy Harper* (1909), to be issued by Eyre & Spottiswoode, on whose board Greene sat – and talked at such length that when the restaurant closed they transferred to the pub across the way.

There were other negotiations in train that would have a profound effect on Orwell's personal life. By the summer of 1944 Orwell and Eileen had been married eight years. Orwell had been unfaithful to his wife – there is evidence of an affair with his *Tribune* secretary Sally McEwan during this period, which upset Eileen greatly – but it was a durable relationship, characterised by Orwell (Eileen's views are not recorded) as 'a proper marriage', by which he seems to have meant one involving a good many rows and disagreements but always redeemed by the underlying bond. Whether or not Orwell was, as he claimed, sterile, Eileen's health may have prevented her from bearing a child. Quite apart from the intense depression into which she had plunged following her brother's death and the fatigue of her job, she was increasingly unwell during the later stages of the war with internal trouble that would later require a hysterectomy. It is a measure of the Orwells' intense desire to have children that despite their poor health and the precariousness of their life in London they should have decided to adopt a child. The facilitator was to be Gwen O'Shaughnessy, who dealt with unmarried mothers in her Newcastle medical practice and could negotiate on their behalf with the local adoption agency. To Orwell it must have seemed a logical step. His next letter to *Partisan Review*, written while the adoption process was continuing, carries an odd little scene attesting to the way in which he noticed children and the anxieties he felt for their welfare. Returning home at midnight on the tube, wandering through the vast, recumbent crowds of people who continued to sleep there at night – the earlier terrors of the Blitz had been replaced by the menace of the new V1 flying bomb – he came upon a little girl of five minding her younger sister. The smaller child – she might have been two, Orwell thought – had got hold of a scrubbing brush with which she was scraping the stones of the platform and then sucking the bristles. Orwell intervened and issued instructions to the older girl. 'But I had my train to catch, and no doubt the poor little brat would again be eating filth in another couple of minutes.'

Richard Horatio Blair, as he was subsequently named, was born illegitimately in the Newcastle area on 14 May 1944. The paperwork covering his adoption having been completed, he was first taken, aged three weeks, to the O'Shaughnessys' family house, Greystone, twenty-five miles south of Newcastle, until arrangements could be made to transport him south. Eileen, the Orwells agreed, would give up her job at the Ministry of Food to look after him. In the event, Richard's transfer to London took several months to accomplish, but the effect of his arrival on the adoptive parents is attested to by their friends. Eileen, though worried that she might not love him enough, 'wanted to live' once more. In Orwell, on the other hand, the prospect of parenthood awakened an odd, formal side. According to Lettice Cooper, the two things he wanted for his adopted son were a cream perambulator with a gold line round the side of the kind pushed by Edwardian nannies and to have his name put down for Eton. It also stirred the deep reservoir of superstition that always lay beneath the rational surface of his mind. Late July found him writing to Rayner Heppenstall with a request for Heppenstall, supposedly expert in these matters, to draw the baby's horoscope ('. . . he is an adopted child,' Orwell explained, wondering if this factor would make any difference to the astral verdict). What Heppenstall divined is not recorded. While one or two onlookers, for example David Holbrook, later detected a faint half-heartedness in Orwell's dealings with Richard, his affection for the baby was engagingly transparent, as was his willingness to involve himself in the routines of childcare.

Much of the delay in getting Richard down to London was caused by an abrupt change to the Orwells' domestic circumstances. At the end of June a V1 fell on Mortimer Crescent. No one was hurt, but extensive damage made the house uninhabitable. The Orwells decamped to Inez Holden's flat in George Street while they looked for a replacement. All this, though, was overshadowed by another bombshell, dropped a few days before. Cape had suddenly changed tack and decided not to publish *Animal Farm*. Writing to Moore, Jonathan Cape explained that the decision had been taken on the advice of a senior official in the Ministry of Information. Such flagrant anti-Soviet bias was unaccept-able: and the choice of pigs as the dominant class was thought to be especially offensive. The 'important official' was, or so it may reasonably be assumed, a man named Peter Smollett, later unmasked as a Soviet agent. The fact that a Communist spy, secretly placed in the upper reaches of the government intelligence network, should be able to influence British publishers in their choice of books may seem extra-ordinary six decades later, but this was wartime London, subsequently revealed as a hive of espionage whose consequences were felt in practically any government-run institution. Orwell himself had come across Guy Burgess, as had countless other people who at this point regarded him as no more than a rather rackety nuisance. Again Orwell's frustration seeped out in print. The 'As I Please' column of 7 July touched on the subtle network of unseen alliances that governed wartime censorship. Hardly anything was officially proscribed, Orwell suggested, and yet the 'advice' covertly tendered by officials, and the eagerness with which this advice was accepted, meant that nothing that was actually offensive to the governing class ever got into print. 'Circus dogs jump when the trainer cracks his whip,' Orwell concluded bitterly, 'but the really well-trained dog is the one that turns his somersault when there is no whip.' The manuscript was immediately sent to Faber, where Orwell imagined that Eliot would be on his side, even if – this was apparently Eliot's own warning – he might not be able to persuade his fellow-directors. And yet, as a letter of mid-July makes clear, Eliot himself was doubtful of the novel's merits. It was a distinguished piece of writing, he conceded, but he doubted 'that this is the right point of view from which to criticise the political situation at the present time'. The book's 'positive' point of view, 'which I take to be generally Trotskyite', Eliot found unconvincing. As the most intelligent animals on the farm, the pigs were clearly the best qualified to run it. In fact there could not have been an Animal Farm without them. What was needed, it might be argued, was 'not more communism but more public-spirited pigs'.

Four months had now passed since *Animal Farm*'s completion, but there was still no sign of anyone prepared to publish it. From Orwell's standpoint, the situation was becoming desperate. There were still irons in the fire with other mainstream publishers – at some point in the summer the manuscript was offered to William Collins, who turned it down not out of political squeamishness but on grounds of length: at 30,000 words the book was half the size of the average commercial novel. But Orwell had begun to explore less conventional routes. An approach was made to André Deutsch, still employed by Nicolson & Watson but itching to start up on his own. Deutsch declined, however, fearing that he would not be able to launch it with sufficient bombast. A scheme by which Orwell would publish it himself as a two-shilling pamphlet on money borrowed from David Astor (Astor was prepared to put up a £200 loan but doubtful of the plan's merits) and paper supplied by Paul Potts' tiny Whitman Press had reached the stage of Potts travelling to Bedford to negotiate with the printers. Potts, reading the manuscript for the first time on the train, found himself tempted to look under the seat 'to see if there was any more dynamite about'. Then, finally, a dialogue was opened with Warburg. On 18 July Orwell could tell Moore that he thought Warburg would publish it if he could see his way to getting the paper. Even then, though, the pamphlet idea lay in reserve – a course which, had he been compelled to take it, would have appealed to Orwell's historical sense. He remained a connoisseur of underground literature of this kind, providing regular surveys of con-temporary specimens to *Tribune* and bequeathing a sizeable collection to the British Museum on his death.

Beyond the immediate saga of *Animal Farm*, his life was stretched in half a dozen directions. Richard was still at Greystone, which required trips to the north-east. *Tribune* work and *Tribune* reviewers continued to eat into his evenings. On a basic level he and Eileen needed some-where to live that would be suitable for a baby. 'Life is pretty full up now,' he told Rayner Heppenstall, as if it had ever been anything less, excusing himself for his reluctance to fix up engagements out of town. Even his lunch hours were taken up with strenuous manual labour. In the early part of 1944 Orwell had completed the longstanding project of getting the majority of his books up from Wallington. No sooner had this been accomplished than the bomb fell on Mortimer Crescent. 'The place is no longer habitable,' Inez Holden wrote in her diary in early July, 'but he goes each day to rummage in the rubbish to recover as many books as possible and wheels them away in a wheelbarrow.' Meanwhile he was somehow finding the time to complete other substantial pieces of work. The 'English People' essay for Collins, for example, was finished by the early summer although, paper shortages being what they were, it would not be published until 1947. Essentially a watered-down version of *The Lion and the Unicorn*, it generalises shrewdly about such English characteristics as gentleness and class while betraying its less abrasive edge in areas such as the need for greater democracy in education. 'A completely uniform system of education is probably not desirable,' Orwell somewhat innocuously concludes. His thoughts on 'The future of the English people', too, verge on the simplistic. 'They must breed faster, work harder, and probably live more simply, think more deeply, get rid of their snobbishness and their anachronistic class distinctions, and pay more attention to the world and less to their own backyard.'

Throughout the summer of 1944 the fate of *Animal Farm* hung in the balance. In mid-August there were still worries about Warburg's paper supply. As negotiations continued Orwell finished the final essay that would go to make up *Critical Essays*, 'Raffles and Miss Blandish', a pointed comparison of the new breed of hard-boiled American detective fiction with E.W. Hornung's 'amateur cracksman'. Searching a little way beyond the area in which they had lived since their arrival in London over four years before, he and Eileen had also found somewhere to live. Number 27b Canonbury Square lay on the top floor of an Islington apartment block – not traditional terrain, but near to central London and not uncomfortably removed from friends such as Powell and Muggeridge. Acquaintances who had blanched at the privations of Wallington or the Mortimer Crescent basement were pleasantly surprised by Canonbury Square. As a district Islington was famously run down, and the block's entrance was 'very squalid', one friend remembered, 'but once you got up there it was a very nice flat', with a long sitting room uncluttered by the Orwells' collection of furniture. Eileen, who professed 'in some ways' to like it very much, volunteered that 'the outlook is charming, and we have a flat roof about three yards by two which seems full of possibilities'. It was also full of holes, although this was felt to be a minor inconvenience. Moving in took some time – it was not until early October that Orwell felt able to tell Moore that Canonbury Square was now his permanent address – and was further complicated by a two-week holiday that Orwell took at the start of September; no hard evidence remains, but this was probably his first visit to the Scottish island of Jura. But by mid-autumn the flat was sufficiently established as their new base to be used for entertaining friends. As ever the meal at which Orwell most liked to dispense hospitality was tea – the tea itself brewed up in an immense metal teapot that held nearly a gallon of liquid, with huge leaves floating on the surface. As in Kilburn, Orwell's 'practical' side was much in evidence, although proof of his dexterity was sometimes curiously lacking. Needing bookshelves for the library to be transported from Mortimer Crescent by way of the Strand, and in the face of severe wartime restriction, he applied to Michael Meyer, whose timber-merchant father produced several lengths of prime cherrywood. Invited to view the finished product, Meyer thought it 'awful beyond belief'. Orwell had whitewashed the wood and not put in enough supports, so that the shelves 'curved like a hammock'.

By now, *Animal Farm*'s future was finally secure. Warburg undertook to publish it in March the following year, paying an advance of £100 on future royalties with an option on future books ('quite satisfactory,' Orwell thought). In fact, such were the difficulties under which Warburg laboured that the novel would not see the light for nearly a year after the agreement was reached. High in his Islington eyrie – with its flights of echoing stone stairs, the block undoubtedly gave something to Victory Mansions in *Nineteen Eighty-Four* – Orwell settled down to a hard autumn's work. Again one is struck by the range of his interests, application, sheer indefatigability. The essay on 'Tobias Smollett: Scotland's Best Novelist', written for *Tribune* in the early part of September, is a good example of the kind of work Orwell was capable of throwing off with apparent casualness: a magazine essay, written under magazine essay conditions, probably in the course of a single morning, but conveying the point about Smollett and his place in the history of the novel with maximum attack. Simultaneously he was conducting a vigorous social life, lunching with Eliot, with whom he remained on good terms despite the *Animal Farm* débâcle, going with Michael Meyer to the Olivier/Richardson season at the New Theatre. Here, having lunched in Soho they sat through consecutive performances of *Henry IV* Parts One and Two, emerging in a state of near-exhaustion for dinner at the Hong Kong restaurant in Shaftesbury Avenue.

Meyer remembered the trip less for the opportunity to savour wartime Shakespeare than for blatant evidence of Orwell's ill health. Lunch finished late, requiring them to walk the 500 yards to the theatre at a 'rather fast' pace. Once he had taken his seat, Orwell's chest could be heard 'whistling' as he breathed for the next five minutes. The war, meanwhile, was clearly moving towards its final phase. Ever scrupulous where ancient predictions were concerned, Orwell spent part of a *Partisan Review* letter reflecting on the mistaken forecasts of the past few years, not so much out of a desire to correct them but from a wish to explain why they were wrong. The shift in political power he had envisaged had simply not taken place. Orwell feared that he had over-emphasised the anti-Fascist character of the war, exaggerated the degree of social change that was actually occurring and underrated the enormous strength of the forces of reaction. The latter were painfully evident in the world of literature. Reviewing *Four Quartets* for the *Manchester Evening News* early in October he returned to the vitiating effect of Eliot's Anglo-Catholicism. The Eliot of *Prufrock*, who frankly despaired of life, had shown a greater power and gaiety than the subdued pursuer of spiritual truth. The review appeared before Orwell and Eileen's meeting with Eliot; the poet would have been able to eat his lunch in full possession of Orwell's low opinion of his work. But this, it can be said, was characteristic of Orwell's view of friendship. He was not disinterested about his friends, could always be relied upon to promote their work or to dispense such patronage as lay in his gift – the reorganisation of *Tribune*'s literary pages, for example, led to Rayner Heppenstall being given his own regular slot. Equally, he continued to behave as if his estimate of a writer's work as set down on the page and his behaviour face to face were entirely separate things. Not everyone was able to approach this separation with the same equanimity.

By the middle of October, number 27b was more or less habitable, apart from the absence of carpets, and Orwell made the trip up to Newcastle to fetch Richard. Eileen had given up her job at the Ministry of Food and settled down to prepare for a regime of full-time childcare. Each in their own way was exalted by these new responsibilities. 'I'm no judge but I think he is a very nice child and quite forward for his age,' Orwell reported at the end of the month. Friends who re-encountered them in the autumn of 1944 noted how they had suddenly become a family. Lady Violet Powell remembered Orwell and Eileen turning up for dinner one night at the Powells' house in Chester Gate with Richard in a carry-cot. 'George is a good nursemaid,' Eileen explained. But George's mind was already bowling off along avenues whose end would not be reached for several more years.

To read Orwell's journalism and letters to friends from the fag-end of the war is immediately to become aware of the way in which the themes of *Nineteen Eighty-Four* were crowding in on his mind. Unquestionably the novel had already begun to take shape. He had admitted as much in a letter from earlier in the year to Gleb Struve, then teaching at the University of London's School of Slavonic and East European Studies. Struve had sent a copy of his *25 Years of Russian Literature*, which provided Orwell with his first introduction to Zamyatin's totalitarian dystopia *We* (1920–1). 'I am interested in that kind of book,' he wrote prophetically to Struve, 'and even keep making notes for one myself that may get written sooner or later.' The notes lay everywhere to hand, in his reviews and *Tribune* pieces. Reviewing Alfred Noyes' *The Edge of the Abyss* in the *Observer*, shortly after the letter to Struve, he returned to his longstanding belief that at the heart of totalitarianism lies displaced, or extinguished, religious sensibility. The real problem of the age was to renew the sense of absolute right and wrong when the belief on which it had once rested – the conviction of personal immortality – has been destroyed. He took up the theme again in an 'As I Please' column about Catholic doctrine. There was little doubt, he thought, that the cult of power worship was bound up with modern man's feeling that life here and now is the only life there is. Orwell did not want the belief in personal immortality to return, but he realised that the hole left by its absence was growing ever more conspicuous. Above all, there was a memory of the Blitz, confided to his *Tribune* readers in April 1944. Here Orwell, sheltering in the Café Royal, got talking to a young man selling copies of *Peace News*, who tried to convince him that whatever the oppression of a totalitarian government, one could be free 'inside'. The memory prompted this sketch of what, to him, seemed a quite unattainable mental liberty:

> Out in the street the loudspeakers bellow, the flags flutter from the rooftops, the police with their tommy guns prowl to and fro, the face of the leader, four feet high, glares from every hoarding; but up in the attics the secret enemies of the regime can record their thoughts in perfect freedom – that is the idea, more or less.

It was an idea that *Nineteen Eighty-Four* was, above all, determined to disprove.

What kind of future did Orwell envisage for himself and his family in the winter of 1944–5? The probable shape of the post-war world filled him with gloom. Attending a meeting of something called the 'League for European Freedom' in January 1945 – an 'all party' organisation which turned out to be dominated by anti-Soviet Conservatives – he saw only a covert defence of vested interests. He was all in favour of European freedom, he told his *Tribune* readers, but freedom needed to be preached elsewhere, notably in India. The Tehran conference, at which Churchill, Roosevelt and Stalin had effectively parcelled up the world into spheres of influence, seemed to him only a 'sordid bargain', which harboured the seeds of all kinds of future trouble. Personally, though, he seemed content. Now in his early forties, he was overworked and not in good health and yet London, after half a decade of war, was full of debilitated ghosts wrecked by years of upset and poor food. The Orwells were no worse off than many of their friends. Despite the unhappiness brought about by Orwell's relationship with Sally McEwan, they were united in their absorption in Richard. Orwell evinced a 'passionate' interest in the child, Eileen told Moore. Friends from this period in his life stress the 'cosiness' of the Orwells' domestic interior – the kettle dispensing tar-black tea, the Edwardian bill-of-fare. The intimacies of family life were something that Orwell craved. Already, though, there is a sense that the life he was leading in London, with its hectic round of professional and social engagements, always ending with the typewriter thumping on into the night, could not be indefinitely sustained. Anthony Powell noted how Orwell's immediate response to the fame that came his way after the publication of *Animal Farm* was to retreat from a world in which his marginal, outsider status could no longer be guaranteed. There was also a suspicion that he was spreading himself too thin, expending his energies on journalism when more serious tasks lay to hand. In one of the last letters that she wrote him, Eileen confided that she would like to see him stop living a 'literary' life and start writing again – a fine but revealing distinction. Such a switch of focus would be better for Richard, too, she thought, so there was no prospect of conflict. Orwell's mind was moving in the same way. The idea of the Scottish island, where he could devote himself to his novels while the real business of the world went on elsewhere, had been in his mind since the early 1940s. It is probable that he first visited Jura, the Hebridean outcrop that was to become his home, in the early autumn of 1944. None of this is conclusive proof of any long-term plans, here in war-torn Islington with eight months of the conflict still to run, but clearly there were schemes afoot involving a new life that he, Eileen and Richard could live together. It was a future that in one vital, tragic respect would never be realised.

He was still working extraordinarily hard. *Animal Farm*'s successor lay some way off – he returned a contract to Warburg unsigned, telling Moore that he didn't know when he would write another novel. For now, his spare hours were taken up with endless pieces of journalism. His regular three articles a week, quite apart from other work, made it impossible for him to take on anything else, he explained to his successor in the Indian Section, regretfully declining an invitation to broadcast on Housman. As ever he was susceptible to the entreaties of literary friends he thought needed encouraging, producing 'In Defence of P.G. Wodehouse' for Kay Dick's *The Windmill* (Wodehouse, interned by the Nazis at the beginning of the war, had been pilloried in the press for some supposedly defeatist radio broadcasts) and approaching the Royal Literary Fund in support of a grant for the eternally indigent Paul Potts. Mid-February 1945 brought an offer of the kind he had yearned for during the preceding stages of the war: to go to France as a war correspondent for the *Observer* and the *Manchester Evening News*. Arrangements were swiftly put in place. Eileen and Richard would stay at Greystone, looked after by the O'Shaughnessy nanny, while Orwell, initially based in Paris, would spend a couple of months reporting on conditions in liberated France and, he hoped, following the Allied trail eastwards in Germany. By the last week in February he was installed at the Hotel Scribe, a popular resort for literary men in transit – he met Ernest Hemingway, Harold Acton and made his first acquaintance with the young philosopher A.J. Ayer – and sending back dispatches on French public opinion and the political aims of the French Resistance. He dined with Wodehouse, who was grateful at this point for any support he could get, although subsequently more equivocal about Orwell's defence of him.

Frequent letters came from Eileen, whose position, despite the attentions of the O'Shaughnessy family nanny Joyce Pollard, was increasingly fraught. Now obviously unwell, she was obliged to go to London to complete the legal formalities surrounding Richard's adoption, including an appearance before a judge. This went off satis-factorily, only for her to fall ill. Medical examinations, organised by

Gwen O'Shaughnessy, revealed the cause of Eileen's ill health to be tumours on her uterus. She was advised to have an immediate hysterectomy. Orwell meanwhile had sent no news, she told Leonard Moore, being largely confined to a hotel full of war correspondents. An additional inconvenience came to light when Eileen called at Canonbury Square and discovered a pile of unforwarded mail supposed to have been sent on by Georges Kopp. In Paris Orwell was chafing at the restrictions of life in a single French city and trying to fix up a trip to Cologne. He intended to get back to England by the end of April, he told Sally McEwan ('Dear Sally'), in a letter sent in the second week of March, and was clearly missing his adopted son. 'I hear that he has 5 teeth and is beginning to move about a lot.' A letter to Roger Senhouse, Warburg's partner, provided final, scrupulous corrections to the proofs of *Animal Farm*. Napoleon should not be described as flinging himself on the floor when the windmill was blown up, he instructed. This was unfair to Stalin who, to do him justice, had remained in Moscow during the German advance.

In the light of what came after, the stream of letters that Eileen sent from Greystone in the last week of March make poignant reading: small things and large things mixed together; concern for those around her; unwillingness to make a fuss; deeply felt emotion. A letter of 21 March sets out the immediate problems of her health. Hearing of her being taken ill when she was in London, Orwell's *Tribune* colleagues had rallied round with offers of help, even to the extent of summoning him back from the continent. The offers were declined. What Eileen did want was Orwell's agreement that she should undergo expensive surgery and recuperation (the operation itself would cost 40 guineas). Ivor Brown at the *Observer*, to whom the question of getting in touch with Orwell was referred, suggested sending a message via Cable & Wireless, but in the end Eileen declined. The operation must go ahead as soon as possible. 'Obviously I can't just go on having a tumour or rather several rapidly growing tumours.' The second half of the letter strikes a plaintive note, in which solicitude for Orwell comes mingled with desperate awareness of her own needs and all kinds of inchoate plans for the future. There was a plan in existence to borrow Inez Holden's cottage in Hampshire, while mention of an estimate for 'repairing Barnhill' shows that at least some interest had been expressed in Jura. It was essential, Eileen thought, that Orwell should write a book again and that they should get out of London to a place where life, even on £200 a year, would be infinitely preferable. 'I don't think you understand what a nightmare the London life is to me,' she lamented. 'I know it is to you, but you often talk as though I *liked* it.' All these years, Eileen concluded piteously, 'I have felt as if I were in a mild kind of concentration camp'.

Although, or perhaps because, it was written in exceptional circumstances, in a state of high emotion, this sheds penetrating rays of light on Orwell's relationship with Eileen: hints of old arguments (a reference to Orwell's 'disapproving' of her operation, which suggests that it had surfaced before), exasperation combining with deep regard. Eileen did not resent her husband's occasional aloofness or his absence at a time of personal crisis. She merely wanted a better life for them both. She was convinced of his innate dependability. 'George, however, is due home in the latter half of this month,' she told another correspondent, '& he is a curiously reliable man.' Other attempts to contact him in Cologne failed. There were further letters, to Moore and to her friend Lettice Cooper, suggesting that the surgery would be 'a very good thing'. She had been ill for a long time: now there was a prospect of relief. With the ironical affection that characterised her relationship with Orwell, she could even joke about the 'mercy' of his foreign trip. 'George visiting the sick is a sight sadder than any disease-ridden wretch in the world.' The operation, to be carried out at the Fernwood House Hospital, Newcastle, was set for 29 March. Shortly beforehand Eileen began a letter to her husband, to be completed after it was over, she explained, and got off quickly. It was a nice room, she told him, on the ground floor with a view of the garden: not much in it except daffodils and, she thought, arabis, but a nice little lawn. The anaesthetic took effect and she was borne away into the operating theatre. Shortly afterwards, six months short of her fortieth birthday, she was dead.

Orwell had not known about the impending operation until two days before it took place. By the time of Eileen's death he was back in Paris, having filed a dispatch on the devastation wreaked on Cologne by the Allied bombing, fallen ill and been admitted to a local hospital. Still unwell – whether suffering from bronchitis, pneumonia or some kind of haemorrhage – he received the bolt from the blue that was Gwen O'Shaughnessy's cable. He flew back to London immediately, calling on Inez Holden – on whose doorstep he materialised as a gaunt, grief-ravaged spectre – before heading north. One of the most pervasive myths attached to Orwell's relationship with Eileen is the idea that he was unmoved, or rather rendered stoical to the point of indifference, by her death. The letters written from Greystone early in April are those of a shocked and bitterly unhappy man, desolate above all that the happiness Eileen had looked forward to – the house in the country and care of Richard – had been denied her. Paul Potts, who saw him either immediately before or after the funeral, remembered his deep distress, eventually prompting the confidence that 'the last time he saw her he wanted to tell her that he loved her much more now since they'd had Richard, and he didn't tell her, and he regretted it immensely'. He didn't want to bore him with his private affairs, he told one correspondent, 'but my wife has died very suddenly and in particularly distressing circumstances, and it has upset me so much that I cannot settle to anything for the time being'. Once Eileen's funeral had taken place – she lies in St Andrew's and Jesmond Cemetery, Newcastle upon Tyne – and arrangements had been concluded for Richard's care (he would spend the next couple of months with the Kopps, who lived only a step away from the Canonbury Square flat) he decided that the only way he could come to terms with the loss was to resume his job in Occupied Europe.

Back in London he called in at Secker & Warburg, tried and failed to meet up with Anthony Powell and then returned to Paris, where he remained until the end of May. Aunt Nellie, writing to Marjorie Dakin, was impressed by what to a contemporary observer may look like remorselessness. 'How wonderful he is – there is his article in the Observer today and I know he had to rush over for Eileen's funeral & then arrange a temporary haven for little R.' If there was solace, it would come in work. Orwell's early *Observer* pieces had been fairly anonymous pieces of reportage. Now, following the Allied advance east in the second half of April he produced an incongruous account of the aftermath of the US 12th Armored Division's passage through a village to the west of Nuremberg: shell craters all around, houses burning, prisoners being brought in, but the villagers almost entirely uncon-cerned. The war was nearly at an end, the devastation in Germany far worse, Orwell thought, than people in England grasped. His foreign trip had been 'quite interesting', he told Lydia Jackson in the course of a letter about the re-letting of the Wallington cottage, which she was currently occupying with her friend Patricia Donoghue. David Astor's later verdict was that the tour was 'ill-conceived': Orwell had wanted to inspect a country under the conditions of dictatorship, but by the time he arrived there the dictatorship had vanished. The best piece of writing about his experiences appeared not in the *Observer* but in *Tribune*, six months later. 'Revenge is Sour' records his presence in a former concentration camp watching a Jewish man confront an SS guard, and standing over the corpse of a German soldier outside Stuttgart with a Belgian journalist whose belligerence was extinguished by the sight of *'ce pauvre mort'*. In the third week of May he drove through the area to the south of Salzburg recording the final round-up of the German army: an endless succession of fields full of men sunbathing or laundering their clothes in streams, tens of thousands of neatly parked vehicles and hundreds of piled corpses. By 24 May he was back in London.

Orwell's immediate priority was to find someone to look after Richard. His first thought on Eileen's death had been to take Richard to live somewhere in the country. Back in the Islington flat, and interested in the forthcoming general election, he realised that he had too much to keep him in London and began the search for a resident nurse-cum-housekeeper. Work reached out from all sides. By mid-June he could tell Warburg that he had written the first pages of a new novel. There was a new highbrow magazine, *Polemic: A Magazine of Philosophy, Psychology and Aesthetics*, edited by Humphrey Slater, for whom he contracted to write four articles ('Notes on Nationalism', written while he was still in Germany, would appear in the October issue). For the *Observer* he trailed through various London constituencies in an attempt to grasp the public mood. This was something of a let-down. In his article of 24 June he reported that he had not yet heard a spontaneous remark or, for that matter, seen a person stop to look at an election poster, but he remained convinced, despite this inertia, that the prevailing attitude was 'serious and democratic'. Another *Observer* piece a week later noted presciently that Labour was gaining ground and that any upsurge in Liberal support would split the Tory rather than the Labour vote, while a review of a Catholic work on democracy and social justice made a point that would by now have been familiar to anyone who had followed the progress of Orwell's thought during the second half of the war. Material progress, necessary if the average human being was to be anything better than a drudge, had been won at a fearful cost. Somehow, in the absence of religious belief, the religious attitude to life must be restored.

His domestic life was beginning to renew itself. By the end of June he had found a housekeeper-nurse for the burgeoning (he now weighed 25 pounds) Richard: a young woman named Susan Watson, separated from her Cambridge don husband and with a small daughter of her own, who was prepared to look after the child for £5 a week plus her board. In early July the boy was brought back from Greenwich, where he had been staying with Gwen O'Shaughnessy. *Animal Farm* was set to appear at the end of August. The saga of its path to publication had dragged on for so long that Orwell might have feared that some of the impact, at least on his friends, would have been lost. He need not have worried. Like Michael Meyer, they were overwhelmed by it. There were other less obvious compliments, equally well received. Some time around publication the book was read by the Powells' seven-year-old nephew Ferdie Mount, who commented appreciatively that there were 'no difficult words in it'. Orwell was delighted.

The case against

A critic – let us call him Comrade X, writing a book entitled something along the lines of 'Twentieth Century English Novelists: A Marxist Guide' – might put it like this:

As a novelist, Orwell scarcely begins to exist. His early books – from *Burmese Days*, say, to *Coming up for Air* – are derivative (Maugham, Gissing, Wells) and something worse than this: projections of his own self-pity, in which the writer's life is used, quite unmediated, for the purposes of art. The results are not only clumsily executed but lack all artistic conviction. *A Clergyman's Daughter*, for example, is simply three or four stretches of personal experience – the small-town Suffolk life, the tramping adventures, the private school teaching – thrown disconnectedly together in an unconvincing story about a woman who loses her religious faith. As for the later work, *Animal Farm* is an ingenious fable, but Swift had been there before. And half a century after its publication, *Nineteen Eighty-Four* is merely an exercise in emotional vulgarity, all flaring surfaces and bogus special effects, its bleakness coexisting with an altogether ghastly brand of guilt-ridden upper-bourgeois sentimentalising of the working class. 'If there is hope, it lies in the proles,' Winston decides. As any student of social determinism can tell you, the only reliable agent of societal change is the radical middle classes.

   As an essayist and polemicist, Orwell achieves his effects through a series of confidence tricks. One need only examine his diaries alongside the 'official' versions of the events they describe to appreciate the liberties he was prepared to take with observable fact. Exaggeration, selectiveness, outright misrepresentation: Orwell is guilty of them all. The opening chapter of *The Road to Wigan Pier* is a pattern example of how his careful use of pejorative language is capable of hoodwinking the reader. 'Such, Such Were the Joys' is worse than this: thirty years of brooding and reality-erasure put to work to demonise – what? A snobbish pre-school master's wife who made the mistake of offending a hyper-sensitive twelve-year-old boy! There were better targets than Mr and Mrs Wilkes, better targets than the Brookers in their dismal lodging house where the tablecloth was never changed, but no, they had offended Orwell's gargantuan sense of personal myth – a kind of eternal *nemo me impune lacessit* – and all slights were to be repaid with compound interest.

As a political thinker, Orwell is hopelessly naïve. His hastily assembled view of the left-wing movements of the 1930s again mixes that absurd sentimentality about every aspect of working-class life with huge amounts of personal prejudice. In Spain he persisted in regarding the Trotskyist splinter group whose colours he fought under as a key player in proceedings, whereas its role was merely incidental. Back in England he completely misread the national mood both in the run-up to the war (when he was seriously advocating some kind of underground resistance movement) and in the post-Dunkirk era when he imagined the country to be gripped by proto-revolutionary fervour. His views on the ethical questions that war produced – notably the idea of non-resistance – are extremely reductive. How could someone who had pacifist friends, and was made wretched by the thought that he might have killed a Fascist soldier with a hand grenade, seriously equate non-violence with 'objective pro-Fascism'? Or affect such hard-headed nonchalance about the saturation bombing of German cities? Above all, perhaps, Orwell remains permanently detached from the practical realities of politics, always believing that emotional conviction alone will magically get things done. His post-1945 manifesto for what the Attlee administration should be seen to be doing if it meant business is rather like one of Tony Benn's 1980s wish-lists: slogans parroted by people who have no idea of the effort involved in putting a catch-phrase into practice.

As a human being Orwell was, well, a preliminary list might read: secretive, incompetent, womanising, offhand, anti-Semitic and homophobic. The late-period photographs of Orwell bending fondly over his lathe are misleading: the real-life Orwell was highly impractical – a botcher of shelves, a misreader of tide-tables, a vague, hopeless presence, fluttering diffidently about on the edge of things. Orwell's dealings with the opposite sex, on the other hand, form a high old catalogue of duplicitousness, evasiveness, treachery and the eternal self-pity. Even coming across a childhood sweetheart nearly thirty years later he couldn't resist suggesting that she had 'abandoned' him to Burma, whereas in reality Orwell had abandoned himself. Naturally, none of these failings invalidates anything that Orwell wrote – as he himself remarked, the second-best bed in Shakespeare's will left to the author's wife, does not invalidate *Hamlet* – and yet there is a way in which the stage-management Orwell lavishes on his life is subtly transferred to his art. Remembering the occasion on which he found him in his son's bedroom ostentatiously standing to one side while the child played with a nine-inch Bowie knife, Anthony Powell decided the scene was 'much too big to be ignored'. Orwell had set up the scene in order to be detected, and to appear to advantage in it. This kind of manipulation is a feature of his work. Reading 'A Hanging' the reader recalls only the appalled observer, not the servant of British Imperialism who, in his attendance at the Burmese jail, was merely doing his job, and continued to do it for a good four and a half years. The factor that made Orwell such a good critic of authoritarian regimes was his own pronounced authoritarian streak. It took one to know one.

And then there is the question of Orwell's reputation, burnished up and inflated out of all proportion by people he would probably have regarded with infinite disdain. What would we think of *Nineteen Eighty-Four* if a gaggle of transatlantic spook-hunters and CIA opinion-formers – that epic 'free world' conspiracy that takes in everyone from Senator McCarthy to the brave boys at *Encounter* – hadn't decided that it was *the* political text of the Cold War decades? Orwell dominates the NATO landscape because a gang of right-wing politicians and their media accomplices decided that he should do. This conspiracy, queerly, was responsible for a wide-ranging *literary* fraud. Once established, his significance naturally had to be pushed back in time, with the result that Orwell's four third-rate novels now crowd out the real heroes of the 1930s. This, though hardly anyone now remembers, was the age of Walter Greenwood, Jack Hilton, Lewis Grassic Gibbon and the first stirrings of a genuine working-class literary movement. But the figure who survived, who walked through into the textbooks and the reading lists, was the tall ex-public school boy who, try as he might, could never shake off his origins or his prejudices, who even below stairs in a Paris hotel could imagine that one of the waiters resembled an Eton boy, and whose misleading perceptions of an entire political and literary era are now our own.

Part Five
1945–1950

16

The Last Man in Europe

To write in plain, vigorous language one has to think fearlessly,
and if one thinks fearlessly one cannot be politically orthodox. –
'The Prevention of Literature', January 1946

It is only that I just feel desperately alone sometimes. I have
hundreds of friends, but no woman who takes an interest in me. –
Letter to Anne Popham, 15 March 1946

The majority of English writers picking up the pieces of their professional careers in the aftermath of six years' war service were
conscious of sharply diminished prospects. Walking into his agent's
office after returning from an intelligence posting in the Middle East,
Alec Waugh was told flatly that a new echelon of younger writers had
come along and that he would have to be 'regraded'. Anthony Powell
took five years to complete the novel that would begin his great post-
war sequence *A Dance to the Music of Time*. Professionally the talk was
of paper shortages and government restrictions. A book could take two
years to emerge from the laggardly post-war production processes.
Occasionally it would never emerge at all. In contrast, Orwell's professional horizons had never looked better. By his previous standards,
Animal Farm was a spectacular success: 4,500 copies sold in the six
weeks following publication, another 10,000 ordered for October.
Within eight months of publication nine translations were in progress
across Europe and beyond. In America, where it appeared at the end of
August, strong early sales were followed by a Book of the Month Club
selection the following spring, guaranteeing a circulation of several
hundred thousand.

To a world waking up to the political arrangements of the post-war
age, Orwell's 100-page fable about a gang of animals who take over
their farm and are then swindled back into slavery seemed a work of

extraordinary resonance. Fan letters poured in from acquaintances such as E.M. Forster and Evelyn Waugh. The Queen was known to have read a copy. Senior literary figures who had regarded him as not much more than a maverick left-wing journalist now made personal enquiries. 'Who is he? What is he like?' the veteran man of letters Logan Pearsall Smith demanded of his former secretary Cyril Connolly in a telephone conversation on what turned out to be the day before his death. Anxious to get off the phone, Connolly promised that he would tell him on the following day, when they were due to meet at tea. 'No. Tell me now,' Pearsall Smith urged. Again Connolly demurred. Pearsall Smith's final words to him – among the last words that he spoke – were that Orwell 'beat the lot of you'.

Characteristically, Orwell's own reaction to *Animal Farm*'s success was an odd mixture of satisfaction and unease: concern that it should be read by the right audience mingled with an anxiety over some of the uses to which it might be put. Money from translation rights was of little concern to him, particularly if the translators were from Slav countries about to recede from view behind the Iron Curtain. He was more concerned that the novel should simply exist in those areas, he told Moore. But he kept a fond eye on its commercial prospects, reporting – again to Moore – a meeting with representatives of Metro-Goldwyn-Meyer and suggesting that it would make a good Disney cartoon (an animated version did appear some years after his death). Professionally and materially – his lifetime earnings from the novel amounted to something over £12,000 – life would never be the same again, and yet Orwell was nervous of the wider political response, fearing – correctly, as it turned out – that a left-wing critique of Stalinism might be misrepresented by the post-war Right as an attack on Socialism *per se*. A.J. Ayer remembered him six months before at the Hotel Scribe worrying that the book might play into the hands of English Conservatives. Mindful of the danger of being adopted as a talisman of the Right he lost no opportunity over the next six months to state his political position. The Duchess of Atholl, a Unionist MP who had gained some notoriety in the 1930s by opposing Franco, soliciting support for her League of European Freedom, was politely rebuffed. 'I belong to the Left and must work within it,' he told the Duchess, 'much as I hate Russian totalitarianism and its poisonous influence in this country.'

The political situation, both at home and abroad, needed constant vigilance. Stepping through the litter of Fleet Street on the day in

August 1945 that the Japanese surrender was announced ('It annoyed me rather. In England you can't get paper to print books on, but apparently there is always plenty of it for this kind of thing') Orwell's immediate concern was to monitor the effectiveness of Attlee's newly elected Labour government. He approved of the Labour landslide and the eviction of Winston Churchill – that the British electorate could throw out a prime minister who had enjoyed almost dictatorial powers showed that the country had gained something by not losing the war, he thought – but the cautious gradualism that typified Labour's attitude to reform awakened the gravest suspicions of compromise and sell-out. As Orwell's parliamentary colleagues on *Tribune* could have told him, the wholesale reform of the country's institutions that he envisaged from a Labour government that 'meant business' was unlikely to happen, and certainly not at the pace he desired. Major Freeman's moving of the address in reply to the King's Speech at the opening of the first post-war parliament struck an appropriately martial note ('Today may rightly be regarded as D-Day in the battle for the New Britain') but as one post-war historian remarked, no one appeared to think that it was seriously meant. To add to this is the sense that whatever might have been embarked upon by governments in the post-war years would never be enough to satisfy Orwell. The ghouls he had derided in the wartime visit to watch Cripps in action continued to gibber.

Orwell's interest in the political arrangements of the immediate post-war era seems much more muted than his absorption in the manoeuvring in the old Churchill-led coalition. He had no great opinion of Attlee. His political energies, after 1945, were mostly directed at specific causes and individual cases. Anthony Powell has a characteristic glimpse of him from this time going off to address protest meetings ('. . . probably a blackguard but it was unjust to lock him up . . .') in a spirit that mixed dutifulness with down-to-earth scepticism. What was the meeting like? Powell would ask afterwards, to be told that 'the usual people' had turned up. 'There must be about two hundred of them altogether. They go round to everything of this sort. About forty or fifty turned up tonight, which is quite good.' Orwell's letters from the winter of 1945–6 are full of references to the Freedom Defence Committee, on to which he had been inducted in the role of vice-chairman by George Woodcock. Originally founded in 1944 as the Freedom Press Defence Committee to fight legal action against the editor of the anarchist Freedom Press, the FDC took a particular interest in the cases of political prisoners held under the wartime legislation. In the same stretch of time he was writing to Michael Foot, now Labour MP for Devonport, to see if he could obtain permission for his friend Karl Schnetzler to visit Germany, signing a Revolutionary Communist Party round-robin about the Nuremberg trials and writing a *Tribune* article in defence of pacifist newspaper-sellers had up for obstruction in Hyde Park. Plans for a pro-democratic European ginger group, fronted by himself and Koestler, reached the stage of putting out feelers to similarly constituted American groups. Meeting Francis A. Henson of the International Rescue and Relief Committee in March 1946, Orwell reported that its anti-Stalinist agenda was 'along much the same lines as our own'.

At the heart of this passionate attempt to come to terms with a new world order and to deal with some of the human casualties left in its wake is a marked paradox. Part of Orwell, clearly, was fighting a one-man battle against the forces of post-war darkness. Tosco Fyvel, who took over from him as literary editor of *Tribune* in the autumn of 1945, remembered his friend calling in at the office 'looking thinner and more raggedly dressed' and embarking, even as he entered Fyvel's room, on some statement about the political situation. As Fyvel noted, this was his way of making human contact. The aftermath of Nagasaki and Hiroshima produced a *Tribune* essay on 'You and the Atom Bomb', noting presciently that nuclear warheads had the capacity to prevent large-scale warfare while preserving indefinitely 'peace that is no peace'. Another part of him, though, was planning his retreat. He spent two weeks on Jura in September, after which the plan to remove himself to the Inner Hebrides became something sharp, hard and tangible. Although it went back to the early 1940s, the vision of the remote island fastness was unwittingly sustained by David Astor, Orwell's patron at the *Observer,* whose family owned land in the area. By his own admission, Astor took some time to appreciate the seriousness of Orwell's interest in abandoning literary London for a remote eyrie where he could write and ponder undisturbed. As he discovered, having recommended Jura on account of its natural beauty and character, to establish his friend on the island needed careful reconnoitring. On the one hand, tenancies were difficult to come by. On the other, Orwell himself needed tactful management: 'he wasn't someone you could offer a present'. Investigation by Astor produced a family named McKinnon who, after some pressing, offered to rent Orwell a room. Further research turned up a farm on the northern part of the island, owned by an Old Etonian named Robin Fletcher and his wife Margaret. Barnhill was a remote spot, seven miles from the Fletchers' house at the hamlet of Ardlussa and, owing to the lack of wartime inhabitants, fallen into disrepair. But with four bedrooms and plenty of space downstairs it was a decent size. Robin Fletcher met Orwell in London and explained some of the disadvantages, but these were waved away. Orwell spent the autumn of 1945 planning his departure.

Why was he so intent on moving himself several hundred miles to the north-west, beyond the reach of telephones, literary editors and, above all, his friends? Most of the people who knew Orwell at this time – and the mid-1940s was a period when observers began to take note of him, write him up in their diaries and speculate about his habits – diagnosed a short-term response to the exhaustion of six years' hard work, anxiety and bereavement. David Astor noted how 'frightfully tired' he seemed at the war's end. Emaciated and frail-looking, he was clearly in poor health, although as Astor notes 'he didn't talk about it at all'. Yet the retreat to Jura seems symbolic of something deeper. Orwell, one friend suspected, 'could thrive only in comparative adversity' (Richard Rees' line about the 'fugitive from the camp of victory' makes the same point metaphorically). There was also a pressing, practical need to get away from the distractions of London literary journalism to an environment where sustained writing could be done. The volume of literary work that Orwell produced in the winter of 1945–6 was startling, even by his exacting standards. In addition to his *Tribune* articles, he was still writing regularly for the *Manchester Evening News*. Towards the end of the year he compiled a series of chatty 'domestic' essays for the London *Evening Standard* on such topics as nice cups of tea and pubs. He was still producing his three-monthly letter for *Partisan Review*, as well as substantial pieces for *Horizon*, *Polemic* and the American journal *Commentary*. Undoubtedly there was something calculated in Orwell's eagerness to accept the mass of commissions that came his way in the wake of *Animal Farm*'s success – in the year following Eileen's death he produced around 130 pieces of literary journalism, in other words an article every two to three days – as a means of cutting himself off from sides of his emotional life that he preferred to keep at one remove. At the same time he was busy fashioning the domestic routine that could enable an output of this kind to be maintained.

By the autumn of 1945 the life of the Islington flat, which now contained himself, Susan Watson and Richard (Susan's daughter was away at school, though she later came to stay on Jura), was beginning to take coherent shape. In her late twenties, prepared to regard Orwell as a father figure, Susan Watson took to her new employer, noting his gentleness towards his adopted son, his transparent loneliness, and his tactfulness over her disability (a sufferer in childhood from cerebral palsy, Susan walked with a limp). She was reassured, too, by the tone of her job interview. Could she cook? Orwell wondered. Not very much, she suggested. Never mind, he gamely deposed, they could live off fish and chips. The impression Susan picked up during her early days at Canonbury Square confirmed this good opinion – a kindly man, clearly in bad health, heedless of his personal appearance (she remembered his cheap haircuts, which simply involved a razor applied to the back of his neck). He was good with Richard, if somewhat baffled by the processes of child development. Geoffrey Gorer, by now doing anthropological work amongst primates, was summoned to see how the fifteen-month boy compared to his chimpanzees. In a somewhat avuncular manner Orwell reciprocated the pleasure Susan took in his company. 'I have a *dear* little housekeeper,' he wrote in a letter to a friend, left absent-mindedly on the typewriter for Susan to read when she cleaned his study. The routines instilled were those of a bachelor from a vanished age: work; lunch out; more work. The Islington ménage brought out Orwell's homely, Edwardian side: high teas of sandwiches and cake, Orwell smoking endless cigarettes as he infused tea that had the consistency of treacle. After tea he would bathe Richard and put him to bed before retiring to the study for a final session that could go on into the small hours. Absorbed in his work but relaxed in the security of his new domestic environment, he could unbutton himself in Susan's company. On one occasion, seeking to extend the lifespan of Orwell's exiguous wartime wardrobe, she tried to dye his Home Guard beret. Unfortunately the hat shrank beyond utility. Presented with it, Orwell balanced it on his head, plucked an antique Burmese sword from a display bracket on the wall and executed what Susan described as 'a kind of waltz'. From Susan's point of view there was a single drawback to the job. She and Avril – the latter ten years older, childless, but with emphatic notions about infant discipline – did not get on.

Some idea of the interiors of Canonbury Square and the life that went on within it can be gleaned from a series of photographs that Vernon Richards took there in the early spring of 1946. Pictured examining one of the Burmese swords, working at lathe or typewriter, sitting before a varnished scrap-screen or dealing with Richard, Orwell has an intimacy not always seen in the handful of photographs of him that survive. To register the countless testimonies to Orwell's aloofness and self-absorption from this time is to ignore the depth and variety of his friendships: staring at the windows of the Islington newsagents with Paul Potts (at one point they came upon an advertisement offering 'Rooms to let – all nationalities welcome'. 'That's a real poem for you,' Orwell exclaimed); jumping up from a tête-à-tête with a woman friend with a cry of 'Let's ring up Tony Powell'. The Powells, then living in Chester Gate, were also able to help Orwell professionally, providing – at a time when secretarial help was in short supply – the figure of Mrs Miranda Christen, whom Anthony Powell knew from his Duckworth days in the 1930s. Among other exploits, Mrs Christen had married a German and spent the war in Sumatra, unmolested by the Japanese occupiers.

And yet for all the warmth of Susan Watson's memories, there is also a sense of something ramshackle and knocked out of kilter about these post-war Islington days, the thought of people doing their best in deeply unpromising circumstances. Tosco and Mary Fyvel, visiting Canonbury Square to renew a friendship that had lapsed during the latter part of the war, were shocked by the atmosphere of 'utter cheerlessness'. A solitary coal fire burned in the sitting room; otherwise the flat was unheated. There were gaps in the bottoms of the doors – surroundings, Fyvel thought, of strange and almost deliberate discomfort. Orwell's treatment of Richard seemed to combine lavish affection with comical cack-handedness. He asked Mary Fyvel if she would like to watch Richard have his bath. Mary suggested that it would be a good idea to close the bathroom window, which was admitting freezing January air. Orwell agreed enthusiastically. The bath over, he picked up Richard, draped him – undried – in a flimsy towel and carried him off along the icy passage to the sitting room. Again, advice on the correct procedure was gratefully received. Despite these oversights, Richard seemed a particularly healthy child. Orwell accepted compliments on his upbringing with suitable gravity. 'Yes. You see I've always been good with animals.' But there was no getting away from the pervasive sense of bleakness, the Fyvels thought. Susan had made attempts to cheer the place up, buying a green hessian cover for Orwell's bed and hanging up prints, but the overall effect was still dispiriting. Orwell's small work-room seemed 'quite emphatically bleak', crammed with table and typewriter, and a filing cabinet filled with Communist pamphlets. Such traces of his personality as could be found in the flat consisted of cardboard boxes, one full of fishing flies, the other of comic postcards. There was no wine or drink. It was also a place of ghosts. The bedroom contained wardrobes full of Eileen's clothes (Susan was told she could take what she liked). Her portrait sat on the nursery mantelpiece. It had not been an ideal marriage, Orwell explained, and he didn't believe he had treated her very well at times. Whatever the extent of his grief and the measure of his self-recrimination, Eileen – visibly and invisibly – dominated the flat.

All this sets in context, if not by any means explaining, the emotional confusion under which Orwell laboured at this time. His habitual ingenuousness with the opposite sex now heightened by the trauma of unexpected widowerhood, he spent the winter of 1945–6 making proposals of marriage to a series of younger women, some of whom he barely knew, none of whom found him in the least attractive and all of whom spent their time fending off his advances. One of these – the chronology is confused, in fact the relationships appear to have proceeded simultaneously – was Celia Paget, the twin sister of Arthur Koestler's wife Mamaine, whom Orwell knew additionally through her work as an editorial assistant on *Polemic*. Celia was impressed by Orwell's personality ('this terrific quality which one just spotted') while not wanting to have anything to do with him romantically. Orwell was unexpectedly direct in his approach. He would like her to marry him, he explained, but if not perhaps they could have an affair? Celia found herself in a quandary. To embark on an affair, she reasoned, implied a deep level of emotional commitment, and if one were to become deeply emotionally involved with someone, then why not marry them anyway? The situation was not helped by Koestler, who was strongly in favour of Orwell's suit and suggested that his sister-in-law might be able to 'pep him up a bit'. In the end she wrote an equivocal reply and the two remained friends until the end of Orwell's life. Celia Paget was at least someone whom Orwell knew in the course of his personal and professional life. His acquaintance with Anne Popham, on the other hand, was limited to their occupying flats in the same block and meeting casually at supper at V.S. Pritchett's. Returning to London for a few days' leave from her job with the Control Commission in Occupied Germany in the early spring of 1946, Miss Popham got into conversation with her neighbour on the stairs. Shortly afterwards there arrived a brisk, businesslike letter ('Dear Miss Popham') inviting her to tea. The tea having been drunk, Orwell drew her to one side and said something along the lines of 'Do you think you could take care of me?'

Alarmed at this full-frontal assault, she protested that they didn't know each other and that, given the demands of her job in Germany, their slight acquaintance had little chance of developing into something stronger. An exchange of letters followed in which Orwell stressed the advantages that might accrue from being a literary man's widow. Miss Popham recalled that she 'never felt at ease with him'.

By far the most important of these proposals, in the light of what came later, was to the girl that Orwell had known slightly since the early years of the war. Sonia Brownell was now in her late twenties. Like Orwell's, her background was Anglo-Indian. It was also traumatic. After burying one rackety husband and leaving a second, her mother was forced to return to the old country and open a boarding-house in South Kensington. At the age of six Sonia was dispatched to the Convent of the Sacred Heart at Roehampton. She hated the nuns so much that in later life she took to spitting in the street when one passed. 'I'm so bored I wish I'd been birth-controlled so as not to exist,' she once remarked in the hearing of a horrified teacher. At the same time an exacting Convent education seems to have invested her with the gargantuan sense of 'conscience' that characterises her later life. There was also a terrifying incident in her teens when her three companions on a Swiss boating trip drowned, Sonia only surviving by pushing away a boy whose struggles threatened to drag her under. According to her brother Michael, who as a psychiatrist took a professional view of his sister, this remained the dominant memory of her life. Thirty-six years later, for example, reviewing a book of Alberto Moravia's short stories, she produced this startling image of the aimless, stultified lives lived out by Moravia's cast:

> But how well they describe it! Often with the force of the trapped who have no alternative but to become traps themselves, like drowning people who struggle against their rescuers: and, as drowning people are said to do, they see everything leading to their predicament with absolute clarity. But what help is that to them?

Bright, beautiful and – one gathers – irrevocably damaged by her formative years, the late-teenage Sonia escaped from a secretarial job to pre-war Fitzrovia, was taken up by the painterly bohemians who hung around the Euston Road art school (two of her early boyfriends were the artists Victor Pasmore and William Coldstream) and, at least in terms of her reputation, never looked back. By 1940, still only twenty-one, she was one of Connolly's glamorous *Horizon* sorority (other assistants included Lys Lubbock and Janetta Woolley), returning after war work to the post of editorial secretary and, ultimately, to virtual control of the magazine while Connolly idled elsewhere. Connolly, for whom she had a profound intellectual respect, may have formed her opinions but as her biographer Hilary Spurling shows it was Peter Watson, *Horizon*'s wealthy homosexual proprietor, on whom she lavished her real affection. To mark this intensely serious and well-meaning bearer of slippers to the feet of great, or even mildly interesting, men down as a kind of high-class literary groupie would be a mistake. Friends who came across her in her early 1940s Euston Road–*Horizon* stage stress her sense of duty, her capability, shrewdness at dealing with Connolly's contributors, even if, as one of her fellow-assistants conceded, this encouraged her tendency to bossiness. Even in her early twenties the almost Manichaean separation of Sonia's character was sharply in evidence, an anxiety to please frequently cancelled out – often in the space of a few moments – by grievous displays of sulks or bad manners: 'intriguing, delightful, intelligent, quick' on the one hand, 'bitchy, fearfully unpleasant and rude' on the other. Many years later Anthony Powell put elements of her into Ada Leintwardine, secretary to the ancient, *affairé* don Sillery in *Books Do Furnish a Room*: brisk, capable, informed, wanting to help. Highly attractive to men – Julian Maclaren-Ross was obsessed with her for years – she was also famous for holding them at arm's length, embarking on physical relationships on the instant and then abandoning them in equal haste out of boredom, indifference or disgust.

Orwell had met Sonia in the early days of the war: as Celia Paget put it, she 'couldn't not have come across him' through the *Horizon* connection. Sonia herself remembered their first meeting as taking place at one of Connolly's dinner parties. Her initial impression had been far from positive: Orwell had remarked that one should never write anything the working classes don't understand, or use adjectives; there was also a complaint about 'foreign stuff in the food'. Their formal reintroduction seems to have come around the end of 1945 when, in her capacity as his editorial secretary, Connolly brought her round to Canonbury Square for a drink. In fact there was no drink and Susan Watson had to go out for a bottle of sherry. There may have been an earlier re-encounter at one of Connolly's parties: a friend of Orwell's remembers introducing her to him at a *Horizon* dinner because he 'needed looking after'. While the details of what at this stage was a fragmentary relationship are difficult to piece together, her sense of duty was awakened by the plight of the widowed man and his child. Sonia volunteered to baby-sit on Susan's days off, which required a considerable amount of will-power ('Oh the smell of cabbage and unwashed nappies'), and also was a frequent visitor to the flat: on one of her own visits Anne Popham discovered her talking to Orwell about Mallarmé and apparently very much at home. There was certainly a brief affair, again dutifully conducted on Sonia's side (she confessed to Lucian Freud that she was 'appalled' when Orwell began making advances) which fizzled out after the inevitable proposal. Like Celia, Anne Popham and possibly one or two other young women met at parties around this time, Sonia – sought after, absorbed by her work with Connolly and Watson – did not particularly wish to be married. And she particularly did not wish to be married to Orwell.

These romantic misadventures, conducted almost simultaneously in the winter of 1945–6, are not easy to explain. Undoubtedly Orwell was keen to, or was compelled to, dramatise certain aspects of his life, to create roles for himself which other people could admire and, as the roles broadened out into dramatic tableaux, occasionally participate in themselves. In his relations with Celia Paget, Anne Popham and Sonia Brownell he seems to have figured as the dispossessed solitary, the lonely man needing a woman's love to turn him round. But there were other roles. Visiting the Powells' house in the following year, Orwell was left upstairs in the nursery with their infant son John. When Powell came back to the room after fetching a book they wanted to consult, Orwell was staring intently at a picture on the farther wall. Powell, noting that John was stirring, went over to the cot to straighten the coverlet. His hand touched a hard object. This turned out to be an enormous clasp-knife. Powell having expressed surprise, Orwell looked away, embarrassed. 'Oh, I gave it him to play with,' he said. 'I forgot I'd left it there.' As Powell observed, reflecting on the incident thirty years later, all this was much too big to be forgotten. Why take such pains to avoid being found playing with a child? And why leave the knife behind as evidence? What, if it came to that, was Orwell doing with an implement that looked as though it could be used for disembowelling deer? Powell's conclusion was that the whole thing had been staged for their mutual benefit – a kind of 'Victorian group picture' depicting the strong man touched by infant vulnerability but unwilling to confess his weakness, which made a huge appeal to his imagination and way of regarding the world. Yet, as Powell noted, 'he had to be discovered for the incident to achieve graphic significance'.

One makes these points as a means of stressing – something not always remembered when the 'secular saint' aspect of Orwell's life is under discussion – that Orwell was just as given to calculation as anyone else, and that the situations he was capable of stage-managing – emotional and otherwise – called for a certain amount of deviousness. In a curious way the episode of the clasp-knife makes him seem less rather than more odd, more driven by inner psychological force. So, from a slightly different angle, does the variegated nature of the life he was leading in the immediately post-war era, taking place on an infinite number of levels – from prowling the Islington back streets with Paul Potts to lunching with Bertrand Russell at the Ritz (he dressed for this engagement in a brown herringbone suit, and Susan Watson was dispatched to buy a pair of working-men's braces) – but always reduced to the qualities of decency and kindliness which he sought in the people with whom he mixed.

Late September found him writing to Kay Dick to lament his inability to produce another contribution for the *Windmill*. He had an idea for a story about a man who grows so tired of fighting the weeds flourishing in his garden that he decides to have a garden filled with weeds, only for the flowers and vegetables to spring up of their own accord. Surrounded on all sides by journalistic commitments, such bagatelles were difficult to accomplish. Mid-October brought the proofs of *Critical Essays*, which Warburg planned to publish early in 1946. Ill at the end of the month, apparently with bronchitis, he was in the unusual position of being forced to turn work down, declining Warburg's invitation to read a manuscript and a proposed commission from the BBC's Latin American Service. But he was still anxious to help his friends, reviewing Herbert Read's essays for *Poetry Quarterly* and appraising Cyril Connolly's collection *The Condemned Playground* for the *Observer*. Connolly's near-blanket dismissal of modern English writing and his insistence on the superiority of the American novel he found too sweeping, but he agreed with Connolly's conclusions about the weakening effect of class on home-grown art. 'Almost certainly he is right in saying that the rigid English class system, which narrows the range of nearly everyone's experience, is responsible for the thinness of subject matter in the average novel . . .' It was also, and perhaps yet more ominously, 'responsible for the present decadence of the English language'.

However generally well disposed to Connolly and other con-temporaries, Orwell was still capable of separating a good friend from a poor piece of work. Occasionally this determination to say what he thought about an inferior performance while remaining on friendly terms with the performer – or rather his belief that the two things were scarcely connected – could reach faintly bizarre heights. At the end of November, for example, he wrote a scathing review of Koestler's play *Twilight Bar*. Some weeks later the two spent Christmas together in Wales. No reference was made to the review until the very end of the holiday when Koestler, driving his friend back to the station, wondered 'jocularly' whether the criticism hadn't been a bit too severe and might have been toned down. Orwell replied that this hadn't occurred to him, but eventually conceded that perhaps in the circumstances he could have softened his asperity. In some ways this is a classic Orwell moment, repeated in various guises throughout his life: a scrupulousness about thought and feeling that, put through the mangle of ordinary human experience, can sometimes look almost unworldly. Ideally a relationship between two writers founded on integrity and common sense should be able to survive the knowledge that one of them has written something disparaging about the other's work. Faced with the same situation himself, you feel, Orwell would barely have noticed. It was only when he thought dishonesty involved that he took exception to hostile comment. But not everyone – certainly not Koestler – was Orwell in this respect. Then again, Orwell had the knack of attracting people who admired his work almost without reservation. From his point of view such embarrassments could nearly always be avoided for the simple reason that they were never likely to arise.

Another whiff of Orwellian unworldliness rises from an essay written for *Tribune* at the very end of 1945 on the tour of England then being undertaken by the Moscow Dynamo football side. International soccer, for Orwell, was simply nationalism in disguise – young men kicking each other in front of thousands of baying spectators in a pantomime representation of wider political conflicts. The pivotal role played by football in early twentieth-century working-class life scarcely occurs to him. Coming from a writer so consistently engrossed in the ebb and flow of popular culture this apparent myopia is unusual, but it demonstrates the way in which greater abstracts were beginning to dominate his thinking at the expense of detail. The theoretical foundation on which an essay such as 'The Sporting Spirit' could be erected had been shifted into place shortly before in the *Polemic* essay 'Notes on Nationalism'. Orwell enjoyed writing for *Polemic*, of which he had a favourable opinion ('I have great hopes that it will develop into something good,' he wrote early in 1946). Edited by Humphrey Slater, whom he had met in the early years of the war, probably through Inez Holden, with whom Slater had a longstanding affair, it combined high intellectual content (A.J. Ayer was an early contributor) with a definite air of smartness, enhanced by Ben Nicolson's imaginative design. 'Notes on Nationalism' forms the final part of the triptych begun by *The Lion and the Unicorn* and carried forward by the still-unpublished *The English People*. Defining various types of nationalism 'now flourishing among English intellectuals' – 'positive', 'transferred' and 'negative' – Orwell concludes by attributing its worst follies, once again, to the breakdown in patriotism and religious belief. The piece develops into an assault on quietism. The ivory tower line that because no point of view is altogether unbiased one ought to keep out of politics is unacceptable. In the modern world, no one capable of being described as an intellectual *can* keep out of politics. All one can do is to recognise that some causes are objectively better than others, even if advanced by bad men, and to make a genuine moral effort to overcome the nationalist loves and hates that are a part of the average person's make-up.

From the angle of the end-of-year savant, this kind of moral purpose was in short supply. 'Old George's Almanac', written for *Tribune*'s Christmas number, offered a range of predominantly gloomy predictions on the course of world affairs. For the UK Orwell prophesied a series of privations, including chronic food shortages, unofficial strikes and savage battles over nationalisation, while conceding that this still provided a cheerier vista than the Christmases of the previous six years. On his way to spend Christmas with the Koestlers in Wales, he met Celia Paget at Paddington and she was struck by the 'tall, slightly shaggy figure' she found walking the platform and also by his transparent affection for Richard, now eighteen months old, who accompanied them on the trip. Richard 'simply adored George'. Apart from the slight tension produced by the *Tribune* review, the week went well. In particular Celia remembered a conversation in which they discussed the qualities they would most like to have if it were possible to choose. Orwell maintained that he would like to be irresistible to women. He reported to friends that he had enjoyed himself, taking Richard to parties and encouraging him to sit up at table in an adult chair. Returned to London, he was full of plans. *Critical Essays*, published in January 1946, brought together the essays on Dickens and 'Boys' Weeklies' from the now out-of-print *Inside the Whale* with half a dozen of his best *Horizon* pieces and the essay on Dali that had been nervously excluded from the *Saturday Book*. There was an unrealised scheme to produce a book about nursery rhymes, possibly with the expert help of Eric Partridge. Meanwhile Jura was looming through the January fogs. Early in the New Year he asked Secker & Warburg for £300 as an advance on the as yet unwritten novel, this being the amount that Orwell calculated he could otherwise have made from six months' journalism. Spring, he was certain, would see him heading north.

The end of the war had brought all kinds of old friends back into his orbit. One of them was Dennis Collings, caught in the Far East by the Japanese advance and eventually interned in a Japanese prisoner-of-war camp where he escaped the worst brutalities through his status as a translator. Michael Sayers, briefly back in London after spending the war in America, found his old flatmate looking 'terrible' and prophesying universal destruction at the hands of the atom bomb ('It will blow up all of us'). Orwell presented Sayers with a copy of Zamyatin's *We*, which he contrived to lose on the trip back across the Atlantic. Peace had also brought many of Europe's literary and political notables to London, several of whom came Orwell's way in the early part of 1946. In January, for example, he lunched with Negrin, the former Spanish Socialist Prime Minister (he had not managed to get him alone, he reported to Koestler, but believed he was not a Russian stooge). Shortly afterwards he lunched with Ignazio Silone, taxing the Italian novelist with a published statement saying that he accepted the need for a united front with Communism. Both these encounters took place in the context of his political work with Koestler and the series of cases in which he was involved on behalf of the Freedom Defence Committee. There were some steps, however, which he was not prepared to take. An invitation to address the pacifist Peace Pledge Union was declined. And the book, above all, had come to dominate his thoughts. He didn't suppose he would finish it in the six months he was allowing himself off from regular commitments, he suggested to Moore, but he would be able to break its back.

All this – the ceaseless journalism, the political lobbying, the Jura plans – took place against a backdrop of increasing personal frailty. Towards the end of February, shortly after his marriage proposal to Anne Popham, Orwell suffered a tubercular haemorrhage. Susan Watson, working in the kitchen at Canonbury Square, found him walking along the passage with blood coming from his lips asking could she help? As instructed, Susan fetched a jug of iced water and a block of ice, wrapped the ice and placed it on Orwell's forehead and then sat holding his hand until the bleeding stopped. What followed was an extraordinary catalogue of evasions and refusal to face facts. Plainly Orwell was seriously ill. There could be only one explanation for a haemorrhage of this kind, and that was TB. Deeply concerned, Susan called a doctor but did not feel it was up to her, as Orwell's employee, to explain the precise nature of his illness. Orwell himself was similarly delphic in his responses, with the result that the doctor diagnosed a bad case of gastritis. Orwell spent the next two weeks in bed, relying on Susan to make his excuses to editors by telephone and keeping up the pretence in written communications to friends. Writing to George Woodcock in mid-March, about the case of a man who had married a German woman and wanted to get her back to England, he remarked only that he was 'sick in bed, but somewhat better'. To Anne Popham, by now back in Germany, he stuck to the myth of the severe stomach complaint – 'quite an unpleasant thing to have, but I am somewhat better and got up for the first time today'. The most obvious question to ask about this episode is: who did Orwell think he was fooling? Not himself at any rate. The explanation of his reluctance to acknowledge, even to a doctor, how ill he was has everything to do with *Nineteen Eighty-Four*. A diagnosis of TB would have meant immediate hospitalisation – the fate that awaited him when *Nineteen Eighty-Four* was completed. At other times he seems perfectly conscious of his condition, telling Susan that he thought he would survive until Richard was thirteen.

The letter to Anne Popham which looks back to the ill-fated proposal is a revealing document: candid, plaintive, not unlike the letters of a dozen years before to Brenda Salkeld, on the one hand faintly desperate, on the other curiously resigned. As to the idea of marriage, Orwell had thought it 'just conceivable' that she might accept. Now he realises that he is not suited to someone who can still expect to get something out of life, in contrast to his own destiny of work and seeing that Richard gets a good start. It was only that he felt terribly alone sometimes, he concluded. 'I have hundreds of friends, but no woman who takes an interest in me and can encourage me'. There was a typical postscript: 'I am not sure how to stamp this letter, but I suppose threepence is right?' By the end of March he was back to something approaching normality, although telling Koestler that he felt 'desperately tired and jaded', well enough to make arrangements for a removal firm to be summoned to Wallington to assess what needed to be taken to Jura. Apart from the gap caused by his fortnight in bed, his work-rate had barely faltered. Some time in the early spring he wrote the introduction to *The Position of Peggy Harper*, long promised to Graham Greene, although as Greene left Eyre & Spottiswoode shortly afterwards the reprint of Leonard Merrick's shabby-genteel Edwardian classic never appeared. There was also a script for Rayner Heppenstall's BBC radio production *The Voyage of the Beagle* and – one of Orwell's more exotic commissions – a pamphlet on the subject of 'British Cookery' sponsored by the British Council, presumably on the strength of one of his *Evening Standard* essays, 'In Defence of English Cooking'. This, too, never saw the light in Orwell's lifetime, its sponsors eventually deciding that the distribution of such a booklet across Europe at a time of widespread food shortages would be insensitive.

Logistically, the Jura expedition was turning into a nightmare. He had hoped to get away by the end of April. There were still repairs to be done at Barnhill and the furniture was a problem. Additionally Susan was ill and might have to go into hospital, he told Inez Holden early in the month; he also made some fond remarks about Richard's progress. On 10 April he went to Wallington to examine the furniture and books before the Pickford's men arrived. It was the first time he had been to the cottage since Eileen had died and he expected it to be horribly upsetting. In the end only the sheaves of old letters, discovered as he went around packing up, rose to distress him. A week later, alone in the flat with Susan and Richard away in the country for the Easter weekend, he wrote another long letter to Anne Popham, a kind of rumination addressed to himself. The gist of it was that he wanted someone to share 'what is left of my life, and my work'. If he could live another ten years he thought that he had three worthwhile books in him, and he wanted peace and quiet and someone to be fond of him. The letter ends with another nature report, of going to a small, disused reservoir in Wallington and seeing the tadpoles foaming. He and Eileen used to have a small aquarium, he reminisced, made of a seven-pound pickle jar, and 'each year watch the newts grow from little black blots in the spawn to full-grown creatures . . .' There was a lot about Eileen in the letter – an acknowledgement of unfaithfulness and bad treatment, but also a conviction that they had shared a 'real marriage'. Whatever Anne Popham made of this proposal-cum-meditation she was not to be shifted.

He was still keenly observing the Attlee administration's first year in office. Everyone seemed to like the Labour government, he reported to *Partisan Review* early in May, but in terms of social readjustment it was difficult to detect any symptom by which one could infer that the country wasn't being run by Conservatives. He was alarmed by Communist infiltration of the parliamentary party – twenty or thirty MPs could be marked down as fellow-travellers, he calculated – and worried by the apparent re-emergence of snobbery. A walk past St Paul's Cathedral, where some ceremony was going on, had produced a sudden vista of top-hats, the first he had seen in large numbers for over six years. Jura lay before him – he had told Moore that he intended to leave on 10 May – but there came another change of plan when his elder sister Marjorie Dakin, who had been ill with pernicious anaemia, died unexpectedly of kidney disease. In recent years Orwell's formerly close connection with 'Marje' – the Dakins had been a great standby in his apprentice days – had lapsed a little, but he would have been conscious that with her passing only two members of their original family unit remained. He went to Nottingham for the funeral, returning to London for a week before moving north to Biggar, thirty miles south of Edinburgh, now the home of Georges and Doreen Kopp. Here he began to keep a diary again, watching the sowing of a field of wheat with his usual absorption in detail ('It is scattered pretty evenly, the grains being generally about 3 inches apart'). During the week he travelled south to visit Eileen's grave at Jesmond. The polyanthus rose on the grave had rooted well, he noted. She had been dead just over a year. Then, on 22 May, by train, ferry, bus and car, he made his way to Jura.

Seven miles from the nearest village, in sight of the sea, set amidst treeless heaths and farmland, Barnhill would have made an excellent refuge for a fit young man of the kind that Orwell patently was not. Perhaps divining this, his landlady, Mrs Fletcher, was anxious about her solitary middle-aged tenant's ability to cope. However, solicitous offers of help were abruptly turned down. Orwell was determined to be his own man. Despite this resolve, living conditions on Jura made at least some form of semi-communal existence unavoidable. Groceries, for example, had to be collected from Ardlussa, having been ordered in their turn from Craighouse. The official postal service got no further than the Fletchers, who delivered the Barnhill mail by car once a week. Orwell's solution to the transport problem showed a reversion to type. He bought a motorbike, with whose malfunctions he could often be seen tinkering at the side of the makeshift Jura roads. Mrs Fletcher's anxieties were somewhat reduced by the arrival of Avril, a week later, to stay and keep house. Susan Watson and Richard were to follow later in the summer.

Orwell's retreat to Jura is often represented as the visible symptom of a profound inner malaise, if not a death-wish: a sick, tubercular depressive deliberately exiling himself to a rain-swept extremity of the British Isles where he could, literally, sit and rot, risking his TB-ravaged lungs every time he drove his motorbike over the local pot-holes. In fact the climate was temperate and probably better for Orwell's health than smoke-blackened London. Jura's drawback was its remoteness. A letter from the following year inviting Sonia Brownell to stay, and outlining alternative routes from Glasgow, takes up nineteen printed lines. From Glasgow to Gourock by train. Boat to Tarbert. Bus to West Tarbert. Another boat to Craighouse, followed by a seventeen-mile taxi trip after which, depending on the state of the road, the visitor might well have to get out and walk. This self-imposed seclusion was Orwell's delight, but it offered a severe obstruction to the company he still wished to have around him. Michael Meyer was not the only friend who, forwarded details of the forty-eight-hour trip, cried off on grounds of inaccessibility. But however badly located from the point of view of Orwell's delicate state of health, Barnhill itself – especially in summer – was a pleasant place in which to live: a large kitchen-breakfast room with separate pantry and laundry, a substantial dining-cum-sitting room and, above, four smallish bedrooms. A single field separated the house from the sea, and there were outbuildings, a vegetable garden and two further fields farmed by Barnhill's neighbours, the Darrochs. Yet using the site for anything more than an extended holiday would require careful planning. Fuel was an abiding problem. There was little wood on the largely treeless island. Peat could be had but the cutting season was over by the time Orwell arrived. Coal had to travel the seven miles from Ardlussa. The water supply was also erratic, provided from a tank up the hill which was liable to run dry at high summer. Orwell got on well with the Darrochs, Donald and his sister Katie, who lived a mile and a half away and sold him milk until such time as Barnhill obtained its own cow. Impressed by his friendliness and courtesy, the Darrochs were struck by his obvious ill health. 'You could tell that he wasn't very well.'

Orwell liked Jura. His diaries are full of accounts of practical tasks accomplished – a trestle on which to saw logs, a sledge – and fascinated nature notes: an engorged tick cut open to reveal dark, viscous blood, a snake which he chopped in half and tried to examine, only to find the head still attempting to bite him. A fortnight into his stay there was still no hot water but he was managing to get copies of the *Observer* only a day late, which, as he told David Astor, wasn't bad. The transport problem looked as if it had been solved by the purchase of a Ford van, bought from the Kopps, but this was in poor condition. Rayner Heppenstall, booked for a visit in early July – in fact like many proposed guests he never made it – was told that he might have to accomplish the last leg of his journey on foot. Still settling in and taking stock of his surroundings, Orwell was happy to defer any thought of work until later in the summer, content to fill his journal with notes on geese husbandry (the Barnhill flock produced as much as two pounds of droppings per head a day, he estimated from the dung heap) or accounts of the difficulties involved in extricating a cow from a bog. He was having a splendid time, he informed Warburg a month after his arrival, might start on the novel in July but at this point was not even tying himself down to that. Avril, too, was having the time of her life, feasting on the fresh fish, seafood and venison given to them by the Fletchers and telling her brother-in-law Humphrey Dakin that 'I am really enjoying it all immensely'.

Avril's letter reveals that there was a third person staying at Barnhill. This was Paul Potts, whose presence was largely the cause of Heppenstall's absence, Heppenstall not relishing the fruitless arguments that any conversation between the two of them was likely to produce. Many of Orwell's friends – much of Fitzrovian literary London, if it came to that – took the same line on Potts. Orwell's attachment to this legendary Soho figure, whose accomplishments included stealing the young Iris Murdoch's typewriter on the grounds that his need of it was greater than hers, is one of his most revealing friendships. There was something in Potts's combination of irascible self-righteousness and gentle whimsicality that appealed to his less conventional, anarchistic – perhaps the best adjective would be 'Whitmanesque' – side. Avril's letter gives a fair idea of Potts's own otherworldliness: she notes that he took any witty remark in all seriousness while suffering 'fits of temperament'. Indulged by Orwell, tolerated for the moment by Avril, grateful, as a man of spectacularly improvident habits, for the free board and lodgings, he wandered happily around Jura for several weeks and was dislodged only by the arrival of Susan Watson and Richard, whom Orwell fetched from London at the beginning of July. Undoubtedly Susan's appearance produced an air of tension. There were petty disagreements with Avril, who disliked Susan calling her employer 'George' instead of 'Eric' and on one occasion, irked by some domestic oversight, expostulated 'Call yourself a nurse and you can't darn socks!' Both women were eventually united in their dislike of Potts, to whose general intractability was added the crime of cutting down the area's solitary nut tree in the mistaken belief that it would make good firewood. Matters came to a head when Susan, apparently innocently, kindled the fire with what turned out to be a Potts manuscript in progress. By the next morning Potts had disappeared.

Quite probably Orwell never noticed the successive phases of Potts' discomfiture, culminating in his moonlit flit. He was, as ever, engrossed, first by the Jura routines – a lobster needed a cubic foot of fresh sea-water every twenty-four hours, he noted in an account of lobster creels – and second by the prospect of resuming work. A letter to Anne Popham from early August acknowledging her decision to decline his offer of marriage reveals his output over the past two months to have been a single magazine article, possibly 'Politics vs Literature'. After long years of overwork the rest had done him good, he believed. Certainly he had survived ten weeks on the island without catching a cold, despite being regularly soaked to the skin. A few days later he told George Woodcock that he had 'just started' another novel. The prediction, made four months back to Leonard Moore, that he could break its back in the course of a summer and early autumn on Jura was over-sanguine. In fact *Nineteen Eighty-Four* would occupy him almost to his death.

What was in his mind when he began it? It is easy enough to isolate some of the novel's 'influences' for references to them dot his writings from the period. Since his childhood worship of H.G. Wells he had been fascinated by the idea of the 'dystopia', a futurist society in which all the best-laid plans have gone wrong. In this respect *Nineteen Eighty-Four* is an obvious successor to dystopian landmarks such as Zamyatin's *We*, or Jack London's *The Iron Heel*, which features a society run by a small group of tyrants known as 'Oligarchs', served by a proto-SS called the 'Mercenaries'. Orwell had spent much of an introduction to a reprint of London's collection of Yukon tales *Love of Life and Other Stories*, written towards the end of 1945, drawing attention to this book. There are other, equally plausible, twitches on the thread. Some years ago, for instance, a literary scholar rooting through a 1934 number of the *Chronicle*, the magazine of Sunderland Church High School, came across a poem entitled 'End of the Century: 1984'. A clever futurist satire in three parts ('Death', 'Birth', 'The Phoenix') and containing lines about 'sun-bronzed scholars' who 'turn their thoughts to telepathic station 9'; its author was a twenty-nine-year-old former pupil of the school named Eileen O'Shaughnessy. Or there is an extremely odd period curio, which Orwell could hardly have failed to notice on its appearance in 1937 as it was published by Gollancz and later reissued by the Left Book Club, Murray Constantine's *Swastika Night*. Though not a particularly good novel, *Swastika Night* offers an uncannily suggestive glimpse of the landscapes of *Nineteen Eighty-Four*. Constantine (the pseudonym of a prolific 1930s novelist named Katherine Burdekin) envisages a society which has been under Nazi rule for 700 years and a world divided between German and Japanese empires, permanently at war in their colonial possessions. A young English dissident, entrusted by one of the German ruling class with the only extant copy of a 'true' history of the world, discovers that Hitler was not a god and that there had in the past existed entities such as 'memory' and 'socialism'. In several key details – the constant rewriting of history, the state of permanent warfare, the demonisation of 'the four arch-fiends' (whose number includes Lenin and Stalin) – the novel anticipates Orwell by nearly a decade.

And yet, in the last resort, influence-mongering of this kind has a limited value. Orwell, it is safe to say, did not write *Nineteen Eighty-Four* because he had read a poem that his wife had written for her old school magazine or browsed through an obscure novel that came his way through the Left Book Club. Rather, he had spent the late 1930s and early 1940s conceiving a vision of totalitarianism and its implications for human existence: the things he picked up along the way fed his imagination, brick upon brick piled upon the original foundation. Significantly, the novel's themes are endlessly reflected in the journalism that Orwell produced in the two years before he began work on it. 'The Prevention of Literature', which appeared in *Polemic* in July 1946, notes that the organised lying practised by totalitarian states is not a temporary expedient in the matter of military deception and false intelligence, but something integral to totalitarianism, its defining characteristic. Increasingly, Orwell's concern with 'truth' had taken him back to language. The same essay notes that 'to write in plain, vigorous language one has to think fearlessly, and if one thinks fearlessly one cannot be politically orthodox'. 'Politics and the English Language', written for *Horizon* at practically the same time, fore-shadows the basis of 'Newspeak'. The English language becomes ugly and inaccurate because people think foolish thoughts, but the sloven-liness of our language makes it easier to think them. Ultimately the nature of language has economic and political causes. No sharper reason exists for perverting the truth.

At the heart of *Nineteen Eighty-Four* lies a connection between language and morality. But also lurking there is a connection to every other novel that Orwell wrote. While the futurist setting, and a lurid, unvarnished quality inseparable from the circumstances in which it was written, encourage a view of something discrete and self-sustaining, in many ways the novel conforms to a pattern established many years before. The opening scene in which Winston Smith is forced out of bed and compelled to perform physical jerks by the barking voice of the telescreen bears several resemblances to Dorothy's awakening in *A Clergyman's Daughter* or George Bowling's lurch into consciousness at the start of *Coming up for Air.* Just as much as Flory or Gordon Comstock, Winston Smith is a projection of Orwell himself: dreaming of days in an unspoilt Thames Valley, of fish swimming in pools beneath the willow tree. He is also, however starker the realities facing him, a very typical Orwell hero – the rebellious solitary more or less alone in a hostile world, consumed with self-pity, planning an escape, a future that depends not on selfishness but a genuine abnegation of self. The message for Winston corresponds to the words that Orwell puts into Shakespeare's mouth in 'Lear, Tolstoy and the Fool': if you live for others, then you must live *for others*, and not as a roundabout way of getting advantage for yourself.

The fresh start on *Nineteen Eighty-Four* was interrupted by a trip to Glasgow to fetch Susan's daughter, a lengthy saga of punctured motorbike tyres and missed ferries. Orwell ended up taking a bus to Port Ellen to wait for the following morning's boat, only to find a cattle show in progress and the hotels full. He spent the night in a cell at the local police station. A fortnight later he watched with interest as most of the population of Ardlussa arrived to harvest the field of corn in front of Barnhill. The scene led him to reflect on Jura and the extreme primitiveness of conditions on the island. Even when a field had been ploughed by tractor, the seed was still cast by hand. Yet despite having to work hard, the crofters seemed in every way better off and more independent than their town equivalents. A better local infrastructure and less exigent landlords would have made their situation almost comfortable. Meanwhile the sheets of *Nineteen Eighty-Four*, stacking up in the study-bedroom, were not without their readers. One of the earliest was a young man of twenty-three named David Holbrook, Susan Watson's boyfriend, lately arrived on the island for a visit.

Holbrook, sneaking upstairs with Susan for surreptitious glances at the manuscript, was not impressed: 'Pretty depressing stuff. There was this man Winston . . . and these dismal sexual episodes. It just seemed depressingly lacking in hope . . .' Unhappily Holbrook's entire visit was an exercise in disillusionment. A fan of Orwell's since his schooldays, he arrived on Jura expecting 'brilliant conversations' and the opportunity to 'talk to him about writing and culture'. The reality was sharply different. Orwell turned out to be hostile and grumpy, living in a closed world, Holbrook thought, and always going on about the locale's 'bloody birds'. Barnhill, too, seemed thoroughly ramshackle and down-at-heel. Holbrook noted Orwell's habit of 'breaking things', notably the motorbike. Sensing Orwell's disapproval of their relation-ship, he and Susan would escape for long walks, returning to sit glumly in the kitchen while Orwell and Avril embarked on dispiriting, monosyllabic conversations as they got on with the household tasks.

The problem, as Holbrook swiftly divined, was that Orwell had got wind of his Communist Party membership and regarded him if not exactly as a spy then as someone to be regarded with deep suspicion. Time had not softened Holbrook's memory of these asperities when, years later, he wrote an unpublished autobiographical novel which includes a section set on Jura. *The Inevitable Price* is a fascinating document, if only for its sustained exposure of an Orwell markedly different from the man who marches through the recollections of his friends. 'Paul Grimmer', Holbrook's alter ego, turns up on Jura to visit his girlfriend 'Brigid', employed as housekeeper to a writer named 'Gregory Burwell'. Dropped by the taxi-driver three miles from his destination, he arrives to find Burwell ('a black oil-skinned figure crouched behind one corner of the stone house, peering along the barrel of a shot-gun') shooting a goose. Eyeing up this tall, lugubrious man, Paul decides he has 'the most mournful face he had ever seen'. Burwell greets Paul without enthusiasm. Asked to explain why the goose had to be shot, there follows 'a curious grinding noise', the sound of Burwell 'explaining a subject, without human interest, but in exasperating detail'. Inside the farmhouse – Brigid and Burwell's son 'David' are visiting crofter friends – Paul is introduced to Burwell's sister 'Olwyn' and made to feel, if anything, even less welcome. He sits listening to their dejected conversation ('The couple's gloomiest pleasure was in undermining all possibilities: they liked everything to be inaccessible, broken, beyond repair, unattainable. There was no help to be had, no support, no community, no human succour') before escaping in search of Brigid. Similar scenes follow: Burwell miserably carving the goose that has been thoroughly incinerated by Olwyn; hoarsely venturing small-talk about the local fauna. Paul is shocked to find 'this well-known author, whose books he had read and admired and even found sensitive at times, such a bore, and so ponderously remote . . .' Burwell seems to take no interest in David, while Olwyn (nicknamed 'Old Witchy' by the younger element) merely nags him. It is left to Brigid to stimulate the child's imagination. She and Paul take their revenge by sneaking upstairs to snoop on Burwell's writing and make love on the study floor, mimicking the roles of housekeeper and footman on the day when the laird and his beaters come to tea and they are confined 'below stairs' in the kitchen.

This is a loaded account – Holbrook accepted that people who 'weren't carrying on with his nursemaid and weren't members of the Communist Party' might have seen Orwell differently – but the occasionally extremist nature of Orwell's detached self-absorption has other chroniclers. The inevitable explosion was ignited by Susan's discovery that she could no longer stand being on the same premises as Avril. She and Holbrook left together, turning up at Ardlussa with suitcases; Mrs Fletcher put them up for the night, before they continued their journey to the mainland. None of this, significantly, found its way into Orwell's diary, which concentrates instead on the weather, the practicalities of manufacturing a tobacco pouch out of rabbit skin and the visit of the estate carpenter to put in a new sash window for the Darrochs. Autumn came and he planned a short trip to London, aiming to leave in mid-October and be back by the middle of the following month. He had done fifty pages of the novel, he told Humphrey Slater at the end of September, arranging a lunch date for a fortnight hence. That Orwell envisaged a long-term occupancy of Barnhill seems clear from his plans to ship in more furniture, in particular tables and chairs, and possibly even install a forge and an oil engine capable of running a circular saw. Undoubtedly, as he packed up his things and noted the depredations of rats in the byre, he saw it as the beginning of a new phase in his life, successfully reconnoitred.

17

Islands

I know that if I return to London and get caught up in weekly articles I shall never get on with anything longer. – Letter to Anthony Powell, 8 September 1947

We have made ourselves quite comfortable here. – Letter to Helmut Klöse, 19 September 1947

Back in London in the autumn of 1946 Orwell threw himself into his old routines, taking up the 'As I Please' column for *Tribune* and resuming his weekly spot in the *Manchester Evening News*. He had been away six months and there was much to catch up with, a whole range of alliances – social and professional – to reforge. Three lunch engagements were already booked for the following week, he explained to Julian Symons in early November, deferring their meeting for a fortnight. There were other reunions, culminating in a lunch at the end of the month with Graham Greene. Much of Orwell's time was taken up with literary business. A decade and a half into his career, he had suddenly become a solid commercial proposition. Translations of *Animal Farm* were appearing all over Europe (early 1947 brought Dutch and Ukrainian editions). Eager to profit from this interest, Secker & Warburg were keen on the idea of a uniform edition of his works. Orwell agreed, while refusing to sanction reprints of *A Clergyman's Daughter*, *Keep the Aspidistra Flying* or *The Lion and the Unicorn*. In some ways this disparagement of his early work is odd. Orwell had worked up a 'bloody sweat' on *Aspidistra* and tried to produce something that could be regarded as a work of art. Eleven years later he preferred to tell friends that the novel had been written merely because he was hard-up and needed Gollancz's £100 advance. Yet this lack of vanity extended even to those novels which he was prepared to allow back into print. He turned out not to possess copies of *Burmese Days* and *Coming up for*

Air; the latter proved so difficult to get hold of that it had to be advertised for. There were other signs of his growing status. His radio adaptation of *Animal Farm* was in the pipeline, to be produced by Rayner Heppenstall. There were even plans to visit America in 1948, if only to spend some of the US royalties that currency restrictions kept on the farther side of the Atlantic. There was a problem with Gollancz, understandably reluctant to let such a valuable property out of his hands, but Orwell was adamant that he wanted to stay with Secker & Warburg. He wanted Warburg to be his regular publisher, he told Moore, because although he might not sell as many books as the streamlined operation in Henrietta Street, 'I can trust him to publish whatever I write.'

Not all the Islington routines were capable of resuscitation. Susan Watson never came back, although there was no rancour in their parting; Orwell accepted that the tensions of Jura might well have been unendurable. Avril continued to look after the two-year-old Richard. Orwell had turned forty-three in the summer, an age at which most mid-twentieth-century writers would have expected to have thirty or even forty years of literary life before them. But he was tired, conscious of waning powers. Two things now dominated his life, each linked to the other: his failing health and his intense desire to finish *Nineteen Eighty-Four*. There is no way of knowing quite how ill Orwell was at this time – he was keen to keep away from doctors – but the London of 1946–7, caught in one of the hardest winters for years, was perhaps the worst environment he could have chosen in which to spend the next six months. A year later he told Julian Symons that he believed his health problems 'really started in the cold of last winter'. In fact his lungs had been quietly hardening – he was later discovered to have a fibrotic form of TB – for some time, but the arctic freeze-up of early 1947, compounded by Dickensian fogs, food shortages and power shutdowns, could only have made them worse. He seems to have admitted to himself that he was seriously ill, while being content to postpone any kind of treatment until the novel was finished. Orwell's determination to maintain his punishing schedules while physically exhausted had been noticed on Jura by Susan Watson. She remembered him working in bed, lying on the iron bedstead in a dressing-gown, the smoke from his cigarettes clogging an atmosphere already polluted by a defective fire-grate and a paraffin heater.

He was a driven man. But why did he drive himself into areas from which he could easily have kept his distance? By late November he was 'swamped under work' but still managing to take his customarily benevolent interest in his friends' careers: producing a list of 'important' English books for a friend of Helmut Klose (Klose was a German anarchist who had fought on the Aragon Front in Spain) who aimed at starting a publishing house in Düsseldorf, putting Paul Potts in touch with Moore in an attempt to settle a dispute with Nicolson & Watson, trying in the following spring to transfer his *Manchester Evening News* column to Julian Symons. (Orwell, Symons remembered, was 'determined to do something for me. The editor had never heard my name, but allowed himself to be persuaded into giving me a month's trial.') There were domestic cares, too, notably another instalment in the long-running quest to find decent footwear, a saga in which both Warburg and Dwight MacDonald, formerly co-editor of *Partisan Review* but now in charge of the New York journal *Politics*, took part. The 'As I Please' columns from late 1946 cover a bewildering range of topics: the jury system, four-letter words in literature, 'good bad books' (one of his favourite subjects both in talk and journalism), the difficulty of finding a laundry. His Christmas column was prompted by an advertisement suggesting that the four things needed for a successful Christmas were a roast turkey, a Christmas pudding, a dish of mince pies and a tin of the advertiser's liver salts. Given the world situation it would hardly be possible to have a 'proper' Christmas, he mused, even if the materials were available. However, he wished his readers an 'old-fashioned' Christmas, and meanwhile half a turkey, three tangerines and a bottle of whiskey at not more than double the legal price.

He celebrated the New Year by making a brief trip to Jura to carry out winter planting. The expedition had been planned to allow him to reach Barnhill on New Year's Eve, but a missed bus obliged him to spend two nights in Glasgow. After a rough crossing from Tarbert, during which he was severely seasick, the weather turned suddenly spring-like, only for rain to set in with a wind so violent that it was difficult to stay on one's feet. Inspecting the garden, he discovered that the rabbits had eaten most of the vegetables. He planted fruit trees and roses, drew a map to show the layouts and carefully itemised the food supplies that would be needed on his return in the spring. By 9 January he was back in London, in time to hear the Third Programme adaptation of *Animal Farm*. This was well received – several fan letters and good press notices, he reported to Heppenstall; the sole dissenter, ironically enough, being the *Tribune* critic. There was still no let-up in the weather. Large-scale power cuts closed the London weekly papers for a fortnight, and one 'As I Please' ended up being printed in the *Daily Herald*. These privations were relative, Orwell supposed – all this would presumably be reckoned 'normal' in post-war Paris, he proposed to Dwight Macdonald. All the same, writing in *Tribune* about the shortage of firewood, he was able to relate, not without a certain pride, that he had 'kept going' for a day on the warmth of a blitzed bedstead. Avril recalled that at one point it got so cold that some of Richard's toys went the same way. Frowsting in the Islington flat he was combining his regular commitments with more substantial work: 'Lear, Tolstoy and the Fool' for *Polemic* (a shortened version, intended for *Politics*, failed to appear), another long essay on the political savant James Burnham for the American *New Leader*. (Burnham had predicted another war within the next few years; Orwell, while accepting that Burnham was not pro-Stalin, judged that 'the note of fascination is still there'.) It was probably at about this time that he produced the introduction to *British Pamphleteers Volume I*, a collection assembled by Reg Reynolds which would be published at the end of the following year. Increasingly, though, his mind was set on the return to Jura. His friends seem to have realised that in future he would be a vagrant figure, returning to London only when he had good cause. However tinged by retrospect, there is an odd sense of finality about some of their glimpses of him at this time, the sense of bridges being burned. Tosco Fyvel's last memory of Orwell was of having dinner at the home of their *Tribune* colleague Evelyn Anderson in Bayswater. Before their arrival the fog had been so bad that the Fyvels were obliged to abandon their car. Emerging from the Andersons', they found conditions worse than ever. The Fyvels decided to stay the night with their hosts. Orwell, taking this as a challenge, was determined to walk home to Islington. Fyvel's abiding memory was of 'his tall figure, looking grim and sad-faced, as he strode off and disappeared into the fog'.

There were still difficulties with Gollancz, who had pointed out that legally he had an option on Orwell's next two works of fiction (Orwell thought that only a single book was covered by this pre-war agreement, and that one of the options had been worked off by Gollancz's rejection of *Animal Farm*.) It was not until the end of March, after several letters had been exchanged, that Gollancz was finally persuaded to release him from the contract. He was planning to leave for Jura in the second week of April, he told Brenda Salkeld in March, this time taking a speedier route by plane from Glasgow to Islay. Meanwhile London was still bitterly cold: no fuel left at all, he reported to Brenda. One of the final

'As I Please' columns for *Tribune* at the very end of March strikes a typical Orwell note: intentness, self-absorption, love of nature jumbled unselfconsciously together. For the last five minutes, he revealed, he had been staring out of the window into the square, keeping a lookout for signs of spring. Any hints were of the vaguest kind – a thinnish patch in the clouds with the faintest thought of blue behind it, a sycamore tree with a few notional buds. A careful search of Hyde Park two days before had yielded better results, in the shape of a hawthorn bush that was 'definitely in bud' and some birds who, if they were not actually singing, 'were making a noise like an orchestra tuning up'.

The following week's column, discussing press freedom in the event of nationalisation, patent medicines, tobacco-growing and pidgin English, was his last. He left for Jura on 10 April and would never see London again except from the window of a hospital room. There is an odd deliberateness about the way in which, over the following months, Orwell cut himself off from his old London haunts, and indeed the south of England generally. Both the lease on the Islington flat and the Wallington tenancy – the latter dated back to 1936 and the early days of his marriage to Eileen – would soon be given up. Books and furniture went north. Meanwhile he was determined to convert Barnhill into an all-year-round dwelling place rather than makeshift spring and summer quarters. A letter to Helmut Klöse from later in the year – 'We have made ourselves quite comfortable here' – implies settlement, permanence, the eye to the long term trained here on the Inner Hebrides. Orwell being Orwell, and prone to long, lugubrious brooding on the perils of international power politics, there was also the thought that, in the last resort, Jura might provide a refuge. One of his old Home Guard comrades, who re-established contact a couple of years later, remembered him prophesying a nuclear holocaust and maintaining that Richard would be 'safer' in the far north. On a more mundane level he appreciated the advantages that Jura offered to a two-year-old boy: unlimited space, a healthy environment, fresh air and good food. Richard himself recalled the island as a kind of lost idyll: 'marvellous for a child, with acres of land to roam'. With other children at the Fletchers' and a stream of visitors to Barnhill, he was not aware of isolation or loneliness. Perhaps the single most obvious drawback was the distance from medical help. Islay, home of the nearest doctor, was thirty miles away.

No doctor was allowed anywhere near his father. Orwell arrived back on the island on the evening of 11 April 1947, having flown across a Scotland whose high ground was still streaked with snow. The trees and bushes planted in January had survived, he noted; a single primrose seemed to be the extent of the wild flowers. He had been ill in the week before departure. New arrivals to Jura in the early summer of 1947 were struck by his obvious weakness. Bill Dunn, an ex-serviceman who had lost a limb in the war and was lodging with the Darrochs while he took up Robin Fletcher's offer of agricultural work, realised immediately that 'he didn't look well'. There are other Jura testimonies to a visibly sick man, gaunt and preoccupied, who already looked as if he had only a short time to live. But Orwell had other goals in mind, beyond the completion of *Nineteen Eighty-Four*. One of the first letters he wrote after returning to Barnhill, following up an invitation issued a short time before, was to Sonia Brownell discussing a possible visit. Clearly the plan to inveigle Sonia to Jura had been thoroughly researched, as Orwell also revealed that he had written to her great friend Janetta Woolley (forename characteristically misspelled) asking if she could join the party with her baby daughter. However warmly intended, the letter, with its formidable list of directions, failed to entice ('The room you would have is rather small, but it looks out on the sea,' Orwell promised) and Sonia, as did Janetta, stayed away.

There was much to do before he could resume work on his novel. The week after his arrival was taken up in digging, planting bulbs and constructing a hen-house – this despite the fact that he was 'still not feeling well enough to do much out of doors'. Shortly afterwards the weather turned and a gale blew up, wrenching the hen-house off its base. Subsequently, continuous rains set in. Richard, having gashed his scalp the previous week – it took a day to procure medical help – now went down with measles. Orwell tried to amuse him by making a jigsaw, only to find that the blade of his coping-saw was broken and he could only cut the pieces with a straight edge. There is a curious absorption in Orwell's domestic diaries. Plainly he was fascinated by Jura, and relished both the mundane tasks and the natural life of the island. Green plovers, spring ploughing, the dispatch of a mouse that had got into the larder: all this is dutifully, but one imagines delightedly, set down. He was still not well enough to do much, in bed for three days at the end of May and dosing himself with M&B tablets. But as the weather improved, so did his health. There are references to his 'struggling' with *Nineteen Eighty-Four*, and by the end of May he could tell Warburg that he had made a fairly good start and completed nearly a third of a rough draft. This was less than he had hoped, he admitted, but the wretchedness of his health had stopped him from writing more.

The Orwell of two or three years before would not perhaps have acknowledged this: one of the features of Orwell's second stay on Jura was his readiness to admit his failing health not only to himself – always difficult enough – but to other people. Summer visitors began to arrive, notably Richard Rees, who from now on seems to have appointed himself Orwell's unofficial guardian on Jura. He spent much of the rest of the year at Barnhill, and took a keen interest in the life of the island. It was he, for instance, who suggested that Bill Dunn might like to farm land at Barnhill and put up £1,000 to fund the venture, with himself as sleeping partner. Rees, too, is a key witness to the life of Barnhill and Orwell's reaction to some of its minor excitements. In early July Avril dislocated her shoulder jumping over a wall. Rees remembered Orwell instantly deferring to his own (presumed) expertise, rushing back to the house to call him to help. 'You've done first aid, haven't you?' (Rees had served with an ambulance unit on the Madrid Front). 'You'll be able to get it back. You just have to jerk it sharply upwards, isn't that it?' Rees was unable to get it back (Orwell made no attempt). The Islay doctor proved similarly unsuccessful. Rees, Dunn and Donald Darroch ended up having to convey Avril by road and boat to the mainland for treatment.

Orwell was still hoping to finish *Nineteen Eighty-Four* early the following year. But the fine summer weather was a distraction, encouraging picnics and sailing trips, camping at Glengarrisdale on the Atlantic side of Jura and fishing for trout in Loch nan Eilean. A storm hit the island with such ferocity that a small patch of the garden appeared to have been struck by lightning. There were more guests – his dead sister Marjorie's three children – and he seems to have made a conscious effort to entertain them. The junior Dakins – teenage Lucy, her elder sister Jane, who had just left the Women's Land Army, and their brother Henry, on leave from the army – got on well with their uncle and enjoyed his company, while noting the occasional awesome level of detachment. This was particularly evident in a mid-August boat trip to Glengarrisdale, when on the return journey they were nearly drowned in the famous Corryvreckan whirlpool. Orwell's account of the incident is laconic, while admitting the danger they had been in. It was left to his nephew to provide what, in retrospect, seems a pattern account of Orwell being Orwell.

The six of them – Orwell, Avril, the Dakins and Richard – had spent two or three days on the coast – there was an ancient shepherd's hut to provide shelter – before deciding to return home. Avril and Jane opted to walk; the others took the small motorised boat. Asked previously if he had consulted the tide tables, Orwell had remarked airily 'Oh yes, yes, I've looked it all up.' A slight misreading was enough to put them in grave danger. The waves grew bigger. Then, as they drifted towards the edge of the whirlpool, there was a cracking noise, and the engine sheared away from its mounting and disappeared into the sea. Perhaps they ought to row out, Orwell suggested. However, taking to the oars produced no visible effect. Suddenly a seal popped up in front of them. 'Curious thing about seals,' Orwell remarked. 'Very inquisitive creatures.' By this stage the whirlpool had begun to recede. Oar power brought them to a rocky outcrop a mile from the Jura coast. As they reached the cliff Henry leapt out, but as the boat went down it rolled against the edge of the cliff and turned over. Orwell, Lucy and Richard managed to extricate themselves from beneath it and were hauled up on to the rock. There, exhausted and shivering, they tried to establish the best course of action. Proposing that they ought to have something to eat – a single cold potato which had been salvaged from the boat was fed to Richard – Orwell tramped off. Half an hour later he was back, empty-handed, but clearly enthused by something he had seen on the way. 'Extraordinary birds, puffins . . . They make their nests in burrows . . . I did see some baby seagulls, but I didn't have the heart to do anything about it.' Eventually they were rescued by a passing lobster boat whose crew had seen a fire they had lit, taken back to the Jura coast and obliged to walk the four or five miles back to Barnhill. The contents of the boat were lost for ever.

To the Dakins the incident seemed to sum up a good deal about their uncle: 'typical of him', Lucy thought, 'sweet and kind but in another world'. The others noted his hard work ('colossal amounts of typing') and wretched appearance, the perpetual cough made worse by chain-smoking, an obvious debility that was never discussed. Richard, then aged three, had only vague memories of the accident, other than that the soaking did Orwell's lungs no good. Within a couple of months he was seriously ill. By the end of August a drought set in, drying up the runner beans and the late peas and turning the local river, the Lealt, into a series of disconnected pools full of wary, irretrievable fish. There had been no water in the taps for nearly a fortnight, he told Brenda Salkeld at the start of September: the household had been forced to carry buckets back and forth from the well 200 yards away. At this point he seems to have been planning to return to London in November. The rough draft would be finished in October, he told Warburg. Mrs Christen, to whom he had sublet the Islington flat, had been typing it up since the early summer, occasionally calling on the Powells in Chester Gate to keep them abreast of the plot. At the same time he was wary of staying for more than a few weeks. He knew that if he got caught up once more in the world of journalism he would never get on with anything more substantial, he told Anthony Powell, ending rather ominously: 'One just seems to have a limited capacity for work nowadays and one has to husband it.' Already the autumn was setting in, with rain blowing east from the Atlantic. Writing to Powell, regretfully declining a request to review a new edition of Gissing's *A Life's Morning* for the *Times Literary Supplement,* where Powell was now fiction editor, he noted the gloom of the October afternoons, the lamps lit at half-past five, enveloping blackness waiting to move in. There were advantages, though, in this remote, island life. They had more coal than in London and in contrast to Canonbury Square the roof was at least waterproof.

For all his distance from the torn and cratered landscape of post-war London, the world Orwell was creating on his desk placed him at the heart of his old metropolitan life. The topography of *Nineteen Eighty-Four* would be instantly recognisable to anyone who, like Orwell, had spent the war years wandering around the three or four square miles centred on Oxford Street and its immediate hinterlands. The Ministry of Truth, for example, in which Winston labours at his falsification of the past, 'an enormous pyramidal structure of glittering white concrete', can be identified with the University of London Senate House, where the Ministry of Information had been based during the war. Its interior, on the other hand, reproduces the BBC studios at 200 Oxford Street. 'Victory Square' is Trafalgar Square, where Nelson has been replaced by a statue of Big Brother. There is an eerie scene in which Mr Charrington, the junk shop proprietor who furnishes Winston and Julia with their love-nest, recites the nursery rhyme 'Oranges and Lemons' and is asked by Winston to explain the line about 'the bells of St Martin's'. Winston realises that the church in 'Victory Square' has been turned into a propaganda museum full of waxwork tableaux depicting enemy atrocities. Even Mr Charrington's shop looks as if it has its origins in an *Evening Standard* piece from the autumn of 1946. The geographical precision which can be brought to *Nineteen Eighty-Four* – where once again like Gordon and Rosemary, hero and heroine end up at a version of Burnham Beeches – is intriguing in itself, but there are wider implications. Like the political arrangements beyond it, the landscape of the novel is a projection from existing material, anchored in the physical present and the physical present's consciousness. Previous dystopias had tended to be set on remote islands or in transparent never-never lands. The appeal – and the resonance – of *Nineteen Eighty-Four* to many of its original readers stemmed from the fact that it depicted a world that, by and large, they already knew.

A departure date for the London trip was set for early November. Late October found Orwell carrying out the round of pre-winter tasks: pruning the gooseberry bushes and manuring the apple trees. But his health was in steep decline and he knew it. By the end of the month he was confined to bed with what he told Moore was 'inflammation of the lungs'. He was reluctant to abandon the idea of travelling south – there were things to sort out with Moore, and others – while acknowledging that it would be several weeks before he would be fit to travel. By 7 November, the date on which he had planned to set out, the prospect of moving from Jura seemed yet more remote, 'unless for a very short business trip'. His overriding need was to stay in bed and try to get himself into some sort of shape. By this stage the draft of *Nineteen Eighty-Four* was practically finished. Mrs Christen, who had continued to type up batches of material sent to Canonbury Square, remembered that the initial manuscript stopped a few hundred words short of its eventual end. But it was clear that Orwell would be able to do no more work on it until at least the New Year.

It was obvious to everyone – to Rees, who was still staying at Barnhill, and to Orwell himself – that he was seriously ill. His letters to friends from the early winter are full of foreboding as to what the year spent 'staving off' might have done to him, and faint hopes that he might still be well. He had been very bad for several months, he acknowledged to Koestler, speculating that he might need a month's enforced rest in a nursing home. By the end of November he was suggesting to Anthony Powell that, though still ill, he might be getting a little better. Eventually, in early December, a chest specialist was summoned from Glasgow and Mrs Fletcher prepared a room at Ardlussa where he could be examined. The doctor confirmed what Orwell had feared: 'seriously ill', he reported to Moore; 'TB, as I suspected'. But this was not the whole story. The doctor who examined him was so alarmed by his state that he suggested that it might be better to keep him at Ardlussa: the trip back to Barnhill over the primitive

Jura roads was quite capable of setting off a haemorrhage. Characteristically, Orwell refused and was driven home by Rees, but the gravity of the situation impressed itself on him. He was resigned to spending several months in a sanatorium, though keen to assure his friends – he was probably right – that the time spent on Jura was not responsible for his damaged lungs. A fortnight later, in the week before Christmas, he was removed to Hairmyres Hospital near Glasgow. A letter sent to the *Observer* a couple of days later strikes the usual indefatigable note. The paper had invited him to go to South Africa to report on the forthcoming general election. This, Orwell acknowledged, was beyond him. On the other hand he wondered if they would let him have some books to review.

He was entering the final phase of his life: a world of hospital beds, enforced idleness and long hours of brooding. Of the next twenty-four months, only four would be spent outside a medical ward. How much did he know, or suspect? In the dead weeks of late 1947 when he lay in bed at Barnhill he had several long conversations with Robin Fletcher. There was an affinity between the two men: though his landlord was some years younger, both were Old Etonians. Robin Fletcher was sure, as he put it to his wife, that Orwell *knew*, and that his solitary wish was to get his novel finished while there was still time. Certainly he was very seriously ill. Bruce Dick, the consultant who examined Orwell at Hairmyres, diagnosed 'chronic' tuberculosis, consisting of a largish cavity in his left lung and a small patch at the top of the right. Provided that he could be induced to rest, however, his prospects were not uniformly bleak. Fibrotic TB hardens the lungs rather than causing them to disintegrate at breakneck speed to produce the 'galloping consumption' of the Victorian novel. Orwell had already survived for some years. Given suitable conditions, there was a good chance he could survive for several more. As for treatment, although the first stirrings of the new wonder drug streptomycin could be heard on the other side of the Atlantic, all that could be done at present was to 'rest' Orwell's worst-affected lung and give the lesions a chance to heal. This was done by paralysing the phrenic nerve by piercing it with a pair of forceps, collapsing the lung and then pumping in air. It was a painful intervention requiring regular 'refills' and Orwell, though never complaining, came to dread it. There was also a need to build him up: he had lost a stone and a half in weight over the preceding weeks. But already, a fortnight into his stay, he claimed to be feeling better: no longer subject to night-sweats and with a better appetite. He liked the hospital, he told Gwen O'Shaughnessy, with whom Mr Dick had been in professional communication. Everybody was very kind and the amenities even extended to a New Year party where all the beds were dragged into a single ward and the patients entertained by singers and a conjuror. If there was a drawback it lay in the sparse visiting times – an hour three afternoons a week with an extra session on Tuesday evenings. There was little chance of seeing friends, although several people made the long trip up from London. The person whom he most wanted to see he scarcely dared let into his presence. The possibility of Richard contracting the disease terrified Orwell, to the extent that if the boy held out his hands he would try to push him away.

Flat on his back, with only one lung working, he took solace in letters to friends. He was not feeling quite so death-like, he told Symons early in the New Year, and was eating more. *Nineteen Eighty-Four* was 'a mess' and would not be touched again until he was well. There was a typical letter to George Woodcock on Freedom Defence Committee business. It was time something was done to counter the continual demands to outlaw Sir Oswald Mosley and his supporters (Mosley had spent the war in Holloway but was now politically active once more). *Tribune*'s attitude he thought shameful. The fellow-travelling Labour MP Konni Zilliacus, with whom he had several times crossed swords in the past, had appeared in its columns demanding what amounted to Fascist legislation. The point, Orwell argued, was that Mosley would never attract mass support. No one, not even a Fascist, should be prosecuted for expressing an opinion when it could be shown that there was no substantial threat to the state. Meanwhile, his own condition was showing signs of progress. The treatment would probably take a long time, he told Helmut Klöse, but the doctors seemed optimistic about their ability to patch him up. He was even putting on weight.

Orwell's principal confidant seems to have been David Astor, who came several times to see him and discussed his condition with the hospital staff. (In the course of these conversations it came out that Bruce Dick had served with the Nationalist side in Spain.) Alerted to developments in pulmonary medicine on the further side of the Atlantic, the Hairmyres staff was keen to treat Orwell with streptomycin. There were, however, various impediments. The drug was expensive, procurable only in the US and, given that it had only been discovered three or four years previously, in the very early stages of use, so there was no real agreement as to what kind of dosage should be administered to patients. In response to a letter from Orwell, written on 1 February 1948, Astor volunteered to take the case up: a task that, in the regulatory labyrinth of the post-war era, needed all his ingenuity and high-level contacts. In the end the request for permission to import went as far as Orwell's old *Tribune* editor, Aneurin Bevan, by now Secretary of State for Health in the Attlee government. By the middle of the month the first 70-gram shipment was on the way – not before time, Orwell thought, as he believed that the doctors' confidence had slipped back a notch or two. He had stopped gaining weight, he noted, and fancied he was getting weaker, 'though mentally I am more alert'. He was, he discovered when the streptomycin arrived, a virtual guinea-pig. His doctors had no experience of using the drug and simply administered it to him in what turned out to be hugely excessive doses. There were distressing side-effects, including sore throats and flaking skin (all of which Orwell recorded dispassionately in his diary) but the general effect on his condition seemed positive. He felt much better and even started to do a little reviewing. The progress of his pro-fessional life was brought back into focus by a visit from Warburg, who brought specimen bindings for the proposed uniform edition of his work. Perhaps remembering the long, speculative conversations with Jacintha Buddicom from thirty years before, Orwell professed himself 'dismayed' by the light green covers that Warburg dangled before him. A uniform edition should be 'chaste-looking', he complained, preferably dark blue. Perhaps Warburg could try and get hold of some darker stuff?

Spring was coming. Lying in the hospital bed he found his mind moving backwards. Astor had invited him to stay at his home in Oxfordshire during the summer. He was captivated by the prospect of fishing in the Thames. He had caught some good fish at Eton, he reminisced, 'but hardly anyone outside college knew the place, as it was in the backwater joining College Field'. Celia Paget had worked in Paris, which prompted several elegiac sorrowings over past time, and a world that in the light of recent Parisian history now seemed extraordinarily remote. He was also concerned, in his characteristic, ruminative way, to analyse the effect of illness on his mental state. Weak and without appetite, if not actually in pain, you had the impression that your brain was functioning quite normally, he decided. It was only when you began to write that you realised the extent of the deterioration inside your skull. Yet his own mind was moving back into gear, planning to review a reissue of Oscar Wilde's *The Soul of Man under Socialism* for the *Observer* and meditating a long essay for Dwight

MacDonald on a writer who was coming to occupy an ever more significant place in his private literary pantheon. This was his late-Victorian hero, George Gissing. Orwell's career is dotted with literary enthusiasms, each of them capable of spilling over into his work. In the early 1930s it had been Joyce. The weeks spent re-reading Dickens in the Moroccan winter of 1938–9 had produced his first substantial piece of literary criticism. But there is an eeriness about the Gissing fixation that coloured the last years of his life. Irrespective of the similarities between their work – both were social investigators with an eye for low-life detail, each was a brilliant Dickensian – they died at the same age of lung disease. Whether or not Orwell was aware of the physical connection, he spent much of the late 1940s in pursuit of his Victorian avatar: seeking out copies of *New Grub Street* for friends, trying to get Gissing's novels reprinted, mentioning at one point a publisher's idea that he should write a biography. With its fascinated glimpses of urban working-class life and grimy backdrops, *Nineteen Eighty-Four*, too, is demonstrably a novel written in Gissing's shadow.

Come April his health seemed definitely to be improving. Despite his severe reaction to the streptomycin overdose – which induced rashes, ulceration and hair loss – he had put on 3 pounds in weight. Three sputum tests in a row had proved negative. The mild spring weather made him long to get out of bed, if only to sit in a chair. There was a hope that he could be discharged in summer, he told Moore. Past life continued to stir before him. Settling down to sleep one night, he had a curious dream of being shown a government document so secret that the minister or secretary responsible for it had orders not to let it out of his hands: Orwell had to come round to the further side of the desk and read it over the man's shoulder. Considering the incident – and the diary is much annotated, showing how hard Orwell had tried to remember it accurately – he realised that the man must have been Cripps' secretary, David Owen, and that the document concerned post-war British policy towards Burma. There was a vague memory, too, of telling a Burmese contact in London that he should not trust the British government. Had he given this warning it would have amounted to a betrayal of trust. Perhaps this was why until now the memory had lain dormant in his mind. But why should it return to haunt him five years later?

He was definitely better, reporting to Astor early in May that he was allowed to leave his bed for an hour a day and even put on a few clothes. Another sputum test had shown up negative. There was a plan that he could be discharged and stay somewhere near the hospital, perhaps in Richard Rees' Edinburgh flat, and receive treatment as an out-patient. Shortly afterwards he told Moore that the doctors thought he should stay until August; he felt so well, however, that he thought he might get on with the second draft of *Nineteen Eighty-Four*. He was pining to be back on Jura: his letters are full of wistful remarks about Barnhill or, in a letter to Michael Kennard, a young protégé of Warburg's who was staying on the island, details of the local fishing. By the end of May, although 'frightfully weak and thin', he was getting up for two hours a day and taking laborious walks – he was still very short of breath – in the hospital grounds. In this improved state he was keen to work. Books for review piled up at his bedside: Graham Greene's new novel, *The Heart of the Matter*, an 'interim' biography of Attlee by the young Labour MP, Roy Jenkins. *The Heart of the Matter*, dragging him back once more to the question of 'belief' in a world where there was no prospect of an afterlife, prompted a mordant attack on Greene's Catholicism, a world in which hell resembled 'a glorified nightclub'. Greene's cult of the sanctified sinner seemed to him to be merely 'frivolous'; when people really believed in hell, he maintained, they were not so fond of striking stylish attitudes on its brink. On the long summer afternoons he played croquet and was interested to talk to one of his fellow-patients, the editor of the boys' weekly the *Hotspur*. Early in July, a week after his forty-fifth birthday, he told Julian Symons that the doctors seemed to think he was 'pretty well all right now', though he would have to take things extremely quietly for a long time. A few days before the end of the month he made the long journey westward to Jura.

Was all the talk about being 'pretty well all right' simple self-delusion? Orwell's doctors agreed that when he left Hairmyres he was substantially better. Bill Dunn noted how well he seemed in comparison to the frail spectre that had left the island eight months before. Yet being diagnosed as free of TB germs did not mean that he would necessarily recover. In the years before he had received proper treatment, the arteries in his lungs had become dangerously exposed. A period of quiet convalescence might have maintained his improvement. However, this was exactly what Orwell was secretly scheming to deny himself. Back on Jura and 'very glad to get home', he gratefully resumed his domestic diary, inspecting the state of the garden and making lists of items required. The house that summer was full of visitors. Inez Holden came to stay for several months, annoying Avril by bringing many unnecessary items, including a female cat which over-stimulated the local toms. Richard Rees had the additional excuse of his partnership with Bill Dunn, the visible sign of which was the purchase of a farm truck. So great was the press of guests that at one point they overflowed into tents in the Barnhill garden. In his semi-invalid state Orwell pottered about the garden and played with Richard, even allowing him to smoke a cigarette in the hope that this might curb his interest. The experiment worked. Richard was violently sick. A fortnight later bad weather set in. The six hours of each day that Orwell had been ordered to spend in bed proved no hardship. He was ill towards the end of September – the note 'Unwell. Stayed in bed' chimes through the diary like the responses to a litany – recovered, but went back to Hairmyres to be examined. Mr Dick declared himself pleased, but Orwell was aware that any kind of exercise exhausted him. Even going out in the evening to milk the cows gave him a temperature, he told Astor. There was a plan to visit London, but everything was subordinate to the book. It was the worst possible time to be making the mental and physical effort needed to finish *Nineteen Eighty-Four*. As the pages of the second draft piled up, so did the signs of increasing feebleness. 'Pain in side very bad.' 'Pain in side very bad on & off.' Unquestionably the lurid and faintly unreal quality that the novel possesses – a ragged sense of a mind running out of its natural groove – derives from the mental state in which the final version of it was written: a desperate race towards a finishing line that would carry its own built-in defeat. By the end of October the manuscript was nearly complete and ready for typing. Here another problem presented itself. In bed most of the time, Orwell flinched from the effort of typing a fair copy. Worse, it was 'an unbelievably bad ms'. No one else would be able to do the work without on-the-spot guidance. Could Warburg find anyone – ideally a typist who could stay at Barnhill and complete the work under his supervision? Mrs Christen, who might perhaps have been inveigled north, had returned to the Far East. Warburg said he would try.

Already here in October, a bare three months after his discharge, Orwell knew that his condition had rapidly deteriorated. He was resigned to spending the worst part of the winter in a sanatorium. Waiting for the result of Warburg's attempt to procure a typist, he mused over Sartre's *Portrait of the Anti-Semite*, which the *Observer* had sent him for review. It was 'nonsense', he thought, for his Jewish friend Tosco Fyvel to claim that Eliot was anti-Semitic. Doubtless there were anti-Jewish remarks in his early work, but such things were common-place at the time. A distinction had to be made between what was said before and after the first evidence of Nazi policy towards the Jews. All the same, Orwell admitted, if six million English people had recently been killed in gas ovens, he imagined he would feel insecure if he even saw a joke in a French comic paper about Englishwomen's buck teeth. Roger Senhouse wrote in early November, still in search of a 'Scots lassie' who could do the work, but the pursuit was proving difficult. Stenographers were in short supply, even in London. To find someone prepared to travel to the Inner Hebrides at the onset of winter was nearly impossible.

Meanwhile the weather was bad and now the roof leaked. To walk even a few hundred yards incapacitated him, Orwell discovered. He could not so much as pull up a weed in the garden. 'Whatever I do, it seems my temperature rises,' he told Avril. There was still no typist, so in mid-November he began on the 'grisly job' of typing it himself. Orwell knew exactly what he was doing – he was already fixing up a sanatorium bed through Mr Dick and Gwen O'Shaughnessy – making a final effort that would have a shattering effect on his already weakened frame. Sitting up in bed, the paraffin heater wheezing at his side, still smoking his endless hand-rolled cigarettes, he laboured on. Ironically, it could all have been avoided. Leonard Moore, whose help Orwell had enlisted, had managed to find a typist but feared to close on the deal in case Senhouse, working through his niece in Edinburgh, also came up with someone. Orwell was beyond help even had it arrived. In any case the work was nearly done. He would send off the manuscript on 7 December, he told Moore. 'Feeling unwell', 'feeling very unwell', runs the diary. By the middle of the month the work was complete. He could not write anything, he was very ill, he told Fyvel, announcing his departure early in the New Year to a sanatorium in the Cotswolds. The diary lapses, although shortly before Christmas he marshalled his resources to write to Astor apologising for his inability to fulfil his *Observer* commitments. 'I just must try & stay alive for a while because apart from other considerations I have a good idea for a novel.'

He spent Christmas and New Year in bed. Then one evening in the first week in January Bill Dunn drove him down to Ardlussa on the first stage of his journey to Gloucestershire. The weather had been bad and Dunn's Austin 12 got bogged down. The farm truck was summoned, and Orwell and Richard sat together in the car, as the rain drummed on the roof, talking and eating boiled sweets. He was quite cheerful, Richard remembered, anxious amid the cold and the icy Jura rain to make it appear that there was nothing wrong.

Orwell's things

Most writers, either unconsciously or not, accumulate property around them. To read more than a page of Evelyn Waugh's diaries is to be plunged immediately into a world of antique Burges washstands and high-grade cigars. Thackeray's first act on acquiring the gentleman's mansion that he thought commensurate with his ancestral dignity was to stock it with vintage wines and fine bindings. The sale of number 2 Palace Green, Kensington's effects after his death was an auctioneer's dream. Orwell's life, on the other hand, seems ominously short on paraphernalia, possessions, aspects of his personality focused on or expressing themselves in things. Practically the only photographs of him to contain artefacts above the level of a beach towel are the ones taken by Vernon Richards in the Canonbury Square flat in 1946. The Orwell who stands drawing an ancient Burmese sword from its scabbard, working at his lathe or lighting a cigarette with a little flash of flame looks oddly puzzled, as if he has only just stumbled upon these objects for the first time, can't quite fathom how they operate, what makes them tick.

So what were Orwell's things – the items that lay on the desk beside him as he wrote, on his bedside table, on stray surfaces in the dozen or so habitations that he occupied at one time or another in the years of his maturity? Anthony Powell's account of the Kilburn maisonette during the war perhaps offers a hint of the ideal environment Orwell would have liked to create around himself in more propitious circumstances – the dark, heavy furniture, the family portraits on the walls – like an eighteenth-century squire's drawing room set down in London NW6. But this kind of lifestyle takes time, care and money to assemble. Time, care, money . . . and things. The clothes we know about, those spreading hats unpacked from the Burma trunks that the Portobello Road children remarked on, the pairs of flannel trousers and the shabby jackets that looked more distinguished the shabbier they became. The books and the pamphlets are docketed and accounted for. What about the rest? What about, to take an obvious category, the tools of his professional trade, the legendary implements about which so much posthumous fuss is made? (The Royal Society of Literature, for example, gives incoming fellows bidden to sign the roll the choice of Dickens' pen or Byron's quill.) Most of the early letters are written in fountain-pen and ink; in several of the early notes to Leonard Moore Orwell apologises for using a disposable 'post-office pen'. In the post-war era he took to a Biro – then a newfangled accessory on a par with a modern-day Rolex watch – which cost all of £3 and was lent to friends commissioned to indict 'must do' lists as he lay in his hospital bed. His manual typewriter – rather suitably, in the light of his faint anarchist leanings – was later bestowed by Sonia on the 1960s hippy-radical news-sheet, the *International Times*.

Orwell took an occasional interest in other writers' possessions: as we have seen, visiting the Brontë museum at Haworth during the *Road to Wigan Pier* trip he was struck by Charlotte Brontë's tiny, cloth-topped boots. His own leavings are painfully small. He left hardly any manuscripts: a few pages of *Keep the Aspidistra Flying*, and partial revised typescripts of *Nineteen Eighty-Four* and *Animal Farm* are all that survive. With the exception of the Burma gear, he was not a great one for souvenirs: his solitary memento of Spain was an oil-burning peasant's lamp. The fishing rods that lay in the corner of his room at UCH were given to Warburg's protégé Michael Kennard, now dead; no one knows what became of them. That elemental biographer's urge to fetishise – the lock of some Romantic poet's hair, the page from some literary doodler's sketchpad – has scant chance of succeeding with Orwell. Not long ago a squat, bulky item turned up along with the piled review copies on the doormat. Torn open, it contained a large, gunmetal stapler – 'Orwell's stapler', according to the friend who had bought it (at considerable expense) at a *Tribune* fund-raiser. Though treated with every respect – I certainly wouldn't dream of stapling anything with it – there is nothing to differentiate it from any other example of its genre, nothing that an insurance agent would care to put a value on. This, you feel, is rather typical of Orwell, the approach he took to life and the things – mostly abstract things – he cared about. In the end, only the books endure.

18

Endgame

Of course I've had it coming to me all my life. – Letter to Jack
Common, 27 July 1949

It will probably be a rather macabre wedding. – Malcolm
Muggeridge, diary, 5 September 1949

Escorted by Richard Rees, he went south by train. No sooner had they
cleared the Glasgow suburbs than Orwell, thinking back to the climatic
conditions he had left behind on Jura, remarked that the weather
seemed to be just the same in England. Rees's astonishment at this
stupendous piece of ignorance left him unmoved: he was more
interested to be told that the part of Scotland through which they were
travelling was the home of Burns, Walter Scott and Carlyle. Then, as
the train continued its criss-crossing, irregular progress over the border,
Orwell ventured a second almost classically ingenuous comment. Was
it possible, he wondered, for the trains of one railway company to run
on the tracks of another? A dozen years later the conversation was still
fresh in Rees's mind. The rest of the journey proceeded without
incident. Some time late on 6 January 1949 they arrived at Cranham,
where Rees delivered his friend into the care of the medical staff.

On the previous day Bruce Dick, the consultant at Hairmyres, had
written to David Astor about Orwell's case. It was obvious, Dick
thought, that the patient had suffered a fairly acute relapse over the
autumn and winter. When seen by the Hairmyres doctors in September
he had seemed 'as good as when he left us', physically capable of the
semi-invalid's life of pottering around Barnhill. Now it seemed plain
that he would need to live a more sheltered life. 'I fear the dream of Jura
must fade out,' Dick concluded. Cranham, where the laborious task of
attempting to restore Orwell's health would begin, had a fairly austere
reputation. High up in the Cotswolds and inconveniently sited – nine

miles from Stroud and inaccessible by public transport – it was built to a chalet-style design: in reality a series of wooden huts, 15 feet by 12, and, beyond, a glass-covered veranda. It was a private establishment, costing 12 guineas a week, but, Orwell noted, extra for medicine and operations. He was, it soon became evident, desperately ill. Within a week the doctors had begun administering para-amino-salicylic acid – like streptomycin a drug so new that there was no agreement on the proper dosage. Yet he remained curiously optimistic about his prospects, telling Moore, the day after his admission, that 'I daresay in a month or so I shall be fit to begin working again.' Clearly at this stage he still envisaged the world of southern sanatoria as a stop-gap expedient, as a letter to Reg Reynolds, discussing a proposed second volume of *British Pamphleteers*, gives Barnhill as his permanent address. Cranham, he told Rees, was not as bad as he had feared: warm, centrally heated and with reasonable food suited to his improving appetite. But short-term plans – in particular to keep up Barnhill for the summer – jostled with an awareness of how serious his situation had become. His aim, he told Rees, was to stay alive for another five to ten years. This, he appreciated, would mean having medical attention near to hand: on Jura 'I am just a nuisance to everybody when I am ill, whereas in a more civilised place this doesn't matter.' His early optimism about his condition and his chances of being allowed out for the summer was misplaced. He spent eight months at Cranham and eventually left it for a bed from which he would never rise again.

The typescript of *Nineteen Eighty-Four* had been with Secker & Warburg for several weeks. Warburg, who had read it within days of the parcel arriving, was devastated by what he found. The internal memorandum he circulated in mid-December 1948 seems practically awestruck. First and foremost, the novel was 'amongst the most terrifying books I have ever read'. The object of its satire was the Soviet Union 'to the nth degree'. Additionally, Orwell's invention of 'Ingsoc' as the theoretical framework on which life in Oceania is based, represented 'a deliberate and sadistic attack on Socialism and Socialist parties generally'. The book was worth a million votes to the Conservative Party, and could plausibly be issued with a preface by Winston Churchill. The final section, describing Winston's torture and subsequent rehabilitation, seemed to him Dostoevskyan in its repudiation of hope. Like many later critics, Warburg diagnosed a physical explanation for the sickly, lurid quality he judged the novel to exhibit. 'I cannot but think,' he concluded, 'that this book could have been written only by a man who himself, however temporarily, had lost hope, and for physical reasons which are sufficiently apparent.' He prayed that he would be spared reading anything like it for years to come. As for the novel's commercial prospects, David Farrar, Warburg's associate, prophesied that *Nineteen Eighty-Four* had the potential to do for Orwell what *The Heart of the Matter* had done for Graham Greene. If they failed to sell between fifteen and twenty thousand copies, they 'ought to be shot'.

In fact, though he immediately isolated several of the novel's characteristic effects, Warburg was wrong about *Nineteen Eighty-Four* on two counts. It is not exclusively anti-Communist but anti-totalitarian. This is a point that Orwell himself was concerned to labour for the rest of his life. There was an exchange of correspondence to this effect later in 1949 with Sidney Sheldon, then a young Hollywood screenwriter, who proposed – in the end unsuccessfully – to adapt the novel for the Broadway stage. *Nineteen Eighty-Four* was being promoted in the United States as an anti-Soviet tract. Sheldon, who had read it carefully, was concerned to give his adaptation an anti-Fascist slant: Orwell supported him in this. Neither is the novel altogether without hope. The proles, in which 'hope' resides, are a debased and powerless lower order, but it is their innate humanity, the sense of a genuinely popular culture running on in silent defiance of the lofted torches and marching feet, that redeems the nightmare landscape on which Oceania, the world of Big Brother, the Thought Police and the Ministry of Love, is fashioned. And – a point always worth making about *Nineteen Eighty-Four* – it *is* a nightmare landscape, a world whose horrors are driven home on the one hand by their utter inescapability, and on the other by the fact that they take place not in some Swiftian fantasy land but in an environment that is recognisably our own. When he came to read a proof copy of the novel some months later, Orwell's friend Malcolm Muggeridge found it 'rather repugnant', bearing little relation to life or 'anything that could happen', and containing horrors that were merely 'silly'. Subsequently he and Anthony Powell were highly amused by a report, conveyed to them by Warburg, that a number of booksellers given advance copies had been so frightened that they were unable to sleep. The reaction of a blasé journalist like Muggeridge, whose public and private utterances of the period are characterised by a refusal to be impressed, is understandable, and yet it ignores the dreadful twinge of recognition that the novel habitually produces, the thought that this is not some alternative world hauled down out of the sky but a vivid projection of existing tendencies and states of mind.

Essentially the world of Winston Smith is the world of wartime London cranked up a gear or two. England, rechristened Airstrip One, is part of Oceania, an agglomeration of international territories jostling for precedence with its rivals, Eurasia and Eastasia, and at this stage at war with Eurasia. It is a world of tireless, omnipresent propaganda and surveillance: Big Brother's poster on every street corner, daily 'two minute hates' to boost morale, telescreens constantly monitoring every public and private act. Winston Smith, Orwell's desiccated thirty-nine-year-old hero, is only a minor cog in this streamlined bureaucratic machine, but the part that he plays is a vital one: sitting in a cubicle at the Ministry of Truth falsifying back numbers of the *Times* and in some cases literally airbrushing people out of his history. Significantly, some of the novel's most revealing procedural passages come in the lunch-hour conversations Winston has with his fellow-workers in the Ministry's grim canteen, for they reveal *Nineteen Eighty-Four's* grounding in the corruption of language. His colleague Symes, for example, at work on the latest dictionary of 'Newspeak', the savagely reductive formal tongue of Oceania, exults in the constricting effect that his manipulations have on thought: 'In the end we shall make thoughtcrime literally impossible, because there will not be words in which to express it.' There will, to anticipate modern literary theory, be nothing beyond the text. By this stage, however, Winston is secretly engaged on his own thoughtcrime, buying an ancient vellum-bound notebook, a relic of the days before death squads and the dominion of the 'Party', on which, involuntarily, he finds he has scrawled the words DOWN WITH BIG BROTHER. Launched on a passionate but essentially loveless affair with Julia, the dark-haired 'girl from the fiction department' (a branch of the Ministry of Truth involved in producing state-sanctioned pornography for the proles), he finds himself approached by O'Brien, previously a fabulously remote member of the Inner Party, who, divining his rebellious streak, lends him a copy of *The Principles of Oligarchical Collectivism*, the book by the arch-traitor Emmanuel Goldstein which explodes the premises on which Oceania's autocracy is based. O'Brien, it turns out, is merely an *agent provocateur*. Their cover blown, their hide-out above Mr Charrington's junk-shop raided, Winston and Julia are dragged off to the Ministry of Love. Tortured and humiliated by the horrors of 'Room 101', Winston is eventually forced to recant. Or rather, it is worse than this, for he ends up believing that what he has done is wrong. 'He had won the victory over himself. He loved Big Brother.'

Thus framed, the point that *Nineteen Eighty-Four* labours is the one that had animated Orwell's journalism since the early years of the war. Its origins can be detected even before that in the scene in *Coming up for Air*, where George Bowling asks Porteous, the retired schoolmaster, what he thinks of Hitler. Porteous is properly dismissive of this transient modern phenomenon, causing Bowling to reflect:

> 'I think you've got it wrong. Old Hitler's something different. So's Joe Stalin. They aren't like these chaps in the old days who crucified people and chopped their heads off, and so forth, just after the fun of it. They're after something quite new – something that's never been heard of before.'

Subsequently Bowling imagines that 'I can see the war that's coming and I can see the after-war, the food-queues and the secret police and the loudspeakers telling you what to do.' In other words, the world of *Nineteen Eighty-Four*. Any military regime at war with its neighbours will commit acts of cruelty and spread false intelligence. A totalitarian regime does these things to sustain something integral to itself, to wield power for its own sake. As it calls into question the historical justification on which this power is based, objective knowledge must be destroyed, and the means to destroy it lie in language. Perhaps the most revealing moment – the scene in which the last fragment of the jigsaw snaps into place – comes when O'Brien demands of Winston if he begins to see what kind of world 'we' are creating. It is 'the exact opposite of the stupid hedonistic utopias that the old reformers imagined' – a world of fear and treachery and torment, devoid of art, literature, science, love and laughter, dominated by the much greater intoxication of power. By comparison the ancient tyrants whom Porteous blandly invokes as Hitler's forebears were simple hooligans. The totalitarians of the twentieth century were engaged on something that was much more insidious – not to tell a man that $2+2=5$, but to convince him that it was so.

There is something sacerdotal about O'Brien as he pronounces this analysis – and a few pages before he has in fact remarked that 'We are the priests of power. God is power' – but there is also something schoolmasterly, the sense of a patient, occasionally exasperated instructor urging on a student who may still 'make good' if he is sufficiently goaded. Orwell even notes that he 'assumed again his air of a schoolmaster questioning a promising pupil'. But the faint gestures towards his own early life – Mr Wilkes, perhaps, catechising contenders for the Harrow History Prize – make perfect sense in the novel's wider context. As his last completed book, *Nineteen Eighty-Four* reveals Orwell's work to be a kind of palimpsest, an endless scroll constantly refined and brought up to date, in which early entries re-emerge to assume an unexpected resonance. The early sections, in particular, can be read as a deliberate re-framing of the landscape of *Keep the Aspidistra Flying*. As Winston looks out of the window of Victory Mansions in the opening chapter, 'Down in the street little eddies of wind were whirling dust and torn paper into spirals.' (Compare this with the ribbon of paper that 'fluttered fitfully like a tiny pennant' outside Mr McKechnie's bookshop.) Later Winston steals adventurously into a prole pub ('Behind his back he could feel everyone eyeing his blue overalls. A game of darts going on at the other end of the room interrupted itself for as much as thirty seconds'), recalling Gordon and Ravelston's excursion to the working-class drinking den. Winston's careful hoarding of his cigarettes exactly matches Gordon's, for all that the cause is rationing rather than poverty. And every so often comes a twitch – subtle, but unmistakable to anyone who knows Orwell's work – on the thread of his own memory. 'Want to see the hangings! Want to see the hangings!' chants the daughter of Winston's neighbour Parsons, referring to the execution in the park of Eurasian prisoners with round Mongol faces. Orwell had attended a very similar occasion a quarter of a century before. Finally there is an extraordinary moment, like a bullet winging its way back across time, when Winston summons up the vision of Mrs Parsons in her slatternly kitchen, 'a woman with a lined face and wispy hair, fiddling helplessly with a blocked waste-pipe'. Orwell had seen such a face years before as he walked up the back-alley in Wigan.

For the moment the novel lay quietly ticking on Warburg's desk and that of his American publisher, Harcourt Brace and Company. Each of the preliminary soundings Warburg took in the book trade produced the same result. The novel would be a bestseller, guaranteed to whip up controversy on both sides of the Atlantic (even Muggeridge told his diary that he 'knew it would sell'). Its author, meanwhile, was in a bad way. The Fyvels, who came over to see him early in the New Year, bringing with them Olga Miller, who wrote satirical verse for the *New Statesman* and was known to Orwell from his *Tribune* days, were shocked by their visit. Orwell seemed so much worse, so much thinner and frailer than they had expected. Mentally he seemed in perfect control. Physically, however, he was 'terribly emaciated, his face drawn and waxen pale'. But he was pleased to see them, and happily allowed himself to be twitted by Mary Fyvel on the subject of his royalties from *Animal Farm*. There would be no more worries about the depredations of the Inland Revenue, she suggested. It was fairy gold, Orwell told her, fairy gold. And yet he was now a moderately well-off man, able to pay for private medical care, beginning to make proper arrangements through his accountants, Harrison, Son, Hill & Co., to spread his earnings, although the immediate consequences – the upper rate of income tax was then above ninety per cent – was that the taxman demanded half of his previous year's income.

Fyvel's account of the visit raises a concern voiced by several of Orwell's friends in the spring of 1949. This was the non-effectiveness of the treatment he received at Cranham, and what seemed to the non-medical eye to be the sanatorium's very visible shortcomings. The Fyvels noted a prevailing air of bleakness. Another friend remembered 'the horrible hut he had at Cranham' and the unappetising-looking food. Orwell's niece Jane, who arrived as part of a Dakin family visitation – the Dakins lived not far away, at Bristol – recalled being 'rather horrified . . . it seemed rather stuffy and untidy and rather cluttered'. Orwell himself complained to Richard Rees – something also noted by Pamela Warburg – that the chief doctor, a man named Hoffman, had yet to meet him and that medical attention was confined to a female subordinate looking in every morning to ask him how he felt. Curiously, no one had yet taken a stethoscope to his chest. 'However, I suppose they know best.' Six months before, the tenants around Barnhill had noted the improvement produced by his stay at Hairmyres. Now he seemed almost cadaverous. Brenda Salkeld, in particular, returned from a trip to Cranham convinced that he was going to die. Only Richard, who was brought to see him from temporary lodgings at the nearby anarchist commune of Whiteways, was puzzled by the spectacle of the tall, emaciated but apparently uninjured man who lay all day in his bed. 'Where does it hurt, daddy?' he would enquire.

The Fyvels had noted the gap between Orwell's apparent mental vigour and the waning of his physical powers. It was a contrast that occurred to Orwell. Writing to Anthony Powell early in February – Powell was hard at work on *A Question of Upbringing*, the first volume in his gigantic *Dance to the Music of Time* sequence – he noted wistfully that 'It's a god-awful job getting back to writing books again after years of time-wasting, but I feel now I've broken the spell and could go on writing if I were well again.' There were few signs of improvement. Although 'well looked after', he had gained only four ounces in weight, he told Julian Symons. A letter to Celia Paget had to be cut short: 'I feel so lousy I can't write any more.' Yet there were good days. On the third Saturday in February Powell and Muggeridge walked the nine miles from Stroud to visit him. Muggeridge thought him 'in very good shape in the circumstances . . . the same old crusty, loveable egotist' and noted the avidity with which he talked. He wanted to live another ten years, he confided: there were books to write, Richard's childhood to watch. Muggeridge was 'not sure he will pull this off'. Much of the conversation turned on Gissing: 'he rather sees himself in Gissing's position,' Muggeridge shrewdly noted. The two hours passed swiftly in a haze of cigarette smoke and alcohol fumes, the latter rising from a bottle which Orwell produced from under the bed.

In contrast to the delays that had afflicted *Animal Farm* five years before, production arrangements for *Nineteen Eighty-Four* were well in hand. American proofs had already arrived by the end of February. Orwell spent the first few days of March dealing with queries from Roger Senhouse. Despite his feeble state he was longing to resume work, planning an essay on Evelyn Waugh and still envisaging an early-summer discharge. The doctors said he would have to stay in bed for another two months, he reported. It was a great bore, he told Michael Meyer, now teaching at a university in Sweden: 'I cannot resign myself to living a sedentary life, which I suppose I have to from now on.' Friends rallied round – Rees offered to lend him money, Astor offered to procure an early version of the tape-recorder for him to dictate into – but Orwell's chief concern seems to have been his separation from Richard. He was worried that the child would grow away from him, he told Rees, or come to think of him merely as a person who was always lying down, unable to play. By the end of March he was definitely worse, spitting up quantities of blood and forbidden to type, depressed and noting ominously that 'there is evidently nothing very definite they can do for me'. There had been talk of the 'thorax' operation, but the surgeon had cried off: the patient had to possess one sound lung. The projected essay on Evelyn Waugh realised only notes and an aborted draft. One regrets it was never finished, as Orwell's view of 'the English novelist who has most conspicuously defied his contemporaries' would, on the strength of its surviving fragment, certainly have been worth reading. There were at least two face-to-face meetings with the essay's subject. Waugh, who lived at nearby Dursley, was persuaded by Connolly to visit Cranham. No record of the conversation survives, but Waugh, detecting sanctity in the ravaged figure on the bed, reported that Orwell was 'very near to God'.

By early April the blood-spitting had stopped, but he confessed to 'feeling ghastly most of the time'. The fact was, he admitted to Rees, he was in a bad way. The doctors were thinking of trying streptomycin again. There was another foreshadowing. If things went badly he would ask Rees to bring Richard to see him once more 'before I get too frightening in appearance'. Indications of *Nineteen Eighty-Four*'s probable impact were everywhere to hand, in particular its selection by the American Book of the Month Club, despite his refusal to remove the long extracts from *The Theory and Practice of Oligarchical Collectivism*. Work proved increasingly beyond him. He managed a review of Winston Churchill's *Their Finest Hour* for the *New Leader*, but Dr Hoffman was deputed to send telegrams declining other offers. At the end of March Orwell had a visit from Celia Paget. She could now be reckoned one of his close friends – they had known each other since the Welsh Christmas of 1945 – but the visit was primarily on official business. Having spent a year or so in Paris, following her time at *Polemic* – now defunct – she was back in London working for an organisation called the Information Research Department (IRD). Established in 1948 by the Attlee government, the IRD was an offshoot of the Foreign Office whose brief was to support democratising influences across Europe by issuing pamphlets about Communist influence and to brief the UK's representative at the United Nations to counter Soviet misrepresentation. Given the political climate – this was the height of the early Cold War era, when reds were thought to lurk beneath every bed – this involved the IRD's small staff (Celia shared a room with her boss, the later scourge of Soviet despotism, Robert Conquest) in a labyrinthine exercise in intelligence gathering: establishing in advance that the experts they approached to write for them did not harbour secret Communist sympathies. The process was fraught with difficulty. Many of its pitfalls were only revealed years later: Celia Paget remembered once seeking an opinion on something she had written from Guy Burgess, then of the Foreign Office's China Desk. The IRD's motives in contacting Orwell were threefold: to see if he would write a pamphlet himself; to invite him to recommend other potential helpers; and to advise on public figures whose covert political sympathies would make their involvement either invidious or downright dangerous.

Operating under this remit, the IRD could have been set up with the express intention of stirring Orwell's interest. He immediately recommended potential pamphleteers and wrote within the week to Rees, then back on Jura, asking him to send up a notebook which contained a list of crypto-Communists and fellow-travellers which he wanted 'to bring up to date'. This is the first reference to Orwell's 'list', notorious since its (partial) public unveiling in 1991. Clearly kept up and added to over a period of several years, it harboured 135 names – a few of them kept back even now from public gaze for fear of libel proceedings. Thirty-five of these were subsequently sent to Celia Paget: 'not very sensational', Orwell thought, 'and I don't suppose it will tell your friends anything they don't know'. Despite the furore that surrounded publication of the list – the Labour MP Gerald Kaufman declared that 'suddenly, it turns out that Orwell himself was hounding those whose thoughts did not chime in with his own' – 'not very sensational' is a fair enough description both of the roster sent to the IRD and the exercise on which Orwell and Rees were engaged. *Pace* Kaufman, no one was being hounded – this was merely a private endeavour, not without its light-hearted side, carried on by two men with little direct political influence. Moreover, in the context of the time, and the remit of the IRD, it could be regarded as a highly necessary undertaking.

To examine the list with the benefit of half a century's hindsight is to turn up some notably implausible fellow-travellers – Priestley, for example, or the mountainous Liverpudlian MP Bessie Braddock. At the same time there are plenty of people who by the standards of contemporary left-wing politics were little more than Communist stooges: Tom Driberg, for instance, who was known for his regular lunch dates at the Russian embassy, or Peter Smollett OBE, head of the Ministry of Information's Russian Department during the war, in all probability the man who advised Cape not to publish *Animal Farm*, and who was exposed after his death as a spy. Even Priestley, for all the popularity of his war broadcasts, was capable of publishing a book like *Russian Journey* (1946), which among other claims, denied the existence of the Soviet secret police. Consider the career of John Platts-Mills, whose appearance on the list was revealed only after his death, at the age of ninety-five, in 2001. At this point an Independent MP for Finsbury – he had been expelled from the Labour party a year before for refusing to apologise for a telegram in support of the Italian Socialist leader Nenni's pact with the Communists – Platts-Mills was an unshakeable Commons apologist for Stalin, a tireless supporter of Eastern European 'friendship movements' and unable, even in the Khrushchev era, to bring himself to accept the truth about Stalinist atrocities. Even confronted by a Platts-Mills, or a Zilliacus, Orwell strove for objectivity. 'The whole difficulty is to decide where each person stands,' he told Rees, '& one has to treat each case individually.' To talk about 'hounding', too, is perhaps to ignore the NKVD file on Orwell himself, which exists somewhere in the vast mass of pre-*glasnost* Russian archives.

The second course of streptomycin produced 'ghastly' results – presumably some kind of allergic reaction – but by mid-April he claimed to be feeling a little better. In this state he wrote a sombre letter to Gwen O'Shaughnessy effectively summarising his position and making arrangements in the event of his death. Nothing could be done for him medically, he feared, except to keep him quiet. Possibly he would be allowed to Jura for a week or two in the summer. The winter would have to be spent somewhere warm, and with medical help close to hand. Were he to die, decisions about Richard's upbringing should be left to her and to Avril, Gwen having the casting vote should there be any dispute. There would be substantial tax owing on his estate but this could easily be met from the large sums of money he expected to make from *Nineteen Eighty-Four*. Meanwhile, when in London he intended to solicit 'an expert opinion on how long I am likely to live'. The implication of this and other statements to friends is clear: despite occasional flashes of optimism, Orwell was in no doubt about the seriousness of his condition. It would not surprise him, he told Astor, if the *Observer* profile planned to mark *Nineteen Eighty-Four*'s publication should have to be reworked as an obituary. Even the prospect of a few years' grace was hedged with qualifications. He could stand the thought of another five years as an invalid if he could work, he confided to Anthony Powell, but at the moment he was fit for nothing.

Advance copies of *Nineteen Eighty-Four* were already being dispatched. The names featured on Orwell's complimentary list – they included Eliot, Henry Miller, Edmund Wilson and Aldous Huxley – are an eloquent testimony to the intellectual reputation he now commanded. But his physical state was 'ghastly': too feverish even to go to the X-ray room and stand against the screen. There was little doubt that when a picture could be taken it would show serious deterioration in both lungs. As it was, though, he thought he might still survive. Dr Kirkman, Hofmann's deputy, would only say that she didn't know.

Anxious to find out where he stood and with, as he put it, 'the strongest reasons for staying alive', Orwell determined on a second opinion, either from a specialist supplied by Warburg or from Dr Morland, the man who had attended him in pre-war days. He was adamant that he wished to be told the truth: '. . . I don't want to be cheered up but to be given an expert opinion on whether I am likely to stay alive, & if so, how long'. One of Orwell's reasons for wanting to stay alive was perhaps less obvious than his desire to write more books and to watch Richard grow up. But it became clear in the identity of the person to whom he wrote immediately after Morland's visit on 24 May. The specialist had concluded that he was 'not so bad', Orwell reported to Sonia Brownell, but it would mean complete rest for a long time, possibly as much as a year. Morland's report to Warburg was couched in the same relatively optimistic tones. The patient's left lung was badly affected, the right lung less so. There was little chance of a cure, but with rest he might aspire to the condition of a 'good' chronic: living an extremely sheltered life and perhaps doing a few hours' work a day. Morland made the point that must have occurred to Orwell himself – that his health would not have broken down so spectacularly had he not over-taxed himself the previous winter.

In mid-June, on the eve of *Nineteen Eighty-Four*'s publication, Warburg paid him another visit. An internal Secker & Warburg memorandum, written shortly afterwards, notes Orwell's 'shocking' state of health and rates his medium-term chances of survival at 50–50. But he was full of ideas – a book of essays, a new short novel with a Burmese background (Orwell did manage to sketch a few notes for the provisionally titled 'A Smoking-Room Story' around or before this time). Naturally a certain part of Warburg's anxiety on his friend's behalf stemmed from his desire that Orwell should stay alive to write him more books: Muggeridge, some months before, had noted the 'plaintive' tone that came into his voice when Orwell's prospects were discussed. The reviews of *Nineteen Eighty-Four* had begun to roll in: awed and approving, apart from occasional reservations about its starkness ('. . . the nature of its fantasy is so absolutely final and relentless that I can recommend it only with a certain reservation,' Diana Trilling wrote in the American *Nation*) and predictable hostility from the Far Left (it was eventually reviewed in *Pravda*, whose critic diagnosed a 'filthy book' slobbering with 'poisonous spittle'). Gratified by the wave of enthusiasm, and feeling slightly better, Orwell had a more personal quarry in view. Once he was well and about again, he remarked innocuously to Astor, he intended to get married. 'Apart from other considerations, I think I should stay alive longer if I was married & had someone to look after me.' A second courtship of Sonia proceeded throughout the summer – she visited him several times at Cranham – culminating in another proposal. It coincided with a further collapse in Orwell's condition. He was suffering 'flare-ups', one of which produced a touch of pleurisy which left him feeling 'absolutely ghastly'. A note of fatalism enters one or two of his letters from this time. 'Of course I've had it coming to me all my life,' he told Jack Common. Morland, who came to see him at the end of August, though noting no apparent deterioration, suggested that a change of hospital might do him good. Early in September he was removed by private ambulance to Morland's own fiefdom of University College Hospital. A stone's throw away, the Ministry of Truth loomed above the Bloomsbury skyline.

University College Hospital lay in familiar territory: not far from the *Adelphi* offices where nearly twenty years before he had smoked cigarettes in front of the gas fire with Jack Common. The idea, he reported to Rees, was that he should stay at UCH for a couple of months, going on to spend the winter in some more temperate climate: Capri and Switzerland were among possible destinations. He felt ghastly, he told Astor on 5 September, while marvelling at the comfort of his journey up from Gloucestershire 'in the most ritzy ambulance you can imagine'. There was a much more salient piece of news to convey. At some time in the past few weeks he had proposed to Sonia and been accepted. Their plan was to get married 'while I am still an invalid'. Among other advantages a legal union would make it easier for Sonia to look after him if they went abroad later in the year.

Orwell's desire to marry Sonia, and her willingness to accept him, has always been regarded as the last great enigma of his life, and yet the motivation is readily understandable on both sides. Undoubtedly Orwell was highly attracted by the lively and efficient girl fifteen years younger than himself. There have been attempts to write up Sonia as Julia – described as 'a bold-looking girl of about twenty-seven, with thick, dark hair, a freckled face, and swift athletic movements'; several of Sonia's friends remarked the similarity of vocal tone. Literary insiders of the time noticed that, in a curious way, their relationship was – the phrase is Muggeridge's – 'the coming to life of the love affair in *Nineteen Eighty-Four*'. But there was also a more prosaic urge: he wanted someone to look after him, and the thought of an obliging helpmeet clearly crowded out any romantic aspirations (according to Sonia's account of the proposal, his next words were 'You must learn to make dumplings'). On Sonia's side a sense of duty mingled with a strong interest for self-preservation. After nearly a decade in the saddle, Connolly was losing interest in his creation: *Horizon*'s days were numbered. On the rebound from an intense love affair with the French philosopher Maurice Merleau-Ponty, Sonia was also in search of a focus for her life. 'When *Horizon* folds up I'll marry George,' a friend remembered her saying at the time. Undeniably these words were said, but it would be wrong to deduce from them that Sonia regarded marriage to Orwell as merely expedient. Friend after friend stresses her organising, practical side, that she 'liked looking after people', while acknowledging her relish of the power it brought. 'She loved it,' her great friend Janetta, now married to the writer Robert Kee, observed of her dextrous management of Orwell's hospital routines, 'and it was all to do with being in control.' Certainly, Orwell approximated to an ideal she had been stalking since her Euston Road days, what Stephen Spender, who observed her for forty years, called 'Sonia in pursuit of her genius', the great man whom she could comfort and revere.

There was an air of fantasy about the relationship, in particular its presumed destiny – a cottage in the country where Sonia could deal with her husband's post and cook his meals while Orwell languished in a bath-chair – but also a sharp awareness of the long-term benefits which might accrue. To mark Sonia down as an impenitent gold-digger, staking her claim with the purchase of a lavish engagement ring, is nonsense. At the same time, here in the autumn of 1949 with 25,000 copies of *Nineteen Eighty-Four* in print in England and American sales booming it was clear that Orwell's leavings would be worth having. Perhaps in the end Sonia's motives were not explicable even to herself. Asked point-blank later in life by a friend she replied simply: 'I don't know ... I felt sorry for him.' Julian Symons' theory was more straightforward. She had married Orwell, he explained to a lunchtime audience of Powell, Muggeridge and Fyvel, because Cyril Connolly had told her to.

News of the impending nuptials travelled to literary London in the slipstream of Orwell's ambulance. Muggeridge noted in his diary on 5 September that Powell was intrigued by 'the curious information I had received that George Orwell is going to marry a girl called Sonia Brownell who is connected with bringing out the magazine *Horizon*'. Sonia's old Euston Road reputation and her fondness for the society of painters preceded her. 'She is what Tony calls an "Art Tart",' Muggeridge noted, going on to speculate that 'it will probably be a rather macabre wedding, I should suppose'. Nonetheless, like most of Orwell's acquaintance, Muggeridge was absorbed by the spectacle of love flourishing across a hospital bed, and regretted that he had failed to attend a party of John Lehmann's later in the month where Sonia had been present. The prospective bride, meanwhile, had made herself thoroughly at home at UCH, arriving daily from her flat in nearby Percy Street to deal with Orwell's business affairs, write letters on his behalf and supervise his visitors in a way that some thought reminiscent of a bossy hospital nurse. Room 65, Orwell's home during the time he spent at the hospital, was relatively small, furnished according to the standard hospital pattern – a high bed which could be tilted, a bedside table with telephone, dressing table, armchair, one or two upright chairs and a commode. The heavy white china crockery was taken away to be boiled after use. Hospital staff remembered him as courteous but uncommunicative, sitting up in bed wrapped in an old camel-coloured woollen cardigan – outwardly placid but inwardly raging against his plight, a nurse thought. His delight in visitors was most apparent when Richard was brought to see him, although his condition meant that these appearances were few.

The post continued to bring acclamatory letters from his peers: there was fan mail from John Dos Passos and Aldous Huxley. He believed, or affected to believe, that he was improving: 'distinctly better since being here,' he told Richard Rees, although the only new treatment consisted of making him lie throughout the night and part of the day with his feet higher than his head to help improve the production of sputum. It was going to be a very slow business, he suggested to Rees, '& lord knows when I shall be able to get up or work again'. Muggeridge, visiting him in the last week of September, thought differently. 'He looks inconceivably wasted, and has, I should say, the appearance of someone who hasn't long to live'. Their talk was interrupted by the arrival of Sonia, who disconcerted Muggeridge by watching for a long time through the glass window in the door before coming in. Muggeridge's account of Sonia is characteristic of that of several of Orwell's male friends: appreciative but patronising. She was 'a large, bouncy girl, quite pleasant', Muggeridge thought, who, dressed in a tweed suit, would be the epitome of a village do-gooder, but instead had opted to 'mess about' with *Horizon* and 'intellectual circles'. Orwell, Muggeridge thought, seemed 'more peaceful than he was' but still turned in on himself, 'his mind still going over the old political questions . . . Always feel affectionately towards him,' Muggeridge concluded.

A week later Muggeridge received a letter from Sonia stating that the marriage was fixed for 13 October. 'To George's great delight', as he could not be moved from his hospital bed, a clergyman would have to be in attendance. For once Orwell had begun to take an interest in his personal appearance, commissioning Powell and Muggeridge to procure something that he could wear in bed. With clothing still in short supply, the choice lay between a Jaeger coat with a tying belt or a crimson corduroy jacket. Orwell decided on the jacket. Sitting up in bed, Powell thought, 'he had an unaccustomed epicurean air', cheered by the prospect of marriage and the conviction, however fanciful, that no writer can die while a book remains unwritten within him. Visiting him with Powell early in October, when the question of the jacket was discussed, Muggeridge noted that he was in 'quite good form', pleased that UCH had a resident chaplain who would officiate. 'Death-bed marriages', as he put it, were not very common. The wedding took place a few days later in Room 65. The Revd W.H. Braine conducted the service. David Astor was best man. Robert Kee gave away the bride. Janetta acted as witness. Robert Kee retained a mental photograph of Orwell 'in bed, but wholly participating and showing real attachment to Sonia'. Janetta found herself standing by a small table just inside the door, desperately upset but at the same time – despite a suspicion of marriage, Christianity and all its appurtenances – deeply moved. Subsequently the wedding group, minus the groom, moved on to the Ritz for a lunch hosted by Astor. The aftermath of this 'strange wedding party' was witnessed by Frances Partridge, who with her husband Ralph turned up later at the house in Sussex Place which the Kees shared with Cyril Connolly. Orwell was said to have a 50–50 chance of recovery, she noted, 'and as he is much in love with her everyone hopes that marriage will give him a new interest in life'. A halo of emotion still lingered in the air. The Kees were obviously 'much moved'. News of the marriage, once relayed to the wider world, occasionally provoked a less charitable reaction. Five days later Frances Partridge returned to the subject. 'Many people regard the Orwell marriage cynically and remind one that Sonia always declared her intention of marrying a great man.' She judged her impulse as 'neurotic' – a union with 'a bed-ridden and perhaps dying man is as near no marriage at all as it's possible to get'. The same thought occurred to Muggeridge. 'Whole affair is slightly macabre and incomprehensible,' he decided.

The effect on Orwell was, for a brief period, intensely therapeutic. Anthony Powell thought that in some respects 'he was in better form than I had ever seen him show', irradiating flashes of 'the old Wodehousian side'. Muggeridge, too, detected a change for the better. Visiting him in the last week of October, he found him 'remarkably cheerful'. The two men embarked on a long argument about whether old people should be allowed to commit suicide. 'Health and beauty' were essential to the good life, Orwell maintained. He was annoyed by an advertisement in an evening paper that showed the god Zeus modelling a pair of socks: such 'blasphemy' offended him far more than mockery of Christianity, he explained. Muggeridge also left a neat cameo of Sonia's forthright and less engaging side, declaring as Orwell's supper was brought in that he had had a wonderful life, waited on hand and foot, compared to her struggles with the temperamental Connolly.

But the improvement was short-lived. By mid-November he had relapsed, 'desperately ill', Janetta Kee recalled, propped up against the pillow with Sonia at his side. Janetta's five-year-old daughter, sitting on the end of the bed as her mother talked, was curiously cheered by the experience. Ever solicitous of children, Orwell took an interest in the toy she had brought and did his best to relieve what must have been a notably grim atmosphere. He had got so thin, he told Celia Paget, 'that it's below the level at which you can go on living'. Requests for articles and interviews were declined, the importunate waved away. A steady stream of visitors filed across the Bloomsbury squares to visit, often passing each other in corridors and doorways as they went back and forth (Celia remembered coming into the room once as Lucian Freud was leaving it), drawn from every compartment of Orwell's life: Stephen Spender and his wife Natasha, Potts, old comrades from Spain and the St John's Wood Home Guard, *Tribune* friends. Some faces came from even further back. His old tutor Andrew Gow arrived unexpectedly, claiming to have discovered Orwell's presence on the ward while visiting a sick colleague. Orwell's acquaintance with Freud, met long before at the Café Royal, is a good example of how he kept up his bohemian links. The two men never knew each other well – the young artist was drawn into Orwell's world by Sonia – but here in the last few months of his life, Freud became a regular visitor.

As Christmas came Orwell grew yet weaker. His doctors acknowledged that little could be done with such an advanced case of bilateral pulmonary tuberculosis. He was not in pain, a junior doctor believed, but ever more conscious of his frailty. Penicillin injections proved problematic as little surplus flesh remained in which to jab the needle. He was given insulin to ginger up his appetite, but to little effect. After listening to the King's Speech on Christmas afternoon Powell and Muggeridge walked round to the hospital. Alone in his room, Christmas decorations suspended above his bed, Orwell looked, Muggeridge thought, like a picture he had once seen of Nietzsche on his deathbed. There was a kind of rage in his expression as though the approach of death made him furious. 'Poor George,' Muggeridge apostrophised his friend. 'He went on about the Home Guard, and the Spanish Civil War, and how he would go to Switzerland soon, and all the while the stench of death was in the air, like autumn in a garden.'

The Swiss plan, ventilated on several occasions in the previous months, had now begun to take coherent shape: transfer by plane to the Montana sanatorium in the Swiss Alps. There was little prospect that the change of scene and the fresher air would have any effect on his lungs, his doctors later conceded: the objective seems to have been to enable him to die as peacefully and contentedly as possible. Jon Kimche, by virtue of his Swiss extraction, made the necessary arrangements with the embassy. Sonia engaged Lucian Freud, avid in the era of post-war travel regulation for any kind of foreign jaunt, to join the party in the role of surrogate male nurse. Meanwhile the festive season flowed on around them. Avril had not seen her brother for several months, but in the New Year she and Richard travelled down from Jura for a short stay in London. On 2 January the Powells had the five-year-old boy to lunch in order to take him to the zoo. Was there anything he particularly wanted to see? Lady Violet enquired as they walked up to the park. 'Lions and tigers,' he answered. There was a pause. 'They are in cages aren't they?' Orwell telephoned that night to say how much Richard had enjoyed the expedition, and that he wished he could have been there himself. Vernon Richards, visiting him a day or so later, recalled how his 'thin, drawn face lighted up and his eyes shone' as he described Richard's account of the trip. But it was all fading away: Richard, Sonia, the manatees he remembered from his own visits to the zoo. Muggeridge, visiting him on 12 January, found him talking miserably to Richard Rees, more deathly than ever and still losing weight from an already skeletal frame. Fishing rods for the Swiss trip lay in the corner of the room. Still the visitors came and went. Denzil Jacobs, to whom he taught the techniques of street-fighting nearly a decade before, remembered him talking of Jura and the certainty of nuclear holocaust. 'I've made all this money,' he remarked, 'and now I'm going to die.'

The Swiss trip was now scheduled for Wednesday, 25 January. How was he? his old Spanish comrade Stafford Cottman asked when he telephoned to make arrangements to see him before he went. 'I'm frightful,' Orwell told him, 'I look like a skeleton.' On Wednesday, 18 January, in the presence of a nurse and a solicitor, he made a will leaving the bulk of his estate to Sonia and appointing Richard Rees as his literary executor. On the following day Muggeridge came to say goodbye. 'He looked at his last gasp.' When Celia Paget rang wondering if she could see him he explained about the Swiss trip and advised her to come on the following Monday. Celia assumed this meant his condition was improving. Presumably the UCH doctors thought that he was getting better. Orwell swiftly disillusioned her. 'Either that or they don't want a corpse on their hands.' Fyvel, who visited on Friday, 20 January, remembered 'a nice and easy conversation in which we recounted our early schooldays': even here, apparently, the shades of Flip and Sambo still stalked Orwell's consciousness. Sonia, witnesses suggest, had been suffering from a cold during the early part of the week and was not at her usual post. But she spent much of the Friday seated by the high hospital bed and its wasted occupant. Then in the early evening she went away. Though he was wretchedly ill Orwell's condition was not giving cause for immediate concern. One of his peripheral worries about Switzerland – he had been similarly anxious about Spain – was the quality of the tea. How would he get the 'proper' brands he liked? Paul Potts, who turned up later in the evening, had brought a packet with him. Looking through the glass window of the door of Room 65 he saw that his friend was asleep, and decided to leave the gift propped against the jamb. With the possible exception of a passing nurse, he was the last person to see Orwell alive. Some time in the small hours of Saturday, 21 January an artery burst in his lungs. Within a few moments he was dead.

19

Epilogue: And Sonia

February 19th, 1953
Found the P.M. absorbed in George Orwell's book, 1984.
   'Have you read it, Charles? Oh, you must. I'm reading it for a second time. It is a very remarkable book.' – Lord Moran, *Winston Churchill: The Struggle for Survival 1940–1965* (1966)

'G. Orwell dead,' Evelyn Waugh wrote to his friend Nancy Mitford late in January 1950, 'and Mrs Orwell presumably a rich widow.' Orwell died young. Many of his friends survived him for nearly half a century. A few of them survive him still. Cyril Connolly lived on into his seventies; Julian Symons into his eighties; Anthony Powell into his nineties. On the most basic level the effect that Orwell had on their lives can be glimpsed in the books they wrote after his death. Paul Potts' rambling memoirs are full of scraps of remembered conversation, hoarded across the years. In his conscience-of-a-generation role, Orwell makes several appearances in Symons' collection of imaginary character sketches *Portraits of the Missing* (1991), brought in for example to denounce the wartime political opportunist 'Rupert Loxley' on the grounds that 'If the Germans were in power and the right sort of people were going to the parties they gave, your friend Loxley would be there too. He'd call it accepting reality, something like that.' The three volumes of Anthony Powell's *Journals*, produced in his Somersetshire-bound old age, are full of shrewd reflections on 'George', George's undoubted taste for power and what George might have thought. Orwell's books sold in their millions, the writer acquired an almost mythic status in the public imagination, but the man himself stayed green in their memory. Connolly's reviews of the pieces of Orwelliana that came his way in the decade or so before his death in 1974 are stalked by the ghost of Orwell's personality, and a relationship that began 'with his comments on a poem I wrote when I was thirteen on the

419

death of Lord Kitchener and ends with the label on a basket of fruit sent to University College Hospital in 1949'.

Avril Blair, clearly invigorated by the open-air life of the Inner Hebrides, married Bill Dunn a year or so after her brother's death. The two of them moved to another property on Jura and made themselves responsible for Richard's upbringing and education; Avril continuing to keep a vigilant eye on the misrepresentations of biographers. As early as June 1950 she wrote to David Astor, apropos an article by Tosco Fyvel in the *World Review*, complaining that 'this insistence on Eric's unhappiness at school, & the unsuitability of his education, is a reflection on our parents, who, in actual fact, made every kind of sacrifice to give him what they thought & hoped would be a good education'. Avril died in 1978.

Of all those affected in one way or another by Orwell's death, it was Sonia on whom his legacy placed the heaviest burden. Unprepared for the late-night news from the hospital, guilty at not having been present, she was inconsolable. Janetta Kee, whom she contacted early the following morning, remembered her being 'in the most terrible . . . appalling state'. Sonia's unfeigned grief won over several of Orwell's friends who had previously regarded her influence with faint suspicion. Muggeridge, for instance, wrote that he would always love her for her 'true tears'.

At an early stage – there was something uncomfortably prescient in Waugh's remark – opinions of Sonia split up into two implacably opposed camps. To her friends, a distinguished array of literary and artistic notables picked up in the forty years between her Euston Road début and her death in 1980, she was a loyal custodian of her husband's memory, an unobtrusive supporter of good causes and deserving cases, good-natured – despite well-attested bouts of fractiousness – and well-meaning. To her enemies – a category which includes at least two Orwell biographers – she was simply a gold-digger who spent the material rewards of a relationship conducted across a deathbed on three decades' self-indulgence. In these contending hands even the events surrounding Orwell's death have acquired a dreadful symbolic significance. Where exactly was she, for example, at the moment Orwell died? According to Michael Shelden's biography of 1991, in a nightclub with Lucian Freud and their mutual friend Ann Dunn. And yet the image of the carefree socialite, carousing into the small hours while her husband haemorrhaged to death half a mile away, has been endlessly denied. According to Ann Dunn she and Freud had dined together and then invited Sonia, exhausted from a day at the hospital, to join them at a small supper club opposite her flat in Percy Street. Sonia then telephoned the hospital and returned 'in a state of shock' to report that Orwell was dead. The same starkly opposed views attend the holiday she took in the south of France shortly afterwards. To Shelden this involved 'chasing her lover on the Riviera', but it was remembered by Janetta Kee, who accompanied her, as 'very humble and low key'.

Whatever may be said about Sonia, she was a diligent guardian of Orwell's interests – 'assiduous in her attention to every detail in the considerable amount of work involved in the administration of Orwell's affairs', according to the literary agent who succeeded Leonard Moore in charge of the Orwell estate. As for the proceeds, Sonia's conspicuous generosity towards other writers, and on occasion their dependants, stemmed from the conviction that the money was held on trust, that her duty to Orwell was to lay out his posthumous income in ways of which he would have approved. When Francis King remarked on the care lavished on the late J.R. Ackerley's sister Nancy, including the redecoration of her flat, she commented, 'Well, the money isn't really mine.' She was a notable supporter of Jean Rhys, paying for her to stay in hotels, quietly supplying her wants and often passing off her own kindnesses as other people's. Beyond the good works she made a not inconsiderable contribution – a form of words her late husband would have hated – to the cultural world of her time, working as an editor at Weidenfeld & Nicolson, where she has some claims to have discovered the novelist Nigel Dennis, co-editing the Paris-based journal *Art and Literature* and putting in long hours of work on the four-volume 1968 edition of Orwell's *Collected Journalism, Letters and Essays*. The aspiring talents she encouraged were always grateful for her interest while occasionally disposed to mock her in print. Angus Wilson, for example, who caricatured her mercilessly in *Anglo-Saxon Attitudes* (1956), was careful to acknowledge a debt. It was to Cyril Connolly, he later noted, 'and his then secretary, Sonia Brownell, that I owe my first appearance in print'.

Beneath the volatility, the imperiousness and the occasional starring performance as 'the widow Orwell' lay a rather unhappy woman: warm-hearted, passionate, impulsive, but also fraught, insensitive and fond of one drink too many. Emotionally there were great cracks and crevices into which the unwary could tumble. Several people have remarked her nervousness in the company of heterosexual men. Her male dinner guests, Francis King remembered, were invariably either homosexual or safely uxorious. There was a brief and unfortunate second marriage in 1958 to Michael Pitt-Rivers, who had spent eighteen months in prison for some widely-publicised homosexual offences. Frances Partridge's mid-1960s diaries contain bracing accounts of Sonia in action. Watching her as she conversed with the other guests at Charleston and noting the 'safe' artistic preferences expressed, Partridge complained that her mind worked 'in such a boring, intensely conventional way'. In November 1965 Sonia collapsed dead drunk on the floor at Janetta's. A conversation, or rather monologue, into which the diarist found she could scarcely interject a word, produced the following reflection: 'I've never been so browbeaten, bossed and bully-ragged in my life . . . I can only think she hadn't a clue about what I feel about her, that I really despise her pretentiousness, and now had added to my picture of her a full awareness of her crude, raw, arrogant, insensitive bossyness.' Happily all this was 'so awful' as to be almost funny.

Towards the end it all went badly wrong. For reasons which none of her friends could really understand, but apparently urged on by her accountants, she fetched up in Paris – ill, separated from her friends, and strangely hard-up. According to the novelist David Plante 'there was something manic in the move, as if Paris were a solution to a problem which had no other solution'. Friends were informed that she intended to get a job working for a French publisher, but no one understood why she should be living in self-imposed exile. Neither could anyone understand why she was short of money. For many years Orwell's financial affairs had been in the hands of George Orwell Productions, a company formed immediately before his death and administered by his long-term accountant Jack Harrison of the firm of Harrison, Son, Hill & Co. In the 1970s, when according to Secker & Warburg the annual income from Orwell's foreign sales regularly topped six figures, Sonia's monthly allowance was £750. Increasingly ill – she was later diagnosed with cancer – Sonia spent her declining years in pursuit of legal redress for what she imagined was embezzlement. Her state of mind became desperate. 'Once I win – and I've put everything I've got into winning – I'll kill myself,' she once said. In the event she died of natural causes, late in 1980, with Bernard Crick's biography, which she hated, in the bookshops. The court case was settled shortly before. Most of the money turned out to have been lost by the accountants in inept investments. Visiting her in hospital and staring at her gaunt, distorted face, Plante kissed her, whereupon she burst into tears and suddenly 'looked very beautiful'. After her death the solicitor informed her co-executor Hilary Spurling that there was barely enough money left to pay for the funeral.

Writing up his diary on 17 December 1980, after attending the ceremony at the Roman Catholic church in Cadogan Street, Stephen Spender thought about his dead friend. Remembering Sonia as the beauty of the pre-war Euston Road, he recalled an impression of 'someone always struggling to go beyond herself, to escape from her social background, the convent where she was educated, into some pagan paradise of artists and "geniuses" who would save her'. Passionate loyalties contended with passionate disloyalty, the result, he believed, of people falling short of the ideals she had conceived of them. 'She had a feeling, perhaps, with some people, that she'd invented them, and they'd jolly well better recognise this.' Under the veneer of sophistication, she was not in the least sophisticated. People understood this, but no one knew what lay beneath this second layer of innocence. What did Sonia want? No one had ever found out, Spender concluded. The likeliest answer was 'the love of a great and maligned genius' whose honour she could defend. Did she ever obtain it? As in so much surrounding Sonia, let alone the man who had pre-deceased her thirty years before, there is no answer.

Orwell's dream

And perhaps at the very end his mind moved back, back through the cloud of the years, to older and even older memories: to the rain falling over the grey sea off Jura; to the thump of the bombs going off in the streets beyond Piccadilly; and the lofted torches in the great square at Barcelona; and the electric shock of the bullet slamming home; and Eileen's face under the church gate; and Eileen at the supper table in Hampstead, and out riding at Blackheath; and the smell of the hops in the Kentish fields; and Pétain with his spreading moustache; and the flying fish in the bay at Colombo; and picking mushrooms up on the hills above Henley; and roaming through the silent dormitories at dawn on a summer day; and the portraits of the Blairs in their frames; and the shallows near Jordan; and his mother's shadow falling across the garden; and the sound of the nightjars on summer evenings in the lanes; and the woods and the streams of Oxfordshire.

Appendix I – *Orwell and his publisher*

Between 1933 and 1940, beginning with *Down and Out in Paris and London* and ending with *Inside the Whale*, Orwell published seven full-length books with the firm of Victor Gollancz Ltd. The substantial volume of material that survives, now in the archive of the Orion Publishing Group, can be divided into three main categories: letters, postcards and telegrams exchanged between Orwell and Gollancz, and between Gollancz and Orwell's agent, Leonard Moore; readers' reports and other internal memoranda relating to individual books; and miscellaneous items, such as the letter received shortly after the publication of *Down and Out* from the secretary to the editor of *The Times* asking, apropos Orwell's reply to the outraged restaurateur, M. Possenti, if 'George Orwell' and 'E.A. Blair' were the same person. Understandably the files of correspondence continue long after Orwell's death, when Gollancz was regularly addressed by scholars and bibliographers. There is, for instance, a somewhat terse letter from 1952 informing an American journalist that a meeting with the author of *Nineteen Eighty-Four* would be impossible to arrange. Taken together they shed considerable light both on Orwell's relationship with Gollancz and the publishing processes in which the two were involved.

In later life – he died in 1967 – Gollancz was disposed to play down his personal connection with Orwell, representing himself to enquirers as a business associate rather than a genuine friend and remaining sensitive to any discussion of the circumstances of *Animal Farm*'s rejection in 1944. Nonetheless, the surviving correspondence makes plain his enormous enthusiasm for Orwell's work. In a letter of February 1935, for example, three-quarters of the way through a re-read of *Burmese Days*, he could tell the author that 'It is, if I may say so, an exceptionally brilliant book.' A letter from January 1936 dilates on the merits of *Keep The Aspidistra Flying*: 'I daresay there are plenty, but I can think of no other English novel which deals with the central question of money; and I think you have dealt with it extremely well.' This pitch of enthusiasm was maintained. At the start of the war-time boom in book sales he wrote anxiously to enquire if Orwell had anything on the stocks. Subsequently, when it became clear that Orwell's later work would be going to Secker & Warburg, he fought a long, if unsuccessful, rearguard action in defence of what he obviously regarded as a jewel in the Henrietta Street crown.

However great his zeal on Orwell's behalf, Gollancz was also a sharp operator. In this context the early negotiations with Leonard Moore over the manuscript of *Down and Out*, dating from mid-1932, are especially revealing. Moore began by proposing an advance of £70. Gollancz countered with £40. Moore then reduced his demand to £50. Gollancz stuck to his original offer. In the end Orwell and his agent had little choice but to accept. Yet from Gollancz's point of view, Orwell could be an equally tricky customer. The correspondence generated by *Aspidistra*'s stuttering progress to the printer is a case in point. The delays, legal ramifications and bad feeling that (temporarily) poisoned Orwell's dealings with Victor Gollancz Ltd were mostly the fault of the author. Orwell's misleading assurances that the novel's spoof advertising posters bore no relation to real-life slogans were only exposed by chance, when Gollancz sent a proof copy to their press agents, the Fanfare Press. The low opinion Orwell subsequently conceived of Gollancz's deputy chairman, Norman Collins, based on what he assumed was Collins' inefficiency, is misplaced. Collins, as his tactful letter to Moore makes clear ('Please don't regard even this as a sign of messy or slipshod procedures on our part. It is simply that the author has evidently been too close to the work') was only doing his job.

Above all, the Gollancz papers make plain the circumstances surrounding the genesis and publication of *The Road to Wigan Pier*. Orwell was not given a specific commission to travel north in early 1936 and write a book based on his experiences. Neither was what he might or might not write at this stage connected with the embryonic Left Book Club. In fact for most of that year he and Gollancz were not even in contact. A letter from Gollancz to Moore dated 29 October 1936, written as the publisher began to draw up his list of titles for the following spring, asks simply 'What about George Orwell?' adding that 'I haven't heard from him since he went up north.' At this stage in the book's development, Moore was only a little better informed himself. 'It is not a novel but a sort of book of essays,' he replied a week later. The thought that *The Road to Wigan Pier* might do for the Left Book Club seems to have taken root in this exchange, as Gollancz's next letter, dated 6 November, notes that he 'might consider it' for selection. The advance was £100, confirmed in a letter of 24 December. All Orwell's other earnings from the book came in Left Book Club royalties.

Amid the to-and-fro of negotiation and the lengthy memoranda from Harold Rubinstein, Gollancz's legal adviser, are a handful of tantalising biographical fragments. On 28 July 1932, for example, as discussions of *Down and Out* proceeded, Moore advised Gollancz: 'If I could hear from you by tomorrow, Friday, I shall be glad as Blair is going abroad.' Where exactly was Blair going? And for how long? A lettercard to Moore sent from 36 High Street, Southwold and dated 4 August notes that 'The above address will find me at any time during August and September'. The only time at which Orwell could have been out of the country was 29 July to 3 August, but there is no record of where he went, not even a postcard to Eleanor Jaques, to whom he wrote constantly in the second half of 1932. Did he, when it came to it, go abroad at all, or was Moore using the fiction of his client's impending absence as a ruse to force Gollancz's hand? As with so much of Orwell's life at this time – the rumoured engagements and the uncharted friendships – we shall probably never know.

Appendix II – *Dear Malcolm . . . Yours George*

Malcolm Muggeridge (1903–1990) was a punctilious observer of the last year of Orwell's life. Indeed his compendious diaries – for all their rigorous puruit of Muggeridge's own agendas – are a vital source for any reconstruction of Orwell's final months at University College Hospital. Until recently the public record of this friendship has been one-sided. We know of it only what Muggeridge chose to tell us. However, the discovery of unpublished correspondence between Orwell and Muggeridge sheds new light both on their relationship and the development of Orwell's political thinking in the year or so before his death.

On the face of it, the two were unlikely soul-mates. Muggeridge, at this point in his career, was a *Daily Telegraph* leader-writer and already enjoyed some reputation (a reputation that was vastly to increase in the following decade) as a controversialist. What united them was a love of literature, a consuming interest in politics and a profound suspicion of the influence of the Soviet Union on international affairs. Muggeridge's trail-blazing exposé of the Russian experiment, *Winter Journey*, had appeared as long ago as 1933. Orwell had reviewed Muggeridge's *The Thirties* on its appearance in April 1940, finding its closing chapters 'deeply moving' and acknowledging a link between Muggeridge's attitude to the war and the sentiments he had expressed in 'My Country, Right or Left'. 'It is the emotion of the middle-class man, brought up in the military tradition, who finds in the moment of crisis that he is a patriot after all . . . As I was brought up in this tradition myself I can recognise it under strange disguises, and also sympathise with it, for even at its stupidest and most sentimental it is a comelier thing that the shallow self-righteousness of the left-wing intelligensia.'

Muggeridge spent the war years working for the British secret service in East and North Africa, Italy and France. In recognition of his work the French government subsequently awarded him the Legion d'Honneur and the Croix de Guerre avec Palme. His friendship with Orwell seems to have begun after his return to England in mid-1945. Its rapid development can be tracked in a typewritten letter from Orwell dated 25 September 1945, sent from the Canonbury Square flat, inviting him to lunch with Julian Symons, with whom he assumed Muggeridge would have much in common ('I know you would like him. I think he is one of the most gifted of the writers now in their thirties. I know he would like to meet you too.') Clearly Orwell was also moving to some extent in the Muggeridge family circle, as there are references to 'a nice letter from your son [possibly John Muggeridge] which I am answering.' In a later, handwritten, note sent from the Cranham sanitorium in February 1949, Orwell wonders if Muggeridge's elder boys would like to come and stay in Jura during the summer holidays: 'Of course it's kind of rough, because there are generally a number of people staying there in the summer, which means sleeping on camp beds etc, but they would probably enjoy catching fish + shooting rabbits + so on.'

Of particular interest, though, is a long typed letter sent from Jura in early December 1948, shortly after Orwell had finished work on *Nineteen Eighty-Four*. Here Orwell confesses to having disapproved of Muggeridge's study of Samuel Butler, which he had recently read, 'because I thought it would give a false impression to anyone who didn't know Butler's work already.' Not only was Butler a much kindlier and more unassuming person that Muggeridge made out, Orwell suggested, but he was 'very nearly the only writer of the later part of the nineteenth century who could write in a plain straightforward manner.' As ever, Orwell uses Butler to draw a contemporary distinction:

I know that you feel people like Butler, who are disintegrators, prepare the way for dictatorship etc., and I can see the connection beteween Butler's revolt against his parents and your experiences in Moscow. But I do earnestly think that you are wrong. The real division is not between conservatives and revolutionaries but between authoritarians and libertarians.

The remainder of the letter discusses his shattered health and its causes ('I daresay I was turned out [of hospital] too soon and didn't take things easily enough at first') the beauty of the Jura winter ('wonderful still sunny days with the sea like glass and wonderful colours in everything, bright brown bracken and the sea a sort of bluish green'), *Nineteen Eighty-Four* – inevitably Orwell was 'not pleased with it, but I think it is a good idea' – and his infant son: 'He gets a horrible low-class comic paper every week from Dundee and likes to have it read to him, but doesn't show any desire to learn to read himself.' Significantly, Orwell seems to assume at this stage that he could expect to recover. The Islington flat was to be given up 'because I never use it and it is simply an expense. But I shall have to have a pied a terre in London again later.'

There is a final, typed letter – presumably dictated to Sonia – sent from University College Hospital in the autumn of 1949. In it Orwell thanks Muggeridge for a wedding present of some volumes of Surtees: 'I was really charmed to get these very rare books with their lovely illustrations.' The letter is undated, but appears to have been composed either late in October or early in November as Orwell refers to, and in fact encloses, the magazine advertisement for Wolsey Socks ('Fit for the Gods') which Muggeridge mentions in a diary entry of 25 October. 'I think you will agree that it is in a way really blasphemous. Please come and see me soon. Thank you so much again, Yours, George.'

Notes and Further Reading

The chief source for this biography is Peter Davison's twenty-volume *George Orwell: Complete Works* (Secker & Warburg, 1998 and subsequent corrected paperback editions). As a general principle I have tried to indicate within the text the origin of quotations from Orwell's writings and when and to whom particular letters were written. In cases where the circumstances seem to demand greater explanation – for example letters written in the 1940s referring to events that had taken place many years before – I have supplied fuller references.

Certain works are cited so frequently that I have identified them simply by author or abbreviated title. Unless otherwise stated the place of publication is London.

CW   Peter Davison, ed. *George Orwell: Complete Works*, twenty volumes, 1998
Buddicom   Jacintha Buddicom, *Eric and Us*, 1974
Coppard/Crick   Audrey Coppard and Bernard Crick, eds. *Orwell Remembered*, 1984
Fyvel   T.R. Fyvel, *George Orwell: A Personal Memoir*, 1982
Infants   Anthony Powell, *To Keep the Ball Rolling: The Memoirs of Anthony Powell, Volume I: Infants of the Spring*, 1976
Muggeridge   Malcolm Muggeridge, journals 1948–50 (three volumes, unedited typescripts)
Rees   Richard Rees, *George Orwell: Fugitive from the Camp of Victory*, 1961
Stansky/Abrahams   Peter Stansky and William Abrahams, *The Unknown Orwell*, 1972
Wadhams   Stephen Wadhams, ed. *Remembering Orwell*, Harmondsworth, 1984

1. An Oxfordshire Tomb

Cyril Connolly's review of *The Unknown Orwell*, which originally appeared in the *New York Times Book Review*, is reprinted in *The Evening Colonnade* (1973), 335–9. George Summers' account of his dealings with Orwell (of whom he also remarked, 'I hated his guts') is taken from an interview with the author, Blewbury, Oxfordshire, 16 February 2000.

For accounts of Orwell's funeral and burial, see Wadhams, 218–20, Muggeridge, 26 January 1950 and Anthony Powell, *Faces in My Time* (1980), 220–1. David Astor's recollections come from an interview with the author, London, 14 March 2000. Lady Violet Powell's comment about the 'publishers' party' atmosphere was made in a letter to the author, 11 March 2000. The recollections of Janetta Parladé (formerly Kee and Woolley) are taken from an interview with the author, London, 25 May 2000.

2. A Question of Upbringing

For a detailed account of the Blair family background, see Stansky/Abrahams, 23–9. Plant senior's comments on the destruction of the English gentry are taken from Evelyn Waugh, *Work Suspended and Other Stories* (Harmondsworth, 1967), 112. Avril Blair recalled the legend of the Reverend Blair's courtship in 'My Brother, George Orwell', a BBC radio broadcast from 1960 reprinted in *Twentieth Century*, March 1961, and in Coppard/Crick, 25–32. Eileen Blair confided the story of the pawned fish knives to the Powells, *Infants*, 136. The account of Richard Blair's attitude to his tradesmen is taken from an interview with his former grocer, Mr George Bumstead, Southwold, 28 November 2000. For Ida Blair's diary, see Coppard/Crick, 19–20.

For Orwell's questioning of Richard Rees, see Rees, 144. Orwell's claim to have 'disliked' his father appears in 'Such, Such Were the Joys', *CW*, XIX: 379. For Richard Rees' memory of his relationship with Avril, see Rees, 93–4. The visitor to Jura who overheard the conversation about the plucked goose was David Holbrook, interview with the author, Cambridge, 14 November 2000. The comments on Richard and Ida Blair are taken from an interview with Mrs Esmé Goldsmith (née May), 14 February 2001. The description of Mrs Blair is Ruth Pitter's, quoted in Stansky/Abrahams, 33. For Avril's memories of *Down and Out in Paris and London*'s reception by the senior Blairs, see 'My Brother, George Orwell', in Coppard/Crick. On Orwell's rebelliousness, see Kay Ekevall, quoted in Coppard/Crick, 105.

For Humphrey Dakin's impression of the pre-teenage Orwell, see Stansky/Abrahams, 37. The review of Osbert Sitwell's *Great Morning* is reprinted in *CW*, XIX: 95–8. Orwell remembered the popular songs of the Edwardian age in an *Evening Standard* essay of 1946 ('Songs We Used to Sing'), *CW*, XVIII: 49–51. The letter to Jacintha Buddicom about the 'young days' is in *CW*, XX: 42. Avril's memories of Orwell's childhood are taken from Coppard/Crick, 26–7. For her comments to Jacintha Buddicom, see Buddicom, 19. Orwell's account of his early attempts to write is taken from the essay 'Why I Write', *CW*, XVIII: 316–21.

For background to Orwell's time at St Cyprian's, see Stansky/Abrahams, 38–83. For the memories of his contemporaries, see Cyril Connolly, *Enemies of Promise* (Harmondsworth, 1961), 174–93, and the review of *The Unknown Orwell* quoted above, and Wadhams, 4–11. Jacintha Buddicom's description of her first meeting with Orwell and her recollections of the Blairs are in Buddicom, 11–18. For some accounts of the weeks preceding and following the start of the Great War, see Powell, *Infants*, 57–8, and Alec Waugh, *The Early Years of Alec Waugh* (1962), 56–7. Avril's memory of knitting the school scarf is in Coppard/Crick, 26.

Orwell's letters to Connolly from 1938 are in *CW*, XI: 175, 253–4. For accounts of St Cyprian's by distinguished former pupils, see Henry Longhurst, *My Life and Soft Times* (1972) and Gavin Maxwell, *The House of Elrig* (1965). John Wilkes' memory of his mother's 'great respect' for Orwell is in Wadhams, 10. For other accounts of contemporary prep-school life, see Powell, *Infants*, 61–5 and Alec Waugh, op. cit., 17–27. Jacintha Buddicom's opinion of Orwell's attitude to St Cyprian's is in Buddicom, 42–53. See also Robert Pearce, 'Truth and Falsehood: George Orwell's Prep School Woes', in *Review of English Studies*, 1992, 367–86. For Alaric Jacob's memories of 'St Saviour's', which he entered in 1917, see *Scenes from a Bourgeois Life* (1949), 53–9. Curiously, the final sentence echoes Orwell's own valediction: 'I gloomed a year away and greyly suffered to find myself a failure at fourteen.' Malcolm Muggeridge's reflections on 'Such, Such Were the Joys' are taken from Muggeridge, 20 February 1950. For Robert Pearce's comments on the bed-wetting and beating episodes, see the essay cited above. For Connolly on the Wilkeses, see the review of *The Unknown Orwell*, cited above. Jacintha Buddicom's account of Blair family routines is in Buddicom, 16–19. Connolly's memory of the Wellington scholarship exam is in *Enemies of Promise*, 188–9.

3. Eton Medley

On Orwell's time at Wellington, Buddicom, 57, and Michael Meyer (the Old Wellingtonian whose tie Orwell recognised), interview with the author, London, 16 February 2000. For some contemporary views of Eton, see Anthony Powell, 'The Wat'ry Glade', in Graham Greene, ed. *The Old School* (1934) and Connolly, *Enemies of Promise, passim.* There is a good description of the atmosphere in College in Christopher Hollis' contribution to Coppard/Crick, 37–50. Jacintha's view of Orwell's attitude to Eton is in Buddicom, 58. John Wilkes' comment appears in Wadhams, 11. The conversation about 'Oxford and the wonderful time we should have when we got there' is recorded in Buddicom, 73. Orwell's account of his discovery of Lawrence's 'Love on the Farm' – its original title was 'Cruelty and Love' – comes in a review of *The Prussian Officer* in *Tribune*, 16 November 1945, CW, XVII: 385–8.

For Denys King-Farlow's memories of Orwell at Eton, see Coppard/Crick, 54–61. Steven Runciman's remarks on Huxley are taken from Wadhams, 21. For Hollis' recollections, see Coppard/Crick, above. The letter from Jacintha's Aunt Lilian commenting on 'Eric's cough' is reproduced in Buddicom, 58–60. Connolly's account of Orwell's passion for Eastwood – the original Orwell letter is lost, but part of it was quoted in a letter to Connolly's friend Terence Beddard, Easter 1921 – is in CW, X: 79–80. For Prosper Buddicom's diary of the spring holidays of 1920, see Buddicom, 99–101. For the stay in Rickmansworth and the discussion of Orwell's future, ibid., 113–17. Sir Anthony Wagner's recollection of Orwell as fag-master is quoted in Powell, *Infants*, 140.

Christopher Eastwood's view of Etonian snobbery is in Wadhams, 17. For Hollis' account of the peace celebrations of 1919, see Coppard/Crick. The opinion of the Provost (M.R. James) is taken from a letter quoted in Michael Cox, *M.R. James: An Informal Portrait* (Oxford 1983), 203. Details of Sir Alec Douglas-Home's Eton career can be found in D.R. Thorpe, *Alec Douglas-Home* (1996), 23–7. Orwell's public school manner was recalled by David Holbrook, interview with the author, Jack Common (Coppard/Crick, 139–43) and Peter Vansittart, interview with the author, Kersey, Suffolk, 15 October 2001. Stafford Cottman's memory of being asked to sing the Eton boating song in a Spanish trench is in Wadhams, 81. The 'joy' in Orwell's expression when he discussed the probable demise of Eton was detected by Peter Vansittart. For Richard Rees' incautious use of the word 'tug', see Rees, 143. David Astor made this comment on Orwell's view of Eton in an interview with the author, London, 14 March 2000. For the birching incident, see John Heygate, *Decent Fellows* (1930), 121–2. The parting gift to Anthony Wagner is recorded in Powell, *Infants*, 140.

Orwell's face
For Richard Rees on Dorothy Hare's features, see Rees, 36. For Powell's comments, *Infants*, 132–3. Paul Potts's memoir, 'Don Quixote on a Bicycle', originally appeared in the *London Magazine*, March 1987, subsequently became a chapter in *Dante Called You Beatrice* 1961 and is reported in Coppard/Crick, 248–60.

4. White Man's Burden
Orwell's letter about the Southwold crammer is quoted in Buddicom, 44. For Jacintha's memory of him staying at Quarry House in April 1922, ibid., 140. On the entry procedures to the Burma Police, see Stansky/Abrahams, 144–6. The episode involving Mr Hurst and the dead rat is recalled by R.G. Sharp in Coppard/Crick, 61. For Jacintha's memories of the summer of 1922, see Buddicom, 141–2. On the two incidents which Orwell remembered from the Burma voyage, see the 'As I Please' column of 5 July 1947 (*CW*, XIX: 5–6) and a *Time and Tide* 'Notes on the Way' contribution of 30 March 1940 (*CW*, XII: 121–4). For Roger Beadon's description of Orwell's arrival in Burma, see Stansky/Abrahams, 50–1.

For a recent analysis of the background to early twentieth-century Burmese history, see Thant Myint U, *The Making of Modern Burma* (Cambridge, 2001). The crime statistics are taken from the annual *Report on the Administration of Burma*, 1923–4, 1924–5 and 1925–6 (Rangoon, 1925–7). For some contemporary expatriate reactions, see Derek Brooke-Wavell, ed. *Lines from a Shining Land* (Britain–Burma Society, 1998). The review of C.V. Warren's *Burmese Interlude* appears in *CW*, XI: 109.

The comments on the reputation of the Burma Police at this time are taken from a privately printed memoir by Alfred White, kindly lent to the author by the former's granddaughter, Tiffany White, 86–7. Roger Beadon's memories are in Coppard/Crick, 62–5, and in Wadhams, 23–4. Jacintha's account of the three letters sent home from Burma is in Buddicom, 143–4. The reference to the 'police officer at Twante' comes from Alfred White's memoir, cited above, 40–1. Hollis' account of meeting him in Rangoon is in Coppard/Crick. For Maung Htn Aung's memory of the Pagoda Road railway station incident, see Stansky/Abrahams, 171–2. The BOC refinery chemist, L.W. Marrison, is quoted in Coppard/Crick, 65–7. For Beadon's memory of visiting Orwell's house at Insein, ibid., 64–5. For the 'older colleague' who met Orwell with his Limouzin relatives at the sporting event, see Stansky/Abrahams, 166. May Hearsey's recollections are in her *Land of Chindits and Rubies* (1982), 94–5. I am grateful to Peter Davison for drawing my attention to this work. George Stuart's memories of Orwell in Burma are in the Orwell Archive, University College London (see *CW*, X: n.506). The remark about a Burman needing two names was made to Lady Violet Powell, letter to the author, 1 July 2000.

For Orwell's memories of the Western popular songs introduced to Burma, see 'Songs We Used to Sing' (*CW*, XVIII: 49–51). The fascination exerted on him by Margaret Kennedy's *The Constant Nymph* is recalled in a letter to Brenda Salkeld (*CW*, X: 346–7). For the review of *The Prussian Officer*, see *CW*, XVII: 375–8.

The description of Wellbourne comes from Alfred White's memoir, 86–7. The report of Major E.C. Kenny's dispatch of the elephant at Takton is printed in the corrections to Volume X of Davison. I am grateful to Peter Davison for supplying me with details of the names pilfered by Orwell from the *Rangoon Gazette*. The tentative identification of Mr Macgregor with Colonel F.H. McGregor, Commander of the Rangoon Third Field Brigade, was made by his granddaughter, Pauline McGregor-Currien, in a letter to the author of 4 March 2001.

For the letter to Jack Common on the inadequacies of most anti-Imperial polemic, see *CW*, XI: 221–3.

5. Cross-Channel

Orwell remembered the Marseilles protest march of August 1927 in an *Adelphi* article of May 1932 (*CW*, X: 244–5). For Avril's account of his homecoming, see 'My Brother, George Orwell'.

R.G. Sharp's memory of Orwell's return to Southwold is in Coppard/Crick, 61. For Jacintha's account of Orwell's stay in Shropshire, Buddicom, 145. Mr Denny's dealings with him are outlined in Coppard/Crick, 83–5. Esmé Goldsmith (née May) described her first meeting with Orwell in an interview with the author, 14 February 2001.

For Orwell's visit to Cambridge in the autumn of 1927, see Bernard Crick, *George Orwell: A Life* (1980), 105. Ruth Pitter's memories of

Orwell can be found in Coppard/Crick, 68–75. She is also quoted in Stansky/Abrahams, *passim*. Orwell's account of the borrowed ladder is in an 'As I Please' column of 20 May 1944 (*CW*, XVI: 231). For the Eton dinner, see Stansky/Abrahams, 199.

On Paris during Orwell's time there, see Vincent Cronin, *Paris: City of Light 1919–1939* (1994), 139–54, and Richard Mayne, 'A Note on Orwell's Paris', in Miriam Gross, ed. *The World of George Orwell* (1971). Orwell refers to his possible sighting of James Joyce in a letter to Celia Paget of 20 January 1948 (*CW*, XIX: 257). John Dos Passos' remarks are quoted in Cronin, op. cit. For the letter from L.I. Bailey of the McClure agency, see *CW*, X: 113. Ruth Graves' letter of 23 July 1949 is printed in *CW*, XX: 150. Orwell mentions his fondness for the Jardin des Plantes in a letter to Celia Paget of 23 May 1948, *CW*, XIX: 344–5.

Orwell's account of his presence at Foch's funeral is in an 'As I Please' column of 24 January 1947 (*CW*, XIX: 25). Mabel Fierz' memories of his Parisian experiences are in Coppard/Crick, 95. For Orwell's annotations to the copy of *Down and Out in Paris and London* presented to Brenda Salkeld, see Michael Shelden, *Orwell: The Authorised Biography* (1991), 145–6. There is a useful discussion of the background to and dating of 'How the Poor Die' in *CW*, XVIII: 455–9.

Orwell's voice
The account of Orwell's vocal style is taken from the following sources: Michael Meyer, interview with the author; William Empson ('Orwell at the BBC', in Gross, ed. *The World of George Orwell*); Anthony Powell, *Infants*, 131–2; David Astor and Lucian Freud to author (the latter via William Feaver).

6. Down There on a Visit
For Richard Rees' first meeting with Orwell, see Rees, 141–2. On his 'Bohemian Toryism', ibid., 46. Jack Common's account of the *Adelphi* encounter is in Coppard/Crick.

For information on Southwold life in the 1930s I am grateful to Mr Ronnie Waters, Mrs Winifred Cook, Mrs Rita Field, Mr Dudley Crick and Miss Norah Denny for letters to and conversations with the author. 'Miss Avril Blair' is listed as proprietress of 'The Refreshment Rooms', 5 Queen Street, Southwold, in *Kelly's Directory* for 1933. For Avril on Orwell's attitude to Southwold, see 'My Brother, George Orwell'. I am indebted to Mr Anthony Bateman for supplying details of Orwell's connection with the Morgan family of Southwold in a letter to the author, 18 July 2002.

Brenda Salkeld's exasperation at Orwell's tramping excursions is quoted in Shelden, *Orwell*, 157. For Humphrey Dakin's reminiscences of his stay at Bramley, see Stansky/Abrahams, 231–3. Esmé Goldsmith's recollections of Orwell at work on *Down and Out* are taken from an interview with the author, 14 February 2001. Mrs Dora Hammond (née Georges) provided information on Orwell's relations with the Morgan family of Walberswick in a letter of September 2001 and in an interview with the author, 16 October 2001. Richard Peters' memoir is reproduced in Coppard/Crick, 90–4, as is Mabel Fierz' account of her first meeting with Orwell and subsequent relationship (94–8). For the account of 'Laurel' undertaking the role of a male charwoman in the East End, see Stella Judt, 'I Once Met: George Orwell', in *I Once Met* (1996), 59–60.

Orwell's hop-picking diary is reproduced in *CW*, X: 228–31. I owe the juxtaposition of Orwell's presence in Billingsgate in late September 1931 and the unfolding crisis at the Bank of England to David Kynaston, *The City of London, Volume III: Illusions of Gold: 1914–1945* (1999), 246–7. Alec Waugh recalls the contemporary reaction in *A Year to Remember: A Reminiscence of 1931* (1975), 149–52. For Mabel Fierz' memory of badgering Leonard Moore to read the manuscript of 'A Scullion's Diary', see Coppard/Crick. Orwell's time at the Hawthorns is remembered by his pupil Geoffrey Stevens in Wadhams, 51–4.

David Astor recalled Orwell's remark about the test of a person's honesty in an interview with the author, 14 March 2000. Avril's memory of the refurbishment of Montague House is in 'My Brother, George Orwell'. The noise of Orwell's typewriter was recalled by George Bumstead, interview with the author, Southwold, 28 November 2000. The details of Eleanor Jacques' unwillingness to marry Orwell and her memory of the Blair/Orwell transformation are taken from an interview with her daughter, Susannah Collings, Southwold, 20 November 1999. For Richard Rees' comment, see Rees, 44.

7. Clergymen's Daughters

For Avril's recollections of Richard and Ida Blair's reaction to *Down and Out in Paris and London*, see 'My Brother, George Orwell'. On Orwell's personality in the early 1930s, Rees, 143.

Ruth Pitter recalls her visit to the Ealing hospital in the interview reprinted in Coppard/Crick, 72. The account of Victor Gollancz and the early years of Victor Gollancz Ltd is largely taken from Ruth Dudley-Edwards, *Victor Gollancz: A Biography* (1987). For the incident on Southwold Common involving Dorothy Rogers, George Summers, interview with the author, 16 February 2000.

Orwell and the rats
For details of the Burmese rat culls, see the volumes of the *Report on the Administration of Burma,* quoted above. Bob Edwards recalls Orwell's 'phobia' in a BBC radio broadcast reprinted in Coppard/Crick, 147–8.

8. A Room with a View
On the atmosphere of Warwick Mansions and the Westropes', see Jon Kimche, quoted in Wadhams, 54–5. For Orwell as bookseller's assistant, see Kimche, ibid., and Peter Vansittart, *Paths from a White Horse* (1986), 91, and interview with the author, 15 November 2001. On the 1930s background, see Alec Waugh, *The Best Wine Last: An Autobiography through the Years 1932–1969* (1978), 53, and, pre-eminently, Valentine Cunningham, *Writers of the 1930s* (Oxford, 1988). The *Sunday Times* Book Club exhibition programme is repro-duced in Rupert Hart-Davis, *The Power of Chance* (1991). For the origins and influence of the Independent Labour Party, see Kenneth O. Morgan, *Labour People* (Oxford, 1987), *passim*. For Orwell's acquaintance with Reg Groves, Crick, *George Orwell: A Life,* 175.

Kay Ekevall's reminiscences are printed in Wadhams, 56–60, and in Coppard/Crick, 98–106. The readers' reports on *A Clergyman's Daughter* are in the archive of Victor Gollancz Ltd, currently the property of the Orion Publishing Group. For the reviews, see Jeffrey Meyers, ed. *George Orwell: The Critical Heritage* (1975), 58–64. On the critical reaction to *Burmese Days,* ibid., 50–3. Connolly remembered his reunion with Orwell in a note on some Orwell letters published in *Encounter*, January 1962. Mrs Obermeyer's recollections of the party are in Crick, 172.

The portrait of Eileen is taken from the following sources: Lady Violet Powell, letter to the author; Fyvel, *passim*; Lydia Jackson and Stafford Cottman, quoted in Fyvel, 134; interview with Lydia Jackson in Wadhams, 66–8; Kay Ekevall, quoted in Wadhams, 58. Rayner Heppenstall's memories of the Lawford Road flat are in *Four Absentees* (1960), reprinted in Coppard/Crick, 106–15. Michael Sayers' comments were made in an interview with the author, 30 September

2002. For A.D. Peters on the craft of newspaper serial writing, see Alec Waugh, *The Early Years of Alec Waugh*, 208.

9. English Journeys

Details of the letters sent to Orwell by Victor Gollancz Ltd during the Wigan Pier journey are supplied in *CW*, X: 413–14. Peter Davison discusses the background to *The Road to Wigan Pier*, ibid., 529–32. A copy of the letter from Gollancz to Moore, dated 29 October 1936, wondering what Orwell is up to is in the Gollancz archive.

For the background to the working-class literary movement of the 1930s, see Cunningham, *Writers of the 1930s, passim*, Andy Croft, *Red Letter Days: British Fiction in the 1930s* (1991), and D.J. Taylor, 'Depression Britain', in Malcolm Bradbury, ed. *The Atlas of Literature* (1996), 208–11. Jack Hilton's comments on *The Road to Wigan Pier*, taken from his unpublished autobiography, are in Croft, 253–4.

For Jerry Kennan's recollections of Orwell in Wigan, see Coppard/Crick, 170–3. The comment about the Frosts' establishment, made by Sidney Smith, is in Wadhams, 61. The Deiners' memories of Orwell's time in Liverpool, originally recorded for Melvyn Bragg's 1970 BBC *Omnibus* programme, are printed in Coppard/Crick, 134–6. For Humphrey Dakin on Orwell's stay at Headingley, ibid., 128. The account of the argument with the Sheffield Communist is in Rees, 146. On Orwell in Barnsley, see Irene Goodliffe (née Gray), Wadhams, 64–5.

The description of the Stores, Wallington, is taken from an interview with Celia Goodman (née Paget), Cambridge, 14 November 2000, and the recollections of Wallington neighbours, Wadhams, 114–17. For Jack Common's memories of Orwell at Wallington, see Coppard/Crick, 142–3. On the exchange of letters with Anthony Powell, *Infants*, 133–4. For Wallington memories of the wedding day, Wadhams, 115. Mark Benney's account of his visit to Wallington with Richard Rees is in *Almost a Gentleman* (1966), 107–8. For Lydia Jackson's memory of Eileen's 'dissatisfaction', ibid., 68.

Andy Croft's comment on Orwell's 'exaggerated panic' over left-wing writing of the 1930s is in *Red Letter Days*, 26. On the background to the Left Book Club, see Paul Laity's introduction to his *Left Book Club Anthology* (2001) and Ruth Dudley-Edwards, *Victor Gollancz*. On the preliminaries to the Spanish trip, see Fenner Brockway's recollections in Wadhams, 72–3. Crick quotes Jack Common and Philip Mairet in *George Orwell: A Life*, 205–6.

Orwell and the Jews
The correspondence between S.M. Lipsey and Victor Gollancz is in the Gollancz archive. See also Dudley-Edwards, *Victor Gollancz*. For Tosco Fyvel on Orwell's interest in Jewishness, see Fyvel, *passim* and especially 178–82.

10. **Spanish Bombs**
For Orwell's visit to Henry Miller's studio, see the extract from Alfred Perlès' *My Friend Henry Miller* (1955), reprinted in Coppard/Crick, 143–6. Orwell recalls the dispute with the Parisian taxi-driver in an 'As I Please' column of 15 September 1944 (CW, XVI: 402–3). For accounts of Orwell's arrival in Spain, see Jennie Lee, letter quoted in CW, XI: 5. McNair and Alba are both quoted in Wadhams, 73–5.

Kenneth Sinclair-Loutit's memories of his enlistment are taken from an unpublished memoir in the possession of the author. For Orwell's comment to Anthony Powell about the loyalties of native Spaniards, see the latter's *Journals 1982–1986* (1995), 54. On the background to the war, see Paul Preston, *The Spanish Civil War* (1986), *passim*, and Martin Blinkhorn, *Democracy and Civil War in Spain 1931–1936* (1988). Sinclair-Loutit's account of his 'interview' is taken from his memoir, as is the comment about Orwell 'serving no useful military purpose'. For the recollections of other members of the ILP contingent quoted here, see Robert Edward in Coppard/Crick, 146–7, Stafford Cottman, ibid., 151. Frank Frankford and Jack Branthwaite's memories are in Wadhams, 82–5. On Orwell's lack of political consciousness, see Harry Milton's remarks in Wadhams, 81–2. The ILP *New Leader* account of the Huesca Front sortie is reprinted in CW, XI: 18–20. For Milton's warning about the International Brigade, see Wadhams, 85. For Rees on Eileen in Barcelona, see Rees, 147.

11. **Barcelona**
Eileen's relationship with Kopp is explored by Michael Shelden, *Orwell: The Authorised Biography*, 288–9. For Branthwaite's memory of the shot coming through the window of the Hotel Continental, see Wadhams, 87. For Kimche's recollections, ibid., 88–9. Kenneth Sinclair-Loutit's description of his meeting with Orwell in the POUM café is taken from his unpublished memoir. For eyewitness accounts of the morning of 20 May, see Wadhams, 89–91.

For Orlov and the 'liquidation' of POUM, see Christopher Adams and Vasili Mitrokhin, quoting John Costello and Oleg Tsarev, *Deadly*

Illusions (1993). On the Orwells' escape from Barcelona, see Stafford Cottman and Fenner Brockway's reminiscences in Wadhams, 95–6.

Orwell in view
For the cine films of inter-war Southwold referred to here, see the video cassette *Barrett Jenkins' Southwold*, East Anglian Film Archive, n.d.

12. Wintering Out

For Malcolm Muggeridge's memory of Orwell talking about the Home Guard and Spain, see Muggeridge, 25 December 1949. 'Looking back on the Spanish Civil War', appeared in *New Review*, 1943, XIII, 497–511. Kenneth Sinclair-Loutit's view of Orwell's position on Spain is taken from his unpublished memoir. For a left-wing analysis, see Sam Lesser, in Wadhams, 96–9. Christopher Hitchens discusses the Raymond Williams quotation in *Orwell's Victory* (2002), 50–1.

Details of Kingsley Martin's career and temperament are taken from C.H. Rolph, *Kingsley: The Life, Letters and Diaries of Kingsley Martin* (1973). Gollancz' letter of 5 July 1937 is in the Gollancz archive, and see *CW*, XI: 37–8.

In *Four Absentees*, Heppenstall dates the Hampstead encounter to 17 January 1938, but in Jonathan Goodman, ed. *The Master Eccentric: The Journals of Rayner Heppenstall* (1982), he refers to 'a night in 1937'. For Anthony Powell's memory of a shabbily dressed Orwell turning up at smart parties, see *Infants*, 137.

For the *Daily Worker* controversy with Frankford and Orwell's reply, see *CW*, XI: 82–5. Powell refers to his correspondence with Frankford in his *Journals 1987–1989* (1996), 221. Heppenstall's description of his visit to the Stores, reprinted from *Four Absentees*, is in Coppard/Crick, 114. On Raymond Mortimer's letter, *CW*, XI: 116.

For Orwell's time at Preston Hall, see Wadhams, 107–8. Lydia Jackson's account of her visit is in *CW*, XI: 336. On L.H. Myers, see Adrian Wright, *Foreign Country: The Life of L.P. Hartley* (1996), 98 and 130–1, and G.H. Bantock, 'L.H. Myers and Bloomsbury', in Boris Ford, ed. *The Pelican Guide to English Literature, Volume 7, The Modern Age* (Harmondsworth 1961), 288–97. I am also grateful for the recollections of Frances Partridge, interview with the author, London, 13 June 2001.

Evelyn Waugh's account of his exploits in the Fez brothels is taken from Mark Amory, ed. *The Letters of Evelyn Waugh* (1980), 82. The description of the Sitwell visit is drawn from Sarah Bradford, *Sacheverell Sitwell: Splendours and Miseries* (1993), 277–9.

For Anthony Powell's remarks about the poor prospects for authors in the publishing season of spring 1939, see *Faces in My Time*, 74. The account of the pennies thrown into the sea at Southwold is in Rees, 145. Stephen Spender's diary entry is reproduced from S. Schimanski and H. Treece, eds, *Leaves in the Storm* (1947), 5–6.

13. Life during Wartime

The quotations from Stephen Spender's journal are taken from *Leaves in the Storm*, op. cit., 14 and 16. For the Evelyn Waugh letters quoted here, see Amory, 137 and 578. The history of *Horizon* is covered in Michael Shelden's excellent *Friends of Promise: Cyril Connolly and the World of Horizon* (1989).

For Fyvel's account of his first meeting with Orwell, see Fyvel, 98–102. On his memories of Orwell and Eileen, ibid., 108–9. For reviews of *Inside the Whale*, see Meyers, ed. *George Orwell: The Critical Heritage*, 175–90.

The account of Orwell's time in the St John's Wood Home Guard is taken from an interview with Denzil Jacobs, London, 13 June 2001. For a description of the days spent at Scarlett's Farm and Eileen's reaction to the death of her brother, see Fyvel, 103–16.

Orwell's paranoia

For Jacintha Buddicom's memory of the Burma letter ('I got the impression that perhaps correspondence might be censored'), see Buddicom, 143. For the 'enemy' who might cut out a name seen in print, Rees, 44. For Kimche's recollections, see Wadhams, 55. Isaac Deutscher's memory of their time as war correspondents is in his essay '1984 – The Mysticism of Cruelty', *Heretics and Renegades and Other Essays* (1955), 48n.

14. London Calling

For Frances Partridge's account of January 1941, see *A Pacifist's War: Diaries 1939–1945* (1978), 75–6. Powell's description of the meeting at the Café Royal is in *Infants*, 130–1. On the dinner invitation from L.H. Myers, Peter Vansittart, interview with the author, 15 October 2001. Mark Benney reproduces the interview with Alan Clutton-Brock in *Almost a Gentleman*, 166.

For details of the BBC's Indian Section, see CW, XIII: 3–13. Inez Holden's description of the dinner with Wells and Empson is reproduced in Crick, *George Orwell: A Life*, 293–4. On his continuing enthusiasm for Wells' early work, Anthony Powell, *Journals 1982–1986*, 248–9. The (slightly disparaging) account of Orwell's recruitment by the BBC as part of a 'jobs for the boys' initiative comes from C.H. Rolph, *Further Particulars* (1988), 102. For recollections of Orwell's BBC days, see Jennifer Rolph, quoted in Rolph, above, 155, and Sunday Wilshin, in Wadhams, 126–7.

Anthony Powell's description of Eileen in the early war years is taken from *Infants*, 136. For his account of the night spent in the Kilburn basement, ibid., 136–7.

15. Gains and Losses

Michael Meyer's memories of Orwell's summary of the plot of *Animal Farm* are taken from his *Not Prince Hamlet: Literary and Theatrical Memoirs* (1989) and interview with the author, London, 16 February 2000. On the background to Orwell's appointment at *Tribune*, see Fyvel, 125–6. For the argument with Bevan, ibid., 140. On the controversies stirred up by Orwell's anti-Soviet stance, Michael Foot, interview with the author, London, 8 October 2002. For the recollections of *Tribune* contributors, see Wadhams, 139–40, and Peter Vansittart, interview with the author. On Orwell's influence on the young at this time, David Holbrook interview with the author, 14 November 2000.

The account of Orwell's social circle in the mid-1940s is drawn from a variety of sources. Avril's memory of Ida Blair's death is taken from 'My Brother, George Orwell', Coppard/Crick, 29. The description of Avril given by Anthony Powell to Muggeridge is in Muggeridge, 2 January 1950. Henry Dakin's account of his stay with Orwell and Eileen is in Wadhams, 129–30. On Orwell's bohemian connections, Lucian Freud to the author (via his biographer, William Feaver), Anthony Burgess, *Little Wilson and Big God* (1987), 290–1. I am grateful to Paul Willetts for allowing me to make use of several details amassed while researching his forthcoming biography of Julian Maclaren-Ross. Jack Branthwaite remembers his stay at Wallington in Wadhams, 99–100.

For Francis Wyndham's meeting with Orwell, interview with the author, London, 18 September 2000. For the bus journey back from the Connolly party, see Janetta Parladé, interview with the author. On the meeting with Alick Dru, Anthony Powell, *Faces in My Time*, 184–5. On his 'officer-like tendencies', Peter Vansittart interview with the author, 15 October 2001. John Morris' recollections, reprinted from a September 1950 contribution to *Penguin New Writing*, are in

Coppard/Crick, 171–6. For the friendship with Michael Meyer, *Not Prince Hamlet*, *passim*, and interview with the author 11 February 2000. Powell comments on Orwell's air of 'unreality' in *Infants*, 133.

The saga of *Animal Farm*'s progress towards publication can be followed in *CW*, XIV. Michael Meyer, who later had dealings with the firm, was adamant that the manuscript was offered to William Collins Ltd. See also Ion Trewin, 'Andre Deutsch: A 70th Birthday Tribute', *Publishers' Weekly* n.d. On Potts' involvement, see the extract from *Dante Called You Beatrice* (1960) reprinted in Coppard/Crick, 248–60. Inez Holden's account of his trips from Mortimer Crescent to the Strand is in *Leaves in the Storm*, 245. Descriptions of the Canonbury Square flat are taken from interviews with Celia Goodman (14 November 2000) and Michael Meyer, *Not Prince Hamlet*. The latter is also the source of the anecdote about the bookshelves and the trip to see *Henry IV* Parts I and II.

Lady Violet Powell remembered the Orwells' visit to Chester Gate with Richard in a letter to the author of 1 July 2000. The friend to whom Orwell confided details of the affair with Sally McEwan was Celia Paget (see Shelden, *Orwell: The Authorised Biography*, 419). For Anthony Powell on Orwell's 'retreat', see *Infants*, 138.

Inez Holden's account of Orwell's return to London after Eileen's death is in Shelden, *Orwell*, 417. See also Potts, in Coppard/Crick, 251 and Wadhams, 145. Astor's verdict on the European tour is taken from an interview with the author, 14 March 2000. For the seven-year-old Ferdinand Mount's enthusiasm for *Animal Farm*, Lady Violet Powell, letter to the author.

16. The Last Man in Europe

On the literary scene of the immediately post-war era, see Alec Waugh, *The Best Wine Last*, 235, Powell, *Faces in My Time*, 196–202. Cyril Connolly's conversation with Logan Pearsall Smith is taken from Shelden, *Friends of Promise*, 151–2. For A.J. Ayer's memory of Orwell at the Hotel Scribe, see Wadhams, 168. On John Freeman's moving of the address in reply to the King's Speech in the first post-war parliament, see Anthony Howard, 'We Are the Masters Now', in Michael Sissons and Philip French, eds, *Age of Anxiety* (Oxford, 1963). Powell's memory of Orwell going off to address protest meetings is in *Infants*, 140.

For Orwell's visits to the *Tribune* offices in the winter of 1945, see Fyvel, 143. On the preliminaries to Jura and Orwell's state of health, David Astor to the author 14 March 2000. Michael Sayers remembered his reunion with Orwell in an interview with the author, 30 September 2002. Susan Watson's memories of the Islington household are in Wadhams, 156–62. Paul Potts' account of Orwell looking at the windows of the Islington newsagent's is taken from his *To Keep a Promise* (1970), 71. The memory of Orwell leaping up to telephone Powell is in Celia Goodman's' interview with the author, 14 November 2000. I am grateful to the late Lady Violet Powell for information about Miranda Christen, later Wood. See also the latter's memoir in *CW*, XX: 300–6. For an alternative view of the Canonbury Square establishment, see Fyvel, 147–50.

The account of Celia Goodman (neé Paget)'s early dealings with Orwell is taken from her interview with the author. In addition, see Wadhams, 162–5. For Anna Popham's memories, see Wadhams, 165–7. On Sonia Brownell's early life, see Hilary Spurling, *The Girl from the Fiction Department: A Memoir of Sonia Orwell* (2002), *passim*. The memory of her combination of good and bad qualities is Janetta Parladé's, interview with the author, London, 25 May 2000. For her first meeting with Orwell and the quote about 'unwashed nappies', see Shelden, *Friends of Promise*, 159–60. The friend who introduced Orwell to her in 1945 was Michael Sayers (interview with the author, 30 September 2002). For Susan Watson's account of her visit to the flat with Connolly, see Wadhams, 162. For her horror at Orwell's advances, Lucian Freud to author (via William Feaver). Powell records the incident with the knife in *Infants*, 140–1. John Powell dates this to the winter of 1946–7. For Koestler and the conversation about *Twilight Bar*, see Coppard/Crick, 168. Celia Paget's account of the Welsh Christmas is in Wadhams, 162–4.

On Orwell's illness of early 1946, see Susan Watson, Wadhams, 162–3, and Fyvel, 151. For Margaret Fletcher Nelson's memory of his arrival on Jura, Wadhams, 170–4. For Katie Darroch's reminiscences and the row between Avril and Susan, ibid., 174–5 and 177. Potts' memory of cutting down the nut tree is in Coppard/Crick, 259. For Eileen's poem in the Sunderland High School *Chronicle*, see Sally Conian, 'Orwell and the Origins of *Nineteen Eighty-Four*', *Times Literary Supplement*, 31 December 1999, 14. For David Holbrook's memories of his stay on Jura, Wadhams, 178–81.

17. Islands
For Susan Watson's memory of Orwell's working routine on Jura, see Fyvel, 159–60. Julian Symons remembers Orwell's efforts on his behalf

in *Notes from Another Country* (1972), 140–1. Avril recalled Orwell chopping up Richard's toys for firewood in 'My Brother, George Orwell', Coppard/Crick, 30. The fog-bound Bayswater dinner is described in Fyvel, 152. On the supposed safety of Jura, Denzil Jacobs, interview with the author, 13 June 2001.

For Bill Dunn's recollections of Orwell's second stay on Jura, see Wadhams, 182–3. The account of Avril dislocating her shoulder is in Rees 152. Henry and Lucy Dakin's description of the Corryvreckan episode is in Wadhams, 188–92. For Mrs Fletcher Nelson's reminiscences of Orwell at this time, ibid., 198. On Orwell's interest in Gissing, see Peter Morton, 'Allusions to Gissing in the Complete Works of George Orwell', *Gissing Journal*, xxxvi, no.1, 25–9, January 2000. For Avril's memory of the remark about his temperature, see 'My Brother, George Orwell', Coppard/Crick, 31. On the departure from Jura, Wadhams, 201–2.

18. Endgame

For the train journey south, see Rees, 151. Warburg's memorandum is reproduced in *CW*, XIX: 478–81. For Farrar's reaction, ibid., 482. On the plan to adapt *Nineteen Eighty-Four* for the Broadway stage, Sidney Sheldon, letter to the author, 27 January 2000. Malcolm Muggeridge's comments about the novel are taken from Muggeridge, 14–15 March 1949. For Warburg's report of the booksellers' reaction, ibid., 23 March 1949.

An account of Tosco and Mary Fyvel's visit to Cranham is in Fyvel, 162. For other recollections: Celia Goodman, interview with the author, 14 November 2000; Jane Morgan (née Dakin), quoted in Wadhams, 203–4; Richard Blair, ibid., 203. Muggeridge's account of his and Powell's visit is in Muggeridge, 19 February 1949. Evelyn Waugh's belief that Orwell was 'very near to God' is quoted by Connolly in his *Sunday Times* review of *George Orwell: The Collected Essays, Journalism and Letters*, reprinted in *The Evening Colonnade*, 343–9.

Celia Goodman's view of 'The List' is taken from an interview with the author, 14 November 2000. The summary of John Platts-Mills' career is drawn from his *Daily Telegraph* obituary of 27 October 2001. The Secker & Warburg internal memorandum of 15 June 1949 is reproduced in *CW*, XX: 131–3.

On Orwell's marriage to Sonia Brownell, see Spurling, *The Girl from the Fiction Department*, 94–7, Janetta Parladé (then Kee), letter to the author, 25 May 2000, Julian Symons, quoted in Muggeridge, 15 November 1949. See also Muggeridge, 15 September 1949. For the memories of the UCH staff, Wadhams, 214.

On Orwell's condition in late September, see Muggeridge, 27 September 1949. On the wedding preparations, see Powell, *Infants*, 141–2, Muggeridge, 6 October 1949; Sonia's letter is quoted in the entry of 4 October 1949. The account of the wedding draws on interviews with David Astor, 14 March 2000, and Janetta Parladé, 25 May 2000, and a letter to the author from Robert Kee, 17 February 2000. For Frances Partridge's reaction, see *Everything to Lose: Diaries 1945–60* (1985), 13 and 18 October 1949.

For Powell's comments on the apparent improvement in Orwell's health, see *Infants*, 141, corroborated by Muggeridge, 25 October 1949. For other accounts of visits to UCH, Janetta Parladé, interview with the author, 25 May 2000; Nicky Gathorne-Hardy, interview with the author, 28 August 2002; Celia Goodman, interview with the author, 14 November 2002. On Powell and Muggeridge's Christmas visit, Muggeridge, 25 December 1949.

On the plans for the Swiss trip, Jon Kimche, Wadhams, 215. For Avril's journey to London, 'My Brother, George Orwell', in Coppard/Crick, 32. Details of the excursion to Regent's Park Zoo were provided by the late Lady Violet Powell, letter to the author, 11 March 2000. Vernon Richards' recollection of his last meeting with Orwell is in the *Freedom* obituary, 4 February 1950, reprinted in *George Orwell at Home (and among the Anarchists): Essays and Photographs* (1998). For final visits and telephone conversations: Muggeridge, 12 January 1950; Denzil Jacobs, interview with the author, 13 June 2001; Stafford Cottman, Wadhams, 215; Muggeridge, 19 January 1950; Celia Goodman, interview with the author, 14 November 2000; Fyvel, 167–8; Paul Potts, Wadhams, 216.

19. Epilogue: And Sonia

For the Evelyn Waugh letter to Nancy Mitford, see Amory, ed. *The Letters of Evelyn Waugh*, 319–20. Avril's letter to David Astor is among the additions to Peter Davison's revised edition of *CW*.

The portait of Sonia is assembled from the following: Janetta Parladé (then Kee), interview with the author, 25 June 2000; Muggeridge *passim*; *Times Literary Supplement* correspondence provoked by Michael Shelden's *Orwell: The Authorised Biography*, 25 September to 9 November 1991; Hilary Spurling, *The Girl from the Fiction Department*, *passim*; letter to the author from Francis King, 12 February 2000; Margaret Drabble, *Angus Wilson: A Biography* (1995); David Plante, *Difficult Women* (1983), 65–101; Miriam Gross, interview with the author, London, 14 February 2000; Frances Partridge, *Other People: Diaries, 1963–1966* (1993); Francis Wyndham, interview with the author, 18 September 2000; Stephen Spender, *Journals, 1939–1983* (1985), 433–5.

Index

Waugh, Evelyn 21, 73, 83, 129, 150,
161, 197, 202, 258, 272, 276, 277,
300, 356, 398, 407–8, 419, *Decline
and Fall* 38, *Labels*, 83, *Sword of
Honour* trilogy, *Unconditional
Surrender*, 276, *Work Suspended*,
13–14
We (Zamyatin) 342, 368, 375
Wedgwood, Veronica 334
Wellbourne, Colonel 79
Wells, Dennis 286
Wells, H.G. 26, 93, 236, 303, 305,
332, 375, *A Modern Utopia* 45,
Kipps (film), 293, *Love and Mr
Lewisham*, 305, *Outline of World
History*, 312, *The Country of the
Blind* 26,*The History of Mr Polly*, 93,
261, *The Sleeper Wakes*, 280
West, W.J. 6
Westrope, Francis and Myfanwy 142,
147, 151, 155, 167, 258, 259, 292
White, Alfred 70
Whittome, Maurice 91
Wickham-Stead, Henry 323
Wilde, Oscar 393

Wilkes, John 32, 43
Wilkes, Mr and Mrs Vaughan 24–6,
29–37, 292
Wilkinson, Ellen 152
Williams, Raymond 242
Wilson, Angus 276, 421, *Anglo-Saxon
Attitudes*, 421
Wilson, Edmund 410
Windmill 331, 344
Wintringham, Tom 298
Wodehouse, P.G. 344, *A Damsel in
Distress*, 149
Woodcock, George 277, 316, 357,
370, 375, 391
Woolley, Janetta (see also Kee) 331,
364, 375
Woolsey, Gamel 135
Woolton, Lord 295
World Review 420
Wyndham, Francis 331

Young, Desmond 250

Zamyatin, Yevgeny 342, 368, 375
Zilliacus, Konni 391